YOM-TOV LIPMANN HELLER

Publication of this book is
largely due to the generous support of the
MICHAEL AND MORVEN HELLER
CHARITABLE FOUNDATION
whose trustees have a special interest in
Yom-Tov Lipmann Heller.
It was also awarded a grant by the
KORET FOUNDATION

THE LITTMAN LIBRARY OF
JEWISH CIVILIZATION

Dedicated to the memory of
LOUIS THOMAS SIDNEY LITTMAN
who founded the Littman Library for the love of God
and as an act of charity in memory of his father
JOSEPH AARON LITTMAN
and to the memory of
ROBERT JOSEPH LITTMAN
who continued what his father Louis had begun
יהא זכרם ברוך

'Get wisdom, get understanding:
Forsake her not and she shall preserve thee'
PROV. 4: 5

The Littman Library of Jewish Civilization is a registered UK charity
Registered charity no. 1000784

YOM-TOV LIPMANN HELLER

◆

Portrait of a Seventeenth-Century Rabbi

◆

JOSEPH M. DAVIS

The Littman Library of Jewish Civilization
in association with Liverpool University Press

The Littman Library of Jewish Civilization
in association with Liverpool University Press
4 Cambridge Street, Liverpool L69 7ZU, UK

www.liverpooluniversitypress.co.uk/littman

Managing Editor: Connie Webber

Distributed in North America by
Oxford University Press Inc., 198 Madison Avenue,
New York, NY 10016, USA

First published in hardback 2004
First issued in paperback 2005

Catalogue records for this book are available from the
British Library and the Library of Congress

ISBN 978–1–904113–32–4

Publishing co-ordinator: Janet Moth
Design and production: Pete Russell, Faringdon, Oxon.
Copy-editing: Lindsey Taylor-Guthartz
Proof-reading: Tamar Wang
Indexes: Joseph Davis
Typeset by Footnote Graphics Limited, Warminster, Wilts.

Printed and bound by CPI Group (UK) Ltd, Croydon, CR0 4YY

For Susan
with all my love

Motionless he sat, his spectacled eyes fixed upon the printed page. Yet not altogether motionless.
STEFAN ZWEIG, 'Buchmendel'

Acknowledgements

In the course of writing this book I have had the help of many persons and institutions whom it is a pleasure to acknowledge. The book began as a Ph.D. dissertation at Harvard. I have benefited greatly from the insights and inspiration of the late Professor Isadore Twersky. I thank Professor Bernard Septimus for his many cogent suggestions, criticisms, and advice. I am grateful as well to my many other teachers, too numerous to name, whose devotion to history and to Jewish texts inspired my own. My dissertation research was supported by grants from the Memorial Foundation for Jewish Culture and Harvard University. The manuscript of this book was awarded a publication prize by the Koret Foundation, and I thank the foundation both for their financial support and for their encouragement.

The present work is the second biography of Heller to be written (leaving aside short essays), but the first to be published. In about 1932, towards the very beginning of his career, the great Jewish historian Israel Hailperin wrote a monograph on Heller, who was one of his ancestors. The work contained a narrative of Heller's life, together with appendices, such as a bibliography of his major writings, and an annotated text of *Megilat eivah*. Only the bibliography ever appeared in print.

In summer 1988, before I began writing my dissertation, I made some efforts to find the manuscript of the monograph, which Hailperin mentions in the bibliography. With the help of Israel Bartal and Adam Teller, I spent a fascinating but fruitless afternoon rummaging through Hailperin's papers in a warehouse in Jerusalem; alas, the manuscript was not there, and I gave up the search. Years later, Elhanan Reiner and Moshe Rosman led me to the actual location of the manuscript, in the Dinur Institute in Jerusalem. I have made extensive use of it. The youthful work already shows Hailperin's sharp historical insight, and his extraordinary command of Jewish historical literature. I thank all these scholars and the Dinur Institute for their gracious help.

A significant figure in his own day, Heller's fame has been kept alive in subsequent generations by his very numerous and very devoted family. Each year, many of his descendants observe a ritual that he instituted in commemoration of his arrest and imprisonment in 1629. I am not a descendant of Heller, but my first knowledge of him came from a member of his family, Marcia Lapidus Kaunfer. My interest in the man was initially sparked by the tradition, preserved in her family, that the turkey is not a kosher bird, a view that is said to have passed down orally, generation to generation, from Heller.[1] Recently I was privileged to partici-

[1] See Zivitofsky, 'Is Turkey Kosher?'.

pate in an annual Heller celebration in Baltimore. I thank all of the members of the extended Heller family who have encouraged me in this project over many years. Special thanks go to Michael Heller, who provided both encouragement and important financial support towards the publication of this book.

I have received invaluable assistance from the staffs of the following libraries and institutions: Harvard University, Washington University in St Louis, the University of Maryland, Brown University, the University of Pennsylvania and its Center for Judaic Studies, Gratz College, the Jewish Theological Seminary of America, the Leo Baeck Institute, YIVO, the New York Public Library, the Jewish National and University Library, the Makhon Letatslumei Kitvei Yad, the Central Archives of the Jewish People, the Dinur Institute, the British Library, the Bodleian Library Oxford, the Židovské Muzeum in Prague, and the Haus-, Hof- and Staatsarchiv in Vienna. I am very grateful to them all for their hard work and kind assistance.

Certain parts of the book have been presented as lectures at Reed College, Young Israel Synagogue of St Louis, Brandeis University, Harvard University, the AJS Annual Conference, the Sixteenth Century Conference, and two international conferences: Jewish Responses to Early Modern Science: Jewish Treatments of Science from *De revolutionibus* to the *Principia* and Beyond, held at Tel Aviv University and the Van Leer Institute in Jerusalem, and Gezerot Taḥ-Tat: European Jewry in 1648–49: Contexts and Consequences, held at Bar Ilan University. I thank the members of the audience in each of those places for their suggestions and criticisms.

I have also received help and support from Israel Bartal, Dean Bell, Philip Benedict, Robert Bireley, Stephen Burnett, Yisrael Dubitsky, Noah Efron, Edward Fram, Christopher Friedrichs, Gilad Gevaryahu, David Weiss Halivni, Gershon Hundert, Ephraim Kanarfogel, David Malkiel, Adam Mintz, Aryeh Motzkin, Elhanan Reiner, Moshe Rosman, David Ruderman, Marc Saperstein, Jacob J. Schacter, Hayyim Sheynin, Stephanie Siegmund, Joaneath Spicer, John Spielman, Frank Sysyn, Elliot Wolfson, and Kristen Zapalac. I thank all of these scholars wholeheartedly. Many members of my family, including my children Leon and Miranda, have helped me with this book in innumerable ways. A number of people read drafts and gave useful suggestions, criticisms, and encouragement. I am very grateful to the staff of the Littman Library of Jewish Civilization for their encouragement and for their patient and careful work in the editing and production of this book. Others whom I have forgotten to list will (I hope) forgive my poor memory and know that their help, as well as that of all those whom I have mentioned, has been very precious to me. Any errors in the book are of course my own.

An earlier version of Chapter 9 appeared as a separate article: 'Ashkenazic Rationalism and Midrashic Natural History: Responses to the New Science in the

Works of Rabbi Yom Tov Lipmann Heller (1578–1654)'.[2] I thank the editors and publishers for their permission to use the material again here.

My parents have encouraged me in this work over a long period and in many ways. I am very grateful to them.

Without the help and support of my wife Susan, no part of this work would have been possible, and it is dedicated to her.

[2] *Science in Context*, 10 (1997), 605–26.

Contents

List of Abbreviations xiii

Note on Transliteration and Place Names xiv

Map: The World of Yom-Tov Lipmann Heller xvi–xvii

INTRODUCTION 1

A Rabbinic Life 1

The Six Pillars 4

Philosophy and Mysticism in Ashkenazi Culture 5

Social Rabbis 7

The Politics of Seventeenth-Century Jews 9

Persecutions and Plagues 11

Satan in Goray 13

PART I

THE LADDER OF ASCENSION

1578–1617

1. The Orphan 19

The Orphan 19

Wallerstein, 1578 20

Marriage into a Prominent Family 23

The Maharal of Prague 26

The New Curriculum 31

The Examination of the World 35

2. The Exile of a Philosopher 39

The Flowering of Philosophical Study among Ashkenazi Jews 39

Joseph ben Isaac Halevi and *Givat hamoreh* 44

'A Dwarf on the Shoulders of a Giant' 45

The Plague of 1611 47
The Exile of a Philosopher 48

3. Two Kabbalists 51
Isaiah Horowitz and the 'Repudiation of Philosophy' 51
Heller as Kabbalist 54
On Magic, *Magidim*, and the Individual Self 56
On Esotericism, Non-Kabbalistic Judaism, and the Purposes of Prayer 59
In Defence of Philosophy 63

4. *Tosafot yom tov* 66
The Maharal and the Revival of the Mishnah 66
On Rashi, Tosafot, and the Seventy Faces of Torah 70
The Exegetical Experience 79
Letter to Worms, 1616 82

5. Jews and Non-Jews 83
The Nikolsburg Wine Controversy of 1616 83
On Non-Jewish Bread and Non-Jewish Books 87
Humanizing the Non-Jews 92
Against Trinitarianism, 1619 96
On Unity 97

PART II
THE TRIAL
1618–1630

6. Prague in Wartime 101
The Defenestration of Prague, 1618 101
Letter to Vienna, 1619 101
Fears 104
Prague, 1620: Habsburg Loyalist 106
On Providence and Miracles 109
Jacob Bassevi 112
The Plague of 1625 113

7. The Chief Rabbi 117

'Who are the Kings? The Rabbis.' 117
Rabbinical Activism and Educational Reform 119
'Delights of the King' 121
Against the *Shulḥan arukh* 122
On Humility 126
Interpretations and Decisions 127
The Constitutions of the Jews 129
The Title Page 131
Letter to Frankfurt, 1628 132

8. The Trial 136

The Arrest 136
In the Prison of Vienna 138
Deliverance 142
Explanations 146
On Politics 152
Again on Non-Jews 153
A Day of Remembrance 155

PART III
CHANGE AND DEFEAT
1631–1654

9. The Sermon 159

From Prague to Poland 159
'The Lessening of the Moon' 161
Midrashic Natural History 164
On the New Astronomy 166
On Change 168
The Maharal and the Illusion of Self 171
The Acceptance of Suffering 172

10. Attacks and Retreats 175

To the Edge of Europe 175
Again on the *Shulḥan arukh* 178

On Honour 181
The Ban on the Purchase of Rabbinical Office 183
The Permission to Publish Kabbalah 189

11. A Rabbi's Autobiography 192
The Coronation, 1644 192
Deliverance Narrative and Autobiography 193
On Silence 197
Family 199
On Himself 201

12. The Massacres of 1648 205
The Twentieth Day of Sivan 205
Fasting and Silence 206
Two Kinds of Messianism 209
Demonizing the Cossacks 211
The Absence of the King 213
'You have become a plague' 219
Letter to Chęciny, 1651 220

Yom-Tov Lipmann Heller's Extant Works and Writings 225
Bibliography 232
Index of Personal Names 275
Index of References to Yom-Tov Lipmann Heller 282
Index of Subjects 287

Abbreviations

EJ	*Encyclopaedia Judaica* (Jerusalem, 1971–2)
Hailperin MS	Israel Hailperin, 'Rabbi Yom Tov Lipmann Heller (Tosafot Yom Tov): A Monograph with Sources, Tables, and Illustrations' [Rabi yom-tov lipman heler (tosafot yom tov): monografiyah betseruf mekorot, tabelot, vetsiyurim], manuscript, Dinur Institute, Jerusalem, *c.*1932
HHStA	Haus-, Hof- und Staatsarchiv (Vienna)
HUCA	*Hebrew Union College Annual*
JNUL	Jerusalem National University Library
JTS	Jewish Theological Seminary, New York
ŽMP	Židovské Muzeum Praha (Jewish Museum of Prague)

Heller's Works

MalYT	*Malbushei yom tov*
MYT	*Ma'adanei yom tov*
(*DH*)	*Divrei ḥamudot*
(*MM*)	*Ma'adanei melekh*
(*PH*)	*Pilpula ḥarifta*
TosYT	*Tosafot yom tov*

Note on Transliteration and Place Names

Transliteration

The transliteration of Hebrew in this book reflects consideration of the type of book it is, in terms of its content, purpose, and readership. The system adopted therefore reflects a broad approach to transcription, rather than the narrower approaches found in the *Encyclopaedia Judaica* or other systems developed for text-based or linguistic studies. The aim has been to reflect the pronunciation prescribed for modern Hebrew, rather than the spelling or Hebrew word structure, and to do so using conventions that are generally familiar to the English-speaking Jewish reader.

In accordance with this approach, no attempt is made to indicate the distinctions between *alef* and *ayin*, *tet* and *taf*, *kaf* and *kuf*, *sin* and *samekh*, since these are not relevant to pronunciation; likewise, the *dagesh* is not indicated except where it affects pronunciation. Following the principle of using conventions familiar to the majority of readers, however, transcriptions that are well established have been retained even when they are not fully consistent with the transliteration system adopted. On similar grounds, the *tsadi* is rendered by 'tz' in such familiar words as barmitzvah, mitzvot, and so on. Likewise, the distinction between *ḥet* and *khaf* has been retained, using *ḥ* for the former and *kh* for the latter; the associated forms are generally familiar to readers, even if the distinction is not actually borne out in pronunciation, and for the same reason the final *heh* is indicated too. As in Hebrew, no capital letters are used, except that an initial capital has been retained in transliterating titles of published works (for example, *Shulḥan arukh*).

Since no distinction is made between *alef* and *ayin*, they are indicated by an apostrophe only in intervocalic positions where a failure to do so could lead an English-speaking reader to pronounce the vowel-cluster as a diphthong—as, for example, in *ha'ir*—or otherwise mispronounce the word.

The *sheva na* is indicated by an *e*—*perikat ol*, *reshut*—except, again, when established convention dictates otherwise.

The *yod* is represented by *i* when it occurs as a vowel (*bereshit*), by *y* when it occurs as a consonant (*yesodot*), and by *yi* when it occurs as both (*yisra'el*).

Names have generally been left in their familiar forms, even when this is inconsistent with the overall system.

Place Names

Place names are something of a minefield in a book of this sort. The names that were used by Jews living in Yom-Tov Lipmann Heller's time are often not those that contemporary English-speakers would recognize; moreover, names that the latter would recognize (or that are used in the *Encyclopedia Judaica* or other reference works in Jewish studies) are not always those that are in use today. Inevitably, then, the decision about which names to use has not been easy. Where English forms are in common usage, these have been used in preference to native forms. In some instances (for example, Nikolsburg/Mikulov), Germanic names that are perhaps more familiar to readers have been used for places that now use a Slavic name. In other cases (for example, Tulczyn/Tulchin) Polish spelling has been used for places that are now in the Ukraine. The city in Volhynia (now in the Ukraine) that Jews called Ludmir or Lodmir (Volodymir/Włodomierz Wolinski/Vladimir Volinski) has been called by its Jewish name. I trust that the map on pages xviii–xix and the cross-referencing provided in the index will help solve any outstanding problems.

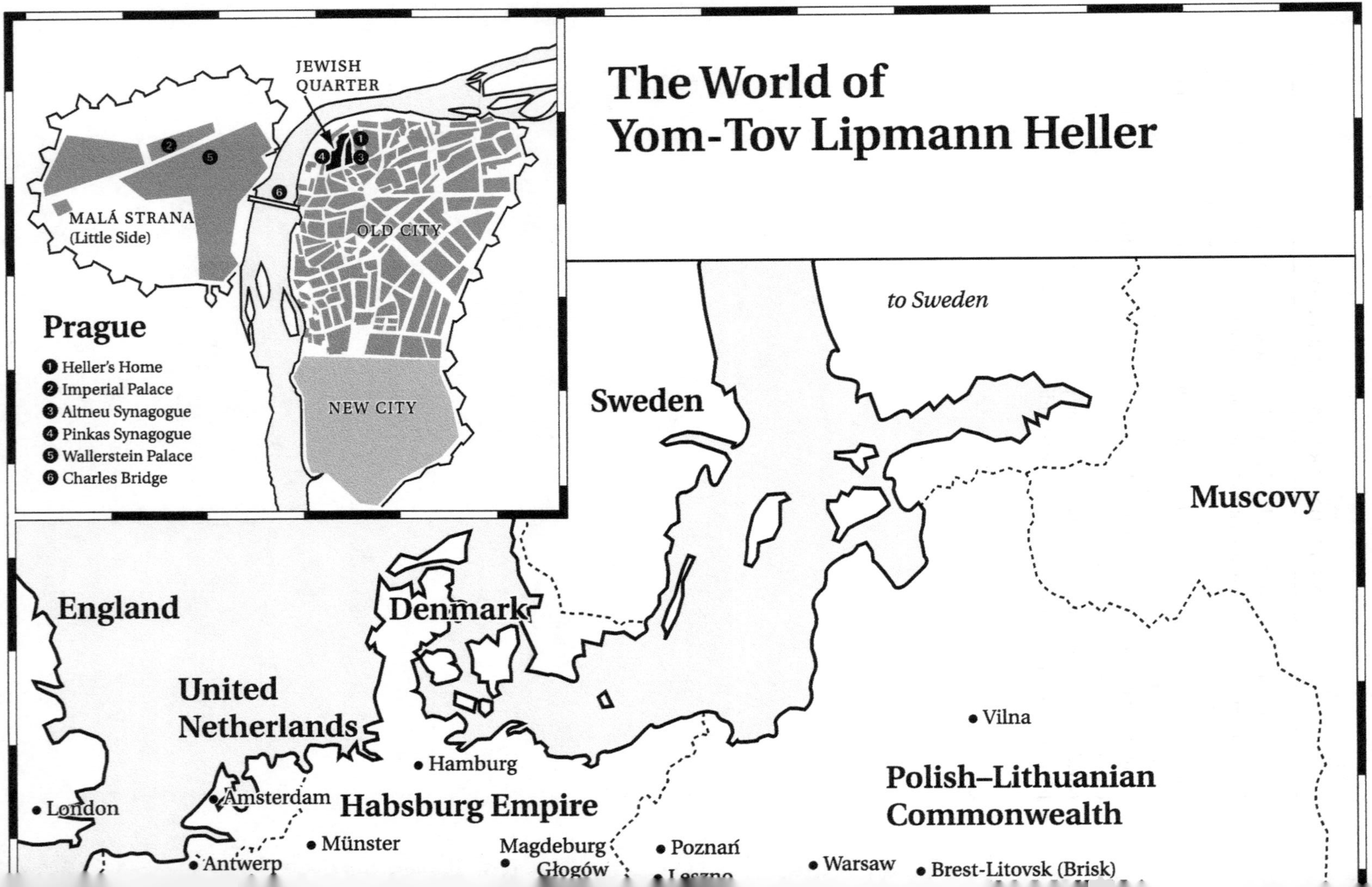
The World of
Yom-Tov Lipmann Heller
Prague
1 Heller's Home
2 Imperial Palace
3 Altneu Synagogue
4 Pinkas Synagogue
5 Wallerstein Palace
6 Charles Bridge
JEWISH QUARTER
MALÁ STRANA
(Little Side)
OLD CITY
NEW CITY
to Sweden
Sweden
Muscovy
England
Denmark
United
Netherlands
Habsburg Empire
Polish–Lithuanian
Commonwealth
Vilna
Hamburg
London
Amsterdam
Münster
Antwerp
Magdeburg
Głogów
Poznań
Warsaw
Brest-Litovsk (Brisk)

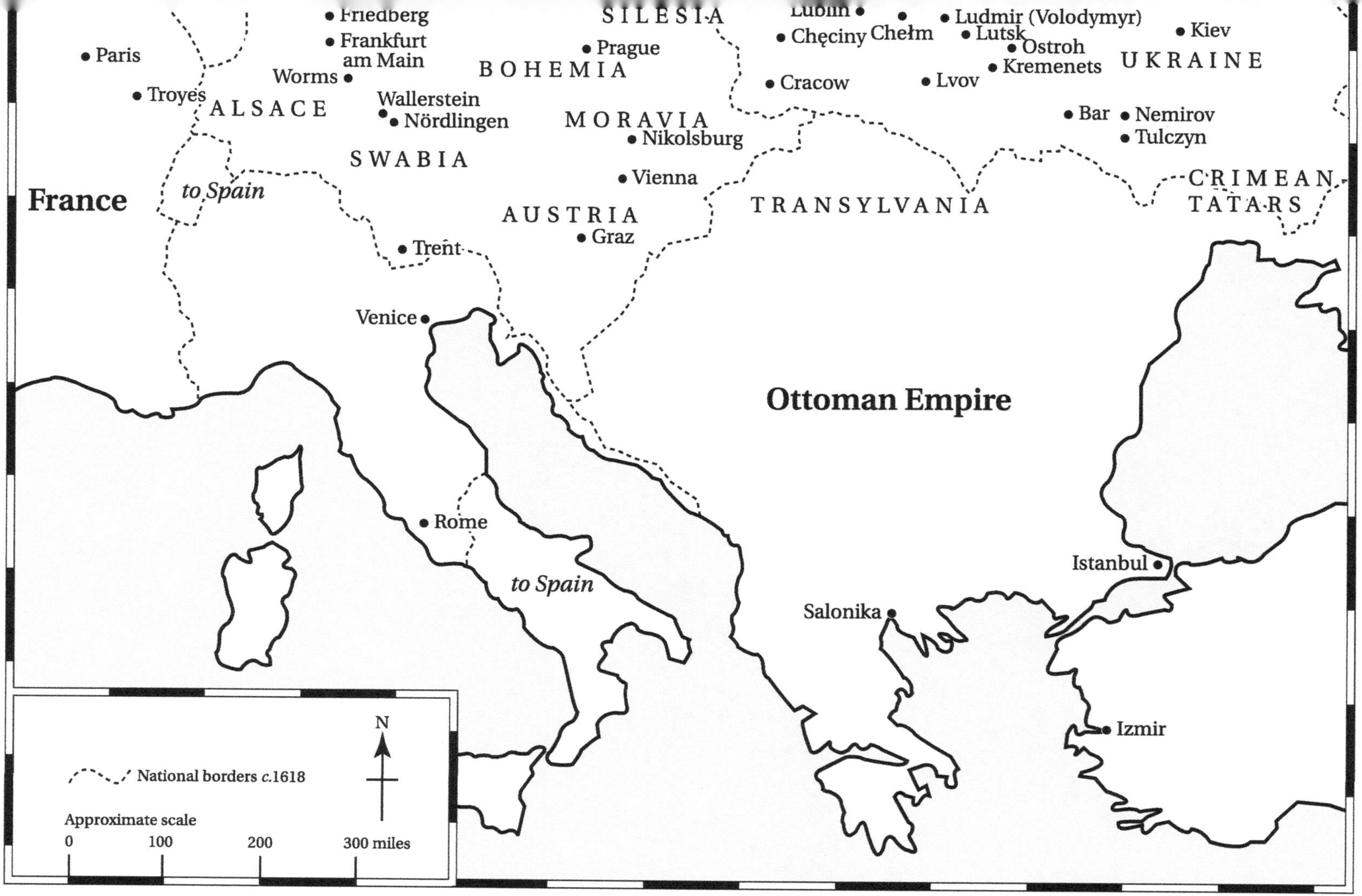
Friedberg
Frankfurt am Main
Worms
Paris
Troyes
ALSACE
Wallerstein
Nördlingen
SWABIA
France
to Spain
SILESIA
Prague
BOHEMIA
MORAVIA
Nikolsburg
Vienna
AUSTRIA
Graz
Trent
Venice
Rome
to Spain
Lublin
Chęciny
Chełm
Cracow
Ludmir (Volodymyr)
Lutsk
Ostroh
Kremenets
Lvov
Kiev
UKRAINE
Bar
Nemirov
Tulczyn
TRANSYLVANIA
CRIMEAN TATARS
Ottoman Empire
Istanbul
Salonika
Izmir
N
National borders c.1618
Approximate scale
0
100
200
300 miles

Introduction

A RABBINIC LIFE

IN MAY 1998 I stood at the grave of Rabbi Yom-Tov Lipmann Heller in the old Jewish cemetery of Cracow. I walked through the cemetery and the long grass, and viewed the many gravestones of the sixteenth and seventeenth centuries. I reflected in my solitude that these stones bear witness to their owners' wishes to be remembered and to be recognized as individuals. Earlier centuries of Jews had been content with more modest grave markers. Not so these men and women, whose names were chiselled on large, fine stones by artist masons. Do not forget us, the gravestones seem to say, and do not think that we were all the same.

It is difficult now at the distance of four centuries to grasp these men and women in their individuality. Almost none left any record of their thoughts or of their lives, save these silent stones.

Heller is an exception. More than anyone else buried in that cemetery, Heller left ample records of himself, a sequence of published and manuscript writings spread over fifty years: books, letters, archival documents, responsa, poems, prayers, sermons, commentaries, and even a memoir.

The present work aims to portray Heller in his individuality and in detail: to narrate his life, to place him in the context of his time, and to see his vision of Judaism, of the world around him, and of the events through which he lived.

Rabbinic biography is one of the oldest projects of modern Jewish historical writing; a call for rabbinic biography was issued in 1783, in the initial prospectus for *Hame'asef*, the first journal of the Jewish Enlightenment.[1] Many great Jewish historians, as well as many lesser ones, have answered the call of the Enlighteners. My grandfather, Louis Finkelstein, and several of my teachers, including the late Isadore Twersky, were authors of important rabbinic biographies. I come to the project by inheritance, so to speak, as well as predilection.

A rabbinical biography should not be merely a summary of a few talmudic decisions supplemented by a small assortment of biographical facts. It must present a

[1] Euchel and Breslau, 'Stream'; cf. Schechter, 'Leopold Zunz', 95.

balanced and rounded view of the subject's life, placing him in the context of a time, a place, and a community. It should follow the subject's development from youth to age, presenting his ambitions and his failures as well as his accomplishments. It should seek to explain the motives of his major decisions—his unconscious motives, if possible, as well as his conscious justifications. It should attempt to see the events of the subject's life from his own point of view, as well as from the author's. The lives of most of the great rabbis of the past, on account of the limitations of the existing records, cannot be written in such an extensive and satisfactory way, but Heller's, as I have suggested, can be, and that has been my aim.

This work has three parts. Part I covers the years 1578 to 1618: Heller's youth as an orphan in the village of Wallerstein in Germany, his move to the city of Prague, his marriage into the Horowitz family, his education, and his early writings. Its title, 'The Ladder of Ascension', is a medieval metaphor for education used by Mordechai Jaffe, one of the rabbis of Prague during Heller's early years.

In Prague, Heller was a part of the brilliant circle of scholars gathered around Judah Loew ben Bezalel, known as the Maharal of Prague (*c.*1525–1609). Like the Maharal, Heller was a rabbinic aristocrat. He came from a distinguished family, and was proud of his lineage. He opposed two efforts at the popularization of Judaism that were being pursued in this period: the popularization of Jewish law in the *Shulḥan arukh*, the monumental code of Jewish law written by Joseph Caro (1488–1575), and the popularization of kabbalah.

Many of Heller's views, including his activist conception of the rabbinate, were based on those of the Maharal. Yet his relation to the Maharal was ambivalent—he did not refer to him as 'my teacher' until the 1640s. Heller had studied with several other teachers, including the Jewish philosopher Joseph ben Isaac Halevi. Heller followed the Maharal in championing the study of the Mishnah, the ancient code of Jewish law, and his *magnum opus*, *Tosafot yom tov*, was a Mishnah commentary. Yet whereas the Maharal had favoured the Talmud commentary of Rashi (1040–1105), Heller emulated that of the Tosafists (twelfth–thirteenth centuries). Furthermore, he opposed the Maharal on several topics, among them his view of non-Jews.

Part II, 'The Trial', focuses on politics between 1618 and 1630. The Thirty Years War began in 1618 and cast its shadow over these years. In this period Heller began to take a leading role in Jewish communal life, becoming chief rabbi of Prague in 1627. His second major work, *Ma'adanei melekh* (Delights of the King), was intended as a response to the *Shulḥan arukh*.

Heller's new role drew him into bitter conflicts. In 1629 he was accused of partiality towards the rich in the distribution of taxes within the Prague Jewish community. A few weeks afterwards, he was arrested by order of the emperor, imprisoned in Vienna, and tried for blaspheming Christianity. He was released from prison only after an enormous fine had been imposed on him, and was deposed from the position of rabbi of Prague.

Part III, 'Change and Defeat', covers Heller's years in the Ukraine and Poland from 1631 to 1654. Several of his views changed during this period. He became convinced of the truth of some aspects of the 'new astronomy' of Tycho Brahe. His social attitudes changed, and he came to accept the authority of the *Shulḥan arukh* (abandoning his work on *Ma'adanei melekh*) and the popularization of kabbalah. His 1645 memoir gives evidence of his changing attitude towards his family. His effort in 1640 to ban the purchase of rabbinical office in Poland involved him once again in communal conflict. The biography ends with the massacres of 1648, Heller's responses to them, his last years, and his death in poverty.

Various interrelated threads weave throughout the work. The first is Heller's commitment to the medieval tradition of Jewish rationalism. From his first extant work, a commentary on a medieval Hebrew philosophical poem, until his last writings, his study of Jewish philosophy shaped his thinking on a wide variety of issues: his thoughts on the nature of Jews and non-Jews, his attitude to education, and his views on messianism, prayer, divine providence, miracles, and politics, among other topics. Heller was a talmudist and also a student of kabbalah, yet he followed those talmudists and kabbalists who had combined those fields of study with appreciation for Jewish philosophy.

I shall contrast Heller's views to those of his kinsman, Isaiah Horowitz (*c.*1565–1626), who rejected the study of Jewish philosophy.[2] Horowitz also supported the popularization of kabbalah and the acceptance of the *Shulḥan arukh*, positions that Heller adopted later and more hesitantly. Both Heller and Horowitz could point to distinguished predecessors within the sixteenth-century Ashkenazi rabbinate, but it was Horowitz, not Heller, who pointed the way towards Ashkenazi culture of the late seventeenth and eighteenth centuries.

Another theme running through the work is Heller's perception of the changing world around him. He was an eyewitness to one of the major events of European history, the beginning of the Thirty Years War in Prague in 1618. Moreover, he wrote a memoir, mainly an account of his 1629 trial, while his two extant sermons also reflect on events in his life. He felt that he and those around him had experienced various miraculous deliverances (from expulsion in 1618, from the war in 1620, from plague in 1625, and from prison in 1629). Although he was aware of the natural (or political) causes of these events, he felt that they must be given expression in rituals of thanksgiving, and (as we shall see) he established an annual family celebration that is observed by his descendants to this day.

[2] At certain points, Heller's views will also be contrasted to those of Isaiah Horowitz's son, Shabetai Horowitz.

A final thread traces the roots of Heller's responses to the massacres of 1648. By this time, he was 70 years old, and had lived through plagues, wars, and the death of several of his children. For many years he had wrestled with questions such as the nature of divine reward and punishment, the differences between Jews and non-Jews, the meaning of suffering, and the meaning of silence. This biography traces Heller's sometimes changing views on all of these questions. His writings and actions after 1648 were in one way a culmination of all of his earlier thought. His last major written work, on the other hand, a liturgical poem commemorating the massacres of 1648–9, may also be seen as a spiritual defeat, in which his hard-won spiritual insight departed from him in his rage and despair.

THE SIX PILLARS

One might say schematically that historical writing concerning early modern Ashkenazi Jews has moved through five stages. The first stage was traditional; the second was born of the Jewish Enlightenment, the Haskalah; the third was socialist and the fourth, Zionist; the fifth stage, which is the present one, is integrationist and academic.

The piety of seventeenth-century Ashkenazi Jews has been praised many times, but never so memorably as by Nathan Neta Hannover (d. 1683). In the last section of his chronicle of the massacres of 1648, *Yeven metsulah*, written in 1653, Hannover described the institutions of the Polish Jewish community—schools, synagogues and prayer societies, communal charity funds, and rabbinical courts. He presented them as expressions of the most fundamental values of Jewish life, the 'six pillars': Torah study, prayer, charity, justice, truth, and peace. Hannover depicted the Polish rabbinate, and specifically Heller's generation of rabbis, the generation of 1648, as men great in Torah who had exemplified the pious ideals of Judaism.[3]

Hannover borrowed the motif of the 'six pillars' from a leading rabbi of the generation before Heller's, Ephraim of Luntshits (Łęczyca, d. 1619). Ephraim of Luntshits was a preacher rather than a chronicler, but his sermons also give a portrait of Ashkenazi Jewish society in his time. This portrait is different in one crucial aspect from Hannover's: Ephraim emphasized the moral deficiencies of the Jews of his day, not excluding the rabbinate. For him, the 'six pillars' represented ideals that Jewish society had failed to reach. He denounced the neglect of Torah and prayer, the mistreatment of the poor by the rich, the injustice of rabbinical courts, and the restless search for prestige.[4] Early modern Ashkenazi Jews were not angels,

[3] Hannover, *Yeven metsulah*, 82–92.

[4] See Ephraim of Luntshits, *Amudei shesh*; H. H. Ben-Sasson, 'Wealth and Poverty', *passim*.

and most were not saints. Some hounded debtors; others slept with servants.[5] Charges of partiality towards the wealthy were not unknown in rabbinical debates of the period.[6]

We should not blind ourselves to Heller's flaws. His support for the institution of the debtors' prison, for instance, surely engendered criticism in his own day and not only in ours.[7] Heller faced bitter opposition throughout the latter part of his life, but we should not jump to the conclusion that his opponents were all villains and men of bad character. At the same time, we must recognize, as Hannover suggested, that the realities of piety shaped medieval Jewish culture and formed the matrix of Heller's life. Heller wrote prayers and contributed to the theory of Jewish prayer. There are testimonies to his (and to his wife's) generosity.[8] Nor can his Torah scholarship be ignored: his Talmud commentary *Ma'adanei melekh* and his Mishnah commentary *Tosafot yom tov* brought him fame and prestige in his life and in later generations.

PHILOSOPHY AND MYSTICISM IN ASHKENAZI CULTURE

In his justly famous multi-volume *History of the Jews*, the great Jewish historian Heinrich Graetz (1817–91) gave a view of the Polish rabbinate that was very different from that of either Hannover or Ephraim of Luntshits. Graetz's history is one of the masterworks of the final period of the Haskalah. It is structured around a number of polarities. Among them are the contrasts of *peshat* (clear and straightforward interpretation) and *pilpul* (complex and far-fetched interpretation), and of philosophy and mysticism. Graetz associated *peshat* and philosophy with Sefardi (Spanish) Judaism, and *pilpul* and mysticism with Ashkenazi, especially Polish, Judaism.[9] He found the piety of Polish rabbis oppressive and their faith superstitious.

There were exceptions, however, to the bleak picture that Graetz drew of Ashkenazi Judaism before Moses Mendelssohn, and one of these was Heller,[10] who embodied, for Graetz, some of the virtues of the Haskalah. He had, for instance, favoured the study of geometry and astronomy. Furthermore, he had opposed those elements of Jewish life that Graetz found most objectionable, namely kabbalah, *pilpul* (so Graetz mistakenly thought), and the *Shulḥan arukh*. The fact

[5] On treatment of debtors, see Fram, *Ideals Face Reality*, 156 ff. On female servants and wet-nurses, see e.g. the precautions ordered by the Va'ad of Lithuania in 1637, in Cygielman (ed.), *Jews of Poland and Lithuania*, 598 (no. 326), from Dubnow (ed.), *Pinkas hamedinah*, 69; cf. the Cracow rule in Cygielman, p. 489. See also Shohat, *Changing Times*, 166–8; E. Horowitz, 'Masters and Servant-Girls', 193–211.

[6] See Zimmer, *Embers of the Sages*, 48, 68, 171.

[7] *MYT (PH) BM* ch. 5 (p. 270), no. 2, discussed in Fram, *Ideals Face Reality*, 156 n. 47.

[8] See below, p. 24, Ch. 12 n. 65.

[9] Cf. Schorsch, 'Myth of Sephardic Supremacy'.

[10] Graetz, *Geschichte der Juden*, x. 39–40 [= *History of the Jews*, iv. 703–4].

that Heller was born in the land of Mendelssohn and Lessing may also have counted in his favour.

Graetz's attack on Polish Judaism was quickly challenged. In his Hebrew translation of Graetz's *History*, Saul Pinhas Rabbinowitz (1845–1910), a Lithuanian Jew and a major Jewish historian in his own right, supplemented Graetz's chapters on Polish Jews with extensive notes in which he debated the portrait that Graetz had drawn. Rabbinowitz shared Graetz's faith in the values of the Haskalah, but claimed that Graetz's preference for German Judaism was mere chauvinism.

Rabbinowitz claimed specifically that Heller was not very different from many other members of the seventeenth-century Polish rabbinate: others too opposed *pilpul*, opposed the spread of kabbalah, and proposed a complex and rationalized Judaism influenced by philosophical teachings.[11]

At about the same time, Graetz's assumption that kabbalah and philosophy are eternal enemies came under attack from another east European Jewish scholar, Samuel Horodetsky (1871–1957). He showed that, among Askhenazi Jews in Heller's time, outright opposition to kabbalah was extremely rare, and that many Jewish thinkers combined kabbalah and Jewish philosophy.[12] Heller himself opposed the popularization of kabbalah, but he did not oppose kabbalah itself; he too joined kabbalah, perhaps uneasily, to Maimonidean rationalism.

The debate between Graetz and Rabbinowitz has continued with variations among later generations of scholars. It was echoed in the 1950s in a debate between two leading Israeli historians, Jacob Katz and Haim Hillel Ben-Sasson.[13] Katz and Ben-Sasson linked the question of Ashkenazi attitudes towards rationalism and Jewish philosophy with the question of attitudes towards non-Jews. Echoing Graetz, Katz argued that Ashkenazi rabbis in the early modern period were isolated (or rather, successfully insulated themselves) from non-Jews, from non-Jewish culture, and from Jewish philosophy. Echoing Rabbinowitz, Ben-Sasson argued that they were involved, occasionally polemically, with non-Jewish culture and with rationalist thought.

In 1972 Ephraim Kupfer, supporting Ben-Sasson's claim, documented a circle of students of Jewish philosophy centred in Prague in the late fourteenth century.[14] Significant shifts took place in Ashkenazi culture between the thirteenth

[11] See Graetz, *Divrei yemei yisra'el*, viii. 91–3, 119–24, 157–9. Rabbinowitz's reference to Heller is on p. 159. Note also Rabbinowitz's study of Abraham Horowitz, *Traces of Free-Thinking*.

[12] See particularly Horodetsky's sketches of Isserles, Jaffe, Edels, and others, collected in id., *History of the Rabbinate*. Like Graetz, Gershom Scholem, whose career began after Horodetsky's, tended to emphasize those kabbalists who were furthest from philosophy; other scholars, such as Alexander Altmann and recently Moshe Idel, have tried to redress that balance.

[13] H. H. Ben-Sasson, 'Concepts and Reality'; J. Katz, 'On Halakhah and *Derush*'; H. H. Ben-Sasson, 'Response'. The debate has been reviewed by David B. Ruderman, in his *Jewish Thought and Scientific Discovery*, 60–87.

[14] Kupfer, 'Cultural Image'.

and the sixteenth centuries. Maimonides' thirteen dogmatic principles came to define the content of Jewish belief, allegorical interpretation of Scripture was hesitantly accepted, and the 1232 ban on Maimonides' *Moreh nevukhim* (Guide of the Perplexed) was forgotten or at least allowed quietly to lapse.[15]

One may continue to debate the centrality or marginality of rationalist trends within the early modern Ashkenazi rabbinate (although I certainly agree with Ben-Sasson, Jacob Elbaum, and others who have stressed its centrality), but one can no longer deny the existence of such trends. In the wake of Kupfer's article has come a series of studies showing the wide impact of the Maimonidean tradition within Ashkenazi rabbinic culture in the later sixteenth century and on into the first decades of the seventeenth.[16] At least within the Ashkenazi rabbinic elite, from about 1550 until about 1650, a basic grounding in Jewish philosophy was the rule rather than the exception. It has been clearly demonstrated in an extensive scholarly literature that, as Rabbinowitz claimed, Heller did not stand alone. Heller was a member—one of the last members—of a century-long intellectual movement that included major rabbis throughout central and eastern Europe.

SOCIAL RABBIS

In the small library of the Prague Jewish Museum I sat and studied the 'Book of Seats' of the Pinkas Shul, Heller's synagogue for many years. It is an enormous volume, with one page for each seat in the synagogue, recording its ownership through the seventeenth and eighteenth centuries. Heller's seat is recorded there: he sat at the front of the synagogue, next to the Holy Ark. His father-in-law, Moses Aaron Ashkenazi, a wealthy merchant and a leader of the community, sat next to him. The poor sat at the back of the synagogue. A detailed social hierarchy, with Heller and his father-in-law at its head, was re-enacted in the synagogue at each prayer service.[17] No understanding of Heller will be complete that does not take into account his sense of social status and of honour. Heller struggled for prestige within the rabbinate; he toiled to find elite families into which to marry his children, and when not accorded the deference to which he felt entitled, he struggled to control his anger.

[15] J. Davis, 'Philosophy, Dogma, and Exegesis'.

[16] Chava Fraenkel-Goldschmidt's 1970 edn. of Josel (Joseph) b. Gershon of Rosheim, *Sefer hamiknah* actually preceded Kupfer's article. See also the literature surveyed in Ruderman, *Jewish Thought and Scientific Discovery*, particularly Kaplan, 'Rationalism and Rabbinic Culture'; Elbaum, *Openness and Insularity*; the articles by Fishman, Efron, Reiner, and Davis in vol. 10 (1997) of *Science in Context*; and Davis, '"Ten Questions"'.

[17] The seating plan of the Pinkas Shul is recorded in its *Pinkas hamekomot*. Cf. Volavková, *The Pinkas Synagogue*, 74–5. On hierarchies in the seating plans of early modern synagogues, see Bonfil, *Rabbis*, 169–70.

What was the position of the rabbinate within Jewish society of the seventeenth century? In the early years of the twentieth century, and especially after the First World War, a new set of questions and a new set of values began to influence the historiography of early modern Ashkenazi Jews. The questions were those of social history and the values those of socialism.[18] Jewish socialists had often assumed that the rabbinate had always been aligned with the wealthiest class. Israel Hailperin's unpublished biography of Heller, written in 1932, was intended to counter that assumption. The biography reveals a historian who was uninterested in Heller's intellectual life but fascinated by his place within society. Hailperin celebrated Heller's work as a social reformer, especially his effort in 1640 to have a *ḥerem*, a rabbinical ban, decreed against anyone who purchased rabbinical office from Polish noblemen—a bold attempt to curb the excesses of the wealthy, in Hailperin's eyes.

In the 1950s Haim Hillel Ben-Sasson, a student of Hailperin, continued his work. Ben-Sasson showed that the Ashkenazi rabbinate in the sixteenth and early seventeenth centuries was divided in its attitude towards wealth. While some rabbis regarded wealth as a sign of divine favour, others, such as Ephraim of Luntshits, opposed and even denounced the wealthy. The tension within the Jewish community between the rabbinate and lay leaders, Ben-Sasson suggested, was not merely personal but systemic. The claims to leadership of rabbis such as Heller were opposed in crucial ways to the claims of powerful Jewish laymen.[19]

Elhanan Reiner has recently offered a counter-argument of exceptional analytic power, suggesting that, within early modern Judaism, we must distinguish not simply two classes (rich and poor), but four: an aristocracy of old rabbinical-mercantile families; a class of secondary religious functionaries, such as preachers, cantors, scribes, and beadles; a class of *nouveaux riches*, and, finally, the poor.

The major conflicts in the Ashkenazi communities of the sixteenth and seventeenth centuries, Reiner argues, were not between rich and poor, but between the old aristocracy and an alliance of the secondary religious elite and the *nouveaux riches*. The old aristocracy, he claims, monopolized the upper ranks of talmudic learning: they were the heads of yeshivas and the chief rabbis of the communities. In order to balance that superior talmudism, the secondary elite cultivated kabbalah and popularized it through preaching. The aristocracy opposed such popularization and cultivated Jewish philosophy as a counterweight.[20]

Similarly, the rabbinical aristocracy opposed the spread of the *Shulḥan arukh*, fearing that its authority would undermine theirs; they insisted on high qualifications for the rabbinate because only they possessed those qualifications, and on control of rabbinical appointments by the *kehilah* because they controlled the

[18] See P. Friedman, 'Polish Jewish Historiography'.

[19] H. H. Ben-Sasson, *Theory and Practice*.

[20] Reiner, 'Changes'.

kehilot. Indeed, the development during the late Middle Ages of the new rabbinate, appointed and salaried by the *kehilah*, is intimately associated with the social polarization of the Ashkenazi Jewish communities.

The Maharal is one of Reiner's premier examples of a rabbinic aristocrat. Heller, the Maharal's disciple, a *kehilah* rabbi who led the attack on the purchase of rabbinical positions, who opposed the *Shulḥan arukh* and the popularization of kabbalah, and who favoured the study of Jewish philosophy, seems to be another perfect embodiment of Reiner's rabbinical elite.

In Prague, Heller lived within the ambit of the extended family into which he had married, one of the most powerful Jewish clans in the city, the Horowitz family. The Pinkas Shul itself was the private synagogue of the Horowitzes. Even when Heller had become the chief rabbi, he was still, in the eyes of many Prague Jews, 'the son-in-law of the distinguished Rabbi Moses Aaron Ashkenazi'.

To this picture of Heller as a rabbinic aristocrat we must, however, add another dimension, that of change over time.

In a passage that Heller wrote in the 1630s after his move to Poland, he discussed, in a certain halakhic context, the question of which Jews deserve 'honour'. In the passage, Heller divided Jewish society into five groups: (1) the deserving poor; (2) the undeserving poor; (3) the sinful wealthy; (4) the pious wealthy, and (5) pious poor folk of good descent. Heller's first four categories correspond roughly to Reiner's four categories, although Heller used a language of 'sin' and 'virtue' that modern historians reject. Heller's fifth category is more complicated: pious poor Jews *of distinguished lineage*.

Living in Poland, without the support of a wealthy father-in-law, after having been forced to pay an enormous fine and to leave Prague, Heller discovered the difference between clan and class. One could suggest that Heller insisted on the honour due to the poor who had distinguished lineage because he now identified with that group. This would tally with reports that he died penniless.

Heller shifted some of his views accordingly. In these same years, after he left Prague, he dropped his objections to the *Shulḥan arukh*, and shortly afterwards much of his objection to the popularization of kabbalah. Heller's preaching of the acceptance of misfortune was more sincere, and his continued search for honour more poignant, than might otherwise appear.

THE POLITICS OF SEVENTEENTH-CENTURY JEWS

In Vienna, reading documents in the archives of the Habsburg emperors, I encountered another kind of seventeenth-century Jew: Heller's cousin Abraham Fränklin. Fränklin was a banker and a court Jew in Vienna and Prague. He knew how to manipulate Jewish law to his purposes, but he was also at home among the laws and bureaucracies that governed the Habsburg empire. He was, in a word, a political Jew.

Much of modern historical writing is associated, in one way or another, with the values of nationalism, and much of modern Jewish historiography with Zionism. Just as socialism focused the attention of Jewish historians on questions of Jewish social history, so Zionism focused their attention on questions of Jewish politics.

The Zionist view of early modern Ashkenazi Judaism, however, has always been ambivalent. While Zionist historiography celebrated the institutions of Jewish autonomy in the Middle Ages, including the *kehilah* and the rabbinate, Zionism regards the entire Diaspora period as a dark one in which Jews were deprived of power.[21] Accordingly Yom-Tov Lipmann Heller is acclaimed as a leader of the powerful Council of the Four Lands, but his role in framing the Jewish response to the massacres of 1648 makes him a symbol of Jewish powerlessness.

Several forces acted in the seventeenth century to distance the rabbinate from politics. Indeed, Heller's view of halakhah, stressing the autonomy of the rabbinate within its limited sphere, may be seen as tending to that direction. His essential stance was to support the *kehilah* as the governing body; the thought of communal dissension, *maḥloket*, horrified him.

Yet Heller was by no means permitted to remain outside politics and political conflict, even had he wished to. As rabbi of Prague he attempted to extend his jurisdiction over lesser Jewish communities, and even over the major Jewish community of Frankfurt. Furthermore, he was involved in that most political of questions, tax assessment, and was implicated in 1629 when the assessment within the Prague Jewish community was challenged as unjust. He saw communal conflict and factional politics as the cause of his dismissal from rabbinical office.

Heller had opinions and loyalties, moreover, not only within the politics of the Jewish community, but in the politics of Christian Europe as well. His faith in the Habsburg monarchs was not shaken by his imprisonment in 1629. In Poland, he transferred that faith to the Habsburgs' allies and relatives, the Vasa kings of Poland.

In a seminal article written in 1961, the Israeli historian Jacob Katz accused the 'generation of 1648', Heller among them, of a lack of 'realism'.[22] Katz's bill of particulars included that generation's view of suffering as a punishment for sin. Partly on account of this view, he argued, the leaders of the Jewish community of 1648 were unable to frame a realistic political response to the massacres. The traditional prayers and the efforts to ameliorate the fate of the survivors characterize a Judaism of powerlessness, whose only true hope was that God would send the messiah. The failure of traditional Jewish politics in 1648, Katz charged, did not lead to its revision. Indeed its main elements—alliance with the king, reliance on

[21] See Myers, *Re-Inventing the Jewish Past*, 116–25.

[22] J. Katz, 'Between 1096 and 1648'.

shtadlanim (lobbyists) and private diplomacy, and avoidance of communal factionalism—remained typical of Jewish politics until the twentieth century.

Katz, writing in Israel in 1961, found a lack of political realism in the generation of 1648, but his quarrel was perhaps with the generation of 1942. In the period of the Holocaust, Jewish confidence in the central government and a political strategy based on intercession and lobbying was shown to have been a tragic error. In the post-Holocaust era, Israel's War of Independence in 1948 crystallized a change in Jewish political style and the development of a new Israeli pattern.[23] Katz was correct when he claimed that the 1648 massacres did not bring about the abandonment of traditional Jewish political behaviour. On the other hand, his claim that the generation of 1648 saw misfortunes only as punishment for their sins is not at all correct. Seventeenth-century Jews—medieval Jews in general—although they believed in divine reward and punishment, also believed in more political and less theological causes of events, as Katz himself admitted elsewhere.[24] We will see that Heller blamed the massacres of 1648 largely on the state of interregnum that followed the death of King Władysław in 1648.

Heller, like other Jews, made conscious political choices, reasonable ones within his frame of reference. His reliance on the Habsburg monarchs may have been naive, like his acceptance of the lobbying process at royal courts, and his insistence on the maintenance of Jewish unity. Yet these strategies had brought success to his cousin Abraham and indeed to entire Jewish communities in Vienna and Prague, even to those of the Habsburg empire as a whole, in this very generation. Nothing in his lifetime—he died in 1654—shook Heller's confidence in these essential principles.

PERSECUTIONS AND PLAGUES

A biography of Heller cannot pass over in silence the persecution of the Jews, including Heller's own imprisonment (the major event in his account of his own life) and the massacres of 1648. Since Salo Baron's path-breaking 1928 essay, however, and even earlier, the 'lachrymose conception of Jewish history', the portrayal of Jewish history as merely a series of persecutions has been attacked on several fronts.[25]

Some historians have emphasized the political achievements of the Jews. Early modern Jews did not only suffer episodes of ghettoization, persecution, and expulsion; they also acquired writs of toleration and, during the seventeenth

[23] Note, however, that Spinoza, writing only twenty or thirty years after the massacres, already derided the Jews for their pusillanimity. See Spinoza, *Theologico-Political Tractatus*, ch. 3, p. 56.

[24] *Tradition and Crisis*, 184.

[25] Baron, 'Ghetto and Emancipation'. Cf. Schorsch, *On the History of the Political Judgment of the Jew*.

century, permission to resettle in areas from which they had previously been expelled. Gershon Hundert has written on the 'advantages of peculiarity' reaped by Jews in early modern Poland, together with certain other ethnic minorities (Armenians, Scots).[26]

A second approach has been to place Jewish suffering more carefully in the context of the suffering of many social, ethnic, religious, and other groups of the period. In itself, this tends to produce a lachrymose history of the world rather than a cheerful history of the Jews. Nevertheless the results can sometimes be startling. Though the Jews of the Habsburg empire suffered during the Thirty Years War, Jonathan Israel has argued that they suffered less than either Catholics or Protestants.[27]

A growing consensus of historians has similarly concluded that there is little evidence of special animus towards the Jews—that is, evidence of greater hatred of the Jews than of other enemies—in the general violence of the Cossack uprising of 1648.[28] Frightful massacres there surely were, but not, with some exceptions, massacres of Jews alone. The Jews were not given quarter: the fortress synagogues of the period provided no sanctuary from the sword. There is no reason to suppose that they suffered less than any other group. However, the portrayals of the massacres as pogroms or as repetitions of the Crusader massacres of 1096 are anachronistic and simply incorrect.

In this revision of the traditional Jewish view of the massacres of 1648, attention has turned once again to Heller, whose own response was one of the key factors informing that view. He saw the events as an outbreak of pure anti-Jewish violence. Heller made this view explicit in a brief letter that he wrote to the Hebrew printer in Cracow, in which he contrasted events in Prague in 1620, during one of the early battles of the Thirty Years War, with the events of 1648:

> The misfortunes that have befallen us since the days of the destruction [of the Temple] . . . have always been on account of the hatred against us, for they wanted to kill us to carry out vengeance. . . . But in the holy community of Prague, it was not so: there the misfortune was only on account of the war . . . 'and when permission is given to the Destroying Angel, [he does not distinguish between the righteous and the wicked', BT *Bava kama* 60*a*]. . . . The present events, however, are like all the past massacres. All the things that they did wickedly to our ancestors they have done wickedly to the children.[29]

[26] Hundert, 'An Advantage to Peculiarity?'.

[27] Israel, 'Central European Jewry', esp. pp. 17–19.

[28] This was the general sense of the 1998 conference on the 1648 massacres held at Bar Ilan University. See the articles in *Jewish History*, 17/2 (2003), a special issue on the 1648 massacres. See also Sysyn, 'Seventeenth Century Views on the Causes of the Khmel'nyts'kyi Uprising'.

[29] See the printer's introduction, Haberman, 'Liturgical and Other Poems', 126. Cf. *Tos YT*, *Avot* 5: 8.

For Jacob Katz, Heller is an example of 'the wilful distortion of the events [of 1648] to fit traditional patterns'. One can only agree with this judgement.[30]

For Yosef Yerushalmi, in his brilliant study of Jewish history and Jewish memory, Heller's comment to his printer is important for another reason: it is a classic expression of the ahistoricism of rabbinic Judaism. Every persecution is the same as all the others; nothing changes; nothing will ever change until the coming of the messiah.[31]

This is a valid insight into the mind of medieval and rabbinic Jews. However, for rhetorical purposes, Yerushalmi has misread and overread Heller's brief and off-hand remark. Most of Heller's writings, it is true, show little awareness of historical change, but on the other hand, his memoir shows concern for the recording of events, sensitivity to their historical context, and efforts to provide rational explanations for them. In this passage, Heller's ahistorical view of Jewish suffering is belied by his claim in the same sentence that the events in Prague in 1620 were different.

Historians have traditionally overemphasized the role of persecution in Jewish history and underestimated that of natural catastrophe. Heller lived in an age of plague. He survived epidemics in 1598, 1606, 1611, 1625, and 1652, while the terrible 1639 plague in Prague killed five members of his family. He did not struggle with the religious problem of suffering mainly in terms of why Jews are persecuted; it was sickness and plague that generally claimed his attention.

Heller did not greatly distinguish the sphere of history from that of nature. As will be seen in Chapter 9, his remarks on science show an awareness of the possibility of historical change within the natural world: new seas, new animals, even new stars. His view of human history, on the other hand, retained an awareness of the degree to which, in the final analysis, persecutions (like plagues) are unpredictable and inexplicable, part of the random flux and mutability of human affairs.

SATAN IN GORAY

In 1933 Isaac Bashevis Singer wrote his first novel, *Satan in Goray*, a historical novel about Polish Jewry during the fever of the messianic movement of Shabetai Tsevi.[32] One of the characters, Rabbi Benish Ashkenazi, is based partly on

[30] 'Between 1096 and 1648', 335; cf. Bacon and Rosman, 'A "Chosen Community"', 208–12.

[31] Yerushalmi, *Zakhor*, 50–2, uses Heller as the best example of medieval Jewish 'resistance to novelty in history'. For discussion of Yerushalmi's view, see Funkenstein, *Perceptions*, 1–21; Chazan, 'The Timebound and the Timeless'.

[32] For literary criticism of Singer's book, see Buchen, '*Satan in Goray*'; Niger, 'On *Satan in Goray*'. On Singer's family and his life, see Hadda, *Isaac Bashevis Singer*. I also benefited from Monika Adamczyk-Garbowska's lecture, 'I. B. Singer's *Satan in Goray* and I. J. Singer's *Brothers Ashkenazi* as Two Symbolic Chapters in the History of Ashkenazic Jewry', delivered at the University of Cracow in 1998.

Heller.[33] Like him, Rabbi Benish is 'an author of commentaries and responsa, [and] a member of the court of the Council of the Four Lands', and (like Graetz's Heller) a student of Maimonides and Jewish philosophy, a proponent of *peshat* exegesis, and an opponent of *pilpul* and kabbalah. He also shares some of Heller's basic ethical values, such as his concern for the sin of controversy.[34]

Singer's image of Heller was influenced by the Haskalah historians discussed above and by the Jewish socialism to which he was attracted as a youth. Rabbi Benish's philosophy of 'common sense and moderation in all things', wrote Singer, appealed to 'the substantial citizens—men of means'. In the catastrophes of the mid-seventeenth century, Bashevis Singer implies, for the poor men and women who suffered those catastrophes, the possibilities offered by Heller's and Benish's version of Judaism were insufficient. The hold of the 'substantial citizens' over the poor was broken. After 1648 Benish Ashkenazi retreats to his private study, as the Jewish communities of Poland dissolve around him.

Heller did not retreat in quite this way, nor did Polish Jewry disintegrate during the messianic reign of Shabetai Tsevi in the way that Singer depicts.[35] The origins of Singer's characters should be sought, however, not only in the seventeenth century but also—and more significantly—in the nineteenth and the twentieth centuries, in the inability of the modern rabbinate in eastern Europe to hold together the strands of Jewish life. Indeed, Benish Ashkenazi reflects some aspects of Singer's own father, a saintly hasidic rabbi who was, however, unable to keep his children within the fold of Orthodox piety. Singer projected his own revolt onto the Shabateans of the seventeenth century.

Every society has its foundation myth, a story that explains how it came into being. For medieval and early modern Jews, this was the story of the destruction of the Temple and the exile of the Jews. For modern Jews one foundation story runs as follows: first, Judaism was medieval—that is, otherwordly, dogmatic, rigidly observant of Jewish law, and isolated from its surrounding culture. Then it became modern—secular, freethinking, careless of Jewish law and ritual, open to the outside world. The turning-point is often taken to be the late eighteenth century, the generation of Moses Mendelssohn.[36] In *Satan in Goray*, Isaac Bashevis Singer sketches an alternative foundation myth. In the Middle Ages, he suggests, Judaism was dogmatic and controlling, but also united and moderate. In the modern age, Jews have become free, but also factionalized, full of conflict and extremism. For Singer, the imaginary fulcrum of this transition is the mid-seventeenth century: the massacres of 1648 and the Shabatean crisis. Hence 'Benish Ashkenazi' is

[33] He is also partly based on Berakhiah Berakh ben Isaac. See below, p. 190.

[34] Singer, *Satan in Goray*, 15, 22, 26.

[35] See Stanislawski, 'The State of the Debate'.

[36] Cf. Meyer, 'When Does the Modern Period of Jewish History Begin?'.

central, and, in history rather than fiction, so is Lipmann Heller. What is central is not Heller's accomplishment but his failure: he was unable to inspire the next generation to hold together the strands that comprised medieval Judaism. He was the last medieval Jew.

Was Heller's generation, the generation before Shabetai Tsevi and before Spinoza, the last of the old world? Against the historiographical trend reflected in Singer's *Satan in Goray*, Jacob Katz argued that 1648 did not mark a major turning-point for the Jewish community, indeed that there was no such turning-point before the Enlightenment of the eighteenth century.[37]

This historiographical debate echoes the great debate among the seventeenth-century Jews themselves. As I have said, medieval Jews recognized only one possible epochal change, the coming of the messiah. In the seventeenth century some Jews, including Heller, denied, while others hotly claimed, that the messianic climacteric was indeed upon them, that the spiritual crisis that they felt in their lives and in their souls was not a private nor a passing disturbance but a changing age of the world.

Heller's failures were real. We must resist the temptation, so rife in rabbinical biography, to focus solely on accomplishments. Heller participated in a lengthy attempt to expand the educational curriculum of Ashkenazi Jews, but that was largely unsuccessful. He was part of a larger effort to block the acceptance of the *Shulḥan arukh*: that was even less successful, and he eventually abandoned it. His attempt to ban the purchase of the rabbinate bore little fruit in the long term. He did not successfully pass on to the next generation his commitment to Jewish philosophy, nor his love for astronomy and natural science. To him were not the laurels of victory, but the dignity of an honourable defeat.

To this defeat we must add one more. In 1646, in an act of great self-effacement, he stifled his objections to the publication of a work of Lurianic kabbalah. This decision, as I have mentioned, may have been influenced by his changed class bias.

It would be wrong, however, to conclude with such a cynical judgement. The act expressed one of the values that Heller held dearest: it was a gesture in support of Jewish unity. Eleven years after Heller's death, the Jewish world achieved a brief moment of maximum unity, during the messianic reign of Shabetai Tsevi in 1665. Beginning in the aftermath of Shabetai Tsevi's apostasy, the unity of modern Jews would be decisively broken; they would reap the rewards and pay the price.[38]

[37] J. Katz, *Tradition and Crisis*, 195–7.

[38] Cf. Liebes, 'Ha-Tikkun ha-Kelali of Rabbi Nahman', 116 [= *Zion*, 45 (1980), 201].

PART I

THE LADDER OF ASCENSION 1578–1617

ONE

The Orphan

THE ORPHAN

IN 1628, at the age of 50, Yom-Tov Lipmann Heller had reached the summit of his ambitions.[1] He was chief rabbi of Prague, then the largest Jewish community in Christian Europe, and had written a major new commentary on Jewish law. He looked back and recalled his family, his birth, and the death of his father:

My father, Nathan Heller . . . was called to the heavenly academy when he was 18 years old. He was a man of great deeds, with consideration for his years, familiar with books and their contents, as I found in his writings which were in his trunk. But I never saw his face, for I was born not many days after the death of his holy body.[2]

'Yom-Tov' is a Hebrew name that means 'festival'; 'Lipmann' or 'Liebmann' was used as its German or Yiddish equivalent: the name, as Heller later wrote, was given to babies for good luck.[3]

Heller was born in 1578 in a village called Wallerstein in the south German region of North Swabia, in the area called the Ries. His family was well connected: 'a family of elders and teachers', one contemporary called them.[4] In his short reminiscence, Heller did not mention his mother; indeed, we do not know her name, but she was a member of the prominent Kolinsky family of Prague, and

[1] There have been a number of previous studies of Heller's life and works: Beit Halevi, *Life of Heller*; Klemperer, 'Rabbis of Prague', 52-66; Spiegel, 'Die Prager Juden', 143–6; J. M. Zunz, *City of Righteousness*, 93–104. On Heller's works, see esp. Zinberg, *History*, vi. 99–101; Tchernowitz, *Rabbinic Authorities*, iii.129–37; and Maimon (ed.), *In Honour of Yom-Tov*: versions of some of the essays in this collection appear in *Sinai*, 35 (1954), 414–56, and Mordechai Hakohen's essay 'His Books and Method of Study', which is perhaps the best in the collection, is repr. in his *Great Men and their Times*, 197–213. Israel Hailperin's biography of Heller, 'Rabbi Yom Tov Lipmann Heller (Tosafot Yom Tov): A Monograph with Sources, Tables, and Illustrations', a manuscript now at the Dinur Institute in Jerusalem, is discussed in my Preface. I thank Elhanan Reiner, Moshe Rosman, and the Dinur Institute for leading me to the manuscript and allowing me to make use of it.

[2] Introduction to *MYT Ber.*

[3] *She'elat gitin* (MS Oxford-Bodleian Heb. 808/1), fo. 2*a*, s.v. *berakhah*.

[4] Joseph Kitzingen, in M. Jaffe *et al.*, 'Pesakim bidevar ḥalitsah pesulah', p. 27.

related to the Oppenheim family of Worms.[5] On his father's side, Heller's first cousin Abraham Fränklin was a son-in-law of the famous Rabbi Judah Loew, the Maharal of Prague.[6]

Heller recalled with fondness his grandfather, Rabbi Moses Fränklin, in whose house he was brought up: 'He raised me as a father', Heller wrote.[7] Rabbi Moses was a respected local scholar: in 1564 he was suggested as an arbitrator during the controversy between Simon Günzburg and the rabbis of Frankfurt.[8] Heller quoted his grandfather only once, in a small passage in his first book. There is a blessing said daily: 'Blessed art Thou, O Lord our God . . . who teaches Torah to His people Israel.' Why does the blessing, Rabbi Moses asked his young grandson, use the present tense: 'teaches'? Was not the entire Torah taught long ago to Moses on Sinai? Rabbi Moses answered his own question: 'The Holy One, blessed be He, gives of His abundance to whomever prepares himself for learning, and teaches literally at every hour and moment.'[9]

WALLERSTEIN, 1578

'A market on a small hill', is how the German geographer Martin Zeiller described Wallerstein in the years before Heller's death. A small Judengasse ('Jews' street') led up the hill from the market. The Jewish community of Wallerstein could

[5] On Heller's mother, see Landau and Wachstein (eds.), *Jüdische Privatbriefe*, Nachträge, pp. e–f, note. In Heller's introduction to Seder 'Tohorot' in *Tos YT*, he reveals that his mother's sister was the mother of Simeon Wolf Oppenheim of Worms. Hailperin MS, p. 11 n. 2, notes the continued intermarriages among the Heller and Kolinsky (or Kelin) families.

[6] On Abraham b. Jacob Fränklin, also known as Abraham Wallerstein, see Wachstein (ed.), *Inschriften*, 46–7, 482–4; Muneles (ed.), *Inscriptions*, 307–8; see also below, n. 16. See also M. Jaffe *et al.*, 'Pesakim bidevar ḥalitsah pesulah', rabbinic responsa concerning a case of levirate marriage to which Abraham Fränklin was a party. Abraham's brother Lipmann was murdered and died childless. Abraham wished to delay the *yibum* ceremony until after the settlement of the estate; after performing the ceremony under pressure, he had it annulled on technical grounds.

[7] In the introduction to *MYT*. According to S. Buber, *Anshei shem*, 90–1 (quoted in various places, including Beit Halevi, *Life of Heller*, 38), Heller had an older brother Joseph, who led a yeshiva in Lvov, and died in 1659. There is a tradition stemming from the editor of the 1709 edn. of *Yalkut shimoni* that Heller's grandfather Moses Wallerstein was the chief rabbi of the Habsburg empire; this is not true. See Weingarten, 'Tombstone', 221–4.

[8] See Zimmer, *History of the German Rabbinate*, letter no. 4 (pp. 12–13), letter no. 8 (p. 21). See n. 27 below on the relationship between Heller's family and the Günzburg family.

[9] Heller's commentary on *Beḥinat olam*, 83, no. 18. The question and the answer, although Heller was unaware of this, stemmed from a passage in the writings of the Maharal. See Maharal, *Netivot olam*, i. 32. Cf. I. Horowitz, *Shenei luḥot haberit*, i. 18*b*. The doctrine of continuous revelation is a corollary of belief in God's unchanging nature.

hardly have numbered more than twenty families.[10] Looking across the valley from his home in Wallerstein, the young Lipmann Heller would have seen the towers and the tall church spire of the Protestant city of Nördlingen, an imperial city of about 9,000 inhabitants. Its tax registers for 1579 listed, among others, 349 weavers, two clock-makers, one lawyer, five gatekeepers, fifty-four butchers—and no Jews. The Jews had been expelled in 1509.[11]

In 1578 violent persecution was the exception in Jewish life in Europe. Jews themselves recognized this: the Maharal of Prague, in a sermon delivered a few years later, contrasted the earlier era of Jewish massacres with his own times, in which expulsion was the worst to be feared.[12] In fact by the 1570s the era of Jewish expulsions, which had begun in the thirteenth century and had nearly emptied western Europe of Jews, had ended. The Jews of Germany in the later sixteenth century were also aided by growing tendencies towards mercantilism (that is, policies that favour merchants and bankers), by the growing use of Roman law, which gave Jews civic rights, and by tendencies in the direction of religious tolerance.[13] The Habsburg emperors, unlike their Spanish cousins, were conspicuously supportive of the Jews. They found them valuable as a source of imperial income, and useful as a pretext for the extension of Habsburg authority throughout the empire. As Manasseh ben Israel wrote in the mid-seventeenth century, the German Jews 'are very much favoured by the most mild and most gracious Emperours, [although] despised of the people'. Rudolph II, who ascended the throne in 1575, held fast to this policy.[14]

Dominating the village of Wallerstein, at the summit of the hill, stood the ancient castle of the Catholic counts of Oettingen-Wallerstein. By the time

[10] Zeiller, *Topographia Germaniae*: *Schwaben*, 211. On the Jewish community of Wallerstein in this period, see Müller, 'Aus fünf Jahrhunderten'; Zimmer, 'R. Jacob Reiner', 128. For the subsequent history of the community, see Ophir *et al.* (eds.), *Memorial Book: Bavaria*, 616–19. On the general history of Wallerstein, see Grünenwald, 'Zur Geschichte' (note the map, p. 5); there are a number of other articles on the town of Wallerstein in that issue of *Nordschwaben*.

[11] See Friedrichs, *Urban Society in an Age of War*; census by professions (1579), 312–18.

[12] 'Derush al hatorah', in *Derashot maharal*, 71, quoted by Jacob Katz in 'Between 1096 and 1648', 328. Katz also quotes from the Maharal's *Derekh haḥayim*: 'Today, we all live in our houses, happy and safe.' Cf. David Gans's characterization of the later 16th c.: 'against the children of Israel, not a dog whet his tongue': *Tsemaḥ david*, introduction to pt. 2, quoting Exod. 11: 7.

[13] Cf. Israel, *European Jewry in the Age of Mercantilism*, 35–69. On German Jews, see also M. Breuer, 'Early Modern Period', 85–250; Scribner, 'Preconditions'; Kiessling (ed.), *Judengemeinden in Schwaben*. For a survey of recent historiographical trends, see Dean Phillip Bell's review essay, 'Creating a Jewish History'. On Rudolf and the Jews, see Hsia, 'Printing, Censorship, and Antisemitism'; Press, 'Kaiser Rudolph II.'.

[14] Manasseh b. Israel, 'To his Highnesse', 12; cf. Hsia, 'The Jews and the Emperors'. Hsia stresses that protection of the Jews was a routine policy of Habsburg officialdom, and was not affected very much by the personal attitudes of the individual emperors.

Zeiller's report was published the castle was in ruins, destroyed in the last months of the Thirty Years War. Count Friedrich V, who ruled there when Heller was born, was described by a contemporary rabbi as 'a righteous gentile, a lover of justice and equity'. When a priest from Wettenhausen agitated in 1577 for the remission of debts to the Ries Jews, Count Friedrich established a debt moratorium as a compromise.[15]

The Jews of Wallerstein were not without influence at court. Heller's cousin Abraham Fränklin was given a 'letter of protection' from Emperor Rudolph in 1603. Abraham did not hesitate to bring suits against Christians, even against noblemen, before the highest imperial court, the Reichshofrat. He was familiar with the processes of imperial law, and stood on his right as a citizen of the empire to the protection of Roman law.[16]

Though not permitted by imperial law, violence against Jews was by no means unknown in the later sixteenth century. Heller's younger cousin, also named Lipmann, Abraham Fränklin's brother died at the age of 24 at the hands of Christians (at whose hands and under what circumstances is not recorded; perhaps they were highwaymen). Whatever the circumstances, the family was assured by the Maharal that the young man was in the company of the great martyrs of Jewish history.[17]

The pattern of Jewish life by 1570, however, was not violent persecution but exclusion and marginalization.[18] Jews were excluded from positions of authority, from schools, from certain trades, from families, from many urban neighbourhoods, from whole cities such as Nördlingen, and from much of that web of relationships that comprised Christian Europe. The separation of Jews and Christians was a consequence of Jewish norms as well: for instance, unlike Italian Jews, the Ashkenazi elite did not as yet care to become expert in high Christian culture. Yet Ashkenazi Jews were less marginal and less excluded than they are often depicted.[19] In 1592 the Maharal had an audience with Emperor Rudolph.[20] That

[15] R. Moses is mentioned once again as a local leader: Zimmer, 'R. Jacob Reiner', 128. Friedrich died in 1579.

[16] HHStA Alte Prager Akten box no. 85, fos. 242–9; Schutzbriefe (Juden) 1603. There are also records of Abraham Fränklin in the HHStA series of Citationes. Cf. Press, 'Kaiser Rudolph II.', 280.

[17] M. Jaffe *et al.*, 'Pesakim bidevar ḥalitsah pesulah', 27.

[18] Cf. Hillerbrand, 'The "Other" in the Age of Reformation'.

[19] There is an excellent discussion of the question of the degree and forms of isolation of ghettoized Jews in early modern Italy in Siegmund, 'La vita nei ghetti'. I thank Professor Siegmund for showing me the English original of the article. Siegmund properly points to the need to investigate class and gender differences in Jewish–gentile contacts. One should note in addition that not all Jews in any of the Ashkenazi lands lived in ghettos.

[20] The interview, which became the foundation for many legends and fictional reconstructions, is mentioned by David Gans in *Tsemaḥ david*. A second account attributed to the Maharal's son-in-

such an audience was exceptional in the history of both rabbis and emperors is clear, but the period was shot through with exceptions. There were, for example, Jewish doctors in Prague and elsewhere who had studied at the University of Padua.[21] Jewish isolation was not absolute: Heller lived for many years in the Jewish quarter of Prague, cut off by walls from the Christian quarters, but almost next door to a church that was anomalously located within the Jewish quarter.[22]

Although officially excluded, Wallerstein Jews did business in Nördlingen: loans made by Heller's family appear in Nördlingen commercial records.[23] The worlds of Jews and Christians intersected one another and intertwined, and neither the Jews of Wallerstein nor the Christians of Nördlingen were able entirely to avoid contact with the other.

MARRIAGE INTO A PROMINENT FAMILY

When he was about 15 or 16—about 1593 or 1594, therefore—Heller was married. It was undoubtedly an arranged marriage. His bride Rachel was the daughter of a wealthy Jewish merchant in Prague, Moses Aaron Munk, also known as Aaron Ashkenazi (surnames were fluid in this period).[24] As was customary, Heller went to live with his bride's family in Prague.[25]

We have, by chance, a description of a Jewish wedding in Prague from just the year before, 1592. The English traveller Fynes Moryson had visited the city's Jewish quarter, and wrote:

law, Isaac b. Samson, was published in the 19th c.; however, Hillel Kieval has argued that it is a forgery: see Kieval, 'Pursuing the Golem of Prague', 17 n. 16. The Jews of Prague, in gratitude, presented Rudolph (it appears) with a beautiful precious stone, engraved with a Hebrew prayer. The stone, now in the Kunsthistorische Museum in Vienna, is illustrated in Mann and Cohen (eds.), *From Court Jews to the Rothschilds*, 110; see also p. 181, no. 115, and the discussion in Spicer, 'Star of David', 213–16.

[21] On Jews at Padua, see Carpi, 'Jews with Medical Degrees'; Ruderman, *Jewish Thought and Scientific Discovery*, 100–17.

[22] Muneles (ed.), *Inscriptions*, 323. Note also Ettinger's comment on the presence of Christian houses and churches in the Jewish neighbourhoods of Ukrainian cities. 'The Jews feared separation' is his conclusion: 'Legal and Social Status', 139 n. 111 [= *Zion*, 20 (1955), 149 n. 111].

[23] See Müller, 'Aus fünf Jahrhunderten', 182.

[24] Just to complete the confusion, he is also called Moses Aaron Teomim, but he must be distinguished from another close relative of the same name. See Landau and Wachstein (eds.), *Jüdische Privatbriefe*, 50 n. 4. Cf. Volavková, *The Pinkas Synagogue*, 127; *Pinkas hamekomot* of the Pinkas Shul, 66, 115, 286–9; Bondy and Dworsky (eds.), *Zur Geschichte der Juden*, 791–2, 877. Moses Aaron was a generous man, who endowed a Jewish hospital in Prague.

[25] Certain documents from Heller's early years are published in Muneles (ed.), *Inscriptions*, 321–4. On the preference of Ashkenazi Jews for early marriage, see J. Katz, 'Marriage and Private Life'.

The Jewes and Christians related to me that the Bryde among them vsed to sett in the Synogog vnder a Rich cloth of State, and to giue her Fayth to her husband in the hands of the Rabby, confirming it by taking a Ringe, and to spend the rest of the day in feasting and daunsing, with the doors open for all Jewes and Christians that would enter, permitting imbraces but no kisses while they daunsed.[26]

By the standards of his society, the young Lipmann Heller was a good catch. He had studied in his early teens at the yeshiva of the respected, somewhat ascetic, Rabbi Jacob Günzburg,[27] and was a promising young scholar from a respectable, well-to-do, and well-connected family.

What sort of a woman was Rachel? Her two later trips from Poland to Prague suggest a woman of independence and determination, although attached to her family and her home. On her gravestone she was eulogized as 'a rabbi's wife who strengthened her husband, [helping him] to study and teach young and old'. She managed the Heller household, and looked after Heller's student-boarders when he later ran a school in his home. 'She brought honour to him', the epitaph continues, 'with her coins, [helping him] to make many books . . . a pious woman, pleasant in her good works . . . and God-fearing. Each day, she did works of charity secretly.' The reference to 'coins' suggests that Rachel helped support the family, perhaps by making small loans on interest, while the mention of secret works of charity suggests an active and generous woman, working to help the needy.[28] Heller's mentions of Rachel in his memoir are unsentimental, perhaps expressing real emotional distance between them.[29]

[26] Moryson, *Shakespeare's Europe*, 491. Christian attendance at Jewish weddings was prohibited by the Prague archiepiscopal synod of 1605 (see Ch. 2 n. 37 below).

[27] Heller's teacher, Jacob b. Asher Ulma-Günzburg (d. 1616), participated in the synod of German rabbis in Frankfurt in 1603: see Zimmer (ed. and trans.), *Jewish Synods in Germany*, 94 n. 83, 98 nn. 101, 104; see also Zimmer, *Embers of the Sages*, 224–5. Günzburg was rabbi in Friedberg after 1597 (that is, after Heller was already living in Prague): see Kober, 'Documents', 29. It is unclear where he lived when Heller was his student. Günzburg's asceticism is singled out for mention in his death notice by the Friedberg Jewish community, published in Löwenstein, 'Günzburg', 2 (1901), 27. Heller usually reserved the title *mori*, 'my teacher', for Günzburg (e.g. *MYT* (*DH*), *Ber.*, p. 10 n. 77). One of the 1619 letters traces the relation of the Günzburg family to Heller: Jacob Günzburg's brother was married to a niece of Heller's mother (Landau and Wachstein (eds.), *Jüdische Privatbriefe*, Nachtrage, pp. e–f). Hailperin (MS, p. 8) suggests that this family connection may have contributed to the choice of Günzburg's yeshiva for the boy.

[28] Rachel Heller's epitaph is in Muneles (ed.), *Inscriptions*, 329. Alternatively, the reference to 'coins' might be to Rachel's charity or even to her dowry. Rachel's 1631 trip to Prague is recorded in *Megilat eivah*, 37; another trip can be inferred from the fact that she is buried in Prague. Presumably the latter trip took place in the months between Heller's death and her own.

[29] Although expressions of emotion towards spouses are by no means so routine in 17th-c. memoirs as they later became, they are not unknown. Moreover, Heller was occasionally willing to express warm emotion, e.g. towards his fellow students (in the dedication of *Tsurat habayit*), and towards his daughter Doberish (writing, to be sure, of her death) in *Megilat eivah*.

On her father's side, Rachel was from a wealthy family; on her mother's side, however, she belonged to the important and powerful Horowitz family. In the 1530s, they had actually attempted to establish official control over the Prague Jewish community, an attempt that ultimately failed after a bitter communal dispute. By the end of the sixteenth century, their wealth had been eclipsed by that of the Meisel family, but they remained at the forefront of Jewish social and religious life in Prague.[30] In documents from 1598 Heller is called Lipmann Munk;[31] living with his wife's family, he was given their surname. According to the rules of extended kinship in the Jewish quarter of Prague about 1600, Heller was also considered a Horowitz.[32]

The Horowitz family had special rights in the governance and ownership of one of the synagogues in Prague, the Pinkas Shul. As we have seen, Heller sat at the front of the synagogue, near the eastern wall close to the Holy Ark, next to his father-in-law. In 1616, in 1618, and again in 1620, he served as a representative of the Horowitz family on the synagogue's board of governors.[33] In the spring of 1604, he gave the synagogue a mantle for a Torah scroll. One can only speculate as to the occasion for the gift—perhaps a birth. He and Rachel had at least ten children who survived to adulthood: at least six daughters (Esther, Nechle, Nisel, Reyzel, Doberish, and Rebecca) and four sons (Moses, Liva, Samuel, and Abraham).[34] There was a healthy birth approximately once every two years from 1598 until 1616.

In the records of the Pinkas Shul, Heller is called 'Lipmann Dayan', and in another place 'Lipmann Apelant'. A *dayan* or *apelant* is a judge in a rabbinical court; Heller had been appointed to Prague's rabbinical court in 1597, when he was only 19 years old.[35]

[30] On the controversy, see Josel of Rosheim, *Historical Writings*, 204–12.

[31] Muneles (ed.), *Inscriptions*, 323.

[32] On the Horowitzes, see Munk, *History of the Munk Family*.

[33] See *Pinkas hamekomot* of the Pinkas Shul, 59–60; Volavková, *The Pinkas Synagogue*, 127; Muneles (ed.), *Inscriptions*, 321–4.

[34] Most of the children appear in *Megilat eivah*. Esther appears in the 1619 letter: see below, Ch. 6 n. 10. Another daughter, claim the genealogists, was the wife of Solomon Zalman b. Joel of Brest-Litovsk (or perhaps of Joel himself?—the genealogists disagree). She was the grandmother of the wife of R. Ezekiel Katzenellenbogen (d. 1749). See Hailperin MS, p. 49 (the Heller family tree). There may of course have been other girls, or even boys as well.

[35] Landau and Wachstein (eds.), *Jüdische Privatbriefe*, Nachtrage, pp. e–f; Hailperin MS, p. 11. See also *Megilat eivah*, 28, which can be taken to mean that he was a *dayan* for twenty-eight years. Since he was no longer a *dayan* after 1625, he must have begun in 1597. On the other hand, he might only mean that he lived in Prague for twenty-eight years (that is how Alexander Kisch takes the phrase in his translation of *Megilat eivah*) and that he became a *dayan* later. See below, Ch. 7 n. 8.

'Whoever has a great family in the community', wrote Ephraim of Luntshits, chief rabbi of Prague in the 1610s, 'takes precedence in every religious matter.' He surely had the Horowitzes in mind. In court, as in the Pinkas synagogue, the young Heller may have been seen—and may even have seen himself—as a representative of the Horowitz family. By 1614, the extended Horowitz family accounted for three or even four out of the six *dayanim* in the rabbinical courts of Prague.[36]

THE MAHARAL OF PRAGUE

Fynes Moryson described the sections of the city of Prague in 1592, the Jewish quarter among them:

> On the West side of the Molda is the Emperours castle, seated on a most high Mountaine, in the fall of which is the suburbe called Kleinseit or little side. From this Suburb to goe into the City, a long stone bridge is to be passed over Molda, which . . . divides the suburbe from the city, to which as you goe, on the left side is a little City of the Jewes, compassed with wals.[37]

In the late sixteenth century Prague was a city of about 60,000; it was the capital not only of the Czech kingdom of Bohemia, but also of Germany, that is, the Holy Roman Empire, and home to the court of Emperor Rudolph II. Nevertheless, Fynes did not think much of the city: 'The streets are filthy, there be diverse market places, the building of some houses is of free stone, but the most part are of timber and clay, and are built with little beauty or Art.'[38]

Close by the river, on the eastern bank, was the Jewish quarter, already ancient in the sixteenth century. The Jewish community was nearly as old as the city itself—a Jewish traveller from Spain had recorded their presence in the tenth century. The community's long history was embellished by local traditions: in the sixteenth century, Jewish visitors were shown a grave that was said to be that of the renowned eleventh-century scholar Rashi.[39]

[36] Ephraim of Luntshits, *Amudei shesh*, beginning of section 'Musar amud hadin', 127. The three judges from the Horowitz family were Isaiah Horowitz, Heller, and Mordechai Lipschitz. Lipschitz had married into the Horowitz family in exactly the same way as Heller: see Landau and Wachstein (eds.), *Jüdische Privatbriefe*, 51, 102. A fourth family member, Pinhas Horowitz, was a court judge for at least some time in 1616; see below on the Nikolsburg wine controversy. The entire rabbinic elite of Ashkenazi Judaism, of course, tended to be closely intermarried. Cf. the close linkages of families of German lawyers, discussed in Strauss, *Law, Resistance, and the State*, 187–9. Cf. *Tos YT*, *Avot* 1: 8.

[37] Moryson, *An Itinerary*, i. 29.

[38] Ibid.

[39] See Ashtor, 'Ibrāhīm' and Ruth Kestenberg-Gladstein, 'Bohemia'. On Rashi's grave, see Gedaliah Ibn Yahya (1515–87), *Shalshelet hakabalah*, 112, quoting merchants of Mantua who visited Prague. Ibn Yahya recounts a legend of Rashi's last days in Prague, which Emma Lazarus later reworked as the poem 'Rashi in Prague'.

With 6,000 Jewish souls, Prague had the largest Jewish community in Christian Europe at the turn of the seventeenth century. The community was still expanding, attracting immigrants, like Heller himself, from smaller towns and villages. The wealthiest Prague Jews were prosperous and favoured by the emperor; the family of Mordechai Meisel built a grand new synagogue and a stately home with Italianate features.[40] But Fynes Moryson found little to praise in the Jewish quarter; he was horrified by the overcrowding.

At Prage . . . [the Jews] are allowed a little Citty to dwell in, with gates whereof they keepe the keyes, and walled rounds about for their safety. . . . Many Familyes of Jewes lived packed together in one little house, which makes not only their houses but their streets to be very filthy, and their City to be like a Dunghill.[41]

Unlike the much-travelled Moryson, the young Heller was very impressed by Prague: by its size, its beauty, its political pre-eminence, and particularly by its scholars. 'City of scribes and sages . . . the holy and beautiful community, the populous town, the metropolis, the capital city . . . Prague', he called it in 1602.[42]

It was indeed a city of scholars, both Christian and Jewish. Rudolph II gathered around himself a galaxy of scholars and scientists from many countries, as well as a formidable group of artists. Outstanding among them were the great astronomers Tycho Brahe and Johannes Kepler (who, like Heller, came to Prague from a small town in southern Germany). Other scholars, such as the magician and mathematician John Dee, came to court as visitors. Rudolph's court in Prague was one of the centres of the late Renaissance.[43] Jews were not excluded; there was the alchemist Mordechai of Nelle, and the Italian Jewish engineer and conjurer Abraham

[40] On the Jewish community, see Heřman, 'La Communauté juive de Prague'; Flatto, 'Prague's Rabbinic Culture', 11–40. See also Palmitessa, 'House, Home, and Neighborhood', 4–6 (population, neighbourhoods), 207–10 (the Meisel house), 77 (building of synagogues). As he remarks, the Protestants of Rudolphine Prague, by contrast, were not permitted to build new churches until after 1609. Muneles (ed.), *The Prague Ghetto* and D. Altshuler (ed.), *The Precious Legacy* have a wealth of visual material and useful essays. On the city of Prague generally, and the place of the Jews within the history of the city, see Fučiková *et al.* (eds.), *Rudolf II and Prague*, and Demetz, *Prague in Black and Gold*. Demetz has a useful discussion of Prague historiography. Note also Z. V. David, 'Jews in Sixteenth Century Czech Historiography'.

[41] Moryson, *Shakespeare's Europe*, 490. On the overcrowding of the Prague ghetto, see Muneles (ed.), *The Prague Ghetto*, 59.

[42] *Tsurat habayit*, 10. Gans's similar idealized view of Prague is discussed in Neher, *Jewish Thought and the Scientific Revolution*, 20–2.

[43] On the Rudolphine court, see Fučiková *et al.* (eds.), *Rudolf II and Prague*; see also Evans, *Rudolph II and his World*; T. D. Kaufmann, *The School of Prague*; Grafton, 'Humanism and Science'.

Colorni, who dedicated his book on secret codes to Rudolph.[44] The chronicler and astronomer David Gans worked briefly with Tycho Brahe himself.[45]

Dunghill though it may have seemed to Moryson, Jewish Prague could boast a large group of scholars of considerable and varied attainments.[46] Besides David Gans, there was the Maharal's son-in-law Isaac ben Samson Hakohen, author of the first commentary on the Midrash on Psalms, and the Maharal's scribe, Ephraim ben Abraham Niderlander, author of an arithmetic textbook. The great preacher Ephraim ben Aaron of Luntshits arrived in 1604. There were men such as the moralist and storyteller Moses Altschul, the Bible commentator Joseph ben Issachar, and the Hebrew grammarian Isaac ben Yekutiel Kuskis. One should not neglect to mention the learned Rebecca Tiktiner (d. 1605), one of the first Jewish women to write a book, the ethical work *Meineket rivkah*.[47] There were also kabbalists, such as the doctor Shabetai ben Akiva Horowitz and Eleazer ben Abraham Altshuler Perles, whose kabbalistic writings include a reference to the possibility of creating an artificial man, a *golem*.[48]

[44] See C. Roth, 'The Amazing Abraham Colorni'. Colorni was in Prague from 1590 to 1598. There is a copy of his book, *Scotographia*, in Harvard's Houghton Library. Cf. also Mendel Isaac of Cracow, 'An Unknown Letter'. Mendel Isaac was an engineer who wanted to build a bridge over the Danube.

[45] On Gans's astronomical and cosmographical work, see Neher, *Jewish Thought and the Scientific Revolution*; Ruderman, *Jewish Thought and Scientific Discovery*, 82–7; Efron, 'David ben Shlomo Gans'; id., 'Irenism and Natural Philosophy'; and id., 'Liberal Arts, Eirenism and Jews'. On Gans's world-chronicle *Tsemaḥ david*, see Šedinová's articles, 'Czech History', 'Non-Jewish Sources', and 'Old Czech Legends'; Degani, 'Structure of World History'; M. Breuer, 'A Sketch of R. David Gans'; id., 'Modernism and Traditionalism'.

[46] A list of Hebrew books published in Prague up to 1657 was compiled by L. Zunz: 'Annalen der hebräischen Typographie'; another very useful bibliography of Prague Hebrew imprints is Muneles, *Bibliographical Survey of Jewish Prague*. The Jewish intellectuals in Prague at the time of the Maharal are discussed by O. Muneles and V. Sadek in Muneles' beautifully illustrated *Prague Ghetto*, and in M. Breuer, 'A Sketch of R. David Gans', 97–102, and id., 'Modernism and Traditionalism', 53; see also Reiner, 'Changes', 62–5. Note also S. H. Lieben, 'Der hebräische Buchdruck'; B. Kisch, 'History of the Jewish Pharmacy'.

[47] Note Ephraim Niderlander's correspondence with the Viennese Christian Hebraist Sebastian Tengnagel; see A. Z. Schwarz (ed.), 'Aus der Brief-Sammlung Sebastian Tengnagels', 73. On Ephraim of Luntshits, see Bettan, 'Sermons'; H. H. Ben-Sasson, 'Wealth and Poverty'; Elbaum, *Openness and Insularity*, 97–105, 176–8, 235–47. On Moses Altschul, see Rosenfeld, 'The Brantspiegel'; Gaster, 'The Maasehbuch and the Brantspiegel'. For the reputation of Kuskis (d. 1600) as a grammarian, see Reif, *Shabbethai Sofer and his Prayer Book*, 7. His son-in-law, Eleazer b. Abraham Perles Altshuler, writes in the introduction to Kuskis's commentary on the Song of Songs (Altshuler, *Naḥalot avot*): 'all the seven sciences were ready . . . on his lips'. A full study of Rebecca Tiktiner is still a desideratum. For now, see Shmeruk, 'The First Jewish Woman Writer in Poland'. See also Muneles (ed.), *Inscriptions*, 161.

[48] On Shabetai ben Akiba Horowitz, see Horodetsky, *Jewish Mysticism*, iv. 20–30; Sadek, 'Le Système cosmologique'. On Altshuler, see Brik, 'R. Eleazar Altshul-Perles' and Reiner, 'Biography'. The reference to a *golem* is in E. Altshuler, *Dikdek yitsḥak*, 14*b*.

At the centre of this group of scholars was of course the chief rabbi himself, Judah Liva (or Loew), known as the Maharal.[49] He later became famous thanks to the legend of the *golem* of Prague, of which he is the hero; but in his own day he was well known as a scholar.[50] As Abraham Rapoport wrote from Lvov, 'God has granted [the Jewish scholars of Prague] wisdom and understanding to comprehend every science . . . and at their head is their king, namely the great *gaon* . . . Rabbi Liva.'[51]

We do not know where or precisely when the Maharal was born. In the 1590s, when Heller arrived in Prague, he was probably in his seventies. He had come to Prague in 1573 not as chief rabbi but as head of a yeshiva or *kloyz* (*clausum*, college). He was a controversial man, and twice—once in 1584 and again in 1592—he left the city, though he subsequently returned. He became chief rabbi in 1598. With the exception of halakhic literature, on which he left relatively little mark, the Maharal had no equal among the Ashkenazi rabbis of the sixteenth century: he was the only one to offer a comprehensive theology of Judaism, and he was uniquely skilled as an exegete in moulding Bible verses to his purposes and in drawing unforeseen depths of meaning from seemingly commonplace rabbinic stories.[52] The profundity of his mystical thought had no counterpart within the Ashkenazi world. He strove to overcome the illusion of self, putting forward a goal of mystical self-annihilation.[53]

He was known as 'the Lion', a play on the name Liva, and sometimes compared himself to a lion.[54] His career and his writings were marked by fierce attacks on various opponents. During the first part of his career, when he was rabbi of Nikolsburg in Moravia, he was one of the targets of accusations of illegitimate

[49] There is an extensive literature on the Maharal. Yisrael Dubitsky has made a complete annotated bibliography of the material, which is as yet unpublished. One should note the discussion in Ruderman, *Jewish Thought and Scientific Discovery*, 54–99. The best treatment of the Maharal's life is Sherwin, *Mystical Theology*; the best overall treatment of his theology remains Neher, *Le Puits de l'exil*.

[50] On the development of the *golem* legend, see Goldsmith, *The Golem Remembered*; Kieval, 'Pursuing the Golem of Prague'.

[51] Rapoport, *She'elot uteshuvot eitan ha'ezraḥi*, no. 36.

[52] See Elbaum, 'R. Judah Loewe's Attitude', *passim*.

[53] Rationalist themes in the Maharal's writings have been stressed by some scholars, mystical themes by others. The rational was stressed by Kleinberger, *Educational Philosophy*, summarized in id., 'Didactics'. The mystical was stressed by Sherwin, *Mystical Theology*, and Safran, 'Maharal and Early Hasidism'. See the review by Demetz, 'Die Legende vom Magischen Prag'.

[54] See e.g. the Maharal's 'Derush al hatorah', quoted in Sherwin, *Mystical Theology*, 34. The Maharal's first book was entitled *Gur aryeh* ('Lion Cub'), and his personal seal was decorated with a lion. See HHStA Alte Prager Akten, box 84, fo. 547*b*. In his sermon on the lessening of the moon, Heller also compares the Maharal to a lion: *Derush ḥidushei halevanah*, 15.

birth. In 1584, when invited to give the sermon for the High Holidays at the Altneushul, he used the occasion to return to this old quarrel and to denounce his accusers; he also attacked the communal leadership for their hedonism and their treatment of the poor. He wrote two more fiery sermons on the sins of his generation. In *Be'er hagolah* (Well of the Exile) he joined various Italian and other rabbis in the attack on Azariah dei Rossi (*c.*1511–*c.*1578) for his scepticism about various *agadot*. In *Derekh haḥayim* (The Way of Life) he attacked Eliezer Ashkenazi (1513–85), to whom he referred not by name but merely as 'a certain individual in Poland', for his rationalistic conception of God.[55]

But the Maharal was neither a gadfly nor a crank. Even before his elevation to the chief rabbinate of Prague he was part of the communal leadership, and there, as in Nikolsburg, he took part in establishing communal legislation. His is one of the first signatures on the rules of communal governance that were established in 1579. He wrote a set of rules for the Altneushul and established societies for the purpose of Torah study.[56]

The Maharal, together with his successor Ephraim of Luntshits, must be seen as having created a new, activist model for the Ashkenazi rabbinate.[57] This sort of activism should be distinguished from the judicial activism that focuses on the reinterpretation of Jewish law. Maharal's contribution to halakhic literature was slight; the elements of this new model were, rather, preaching laced with moral and social criticism, supervision of the communal *kehilah* government, encouragement of communal legislation (*takanot*) as a means of reform, and a programme for the reform of Jewish education.

Meeting the Maharal was one of the decisive events of Heller's life. In the introduction to his commentary on the Mishnah, written in 1614, he compares the Maharal to Rabbi Judah the Prince, one of the greatest of the ancient rabbis.[58] It has sometimes been asserted that Heller was the Maharal's student. This is not

[55] See e.g. Sherwin, *Mystical Theology*, 31–4, 58–66, 181–3.

[56] On the Maharal's activism, see Sherwin, *Mystical Theology*, 165–80. The 1579 rules are in Bondy and Dworsky (eds.), *Zur Geschichte der Juden*, 558 (no. 772). The Maharal's Altneushul rules have been published (according to Dubitsky, 'Matter and Form', 58) in Hirschler (ed.), 'These are the Ancient Rules', and again in Anon., 'Rules'. They are also posted at the Altneushul itself.

[57] It is worth stressing that the elements of rabbinic activism are not to be found in the late medieval Ashkenazi rabbinate; one would have to reach back to the 13th-c. Hasidei Ashkenaz to find parallels. Clear parallels, on the other hand, can be drawn with Christian models of clerical activism in this period, especially episcopal activism. See e.g. Evenett, *Spirit of the Counter-Reformation*, 99. Other Ashkenazi rabbis who adopted the model of rabbinic activism include Shabetai b. Isaiah Horowitz in Poznań and Joel Sirkes in Cracow.

[58] Note also the Maharal's paean to R. Judah the Prince in his 'Derush al hatorah vehamitsvot', in id., *Derashot maharal*, 79.

true in the technical sense: he never studied in the Maharal's classes,[59] and always referred to Jacob Günzburg, in whose yeshiva he had studied, with the customary honorific 'my teacher and master'. By contrast, until he was more than 60 years old, he did not use that title to refer to the Maharal, only the less personal 'our teacher'.[60] On the other hand, he referred to the Maharal much more frequently in his writings than to Günzburg. Although Heller did not attend the Maharal's Talmud classes, he listened to his sermons, read his books, and wrestled with the Maharal's teachings throughout his life. Heller's praises of the Maharal may have been based rhetorically on the image of Rabbi Judah the Prince, but his mental image of Rabbi Judah himself and of the other ancient rabbis, his notion of what it meant to be a rabbi at all, was surely modelled on the Maharal.

THE NEW CURRICULUM

It was the ancient custom, the Mishnah recounts, for the High Priest in Jerusalem to spend the entire week before Yom Kippur within the Temple, in a room known as the Chamber of Parhedrin, preparing for the holiday. On the night before Yom Kippur he would stay awake, and if he began to fall asleep the young priests would snap their fingers before him and say, 'My lord High Priest, arise and drive off [sleep] on the [cold] pavement.' Moses Isserles, the rabbi of Cracow (d. 1572), the great codifier of Ashkenazi law and custom, commented:

> They would place [the High Priest] in the Chamber of Parhedrin, for . . . it was decorated with pictures of the Garden and the World, so that he could sit there like Adam. . . . As it is written, '. . . whatever Adam called every living creature, that was its name' (Gen. 2: 19), for [Adam] was wise, and understood the nature of things. . . . And if [the High

59 This observation has been made frequently. Extremely little is known about the Maharal's school, the Prague *kloyz*. If it resembled later institutions of this type, however, it may have had students who had already finished yeshiva; it is then at least possible that Heller and his *ḥevrah* were associated with the Maharal's *kloyz* in some way. See Reiner, 'Wealth, Social Status, and Torah Study', esp. pp. 295 ff. Note that the Maharal himself was not in Prague from 1592 to 1598.

60 In his earlier works, Heller typically refers to the Maharal as *rabenu* ('our master'), without any other honorific or name, e.g. *Tos YT*, *Nega'im* 4: 1, *MYT* (*DH*), *Sefer torah* (in the Vilna Talmud, after tractate *Menaḥot*), p. 229 n. 88, or else (as in *MYT*, loc. cit. in a second reference to the Maharal) *rabenu morenu harav rabenu liva zikhrono liverakhah* ('our master and teacher, the rabbi our master Liva, of blessed memory'). Similarly, in *Derush ḥidushei halevanah* (p. 15): *rabenu hagaon morenu liva perag zikhrono liverakhah* ('our master, the genius, our teacher, Liva of Prague, of blessed memory'), as well as in his responsum written in Ludmir (hence, between 1634 and 1643), published in Rapoport, *She'elot uteshuvot eitan ha'ezraḥi*, no. 40. However, in a responsum dated 1640, published in Joshua b. Joseph, *She'elot uteshuvot penei yehoshua*, no. 53, Heller did finally refer to the Maharal as 'my master and teacher' (no doubt to give added emphasis to his reliance in that decision on the Maharal's published 'Responsum on a Deserted Wife').

Priest] wished to sleep, [that is,] to drown in ignorance . . . they would have him walk on the pavement, so that he might reflect on the various measurements of the sanctuary and the other buildings which he would see in the courtyard, from which he might attain knowledge and understanding.

Isserles imagined the High Priest as man before the Fall, assigning each thing its proper name, and the Temple as a Renaissance 'memory palace'—no barbarous shrine but a microcosm whose images and proportions were designed to impart to its viewer the knowledge of 'the nature of things'.[61]

It seems incongruous to juxtapose the words 'Ashkenaz' and 'Renaissance'.[62] Where, one might ask, are the artworks of the Ashkenazi Jews, their music, their poetry, their palaces?[63] Yet Renaissance humanism was not satisfied with the painting of portraits in oils, the writing of books, the carving of sculptures out of marble blocks; it was the shaping of lives that it desired. Likewise in Judaism in the sixteenth and seventeenth centuries, great efforts were focused on the production and education of a new type of person and life: the man of all-encompassing knowledge. This was the tradition within which Heller was brought up and the ideal for which he was trained.[64] This ideal, new to Ashkenazi culture in the sixteenth

[61] *Torat ha'olah*, iii. 59, based on Mishnah, *Yoma* 1: 1, 1: 7. Cf. J. Ben-Sasson, *The Thought of R. Moses Isserles*, 235, on Isserles' notion of a mental or imagined Temple; cf. pp. 23–6, 243–7. The occult philosophy of the Renaissance was fond of microcosmic buildings, and of using them as short-cuts to universal knowledge: see Yates, *Art of Memory*, 129–59; cf. Idel, 'Magic Temples and Cities'; see also Yates, *Occult Philosophy*, 29–30.

[62] On the meanings of the term 'Renaissance' as applied to this period, see Ferguson, *Renaissance in Historical Thought*; Porter and Teich (eds.), *Renaissance in National Context*; and the forum of articles and essays in the *American Historical Review*, 103 (1998), 51–124. Starn, 'Renaissance Redux', 124, describes the Renaissance as 'a network of diverse, sometimes converging, sometimes conflicting cultures', a suggestion that may be useful in our attempt to locate Ashkenazi Judaism within the cultures of early modern Europe.

[63] Compare Kupfer and Mark, 'Renaissance in Italy and Poland'; Elbaum, 'Influence'; Shulvass, 'Ashkenazic Jewry in Italy'; Shmeruk, *Yiddish Literature*, 72–9, 89–104. On the general problem of the place of the Renaissance in Jewish history, see Bonfil, 'How Golden was the Age of the Renaissance'.

[64] The student of one of Isserles' students, Jacob Koppelman, wrote in one place, 'To the degree that each person has a stronger intellect, he will do more actions and execute more plans than one with an intellect that is weaker. . . . And all the more so, the Holy One blessed be He does many different acts, for He is a simple Intellect and has no materiality at all; He is entirely Intelligible and therefore a fortiori He does many different acts' (Koppelman, *Ohel ya'akov*, i: 12 (p. 18*b*)). This is an interesting text from several angles, not least the bland description of God as an Intellect, but what is most significant is the human ideal that Koppelman suggested: Protean man, whose excellence is in the multiplicity of his actions. Cf. Juan Luis Vives's famous speech in praise of Protean man, printed in e.g. Cassirer *et al.* (eds.), *Renaissance Philosophy of Man*. On the ideal of the *ḥakham kolel*, the Jewish *homo universalis*, see Tirosh-Rothschild, *Between Worlds*, esp. pp. 15–19, 66–73, 133.

century, was expressed through the demand for a new curriculum of studies. One of the leaders of this movement of educational reform was the Maharal.[65]

The education of Ashkenazi Jews in the Middle Ages consisted of essentially only two parts. After being taught to read Hebrew letters, students would study the Pentateuch, sometimes (by the end of the Middle Ages) with Rashi's commentary. Ordinarily, the lesson would be the beginning of the weekly Torah portion; no attempt was made to cover the entire Pentateuch.[66] Later, at the young age of 8 or 9, students would begin to study Talmud. Classes were of two kinds, the first emphasizing practical questions of Jewish law, the second emphasizing interpretative problems. Special problems were sometimes created and solved in class through the method of interpretation known as *pilpul*. Talmud and Jewish law remained the sole object of study for all older students.

The Maharal made various objections to the old educational system, including its methods (for instance, he opposed *pilpul*) and its contents. The entire Hebrew Bible, he argued, should be studied. Students should also study Hebrew grammar; the Mishnah, the ancient code of Jewish law on which the Talmud is a commentary, should be studied in the years between Bible and Talmud, and finally philosophy and science should be studied as well.[67]

The chief rabbi of Prague from 1592 to 1598, during Heller's first years in the city, was Mordechai Jaffe, a student of Moses Isserles. Jaffe also supported the wider curriculum, comparing it to a ladder (a Neoplatonic image), which he identified as Jacob's ladder from the famous Bible story:

Every student . . . who wishes to ascend 'the ladder which stands on the earth, but whose head reaches to the Heaven' (Gen. 28: 12) must ascend to the . . . uppermost heights on which God, may He be blessed, stands. . . . First [the student] must learn the sciences of philosophy and nature . . . all of which are included in . . . the *Guide of the Perplexed* [by Maimonides]. And afterwards he must ascend and study . . . astronomy . . . And afterwards he must ascend even higher and enter into the wisdom of the kabbalah; then he will merit the apprehension of the First Cause, Who stands above [the spheres].[68]

[65] See Assaf (ed.), *Sources*, i. 40–106; Kleinberger, 'Jewish Education'; Bonami, 'Theological Ideas', 135–52; for the wider context of medieval Jewish curricular debates, see Rappel, *The Seven Sciences*. The curricular reform movement is too often associated only with the Maharal. David Fishman, focusing on the study of astronomy, has emphasized the role of Moses Isserles: see Fishman, 'Rabbi Moshe Isserles'. Elhanan Reiner has interpreted the expansion of the Ashkenazi curriculum within a class context as an attempt to retain elite control over the rabbinate: see Reiner, 'Changes', esp. pp. 45–6.

[66] See Kanarfogel, 'Role of Bible Study'.

[67] See Kleinberger, 'Didactics'; id., *Educational Philosophy*; Reiner, 'Changes', 64–7.

[68] M. Jaffe, *Levush*, introd. The passage is discussed at length in Kaplan, 'Rationalism and Rabbinic Culture'. On the image of the ladder, see Altmann, 'The Ladder of Ascension'; cf. Yates, *Occult Philosophy*, 56.

Note the autobiographical introduction of Judah b. Nathan Ashkenazi to his notes on the Jewish

From one point of view, Jaffe's proposed curriculum is very broad: the rabbinic scholar must apprehend the entire world and every type of knowledge. From another point of view, though, it is very narrow, as the humanistic curriculum (grammar, rhetoric, poetry, history) is totally excluded. Equally important, Jaffe does not recommend Jews to study any works written by non-Jews. His student studies the entire universe, but entirely from medieval Hebrew textbooks.

The movement of curricular reform put forward by Isserles, Jaffe, and the Maharal paralleled other efforts to expand and reform European curricula in this period. Much of what distinguished a gentleman of the sixteenth century from his predecessors in the fifteenth was that he had studied fields such as natural philosophy or alchemy, and classical authors such as Tacitus or Terence.[69] On many points, it has been frequently noted, the Maharal's views parallel the reforms initiated by John Comenius, the Czech Protestant educator of the next generation.[70] Comparison could also be made to the reforms of Peter Mohyla, archbishop of Kiev in the 1630s. Mohyla came from a culture—Slavic Orthodoxy—with an educational tradition that, like the Jewish tradition, was very far from the classical curriculum of the Latin West. However, Mohyla's success in establishing the Kiev Academy in 1631 contrasts with the Jewish reformers' inability to gain stable institutional support for their new curriculum.[71]

At the age of 20 Heller published his first book. The work reveals the profile of his education. It is clear, first of all, that he had already begun his study of Jewish philosophy, as he refers in the commentary to Maimonides' *Guide*, to Bahya ibn Pakuda's *Ḥovot halevavot* (Duties of the Heart), and also to the work known as *Musarei hapilosofim* (Ethics of the Philosophers).[72] He had acquired a competent knowledge of the basic doctrines of medieval Jewish philosophy and medieval Aristotelianism. His familiarity with kabbalah, on the other hand, was as yet slight; he did not quote from any of the major kabbalistic works.

calendar and lunar astronomy (pub. together with the astronomical section of Jaffe's *Levush*, 'Levush eder hayakar', 1*b*), trans. in my thesis, 'R. Yom Tov Lipmann Heller', 397–8. Ashkenazi was a student of Jaffe's; his education conformed closely to the model suggested by Jaffe here. See Ch. 3 n. 59.

69 Cf. Stone, *Crisis of the Aristocracy*, 672–83.

70 Adini, 'Education for Perfection'; Kulka, 'Comenius and Maharal'.

71 Kleinberger, 'Didactics', 32, has characterized the Jewish reforms as 'scarcely more than a literary movement'. On Mohyla, see the special issue of *Harvard Ukrainian Studies*, 8 (1984), nos. 1–2. There is a striking contrast, however, between the Maharal's reforms and Mohyla's. Mohyla introduced the study of Latin and consciously mimicked Western educational systems, especially that of the Jesuits (for example, the performance of school plays). This conscious Westernizing was absent from the effort of the Ashkenazi rabbis.

72 8: 3: 1 (p. 78); 1: 1: 14 (p. 11). *Musarei hapilosofim* is a work by the Islamic philosopher Hunain b. Isaac, translated into Hebrew by the poet Judah al-Harizi.

Heller had of course studied Talmud, the unchanging mainstay of Jewish education among Ashkenazi Jews, but the great talmudist of later years was not yet in evidence. The young Heller quoted a large number of sayings from rabbinic works, but the quotations were mostly well-known talmudic commonplaces.

Heller made his reputation in his late thirties as a talmudist. However, his earlier works were not in rabbinics but in other fields of study: philosophy, Bible, grammar, and kabbalah. In contrast to his limited range of talmudic references, Heller showed an impressive familiarity with the Bible and medieval Jewish Bible commentaries. Besides the Targum and the commentaries of Rashi, Abraham ibn Ezra (1089–1164), and David Kimhi (*c.*1160–1235), he had also looked at commentaries such as that of Levi ben Gershon (Gersonides, 1288–1344) on Proverbs, and that of Sa'adiah Gaon (882–942) on Daniel.

In later years, Heller portrayed himself as having begun intensive study of Mishnah and Talmud only after studying the Bible.[73] His first book is evidence of the truth of that self-portrait. Later in life, he became one of the major voices continuing to agitate for the new curriculum. But he was not only a proponent of this: he was a product of it.

S. J. Rapoport, the great nineteenth-century rabbi of Prague and one of the pioneers of rabbinical biography, wrote: 'No mindless *golem* was the masterwork of the Maharal; not in such work as that did he show his . . . wisdom, but in its opposite, in a great sage . . . his student [Heller].'[74]

THE EXAMINATION OF THE WORLD

The winter of 1597 was cruel, perhaps the coldest in a generation, and it was followed in 1598 by an outbreak of plague, which continued until 1599. The Jews published a booklet of special prayers.[75] The great astronomer Tycho Brahe wrote to his mother: 'Gracious God saved us from great peril . . . last summer and a good part of the winter until Christmas time, with much pestilence and pox throughout the whole kingdom of Bohemia, worse than any of the previous years.'[76]

On 21 January in that cold winter Heller, then a young man of about 20, purchased a four-room apartment in the Jewish quarter of Prague for himself and his

[73] See the introduction to *MYT*. All of these commentaries were published together in the 1525 Rabbinic Bible (*Mikra'ot gedolot*) of Bomberg.

[74] From Rapoport's introduction to K. Lieben, *Gal-Ed*, p. liii, quoted in J. M. Zunz, *City of Righteousness*, 96, and Hailperin MS, p. 79.

[75] Joseph ibn Shraga, *Seder ma'aseh haketoret* (Prague, 1598), prayers in time of plague, listed in Muneles, *Bibliographical Survey of Jewish Prague*, 24. On the weather, see Munzar, 'Weather Patterns', 54.

[76] Letter of 21 Mar. 1600; Thoren, *Lord of Uraniborg*, 506. The letter is translated by John Christianson.

young wife. One room served as a study. The apartment was on the bottom floor of the building next door to his father-in-law's house, two doors down from the church of the Holy Spirit (Heller's building is no longer standing, although the church is still there; churches last longer than Jewish houses).[77]

In that same year, Heller published his first book, anonymously. It was a commentary on a fourteenth-century Hebrew philosophical poem, written by Jedaiah Bedersi (*c.*1270–*c.*1340), a Jewish thinker and poet of Provence, and entitled *Beḥinat olam*, 'The Examination of the World'. A difficult text can act as an opportunity for an interpreter to read his own experiences and concerns into it. In a few passages in this first book Heller's mind shifted to scenes of his childhood. On the line '[The celestial bodies] put me where they wish', he commented that sometimes a person wishes to go somewhere—outside, for instance, to play in the fields—but the celestial bodies prevent it, 'for winter comes, and I am forced to stay at home'.[78] In another passage, he recalled the games that he used to play: 'Little boys hit one another while playing, but for them, this is affection and great love.'[79] Certain passages in Bedersi's poem brought to Heller's mind images of Prague society: 'adulterous women' (courtesans) wearing jewels, wealthy men acquiring property for their heirs to inherit. (This was foolish, Heller declared; the ethic of capitalist accumulation did not meet with his approval.)[80] The mill-wheels spinning in the Vltava reminded him of the heavenly spheres, revolving quietly without change in their perfect circular courses.[81] Repeating the image of the circle, Heller wrote:

> The forms . . . that are made by a compass . . . follow the most exact order; so is the body . . . formed by God in the most perfect beauty. It is known to the sages of anatomy and nature that no smallest point in man is without a purpose. . . . And so is it written in [BT] *Berakhot* [10*b*]: 'there is no artist like our God.'[82]

Heller's vision of the world was based on his reading of medieval Jewish philosophy. It was a philosophy shaped by dogmatic bounds: he affirmed Maimonides' Thirteen Principles of Faith, as did Bedersi.[83] He accepted the philosophical notion of God as the First Cause, the Unmoved Mover. Although he had not read any of Aristotle's works, he quoted Aristotelian commonplaces at second hand: spring is the best of the four seasons; touch is the lowest of the five senses; the spheres are not made of any of the four elements but of the fifth element, the quintessence.[84] 'Your deeds prove . . . to us', Heller wrote, addressing God and

77 Muneles (ed.), *Inscriptions*, 323; *Megilat eivah*, 28.

78 5: 3: 13 (p. 57).

79 5: 2: 5 (p. 53).

80 1: 4: 8 (p. 21); 1: 5: 3 (p. 24). Cf. H. H. Ben-Sasson, *Theory and Practice*, 121–9.

81 5: 1: 1 (p. 51).

82 1: 3: 11 (p. 17).

83 Introd., 5.

84 Unmoved Mover: 8: 2: 22 (p. 77); spring: 6: 3: 3 (p. 66), and cf. 6: 3: 5; touch: 1: 7: 11 (p. 32; note that Heller misquotes Maimonides, and writes that 'sex is shameful'); spheres: 14: 1: 7 (p. 109).

quoting from the classic work of medieval Jewish philosophy, *Ḥovot halevavot*, 'that You are supremely wise, when we see the wondrous order of every existing thing.'[85]

Several kabbalistic teachings appeared in Heller's commentary. He accepted the Neoplatonic view that the soul yearns to return to its eternal source, as well as two kabbalistic doctrines associated with this belief. The first is *gilgul*, the transmigration of souls, a doctrine that will be discussed more fully in later chapters. The second is the belief that the root of the human soul, and hence its ultimate home, is higher than the angels, the supernal Intellects. This teaching recurred in Heller's later writings, and will also be discussed at length later.[86]

Like Bedersi's poem, Heller's commentary concerned itself with mankind, with humanity in general, and not with Jews or non-Jews. Non-Jews as a particular category of people are mentioned only once: Heller repeated the medieval tradition that they would not be resurrected.[87]

The past concerned neither Bedersi nor Heller; neither in Bedersi's poem nor in Heller's commentary was there any reference to biblical or historical events. Of the future, all that he knew was the coming of the messiah and the resurrection of the dead.[88] The future, Heller argued in one place, is undetermined. It will be produced by free human choices; even God's foreknowledge is of a type that does not constrain it.[89]

In keeping with Bedersi's generally pessimistic tone, Heller stressed the dangers that surrounded him. At night, there were bandits.[90] In the summer there were diseases, and in the winter even worse diseases.[91] (Those who are of a cold constitution, Heller wrote, drawing on medieval medical theories, cannot tolerate cold weather.[92]) The conjunctions of the stars and planets could produce 'catastrophes and changes'.[93] Invisible to the eye, there were demons.[94]

These were dangers from outside, but there was also danger from within. 'Satan is the evil inclination', Heller quoted from the Talmud,[95] and declared that worldly pleasures were dangerous. At night in bed, especially after a large meal, he

[85] 8: 3: 1 (p. 78).

[86] *gilgul*: 10: 2: 7 (p. 87); soul above the angels: 1: 1: 14 (p. 11) and elsewhere. This is also a theme in the Maharal's work, particularly *Tiferet yisra'el*, e.g. 288–9. Soul returning to its source: 1: 1: 2 (p. 6), 1: 4: 1 (p. 19). Note also 14: 1: 7 (p. 108): number of angels/Intellects.

[87] 14: 1: 13 (p. 111). Note also 10: 3: 22 (p. 90): Samael is the guardian angel of Esau.

[88] 14: 1: 11–13 (pp. 110–11).

[89] 8: 2: 7 (p. 75). Heller repeated this argument later in *Tos YT*, *Avot* 3: 15 and *Avot* 5: 6. In his Bedersi commentary (and later writings), he does, however, accept the predictions of the coming of the messiah and the resurrection of the dead (14: 1: 11–13, pp. 110–11).

[90] 1: 6: 4 (p. 28).

[91] 6: 3: 4–5 (p. 66).

[92] 4: 1: 4 (p. 46).

[93] 'Bakashat hamemin' 1: 2 (p. 112).

[94] 8: 2: 25 (p. 78).

[95] 10: 1: 7 (p. 81), from BT *BB* 15*a*.

wrote, demons could cause erotic dreams; they were born from the seed spilled by the dreamer.[96]

Beḥinat olam, as Heller read it, offered a response to the misfortunes of the world. The message of the book, he wrote in summary, 'is to teach all of mankind the nature of the world, how it is constructed, where it comes from, and not to run after it'.[97] Disease and plague should teach the wise heart the futility of things of this world, and direct us towards matters of the spirit.

Beḥinat olam is written in an extraordinarily difficult Hebrew style—vague, mysterious, and above all highly elliptical. Heller's skills as an interpreter of texts were already apparent in this youthful work; indeed, on account of the text's obvious difficulties, they were never more apparent. Heller managed to make sense of a great many perplexing passages, including even Bedersi's postscript, called 'Bakashat hamemin', a set of puzzles or riddles, written entirely with words beginning with the Hebrew letter *mem*.

'It gave me a lamp of cups of regrets, bitter within and bitter without. . . . My raiser, my depriver. . . . Its way is the way of madmen . . . It fails its hopeful ones', wrote Bedersi. The solution to the riddle, according to Heller, is time:

> Time may GIVE a man a LAMP of solid gold, that is, great wealth, yet the bowls of the lamp will be CUPS OF REGRETS, for wealth does not permit its owner to sleep, and when the wealth is lost, he will find it BITTER WITHIN AND BITTER WITHOUT. . . . Time DEPRIVES a parent of the children they have RAISED (as the Sages have said, 'The mourning for a young man is not like that [for an old man]'). . . . And it FAILS to save one who HOPES for salvation from it.[98]

96 1: 4: 8 (p. 22). 97 Introd. 3. 98 'Bakashat hamemin' 5: 5–7 (p. 119).

TWO

The Exile of a Philosopher

THE FLOWERING OF PHILOSOPHICAL STUDY AMONG ASHKENAZI JEWS

A few years before Heller wrote his commentary on *Beḥinat olam*, Naftali Altshuler, a Jewish scholar in Cracow, was alarmed:

> Woe is me for this great desecration of the Divine Name! For in our generation many have . . . torn through the fence . . . of Torah and gone outside it. With difficulty you will find one in a city and two in a family who fill their bellies with the wisdom of the Torah and the words of the prophets of God, but only with philosophy and 'he who keeps company with harlots' (Prov. 29: 3).[1]

Clearly Altshuler was exaggerating: it is fantastic to suppose that more Cracow Jews were studying philosophy in 1593 than were studying the Bible. But the very complaint is a testimony to the flowering of philosophical study among sixteenth-century Ashkenazi Jews.[2]

Heller's commentary on *Beḥinat olam*, published in Prague in 1598, joined a growing library of classics of medieval Jewish philosophy (and commentaries on those classical works) that were published by Ashkenazi Jews in the 1590s. Another edition of *Beḥinat olam* had already appeared in Cracow in 1591. In 1593 *Ruaḥ ḥen*

[1] Introduction to N. Altshuler, *Ayalah sheluḥah.*

[2] Ruderman, *Jewish Thought and Scientific Discovery*, 54–63, surveys the recent literature on rationalism in Ashkenazi culture, including my own Ph.D. dissertation, 'R. Yom Tov Lipman Heller', which includes more extensive citations. Beginning in the mid-16th c., there was a revival of Aristotelian philosophy in Germany, mainly in the universities. Although no Jews attended German universities in this period, they were perhaps influenced by this general trend of thought. See Petersen, *Geschichte der Aristotelischen Philosophie* and Beck, *Early German Philosophy*. Charles Schmitt claims that, throughout Europe, Aristotelianism 'revived and was probably stronger . . . in the first half of the seventeenth century than in the first half of the sixteenth': Schmitt, 'Philosophy and Science', 513. Moreover, the Jews who studied medicine at the University of Padua learned Aristotelian philosophy as part of their medical education: see above, Ch. 1 n. 21. On the influence of Spanish, Italian, and Oriental Jews, see Elbaum, *Openness and Insularity*, 33–67. It must be stressed that, in the 16th c., 'Ashkenazi' and 'Italian' Jews formed overlapping groups: there was a significant community of Ashkenazi, i.e. Yiddish-speaking, Jews in Italy. See above, Ch. 1 n. 63.

(Spirit of Grace), an anonymous medieval popularization of Aristotelian philosophy, was printed in Prague, while the following year Mordechai Jaffe's commentary on Maimonides' *Moreh nevukhim* was printed in Lublin.[3]

In the late sixteenth century the impact of the study of Jewish philosophy may be seen throughout the learned culture of Ashkenazi Judaism. It is apparent in the writings of scholars such as Isaac Chajes, rabbi of Prague in the 1570s, who wrote that spiritual life depends on a moderate balance between one's desire for pleasure and one's desire for the good; or the Maharal, who regarded natural science as a necessary part of Jewish education; or Abraham Horowitz, one of Heller's cousins by marriage, although a generation older than Heller, who argued that magnetism cannot be explained by natural science; or Jacob Koppelman, who repeated Maimonides' metaphor of God as a clock-maker; or Moses Isserles, who wrote that 'most of the commandments are for the benefit of the body and the conduct of one person towards another'.[4]

Medieval rationalism, needless to say, is very different from modern rationalism. One who comes looking among the Ashkenazi Jews of the sixteenth or seventeenth centuries for atheism, for opposition to mysticism, for the experimental method in science and a programme of progressive research, will be disappointed. One may find, however, belief in an incorporeal God, an emphasis on natural processes rather than miracles, and the Aristotelian cosmology of spheres and elements, form and matter.

Rationalism was a goal and a set of questions as much as it was a set of doctrines. In Chapter 1 we saw Mordechai Jaffe's call for a new curriculum that would

[3] Also in 1593, Bahya ibn Pakuda's *Ḥovot halevavot*. In 1597 the Lublin press published Joseph Albo's *Sefer ha'ikarim*; in 1599 the Cracow press responded with a commentary on Albo, *Ohel ya'akov* by Mordechai Jaffe's student Jacob Koppelman. That work had already been printed in Freiburg in 1584. Abraham Horowitz's commentary, *Ḥesed avraham*, on Maimonides' work on the Aristotelian theory of the mean (*Eight Chapters*) was also published twice, first in Lublin in 1577 again in Cracow in 1602. *Mano'aḥ halevavot*, a commentary on Bahya ibn Pakuda's *Ḥovot halevavot* by Manoah Hendl b. Shemariah of Beresteczko, was published in Prague in 1612. *Beḥinat olam* was reprinted yet again in Lublin in 1614. Lesser-known medieval works also appeared: Shem Tov b. Joseph Falaquera's *Igeret havikuaḥ* in Prague in 1610, and *Even boḥan* by Kalonymos b. Kalonymos in Hanau in that same year. On Prague imprints, see Ch. 1 n. 46. Polish Jewish imprints are listed in Friedberg, *History of Hebrew Printing*. I am grateful to Professor Stephen Burnett for providing me with a copy of his as yet unpublished list of Hanau imprints.

[4] See I. Chajes (or Hayes), *Paḥad yitsḥak*, 10*a*–*b*; Isserles, *Torat ha'olah*, iii. 38; Maharal, *Netivot olam*, 'Netiv hatorah', ch. 14 (repr. New York, 1969, i. 61); A. Horowitz, *Ḥesed avraham*, 2nd edn., 3*a* (cf. Joseph b. Isaac Halevi, *Ketonet pasim*, 16*a*, discussed in my dissertation, pp. 300–14); Koppelman, *Ohel ya'akov*, 18*b*; cf. Maimonides, *Guide of the Perplexed*, iii. 21. On Koppelman, cf. Ch. 1 n. 64. See also H. H. Ben-Sasson, *Theory and Practice*, 63–5; Elbaum, *Openness and Insularity*, 154–82.

include knowledge of the physical universe. In a work published in 1577, Abraham Horowitz (like Jaffe, a student of Isserles) went into greater detail:

A man should comprehend rationally the nature of every existing thing: the heavens . . . and the spheres . . . the earth and everything that is upon it, the four elements and all that is [composed] of them; how the world was created, what are its parts, and what is its purpose; what the soul is, and whether the human soul is immortal; by what merit a person may attain eternal life, whether by thought or by action; to what the soul will unite after death: whether with the Active Intellect, or with God, may He be blessed. All these investigations and their like are called natural science, that is, *ma'aseh bereshit*, the work of Creation. . . . Without natural science, it is impossible to enter the 'Garden' of theology, as Maimonides wrote in his introduction [to *Moreh nevukhim*].[5]

At least one Ashkenazi Jew asked more radical questions than these. Eliezer Eilburg was a doctor, a German Jew who studied in the Italian city of Ancona in the 1550s; he later lived in Silesia. In an unpublished work called *Eser she'elot* (Ten Questions), written about 1575, Eilburg challenged dogmas such as the resurrection of the dead and Creation, the morality of biblical heroes such as Abraham and Moses, and the truth of biblical stories. He denied that the Jews of the present day were a chosen people, and cast doubt on the accuracy of the Masoretic text of the Hebrew Bible.[6]

Medieval Jewish philosophy before the sixteenth century was almost entirely a creation of Mediterranean Jews, particularly those of Spain and Provence.[7] At the time of Rashi, in the eleventh century, German and northern French Jews had known nothing of philosophy at all, barely even its name.[8] At the time of the

5 *Ḥesed avraham*, 1 in the edn. in the Vilna Talmud, before tractate *Avot*.

6 He also suggested that Maimonides had made use of the so-called 'seventh type of contradiction', namely deliberate contradiction in order to conceal radical doctrines. The text is in JTS MS microfilm no. 2323 (Hirsch 109), fos. 45–77. A longer discussion of Eilburg (or Eilenburg) and his *Eser she'elot* appears in my article, 'The "Ten Questions"'.

7 For instance, Colette Sirat's survey of medieval Jewish philosophy, *History of Jewish Philosophy*, exemplary in its inclusion of even relatively minor figures and works, does not include a single Ashkenazi Jew. On study of Jewish philosophy by Jews of Germany and northern France before the mid-14th c., see Davis, 'R. Yom Tov Lipman Heller', 33–47, 63–72. See also Dan, *Mystical Teachings*, 22–32; Kiener, 'Status of Astrology', 24–9.

8 Rashi glosses *pilosofin* in BT *AZ* 54*b* as 'the sages of the gentiles', and *pilosofa* in *Shab.* 116*a* as 'heretic [*min*]'. In *Sotah* 49*b* (cf. *Men.* 64*b* and *BK* 82*b*) he glosses *ḥokhmah yevanit* ('Greek wisdom') as 'a wise speech [*leshon ḥokhmah*] that the members of the royal court speak but the rest of the people do not understand'. In each case, he is probably eliciting the meaning of the term from its context. Note, by contrast, Tosafot on *Shab.* 116*a*: 'Our master heard [in brackets: from a Jew who came from Greece who said] that in the Greek language, *pilosfos* is a lover of wisdom . . .'. Urbach, *The Tosafists*, ii. 604 n. 27 (and cf. p. 694), identifies the comment as coming from the notes of Samson of Sens, and 'our master [*rabenu*]' as referring to Isaac b. Meir ('the Elder') of Dampierre (fl. *c.*1180).

Maimonidean controversies in 1216–33, certain rabbis in northern France had gone so far as to issue a ban on the study of Maimonides' *Moreh nevukhim*.[9] After Heller's time, moreover, the Ashkenazi study of philosophy declined, although it never disappeared, throughout the seventeenth century. Whereas a constant flow of works of Jewish philosophy was published by Ashkenazi Jews between 1590 and 1620, none appeared from 1620 until Bahya ibn Pakuda's *Ḥovot halevavot* was printed in Sulzbach in 1691.[10] The rationalist trends so visible in Ashkenazi culture of the late sixteenth century were to a large degree forgotten.[11]

In 1590, however, Ashkenazi Judaism was not what it had been in 1100, nor was it yet what it would become by 1700. After the middle of the fourteenth century, the ban on the *Moreh nevukhim* had faded from memory; by 1400, scholars in Prague, in Regensburg, and in the Rhineland were studying this and other works of Jewish philosophy.[12]

Opposition to rationalism among Ashkenazi Jews, one need hardly say, did not disappear.[13] In the 1560s Isserles was criticized for his study of Jewish philosophy by his cousin, Solomon Luria (*c.*1510–73):

[9] See Septimus, *Hispano-Jewish Society*, 49–51, 57–9, 76–9, 82; Davis, 'R. Yom Tov Lipman Heller', 48–75 on the 1232 ban and on other instances of opposition to Jewish philosophy among Ashkenazi Jews of the 12th to 14th cc. (Samson of Sens, Moses Taku, the Rosh).

[10] About 1687, Baer Eybeschuetz (Perlhefter) wrote a commentary on *Ḥovot halevavot*, called *Be'er leḥai ro'i*, but it was never published and is no longer extant. He also wrote a commentary on Maimonides' 'Laws of the Sanctification of the New Moon' in the latter's *Mishneh torah*. See MS Oxford-Bodleian Heb. 1416 and the notice in Neubauer's catalogue. The author is mostly known for his involvement in the Shabatean movement. See Tishby, *Paths of Faith and Heresy*, 296–7 n. 43.

[11] The astronomical papers of Yair Hayim Bacharach (1638–1702) may stand as a symbol of this decline. His wide-ranging readings and interests are noteworthy: see Twersky, 'Law and Spirituality', 454–5. In his 'anger and bitterness', however, Bacharach, one of the major German rabbis of the late 17th c., and a great-grandson of Maharal, destroyed his own writings on astronomy in a fire that he lit himself. See Y. Bacharach, *She'elot uteshuvot ḥavot ya'ir*, no. 219. From about 1700 onwards, there was a revival of interest in science and Jewish philosophy. One may note such figures as Tobias Cohen, Solomon Hanau, Moses b. Hayim Eisenstadt, Meir b. Moses Judah Leb Neumark of Nikolsburg, Jonathan b. Israel of Ruzhany, and Raphael Levi Hannover. It is to be noted that (in contrast to the earlier period) none of these writers was a major talmudist. See Zinberg, *History*, vi. 135–53; S. and H. Schwarzschild, 'Two Lives'; D. Kaufmann, 'Der zweite Corrector'; Langermann, '*Tekunat ha-Hawayah*'.

[12] See Kupfer, 'Cultural Image', and J. Davis, 'Philosophy, Dogma, and Exegesis', and note Jeffrey Woolf's forthcoming article on northern French Judaism in the 14th c.

[13] Reiner argues that opposition to philosophy among Ashkenazi Jews did not continue through the 14th and 15th cc. but resumed in the mid-16th c., on account of the pressure of what he terms the 'New Library', namely the reception of medieval Spanish and Mediterranean Jewish literature. See Reiner, 'Attitude of Ashkenazi Society', 589–603.

> You turn constantly to the teachings of Aristotle, the uncircumcised one. . . . Woe to me whose eyes have seen, whose ears have heard, that the words of the unclean one have become . . . a sort of spice for the Holy Torah in the mouths of the sages of Israel, may the Merciful One protect us. . . . For there is no heresy and destruction like their teachings.[14]

Isserles wrote back that he too rejected the metaphysics or theology of non-Jewish philosophers such as Aristotle, but that he accepted their views on natural science, and that any Jewish scholar was free to study the works of the Jewish philosophers.

A few years before Isserles' and Luria's correspondence, in 1559, the study of Jewish philosophy had been at the centre of a controversy in Prague: Abraham Horowitz, who was a student of Isserles, defended it from the attacks of another young scholar, Joseph Ashkenazi.[15] Unlike Luria, Ashkenazi accused the Jewish philosophers of heresy, arguing that their teachings were opposed to the Torah, and should not be taught.[16] Horowitz, then still a young man, responded mockingly. Ashkenazi had said that 'there is no chapter in the *Moreh nevukhim* in which there is not heresy'. Horowitz pointed out that there were chapters in *Moreh nevukhim* that proved God's existence; were these heretical? Was it heretical to believe that God exists? Was it not Ashkenazi who in his ignorance had an inadequate, even a heretical, conception of God? Ashkenazi retreated to the Land of Israel, where he found support and inspiration among the kabbalists and talmudists of the city of Safed. The defence of philosophy by Horowitz and Isserles was successful, and for more than fifty years philosophical study flourished among the Ashkenazi rabbinate.

[14] See Isserles, *She'elot uteshuvot harema*, nos. 6 and 7 (pp. 23–37). Siev's comments on the text are valuable. For discussions of the correspondence, see H. H. Ben-Sasson, *Theory and Practice*, 33–4; Kaplan, 'Rationalism and Rabbinic Culture', 20–43; Elbaum, *Openness and Insularity*, 156–9. Cf. also the discussion in my dissertation, pp. 134–43, and a more penetrating discussion in J. Davis, 'Philosophy and the Law'. Luria's goal was not to prevent the study of Jewish philosophy (like Isaiah Horowitz a generation later) but to keep the realm of halakhah free of its influence; cf. Ch. 4 n. 28.

[15] Abraham Horowitz's tract, responding to Ashkenazi's charges against philosophy and the *Guide*, was published by Bloch, 'Der Streit'. Horowitz was identified as the author of the tract in Rabbinowitz, *Traces of Free-Thinking*. Part of Ashkenazi's tract, written in the 1570s and reiterating his charges, was published and discussed by Scholem, in 'New Information'. The episode is discussed in Šuler, 'Ein Maimonides-Streit'; Elbaum, *Openness and Insularity*, 160–2; Davis, 'R. Yom Tov Lipman Heller', 130–3; Reiner, 'Attitude of Ashkenazi Society', 589–603, and elsewhere. The conflict should perhaps be seen as a continuation of the conflict between the Horowitzes and their opponents, mentioned above, Ch. 1 n. 31.

[16] See Horowitz's tract in defence of Maimonides (above, n. 15), p. 263 (cf. pp. 273, 346). Ashkenazi is quoted as asserting: 'It is not permitted to study anything except the Talmud'. Cf. Twersky, 'Talmudists, Philosophers, Kabbalists', 437.

JOSEPH BEN ISAAC HALEVI AND *GIVAT HAMOREH*

At the culmination of this rationalist turn in Ashkenazi Jewish culture, in the autumn of 1611, a book entitled *Givat hamoreh* (The Mountain of the Guide) was published in Prague.[17] Its author was Joseph ben Isaac Halevi, a Lithuanian Jew born in Brest-Litovsk (Brisk).[18] His goal was ambitious: to improve and correct Maimonides' four proofs of the existence of God. Joseph Halevi's revisions of Maimonides' proofs, however, were not very far-reaching, remaining for the most part within the confines of conservative medieval Aristotelianism. For instance, he defended the Aristotelian conception of bounded space against the notion of infinite space put forward in the fourteenth century by Hasdai Crescas (and in the seventeenth century by Baruch Spinoza).

Joseph Halevi defended Aristotle's and Averroes' conception of the astral spheres as well, although he was aware of the attacks on Aristotelian astronomy that had recently been made by Tycho Brahe and Johannes Kepler in Prague.[19] He gave a special endorsement to Averroes' views on astronomy: 'He may be relied on here since he testified for himself and said that he only came to this belief after great study over a long time.'[20] There is, however, one novel doctrine in *Givat hamoreh*. Halevi argued that our universe is one of an infinite succession of universes: a finite number of worlds preceded our own, and our world would be followed by an infinity of ever more perfect worlds:

> The worlds that preceded [this one] did not possess exactly the same type of perfection as does this world, and likewise, those worlds which come into being after this one will not possess exactly the same type of perfection as still later worlds.[21]

Halevi believed, that is, in a type of cosmic optimism: not an optimism about this world with its plagues, wars, and other misfortunes, but optimism in regard to the totality of all future worlds. This world is not, for him, the 'best of all possible

[17] The date on the title page is 1 Kislev 5372 (7 Nov. 1611). The publisher was Gershon b. Solomon Popper Katz, a member of the well-known Gerson family of Prague printers. The main study of Joseph Halevi is my own 'R. Yom Tov Lipman Heller', 197–338. See ibid. 209–13 on the previous scholarly literature. Note particularly Zinberg, *History*, vi. 96–7 (original Yiddish edn., v. 119–23); Davidson, 'Medieval Jewish Philosophy', 116, 121, 142 n. 77; Elbaum, *Openness and Insularity* (references in index).

[18] In the introduction to *Ketonet pasim*, written in Brest-Litovsk after he had returned there from Prague, he refers to that city as his 'home' (*moledet*). His father's name was Isaac b. Solomon (*Givat hamoreh*, 3*a*). Both the title page and some of the approbations for *Givat hamoreh* mention his youth (Ephraim of Luntshits refers to it twice).

[19] Cf. below, Ch. 9 n. 35.

[20] *Givat hamoreh*, 20*a*. The question here is the nature of the spheres. Halevi also gave a special endorsement to Maimonides: see below, Ch. 2 nn. 28 and 40. His major hesitation regarding Averroes concerned the latter's notorious doctrine of monopsychism.

[21] *Givat hamoreh*, 19*a*; cf. 12*a*.

worlds'; indeed there is no 'best of all possible worlds', just as there is no highest number. There is, rather, an infinite series of increasingly perfect worlds, guaranteed by the infinity of God's perfection. This theory is not quite identical to any of its many antecedents. Although it is less familiar than any of them, it is not, I think, inferior to them.[22]

Although a short work, *Givat hamoreh* was nevertheless, within the context of Ashkenazi culture, an exceptional one. It was the only work of Jewish philosophy published by an Ashkenazi author that was not a commentary on an earlier work. It was the only one that mounted a technical attack on Maimonides' philosophy. Finally it was the only book published by any Ashkenazi author of the period in which Greek or Islamic philosophers were quoted freely.[23]

'A young man came here to the holy community of Prague', wrote Ephraim of Luntshits, chief rabbi after the death of the Maharal.

> His name was Joseph ben Isaac Halevi, and we did not know him until he began to spread his light, teaching philosophy and theology. Then he became known as one with skill in that science, for he was praised by great scholars of our community whom he had taught the *Guide of the Perplexed*.[24]

'A DWARF ON THE SHOULDERS OF A GIANT'

One of the scholars with whom Joseph ben Isaac had studied Maimonides' *Moreh nevukhim* was Lipmann Heller.[25] Heller read *Givat hamoreh* in draft and contributed some notes to improve the exposition of the material, but added nothing substantial of his own. He improved the exposition of certain arguments and added the full text of certain quotations to which Joseph had only alluded. Heller's notes were intended not only as an improvement to the text but also as a gesture of

[22] A number of sources of the constituent elements of Halevi's theory can be located: Isaac Abarbanel's infinite succession of created worlds, Maimonides' single world that is created in the past but eternal in the future, the astrological theory of cosmic cycles, and the kabbalistic theory of 'sabbatical cycles' (*shemitot*). In the previous generation, Moses Isserles had expressed an almost mystical enthusiasm for the end of the cosmos, interpreting the entire sacrificial system of the Torah as a symbol of that great universal end. See J. Ben-Sasson, *The Thought of R. Moses Isserles*, 60–7. Halevi continued Isserles' focus on the world's temporal limits, and he was equally enthusiastic; but, foreseeing new, better universes after this one, he was more conventionally optimistic.

[23] In *Givat hamoreh*, Halevi quotes Plato (18*b*); many works of Aristotle (3*a*, 3*b*, etc.); Euclid's *Elements* (14*a* etc.); al-Ghazzali (17*a*, 24*a*); Averroes' *Long Commentary* and *Short Commentary* on Aristotle's *Physics* (3*a*–*b*, 22*a*–*b*, etc.) and Averroes' *Long Commentary* on *De caelo* (3*b* etc.). Even Halevi did not quote any Christian philosophers.

[24] From Luntshits's approbation in *Givat hamoreh*, 2*a*.

[25] See Heller's approbation, *Givat hamoreh*, 2*b*.

support; he encouraged Joseph to publish *Givat hamoreh* and had perhaps encouraged him to write it.

The three rabbis of Prague's higher court each gave *haskamot* (approbations) to *Givat hamoreh*: Ephraim of Luntshits, the Maharal's son-in-law Isaac Hakohen, and Heller's relative by marriage, Mordechai Lipschitz. Heller also contributed an enthusiastic *haskamah*. Unintentionally, though, Heller's *haskamah* may have contributed to the censure that the book provoked, for in it he stated distinctly that Joseph ben Isaac might, in a certain sense, be a better philosopher than Maimonides.

A number of the Jewish thinkers of Prague around the beginning of the seventeenth century, basing themselves on some passages in Maimonides' *Moreh nevukhim*, gave expression to their belief in the possibility of intellectual or scientific progress.[26] Joseph ben Isaac was among this group. He wrote, '[It is in] the nature of true knowledge that human reason must struggle to understand a matter truly . . . For this reason you will find that no science is perfected except over a long time.'[27] Joseph even denied the dogma of Moses' superiority to all other individuals, and, notably, his superiority to Maimonides, though he did not go so far as to claim Maimonides' superiority to Moses.[28]

In connection with the notion of intellectual progress, David Gans and Mordechai Jaffe had both quoted the proverb of the dwarf standing on the shoulders of a giant, an image later made famous by Isaac Newton.[29] In his *haskamah*, in an exuberant mood of optimism, Heller now applied the image of the dwarf and the giant to Joseph ben Isaac:

[Let blessings] come upon the head of Joseph and upon the crown prince of his brethren (Deut. 33: 16) . . . Give glory to the Lord your God Who gave us the teacher of righteousness, the great rabbi, the father of wisdom, Rabbi Moses Maimonides . . . of whom the proverb says, 'From Moses to Moses there was none like Moses.' And after him, 'He appointed it a testimony in Joseph' (Ps. 81: 6), the son of Isaac Halevi, standing . . . on the

[26] See the discussion in Breuer, 'Modernism and Traditionalism', 64; cf. p. 81 n. 2. On Maimonides' belief in historical progress, see Kellner, *Maimonides*, 69–82; cf. Nisbet, *History of the Idea of Progress*. Nisbet stresses the ancient and medieval roots of the idea.

[27] *Givat hamoreh*, 20*b*.

[28] See ibid. 30*a*.

[29] See Gans, *Tsemaḥ david*, introd. to pt. 1, and M. Jaffe, *Levush*, 'Oraḥ ḥayim', para. 267, which notes the ignorance of astronomy of some earlier medieval Ashkenazi rabbis. Jaffe's student Jacob Koppelman made use of a similar figure, of a horse and a man: 'When a man rides on a horse at twilight, the horse can see and goes down the road, although the man sees nothing; so should we understand more than the ancients understood': Koppelman, *Ohel ya'akov* on *Sefer ikarim* 4: 4. On some other instances of this proverb in Jewish literature of this period (Azariah dei Rossi, Abraham Azulai), see Zlotnick, 'On the Origins'; Elbaum, 'More on the Image'. For an overview of the use of the saying in general literature, see Merton, *On the Shoulders of Giants*. Note also Levine, '"Dwarfs on the Shoulders of Giants"'.

MOUNTAIN, on the shoulders of the giant, the GUIDE of the Perplexed. As the ancient proverb says, a dwarf who stands on the shoulders of a giant will see farther than the giant.[30]

THE PLAGUE OF 1611

'A stiff and freezing horror sucks up the rivers of my blood', wrote Thomas Dekker in 1602:

I could in this place make your cheekes looke pale and your hearts shake, with telling how some have had 18 sores at one time running upon them, others 10 & 12. . . . I could draw a Catalogue of many poore wretches, that in fields, in ditches, in common Cages and under stalls (being either thrust by cruell maisters out of doors, or wanting all worldly succor but the common benefit of earth and air) have most miserably perished.[31]

The seventeenth century was an age of plague. Escape to neighbouring villages, quarantines, ineffectual medical efforts—all these were well known and fairly regular measures. Yet plague is an event that can never be made routine. The terror of the city of death is instinctive. In the autumn of 1611, just as *Givat hamoreh* was being published, the Jewish community of Prague suffered an outbreak of the plague.

The plague was preceded by political upheaval. At Carnival time, in February 1611, there was a brief civil war, the so-called Passau war, and riots in Prague.[32] Emperor Rudolph II was deposed shortly afterwards, and died in 1612. The Maharal, meanwhile, had died in September 1609. In the Jewish community of Prague and in the empire as a whole, an era had ended.

It is perhaps natural—in any event, it is quite common—to respond to plague with blame and reprisals, or with an attempt to purify the community of sin and uncleanness. The closeness of death makes one rethink the moral compromises that one has made, as an individual and as a community. Penitence and purification are the order of the day. Lawrence of Brindisi, visiting Prague in 1606 after an outbreak of the plague, preached aggressively against the Protestants.[33] Enemies of the Jews in Cracow in 1623 blamed them for the plague there.[34] Plague also divided the wealthy, who could retreat to healthy villages and wait out the infestation, from the poor, who had no such escape. The communal leadership being absent, the poor in the plague-ridden city were relatively free from control (this is the premise of Ben Jonson's 1610 play, *The Alchemist*). Wealthy Prague Jews and rabbis, Heller doubt-

[30] *Givat hamoreh*, 2*b*. Cf. Elbaum, 'More on the Image'.

[31] Dekker, 'The wonderfull yeare', 37–8.

[32] See Palmitessa, 'The Prague Uprising of 1611'; Šedinová, 'Hebrew Literature', 7–11; A. David (ed.), *Hebrew Chronicle*, 62–9.

[33] Parker (ed.), *The Thirty Years War*, 22–3.

[34] Dubnow, *History of the Jews in Russia and Poland*, i. 96.

less among them, would leave the city during a plague.[35] It is to be expected, then, that class relations were strained, and that, on the elders' return, attempts would be made to re-establish order.[36]

Led by the chief rabbi, Ephraim of Luntshits, the Jewish authorities of Prague responded to the 1611 plague by enacting a set of penitential rules, including new fast-days, special prayer services, and an exhortation against oaths and blasphemy. Among the rules was an order that all 'whores' be driven from the Jewish community. The reference is apparently to female servants and wet-nurses who had been accused of illicit sexual relations. Male servants who had made lewd remarks or gestures were also to be disciplined or expelled. Women who peddled goods were no longer to enter the houses of Christians, unless accompanied by a chaperone.[37]

In that same plague season of autumn 1611, Joseph Halevi's *Givat hamoreh* aroused controversy. Sometime in the next year, he was forced to leave Prague; he returned to his native city of Brest-Litovsk. Jewish anti-rationalist rhetoric often associated philosophers and whores. Perhaps the exile of the Jewish philosopher so highly regarded by Prague's Jewish leaders and the exile of some of Prague's Jewish servant girls balanced each other in the accounting of the various parties within the community.[38]

THE EXILE OF A PHILOSOPHER

In a work that he published in 1614 Halevi described the controversy that had led to his exile from Prague and his return to Lithuania (the work was a sermon on an appropriately safe and orthodox topic: the superiority of the Torah to the seven

[35] Note for instance the retreat of the Jewish communal leaders of Prague to neighbouring towns and villages during the 1606 plague. See Ephraim of Luntshits's introduction to *Amudei shesh*, and the colophon of the anonymous commentary on the laws of the Hebrew calendar, MS Oxford-Bodleian Heb. 746/4, 403*a*.

[36] See C. L. Ross, 'The Plague': 'The wealthy purchased virtual immunity from the disease' (p. 439 n. 1). Cf. James Amelang's introduction in id., *A Journal of the Plague Year*. On Jewish responses to the plague, including flight by the wealthy from the cities, see Ch. 6 n. 37 below.

[37] See Rivkind (ed.), 'Pamphlet of Regulations'. Cf. the translation and discussion in S.-A. Goldberg, *Crossing the Jabbok*, 227–8. Goldberg seems convinced that the women spoken of were actual prostitutes, but the text of the rules suggests otherwise. See Wiesner, 'Paternalism in Practice': in Munich in 1580, female servants accused of sexual immorality were threatened with exile. Note also that the Prague archepiscopal synod of 1605 prohibited Jewish women from serving as wet-nurses in the houses of Christians: see Bondy and Dworsky (eds.), *Zur Geschichte der Juden*, no. 1009 (p. 794), quoted in Baron, *Social and Religious History of the Jews*, xiv. 167. Compare also the 1620 rules from Zolkiew, which prohibit women from entering Christian houses unescorted: see Cygielman, *Jews of Poland and Lithuania*, 508 (from S. Buber, *Kiryah nisgavah*, 81–4). Cf. below, Ch. 5 n. 4.

[38] See e.g. the quotation from N. Altshuler above, n. 1.

sciences). The introduction is written in extremely convoluted Hebrew, replete with biblical and talmudic allusions and puns. Halevi cast himself in the role of the biblical Joseph:

It came to pass two years ago that 'the inkpots of Joseph' wrote a book against Maimonides [*ben ma'amin*, lit. 'the believing one'] as if he were his opponent, with open reproach and hidden love, and he sent it from another land to his brothers in Dothan, wise men in their own eyes. And they hated him and regarded him as far from them.[39]

Halevi described his opponents' barbs:

They said to him, 'Shall you be king over kings—that is, [over] the rabbis? Shall you rule over the one of whom the proverb says, from Moses to Moses there has been none like Moses [i.e. Maimonides]?' And one said to another, 'Since this Joseph honours the seven sciences, it is clear that he cannot know what the rabbis have written.' How shall the mind bear and the ear hear . . . the objections . . . and the doubts . . . that one young in years and small among the sages cast against our Rabbi Moses [Maimonides], whose equal there has not been since the days of Moses?[40]

'I answered when they did not ask me; I was present when they did not search for me; I said, Here I am, here I am, to a nation that would not listen,' Halevi concluded.[41]

Halevi portrayed the opposition as centring on his criticisms of Maimonides. Yet the Maharal had once done much the same—that is, he had criticized Maimonides' proofs of God's existence and suggested a revised proof.[42] Halevi suggests that one crucial difference, on which his opponents focused their attacks, was his youth and his lack of talmudic training. The Maharal was a great talmudic scholar, but who was Joseph ben Isaac?

Another difference between *Givat hamoreh* and the Maharal's work may also have been decisive. Jewish philosophy, Halevi wrote in a postscript to *Givat hamoreh*, has four types of opponent. Some find it too difficult; some complain that it has no value for religious life; some object that it does not agree with kabbalah; and some object that it is not Jewish.[43]

Perhaps *Givat hamoreh* had aroused opposition of the fourth kind, opposition to that which is not Jewish. Whereas the Maharal had portrayed himself in his

[39] Cf. Gen. 37: 14, 17–18, and also Mishnah, *Mik.* 10: 1, Job 31: 36, Prov. 27: 5. Joseph means to imply that he had a hidden love for Maimonides, although he appeared to disagree with him.

[40] *Ketonet pasim*, 4*a*.

[41] Ibid., introd. 4*a*. Halevi paraphrases Isaiah 65: 1.

[42] *Netivot olam*, 'Netiv hashalom', i. 224 (ch. 2). Maharal's proposed proof, which he calls 'the proof of our sages of blessed memory', is discussed in Sherwin, *Mystical Theology*, 56–7. Maharal's criticism, like Halevi's, was that Maimonides' proofs are based on the Aristotelian hypothesis that the world had no temporal beginning.

[43] *Givat hamoreh*, 29*b*–30*a*. For a survey of opposition to philosophy among Ashkenazi Jews in this period, see pp. 131–43, 180–95 in my dissertation.

attacks on Maimonides as the defender of biblical and talmudic Judaism, Joseph Halevi had actually announced his preference for Averroes' views over those of Maimonides on certain questions. To attack Maimonides at all was dangerous; the Maharal too had been controversial in his day. But to reject any of Maimonides' views in favour of those of Averroes was intolerable.

Like the women pedlars who had visited the houses of non-Jews unchaperoned, Joseph Halevi had come too close to the non-Jews. Although he polemicized against Christianity (both in *Givat hamoreh* and in another work, now lost, called *Ma'amar ha'aḥdut*, Treatise on Divine Unity), he had not sufficiently guarded himself against the charge that his philosophy was essentially non-Jewish.

Heller never quoted or referred to Halevi in his later writings, and it is not possible to determine precisely what he learned in his studies with him. Perhaps he learned—from Halevi's fate rather than from his lectures—a degree of caution in offending the religious sensibilities of the community. The influence of Heller's study of Jewish philosophy, however, can be seen in many aspects of his thought, as will be shown in later chapters: in his attitude towards non-Jews, his understanding of politics, his attitude towards natural science, and his approach to the problem of evil and suffering. In regard to certain of these questions, he was following in the footsteps of the Maharal; in others, he went beyond the Maharal, opposing his teachings. Although Heller was a disciple of the Maharal, he was also, we must recognize, a student of one of the boldest and best-trained Aristotelians among Ashkenazi Jews—Joseph ben Isaac Halevi of Lithuania.

THREE

Two Kabbalists

ISAIAH HOROWITZ AND THE 'REPUDIATION OF PHILOSOPHY'

A FEW years after the exile of Joseph Halevi, in 1614, yet another member of the Horowitz family, Isaiah ben Abraham Horowitz, was elected to the Prague rabbinate.[1] Isaiah Horowitz was a master of Talmud and Jewish law, learned in the Bible and midrash, and an eloquent preacher—a scholar of much the same Ashkenazi Renaissance type as Heller. He was also a kabbalist. His *magnum opus*, *Shenei luḥot haberit*, finished in 1623, is a sort of encyclopedia of Judaism. It was widely read—Hayim Hameln, husband of the diarist Glueckel (Glikl), for example, had parts of it read to him on his deathbed in 1689—and its influence on Ashkenazi Judaism for generations, even centuries, was considerable;[2] Horowitz himself became known as 'the holy Shelah', a name derived from the initial letters of the words of the title. In one of the book's many parts, Horowitz attacked and rejected Jewish philosophy.

Heller and Horowitz were colleagues in the Prague rabbinate for seven years, from 1614 to 1621. Apart from a brief approbation that Heller wrote in 1636 for Horowitz's commentary on the prayer book, he almost never referred to Horowitz in his writings, nor did Horowitz ever refer to Heller in his.[3] Horowitz was Heller's cousin by marriage and a dozen years his senior; he perhaps served Heller as an inspiring model, or perhaps as a rival.

1 *Shenei luḥot haberit* was published posthumously in 1648. Miles Krassen has translated its first section, as *Shenei Luhot ha-Berit: The Generations of Adam.* On Horowitz and *Shenei luḥot haberit*, see Newman, *Isaiah Horowitz*; Horodetsky, *Jewish Mysticism*, iv. 54–113; and J. Katz, *Halakhah and Kabalah*, 97–100, as well as H. H. Ben-Sasson, 'Horowitz', and Krassen's introduction to his translation.

2 Glueckel bat Judah Leib, *Life*, 109. On the work's reputation in the 18th c., see Gries, *Literature of Pious Customs*, 55–9; Piekarz, *Beginnings of Hasidism*, 102 n. 23.

3 Note that Horowitz recommended Bertinoro's Mishnah commentary but not Heller's *Tosafot yom tov* (*Shenei luḥot haberit*, ii. 31*a*). Heller does not appear at all in the list of citations from *Shenei luḥot haberit* in Newman, *Isaiah Horowitz*, 78–87; cf. p. 100. Horowitz's approbation for *Tosafot yom tov* is quoted below, p. 66. Heller referred to *Shenei luḥot haberit* shortly after it was published in 1648: see *MalYT* 696.

If Heller ever saw the approbation that was given to Horowitz's prayer book by the great talmudist Joel Sirkes (1561–1640), he would doubtless have been taken aback. 'No one who uses this prayer book', Sirkes assured the world, 'will have his prayers rejected.' The prayer book must be published, Sirkes wrote, 'for who is the man . . . who would think to hold back the spread of holiness into the houses of Israel?' Heller's own approbation was much drier: 'I have seen that a number of books have been printed, and this one is not less worthy than they.'[4] Heller was unenthusiastic about the publication of kabbalistic works, as will be seen later. 'A holy and awesome man', Heller called Horowitz in that same approbation. The suggestion is of a man whose religious experience and religious psychology were on an entirely different scale to those of lesser men, such as Heller himself.

Three fundamental divergences in their lives typify the difference between the two men. First, Horowitz became one of the great apostles of the kabbalists of the mystical community of Safed in the Land of Israel, and one of the most important channels of their version of Judaism to the Ashkenazi world. He combined the heritage of the two greatest Safed kabbalists, joining the system of meditative prayer and some of the ritual innovations of Isaac Luria (1534–72) to a kabbalistic theology based primarily on the ideas of Moses Cordovero (1522–70).[5] Second, Horowitz left his rabbinical position in Prague, abandoned his home and his family, and moved in 1621 to the Land of Israel. Heller could only suppose that Horowitz had been specially inspired. 'Undoubtedly', he wrote, 'a supernal spirit entered him, poured out to him, as it were, from Heaven.'[6] Third, Horowitz rejected Jewish philosophy. '[The philosophers'] words are all emptiness', he wrote in *Shenei luḥot haberit*, 'because all of their study is from the point of view of necessity and nature'; but both God and man exercise choice and free will.[7] Again, he said: 'The repudiation and prohibition of the study of philosophy are spelled out in the words of both ancient and recent authorities; to quote all of them would be burdensome, but you may see a few of them.'[8]

Horowitz put together a catalogue of anti-philosophical passages from the Maimonidean controversies and from an array of medieval rabbis, quoting from each at his harshest. Finally, he quoted the sixteenth-century kabbalist, Meir ibn

[4] Sirkes' and Heller's approbations for I. Horowitz, *Sha'ar hashamayim*. In spite of Sirkes' enthusiastic and Heller's unenthusiastic comments, the work remained unpublished for eighty years.

[5] Sack, 'Influence of Cordovero'; Wolfson, 'Influence of Isaac Luria'; Piekarz, *Beginnings of Hasidism*, 209–15.

[6] From Heller's approbation for *Sha'ar hashamayim*. Unlike the Maharal, who is sometimes regarded as an important pre-Zionist thinker, Heller did not stress the theme of the Land of Israel in his writings; cf. Ch. 4 n. 13 and Ch. 10 n. 8. None of Heller's students is known to have emigrated to the Land of Israel.

[7] *Shenei luḥot haberit*, i. 14*a* ('Beit yisra'el', pt. 3).

[8] For his repudiation of philosophy, see *Shenei luḥot haberit*, ii. 31*b*–32*a* (in 'Masekhet shavuot').

Gabbai:[9] 'Philosophy is the adulterous woman of Proverbs, the foreign woman whose words are smooth and who seduces man. . . . The Zohar . . . revealed that there are demons that are sages, and parallel to them on the earth are the Jewish philosophers.' Following all of these 'ancient and recent authorities', Horowitz argued that Jewish philosophy should be removed from the curriculum. The student, he suggested, when he has 'filled his belly' with Talmud, should not study philosophy but move directly to kabbalah.

Isaiah Horowitz's father was Abraham Horowitz, the man who defended Jewish philosophy in 1559 from Joseph Ashkenazi's attack. Although Horowitz senior had mellowed in his last years, the sharp-tongued rationalist remained to the end the man who had triumphed in the cause of Maimonides; he had never rejected his earlier views, and surely had never rejected Jewish philosophy as a whole.[10] Joseph Ashkenazi thus enjoyed posthumous vengeance when Abraham's son Isaiah made the same journey to the Land of Israel that Ashkenazi had made sixty years earlier, and when he condemned, as Ashkenazi had done, the study of philosophy.

In his fight against Jewish philosophy, Isaiah Horowitz had an ally in the Polish rabbinate: Joel Sirkes, the rabbi of Brest-Litovsk and later of Cracow, author of the *Bayit ḥadash*, and the man who would later praise Horowitz's prayer book so extravagantly. Sirkes and Horowitz were students of the same teacher, Solomon ben Judah Leibush of Lublin.[11] Sirkes took up the problem of philosophy in a responsum written in 1618, when he was rabbi of Brest-Litovsk.[12] He was responding to a controversy among the Jews of Amsterdam involving a man named David Farrar, a doctor and former Marrano. (The case foreshadowed in certain respects the excommunication of Spinoza forty years later.) Farrar had given allegorical philosophical interpretations of talmudic passages, and had denied the efficacy of kabbalistic magic. Leone da Modena (1571–1648) in Venice supported Farrar, but Sirkes denounced him.

Kabbalah, it has been suggested—at least seventeenth-century kabbalah—had heretical tendencies. Isaiah Horowitz, for instance, like Cordovero himself, took positions whose radical possibilities would later be worked out by Shabatean heresiarchs: positions such as the annulment of Jewish law in the messianic age, or

[9] Note that Horowitz lists Ibn Gabbai, together with Luria and Cordovero, in the introduction to *Shenei luḥot haberit* as one of the three kabbalists whose thought serves as the basis of the work.

[10] The 2nd edn. of his *Hesed avraham*, published in 1602, suggests no retreat from the orthodox Maimonideanism that he had defended in 1577 in the 1st edn.

[11] This point is made in Shulman, *Authority and Community*, 209. *Bayit ḥadash* is a commentary on the halakhic code *Arba'ah turim* by Jacob ben Asher (1280–1340).

[12] On Sirkes, see Schochet, *Bach*. The responsum (no. 5 in *She'elot uteshuvot habaḥ hayeshanot*) is translated by Schochet, ibid. 250–3. On the Farrar case, see Idel, 'Differing Conceptions', 142–52, Saperstein, '*Hesped*', and the literature cited there. See also Idel, '"One from a Family"', 83; Scholem, *Kabbalah*, 79.

the achievement of spiritual elevation through evil thoughts.[13] Sirkes, however, saw the matter very differently. For him, kabbalah did not tend towards heresy. On the contrary, it was the very essence of orthodoxy; heresy was the denial of kabbalah. Like Horowitz, Sirkes quoted from the anti-rationalist teachings of Meir ibn Gabbai. The essence of heresy, wrote Sirkes, is philosophy:

There is no doubt that this man deserves . . . excommunication. . . . For he . . . slights the wisdom of the kabbalah, which is the very source and essence of the Torah and is entirely God-fearing. It is obvious that such a person deserves excommunication, for there can be no greater mockery of Torah . . . than this. Furthermore, this man is drawn after philosophy, which is heresy itself.[14]

Horowitz's and Sirkes's strictures signalled a crucial turn against philosophy in Ashkenazi Judaism. The publication of works of philosophy ceased entirely among Ashkenazi Jews; none appeared for more than seventy years. The study of philosophy did not altogether cease, but it became marginal and suspect.[15]

HELLER AS KABBALIST

In at least one place, Heller professed his ignorance of kabbalistic matters.[16] In fact, however, like Isaiah Horowitz, Joel Sirkes, and nearly every Jewish thinker in the early seventeenth century, Heller actively studied kabbalah. Only a few Jews were strongly sceptical of kabbalah in the seventeenth century: Heller was not one. Nowhere in his writings did he disparage kabbalistic beliefs or the study of kabbalah. On the contrary, it is clear that he could not conceive of Judaism without it.

It is useful at this point to consider this aspect of Heller's work, although it will require us to deviate somewhat from strict chronological sequence, and to examine a number of passages from Heller's 1628 work, *Ma'adanei melekh* (Delights of the King).

Heller began his kabbalistic studies in the first decade of the seventeenth century. He wrote:

At that time, *Sefer pardes rimonim* [The Book of the Orchard of Pomegranates] by the sage and the great kabbalist, the man of God, Rabbi Moses Cordovero, was published. And since many students used to gather each sabbath to study the [Torah commentary] of Rabbi Bahya [ben Asher], and I among them, my heart was raised to comment on it in kabbalistic matters on the basis of the book I have just named [*Pardes rimonim*], and in the

[13] See *Shenei luhot haberit*, i. 39*b*–40*a* (in 'Sha'ar ha'otiyot', *alef*, in Horowitz's comment on Maimonides' Ninth Principle); Piekarz, *Beginnings of Hasidism*, 211, 354; Gries, *Literature of Pious Customs*, 193–7.

[14] Schochet, *Bach*, 250–1. I have revised his translation slightly.

[15] See above, Ch. 2 nn. 10–11.

[16] *MalYT* 651.

way of the author of *ME* [*Me'irat einayim* by Isaac ben Samuel of Acre], and the kabbalah of Moses Nahmanides.[17]

Three are the pillars on which the knowledge of kabbalah rests, wrote Isaiah Horowitz: Meir ibn Gabbai, Isaac Luria, and Moses Cordovero. In his extant writings, Heller referred to Isaac Luria by name only once, and that only in a short bibliographical aside. He referred to the anti-rationalist Ibn Gabbai when he wished to contest his views.[18] His choice of Cordovero as his guide in kabbalah, together with the thirteenth-century kabbalists Moses Nahmanides, Bahya ben Asher, and Isaac ben Samuel of Acre, was the choice of a moderate, universalist variety of kabbalah not altogether opposed to Jewish philosophy.[19]

Tuv ta'am (Good Sense), Heller's supercommentary on Bahya ben Asher's commentary on the Torah, was never published and there is no extant manuscript. However, Heller's personal copy of *Sefer naftali* (The Book of Naftali) by Naftali Treves, another supercommentary on Bahya ben Asher, is in the British Library, and includes his marginal notes. Another of Heller's works, *Leket shoshanim* (The Gathering of Lilies), written some time after 1612, is an unfinished commentary on a grammar textbook, *Arugat habosem* (Bed of Spices) by Samuel Archivolti (1515–1611) published in 1602,[20] and also includes some of Heller's kabbalistic views.

[17] *Megilat eivah*, 28. As we have seen, Heller was already interested in kabbalistic questions in 1598. His teacher Jacob Günzburg may have had some interest in kabbalah: two of his three published approbations are for kabbalistic works. See Löwenstein, 'Günzburg', 2 (1901), 27. On the Maharal's interest in kabbalah, see below, n. 52. The abbreviation *mem-ayin* is sometimes rendered incorrectly as *Megaleh amukot*, a work by Nathan Spira. The chronology makes this impossible, as Hailperin notes (MS, p. 85): *Megaleh amukot* was not published until 1637. *Me'irat einayim* is a supercommentary on the kabbalistic material in Nahmanides' Torah commentary.

[18] *Tos YT*, introd. to Seder 'Kodashim'. Heller identified a certain man as the author of a Lurianic liturgy. The speed at which Lurianic material became disseminated before 1648 has been disputed: see Idel, ' "One from a Family" '; Wolfson, 'Influence of Isaac Luria'. It is clear that some material would have been available to Heller, had he wished to find it. For Heller's reference to Ibn Gabbai, see below, p. 62.

[19] Heller refers to Cordovero in *Tos YT*, *Suk.* 4: 5, *Yoma* 6: 2, and *Sot.* 7: 6. He had also read works such as *Sefer yetsirah*, *Pirkei heikhalot* (see *Tsurat habayit*, ed. N. Malin, 83); and *Ma'arekhet elokut* (see *Leket shoshanim*, ch. 9, fo. 125*a*). Heller had a copy of the kabbalist work *Sefer hapeli'ah* copied for him (see the colophon of MS Bar Ilan 842), but he never refers to the work in his writings. Note also Shabetai b. Akiba Horowitz's comparison of Moses Cordovero's position among kabbalists to that of Moses Maimonides among Jewish philosophers: *Shefa tal*, 9*b*. On competing currents in 16th- and 17th-c. kabbalah, see Idel, 'Differing Conceptions', 137–200, and id., 'Particularism and Universalism'. On Cordovero's attitude to Jewish philosophy, see Ben Shlomo, *Theology*, 23–43.

[20] Although never published, *Leket shoshanim* has survived in a single manuscript copy, now in the Bodleian Library, Oxford: Heb. 2271. It was written between 1612 and 1630. Archivolti (d. 1611) is given the honorific blessing for the dead; moreover, Heller quotes (fo. 130*b*) David

The kabbalistic doctrines that Heller refers to in his marginalia and in *Leket shoshanim* are mostly commonplace doctrines of medieval Spanish kabbalah, such as the doctrine of the four worlds, the spiritual 'clothing' of the rabbis, and the existence of the ten *sefirot*.[21] (The sin of the builders of the Tower of Babel, he wrote in one place, was their rejection of belief in the *sefirot*.[22])

One of Heller's comments, however, shows the special influence of Moses Cordovero. Heller expounds the Cordoverian concept of 'returning light':

> The kabbalists say that two *sefirot*, Keter and Hokhmah, are completely mercy [*raḥamim*], and Binah has in her the awakening of judgement; and afterwards [through the *sefirot*] until Malkhut, everything is composed of mercy and judgement, although some have a preponderance of mercy and some a preponderance of judgement. But the mystery of the reversal of light, which is the returning light—they said that this is all judgement.[23]

While the harsh and self-absorbed aspect of the divine, the failure of contact of the divine and the human, is symbolized for Heller in the image of the 'reversal of light', the ideal of divine–human relations is conveyed in the traditional image of a kiss:

> The [divine] awakening is not a passivity or a change in God. But it is known to the wise of heart that by performance of the commandments, Israel makes an impression and unites the Supernal Attributes [the *sefirot*], each commandment according to its nature. And they are pure, for water is purified by 'kissing' [coming into contact with ritually pure water]. 'And you who cleave [to the Lord your God are all alive today' (Deut. 4: 4)]. And, 'Let Him kiss me with the kisses of His mouth' (S. of S. 1: 2)—the cleaving of spirit to spirit.[24]

ON MAGIC, *MAGIDIM*, AND THE INDIVIDUAL SELF

The Pinkas Shul in Prague held a relic: the garments of the messianic visionary and martyr Solomon Molcho, who died at the stake in Mantua in 1532. The following is a story that was told in 1666, at the time of the messianic movement of Shabetai Tsevi, twelve years after Heller's death:

Gans's *Magen david*, which he read in 1612. On the other hand, *Leket shoshanim* was written while Heller was teaching his own children Hebrew grammar (as he writes in the introduction), which could not have been after 1630. Heller corresponded with Archivolti: see *Tos YT*, *Tam.* 7: 4.

[21] See *Leket shoshanim*, fos. 126*a*–127*a*.

[22] *Sefer naftali*, 34.

[23] *Leket shoshanim*, ch. 8, fo. 125*a*; cf. Ben Shlomo, *Theology*, 270–4.

[24] *Leket shoshanim*, ch. 12, fo. 126*a*. The last phrase is from Zohar ii. 146*a* (trans. and discussed in Tishby, *Wisdom of the Zohar*, i. 365). Heller leaves out the continuation of the Zohar's language, *ḥad ihu* ('they are one'). He refers to *devekut* again in his supercommentary on Ibn Ezra on Exod. 6: 3. Abraham, Isaac, and Jacob did not know the Name of God by which to perform visible miracles 'for their level did not reach that wonderful unity [*devekut*]'.

> [It was the custom] in that synagogue to display the garments [of Solomon Molcho] . . . But [Molcho's] *arba kanefot* [ritual four-cornered garment] was not on display because Holy Names were embroidered on it with silk. But these names are disarrayed all over [the garment—and therefore are hard to read correctly]. Once the beadle of the synagogue wanted to copy these names, and he became blind. And once . . . the illustrious Rabbi Lipmann [Heller] . . . relying on his virtue, wished to copy these names; and indeed his saintliness saved him and he himself escaped unharmed, but his paper and ink-horn mysteriously vanished. Wherefore he decreed . . . that no man should ever approach to read these Holy Names or copy them.[25]

Many Ashkenazi rabbis were retrospectively viewed as kabbalists and miracle-workers. The Maharal of Prague is a particularly well-known example, and Heller himself was later to be treated in the same way.[26] But this story seems rather to stress Heller's limitations as a kabbalist; it implies that, in the judgement of Providence, he was not worthy to possess the holy names that he had copied.[27]

Like almost any person of his time, Heller believed in magic (he also believed in ghosts). He doubtless participated in the normal rituals and home remedies that kept demons and disease at bay.[28] Heller was of the opinion—unlike Maimonides, but in line with Ashkenazi legal precedent—that magic was permitted; even demon magic, and *a fortiori* kabbalistic magic, based on *Sefer yetsirah*, the ancient 'Book of Creation'.[29] Heller also believed in miracles, as will be discussed in Chapter 6. There is one particular sort of miracle or magic, however, concerning which Heller expressed ambivalence: angelic revelation.

In his 1628 talmudic work, *Ma'adanei melekh*, Heller commented on a remark, in a certain medieval Talmud commentary (Tosafot), that the angels know secret human thoughts. His comment moved cautiously through this problem, offering first biblical and then midrashic proofs for this view. Then he offered a philosophical interpretation of angels' knowledge of human thoughts, based on a

[25] Scholem (ed.), 'Sabbatian Miscellany', 142–4, trans. in id., *Sabbatai Sevi*, 563; I have revised the translation somewhat. On the relics, see Sadek, 'Étendard et Robe', 64; Idel, 'Solomon Molkho', 208–12. Heller mentions them in his writings: see *MYT (DH)*, *Tsitsit*, p. 251 n. 25, p. 253 n. 48, p. 256 n. 58.

[26] See M. Roth, 'Notes', 108–9, for a miracle story concerning Heller, related by Roth's ancestor (and Heller's descendant) Nahman Epstein. On the Maharal legends, see Demetz, 'Die Legende vom Magischen Prag'; Goldsmith, *The Golem Remembered*. For miracle stories concerning David b. Samuel, see Schochet, *Taz*, 58–9.

[27] Another folk-tale about Heller with an anti-magical tendency is recorded in Hailperin MS, p. 51.

[28] Cf. Heller's comment on a folk remedy which saved his wife from choking, published in Simon Cohen, 'From the Library', 104. On ghosts, see *Tos YT*, *Avot* 2: 7.

[29] See *MYT (PH)*, *San.*, p. 237 n. 7; *Ma'amar yom tov* on Exod. 6: 3; *Tos YT*, *Ḥag.* 2: 1; *Mal YT* 404. On magic in early modern Ashkenazi Judaism, see Etkes, 'Magic and *Ba'alei-Shem*'; Trachtenberg, *Jewish Magic and Superstition*.

Neoplatonic view of angels. Finally, however, he quoted two Bible verses in support of the opposite position: 'You [God] alone have known the heart of man' (2 Chron. 6: 30), and 'The heart is deceitful . . . who can know it? I the Lord search the heart' (Jer. 17: 9–10). Perhaps the angels do not know human thoughts; perhaps they are known only to God himself.[30]

The question of whether the root of the human soul is higher than the angels figured prominently, we may recall, in Heller's youthful commentary on *Beḥinat olam*: there he expressed his preference for the kabbalistic view that the human soul is higher than angels. The objection that Heller made now in his closing remarks accorded with the same doctrine: angels cannot know the human soul since it is above them; only God can know it. However, certain seventeenth-century kabbalists supported the assertion that angels *do* know secret human thoughts, claiming that *magidim*, angelic voices, revealed secret thoughts to them. A large proportion of the miracle stories of Isaac Luria, for example, concern his ability to discern a person's thoughts or secret past.[31]

The value of these stories was debated in the early seventeenth century. It may have been stories such as these that David Farrar denied, calling down on himself the wrath of Joel Sirkes. In the first decades of the century, the great doctor Elijah Montalto, listening to these wonder stories while he lay sick in bed in the Venice ghetto, grew angry, and told the storyteller to stop talking such nonsense.[32]

Heller, arguing that angels could not know secret thoughts, was arguing circuitously that kabbalists could not know them either. Hesitantly and delicately, he was expressing scepticism concerning some of the stories circulating about Isaac Luria in these years, and in doing so he was reinforcing the position of the rabbinate against the claims of kabbalistic wonder-workers.

He was also doing something more. Much of the debate within kabbalah in the seventeenth century was concerned with the concept of the self. *Gilgul*, the transmigration of souls, for instance, is in some ways a simple and pious doctrine. In other respects, as it dissolves the traditional notion of the individual self or soul into multiple 'sparks' that are said to travel through multiple bodies, it is mysteri-

[30] *MYT* (*MM*), *Ber.*, p. 13 n. 6. The remark is in Tosafot on *Shab.* 12*b*. Shabetai b. Isaiah Horowitz, *Vavei ha'amudim*, ch. 20, p. 22, refers to the 'well-known question of whether angels know that which is in a man's heart'. Cf. Joseph Halevi, *Givat hamoreh*, 18*a*, on the hierarchy of Intellects.

[31] See Fine, 'Maggidic Revelation'; cf. id., 'The Art of Metoposcopy'; J. H. Chajes, 'Judgments Sweetened'; Dan, *The Hebrew Story*, 243. Note also angelic revelations claimed by the English mathematician and magician John Dee during his visit to Prague: see Shumaker, 'John Dee's Conversations'.

[32] See Benayahu, *Sefer toledot ha'ari*, 41–2, on stories of the Ari circulating in Prague as well as elsewhere by *c.*1605–10 (cf. p. 119). The story of Montalto on his sick-bed comes from Leone da Modena, *Ari nohem*, 80.

ous and frightening, and its moral implications are open to question.[33] It was against such views that Heller asserted the privacy of the individual self, its secret thoughts known only to God.

ON ESOTERICISM, NON-KABBALISTIC JUDAISM, AND THE PURPOSES OF PRAYER

Before Heller was born, Moses Cordovero had challenged the age-old tradition of kabbalistic esotericism, and demanded that kabbalah be taught to the fullest extent possible.[34] During Heller's lifetime, a broadening stream of kabbalistic works was being published for Ashkenazi audiences: mystical classics such as the Zohar, and books of kabbalistic prayer, kabbalistic doctrine, and kabbalistic ethics, such as the prayer book of Naftali Treves, *Nishmat adam* by Aaron Samuel of Kremenets, *Shefa tal* by Shabetai ben Akiba Horowitz, and of course *Shenei luḥot haberit* by Shabetai's cousin Isaiah Horowitz.[35] Kabbalah ceased to be the secret tradition of a tiny elite: by the mid-sixteenth century, even a few Jewish women had begun to study it.[36] Teachings such as the transmigration of souls (*gilgul*) and kabbalistic rituals such as *tikun ḥatsot* eventually became part of the popular culture of the Jews of eastern Europe.

The rise of kabbalah was the most significant change in the intellectual life of Ashkenazi Jews of the seventeenth century.[37] In the sixteenth century, kabbalah had a place in Ashkenazi culture alongside other disciplines and systems of thought, such as philosophy and midrash, and like them was subservient to the central discipline, the study of Talmud. As the seventeenth century progressed, however, kabbalah displaced philosophy and, through a process of reinterpretation, swallowed midrash whole. It became the dominant theology of Jewish pietism; it became, indeed, a force and a system of thought that could challenge Talmud for the pre-eminent place in Ashkenazi Judaism. 'There is no doubt',

[33] See Scholem, 'Transmigration of Souls', esp. p. 325.

[34] See Robinson, 'Moses Cordovero'. Cordovero retained certain restrictions: study of kabbalah should only begin after the age of 20, after ample study of Talmud.

[35] See Horodetsky, *Jewish Mysticism*, vol. iv; Elbaum, *Openness and Insularity*, 183–223; Pachter, '*Sefer reshit ḥokhmah*'.

[36] See J. Davis, 'A German-Jewish Woman Scholar'.

[37] For a general discussion, see Scholem, 'The Sabbatian Movement'; Idel, '"One from a Family"', 79–104; Gries, *Literature of Pious Customs*, 41–91; Elbaum, *Openness and Insularity*, 183–222. Kabbalah had an important place in medieval Ashkenazi culture as well, even outside the circle of the Hasidei Ashkenaz, as Ephraim Kanarfogel has shown in *'Peering through the Lattices'*. One should perhaps speak therefore (as Elbaum does) of the rise of Spanish kabbalah. Against this, one could argue, however, that the limited presence of kabbalah in medieval Ashkenazi Judaism in no way prepares us for its overwhelming importance by the later 17th c.

wrote Naftali Bacharach in 1646, that one who disagrees with the Zohar 'may surely be properly termed a heretic.'[38] In 1647 Shabetai Horowitz echoed him: 'Surely those persons who decline to study kabbalah do not merit a soul', he wrote.[39]

Though a supporter and a student of kabbalah, Heller never impugned the orthodoxy of its Jewish opponents. Indeed, like many Jewish leaders, such as Moses Isserles in a previous generation or Samuel Edels (Maharsha) in his own, Heller opposed the popularization of kabbalah.[40] His acceptance of Cordoverian kabbalah did not extend to this crucial principle. He objected to the displacement of traditional, non-kabbalistic forms of Jewish belief and practice by kabbalistic ones. Halakhah, Bible interpretation, and prayer, he argued, may all be studied, pursued, and performed without reference to kabbalah. By insisting that kabbalah remain merely a secret, esoteric theology, removing it from the sphere of public Judaism, Heller neutralized its radicalism.

In his major work on Jewish law, *Ma'adanei melekh*, Heller recommended various kabbalistic customs, for instance, giving a synagogue twelve windows, not pouring water for hand-washing on to the ground, putting myrtle leaves with the *havdalah* spices, making the ink for Torah scrolls from bark, and so on.[41] Nevertheless, he argued there for the autonomy of the system of talmudic law, and for the limited relevance of the Zohar as a source of halakhic norms.[42] He rejected (as Solomon Luria and Moses Isserles had both done before him) kabbalistic customs that are opposed to laws set down in the Talmud, repeating this principle in several places. Perhaps his strongest statement concerned the separation of milk and meat:

> [Joseph Caro] wrote in his *Beit yosef*... that there are some who are stringent with themselves and do not eat meat after cheese in a single meal because of what is written in the Zohar ... and that it is correct and proper that we be stringent and not eat even chicken [after cheese].... But in my humble opinion ... we should not leave aside any saying ... that is explicit ... in our Gemara [Babylonian Talmud] on account of the Zohar, just as

38 N. Bacharach, *Emek hamelekh*, 7*b*: *bevadai ra'ui likeroto min*. Cf. Huss, '*Sefer ha-Zohar*'.

39 *Vavei ha'amudim*, 54, quoting Cordovero.

40 See Isserles, *Torat ha'olah*, iii. 4; Edels (Maharsha), *Ḥidushei agadot* on *Ḥagigah* 13*a*.

41 *MYT (DH)*, *Ber.*, p. 46 n. 76, p. 76 n. 77, p. 70 n. 24; *MYT (DH)*, *Sefer torah* (after *Menaḥot*), p. 223 n. 21. Note also *MYT (DH)*, *Ber.*, p. 10 n. 73 and p. 15 n. 33 (how to read the Shema); p. 13 n. 6 (Kaddish in Aramaic); p. 15 n. 23 (not to read the Torah with the *ḥazan*). Also p. 24 n. 58 (the Hebrew verses of the Kedushah are to be said out loud, and the Aramaic translation in a whisper); p. 41 n. 17 (text of *Barukh she'amar*).

42 See J. Katz, *Halakhah and Kabbalah*; Rafeld, 'Certain Kabbalistic Elements'; Leiner, 'R. Solomon Luria'; Horodetsky, 'R. Solomon Luria'; Siev, *Rabbi Moses Isserles*, 238–41; J. Ben-Sasson, *The Thought of R. Moses Isserles*, 33–40. Note that Isserles endorses Caro's stringency regarding chicken and cheese.

we do not follow any saying in [rabbinic texts such as] Tosefta or *Torat kohanim* [*Sifra*] or *Sifrei* if the Gemara does not agree with it.[43]

Heller refused to accord the Zohar a position superior to that of other ancient midrashic collections. He was willing, however, to grant its claim to antiquity, ranking its authority above that of the medieval rabbinic works. Heller did not accept either kabbalistic leniencies or kabbalistic stringencies where these ran counter to the plain sense of the Talmud, rejecting them even as expressions of personal piety or stringency, let alone as binding on the entire Jewish people.[44]

Heller also opposed the displacement of non-kabbalistic interpretations of the Bible by kabbalistic ones. In 1602 he published his second book, *Tsurat beit hamikdash* or *Tsurat habayit* (The Design of the Temple), a commentary on the last chapters of Ezekiel. The prophecy, which describes in great detail the prophet's vision of the rebuilt Temple, does not agree completely with other biblical descriptions of the Temple; perhaps for this reason, it was given a mystical interpretation from ancient times.[45] Heller, however, renounced the kabbalistic meaning and held closely to the literal meaning of the passage:

Since [Ezekiel's prophecy] will tolerate the simple interpretation, why should one exhaust himself seeking for an interpretation [that refers to] the supernal beings and spiritual things? Rather, we must accept the simple interpretation. And if the words have an inner meaning and spirituality, is it not also the case that . . . even the things that have happened, from the day that God created man upon the earth, contain intimations and an inner form, although they occurred corporeally, as it is said in the Zohar . . . Nevertheless, the matters that teach the simple sense must come first . . . and after them the inner meaning.[46]

[43] *MYT* (*DH*), *Ḥul.*, p. 371 n. 23. Cf. *MalYT*, para. 173; Heller, *Torat ha'asham* (Jerusalem, 1977), 76: 2 (p. 347). Other kabbalistic practices that Heller rejected include not wearing tefillin on *ḥol hamo'ed*: see *MalYT*, para. 490, and cf. 25: 9 and 31: 2; *MYT* (*DH*), *Tefilin*, p. 241 n. 74 and cf. p. 239 n. 57. Cf. also *MalYT*, para. 651. Heller's rejection of the derivation of halakhic principles from midrashic texts (see *Tos YT*, *Ber.* 5: 4) should be seen in the context of the influence of kabbalistic 'midrashim', such as the Zohar.

[44] *MYT* (*DH*), *Ḥul.*, p. 371 n. 23. Cf. *MalYT* 173 (chicken after cheese); *MYT* (*DH*), *Tefilin*, p. 236 n. 18 (wearing two sets of tefillin); *MYT* (*DH*), *Ber.*, p. 76 n. 77 (how long is a nap?). Cf. J. Davis, 'Philosophy and the Law', 264–5.

[45] It was mentioned as a major Jewish mystical text as early as the 3rd c., alongside the Song of Songs and the opening chapter of Ezekiel, the Vision of the Chariot. See the prologue of Origen's commentary on the Song of Songs, quoted in Peters (ed. and trans.), *Judaism, Christianity, and Islam*, iii. 198.

[46] *Tsurat habayit*, ed. Malin, 86. Note Heller's remark in the introduction that the book began with a diagram of the Temple that he drew for his fellow students. The architecture of the Temple was a topic of much interest in this period; Abraham Portaleone's *Shiltei hagiborim* was published in 1612, for instance. Portaleone, like Heller, focused on the physical aspects of the Temple; his Latin erudition and his historical approach contrast, however, with Heller's text-focused literalism. Cf. above, Ch. 1 n. 61.

Heller affirmed the existence of a non-kabbalistic meaning for every passage in the Bible, as well in the Mishnah (as I shall discuss in the next chapter), the Talmud, and the midrashim. As a midrash, even the Zohar, Heller believed, must have a legitimate non-kabbalistic interpretation.[47] If kabbalah was not to be popularized, then it could not be the only permissible type of Jewish belief; a popular, non-mystical Judaism also had to be permitted. He rejected the popularization of kabbalistic attitudes towards liturgy, and thus also opposed the effort to make them normative. Jewish prayer too must have a legitimate non-kabbalistic interpretation.[48]

Prayer was a special focus of kabbalistic piety. Special meditations, called *kavanot*, 'intentions', directed towards specific *sefirot* and their union, played a central role in kabbalistic mystical and meditative practice. Special kabbalistic liturgies, such as Kabalat Shabat, said on Friday evenings, and Tikun Ḥatsot, said at midnight, spread among Ashkenazi Jews in the early seventeenth century. Circles of pietists were established for the performance of these and other rituals. Isaiah Horowitz was once again one of the major proponents of these innovations.

The question of the relation of kabbalah to prayer is taken up in two comments in *Ma'adanei melekh*. In one Heller discusses the question of *kavanot*, commenting on a discussion of whether one may add further praises of God to those in the traditional liturgy (a question that was revived in the twentieth century, in the context of Jewish feminism). A series of medieval Ashkenazi talmudists ruled that it is permitted, but only during private prayer. Always on the lookout for contradictions between texts, Heller found an implicit contradiction here to the view of Maimonides in *Moreh nevukhim* that further praises of God, presumably even in private, would be theologically repugnant because they suggest an anthropomorphic conception of God. Heller wrote:

Those who know the secrets of the kabbalah take a different view of the divine attributes. And the author of *Avodat hakodesh*, [Ibn Gabbai] has written . . . that only the attributes that are finite [are forbidden] . . . for they refer only to the quality of judgement [*midat hadin*]. . . . But if I follow his view, how will I know which are the finite attributes which are forbidden, and which are the infinite attributes which are permitted? For we have no concern with hidden matters.[49]

This passage implies that while liturgy must be acceptable to philosophical theology, kabbalah may be left to fend for itself.

In a second comment, Heller discusses the purpose of the commandment to pray, addressing one of the central problems in Judaism: since prayer does nothing for

[47] See below, Ch. 9 n. 12.

[48] In *MalYT* 139: 10 Heller claims that the text of the liturgy, as established by the 'men of the ancient synagogue', was intended primarily in its *peshat* meaning—*lo tikenu ela leshon peshat*. Cf. *MalYT* 651 (pp. 131–2).

[49] *MYT*(*MM*), *Ber.*, p. 44 n. 6. Cf. *MalYT* 113: 9.

God, why does He want it? 'And if you shall ask, how do our blessings benefit the Holy One, blessed be He, one may answer: our blessings are only to give us merit, as the sages say, "One who blesses is blessed".'[50] Heller endorsed an anthropocentric conception of prayer: prayer serves to fill man's needs, not God's.

The kabbalists explicitly rejected an anthropocentric notion of the commandments. Their belief, often repeated, was that prayer serves God's needs, not only man's: *mitsvot tsorekh gavo'ah* (the commandments are a necessity of the Supernal).[51] Heller, in the continuation of the comment above, distanced himself from any such conception, making one of his strongest statements of the principle of esotericism: 'The kabbalists have other explanations of all of this, but in a work on the Talmud, we have no concern at all for hidden things.'

In spite of its somewhat bland tone, this comment is forceful in its very brevity. 'We have no concern for hidden things' is a very common rabbinic catchphrase in the Talmud (BT *Ḥagigah* 13*a*). Often it indicates no more than that kabbalistic explanations are only tangentially related to the talmudic discussion at hand. By saying 'In a work on the Talmud, we have no concern . . .' Heller made that catchphrase into a principle of genre distinctions: kabbalah is to be excluded completely and on principle from Talmud commentaries. Furthermore, by emphasizing 'no concern *at all*', he made clear that whatever kabbalistic explanations may exist (and he took care to suggest that there is more than one kabbalistic view), the validity of the anthropocentric view of the purpose of prayer suggested by Maimonides and the medieval Jewish philosophers is not to be questioned.

IN DEFENCE OF PHILOSOPHY

How did Heller conceive of the relation between Jewish philosophy and kabbalah? Did he, like the Maharal, view them as essentially opposed? Or did he, like Moses Isserles, view them as essentially identical, differing only in their vocabularies?[52]

We have seen that in the commentary on *Beḥinat olam*, Heller found and stressed the substantive difference between the philosophers and the kabbalists on the question of the origin of the soul. In one passage in *Leket shoshanim*, however, he claimed that the two bodies of Jewish thought are ultimately in agreement,

[50] *MYT(MM)*, *Ber.*, p. 10 n. 1. Cf. BT *Sot.* 38*b*, and also Abraham Horowitz's reference to Isaac Arama's comments on the true purpose of prayer; A. Horowitz, *Emek berakhah*, 59.

[51] See e.g. I. Horowitz, *Shenei luḥot haberit*, i. 22*a*–*b*. On the origins of the doctrine, see the discussion and references in C. Horowitz, *The Jewish Sermon*, 130–1. See also Faierstein, '"God's Need"'.

[52] On the Maharal's view of kabbalah, see Goetschel, 'Maharal of Prague'; Sherwin, *Mystical Theology*, *passim*. The contrast between Isserles and the Maharal is drawn eloquently by Neher, *Jewish Thought and the Scientific Revolution*, 34–9.

stating in strong terms God's transcendence of any language, and the inadequacy of either philosophical or kabbalistic language to express theological truth. There is a realm of silence, a divine reality that may be pointed to but cannot be truly named. For Heller, at that point, philosophy and kabbalah coincide:

When we say that God created the world, we cannot say it, except by saying that He is the cause[53] of the world. And even though He has no relation[54] or similarity to the effects, nevertheless we say so to negate the view that He did not create the world, the opinion of the Philosopher [Aristotle], who believed in the eternity of the world. And since we cannot expressly teach it, we are forced to say, 'cause'.

And this is the meaning of the great sage, the author of the *Guide*, when he writes that all the divine attributes are negative. 'And all the words of his mouth are in righteousness' (Prov. 8: 8). And see and understand the wisdom[55] of that sage, who did not know and had not heard the words of the kabbalah, but by the force of his reasoning discovered[56] the statement of the Zohar that 'There is no letter or vowel that refers to the Ein[57] Sof.' And understand this.[58]

In *Ma'adanei melekh*, Heller again discusses the problem of philosophy and Torah. His comment is a response to an interpretation by Mordechai Jaffe of the difference between two prayers:

Rabbi Mordechai Jaffe wrote that the [fourth] blessing [of the Amidah], 'You graciously give wisdom to man', refers to the gracious giving [of wisdom] to all mankind, both to Jews and to non-Jews, to whom God gave . . . the wisdom of the seven sciences in which all the world have equal shares. But [the Havdalah blessing] 'You have graciously given *us* the wisdom of Your Torah' refers to the special love and graciousness with which the Holy One, blessed be He, gave us His Torah . . . And [Jaffe] explained this well. . . .

But [Jaffe] continues that the two gifts are not equal, because one is in the things of the world, and the other in the words of the Torah, and between them there is a division like the 'advantage of light over darkness' (Eccles. 2: 13). They do not belong together; one is holy and one profane, and God forbid that they should be grouped in the same class in a single prayer.[59]

[53] The manuscript probably reads *elem* (the first letter is not quite clear). This is a scribal error, influenced by the next word (*olam*). The correct reading might be *ilat*, 'the cause', *etsem*, 'reality', or even *tselem*, 'image'.

[54] Reading *yaḥas* in place of *yaḥad*.

[55] The manuscript reads *y-sh-n-h*. I cannot establish any reading that makes any sense. I have translated according to context.

[56] Reading *himtsi* for *hamevi*.

[57] Reading *le'ein* for *ila'in*.

[58] *Leket shoshanim*, ch. 7, fos. 124*a–b*. Note that Heller does not endorse the legend that Maimonides became a kabbalist in his old age (on which see Scholem, 'From Philosopher to Kabbalist'; Shmidman, 'On Maimonides' "Conversion"'). Cf. Joseph b. Isaac Halevi, *Givat hamoreh*, 30*a*.

[59] Jaffe's position is discussed in Kaplan, 'Rationalism and Rabbinic Culture', 71. Cf. above, Ch. 1 n. 65.

Jaffe's denigration of the 'seven sciences' was not radical; he insisted that they should be studied, and that 'Jews and non-Jews . . . have equal shares' in them. (The seven sciences, the *trivium* and *quadrivium*, are used here to mean all rational knowledge, every science.) In spite of this, Heller felt impelled to voice his disagreement with Jaffe's contrast of the sciences and the Torah, arguing that no sharp distinction could be drawn between the seven sciences and the Torah, and that the seven sciences formed part of Torah:

This does not seem correct to me . . . For why should they not [be classed in the same category]? They share the same matter and form. And in the nature of things, [knowledge of] this world precedes the wisdom of the Torah . . . and it is well known . . . that [the latter] requires [the former]. . . . Although the wisdom of the Torah excels them all, are not the seven sciences all contained within it? . . . 'For she has hewn her seven pillars' (Prov. 9: 1).[60]

[60] *MYT (DH)*, *Ber.* pp. 43–4 n. 43. The passage is also quoted in M. Roth, 'Notes', 104, and discussed in Emanuel, 'Attitude', 56–7. Cf. *MalYT*, para. 294: 'Man's natural wisdom, although it does not have as high a rank as the intellectual wisdom of Torah, is nonetheless important and great in the entire human species, and it is necessary for the wisdom of the Torah which is man's [*asher le'adam*] and it precedes it in time and nature.' See Emanuel, 'Attitude', 58. The opposition of 'nature' and 'intellect' shows the influence of the Maharal. Cf. also the commentary on *Beḥinat olam* 14: 1: 11 (p. 110), where Heller remarks that all the seven sciences (which he lists) will be apprehended 'by means of the Torah, and all the sciences are included in her, as it is written, "She has hewn her seven pillars".' Note also *MYT (MM)*, *Ber.*, p. 73 n. 1.

FOUR

Tosafot yom tov

THE MAHARAL AND THE REVIVAL OF THE MISHNAH

THE crowning work of the first part of Heller's life was his *Tosafot yom tov* (or *Tosefet yom tov*),[1] a commentary on the Mishnah, the ancient rabbinic code of Jewish law. *Tosafot yom tov* was published in parts between 1614 and 1617, and is one of the literary monuments of Renaissance culture among the Jews of Prague.[2]

'The whole world will testify', Heller later wrote in a letter, 'that . . . it is no boast, God forbid, that my *Tosafot* on the Mishnah has spread . . . even to the ends of the earth, the land of the Turks and the Holy Land'.[3] Heller was anxious that the work should be published. Indeed, he invested money in the publication himself, to buy 'fine paper, good ink, and a legible typeface', as his kinsman Isaiah Horowitz noted drily.[4]

As mentioned above, *Tosafot yom tov* is a commentary on the Mishnah. More precisely, it is partly a commentary, partly a digest of commentaries, and partly a supercommentary: that is, Heller sometimes commented directly on the Mishnah, sometimes quoted or summarized comments by earlier rabbis, and often commented on those earlier commentaries. In addition to writing his commentary, he also set out to establish a reliable and exact text of the Mishnah. To this end, he consulted five partial or complete printed editions of the Mishnah and four manuscripts, as well as the textual readings of many commentaries.[5]

Heller made comments on almost every one of the thousands of paragraphs of the Mishnah, discussing hundreds of points of practical Jewish law and explaining scores of difficult words, often by the use of cognates in biblical Hebrew or Aramaic. He quoted etymologies of some of the Greek loanwords in the Mishnah,

[1] On the name of the work, see Haberman, 'Liturgical and Other Poems', 125 n. 1.

[2] On *Tosafot yom tov*, see esp. Hakohen, 'His Books', 146–91; Beit Halevi, *Life of Heller*, 13–22.

[3] Brann, 'Additions', 276. Cf. *Megilat eivah*, 29. Menahem Krochmal also wrote that Heller's and Jaffe's writings 'have spread through all the lands of the Diaspora of Israel' (*She'elot uteshuvot tsemaḥ tsedek*, no. 14, quoted in Roth, 'Notes', 108). In 1650 Moses Porges, a Prague Jew, recommended all who immigrated to the Land of Israel to bring with them copies of *Tosafot yom tov*, among other books. See his *Darkhei tsiyon*, 277.

[4] See Horowitz's approbation.

[5] See J. N. Epstein, *Introduction*, 1282–4.

though he knew no Greek himself.[6] A large proportion of his comments seek to reconcile apparent contradictions in the Mishnah text, while a number raise questions that Heller, as a good pedagogue, left unresolved.[7] Unlike earlier commentaries on the Mishnah, *Tosafot yom tov* did not seek to provide a definitive interpretation of the Mishnah text but to lead the reader into the rabbinic dialectic of the text's disputed meaning.

Exceptionally among rabbinic works of its period, *Tosafot yom tov* went through a second edition in the lifetime of its author.[8] The work gave Heller an immediate reputation, and guaranteed him a lasting one, as a Torah scholar. He quickly came to be identified with his most famous book; in his own lifetime, he was already called Rabbi Tosafot Yom Tov, as if there were no distinction between the man and the book.[9]

One of the best-known aspects—for many scholars, the central and defining aspect—of the European Renaissance was the rediscovery of the ancient texts of Greek and Roman literature. Claudius Salmasius, for example, discovered the poems of the *Greek Anthology* in the library of the Elector Palatine in Heidelberg in 1607. Ashkenazi Jews were likewise excited by the discovery of unknown or neglected ancient Jewish texts. 'Praise be to God', wrote David of Szczebrzeszyn, the author of a commentary on an ancient Targum, published in Prague in 1609, '. . . who brought to our hands this book sweeter than manna, which had been buried and hidden for "times and a time" (Daniel 7: 25).'[10]

Heller's *Tosafot yom tov* played a part in the revival of another neglected ancient text, the Mishnah. It was the first published Ashkenazi commentary on the complete work, for, although the Mishnah is the text on which the Talmud is a commentary, and the Talmud (as we have seen) was the focus of all education

---

[6] *Dem.* 2: 4, *Pes.* 8: 1, *Yev.* 8: 6, *AZ* 1: 3, *Kel.* 23: 3, *Mid.* 1: 3, *Nid.* 2: 5, 8: 1, etc. Cf. *Kel.* 14: 8, 20: 7, *Mid.* 3: 1 on the shapes of Greek letters. Cf. Maclean, *Interpretation and Meaning*, 109–11, on etymology in early modern legal interpretation.   [7] e.g. *Tos YT, Makot* 3: 1.

[8] On the edition, see Friedberg, *History of Hebrew Printing*, 30. The first volume of the 2nd edn. was published in Cracow in Kislev (Nov./Dec.) 1642. The publication may have been associated in some way with Heller's candidacy as rabbi of Cracow; in autumn 1643 he was appointed *rosh yeshivah* as co-rabbi together with Joshua b. Joseph (*Megilat eivah*, 39.) The new edition included many new notes and comments, which Heller had begun during the years in Nemirov, 'after the days', as he wrote, 'of my distress and my misery'. See *Tos YT, Pe'ah* 6: 4; cf. Lam. 3: 19. No doubt he had originally written them in the margin of his own copy of *Tosafot yom tov*. The printer now included them in the text, marking them with the sign of a hand pointing to the note (more recent editions mark them off less impressively with an asterisk and brackets).

[9] Heller is referred to as 'Ba'al *Tosafot yom tov*', e.g. in Rapoport, *She'elot uteshuvot eitan ha'ezraḥi*, no. 40, and by the printer of Buchner's *Oreḥot ḥayim*, nos. 5–8 (p. 20). In one of his *seliḥot* for the massacres of 1648–9 (published in Haberman, 'Liturgical and Other Poems', 135), Heller makes an acrostic of his own name as 'Tosafot Yom-Tov Halevi, called Lipmann Heller'.

[10] David b. Jacob of Szczebrzeszyn, *Perush al targum yonatan*, introd.

among medieval Ashkenazi Jews, the Mishnah *per se* was little studied in the Middle Ages, neither by Ashkenazi nor Spanish Jews.[11] There were very few running commentaries on the entire Mishnah written before the sixteenth century: Maimonides wrote one in the twelfth century; in the fifteenth century, the Italian scholar Obadiah of Bertinoro wrote another. There was none written by an Ashkenazi Jew.[12]

The late sixteenth and early seventeenth centuries, however, saw a revival of interest in the Mishnah. Joseph Ashkenazi (Abraham Horowitz's opponent in the 1559 Maimonides controversy) made a name for himself about 1570 in Safed as an expert in Mishnah, and wrote notes or a commentary; so did Bezalel Ashkenazi in Jerusalem a few decades later. The commentary *Kaf naḥat* by the printer Isaac Gabbai was published in Venice in 1614, the same year that the first volume of *Tosafot yom tov* appeared.[13]

The revival of Mishnah study drew on a variety of religious motivations. We have seen the Maharal's suggestion that Mishnah should be taught to all 8- or 9-year-old boys as a basis for study of the Talmud.[14] Among the kabbalists of

[11] See Albeck, *Introduction*, 237–56; Sussman, 'Manuscripts and Textual Traditions'. In spite of its modest title, Sussman's article surveys the study of Mishnah in the Middle Ages, as well as the production of manuscripts and the transmission of different textual traditions. The relative absence of manuscripts of Mishnah reflects an absence of study. Cf. also Jacob J. Schacter's survey of Mishnah commentaries up to the end of the 18th c., which includes useful characterizations of several, including *Tosafot yom tov*, particularly of their different formal features: see Schacter, 'Rabbi Jacob Emden', 160–77. See also Zaiman, 'Traditional Study'.

[12] On Mishnah commentaries up to the end of the 12th c., see Twersky, *Rabad of Posquières*, 106–10; Urbach, *The Tosafists*, i. 298–312 on R. Samson of Sens; Sussman, 'Manuscripts and Textual Traditions', 234–41. Sussman presents both positive evidence of study of Mishnah apart from Talmud in the Land of Israel and its cultural sphere, and evidence of the absence of geonic study (pp. 237–40). Ta-Shema, 'Torah Study', 110, finds a decline in the study of Mishnah among Ashkenazi Jews as early as the 13th c., the time of *Sefer ḥasidim*, if not earlier. My grandfather, Louis Finkelstein (*Sifra on Leviticus*, i. 2), notes that Rashi in his Talmud commentary refers to *Sifra* as the source of passages that appear both there and in the order 'Tohorot' of the Mishnah, indicating that he knew *Sifra* better than that part of the Mishnah.

[13] Sussman, 'Manuscripts and Textual Traditions', 236 n. 89, takes Bertinoro's commentary as a sign of revived interest in the Mishnah as early as the mid-15th c. A number of other Mishnah commentaries were written in the decades after *Tosafot yom tov* appeared. In 1636 Moses b. Noah Isaac Lipschuetz of Poznań published *Leḥem mishneh* in Cracow. Solomon Adeni and Abraham Azulai, both in the Land of Israel, wrote Mishnah commentaries in the same period (see Zlotnick, 'Commentary of R. Abraham Azulai'; Azulai, *Ahavah bata'anugim*, 22). *Ets ḥayim* by Jacob b. Samuel Hagiz was published in Verona in 1650. Abraham b. Hayim Lisker wrote his commentary, *Be'er avraham*, shortly afterwards; it was not published until 1683, in Cracow, but the approbations date from 1661–3. Cf. n. 75 below on Simeon Wolf Oppenheim's Mishnah commentary of about 1610.

[14] See above, Ch. 1 n. 67, and the Maharal's discussion of the Mishnah in id., 'Derush al hatorah ve'al hamitsvot', *Derashot maharal*, 63, 79.

Safed, on the other hand, Mishnah study was developed into a mystical meditative technique. Moses Cordovero advised his disciples to learn two chapters of Mishnah by heart each week.[15] But *Tosafot yom tov* was intended neither for elementary students nor for kabbalistic adepts. It was, rather, intended for—and had its origin in—societies for the study of the Mishnah.

The Maharal, wrote Heller in the introduction to *Tosafot yom tov*, ordered *ḥevrot* to be established in Prague that would study one chapter of Mishnah each day.[16] *Ḥevrot* are pious societies, parallel to Catholic confraternities, that were developed by Jews during the Middle Ages for many religious endeavours: saying prayers, tending the poor and the sick, and especially burying the dead, the task of the 'holy society' or *ḥevra kadisha*.[17] The institution of societies for Mishnah study had spread from Prague to many places by the time that *Tosafot yom tov* appeared, and they remained a part of the life of east European Jews until the Holocaust (in 1950 Abraham Joshua Heschel recalled having seen in the YIVO Library a prayer-book with the inscription, 'Society of Wood-Cutters for the Study of Mishnah in Berdichev'). Heller wrote *Tosafot yom tov*, he tells us, while he was studying the Mishnah with such a society.[18]

Who would be the Maharal's spiritual heir? Ephraim of Luntshits had succeeded him as chief rabbi. Like him, he was a great preacher, a critic of the rich, and a defender of the poor. Isaiah Horowitz shared the Maharal's charisma and his devotion to kabbalah.[19] With *Tosafot yom tov* Heller established his own claim: he championed the Maharal's Mishnah study societies, and he made the Mishnah in its own right an object of study and interpretative discussion.[20]

[15] See Fine, 'Recitation of Mishnah'. The technique, as Fine shows, pre-dates Vital. Fine mentions the identification (on the basis of anagrams) of Mishnah = *neshamah* 'soul' (p. 196). Note Cordovero's recommendation that Mishnah should be memorized (p. 196). Isaiah Horowitz recommends Mishnah study in *Shenei luḥot haberit*, i. 31*a*, though he does not mention Heller's commentary. On Caro, see Werblowsky, *Joseph Karo*, 258–67. Caro's angel-mentor, for example, called herself 'the Mishnah'. The recreation by the Safed kabbalists of the tannaitic community of Galilean mystics portrayed in the Zohar should also be noted. Fine stresses the kabbalists' belief that they were the *gilgulim*, the transmigrated souls, of mishnaic rabbis (pp. 186–7). Cf. Sussman, 'Manuscripts and Textual Traditions', 236 n. 89. Heller's introduction to *Tosafot yom tov* suggests in passing a messianic motivation, based on a midrashic saying (*Leviticus Rabbah* 7: 3).

[16] See also Ephraim of Luntshits's remarks in *Amudei shesh*, quoted in Assaf, *Sources*, i. 83.

[17] On *ḥevrot*, see Farine, 'Charity and Study Societies'; E. Horowitz, 'Jewish Confraternities'.

[18] See Shohat, 'Study Societies'; Heschel, *The Earth is the Lord's*, 46. Juspa Shammash gives the laws of the *kupat mishnayot* in Worms in the mid-17th c.; the manuscript is reproduced in Eidelberg, *R. Juspa*, 200 (73*a*–*b* of the manuscript).

[19] Horowitz also supported Mishnah study, although not specifically the institution of *ḥevrot*. See *Shenei luḥot haberit*, ii. 31*a*. Note that Isaiah Horowitz's son Shabetai later criticized aspects of the Mishnah *ḥevrot*: see id., *Vavei ha'amudim*, ch. 5.

[20] In *Amudei shesh* (1617), Ephraim of Luntshits also endorsed the *ḥevrot mishnayot*, and he recommended the recently published *Tosafot yom tov*.

ON RASHI, TOSAFOT, AND THE SEVENTY FACES OF TORAH

In the seventeenth century, interpretation and commentary were not only common types of writing, but also in themselves constituted crucial topics of debate. In the arguments between Protestants and Catholics, religious authorities and sceptics, lawyers and historians, astronomers and Inquisitors, the problem of *how* to read was paramount.[21]

In writing his commentary, Heller had to take positions on a vast array of detailed questions as to how particular passages were to be interpreted, and also on several larger questions of how the Mishnah should be interpreted in general. He had to decide to what extent it was to be treated as a perfect, divinely inspired text, and to what extent as a text subject to the human deficiencies of its authors. He had to take positions in the debates of his day on *pilpul* and kabbalah as modes of interpretation. He was also forced to choose whether to argue for a single normative meaning of the text or whether to allow the existence of more than one legitimate reading. Finally, he had to take a stand in the debate over the relative status of two of the great Talmud commentaries of the Middles Ages: Rashi and Tosafot.[22]

Is the Mishnah text perfect? In rabbinic tradition, the text's perfection implies its 'omnisignificance' (to use a term coined by my teacher James Kugel). Every feature, however minor, of the sacred text is regarded as containing significant religious and moral teachings.[23] Jewish tradition is far from unique in this regard. 'We believe', wrote the Jesuit Cardinal Robert Bellarmine, a contemporary of Heller's, 'that no word in Scripture is unnecessary, nor is it incorrectly placed.'[24] Isaiah Horowitz asserted the Mishnah's omnisignificance thus: 'Surely the Holy Spirit spoke through Rabbi [Judah the Prince] . . . and if there is an extra letter or

[21] On the general question of interpretation in this period, see Grafton, 'Renaissance Readers'. On Bible interpretation, see Preus, *From Shadow to Promise*; Steinmetz (ed.), *The Bible in the Sixteenth Century*. On the interpretation of legal texts, see Maclean, *Interpretation and Meaning*. On the interpretation of classical texts, see Grafton, *Joseph Scaliger*, vol. i. On humanism in Prague in Heller's day, see id., 'Humanism and Science'. On interpretation by readers who were not scholars, see N. Z. Davis, 'Printing and the People'.

[22] Note the ground-breaking comparative work by Henderson, *Scripture, Canon, and Commentary*, 89–138. Henderson lists six essential interpretative assumptions held concerning Scripture in medieval Chinese, Islamic, and Christian cultures: that Scripture is cosmically comprehensive, well ordered and coherent, moral, self-consistent, profound, and that it contains nothing superfluous or insignificant. The best overview of traditional norms of Talmud interpretation is Halivni, *Peshat and Derash*.

[23] Kugel, *The Idea of Biblical Poetry*, 104–5; cf. Elman, ' "It is no empty thing" '.

[24] Quoted in Kelter, 'The Refusal to Accommodate', 279.

one missing, or a change in the [customary] order of words, it is all from the hand of the Lord.'[25] This axiom guided Heller too in many places in his commentary.

Consider, for example, the order of the Mishnah's sixty-three tractates. The sequence of topics from one tractate to the next often appears haphazard; a modern surmise is that they are placed simply in approximate order of their length.[26] Heller, on the contrary, felt impelled to explain the sequencing of each tractate, and likewise of each of the six 'orders' into which the tractates are grouped. He further claimed that the six orders are grouped into three matching pairs: for example, the third order, 'Women', is paired with the sixth order, 'Ritual Purity', because, in Heller's eyes, 'The unclean are made impure by the Serpent, which brought uncleanness into the world through Eve, the first woman.'[27]

In other respects, however, Heller stopped short of asserting the Mishnah's omnisignificance. For example, he claimed that, throughout the Mishnah, the phrase 'Rabbi Such-and-Such says' means the same as 'said Rabbi Such-and-Such': in his view, the Mishnah is indifferent to tenses, and the exact word order is not always significant. Neither, he claimed in another place, is the presence or absence of the word 'and' significant: in lists of three items, he said, 'A, B, and C' means the same as 'A and B and C'.[28]

Significantly, Heller did not regard the received (printed) text of the Mishnah as letter-perfect.[29] Take, for instance, a line from chapter 9 of tractate *Sotah*. According to the printed text, a certain Jewish bandit of the Roman period had three names or nicknames: Eleazar ben Dinai, Teḥinah ben Perishah, and ben Haratsḥan. Heller reports an ingenious emendation suggested by his colleague Zanvill Katz, who changed the name Teḥinah to the word *teḥilah*, which means 'first': ben Dinai was first called *ben perishah* ('son of a pharisee'), but was later known as *ben haratsḥan* ('son of a murderer'). Heller remarked that it seemed improbable that a man's name would be changed twice, and suggests instead a variant manuscript text, according to which there were two bandits: Eleazar ben Dinai and another man called Teḥinah ben Perishah, who was later known as 'son of the murderer'.[30]

[25] See *Shenei luḥot haberit*, near the end of the work, in the section 'Torah shebe'al peh', *kelal* no. 2 (in the fourth pagination, 5*b*–6*a*).

[26] See Albeck, *Introduction*, 126; Albeck credits Geiger with the observation.

[27] See his 'Petiḥah' to the six orders of Mishnah, at the beginning of *Berakhot* (in the Vilna edn., p. 31).

[28] *Tos YT*, *Shab*. 1: 11, *Bik*. 3: 3. Note the Talmud's ambiguous discussion of whether or not the order of mishnaic lists is always significant: BT *San*. 49*a*.

[29] As Marc Shapiro has remarked ('The Last Word', 228 n. 128), the belief in the letter-perfection of the Talmud (and Mishnah) text is a dogma whose development among some Jews in the modern period is deserving of study.

[30] *Tos YT*, *Sot*. 9: 9. See also the discussion in Albeck's Mishnah commentary.

Heller was a contemporary of some of the great text editors of the Western scholarly tradition—men such as Joseph Scaliger—and he had an abiding, almost compulsive, interest in editing.[31] He was aware of the mechanics of copying and of the possible associated errors, such as when the copyist's eye skips from the first occurrence of a word to a second one further down, thus omitting some text (this is known as homoeoteleuton).[32] According to Heller, this is what caused the error in the printed text about the bandits. His edition of the Mishnah is quite close to previous ones, but he did recognize the possibility of scribal error.[33]

Heller even applied his skills as an editor to the Bible. His suggestion of a variant reading of a verse of Proverbs (6: 7), 'The ant has no chief [*katsin*]' is quoted by a rabbi of the next generation, Aaron Samuel Kaidanover: 'I have heard that Rabbi *Tosafot yom tov*, of blessed memory, said that the Targum [the traditional Aramaic translation of the Bible] had the reading, "The ant has no harvest [*katsir*]".'[34]

Heller lived in the very first years of Bible criticism. A Catholic contemporary, Jean Morin, was the first scholar to declare that the Septuagint text of the Bible was superior to the Hebrew Masoretic text. (Eliezer Eilburg had hinted at this possibility sixty years before.) Another contemporary, Isaac La Peyrère, a man of Marrano ancestry, was the first to argue against the Mosaic authorship of the Bible.[35] Heller took a fairly broad view of divine revelation (we recall his grandfather's saying that the Torah is revealed each day) and did not perceive Bible criticism as an incipient threat to Jewish belief in the Torah or its divine origin. Heller's attitude is apparent in his notes on the Bible commentary of Abraham Ibn Ezra.

[31] Note, for example, that he interrupts his sermon to correct a reading in a midrash; *Derush ḥidushei halevanah*, 37–8.

[32] See e.g. *Tos YT*, *Ber.* 5: 5, *Torat ha'asham*, 281, *MYT* (*MM*), *Ber.*, p. 11, n. 70. Text entering from margin: *Torat ha'asham*, 76. Two text witnesses can rule out the possibility of scribal error: *Tos YT*, *Nid.* 5: 9. *Bet* interchanging with *kaf*: *Tos YT*, *Eruv.* 10: 8.

[33] On Heller as text critic, see Hakohen, 'His Books', 147–50, and Fogelman, 'Observations', 218–19. For Heller's caution, see esp. *Tos YT*, *Kel.* 16: 8. He was much less cautious in regard to the more recent and less authoritative works: see e.g. *Parashat haḥodesh* (MS 2271), 31*b* for the speculative emendation of medieval rabbinic texts.

[34] *Birkat hazevaḥ*, 162*b* on BT *Arakh.* 33*a*, also quoted in J. M. Zunz, *City of Righteousness*, 97. The Targum has *ḥatsda*, which means 'harvest'. Cf. *Torat ha'asham*, 456, on *ḥatsra* vs. *ḥatsda*. Kaidanover rejects Heller's suggestion, although without any indication that he considers it extraordinary, and suggests that since the letters *nun* and *resh* often interchange in Hebrew, *katsin* and *katsir* can be equivalent. Heller's suggestion is an exception to the general early modern Jewish pattern of support for the Masoretic text, discussed in E. Breuer, 'In Defense of Tradition', 47–70. On attitudes towards the letter-perfection of the Bible text, see Kohen, 'Text Criticism and Belief'; Shapiro, 'The Last Word', 187–207. Another example of Heller's hypothetical reconstruction of a variant text on the basis of a later comment (here, that of Maimonides) that seems to assume the variant text is in *Tos YT*, *Yoma* 6: 2.

[35] See Laplanche, 'Tradition et modernité'; cf. Grafton, *Defenders of the Text*, 204, on the unfortunate Noel Journet, who was burned in 1582 for finding mistakes in the Bible. Eilburg's comment

In one place, Ibn Ezra quotes the comment of a certain 'Yitshaki' (perhaps Isaac ibn Yashush), who argued that Moses could not have written Genesis 36: 31, 'These are the kings that reigned in the land of Edom, before there reigned any king over the children of Israel', nor the list of eight kings in subsequent verses. Heller explains the argument for Yitshaki's view:

[The time of Moses] was [too] close . . . to the time that the family of Esau began to . . . set kings over their lands and their dwellings, for eight kings to have reigned [there] . . . Therefore [the list] was not written in the time of Moses. If it was written afterwards, we must say that it was written in the days of [King] Jehosaphat . . . For in his day, the kingdom [of Edom] ended, as we have said. And if it was written in the days of Moses, he would not have said, 'before [any king] reigned', for in his time there had not yet been any king in Israel.[36]

Heller did not, of course, endorse Yitshaki's argument; he merely reconstructed it. On the other hand, he did not feel the need to distance himself from the argument: Bible criticism was not yet a topic of controversy among Ashkenazi Jews in the seventeenth century.[37]

The controversy in Heller's time focused on another mode of interpretation: *pilpul*, a mode that employs elaborate interpretations to iron out apparent inconsistencies within texts and between texts. *Pilpul* was employed not only to rid the text of the Talmud of subtle, almost invisible inconsistencies, but also to reconcile the medieval commentaries with the Talmud text and with each other—for if all are authoritative, how can they disagree? These pilpulistic interpretations did not necessarily agree with the apparent meaning of the texts, nor with normative law in practice. For this reason, a number of sixteenth- and seventeenth-century rabbis, the Maharal among them, opposed the practice of *pilpul*.[38]

Although he was sometimes drawn towards the pilpulistic habit of constructing elaborate hypothetical arguments—for example, when he discovered a subtle

(placed, to be sure, in the mouth of an unnamed 'adversary') is in JTS MS microfilm no. 2323 (Hirsch 109), fo. 72*a*–*b*. On La Peyrère, see Popkin, *History of Scepticism*, 214–28. On Jewish approaches to biblical authorship up to the end of the 16th c., see Lawee, 'On the Threshold of the Renaissance', 293–306.

[36] *Ma'amar yom tov*, 62–3. I thank Professor David Weiss-Halivni for this reference. On 'Yitshaki', see Ashtor, *The Jews of Moslem Spain*, ii. 293. For a survey of other commentaries on this passage in Ibn Ezra, see Shapiro, 'The Last Word', 201–2.

[37] Note, however, Leone da Modena's possible doubts concerning Mosaic authorship of the Pentateuch, expressed in his pseudonymous *Kol sakhal*: see T. Fishman, *Shaking the Pillars*, 55.

[38] On *pilpul*, see the collection of texts in Rappel (ed.), *Debate over Pilpul*. Cf. M. Breuer, 'Ashkenazi Yeshivot', 75–121; Reiner, 'Changes'. The storm over *pilpul*, it has often been pointed out, parallels in some respects the controversies in the Christian world over the more literal 'French mode' and the freer 'Italian mode' of interpretation of Roman law.

hidden contradiction in Bertinoro's commentary on tractate *Eruvin* and then offered a resolution based on a reinterpretation of a talmudic phrase—he tried to refrain from *pilpul* as a method of interpretation in his written work. 'All of this is forced', he wrote, 'and it is not the meaning of the [Talmud] passage.'[39]

Heller did not believe that contradictions should be resolved through forced interpretations. Many of his criticisms of earlier commentators (for example, of Isserles) spring from his belief that the views of earlier rabbis need not be reconciled.[40] To take another example, one of the accomplishments of which Heller was most proud in *Tosafot yom tov* was pointing out many contradictions between Maimonides' interpretation of the Mishnah in his Mishnah commentary and the interpretation implicit in his code of Jewish law, the *Mishneh torah*.[41] Heller was not willing to assume that Maimonides' views were consistent in the two works.

As a teacher, however, Heller acted differently. As we shall see in Chapter 7, *pilpul* formed a regular part of the daily Talmud class in the private yeshiva that he ran in Prague around 1620. Although he did not believe that *pilpul* could reveal the normative meaning of a Talmud passage, he accepted it as a pedagogic device.[42]

For Heller, the Mishnah was absolutely obligatory as law and absolutely true as a record of fact. In one comment, discussing the architecture of the Temple, he was drawn to an alternative tradition found in the writings of the ancient Jewish historian Josephus, but ultimately rejected it. We must not depart from the teachings of the Mishnah, he concluded.[43]

In another comment, concerning the laws of *kilayim* (mixed crops), he announced that, as a matter of principle, we may base our interpretation on the assumption that the Mishnah is correct. Should a passage seem to make a false claim, he added piously, we should attribute the difficulty to our own ignorance rather than to any deficiency in the text itself. He proudly showed in the passage at hand that a certain geometric calculation in the Mishnah was correct; in this connection he discussed the famous 47th proposition of the first book of Euclid, the Pythagorean theorem, on the basis of which the passage must be understood.[44] The axiom of the Mish-

[39] *TosYT*, *Eruv.* 10: 1. Cf. Hakohen, 'His Books', 154. Heller named his commentary on 'Nezikin' *Pilpula ḥarifta*, 'acute *pilpul*'. Hakohen sees 'a sort of irony' in the title, but see below.

[40] See e.g. *Torat ha'asham*, 185.

[41] See *MYT* (*DH*), *Sefer torah* (in the Vilna Talmud, after tractate *Menaḥot*), p. 229 n. 88.

[42] In the Yiddish *Megilat eivah*: MS Oxford-Bodleian Heb. 2209, fo. 1*a*. Cf. *TosYT*, *Ber.* 2: 1. In *Derush ḥidushei halevanah*, 31, Heller imagines the author of the midrash as a teacher who suggests an interpretation and challenges his students to find verses to support it, in order 'to sharpen them'.

[43] *TosYT*, *Shek.* 6: 3. Contrast Isaac Abarbanel's use of Josephus, discussed in Lawee, 'On the Threshold of the Renaissance', 315.

[44] *TosYT*, *Kil.* 5: 5 (p. 251, col. 1 in the Vilna edn.). Cf. *TosYT*, *Kil.* 3: 1 (p. 228, col. 2). The passage is discussed at greater length in my article 'Philosophy and the Law', 260–3. Cf. Koppelman, *Omek halakhah*, 11*a*.

nah's absolute truth is thus turned about by Heller to justify the new curriculum that is discussed in Chapter 1 above: for if Euclid's theorem was necessary for the comprehension of even a single Mishnah passage, then Torah scholars must study geometry. They must study geography as well, at least the geography of the Land of Israel and the Near East. In one place, Heller revised the interpretation of a Mishnah passage to reflect the realities of geography.[45]

Let us consider now the question of the text's profundity. Do the truths of the Mishnah merely concern topics such as architecture, geometry, and geography? Or does the Mishnah have deep, kabbalistic, meaning? Heller addresses this question in his comment on a story in tractate *Avot* (2: 6): 'Once Hillel saw a skull [*gulgolet*] floating on the water, and he said, Just as you drowned others, so were you drowned, and those who drowned you will be drowned in their turn.'

Heller notes a number of difficulties in this passage, beginning with the problem that, while Hillel's dictum might possibly be true of the particular man whose skull he saw, and even of his particular murderers, it is simply not true in general. Most people who drown are not guilty of having drowned anyone else. One interpretation of which Heller takes note in resolving this problem is a kabbalistic one: Hillel is not speaking about a *gulgolet*, a skull, but about *gilgul*, the cycle of reincarnation. It is not in this life that the drowning victim drowned another, but in a previous life; and it is not in this life that his murderers will be punished, but in a future incarnation.

The revival of the Mishnah was based in part on the kabbalists' interest in that work. Kabbalists were attracted to the Mishnah and its rabbis partly because, endowed with legendary personae as kabbalists, the early rabbis were a counterweight to non-kabbalistic talmudism.[46] Just as Heller, by suggesting that the Pythagorean theorem is necessary to the comprehension of at least one Mishnah passage, tried to legitimize the study of geometry, the kabbalists wished to assert that there is at least one passage (the story of Hillel and the skull) that cannot be understood at all without recourse to kabbalah.

Heller, as we saw in Chapter 1, affirmed the doctrine of *gilgul* and admitted that this passage might be given such a kabbalistic interpretation. He insisted, however, that the Mishnah must at every point have a simple, non-kabbalistic meaning, a *peshat*—the same interpretative principle that he applied to the Bible and to prayers, and (as we shall see) also to the Zohar:[47]

[45] See *Tos YT*, *Shevi*. 6: 1, *Ḥal*. 4: 10, *Pes*. 3: 8, *RH* 2: 4; cf. *Ber*. 9: 2. Hailperin, 'Bibliography', notes the existence (into the 19th c.) of a copy of Eshtor Haparhi's work on the geography of the Land of Israel, with marginal notes by Heller.

[46] Note the 1704 edn. of the Mishnah printed together with the kabbalistic classic *Sefer yetsirah*. There are kabbalistic interpretations of halakhic passages from the Mishnah in many works, e.g. Aaron Samuel b. Moses of Kremenets, *Nishmat adam*, 47 (on 'objects found by the wife'). The conversion of mishnaic rabbis into legendary kabbalists is of course a major feature of the Zohar, and began indeed in the ancient world.

[47] See p. 163 below.

It does not at all seem proper to me [to say] that Hillel's only intention in this saying was [to speak about] the mystery of *gilgul*. For truly that is one of the hidden things which it is proper to conceal except from the few whom God calls (Joel 3: 5). If so, the holy Rabbi [Judah the Prince, the editor of the Mishnah] would not have included this saying . . . in the Mishnah. Just as Scripture does not depart from its simple sense [*ein mikra yotse miyedei peshuto*], so the Mishnah does not depart from its meaning which may be understood by all.[48]

Elsewhere Heller pursued the logic of this interpretative position to its extreme. He comments on the most sacred and most profound word in the Mishnah or in any other text, the name of God, and offers a non-kabbalistic interpretation of its meaning.[49]

In Heller's time, the idea that the Torah has multiple meanings ('seventy faces' in the rabbinic phrase) was widespread.[50] Nathan ben Solomon Spira (*c.*1585–1633) wrote a work, published posthumously in 1637, with 252 interpretations of a verse in Deuteronomy. Heller knew that the Mishnah may be interpreted kabbalistically, or by *pilpul* that strays from the plain meaning and from the law. With these possibilities in mind, Heller extended the idea of 'seventy faces of interpretation' to the interpretation of the Mishnah and Talmud. He suggested, further, that among these interpretations, only one, the *peshat*—the simple or plain sense of the text as defined by grammar and etymology and, especially, proper usage—is legally normative. 'The basis of every language is how the speakers of that language speak it and understand it', Heller quoted from Maimonides.[51] But the explanation of the Mishnah in the Talmud, even when it differs from the apparent sense of the passage, also constituted *peshat* for Heller. As he wrote, the Talmud is the 'right interpretation' of the Torah (i.e. Jewish law).[52] An interpretation of the Mishnah that conflicts with that offered in the Talmud, could not, Heller believed, be the *peshat*, the simple sense. Rather, he compared such an interpretation to *derash*, the free homiletical interpretation of Scripture.

Heller found that Maimonides interpreted the Mishnah in a certain place in tractate *Nazir* differently from how it is understood in the Talmud. Rather than try to reconcile Maimonides' view in this place to that of the Talmud, he justified it

48 *Avot* 2: 6. Cf. *Tos YT*, *Avot* 5: 6. In his *Derush ḥidushei halevanah* (29) he writes, 'although it is obvious that [the Torah] has in it hints and secrets of the kabbalah, nevertheless "Scripture never leaves aside its simple sense" [*ein mikra yotse miyedei peshuto*] . . . How much more so did the sages, when they said what they said (although they did intend to hint at secrets), intend primarily [to be understood] in the simple sense of their words, which are correct, "without anything in them perverse or crooked" (Prov. 8: 8), God forbid.'

49 *Tos YT*, *Suk.* 4: 5. Contrast e.g. I. Horowitz, *Shenei luḥot haberit*, i. 4*b*–5*a*.

50 See H. H. Ben-Sasson, *Theory and Practice*, 34–54; Elbaum, *Openness and Insularity*, 302–24.

51 *Tos YT*, *Ter.* 1: 1. Cf. *Tos YT*, *Ber.* 2: 6, *Tos YT*, *BK* 1: 1.

52 Yiddish *Megilat eivah* in Erik, 'Memoirs', 202.

as opening the door of interpretative freedom. The same text may function either as law or as aggadah; the difference is not in the text but in the reader, in the mode of interpretation:

Just as freedom is given to interpret the Bible [differently from the Talmud], as we see [in] the commentaries that have been written since the days of the Talmud—although one may not decide or interpret any law to contradict the opinion of the authors of the Talmud—so [Maimonides'] words here may be upheld, even though [the passage] is interpreted differently in the Talmud, since there are no legal consequences [of the differences between Maimonides' interpretation and the Talmud's].[53]

Heller thus did not believe that the normative interpretation, the *peshat*, was the only legitimate interpretation. He did, however, identify *peshat* as the only interpretation that was legally normative.

Heller's own commentary aimed to give the *peshat* of the Mishnah, which, we have said, is defined largely by the Talmud. But did he believe that the *peshat* of the Talmud was established by one particular commentary? Specifically, was it established by Rashi's Talmud commentary?

Among seventeenth-century talmudists, a much less rancorous but no less significant controversy than that over *pilpul* concerned the relative status of the medieval Talmud commentaries of Rashi and Tosafot. These were the two commentaries that were commonly studied and are still printed in standard editions of the Talmud. But the rabbis were divided over whether Rashi's Talmud commentary should be regarded as true, perfect, omnisignificant, and entirely normative. Furthermore, if Rashi's Talmud commentary were to be canonized in this way, what then was the status of Tosafot?[54]

[53] *Tos YT*, *Naz.* 5: 5. Cf. Tchernowitz, *Rabbinic Authorities*, iii. 130. Roth remarks justly ('Notes', 90–4) that it is difficult to show that a certain interpretation has no legal consequences. Cf. *Tos YT*, *BK* 8: 7, where Heller writes that the interpretation of Scripture offered in the Talmud is not the closest to the meaning of the text, and *Tos YT*, *Yev.* 2: 8 (discussed in Roth, 'Notes', 97), where Heller enunciates the principle that Scripture must always have a *peshat* meaning—by which he means an acceptable *peshat* meaning—even where the talmudic law is based on a *derash*. *Tos YT*, *Meg.* 4: 9 recognizes the 'seventy faces of Torah', while imposing silence on those whose interpretations might lead to an error in Jewish law. Cf. *MYT (MM)*, *Ber.*, p. 29 n. 5. The kabbalistic notion of infinite meanings of Torah appears in *Leket shoshanim*, ch. 26, fo. 135*b*. Cf. also Sykes, 'Discrepancies', esp. pp. 122–6, on Heller's views.

[54] See Toledano, 'When and Where', 185; cf. Bialer, 'Cracow', 155. Rashi's Torah commentary was apparently canonized in precisely this way during the Middle Ages. By the 13th c., northern French rabbis were suggesting that to disagree with Rashi was heretical: see Davis, 'Philosophy, Dogma, and Exegesis', 216 n. 77. Rashi's Torah commentary was regarded as above criticism, and it was made the basis for dozens of supercommentaries, including one by the Maharal. Heller also treats Rashi's Torah commentary with extreme respect, although it is to be remarked that he chose rather to write a supercommentary on Ibn Ezra. See Emanuel, 'Rashi's Torah Commentary',

Joshua ben Joseph, the second-ranking rabbi in Cracow in the 1630s, wrote an entire book defending Rashi from the criticisms of Tosafot. He told his students, so his great-grandson later reported, that 'Rashi . . . had appeared to him . . . in great joy, and told him . . . Because you saved me from those young lions . . . the Tosafists . . . I will come to greet you in the next world with all my students'. On his deathbed in 1648, surrounded by the great men of Cracow, Joshua announced, 'Make room for our rabbi, the light of our eyes, Rashi. . . . He has come for me . . . to show me the way to eternal life!'[55]

'Every comment [in Rashi's commentary]', wrote Isaiah Horowitz, 'has wondrous secret meaning, for he wrote it with divine inspiration.' 'If you wish to understand the meaning of Rashi', he wrote in another place, '. . . [try to] explain the significance of his every word. . . . And it is proper to rebut the objections that the Tosafists brought against Rashi's comments.'[56]

In contrast, Horowitz's son Shabetai Sheftel told his own children that in studying the Talmud they must always try to reconcile Tosafot with Rashi through skilful *pilpul*. 'Anyone who says that there is something missing in Rashi', he wrote, 'has something missing in his head.'[57]

Isaiah Horowitz and Joshua ben Joseph were following in the path of the Maharal. The troubles with Talmud education, wrote the Maharal, 'are all on account of the study of Tosafot, and all on account of Tosafot having been published together with the Talmud'.[58]

While Joshua ben Joseph, Isaiah Horowitz, and the Maharal all felt a special closeness to Rashi, Heller identified himself with Tosafot, as the title of his Mishnah commentary suggests. Bertinoro's commentary, Heller wrote, was similar to Rashi in its form as a concise running commentary. Heller, by contrast, modelled his commentary on Tosafot. Like Tosafot, he offered somewhat longer, less

443–6. One of the charges brought against David Farrar in 1618 (on Farrar, see above, Ch. 3 n. 12) was his temerity in differing from Rashi: see Brody, 'A Manuscript Miscellany', 96, no. 18. This was one of the controversial aspects of Mendelssohn's Bible commentary as well.

55 See the introduction to Joshua b. Joseph, *Meginei shelomoh*, written by Joshua's great-grandson, Eliakim Getz b. Mordechai.

56 I. Horowitz, *Shenei luḥot haberit*, ii. 30*b*; iv. 20*b*.

57 Shabetai b. Isaiah Horowitz, *Vavei ha'amudim*, 54; cf. Shabetai's ethical will in Abrahams (ed.), *Hebrew Ethical Wills*, ii. 256.

58 Quoted in Assaf, *Sources*, i. 47 from Maharal, *Netivot olam*, 'Netiv hatorah', ch. 5. Cf. Assaf, *Sources*, i. 47 n. 1, where the author notes the publication of an edition of the Talmud without Tosafot, probably under the influence of the Maharal's ideas; see also Marvin Heller, 'Observations'. Elsewhere in the chapter, however, the Maharal wrote very respectfully of the Tosafists. Note the family tradition that the Maharal wrote a double commentary, in the style of Rashi and Tosafot, on Seder 'Zera'im' and Seder 'Tohorot'; quoted in Gottesdiener, *Maharal*, 69. Almost two centuries before the Maharal, the anonymous 'Sefer alilot devarim', 182–3, had already attacked Tosafot and favoured Rashi.

frequent comments; he did not comment on every word. Large parts of Bertinoro's commentary, moreover, are copied from Rashi; Heller quoted frequently from Tosafot. Furthermore, just as Tosafot often challenge Rashi's interpretations, so did Heller in many places challenge Bertinoro. '[My] comments', Heller wrote, 'are in the image and form of the commentary of Tosafot on the Talmud.'

The points at which *Tosafot yom tov* disagrees with Rashi are likewise many; a single example will be sufficient.[59] In explaining details of the prohibition on weaving on the sabbath, the Mishnah states that 'one who makes two *batei nirin* in the *nirin*' has violated the sabbath. Heller wrote:

> I have not been able to understand [Rashi's] comment. When I wished to understand it, I went to watch the craft of weaving. But when I saw it, I did not find that I could fit this comment to it. However, I was able to fit the words [of the Mishnah] with the design of the loom that I saw in a way that is different from [Rashi's] comment.[60]

Thus *Tosafot yom tov* did not follow strictly the path marked out by the Maharal, and indeed its title signalled this departure. Unlike Bertinoro, Heller did not offer a single, seamless interpretation of the Mishnah but rather a range of interpretations offered by previous commentators, authorities whom Heller sometimes defended and often disagreed with. No single commentary, not even Rashi's, was strictly normative for Heller. He consulted the medieval commentaries and often deferred to them but, like the Tosafists in their day, he also found room to disagree and to offer new and original interpretations.

THE EXEGETICAL EXPERIENCE

Heller spent a large part of his life reading, and his claim to distinction rested very largely on the reading that he had done. The sixteenth and seventeenth centuries in Christian Europe have been called an 'age of nostalgia'.[61] Extensive knowledge of ancient texts was valued as it had rarely been before and would not be again. The invention of printing had increased the availability of books, including ancient and medieval works, and allowed the accumulation of large libraries.

Even in an erudite age, Heller's erudition in Jewish texts was impressive. To identify, as Heller often does, a manner of phrasing or a certain rule in one text as the same as that in an unrelated text demands an active knowledge of a very large

[59] Note also *Parashat haḥodesh* (MS Oxford-Bodleian Heb. 2271), 40*b*, where Heller claims that Rashi (like the other Ashkenazi rabbis of his day) did not understand astronomy well. Cf. above, Ch. 2 n. 29.

[60] *TosYT*, *Shab.* 13: 2. The precise meaning of this phrase is unclear: Danby (in his *Mishnah*) translates it as '[He who] makes two loops to the heddles'; Jastrow, *Dictionary*, s.v. *nir*, suggests: 'He who starts a web by making two meshes, attaching them to the cross-pieces', and another suggested translation is 'two warp eyes in the loom shaft'.

[61] J. Friedman, *Most Ancient Testimony*.

body of literature. It is clear that Heller knew the Hebrew text of the Bible and the Mishnah and the Aramaic Targum extremely well, perhaps by heart. He knew a variety of medieval Jewish works almost equally well. In 1650, when he was past 70, he responded to a casual question from a printer concerning a sort of copyright notice that the printer was thinking of inserting in his book by citing responsa of Asher ben Yehiel (the Rosh) and Maimonides' *Moreh nevukhim*.[62]

Much of Heller's reading consisted of commentaries—Bible commentaries, Mishnah commentaries, and so on. Perhaps not surprisingly, a large part of *Tosafot yom tov* is commentary on commentary: Heller corrects the text of Bertinoro's Mishnah commentary, identifies his sources, corrects his interpretative errors, cross-references relevant comments by Bertinoro in other places, explains obscurities, and points out difficulties. Likewise, so numerous are Heller's comments on Maimonides' Mishnah commentary that the printer called special attention to them and suggested that they be collected in a separate volume.[63]

Heller even wrote commentary on commentary on commentary. One of the surviving volumes of his library contains his marginal notes to *Imrei shefer*, a supercommentary by Nathan Spira the Elder on Rashi's commentary on the Pentateuch.[64]

Heller was active in building up his library, and frequently wrote with evident delight of his success in securing a particular work.[65] In his writings he quotes from about 150 books. He kept his library in a special room in his house; it was not necessarily a large collection for the period, but it clearly represented an important investment.[66]

The development of Hebrew printing about the beginning of the sixteenth century did not wholly displace Hebrew manuscript culture, and Heller was particularly proud of his manuscript collection. In the 1630s, when he began an intensive study of the laws of *kashrut*, the dietary laws, he collected manuscripts of certain medieval Ashkenazi works on that topic.[67] He was serious in his approach to the scholar's duty of research: 'An author has an obligation to study and to

[62] The letter appears in Haberman, 'Liturgical and Other Poems', 126. Cf. *Tos YT, Kil.* 2: 5. Cf. the emphasis on memorization among 16th-c. German scholars of Roman law: see Strauss, *Law, Resistance, and the State*, 174.

[63] See the printer's introduction to *Tosafot yom tov*.

[64] The copy is now in the British Library in London. Heller's notes were published in London in 1958 by the Greenwald family.

[65] Cf. Beit Halevi, *Life of Heller*, 17; Hakohen, 'His Books', 150–2. Cf. *Tos YT, Pe'ah* 6: 4; *Mal YT* 267. In *Tos YT*, introd. to Seder 'Kodashim', Heller recounts his purchase of a Mishnah manuscript.

[66] *Megilat eivah*, 28. On libraries and private collections of books in Prague, see Palmitessa, 'House, Home, and Neighborhood', 223–4; Fučiková *et al.* (eds.), *Rudolf II and Prague*, 297–8 (cf. 332–44). Cf. Benedict, 'Bibliothèques'. On another Jewish book-collector in central Europe in these years, see Zimmer, *Embers of the Sages*, 230–1. Cf. Schochet, *Bach*, 69–74; Bonfil, *Rabbis*, 272–80.

[67] See *Torat ha'asham*, 60, 257. Cf. his frequent mentions of 'very old manuscripts' in his possession: e.g. his book of *seliḥot* mentioned in his 1650 letter to the Cracow printer; Haberman, 'Liturgical and Other Poems', 126.

search as far as he is able.'[68] Once he even wrote to Lvov, where there was an old manuscript of a medieval legal code, *Sefer raviah*, by Eliezer ben Joel of Bonn (*c.*1140–*c.*1225), in order to confirm the text of a difficult passage.[69]

Heller not only bought manuscripts and read them but commissioned the copying of new ones, and indeed himself wrote manuscript works—his kabbalistic treatise *Tuv ta'am* and his memoir *Megilat eivah*, which were not intended for publication.[70] In a sense, he also turned his copies of printed books into manuscripts. For him, reading was an active process, not wholly distinct from writing. He read, figuratively and perhaps literally, with a pen in his hand. Not content with merely passively imbibing the contents of a book, he noted many of his comments and disagreements in the margins. Several volumes that Heller owned, with their marginal notations, are still extant.[71]

Reading is typically thought of as a solitary activity, but a large part of Heller's reading was probably done in the company of others. Despite printing, despite manuscripts, Ashkenazi Judaism, like other early modern cultures, was in very large part an oral culture, and Heller's life with books was embedded within that oral culture. He studied Mishnah with one of the *ḥevrot* established by the Maharal, who had generally opposed the tendency of adults towards individual study and had recommended the formation of study groups.[72] We recall that Heller also studied Bahya ben Asher's commentary on the Torah together with a group of this kind. In *Tosafot yom tov* he quotes oral teachings in the names of Enshchen Hefets, Moses Kohen, Zanvill Katz, Isaac Levi, and Meir Bach, and in another work, he referred to 'my friend', Pinhas Horowitz.[73] In 1602 he dedicated *Tsurat habayit* to 'the men of the *ḥevrah*, whose love burns in my heart like fire'.[74]

68 *MalYT* 316: 9.

69 *Torat ha'asham*, 327.

70 Note MS Bar Ilan 842, a copy of the anonymous kabbalistic work *Sefer hapeliyah*, made, according to the colophon, by 'Moses b. Jacob ... of Bystřice, scribe of R. Liva . . . for R. Yom-Tov called Lipmann b. Nathan Heller of Wallerstein'. The durability of manuscript culture is stressed in Rowan, 'Jurists and the Printing Press'.

71 The extant volumes are *Sefer maharil* (in the Klar Library at the Hebrew Union College in Cincinnati), *Naftulei elokim*, and *Imrei shefer* (both in the British Library). Heller's copy of *Kaftor vaferaḥ*, with his marginal notes, was still extant in the 19th c. In various places in his extant writings, Heller also refers to marginal notes (now lost) on *Netivot olam* by the Maharal of Prague (*MalYT* 1: 2) and on the responsa of Solomon Luria (*MalYT* 554). MS Oxford-Bodleian Heb. 775 includes a note (fo. 119*b*) on *Shulḥan arukh*, 'Yoreh de'ah', para. 374, copied from 'the writing of . . . R. Lipmann, the author of *Tosafot yom tov*, in his *Shulḥan arukh*'.

72 'Derush al hatorah vehamitsvot', *Derashot maharal*, 62.

73 *Ber.* 1: 1 (Enshchen Hefets), *Dem.* 1: 2 (Moses Cohen), *Sot.* 9: 9 (Zanvill Katz), *AZ* 2: 5 and *Suk.* 4: 5 (Meir Bach; cf. *Leket shoshanim*, fos. 129*a*, 133*a*, 135*b*), *Zev.* 1: 2 (Isaac Levi). *MYT* (*PH*), *BK*, p. 266 n. 9: 'My friend, R. Pinhas Halevi [Horowitz]'. There were two Pinhas Halevi Horowitzes in Prague at this time: Heller was probably referring to his colleague on the rabbinical court.

74 *Tsurat habayit*, 10.

LETTER TO WORMS, 1616

In the preface to one of the later volumes of *Tosafot yom tov*, Heller tells the following story that merges the themes of manuscript culture, exegetical practice, and family. It concerns Heller's correspondence with his cousin, Simeon Wolf Oppenheim, a learned rabbi of Worms, lately returned to that city after the anti-Jewish riots of 1615:[75]

One of the rabbis . . . who saw [the first volume of] this book said [to me]: I know a secret. I can tell you truly that in the holy community of Worms there is a pious rabbi named Rabbi Simeon Wolf ben Rabbi Judah Liva Oppenheim. And in his hands I have seen . . . a wonderful commentary on the order 'Tohorot' [of the Mishnah] by . . . the famous Rabbi Meir of Rothenburg. . . . If you write a letter to Rabbi Wolf to send you the beautiful words [of that commentary], I know him, and I know how generous he is, so I am certain that he will not refuse . . .

When I heard this good news, I set to work . . . to bring [the commentary] into my hands. I hurried, I did not delay . . . and I found . . . a man from the community of Worms. And I told him words to say, and [gave him] a letter that I addressed to Rabbi Wolf.

Please [I wrote to Rabbi Wolf], if he would be so good as to send me a copy [of the manuscript], the Lord will regard it as charity and as a true kindness to [Rabbi Meir, the author] . . . whose lips will move and whisper [through the study of his commentary]. And if [Rabbi Wolf] were to name a high price, I would accept that, and on the contrary it would be very proper.

And when my words and my letter came to that scholar, he wrote back in a letter, sealed with his seal. We are brothers [he wrote], close kin, and family. For your honour's mother and mine were sisters, of a good family. A great mitzvah has come to my hand, and I will not miss it. All my life I have . . . waited for a time to come when I could perform it. I am sending his honour the entire work, so that he may see it, and I will not take from him a single penny. Rather my reward is in the deed itself, and my work has brought pleasure to my soul.

From time to time [Rabbi Wolf continued], when I have had a thought or an opinion [concerning the Mishnah] that seemed right to me, I wrote it down [in a commentary]. . . . And if his honour agrees with [my comments], then may he . . . hold fast to the quality of humility, and quote [my] words in his book in my name. And it will be enough for me that I have merited that.[76]

[75] On Heller's cousin, Simeon Wolf Oppenheim, see Eidelberg, *R. Juspa*, Heb. sect., 101. He died in 1632: see Berliner (ed.), 'Sefer hazkarat neshamot', 12. A manuscript of part of his Mishnah commentary (on the sayings of Simeon b. Gamaliel) is in the Bodleian Library (Heb. 848). Note also MS Oxford-Bodleian Heb. 953, 1031–2.

[76] *Tos YT*, introd. to Seder 'Tohorot'. Heller did in fact quote his cousin ('Wolf Worms') in the later parts of *Tos YT*, e.g. on *Par.* 4: 3.

FIVE

Jews and Non-Jews

THE NIKOLSBURG WINE CONTROVERSY OF 1616

THE Jewish community of Nikolsburg (Mikulov), in the province of Moravia, was divided over an issue of Jewish law during the first two decades of the seventeenth century. In summer 1616, about the same time that Heller was writing to his cousin Simeon in Worms, the Nikolsburg controversy was brought before Heller and the rabbis of Prague.[1] At the root of the case were issues of non-Jewish wine and Jewish autonomy, and at the root of these issues was the broader question of Jewish–gentile relations.

Non-Jewish wine, that is, wine that has been made or in many cases even touched by non-Jews, is prohibited by talmudic law. It is forbidden for Jews to drink it, or even to sell it. The Nikolsburg controversy sprang from the fact that, in Nikolsburg, Jews were drinking non-Jewish wine.[2]

[1] On Heller's attitude towards non-Jews, see the small gem of an article, Emanuel, 'Attitude'. On Maharal's attitude, see Sherwin, *Mystical Theology*, 83–106; M. Breuer, 'Debate'. Note also the short but incisive characterization of Maharal's views by Rosenberg, 'Exile and Redemption', 415–17. On the general question of Ashkenazi attitudes towards non-Jews, the classic statement is J. Katz, *Exclusiveness and Tolerance*. H. H. Ben-Sasson took an opposing view in his 1959 review of Katz's *Tradition and Crisis*, 'Concepts and Reality'. Cf. Katz's response, 'On Halakhah and *Derush*' and Ben-Sasson, 'Response'. The debate has been reviewed in Ruderman, *Jewish Thought and Scientific Discovery*, 60–4. See also Rosman, 'A Minority'; J. Ben-Sasson, *The Thought of R. Moses Isserles*, 289–91. Further literature is listed in Davis, 'Cultural and Intellectual History', 382–4. In a general way, this Jewish discussion may be compared to European discussions of the humanity of native Americans and other non-Europeans: see e.g. Hanke, *Aristotle*; Cañizares Esguerra, 'New World, New Stars'.

[2] On the issue of non-Jewish wine in the 16th and 17th cc., see J. Katz, *Tradition and Crisis*, 18–23; G. Cohen, 'History of the Conflict'; H. H. Ben-Sasson, *Theory and Practice*, 23–5; Siev, *Rabbi Moses Isserles*, 213–14. Note that Isserles singles out Moravia as an area of singular laxity in regard to the laws of non-Jewish wine. In a similar vein, the Maharal contrasts the laxity of Moravian Jews with the piety of Polish and Ukrainian Jews: see his 'Derush al hatorah vehamitsvot', *Derashot maharal*, 92. Solomon Luria, on the other hand, accuses German Jews in general of being lax in regard to the laws of non-Jewish wine (as well as eating fish cooked in non-Jewish inns): see his responsum no. 72, quoted in Tchernowitz, *Rabbinic Authorities*, iii. 74 n. 1.

Long before 1616, even before Heller was born, the conflict had begun to simmer. Nikolsburg was the largest Jewish community in Moravia, and its rabbi during the 1550s and 1560s was the Maharal, whose theology emphasized the contrast and separation of Jews and non-Jews.[3] The Maharal was therefore greatly exercised over the issue of non-Jewish wine, and took steps to discourage Jews from drinking it. He inserted a special blessing in the liturgy, a *mi sheberakh* as it is called in Hebrew, on behalf of 'the pious ones . . . who refrain from drinking wine that the rabbis have prohibited'.[4]

The Maharal's blessing was not sufficient, however, to convince the Nikolsburg Jews that they should switch to kosher wine. A generation later, therefore, in 1602—after the Maharal had moved to Prague—the pious Jews of Nikolsburg took a more decisive step and approached the *shtadlan* of the community. The *shtadlan* was the liaison between the Jewish community and the non-Jewish authorities—the lobbyist, the 'fixer', a man who could get things done at court; typically he was a wealthy man. The following discussion is based on the account preserved in a long responsum by Aryeh Leib Pisek.[5]

The *shtadlan* approached the lord of Nikolsburg, Maximilian von Dietrichstein, and asked him to ensure by decree that Jews should drink only Jewish wine; in other words, that the Jews should be given a monopoly on the sale of wine to Jews. Dietrichstein willingly granted the monopoly. Only Jewish vintners would be allowed to sell wine to the Nikolsburg Jews; in return, they would pay a tax on each barrel of Jewish wine that they sold.[6] The purchase of the wine monopoly, like the Maharal's institution of regular study of the Mishnah by adults, or like the expulsion of the 'whores' from Prague in 1611, was a part of the larger effort to reform the morals of the Jews of Bohemia and Moravia. Truth to tell, the Jewish vintners had been among those who had proposed this pious initiative, combining, like so many of their contemporaries, good religion with good business.[7]

[3] On the Maharal's views on non-Jewish wine, see Sherwin, *Mystical Theology*, 94–102, based mainly on *Derashot maharal*, 81–94. Sherwin emphasizes the kabbalistic basis of the Maharal's concerns on this question.

[4] See Hailperin (ed.), *Legislation*, 89 n. 8. In Germany, the rabbinic conference of 1582 had threatened those who drank non-Jewish wine with *ḥerem* (excommunication): see Zimmer (ed. and trans.), *Jewish Synods in Germany*, 81. The 1582 synod also established prohibitions on non-Jewish milk and styles of clothing, and on Jewish women visiting Christian houses without chaperones. Cf. the decree of the Friedberg community, discussed in Zimmer, *Embers of the Sages*, 222.

[5] Pisek, *Dimyon aryeh*, 3*a*–4*a*. I do not know the name of the *shtadlan* of Nikolsburg.

[6] On the privileges of the Nikolsburg Jews, see Gold (ed.), *Die Juden*, 418–20. Additional material on the case could perhaps be found in the Dietrichstein archives.

[7] Contrast the reverse approach taken in Mantua in the late 17th c. by Moses Zacuto, who felt it necessary to hold down the price of kosher wine lest poor Jews be forced to drink non-Jewish wine. See his letter printed in *Kerem shelomoh*.

In 1611 Maximilian von Dietrichstein died and was succeeded by Franz von Dietrichstein, a major figure in the Habsburg court and a cardinal of the Catholic Church. As was very often the case, the privileges of the Nikolsburg Jews had to be renegotiated at the time of his succession. One of the issues on the table was the question of the Jewish wine monopoly. Two things were changed during the negotiations: the tax on Jewish wine was increased, and it was transferred from the Jewish vintners to the Jewish community as a whole, the *kehilah*.[8]

Dietrichstein was satisfied; the Jewish vintners were satisfied; but in the Jewish community of Nikolsburg there was controversy. Perhaps, in their heart of hearts, there were Jews in Nikolsburg who felt that Jews were permitted to drink non-Jewish wine. For many seventeenth-century Jews (as Rabbi Pisek remarked), established practice was sufficient to create a right or to permit a certain type of behaviour.[9] This view, however, was never pressed.

Instead, the controversy focused on a new issue: the distribution of the new wine tax. Here the opponents of the vintners found room to make a legal stand, The apportionment of taxes was a recurrent problem in medieval Jewish communities. Ashkenazi Jews in this period knew of two basic systems of apportioning taxes: they could be assessed proportionately to income, or as a fixed sum on each household. The first system was graduated, and favoured the poorer households; the latter system was therefore often favoured by the rich. The Nikolsburg Jews debated these alternatives.[10]

There was much tension between rich and poor in early seventeenth-century Ashkenazi Jewish communities. There were no Levellers among the Ashkenazi Jews, but in Prague, for example, Ephraim of Luntshits directed a steady current of criticism towards the rich.[11] Wine, then as now, served a symbolic function in the conflicts of rich and poor. One of Ephraim's disciples, Alexander Pfaffenhofen of Germany, wrote a book-length poem in 1627, in which a poor man debates with a rich man. The rich man taunts the poor man:

[8] In this controversy, one can see three conflicting conceptions of the Jewish community (which will be discussed below: see pp. 129–31). Talmudic law contravened established practice; hence the rabbis found themselves at loggerheads with the *kehilah* council. The *kehilah* of Nikolsburg was then outmanoeuvred, circumvented, and defeated when the rabbi and his supporters (the vintners and the pietists) won the support of the *shtadlan*, who appealed directly to the Dietrichsteins, feudatories of the Christian king.

[9] Pisek, *Dimyon aryeh*, 11*a*.

[10] The Nikolsburg case parallels in many important respects the conflict of the Jesuit fathers with the Münster city council during these same years, over the local wine tax. The Jesuits, with the support of the imperial court, succeeded in overcoming the opposition of local lay leaders, based on custom. See Hsia, *Society and Religion*, 84–92.

[11] See H. H. Ben-Sasson, 'Wealth and Poverty'; note esp. p. 153, on Luntshits's scepticism of the motives of pious rich men. Cf. id., *Theory and Practice*, 90–110; Sadek, 'Social Aspects'. On the Jewish poor, see Guggenheim, 'Meetings on the Road'.

You absolutely don't know how to drink wine
And when you see someone with a cup of wine, you are jealous.
Wine is something special for you, something that comes once in a blue moon
Because you just drink water and other stuff all year.

No one sees you at a dinner,
Because you are so poor and so low-class that you are never invited.
And if once a year you are at one,
You pour wine into your mouth like an animal.
Because you have no manners or culture.[12]

The tax issue was one that, for obvious reasons, did not lend itself to adjudication by the rabbis of Nikolsburg. It was sent on, therefore, as was the custom, to the rabbis of the largest and nearest Jewish community—Prague.

I have mentioned the responsum by Rabbi Pisek, which was a legal brief rather than a court decision. After narrating the entire sequence of events, he argued that the burden of the new tax should be distributed equally among all the households in the community—the view favoured by the rich Nikolsburgers. The opinions of the *dayanim* of Prague are printed at the back of Pisek's book, listed in order of seniority.[13] First the chief rabbi, Ephraim of Luntshits; then Isaiah Horowitz, the president of the court; and then, in order, Moses ben David Segal, Mordechai Lipschitz, Pinhas Horowitz, and finally, the junior member of the rabbinical court of Prague, the young Yom-Tov Lipmann Heller.[14]

Ephraim of Luntshits's role as a tribune of the poor has been mentioned. Horowitz, on the other hand, like the Maharal, was something of a zealot on the subject of non-Jewish wine. Jews, Horowitz later wrote, should avoid wine that has even been *looked at* by a non-Jew.[15] Ephraim and Horowitz, together with Moses ben David, the third member of the higher court, agreed on a compromise. Although Rabbi Pisek's arguments were correct in principle, they wrote, the accepted custom was to make special allowances for the poor, and to apportion any new tax half as a flat tax and half as a graduated tax. They would follow that even-handed custom.

The three junior members of the rabbinical court dissented. The customary apportionment of new taxes, Lipschitz, Pinhas Horowitz, and Heller all agreed,

[12] Pfaffenhofen, *Sefer masah umerivah*, 284–5. In beer-drinking northern Germany, the status issues involved in wine were naturally somewhat different than in wine-drinking Moravia.

[13] Pisek, *Dimyon aryeh*, 17*a*–18*b*.

[14] Pinhas Horowitz, the Jewish jurist in Prague, is not to be confused with his relative Pinhas Horowitz, a Jewish jurist in Cracow and brother-in-law of Moses Isserles. See Muneles (ed.), *Inscriptions*, 327–8. It is slightly odd that Pinhas Horowitz was among the judges in this case instead of Maharal's son-in-law, Isaac b. Samson Hakohen, who signed, for example, the approbation for the 1616 Prague edn. of Solomon Luria, *Yam shel shelomoh* on *Ḥulin*.

[15] Owing to a printer's error, the passage is not in the 1862 Warsaw edn. of *Shenei luḥot haberit*, but it is in the 1878 Józefów edn., in vol. i, p. 52*a*.

had nothing to do with this case. The expense should not be treated as a new *tax* on the Jewish community, but as a voluntary expense of the community, like building a synagogue. Heller noted that the non-Jews had no desire to prevent Jews from drinking non-Jewish wine. Hence all of the added expense should be apportioned according to a graduated assessment.

Heller's conclusion, however, was different from that of any of his five colleagues. Rather than supporting a simple graduated tax, he suggested that a share of the tax should actually be paid by the Jewish wine merchants themselves. They stood to gain from the new situation, he wrote, and 'in all tax matters, the one who benefits more should rightfully pay more'. The wine merchants said, Heller wrote,

> that they gave the money out of the generosity of their hearts, and this is certainly true, but 'God searches the heart' (BT *Sanhedrin* 106*b*), and my heart and your heart know that they benefited from this. . . . Even though they now cannot sell [wine] to the uncircumcised, their loss . . . will be more than balanced by their gain, since no Jew can buy wine except from them.

Like his colleagues Mordechai Lipschitz and Pinhas Horowitz, Heller expressed support for the position of the poorer Jews of Nikolsburg. He went beyond them, however (in spite of his general disapproval of drinking non-Jewish wine, and his general approval of the new wine monopoly) in displaying a notable lack of enthusiasm for the pious Jewish wine merchants.

As a postscript to the controversy one could mention that the Nikolsburg *kehilah* appointed Heller as chief rabbi in 1624.[16]

ON NON-JEWISH BREAD AND NON-JEWISH BOOKS

The prohibition on non-Jewish wine, for whose enforcement the Maharal showed so much enthusiasm and Heller so little, was one means by which Jews were distinguished from Christians in the seventeenth century. There were many such means, some devised by Jews and some by Christians, some imposed by law and some voluntary. Two of Rudolph II's court painters, Roelandt Savery and Paulus Van Vianen, made some drawings of Prague Jews. In one, a Jewish man wears a Jewish star on his robe—a badge imposed by the Church. In another, a Jewish man wears a *talit*—the distinctive prayer shawl required in the synagogue.[17]

16 *Megilat eivah*, 29.

17 I thank Dr Joaneath Spicer for sharing copies of these drawings with me. The drawings (and the garments depicted in them) are discussed and reproduced in Spicer, 'Star of David'. There is an enormous scholarly literature on the extent, limits, and forms of social differentiation between Jews and Christians in the 17th c.; to repeat, the topic is one of the central themes of Jewish historical writing. See Hsia and Lehmann (eds.), *In and Out of the Ghetto*. An important document for Prague Jews is the regulations passed by the archepiscopal synod in 1605: Bondy and Dworsky, *Zur Geschichte der Juden*, no. 1009 (p. 794).

On his coach trip to Prague, Fynes Moryson's fellow-travellers were not sure, or so they joked, of the Englishman's religion. Was he a Calvinist? Perhaps he was a Jew. No, he was no Jew, Moryson joked back when they stopped at an inn: he would eat what the innkeeper put before him.[18] Dietary laws play a large role in rabbinic Judaism; Jews, as Moryson and his fellow-passengers all knew, did not in general eat food cooked by non-Jews. Food is a recurrent topic in Heller's rabbinic works, which he did not consider either minor or laughable. In *Tosafot yom tov*, he quoted Maimonides' explanation of why the Mishnah begins with the laws of agriculture: 'Since man cannot live without eating, the service of God is impossible without food.'[19]

A small catalogue of foods and food customs can be collected from the pages of Heller's works. Some food customs distinguish rich and poor, others, Jews and non-Jews. Small pike are better than large ones, and therefore, Heller wrote, large pike are sometimes called Jew-fish, because the Jews eat them and the noblemen do not. A Jew is not permitted to sell maggoty fruit or grain, even to a non-Jew. Most salted fish, Heller quotes from a medieval rule, is considered unkosher, because kosher and unkosher fish are salted together, but salted herring is kosher.[20]

Just as the Talmud prohibits wine made by non-Jews, it also prohibits bread baked by them, although the laws on bread are neither so detailed nor so strict as those on wine. Heller discussed this rule in a number of places. Once again he seems unenthusiastic, though to be sure, even Isaiah Horowitz recommended leniency on the question of non-Jewish bread.[21]

In *Pilpula ḥarifta*, published in 1619, Heller discussed the case of Jews who lived in small villages in which there was no Jewish baker. He argued that Jews in such villages were not only permitted to eat bread baked by a non-Jewish baker, but were even permitted to eat the bread of a non-Jewish householder. He based his argument partly on the fact that this is what village Jews did. Established practice created a presumptive right.

> For I have seen Jews who live in villages and small towns who eat bread baked by non-Jewish householders. . . . Therefore I have tried to explain the matter, to defend Israel [from the accusation of having sinned], and to defend the rabbis and the students of rabbis who did not object to this practice.[22]

18 Moryson, *An Itinerary*, i. 26–7.

19 *Tos YT*, introd. to Seder 'Zera'im', 31. Hayim b. Bezalel also emphasized the importance of food laws: see his introduction to *Vikuaḥ mayim ḥayim*, printed in Tchernowitz, *Rabbinic Authorities*, iii. 93.

20 *Torat ha'asham*, 341 (pike and Jew-fish), 60 (herring). Cf. Dirlmeier and Fouquet, 'Diet and Consumption'. Note also Zapalac, '"With a Morsel of Bread"'.

21 *Shenei luḥot haberit*, i. 64*a*. Cf. Ravid, '"Kosher Bread" in Baroque Venice'.

22 *MYT* (*PH*), *AZ*, p. 165 n. 60. Cf. *Torat ha'asham*, 319.

It seems likely that the village that Heller was thinking of was Wallerstein, where he lived when he was a child, and that the rabbi who did not protest against this custom was his grandfather.[23]

The relations of Jews and non-Jews in their many phases form the central theme of Jewish history as it has been written in the modern period. In Heller's writings, the theme was not so central, though it is implied in many ways. Even the choice—so much a part of rabbinic tradition that one is inclined to take it for granted—to discuss only Jewish law and not non-Jewish law, and to write books in the Hebrew language and in the Hebrew alphabet, is an expression of Jewish difference. In the seventeenth century, law and language were two major realms in which emerging national identities were expressed, in works such as Coke's *Institutes* and Martin Opitz's *Buch der deutschen poeterey*.[24]

Heller discusses the differences between Jewish and non-Jewish literature in *Tosafot yom tov*. Commenting on 'the book of medicine', which, according to a passage in the Mishnah, was hidden away by King Hezekiah, Heller wrote, 'Since [the book] was so well known among the Jews that [Hezekiah] was forced to hide it away, it was probably written by the sages of Israel.' Heller could not believe that a book written by a non-Jew would need to have been concealed from the Israelites. For surely, he argued, if the book had not been written by the sages of Israel, the Jews would never have read it in the first place![25]

Books by non-Jewish authors held a precarious place at the margin of Heller's library. Heller could read German, although probably not Latin, and a significant number of classical and Arabic authors had been translated into Hebrew over the course of the Middle Ages.[26] As discussed in the last chapter, he quoted by name

23 In the 1630s Heller again brought up the topic of non-Jewish bread, in a letter to Joel Sirkes in Cracow. Heller argued that if a pious Jew who does not usually eat non-Jewish bread is eating together with a less pious Jew who does eat non-Jewish bread, he is permitted (in certain circumstances) to share the non-Jewish bread of the other. Sirkes took the opposite view. See Heller's responsum in *She'elot uteshuvot ge'onei batra'ei*, no. 18; Sirkes, *She'elot uteshuvot baḥ haḥadashot*, no. 27; Heller answers there in no. 28, and continues the dispute in *Torat ha'asham*, 324–9. Cf. *Shulḥan arukh*, 'Yoreh de'ah', 112: 13. Heller's position (which is also Caro's) is followed by the later commentators.

24 Helgerson, *Forms of Nationhood*. See also the articles in *Harvard Ukrainian Studies*, 10 (1986), nos. 3–4: special issue on 'Concepts of Nationhood in Early Modern Eastern Europe'.

25 *Tos YT*, *Pes.* 4: 9. Cf. *Tos YT*, *Avot* 5: 22, quoted from the commentary *Midrash shemuel* by Samuel di Uceda. Emanuel, discussing the passage in 'Attitude', 55, claims that Heller 'holds back from affirming the value of non-Jewish culture'.

26 Heller's reading knowledge of German, as J. M. Zunz has already noted (*City of Righteousness*, 97), is demonstrated by his references to Josephus' *Jewish Wars*. See *Tos YT*, *Shek.* 6: 3, *MYT (DH)*, *Orlah*, p. 277 n. 34. Heller calls this text *Yosipon laromiyim* ('the Roman Josephus') and gives the place and date of the edition as Strasbourg, 5264 [= 1504]. I have been unable to locate this edition; perhaps Heller made an error in transposing dates between the Latin and Hebrew calendars, and was referring to the 1544 edn.. Elsewhere (*Tos YT*, last comment in *Ta'anit*, 4: 8) he

from about 150 books in *Tosafot yom tov* and his other writings. Only two of them are non-Jewish works, neither, significantly, by a Christian author: *Musarei hapilosofim* (Sayings of the Philosophers) by the Muslim Hunain ibn Ishaq, and Euclid's *Elements*.[27] Yet the significance of these exceptions should not be underestimated. By quoting Euclid in *Tosafot yom tov* and mentioning him by name, Heller was taking a stand. He had asserted this principle two years before, in 1612, in an approbation that he wrote for David Gans's book on astronomy, *Magen david* (Star of David). Gans himself had taken the lead, defending his own extensive use of non-Jewish authors such as Tycho Brahe.[28] Heller used the opportunity offered by the invitation to write an approbation not only to praise the book and the author but also to declare his opinion on the legitimacy of studying non-Jewish science and mathematics, especially Euclid. He wrote:

To know [astronomy], they must lay down the elements and principles, established on the basis of axioms and agreed propositions, derived by one of the sages of Athens, the city of wisdom, whose name was Euclid. True to his name, he wrote the *Elements* to be . . . a key [*aklida* in Aramaic] to all the sciences.

The house of Israel say that they would sin . . . if . . . words written by one of uncircumcised lips and flesh . . . came to their lips. . . . But I will wash my hands in innocence (Ps 26: 6) in studying this book [Euclid] or those like it . . . For they do no damage but are useful in the science of the calendar and the other [sciences] like it, which every wise man must understand, for many commandments, all the Lord's holidays, depend on it.[29]

Heller for the most part accepted the prohibition on non-Jewish books. He did not entertain the thought, for example, that it was appropriate to read non-Jewish poets, such as Ovid or Virgil, or to read the plays of Terence, like the Christian schoolboys of Nördlingen.[30] In his approbation for Gans, to take a second example,

refers to *Sefer yosef ben gurion*—that is, the Hebrew Josippon. J. M. Zunz also notes that Heller's reference to the book of Maccabees (*Tos YT*, *Meg.* 3: 6) may be to a German translation.

[27] One should perhaps add a map of the world to the list of non-Jewish sources from which Heller quotes; it is referred to in *Tos YT*, *Ḥal.* 4: 10 and *MYT* (*DH*), *Ber.*, p. 74 n. 37.

[28] See Gans, *Neḥmad vena'im*, introd., 9*b*. *Neḥmad vena'im* is substantially identical to the final (partially printed) text of *Magen david*; confusingly, these both differ from an earlier manuscript draft, also called *Magen david*, which is still extant. Contrast Abraham Horowitz, who explained in *Ḥesed avraham* that he would refrain from quoting non-Jewish philosophers such as Aristotle by name, in order to avoid prejudicing his audience against the views being quoted.

[29] Approbation for the prospectus of Gans, *Magen david*. The book was never published. There is a unique copy of the prospectus in the Bodleian Library. Neher discusses Heller's approbation in *Jewish Thought and the Scientific Revolution*, 77–81; cf. id., 'New Material'.

[30] Terence: Janssen, *History of the German People*, xiii. 167. It is clear that not all books by non-Jewish authors (or even Christian authors) were regarded equally by Ashkenazi Jews. 'The Jewish reading public . . . was enthusiastic about love and adventure stories', suggests Daxelmüller ('Organizational Forms', 35–6). It is possible, albeit unlikely, that Heller read such stories; it is more likely that he read newspapers, broadsheets, and the like.

he explicitly ruled out non-Jewish books 'concerning faith and the principles and elements of religion'. However, following a path laid out by the Maharal, and before him by Moses Isserles, he permitted non-Jewish books on natural science and mathematics, such as Euclid, the key to them all. In an exchange of letters quoted above in Chapter 2, Solomon Luria had claimed that references to Aristotle could not be used in halakhic arguments. Isserles had argued that they could, subject to two restrictions: first, that only Aristotle's natural science may be used, as distinct from his metaphysics or philosophical theology, and second, that non-Jews should only be quoted from intermediate Jewish sources, such as the medieval Jewish philosophers.[31] Heller adhered to Isserles's cautious rules. In *Tosafot yom tov*, he quoted Aristotle's *Naturalia* by way of Levi ben Gershom's Torah commentary, and without referring to the Greek philosopher by name.[32] Indeed is unlikely that Heller ever read any works by Aristotle himself.[33] He quoted Euclid directly and by name, but explained in a note that mathematics, unlike the natural sciences, is based on indisputable proof.[34]

What distinguished Jews from Christians in the seventeenth century? In part, they were distinguished by what they read. By 1500 more than ten thousand books had already been published; by 1600 that number itself had increased many fold. The new wealth of reading material could be used in many different ways; each literate group in Europe drew its own lines between what was and what was not to be read. For Ashkenazi Jews, the essential distinction was between Jewish and non-Jewish books.[35] Tearing down that barrier eventually became one of the major goals of the Jewish Enlightenment, the Haskalah, in the eighteenth and nineteenth centuries.[36]

[31] See above, p. 43; Davis, 'Philosophy and the Law'.

[32] *Tos YT*, *Neg.* 6: 6. Heller is concerned there with the meaning of the term *bohak*, a kind of skin eruption or discoloration mentioned in Lev. 13: 39 and also in the Mishnah. Heller quotes Levi ben Gershom, who quotes from *De coloribus*, ch. 6 (Aristotle, *Works*, vi. 797*a*).

[33] In the notes that he added to *Givat hamoreh* (5*a*), Heller quoted from Gersonides' supercommentary on Averroes' *Epitome* of Aristotle's *Physics*. In his comments on the talmudic dictum 'One who aligns his bed from north to south will have male children' (BT *Ber.* 5*b*), Heller quoted 'the natural scientists' on the effects of the north and south winds on conception. This teaching is based ultimately, but once again indirectly, on a passage from Aristotle's *Politics* (Book VII, 14: 7). See *MYT* (*MM*), *Ber.*, p. 5 n. 50.

[34] *Tos YT*, *Kil.* 5: 5 (p. 251, col. 1, in the Romm (Vilna) edn. of the Mishnah); cf. above, Ch. 4 n. 44. Contrary to what I wrote in my dissertation, the note was present in the 1st edn. of *Tos YT*.

[35] Jewish or non-Jewish authorship is the central issue. The Maharal also expressed some concern, however, that 'most, nearly all, of our books, especially in Italy, are printed by non-Jews': see Maharal, 'Teshuvot', 282.

[36] Italian Jewish scholars in the 16th and 17th cc., by contrast, were often erudite in Latin literature: see e.g. Weinberg, 'Azariah de' Rossi'. Leone da Modena argued explicitly in favour of reading books in languages other than Hebrew: see Rivkin, *Leon da Modena*, 58. See also Barzilay, 'The

Just as there was no hasidic movement in the early seventeenth century, nor any *mitnagedim* in opposition to it, so there was as yet no Haskalah, nor even a proto-Haskalah. The world of Ashkenazi Judaism was not yet divided into parties; currents of thought had not yet crystallized or broken off into movements. But just as many elements of the later hasidic movement can be discerned among seventeenth-century kabbalists, so can elements of the Haskalah, especially the desire to know that which is universally human, be found among Ashkenazi Jews, men such as Heller, touched by medieval Jewish philosophy and Maimonides.

HUMANIZING THE NON-JEWS

Heller's universalism found most eloquent expression in *Tosafot yom tov*, in a remark made in the commentary on *Avot* on the differences between Jews and non-Jews.

In medieval thought there were two opposites to heaven: there was earth, but there was also hell, Gehinnom. One common medieval Jewish view of non-Jews regarded them as worldly or earthy, in contrast to the spiritual, heavenly Jews. For many Christians, the difference was identical, only with the terms reversed: spiritual Christians and material Jews.

For instance, the universal history written by David Gans, *Tsemaḥ david* (Shoot of David), published in 1592, is divided into two sections, 'to separate the holy from the profane', as Gans wrote.[37] One section was for the non-Jews; one for the Jews. Each spanned the entirety of history, from Creation to Gans's own times. The chronicle of the non-Jews focused on the succession of the kings and emperors; that of the Jews (even in the biblical period) on the transmission of the Torah. The distinction between non-Jews and Jews was the difference between the political and the intellectual, that is, between the body and the spirit.

Another view of non-Jews, far from unknown in medieval and early modern Judaism, associated them with the powers of evil. This demonization of non-Jews is explicit in the Zohar: while the root of the Jewish soul is in the Divinity, the root of the non-Jewish soul is in 'the other side', the *sitra aḥra*, 'the side of impurity'.[38] The division between Jews and non-Jews is the same as that between holiness and

Italian and Berlin Haskalah'. Barzilay, like many other scholars, confounds the issues of secular subject-matter with that of non-Jewish authorship. The second was more controversial than the first.

[37] Gans, *Tsemaḥ david*, introd., 6. Note also Efron, 'Irenism and Natural Philosophy', 641–4, on Gans's largely respectful views on Christians. Cf. n. 28 above.

[38] See the references to the Zohar, below, nn. 39 and 42, and also Nathan b. Solomon Spira's and R. Samson of Ostropol's 17th-c. demonization of Christianity; Liebes, 'The Prophet Jonah', 284; id., 'Mysticism and Reality', 241–3.

unholiness, purity and impurity, between heaven and hell. The zoharic tradition was continued, for example, by Judah Hayat (*c.*1450–*c.*1510), an Italian kabbalist, who denied that non-Jews had any place at all in the 'Garden of Eden', in paradise. But is there not, one might object, an ancient rabbinic saying that 'righteous gentiles have a share in the world to come'? Hayat answered:

When they said that 'the righteous gentiles have a share in the world to come', they meant that they are in the highest level of Gehinnom, and enjoy the pleasure of the Garden of Eden which is next to it, for there is only a hairbreadth between them. But God forbid that they should be in the Garden of Eden.[39]

There is only a hairbreadth of difference, but that hairbreadth keeps Jews separate from non-Jews in the world to come.

Heller rejected this view. He noted in one place that 'it is an established rule' that righteous non-Jew had a share in the world to come,[40] and referred there to another passage in the Mishnah, in tractate *Avot* (3: 14), where he discussed the problem of Jews and non-Jews at greater length:

Rabbi Akiva . . . used to say: Beloved is man, for he was created in the Image . . . as it is written, 'For in the image of God made He man' (Gen. 9: 12). Beloved are Israel, for they are called the children of the All-present . . . as it written, 'You are the children of the LORD your God' (Deut. 14: 1). Beloved are Israel, for to them was given the precious vessel [the Torah] . . . as it is written, 'For I give you good doctrine, forsake not my Law' (Prov. 4: 2).

In his comment, Heller distanced himself from an interpretation with which he did not agree. 'Certain interpreters', he wrote, understand 'man' in the first section of the passage to refer exclusively to Israel; only Israel, according to this interpretation, is 'created in the Image'. Heller rejected this: 'I am astonished', he wrote; 'This interpretation is far-fetched.' On the contrary, he said, when Rabbi Akiva says 'man', he means all human beings, who are all beloved, all created in the Image.[41]

39 The comment is quoted in *Sefer olat tamid*, an alphabetic collection of aggadic and midrashic sayings compiled by Meir b. Leib Anshel Ozers in Prague in 1660—MS Oxford-Bodleian Heb. 925, s.v. *gan eden*, no. 33; cf. no. 13. It is based on the Zohar ii. 268*a*, referred to in L. Zunz, 'Das Gedächtniss der Gerechten', 377.

40 *TosYT*, *San.* 10: 3. On the origins and history of this saying, see J. Katz, 'Three Apologetic Dicta', 177–8; and see generally the sources collected by L. Zunz in 'Das Gedächtniss der Gerechten', 371–89. In Heller's commentary on Bedersi, on the other hand (14: 1: 13 [p. 111]), he denies that the non-Jews will be resurrected. Katz finds a clear apologetic tendency beginning in the mid-17th c., in rabbis such as Menasseh b. Israel and Moses Rivkes; Heller's comment should perhaps be seen in such a context. Cf. Schacter, 'Rabbi Jacob Emden', 697–705. See also Rafeld, 'Controversial Dictum'.

41 *TosYT*, *Avot* 3: 14. The passage is discussed in Greenberg, 'You are Called "Man"'; Emanuel, 'Attitude', 51–4; Wolfsberg 'R. Yom-Tov', 123–4, and cf. Kasher, 'Some Notes', 194–5. See also *MYT(MM)*, *Ber.*, p. 73 n. 1.

The rejected interpretation is in fact that of the Maharal. Heller did not mention him by name, but the Maharal's commentary on *Avot*, *Derekh ḥayim* (Way of Life), must have been open in front of him. The Maharal wrote,

Although it says, 'man', this does not include the entire human species. . . . As we have explained many times, Israel . . . is called man. . . . Still the gentiles have the human form as well, but not the essence of the human form. Although the form exists among them, it has no significance.[42]

The Maharal sought to distinguish carefully between the natural and supernatural orders, between Aristotle and the Torah, and between non-Jews and Jews. As he put it, using the typology of Ishmael and Edom for Islam and Christianity, Ishmael is Israel's 'complementary opposite'; its relation to Israel is that of matter to form. Edom, however, is its 'contradictory opposite'. For the Maharal, non-Jews may be either earthy or demonic.[43]

In contrast, Heller sought to minimize the differences between Torah and science, as described above; between the natural and the miraculous, as will be discussed in the next chapter; between Christianity and Islam; and also between non-Jews and Jews. In all his early writings, he conceived of non-Jews as an undifferentiated group, bound in a single eternal contrast to the Jews, the contrast of perfection and imperfection, of spiritual Jews and material non-Jews. He rejected the Maharal's distinction between 'Edom' and 'Ishmael', Christianity and Islam. For Heller, non-Jews were earthy but not demonic.[44]

[42] The Maharal quotes the talmudic saying, 'R. Simeon bar Yohai said . . . "You are called man, but the idolaters are not called man"' (BT *BM* 114*b*, *Yev.* 61*a*, *Ker.* 6*b*). The context in the Talmud is halakhic, concerning the ritual impurity conveyed by the corpses of non-Jews and the punishment for using the Temple oil to anoint non-Jews (in both cases, the legal result is paradoxical: since non-Jews are not 'men' their corpses are not impure, and the punishment for the use of the oil is less severe). The saying is quoted frequently and given a metaphysical sense in the Zohar: see i. 20*a*; ii. 28*b*, 86*a*; iii. 125*a*, 219*a*, 238*b*, and compare the other references given by Margaliot in his edn. of the Zohar at iii. 238*b*. Aaron Samuel b. Moses of Kremenets uses it similarly in *Nishmat adam*, 8. Heller mentions the halakhic rule at *Ohol.* 18: 7; cf. Emanuel, 'Attitude', 53.

[43] So too for Isaiah Horowitz. He does not discuss 'Ishmael', but he contrasts Pharaoh and the Egyptians, governed by unbridled lust, who are 'like monkeys compared to men', with 'Edom' (Christendom), who is associated with Samael, the Evil One himself. See e.g. *Shenei luḥot haberit*, in the 'Torah or' section: iii. 35*a*–39*a* (on the Exodus stories); cf. 19*a* (on 'Toledot') and 23*b* (on 'Vayishlaḥ'). The connotations or implications of these claims are complicated, however, by Horowitz's kabbalistic radicalism, insistent messianism, and tendency in the direction of antinomianism. The biblical character Lot, another 'monkey compared to a man', was also an ancestor of the messiah, through his descendant Ruth the Moabite (see iii. 12*a*, on 'Lekh lekha'); cf. iii. 74*a* on Balaam/Laban.

[44] The comparison of the Maharal to Luther is made in Ruderman, *Jewish Thought and Scientific Discovery*, 96–8.

Heller's comment, with its implied criticism of the Maharal, was a bold and forthright piece of exegesis. It begins by quoting Maimonides' interpretation of the talmudic dictum referred to above: righteous non-Jews have a share in the world to come, Maimonides wrote, if they observe the 'seven laws of the sons of Noah', the principles of universal morality, out of a sense of divine commandment. The 'image of God', Heller wrote, referring to Maimonides' explanation of that phrase in *Moreh nevukhim*, is the mind with which every human being has been endowed.

Heller did not wish to suggest that non-Jews are the equals of Jews. He stressed at the end of his comment that non-Jews do not bring the mind to its true perfection; that is, they do not know God. For that reason, he suggested, Rabbi Akiva says only 'the image' and not 'the image of God'. Heller distinguished sharply between the lofty potential of non-Jews and their present spiritual state.[45] Still, he stressed that the difference is only one of quantity: that is, a difference in the degree of perfection that has been attained, and not the nature of the perfection or in the attainment itself.[46]

In conclusion, Heller expressed a sense of spiritual obligation or even universal mission towards non-Jews:

> Rabbi Akiva came to instruct all the inhabitants of the world, as we have been commanded by Moses our Teacher, as Maimonides explains. For if we are commanded to impose [the laws of the sons of Noah] by the sword . . . how much more so [are we commanded] to draw them by words towards the will of their Creator and the desire of their Rock. [Therefore Rabbi Akiva] spoke well of them, [saying] that they are beloved, having been created in the image. . . . For it is the law of mankind [*torat ha'adam*] to perform God's laws and statutes out of a sense of commandment, as Maimonides has said . . . and as Rashi [also] explained.

In parallel to the well-known Christian ambition to bring the Gospel to the Jews, certain Jews in Prague, such as Heller, wished to 'draw the gentiles by words towards the will of their Creator', that is, towards the perception of their universal moral duty. Heller placed himself in a tradition of Maimonidean universalism, which implied, in principle if not in practice, a duty to enlighten the non-Jewish world.[47]

45 This is pointed out in Emanuel, 'Attitude', 53.

46 Also on the non-Jews; see *Tos YT*, *Avot* 1: 3, where Heller blurs Tosafot's contrast between Jews and non-Jews; *Tos YT*, *BK* 4: 3, where he quotes Maimonides' justification of Jewish law's preferential treatment of Jews over non-Jews; *Tos YT*, *Avot* 3: 10, where he admits that the non-Jews have their own traditions of learning.

47 Cf. *MYT* (*DH*), *Ber.*, p. 73 n. 25, on the messianic conversion of the non-Jews. The decrees of the Prague archepiscopal synod (above, n. 17) prohibit Jews from teaching Christians the liberal arts; this suggests that Jews (perhaps Gans?) had in fact been doing such teaching. Note that the

AGAINST TRINITARIANISM, 1619

In a number of limited but significant instances, Heller argued against the pious tendency to fortify the legal boundaries between Jews and non-Jews. On another issue, however—the legal status of Christianity—he took a very different line. In the same 1619 volume in which he discussed non-Jewish bread, he also discussed the relation of Christianity, polytheism, and idolatry.

The laws of non-Jewish wine, to return briefly to that issue, are a part of the talmudic injunctions against idolatry and against objects used in idolatrous worship. The custom in the Graeco-Roman world was to pour a libation to the gods before drinking wine. Therefore, the rabbis of the period of the Mishnah decided, non-Jewish wine should always be suspected of having been made into an offering to the pagan gods, and on that account, any commerce in it was prohibited, like commerce in other objects of idolatrous sacrifice.

It did not entirely escape the attention of medieval rabbis, however, that there are differences between ancient pagan religions and Christianity. In spite of certain elements of Christianity that might be construed as polytheistic or idolatrous—the apparent semi-polytheism of the Trinity, the use of images and sacred statuary—there were also differences between Christianity and idolatry that could be regarded as decisive in law. In particular, one line of argument, proposed by the medieval Tosafists and accepted by a number of medieval rabbis, including the great talmudist Asher ben Yehiel (the Rosh, *c.*1250–1327), distinguished polytheism from Trinitarianism, and argued that the latter, which recognizes the existence of the One God, is no sin for non-Jews, although it is not a permitted belief for Jews.[48]

Heller rejected this distinction. In a brief comment in the 1619 volume, he argued that worship of the Trinity is a type of polytheism.[49] Working from the abstract to the concrete, he then argued that Jews renting houses to Christians should try to prevent them from bringing objects of worship, notably the eucharistic wafers, into their houses.[50] This was not a pressing issue in Prague, but further east, in the Ukraine, where many Jews were innkeepers, it was a controversial

notion of universal Jewish mission was also put forward by Hayim b. Bezalel (the Maharal's brother), as discussed in H. H. Ben-Sasson, 'The Reformation', 298. By contrast, I. Horowitz, *Shenei luḥot haberit*, ii. 33*b*, prohibits teaching non-Jews even the 'seven commandments of the sons of Noah'. Horowitz was following Luria, *Yam shel shelomoh*, *BK* 4: 9, discussed in Fram, 'Reappraisal', 162. The various medieval rabbinic views on the topic are surveyed in Broyde, 'Obligation'.

[48] See J. Katz, *Exclusiveness and Tolerance*, 162–5, on the dissociation of Christianity and idolatry; cf. id., 'Three Apologetic Dicta', 184. On Isserles, see also J. Ben-Sasson, *The Thought of R. Moses Isserles*, 126–7, 289–91.

[49] *MYT (PH)*, *San.*, p. 237 n. 5.

[50] *MYT (PH)*, *AZ*, p. 158 n. 9. However, the Rosh argued, and Heller accepted, that the Jewish landlord can in effect disclaim responsibility, since the circumstance is a rare one.

problem. Indeed, one of the enduring grievances of Christians against the Ukrainian Jews was that Jewish landlords did not permit their Christian guests freedom of religion, freedom to perform the rituals that they regarded as essential for their salvation.[51]

Heller offered a talmudic prooftext for this stringent view and argued, perhaps correctly, that the Talmud identifies Christianity and polytheism. The halakhic distinction between Trinitarianism and polytheism, as noted above, is medieval, not ancient. But Heller accepted perhaps thousands of medieval distinctions that are weakly borne out in the Talmud text; why did he reject this one, which was accepted, moreover, by the Rosh, a Talmud commentator whom Heller considered especially authoritative?

Heller quoted from Maimonides' Mishnah commentary, and argued, again no doubt correctly, that Maimonides too identified Christianity and polytheism; but what made him prefer Maimonides' view here to that of Tosafot? In his own Mishnah commentary, a few years earlier, Heller had passed over this comment of Maimonides in silence, and had avoided the entire question of the status of Christianity. Why did he recklessly bring up the topic here—for it was a dangerous topic, and Heller, as will be seen, paid full measure for his comments later in life?

One may cite either character or circumstances. Heller was not generally a defender of Maimonides' halakhic views but he was strongly attached to Maimonidean rationalism, one element of which is a special distaste for any diminution of God's absolute unity, including the doctrine of the Trinity (and, on the other hand, many versions of the kabbalistic doctrine of *sefirot*).[52] But circumstance may also have played a role. It is possible that Heller was influenced by the rebellious, iconoclastic, and anti-Catholic mood of Prague in 1619. When radical Protestants were denouncing the Eucharist as 'idolatry', could Heller remain far behind?[53]

ON UNITY

Heller finished *Tosafot yom tov* on Wednesday, 22 Heshvan (corresponding to 2 November 1616). His last comment in the book was on the topic of peace.

The Mishnah ends with this peroration: 'There is no vessel that contains blessing for Israel except peace, as it is written, "God has granted strength to his people, He has blessed his people with peace" (Ps. 29: 11).' Heller commented:

It is appropriate to end the Mishnah in this way, because the Mishnah is full of *maḥloket*, full of disputes and disagreements among rabbis. Lest you think that these disagreements

[51] Sysyn, 'A Curse on Both their Houses', p. xxiii.

[52] Note Joseph Halevi's attack on Trinitarianism in *Givat hamoreh*, 27*b*. Joseph added that he had written an entire work on this topic called *Ma'amar ha'aḥdut* (now lost).

[53] On iconoclasm in the Prague cathedral in 1619, see Šroněk, 'Sculpture', 355.

brought about fighting or hatred, it must be stated that the Torah, when it is studied for its own sake, and not for self-aggrandizement, is the cause of peace. Therefore it is written, 'God has granted strength'—namely, the Torah, which is referred to as 'strength'—'to his people'—and by that means—'He has blessed his people with peace'. And peace is itself a kind of strength.[54]

However, the passage in the Mishnah does not explicitly mention conflict (*maḥloket*) anywhere, nor does it ever explicitly mention the Torah. The whole question of whether the Torah brings about peace, or whether, if it is studied with self-aggrandizing motives, it can actually provoke conflict has been added by Heller. It is surely not out of place to note that Heller was writing at a time when relations between Protestants and Catholics in Prague and throughout the empire were rapidly deteriorating, indeed a time of imminent religious warfare. Torah may lead to peace; in 1616, when *Tosafot yom tov* was completed, religion in general surely did not.[55]

[54] *TosYT*, *Uktsin* 3: 12 (last paragraph of the last tractate of the Mishnah).

[55] The connection between talmudic *maḥloket* and contemporary religious conflicts within Christianity is made explicitly by the Maharal in *Tiferet yisra'el*, ch. 69.

PART II

THE TRIAL
1618–1630

SIX

Prague in Wartime

THE DEFENESTRATION OF PRAGUE, 1618

THE Thirty Years War began on 23 May 1618, when representatives of the Czech nobility threw three Catholic representatives of the Habsburg emperor Matthias I, two regents and a secretary, out of the left-hand window of the Chamber of the Czech Chancery in the castle of Prague. War spread gradually to the rest of Europe. The entire second half of Heller's life, from 1618 to 1654, was lived in the shadow of war.[1] In 1621 a Prague Jew recalled the events:

> During the reign of Emperor Matthias, Roman emperor and king of Germany, Hungary, and Bohemia, in 378 [i.e. 5378 = 1618], while the emperor travelled from the capital city of Prague to the city of Vienna, some of the noblemen of Bohemia formed a conspiracy. They went up to the castle here in Prague, to the chamber of the imperial councillors. . . . And they took three of them and threw them out of the window into the moat. And they shot arrows [actually, guns] after them, but they escaped. . . . And when [the noblemen] saw that they had angered their king, the emperor, they . . . gathered a large army. And the emperor also gathered his army, and there was fierce war between them.[2]

This is not the place for an account of the complex causes of the Defenestration of Prague, nor the details of the long-accumulated tensions and animosities between Germans and Czechs, Catholics and Protestants, emperor and nobility. Neither can the war's many battles and campaigns, its shifting alliances and complex intrigues concern us here. Our focus is rather on the experiences of Heller and the Prague Jews in wartime.

LETTER TO VIENNA, 1619

On 22 November 1619, 15 Kislev 5380 according to the Jewish calendar, on a Friday afternoon, a bundle of letters was sent by the Jews of Prague to the Jews of

[1] See e.g. Parker (ed.), *The Thirty Years War*, which has references to the extensive literature on the war, and Von Krusenstjern and Medick (eds.), *Zwischen Alltag und Katastrophe*. On Prague Jews during the war, see Popper, 'Les Juifs de Prague'; Spiegel, 'Die Prager Juden'.

[2] Haberman, 'Liturgical and Other Poems', 130–1. Adam Mintz, in 'The Jews of Prague', has argued cogently that the author of the prose account was probably the printer, and not Heller.

Vienna and Nikolsburg. The letters were never delivered. By the time they arrived, Vienna (which since 1612 had been the Habsburg capital) was under attack by the Bohemian army and its Protestant Hungarian allies. A week before, the mystic Jacob Boehme had prophesied that the Hungarians would sweep through to the Rhine and overthrow the empire. The war was going badly for the Habsburgs.

Through chance the letters (there were forty-six) ended up in the archives in Vienna, where they were discovered and published in 1911. The letters give a snapshot of these two Jewish communities in the second year of the Thirty Years War. Among them is one from Heller and his wife Rachel to Rachel's Aunt Edel.[3]

Vienna's Jewish community was small relative to that of Prague. However, it was uncommonly wealthy, and had special political influence on account of its proximity to the Habsburg court. The forty-six letters are mostly to and from members of the rabbinic-mercantile elite. Most are written to relatives, and most of the news is family news: health and sickness, births and weddings. Zangwill Hammerschlag's daughter Rikel is engaged to the son of the great Polish rabbi Joel Sirkes, but the marriage will not be for a year. Samuel ben Gabriel writes to his son-in-law about the birth of latter's baby boy five weeks earlier. The circumcision was held in the Meisel synagogue in Prague. Twenty people came, and Isaiah Horowitz was the *sandek* (godfather).

Hezekiah ben Asher Horowitz apologizes for writing to his father-in-law in Yiddish, explaining that he does so in haste; the sabbath is coming, it is almost sunset, and he has no time to compose a Hebrew letter. (All the letters, both in Hebrew and in Yiddish, are characterized by an elaborate sense of decorum.) The young Hanokh ben Isaac writes in Hebrew—actually in rhymed Hebrew prose!—to the father of his fiancée Bella in Nikolsburg. Dutiful Solomon ben Hayim writes to his mother in Yiddish, but to his father in Hebrew. Solomon's father was the rabbi of Nikolsburg, but had fled to Vienna because of the war. The son writes from Prague that he is going to become a student of Rabbi Lipmann.

Some of the letters discuss the war, mostly the troubles in Moravia and Nikolsburg. The official scribe of the Prague community writes to ask for help in a case of *pidyon shevuyim*, securing the release of a certain Jew taken prisoner in Moravia.[4]

[3] Landau and Wachstein (eds.), *Jüdische Privatbriefe*. Some of the letters (though not Heller's) are translated in Kobler (ed. and trans.), *Letters*, 449–79. They are discussed in Spiegel, 'Die Prager Juden', 115–17, and also (from a very different point of view) in Sheffer, 'Beyond Heder'; see also Wischnitzer, 'A Friday in 1619'. Hailperin discusses the letters (MS, p. 18), and annotated texts of Heller's and Rachel's letters appear on pp. 109–10. Aunt Edel died the next year. On Boehme, see Weeks, *Boehme*, 129.

[4] 'The Jewes are very charitable in workes of Pity, more spetially in ransoming Captive Jewes': Moryson, *Shakespeare's Europe*, 494.

Henele, the daughter of Heller's cousin Abraham, writes to her sister that their brother Samuel arrived from Nikolsburg 'naked and stripped of everything'. She has also heard rumours that the duke of Bavaria has captured Nördlingen. Her thoughts must have been for her family in Wallerstein. 'One trouble always comes after the other', she writes.[5] The price of sending a letter is six kreuzers (pennies).

The letter-writers are pious Jews. They thank God for the good, and are quick to see his hand in the small blessings of their lives. They invoke God's help for their plans and endeavours.

Heller's Yiddish letter to his wife's Aunt Edel concerns negotiations for the marriage of one of his young daughters, probably either Nechle or Nisel.[6]

May you have a very good year, my dear *meḥuteneste* (relative by marriage), Rabanit Mistress Edel. . . . The letters that you wrote three or four weeks ago arrived today. . . . Rabbi Isserl [Edel's son-in-law] let me read them. I am . . . happy to hear that what I had been told is not true, [and that] you have taken the trouble to see to what I wrote you, namely all of the articles as they were written. And especially if my part of the dowry will be no more than 1,000 gulden,[7] then I am content. But if this has not yet been done, then I pray you to see if you can bring it down to 800. And that will not lessen your matchmaker's fee, but to the contrary, it will increase it. The young man, thank God, doesn't lack for money. But I certainly do not want to give my daughter without a dowry, God forbid, in spite of my troubles, which you know full well. For that reason, you will know how to act according to your discretion. In short, I have set the matter in your trustworthy hands.

Give my very warm regards to Mirel.[8] I have not had the time to write to her. Nor have I had a letter from her for a long time. I hope that things are going well for her. And best regards to my son-in-law. And also the same to my old friend, your cousin Rabbi Abraham,[9] although he once set himself far away. Greet him warmly on my account. I am a friend to all good people, as he knows very well. May I be the same to him.

Good Shabbos.
Lipmann Levi Heller

More remarkable than anything that Heller wrote in this missive (one does not know whether to class it as a business letter or as a family letter; it is a letter about

[5] On the destruction in Nikolsburg see Toegel (ed.), *Documenta Bohemia*, ii. 187.

[6] Both Nechle and Nisel were in fact later married to members of wealthy Vienna Jewish families. Hailperin (MS, p. 110 n. 4) claims that the daughter discussed in the letter was only 9 years old. It is not clear to me how Hailperin knew which daughter was referred to in the letter. Heller's letter can be compared to the 1640 letter of Maharal's grandson, Naftali b. Isaac (Hakohen) Katz, to his wife, edited by E. Kupfer, most of which concerns negotiations for their daughter's marriage.

[7] About four years' salary.

[8] Mirel was Rachel Heller's first cousin; her husband, Jacob Koppel Wallerstein, was Heller's first cousin once removed. Their son later married Heller's daughter Nechle. See Landau and Wachstein, *Jüdische Privatbriefe*, 19 n. 19.

[9] Probably Abraham Hayim of Opatów, the rabbi of Nikolsburg, who had fled to Vienna.

what can only be called family business), is what he left out of it entirely, namely the news of his daughter Esther's recent marriage. Perhaps a sort of sourness held him back from expressing his joy, or perhaps a kind of division of labour: the husband to take charge of the negotiations, the wife to tell the happy, gossipy news. Heller's wife Rachel filled in with a postscript:

Dearest Auntie,

What should I write to you? I know that you will do everything in the best way, just as if I were with you. For I know that you have a good heart and that you will not fail me.

You should know that your [daughter] Malka is always with us. Also you should know, my dearest Auntie, that our Esther has been married (in good luck) and that thank God, it was negotiated very well, and she got a good settlement. I had not thought that it would go so well, thank God. So great peace and a healthy year

From your niece Rechel
daughter of Mr Moses Aaron

Greet all our dear people for me. God protect you, my children, God protect you. . . .[10]

FEARS

Anxiety and worry runs like a thread through many of the letters of 22 November. One writer after another complains: Why haven't you written? 'We haven't heard any news of you', Hanokh Hammerschlag complains to his son, and Solomon ben Hayim to his father. 'It is as if you were across the Sambatyon River', writes Solomon Zalman, the son of Isaiah Horowitz. 'I have heard no news of you in seven weeks', Sarel bat Moses Gutman writes to her husband Leib. 'Where in the world are you? . . . I don't eat, I don't drink, I don't sleep, my life is no life.'

Hanokh ben Isaac has heard that the Nikolsburg synagogue has been destroyed. He is anxious because he has heard no news of his future in-laws. 'Are you in Nikolsburg?' he asks. Sarel Gutmans writes to her husband that Frederick and his wife Elizabeth have been crowned king and queen in Prague, and that on Sunday 'a riot almost occurred because of a soldier, and we were in great danger, but it was suppressed at once'.

Every Jewish community in Christian Europe at the beginning of the seventeenth century lived with two fears. The first was the fear of expulsion. The Jews had been expelled from Prague in 1541, and again in 1557 and 1561. They had been expelled in the course of the previous 300 years from nearly all of western Europe.

[10] Heller's letter (letter no. 20) is in the Heb. sect., pp. 28–9. There is a transcription into Roman letters on p. 49, and a facsimile reproduction. Rachel's letter is on p. 29 (transcription, p. 50). I thank Kristen Zapalac for her help in translating the two letters. Esther's engagement is also discussed in the letter of Isserl Lipschitz, Edel's son-in-law (letter no. 21).

If in 1618 they were still allowed to live in Poland, or in certain parts of the empire, who could know how long that would continue? How long might it be before Prague followed the example of Nördlingen? The second fear was of riot and pillage. What would be the fate of the Jews if urban order were to break down? If a city were to be sacked by victorious soldiers, or if riots were to break out, the Jews feared that they would be among the first victims. 'When permission is given to the Destroying Angel, he does not distinguish between the righteous and the wicked', Heller would quote many years later from the Babylonian Talmud, apropos of the war, suggesting that the Destroying Angel does not distinguish Jews from non-Jews.[11]

In the spring of 1611, during the so-called Passau war, there was a riot in Prague's New Town. The violence was directed mainly against the Catholic clergy, the population of the New Town being mainly Protestant. Yet the anxious fear that any civil disturbance would lead inevitably to anti-Jewish violence led the Prague Jews to fear for their own safety. So surprised and so delighted, indeed, were the Jews that the riot had left the Jewish quarter untouched that the rabbis of Prague instituted a special day of thanksgiving to God and composed special liturgical poems to be recited in the synagogue each year in commemoration of the event.[12]

That the fears of the Prague Jews had not been far-fetched was demonstrated by the experience of the Jews of Frankfurt am Main. In 1614 the ghetto of Frankfurt, the largest Jewish community in Germany proper, had been pillaged in the course of an urban revolt led by a man named Fettmilch. The Jews had been taken to the cemetery; they had put on shrouds and waited to be slaughtered, resolved to die as martyrs. When they were merely put on boats and expelled from the city, 'we went out rejoicing and mourning', Elhanan ben Abraham wrote.[13]

In 1616 intervention by the Habsburg imperial court, among others, had brought about the return of the Jews to Frankfurt and to Worms (from which the Jews had also been expelled), and the execution of the rebels of Frankfurt, including Fettmilch. But who would protect the Jews of Prague now that the emperor himself was fighting for his throne?

In a comment in his work *Ma'adanei melekh*, published in 1619, Heller reflected on the nature of different types of peace. His comment is based on a verse in Isaiah

[11] Heller's letter is quoted in the printer's introduction to his *seliḥot* of 1651, published in Haberman, 'Liturgical and Other Poems', 126–8.

[12] A. David (ed.), *Hebrew Chronicle*, 62–9. Cf. above, Ch. 2 n. 32.

[13] See Friedrichs, 'Politics or Pogrom?'; cf. id., 'Anti-Jewish Politics'; Kracauer, *Geschichte der Juden*, i. 358–98. Note also Turniansky, 'An Unknown Historical Song'. Elhanan b. Abraham's poetic narrative of the events (Hellin, 'Megilat vints') is published in the 1768 Offenbach edn. of Gans, *Tsemaḥ david*, in the additional material at the end. It is reprinted in A. Kahana, *Jewish Historical Literature*, ii. 182–93. A new edition by Rivkah Kern-Ulmer has also appeared.

(32: 17): 'The work of righteousness shall be peace, and the effect of righteousness, quietness and confidence for ever.' Heller asked: What is the difference between 'peace', 'quietness', and 'confidence'? He answered, 'When there is quietness, it may yet chance that the sword of war will come. . . . And confidence is when one is confident that no harm will occur even if the sword passes by, or other evil events occur in the world. Yet peace includes all the blessings.' Quietness is a temporary blessing, and some confidence may be had in strong walls or the promises of princes; but the only true blessing is peace itself.[14]

PRAGUE, 1620: HABSBURG LOYALIST

Frederick, the new king of Bohemia, ruled only for a single year or a little more. The tides of war, which ran against the Habsburgs for more than a year after the Defenestration—as mentioned, Vienna itself was nearly lost—turned in their favour. The imperial army invaded Bohemia, and on 8 November 1620, in a short but decisive battle, the troops of the new emperor, the devoutly Catholic Ferdinand II, routed Frederick's army and quickly captured Prague.

The providence that had protected the Jews of Prague in 1611 watched over them in 1620 as well. Desperately short of cash to raise an army, Ferdinand had turned to the Jews for support; in return, the victorious imperial army, as it looted the city, was forbidden to pillage the Jewish quarter of Prague or to disturb the Jews in any way. An officer was assigned to keep the peace. The same Hebrew narrative whose account of the Defenestration we quoted at the beginning of this chapter narrates the events:

> The battle was fought hard on the White Mountain, which is near Prague, until the late afternoon, when the men of the Emperor had the upper hand. They made a great slaughter of the men of Bohemia, ten thousand men. . . . On that night, the imperial army entered the castle . . . And on Monday, the thirteenth of Heshvan . . . and the next day, Tuesday . . . the Old City, where we live, did not surrender; nor did the New City surrender. And we were in great danger until in the evening they surrendered.
>
> But God caused the generals of the army to be gracious and merciful towards us, and they set guards over our streets. For His Majesty, the Emperor—may God reward him—had ordered his generals not to touch any Jew, [and to take] neither his life nor his property, but to guard them carefully. Houses full of booty were pillaged for a month, but against the Jews, 'they did not stretch out their hands' (Esther 9: 10).

In thanksgiving for the deliverance of Jews from the pillaging imperial army, the chief rabbi of Prague, who at this time was Isaiah Horowitz (Ephraim of Luntshits having died in February 1619), declared 14 Heshvan as a dawn-to-dusk fast-day

[14] *MYT* (*PH*), *BB*, p. 359 n. 90.

for the Prague community, to be observed each year on the anniversary. The commemoration was identical to the fast-day decreed by Ephraim of Luntshits himself after the Passau riots in 1611. Just as Ephraim had written liturgical poems to be recited on that fast-day, so liturgical poems were to be written now; but Horowitz delegated the task to his junior colleague, Heller.

Heller wrote a pair of poems, the first on the Defenestration and the second on the battle of White Mountain and the siege of Prague. The two poems, rich in biblical allusion but sparse in factual detail—as medieval Hebrew poetry tends to be—add little to our knowledge of the two famous events that they describe. They do, however, allow some insight into Heller's perception of those events. For him, the essential pattern was that of Jewish fear followed by unexpected deliverance:[15]

> The days became many and great became the troubles;
> Before the first had departed, the next had arrived.
> We hoped for peace, a time of healing, but behold there was terror (Jeremiah 14: 19)
> 'For it is mighty and their anger is hard' (Genesis 49: 7).
>
> . . . .
>
> My voice cried out to God, for I was sunk in the abyss of despair
> He opened for me the strait, He was gracious to me, He gave me joy when I heard the news spoken
> That army officers had come to our streets to guard them, lest they be touched
> 'For Thou ridest upon Thy horses, upon Thy chariot of salvation' (Habakkuk 3: 8).
>
> In the year 381 [= 1620], in the month of Bul [= Heshvan], on the fourteenth day
> At evening time, behold, I found ransom and deliverance.
> Upon my walls, He placed watchmen all the night and the day,
> 'And we are left as a remnant to this day' (Ezra 9: 15).

When Jews escaped major harm in the various riots and civic disorders that wracked the empire in the 1610s, the Jewish eyewitnesses and storytellers of that generation often saw miraculous intervention at work. Christians, of course, did the same for their own escapes. One of the victims of the Defenestration, for example, was said to have been protected by the Virgin Mary as he fell out of the window.[16] 'The Lord of Hosts sent an angel into the midst of the crowd', wrote an anonymous Jewish chronicler shortly after the events of the Passau riot in Prague in 1611, 'and they heard a voice say, "Do not raise your hand against the Jews, by order of our sovereign, the Emperor." '[17] Similarly, Juspa Shamash, the beadle of

[15] Heller's *seliḥot* on the events of 1618–20, together with the Hebrew prose introduction, were published in Haberman, 'Liturgical and Other Poems', 129–33. They are translated in A. Kisch, 'Die Prager Judenstadt', and are discussed in Šedinová, 'Hebrew Literature', 11–17, and id., 'Literary Structure'.

[16] See H. F. Schwarz, *The Imperial Privy Council*, 345.

[17] A. David (ed.), *Hebrew Chronicle*, 67. Cf. Juspa Hahn, writing in 1630: 'We have seen with our own eyes . . . that the living God . . . performs miracles for us at all times' (quoted in Baron, *Social and Religious History of the Jews*, xiv. 227).

Worms, credited the rabbi of the town, Gedaliah, with saving the Jews during the riot in 1615: 'By uttering divine names, he caused the Jewish street to be filled with soldiers marching with arms and all types of weapons.'[18]

By contrast, the Hebrew prose account of the 1620 deliverance of the Prague Jews, quoted earlier, did not credit God with any part in the action at all; he is merely asked to reward Ferdinand for his kindness.

In Heller's poem, there are no angels, no magical soldiers, but he did cast the events of 1618 and 1620 in a providential light. Whereas the sending of officers to protect the Jewish quarter is credited in the prose account to Emperor Ferdinand, Heller attributed it to God. The troubles, he declaimed, were divine punishment for sin; the protection of the Jews was God's answer to the Jews' prayers and repentance. God, not the Habsburg emperor, was the active force in Heller's view of events:

> In chastisement for sin, You have afflicted us, and we are hard pressed,
> For strangers have risen against me, and arrogant men.
>
> . . . .
>
> Trembling from shocking news, tales in twisted bundles,
> I grew faint at the word of the king and his noblemen, spoken and decreed.
> The pure of hands gather strength, wearing sackcloth, turning in repentance
> 'For the trouble is near and there is none to help' (Psalm 22: 12).
>
> . . . .
>
> And all the people saw the works of the LORD, for He is fearsome
> The wealth of the nations has He swallowed, and over them the net is cast
> Yet they stretched not their hands against the Jews. This is the law,
> For I lifted my voice and called out.

One must ask, however, why it was that Heller felt impelled to write a second poem, about the Defenestration. The Prague Jews had not been defenestrated. It is exceptional, even extraordinary, for Jewish liturgical poetry to focus on events of the non-Jewish world, even significant ones. The event that was being commemorated by the community was not the 1618 rebellion, but the deliverance of the Jewish quarter in 1620.

Heller had two motives for retelling the earlier events. First, he wished to take the opportunity to praise God for delivering the Jews from a threat surely more dangerous than that of looting in 1620. At the time that Frederick was crowned there was a Protestant proposal to expel the Jews from Prague, but payment of a hefty ransom secured their safety.[19]

[18] Eidelberg, *R. Juspa*, Eng. sect., pp. 71–2.

[19] Cf. Hailperin, 'Jewish Refugees', 199; Spiegel, 'Die Prager Juden', 115.

Measure out [gold] and bring it here, a great and mighty tribute!
My opponents wished to send me from exile to exile
That was their plot and their plan; nor did they feel any pain for me
For he comes to taunt Israel (1 Samuel 17: 25).

Second, Heller's poem on the Defenestration also allowed him to place the blame for the war where he thought it belonged, namely in the Protestant camp. Although it had been the invading Habsburg troops whom the Prague Jews mostly feared in 1620, he wished to present Frederick and the Czechs in a negative light. Heller rejoiced in the re-establishment of Catholic and imperial rule in Bohemia, viewing Frederick and the Bohemians as rebels against their rightful king. He was a Habsburg loyalist, and the events of 1618–20 had only strengthened his political faith.[20]

When men rose against us, and many were the servants who rebelled,
The earth shook for a slave who would be king, and the riots began.

. . . .

They strayed from the way of understanding, a congregation of shadows, like the blind man who gropes at midday.
Out of the window they threw those who sit in judgement, pronouncing justice,
The great men of the king; and shot arrows after them.

. . . .

Therefore my heart trembled, for great was the confusion
And the cry of the city and its neighbours rose to the heavens.
They stiffened their necks against their king, and he will leave not a soul to live,
For it was from the LORD, to harden their hearts for the war.

ON PROVIDENCE AND MIRACLES

Are wars, victories, defeats, sieges and rebellions, rescues, plagues, and earthquakes all brought about by God? Among the theological questions that were debated in Europe in the sixteenth and seventeenth centuries, few aroused more controversy than this. Theories of divine providence were to the seventeenth century, one might say, what theories of economics were to the twentieth.[21]

[20] I have benefited from reading Adam Mintz's unpublished seminar paper, 'The Jews of Prague and the Battle of White Mountain'. The loyalty of the entire Prague Jewish community to the Habsburgs was demonstrated in public by the elaborate Jewish procession held for Ferdinand during his visit to Prague in 1623. See Putík, 'Origin of the Symbols', 22; Popper, 'Les Juifs de Prague', 135. Note also the harsh words concerning the Protestant general Mansfeld in Katzenellenbogen, *Moledot yitsḥak*, introd.

[21] See e.g. Kocher, *Science and Religion*, 93–118 ('Providence, Natural Causation, and Miracle'); Walsham, *Providence*; Kiefer, *Fortune and Elizabethan Tragedy*. On Providence and the plague, see A. L. Martin, *Plague?*, 89–98, 104–11.

Three theories of causation deserve our special attention. The first credits divine providence with all or nearly all that occurs. The Calvinists, for instance, took a particularly strong view of providence. A second view credits human agency and free will; a third attributes events to fortune, chance or accident, the decrees of the stars and planets. Shakespeare's characters regularly contrast the second view and the third.

Each of these three theories may be applied to all types of events, but each applies particularly to miracles (it should be stressed that public 'miracles' of various types were still relatively common events in seventeenth-century Europe: in Florence in 1630 the relics of St Anthony were seen to cure four hundred people of the plague[22]). Miracles may be seen as free acts of an inscrutable God, or as events brought about by the agency of the pious and of those men and women who can work wonders, but the sceptic who believes in chance would see them only as random strokes of good fortune.

The questions of providence—of astrology and nature, miracles, and free will—were debated by Jews as well as by Christians.[23] The Maharal, for instance, took a position that was more than a little troubling. Commenting on the biblical story in which the sun and moon stopped at Joshua's bidding, he argued that the miracle both occurred and did not occur. For the Canaanites, there was no miracle: the sun had never stopped, and they were defeated in the natural way of warfare. For the Israelites, the sun had indeed stood still. The difference, one might be inclined to say, is one of the perception or interpretation of events, but the Maharal denied this: he denied, that is, that apart from the natural defeat perceived by the Canaanites, or the miraculous victory perceived by the Israelites, there was any 'true event' which the two groups could be said to interpret.[24] For Heller as well, the belief in miracles was one of the foundations of religion. In his interpretation, Pharaoh's folly in the Exodus story was his refusal to recognize that the ten plagues were miraculous events.[25]

[22] De Viguerie, 'Le Miracle dans la France'; Cipolla, *Faith, Reason, and the Plague*, 9.

[23] Note Dan, '"No Evil"', and Rosenberg, 'Exile and Redemption', 399–406. Spinoza's contribution to the debates on free will, miracles, and Nature is well known. On discussions of divine providence among Ashkenazi Jews, see H. H. Ben-Sasson, *Theory and Practice*, 78 ff.

[24] See the Maharal's introduction to *Gevurot hashem*, interpreted variously in T. Ross, 'Miracles'; Shatz, 'Maharal'; Gross, 'Importance de la notion'; L. A. Segal, *Historical Consciousness*, 19–20, 142. On concepts of the miraculous in 16th-c. Jewish philosophy generally, see the discussion in Tirosh-Rothschild, *Between Worlds*, 178–83.

[25] *Ma'amar yom tov* on Ibn Ezra on Exod. 10: 20 (p. 132). Cf. the comment on Exod. 12: 43 and 19: 9. Compare Ibn Ezra's own comment on Exod. 20: 2, and see *Tos YT*, *Ber.* 1: 5, *Avot* 4: 22, and *Avot* 5: 6. See also the longer discussion in my thesis, pp. 425–41.

Yet Heller, in contrast to the Maharal, did not regard all miracles as supernatural. He accepted Nahmanides' notion of a 'hidden miracle'.[26] Moreover, in a discussion of prayer and blessings from the 1620s, he treated miracles which involve an interruption of nature as a subset of the wider class of miracles. An example of a miracle within nature is 'one who was attacked by robbers at night, and was in danger but was saved'.[27] Concepts such as a 'hidden miracle' or a 'decree of heaven' (a *gezerah*, in Hebrew and Yiddish) straddle the boundary of the natural and the supernatural.

In other passages, however, Heller set the natural and the miraculous more clearly apart. For him, as for so many of the people of his time, educated and non-educated, the ordinary type of natural causation was astrological. (David Gans, Heller's older contemporary in Prague, was an exception; he rejected astrology, as did the Maharal.[28]) But Heller accepted that astrological determination is tempered by the miraculous.[29] Divine Providence may overturn the decrees of the stars. In medieval Jewish thought, this was called *shidud ma'arekhet*, 'the shaking of the spheres'. The miraculous is not wholly determined by human action, but it is affected by the power of good deeds and human merit and prayer. Even merit, Heller argued, may be insufficient unless it is activated and reinforced by prayer.

Heller discussed this concept in detail in *Tosafot yom tov*, commenting on the passage:

> Rabbi Meir says, A man should always teach his son a clean and easy craft, and let him pray to Him to whom riches and possessions belong, for there is no craft in which there is not both poverty and riches; for poverty does not come from a man's craft, nor do riches come from a man's craft, but all is according to his merits. (*Kidushin* 4: 14)

Heller's interpretation of this passage recast Rabbi Meir's view. Whereas Rabbi Meir had contrasted providential reward with choice of profession (that is, free will), Heller contrasted providence and prayer, taken together, with astrological determination:

[26] On Nahmanides' doctrine, see Berger, 'Miracles and Natural Order'; Nehorai, 'Theories of Miracles'. Meir Schiff (1607–44) identifies 'hidden miracles' with the 'shaking of the spheres' in his comment at the end of his notes published in the Vilna Talmud after tractate *Ḥulin*, p. 27 col. b, end.

[27] *MYT (DH)*, *Ber.*, p. 71 n. 1. The comment is based on David Abudraham. Cf. also *MYT (DH)*, *Ber.*, p. 72 nn. 9 and 15, based on M. Jaffe, *Levush*, 'Oraḥ ḥayim', 219; *MalYT* 219, no. 5. Contrast the view of Abraham Gombiner, *Magen avraham*, 'Oraḥ ḥayim', 218: 9.

[28] See Gans, *Neḥmad vena'im*, 82*a*; Neher, *Jewish Thought and the Scientific Revolution*, 63–5; cf. H. H. Ben-Sasson, *Theory and Practice*, 81–3. Heller's comments in his notes on Ibn Ezra's Torah commentary (published recently under the title of *Ma'amar yom tov*) suggest that he knew something of the 'science' of astrology. Note Tycho's defence of astrology: Howell, 'Role of Biblical Interpretation', 520–1.

[29] Cf. commentary on *Beḥinat olam*, 8: 2: 11 (p. 75); *Tos YT*, *RH* 1: 2.

I say that . . . prayer is efficacious, and that one needs to pray, because merit does not always change the [decree of the] stars. . . . What would be the purpose of prayer if [everything] depends on the stars, and the world goes according to its custom? . . . But rather, even if the stars do not decree a man's success, and even if he pursues a craft which will not make him rich, 'he should pray to Him to whom riches [belong]'. For there is great salvation before Him, may He be blessed.[30]

JACOB BASSEVI

The mid-seventeenth-century conflict brought a loosening of the European political and social order, both of the protections that it offered and of the restrictions that it imposed. Indeed, the political crises of the mid-seventeenth century in Germany and elsewhere created opportunities for certain relatively small groups and small states to increase their influence. Transylvania, in the first years of the war, and Sweden, at its end, suddenly and quite anomalously made themselves masters of the situation. Likewise, the major organized Jewish communities and their wealthy elite to which Heller belonged, flourished both economically and politically during the war.

The Jews of the seventeenth century, no less than other people, saw opportunities and took them. War drove up the demand for money, and hence could be profitable for those who had cash and extensive financial networks. The confusion and lawlessness of wartime, in the seventeenth century as today, provided many opportunities for windfall profits and quick riches.[31]

An outstanding example of economic opportunism among the Jews of that generation was Jacob Bassevi. At the beginning of the war, Bassevi was already the richest Jew in Prague. In 1622 he went into a partnership with General Albrecht von Wallenstein, who soon became the most important general of the imperial armies.[32] Bassevi and Wallenstein, together with two imperial courtiers and two other bankers, were given the right to mint money in Bohemia. The oceans of coins they minted contributed much to the financial panic and violent inflation that spread throughout Bohemia and Germany and caused much suffering; but the various partners, Bassevi among them, did very well.

An incidental goal of the debased coinage was to provide cash for the buyers of property that was confiscated from the Bohemian leaders after their defeat in 1620.

[30] *Tos YT*, *Kid.* 4: 14. Cf. *MYT* (*PH*), *San.*, p. 234 n. 90, where Heller repeats the view expressed here on *shidud ma'arekhet*, and refers to his discussion here. Cf. also *MYT* (*PH*), *San.*, p. 238 n. 6.

[31] Israel, 'Central European Jewry'; cf. id., *European Jewry in the Age of Mercantilism*, 86–106. Note also Baron, *Social and Religious History of the Jews*, xiv. 224–94. On the Prague Jews, see Popper, 'Les Juifs de Prague'; Spiegel, 'Die Prager Juden'.

[32] The famous general's name Wallenstein, spelled with a 'n', is not to be confused with Heller's home town, Wallerstein, spelled with an 'r'.

Here again Bassevi was active, and the Jewish quarter of Prague was expanded in 1622–3 at the expense of people less fortunate or less politically astute than its leading Jew.[33]

In a variety of cases the Jews were able to turn economic gains such as these into political ones as well and to negotiate improvements in their legal status. Once again, Bassevi provides an example. In a turn of events unheard of in the seventeenth century or before, he was elevated to the nobility and given a coat of arms.[34]

During these years, the Jewish community of Vienna was able to procure the grant of official recognition that had long been denied it. In 1624 the Jews were given permission to build a special Jewish quarter close to the river, 'with beautiful, airy, open streets', Heller later wrote, in the neighbourhood that was later called Leopoldstadt. They also received permission to build a synagogue.[35]

Heller himself benefited as well. After twenty-seven years in Prague as a lower court judge, and after having been passed over in 1623 for the position of chief rabbi, he moved to Nikolsburg in autumn 1624 to be the rabbi there. The Nikolsburg community was recovering from the recent troubles, and Heller stayed for just half a year. He rose quickly in the informal hierarchy of rabbinical posts; in spring 1625, he was appointed as chief rabbi of the newly recognized community in Vienna.

THE PLAGUE OF 1625

Questions of catastrophe and providence arose again for Heller in the autumn of that year. There was a plague in Vienna, part of a European pandemic. Like John Donne in London, Heller preached on the plague.[36]

It is not clear how often Heller gave sermons. He was not a preacher by profession, as Donne was, or as Ephraim of Luntshits had been before coming to Prague. The plague sermon may have been one of his first; he was pleased with it, and published it the following year.

[33] Parker (ed.), *Thirty Years War*, 89; Spiegel, 'Die Prager Juden', 108–11.

[34] On Bassevi, see Kestenberg-Gladstein, 'Bassevi', and the references there; also Popper, 'Les Juifs de Prague', 132–8, Spiegel, 'Die Prager Juden', 138–43, C. Mann, *Wallenstein*, 175–81.

[35] On the Vienna Jews, see e.g. Kaufmann, *Der letzte Vertreibung*; I. Schwarz, *Das Wiener Ghetto*; Grunwald, *Geschichte der Juden*. Heller's reference to 'airy, open streets' appears in the Yiddish version of *Megilat eivah*, in Erik, 'Memoirs', 193–4.

[36] Heller's *derush* on 'Ḥayei sarah' (Gen. 23: 1–25: 18) (1st edn. Prague, 1626), newly entitled *Ma'amar hahoda'ah vehatakanah*, was repr. in a new edn. of *Oreḥot ḥayim*, attributed to the Rosh, ed. Meir Malin (Jerusalem, 1987). For Donne's sermon, see id., *Sermons*, vi. 349–64 (sermon 18, 15 Jan. 1626). Donne chose as his text, 'There was not a house in which there was not one dead' (Exod. 12: 30). On the 1625 plague in Prague, see Gindely, *Gegenreformation*, 270.

Plague evoked a range of responses from early modern Jews.[37] Mention has already been made of the penitential rules that were imposed in Prague in 1611, when the 'whores' were driven out of the community. In 1623 the heartbroken Yehiel Mikhel, the scribe in Cracow, wrote a poem after an outbreak of plague in that city that took, he wrote, 500 Jewish lives. It is our duty, he began, to bless God for evil tidings as well as good; we must praise God with a joyful heart even in our suffering. But he went on to castigate the Jewish community of Cracow and to describe the sins for which, he felt, the plague was a punishment, including the neglect of Torah, swearing, greed, sharp business practices, forgery, pride, adultery, drunkenness, sabbath-breaking, and—singling out wealthy women in particular—gossip, vanity, and the wearing of fine clothes. Money became scarce, he wrote, and food became scarce too, and 'death came in the windows and through the gates'. Teachers died with their students, brides with their grooms, young boys, pious and modest women. And his wife died: 'My wife, my perfect one, my dove . . . my gazelle of love, a woman of valour.'[38]

A few years later, in 1630, a Jewish doctor named David of Landshut was moved by the recent outbreaks to translate a medieval Arabic treatise on the plague into Hebrew, from a Latin translation that he found in Prague. The plagues that he had seen, David added in a marginal note, were much worse than the plagues that Galen and Avicenna discuss. The plague is extremely contagious, he wrote. If we only knew its cause, then we would know how to mitigate its effects. But alas, we do not. He was sceptical of astrological explanations.[39]

Heller, preparing his plague sermon, took as his text part of the synagogue reading for the sabbath on which he delivered the sermon, the first sabbath after the plague quarantine had been lifted by the municipal health officials. He preached on the story of the servant of Abraham (in rabbinic tradition always called Eliezer), who journeys to Aram to find a wife for Isaac (Gen. 24: 10). Using the formal style adopted by medieval preachers, he set forth the textual problems that he would solve in the sermon, some of them grammatical and others involving problems in midrashic commentary, and then began his exposition.

It is a mitzvah, he declares, to give thanks to God for the miracles that he performs for us. That is, it is a religious obligation; it is not merely a pious action undertaken freely. Eliezer serves as a biblical example: he offers a prayer of thanks-

37 See S.-A. Goldberg, *Crossing the Jabbok*, 162–73. Note also Siev, *Rabbi Moses Isserles*, 112–16. Cf. Bondy and Dworsky (eds.), *Zur Geschichte der Juden*, 805–7, no. 1024, from Prague, 1607. Compare these to the range of responses to plague and disaster noted in Cipolla, *Faith, Reason, and the Plague*; id., *Fighting the Plague*; Amelang, *A Journal of the Plague Year*, introd.; Goodman, 'Explorations'.

38 Yehiel Mikhel the Scribe in Cracow, poem. The 1638 regulations on Jewish education in Cracow were introduced as a response to the plague: Cygielman, *The Jews of Poland and Lithuania*, 553.

39 Klein-Franke, 'An Unknown Jewish Translation'.

giving (Gen. 24: 27) after he succeeds in his search for a bride. But immediately Heller reverses his argument: on the other hand, *no* thanksgiving is to be offered for a miracle that is destructive of human life. To prove this point from the story of Eliezer, Heller gives a novel interpretation of the rabbinic legend that God 'shortened the way' for Eliezer, making it possible for him to reach Aram from the Land of Israel in a single day. That miracle, Heller suggests boldly, was an earthquake, and it was a catastrophe for the people of the area.[40] Therefore Eliezer offered a prayer when he had succeeded in finding a wife for Isaac, but offered no prayer of thanks for the miracle of the 'shortening of the way'.

Heller then turns from the biblical text to his own experience. 'A miracle happened to me', he says: he was saved miraculously from the plague. It is likely that here again, Heller understood this as a miracle within the bounds of nature. However far-fetched as biblical interpretation, Heller's telling of the story of Eliezer matched closely his own experience and that of the Jews of Vienna. He knew that the plague had not spared the people of Vienna. From their point of view, no miracle had taken place at all, but a great calamity, and for that reason to offer public thanks would be a mockery.

So far as one can judge from the written text, Heller was not a great preacher: a comparison of his sermon with that of Donne, who was, makes that clear. But in this particular sermon, Heller, more successfully than Donne, focused on a genuine and profound religious problem. Private deliverance, by its very nature, often comes at a time of public suffering. Should one's religious behaviour reflect one's personal religious experience alone, or should the experience of the 'people of the land' be taken into account? Leaving aside the question of why the plague had occurred, Heller concentrated entirely on the question of the appropriate religious response.

The dilemma that he found in the biblical text and in his own life also applied to the political and social position of the Jews of Prague and Vienna in the early 1620s. They were fortunate enough to find some advantage in a situation of dire suffering. Should they now thank God or should they join in the general lament?

Heller struggled to find a resolution for this conflict of obligations. Referring to the talmudic example of 'the divine teacher, Simeon bar Yohai', he declared that one who has benefited from a miracle, even a miracle that caused suffering for others, should make a *tikun* or a *takanah*, a new rule, a new custom, a change in his life. He should 'mend something', Heller wrote, borrowing a phrase from the laws of sabbath prohibitions. Although he refrained from placing blame for the plague on particular sinners or sins, he did not refrain from making it an opportunity for moral improvement in the community.

[40] The discussion may reflect Heller's reading of Azariah dei Rossi's *Me'or einayim*, which contains a long description of the Ferrara earthquake of 1570.

Heller therefore concluded the sermon by instituting a new rule for the new community of Vienna, an addition to the daily morning service. Each morning, before the beginning of regular prayer, a section would be read from the medieval ethical work *Oreḥot ḥayim* (Paths of Life). The new custom would serve to acknowledge the miracle that he and they had experienced, the miracle (within nature) of deliverance from the plague.

SEVEN

The Chief Rabbi

'WHO ARE THE KINGS? THE RABBIS.'

HELLER was chief rabbi of Vienna for exactly two years. In spring 1627 he was elected chief rabbi of Prague. Jacob Bassevi was president (*primas*) of the *kehilah* that year; it is reasonable to suppose that he was instrumental in securing Heller's election.[1]

The Prague rabbinate was the sum of Heller's desire. Although the Vienna community offered to raise his salary, he accepted the call of his earlier home. He left Vienna after Passover, escorted by a great crowd, he tells us, with a detachment of soldiers for their protection. The leaders of the Prague community came to greet him a day's journey from the city.[2] Just as the Jewish community of Prague had celebrated the visit of Emperor Ferdinand in 1623 with a procession and music, so did the communities of Vienna and Prague do honour to their rabbi as he left the former and moved to the latter.[3]

Heller's official duties and privileges as chief rabbi were set out in a contract. We do not have a copy of this, but it was probably very similar to a model rabbinical contract written in Prague about a decade later.[4] His position combined two

[1] Spiegel, 'Die Prager Juden', 184.

[2] *Megilat eivah*, 29. On public honour for rabbis, see Zimmer, *Embers of the Sages*, 255. Little is known of Heller's immediate predecessor in Prague, Moses b. Isaiah Menahem (Moses Mendels). Cf. Klemperer, 'The Rabbis of Prague', 51; Avron (ed.), *Pinkas hakesherim*, 72 n. 223, 120 n. 235; Zimmer, 'R. Eliakim Gottschalk', 142 n. 16. Moses is the author of a liturgical poem, 'Moshel ba'elyonim', to be recited in time of plague. Hayim b. Isaac Hakohen, Maharal's grandson, may also have served as rabbi for some time about 1626–7: see Hailperin, 'Controversy', 118. The diarist Asher b. Eliezer Halevi (*Zikhronot*, 10), claims that Moses Mendels served jointly with Hayim b. Isaac Hakohen, and that the latter moved to the rabbinate in Frankfurt in autumn 1627.

[3] See Putík, 'Origin of the Symbols', 22; Popper, 'Les Juifs de Prague', 135.

[4] J. Katz, 'On the History of the Rabbinate', 290–4, discussed in Reiner, 'Changes', 27–37. Note also (besides Horowitz's contract) the 1644 Frankfurt contract of Mendel Bass, published in *Kerem shelomoh*, 5 (1982); the Friedberg contract in Kober (ed.), 'Documents', 45–6; the contracts in Bloch, 'Vielbegehrter Rabbiner', 127–30; the Cracow rules in Cygielman, *Jews of Poland and Lithuania*, 490 (from Wettstein, *Ancient Matters*, 18–19); and Juspa Shamash's description of the rabbi's duties in Eidelberg, *R. Juspa*, Eng. sect., pp. 18–19. For general information on rabbinic contracts and duties

roles:[5] he was *resh metivta*—the head of the yeshiva, the talmudic academy—and also *av beit din*, the president of the rabbinical court.[6] He was also required to preach, and to supervise the *gaba'im* (deacons) of the synagogues, the butchers, the vintners, the beadles, and the communal scribe—that is, nearly all of the communal personnel, except the doctors, the midwives, and the watchmen.[7]

Rabbis in the early modern period did not have extensive pastoral responsibilities. The Prague model contract permitted but did not require the rabbi to perform weddings and divorces or the naming ceremony for girls.[8] It did not specify the rabbi's salary, but it did give him a fee of half a gulden (about a day's wages) for each court case. There were also allowances for a residence, and for wood.[9] Although it is not mentioned in the contract, rabbis were usually exempted from communal taxes.[10]

Though he was president of the rabbinical court, the rabbi's authority to punish offenders was limited by the contract. The consent of the lay leadership was required for any major fine, and while the rabbi might on his own authority impose a *ḥerem* (excommunication) for 'the desecration of God's name', he was not permitted to do so for 'matters that engender shame to the family'.

in this period, see Schwarzfuchs, *Concise History*, 50–64; Hundert, *Jews in a Polish Private Town*, 92–5; H. H. Ben-Sasson, *Theory and Practice*, 178–94; Bonfil, *Rabbis*, 101–2, 331–5.

[5] As a social group, rabbis may be compared to jurists and lawyers, to pastors and priests, or to theology professors and school administrators. On the first group, see Rowan, *Law and Jurisprudence*; on the second, Vogler, *Le Clergé protestant*, and Schorn-Schütte, 'The Christian Clergy'.

[6] The Ashkenazi rabbinate had gradually become professionalized and regularized from the mid-15th c. onwards. On the new 16th-c. rabbinate, see Yuval, *Sages*, 11–20, 398–404; Zimmer, *Embers of the Sages*, 14–19; Reiner, 'Changes', 35–6. Reiner lists five characteristics of the new communal rabbi: he is appointed by the community; his salary is paid by the community; his contract is for a fixed period; he is one of a series of rabbis hired under the same terms; and his rights as an educator and a judge are exclusive.

[7] On the personnel of the Prague *kehilah* (1692), see Putík, 'Prague Jewish Community', 64; cf. the list of personnel in the 1638 budget of the Poznań Jewish community in Hailperin (ed.), *Jews in Poland*, ii. 247–9.

[8] On the rabbinic courts in Prague, see Heřman, 'La Communauté juive de Prague', 56–7; Jakobovits, 'Die Erlebnisse', 257–61; Adler, 'Das älteste Judicial Protokoll'; Spiegel, 'Die Prager Juden', 152.

[9] The 1644 Frankfurt rabbinical contract places the salary of the rabbi at 100 reichsthalers per year, plus fees; this would have been a respectable salary. The 1638 Poznań budget allocates 230 gulden—a larger sum, perhaps half as much again as the Frankfurt salary—a year for the rabbi. It is not unlikely that Heller supplemented his income by lending money. There is a record of a loan that Heller made in Cracow (in the form of a sale and buy-back, to avoid the prohibition on interest): see Wettstein, 'Conversations', 172–3. However, in *Tos YT*, *Avot* 2: 5, Heller quotes Samuel di Uceda to the effect that a businessman may study Torah, but will not teach. Cf. *Megilat eivah*, 35. Hailperin MS, p. 12, has an intelligent discussion of Heller's finances. On rabbinical salaries in Italy, see Bonfil, *Rabbis*, 157–68, 187–92.

[10] Assaf, *In the Tents of Jacob*, 50; cf. Schochet, *Bach*, 169.

The Prague contract also listed the supervision of lay leaders of the Jewish community as one of the duties of the rabbi. He was given the extremely delicate tasks of excluding from the communal leadership anyone of bad character and anyone who was not financially independent, and also of preventing any member of the lay leadership from acting in his own personal interest, particularly in the assessment of taxes.

To shield himself from charges of favouritism, Heller left the Pinkas Synagogue during his time as chief rabbi. This too is specified in the model contract: the rabbi is required to pray on sabbaths and New Moons in one of the two main synagogues (the Altneushul or the Meisel Synagogue).[11] The model contract also promises that the communal leadership will give full support to the rabbi if he is threatened in any way by the non-Jewish authorities 'or in any matter that pertains to his honour'.[12]

Heller's presumed contract in Prague may be contrasted with Isaiah Horowitz's contract when he became rabbi in Frankfurt am Main in 1606.[13] Frankfurt gave less authority to the rabbi and more to the lay leadership, the *ḥavruta*, as it was called in Frankfurt. For example, Horowitz renounced the right to issue a *ḥerem* without their express consent. He was also prohibited from writing official letters to other communities or to non-Jewish authorities without their consent. Nor was the rabbi of Frankfurt expected to oversee the lay leadership; rather, he was to distance himself from communal politics. In Prague, by contrast, for all that the rabbi's powers were limited in significant ways, he was expected to be deeply involved.[14]

RABBINICAL ACTIVISM AND EDUCATIONAL REFORM

In Vienna and Prague, Heller continued but reshaped the rabbinical activism of the Maharal and Ephraim of Luntshits. He did not follow in their path of social criticism, but school reform and moralistic preaching remained central to his view of the rabbinate.

We have no account of Heller's yeshiva in his days as chief rabbi, but we do have a brief account of the yeshiva that he ran in his house in Prague before he became chief rabbi. Students, including some from other cities, studied and ate at his table.

[11] See *MYT* (*DH*), *Tsitsit* (published in the Vilna Talmud after tractate *Menaḥot*), p. 251 n. 25.

[12] This provision—nearly the last one (no. 36)—of the 1640 contract may have been added as a response to Heller's unfortunate experiences in 1629.

[13] In Horovitz, *Rabbis of Frankfurt*, 322–4; repr. in Newman, *Isaiah Horowitz*, 200–1, and trans. on pp. 38–41.

[14] Cf. Hayim b. Isaac Hakohen's observation in his 1627 letter to the Frankfurt community, quoted in Hailperin, 'Controversy', 118.

Each day, he wrote, they would study a passage of Talmud with the commentaries of Rashi and Tosafot and *ḥilukim* (that is, *pilpul*), and there would be a class in the Rosh's commentary on the same passage. Heller did not continue the Maharal's battles against *pilpul* as a pedagogic technique.[15]

He did, however, continue other aspects of the Maharal's efforts to reform the Ashkenazi curriculum:[16] like the Maharal, he believed that students should work their way gradually from the lower to the higher; that what is most valuable must be approached through studies of less intrinsic value.[17] Such gradualism was controversial during this period, both in theory and in practice; Joseph ben Isaac, for instance, had claimed that the study of Torah does away with the need for an educational ladder.[18]

In particular, Heller continued the Maharal's support for the study of Hebrew grammar, that least attractive and most necessary of Jewish subjects. From the introduction to *Leket shoshanim*, Heller's commentary on Hebrew grammar, we know that he actually taught grammar himself, both to his students and to his own children.[19] In 1627 he was instrumental in having a recent Hebrew grammar textbook reprinted in Prague. His discouragement, however, had become pronounced: 'The grammar of our holy tongue is trampled and abandoned, even though since it

[15] MS Oxford-Bodleian Heb. 2209 (the Yiddish *Megilat eivah*), fo. 1*a*: 'Un gezogt ale tag Pei[rush] [= Rashi], To[safot] un ḥilukim oykh ayn shi'ur Rabeinu Asher iber disem milim.' (Erik mistranscribes the text.) Cf. ŽMP MS 157, p. 3, 'Piresh, Tosfes, unt ḥilukim, un vider shi'urim mit Rabeinu Asher.' The Hebrew text (*Megilat eivah*, 28) has fewer details.

[16] For Heller's views on education, see his *derush* on 'Ḥayei sarah', 12; cf. also *Tos YT*, *Men.* 4: 4; *Tos YT*, *Avot* 1: 1, 1: 4, 1: 6. Cf. M. Roth, 'Notes', 104; Hakohen, 'His Books', 159–60, and the discussion in my dissertation, pp. 383–403.

[17] *Tos YT*, *Avot* 2: 2, 3: 9, 3: 17, 3: 18. 'Nature' is the word used. Heller also sometimes uses 'nature' to mean a person's disposition of passions. The word has a negative sense, and the implication is that education changes or overcomes nature. *Ma'amar yom tov* on Exod. 10: 2: '[God speaks] like a man who boasts of his actions, having changed his nature, being from one of the extreme types of character, such as anger or desire, sadness or happiness.' Also *Tos YT*, *Avot* 4: 1, quoted from *Midrash shemuel* by Samuel di Uceda: 'Human nature tends more towards the evil impulse [than towards the good impulse].' Cf. *Tos YT* on *Avot* 4: 2, from the Maharal: 'All sins . . . are pleasurable to man', and in the *derush* on 'Ḥayei sarah', 8: 'God knew the nature of men, that vows come easily to them, and therefore was not so severe as to punish it with . . . the death penalty.'

[18] *Ketonet pasim*, ch. 6, p. 9*b*.

[19] He writes, 'When one does not understand the grammar of a word properly, various mistakes may occur. This will be understood by those who know . . . the wisdom of this craft. And one who does not know it will not understand even if I explain it in various different ways; therefore I will be brief' (*Leket shoshanim*, fo. 122*a*). The tone of discouragement in this passage should not be missed. Heller's interest in and knowledge of grammar can also be seen from his frequent grammatical comments in *Tosafot yom tov* and in his supercommentary on Ibn Ezra. Cf. M. Roth, 'Notes', 98–104.

precedes every [other subject] in time, it is important. Nevertheless it is like a bride who is insulted in her father-in-law's house.'[20]

Heller availed himself (as the Maharal had also done) of the pedagogic opportunities afforded by the printing press. In addition to the grammar textbook *Siaḥ yitsḥak* (Conversation of Isaac), he himself published a textbook of Jewish law, as will be discussed below. He also published a Yiddish broadside on the laws of kashering meat, intended mainly for housewives. Along with his Vienna sermon of 1625, moreover, he published the Hebrew text of the medieval ethical treatise *Oreḥot ḥayim*, together with his own Yiddish translation. As Heller wrote, *Oreḥot ḥayim* 'is written in a very concise style, and there are many difficult words and sayings in it'. Therefore, he announced, 'for women who do not know the Holy Tongue . . . and especially for the righteous women . . . and also for youths and for the ignorant', his Yiddish translation of *Oreḥot ḥayim* 'will be very, very beneficial'.

'DELIGHTS OF THE KING'

In 1619—eight years before his appointment as chief rabbi of Prague—Heller had begun another project no less important to his career as a talmudist, at the significant age of 40. The Talmud suggests that at 40 years, one who is capable of rendering decisions in Jewish law must begin to do so. Heller comments, ' "Forty years": Rabenu Nissim explains that a man does not have sufficient composure of thought until that age.'[21] Heller had in fact been making judicial decisions since he was 19, but having now reached the age of 'composure of thought', he published his first book in the field of *halakhah lema'aseh*, the law in practice. This new work, which he called *Pilpula ḥarifta*, ('Sharp *Pilpul*'—literally 'hot pepper') was a commentary on the *Digest* of talmudic law by the Rosh.

Pilpula ḥarifta covers 'Nezikin', one of the six orders of the Talmud. When he was a young *dayan* of the rabbinical court of Prague, it is likely that many of Heller's cases were small claims of different sorts: questions of loans, inheritances, contracts, and so on. After twenty years on the bench, he naturally chose the tractate of 'Nezikin', where such matters of civil law are discussed.

The order in which Heller wrote his books was not haphazard. His movement from Bible (the 1602 *Tsurat habayit*) to Mishnah to Talmud reflected, as he himself remarked, the classic rabbinic progression. His first writings, from his commentary

20 Approbation for Isaac b. Samuel Halevi of Poznań, *Siaḥ yitsḥak* (Prague, 1627).

21 *MYT* (*PH*), *AZ*, p. 158 n. 400. Later in the same comment, Heller noted that medieval halakhists disagree on whether a man under 40 might be permitted to render decisions in special circumstances. Clearly this was a delicate issue for Heller, who had been made a *dayan* at such a young age. On the nature of the caseload of the Prague rabbinical court later in the 17th c., see Adler (ed.), 'Das älteste Judicial-Protokoll', 220.

on Bedersi's philosophical poem to his later kabbalistic work *Tuv ta'am*, mirror the ladder of ascension ('Jacob's ladder', as Mordechai Jaffe called it) that leads from philosophy to kabbalah. All of these books taken together, moreover, trace a third pattern, perhaps the most important of all: a gradual movement from theoretical questions to practical ones. Heller's ladder of ascension brought him back from metaphysics to the thick of rabbinical politics.

In 1628 Heller added a second volume, with a new title, *Ma'adanei melekh* (Delights of the King). This second volume covers the laws of prayer (tractate *Berakhot*), kosher and unkosher food (*Ḥulin*), menstrual uncleanness (*Nidah*), and some smaller sections on topics such as the laws of Torah scrolls and tefillin. Unlike the 1619 volume, *Ma'adanei melekh* was written as a double commentary. One section dealt with the textual, philological, and interpretative issues, while the second section (entitled *Divrei ḥamudot*) dealt more narrowly with the issues of law and practice.[22]

Tosafot yom tov was Heller's most popular and best-received book, yet it was intended only as a prelude to what was to have been his truly significant work, *Ma'adanei melekh*. Just as the Talmud was far more significant than the Mishnah in the life of medieval or early modern Jews, so *Ma'adanei melekh* was intended to be a more significant work than *Tosafot yom tov* could ever have been.[23]

AGAINST THE *SHULḤAN ARUKH*

Heller's views on rabbinical authority, as well as his goal in *Ma'adanei melekh*, are set out in his introduction, where he explains his decision to write a Talmud supercommentary. He also explains his opposition to the *Shulḥan arukh*: *Ma'adanei melekh* was written as a competitor to that famous code of law.[24] In Chapter 4 it

[22] The title of this work is problematic. First, the plan of the work, and the names of its sections, were changed between the 1619 and 1628 volumes. Second, the name of the 1628 work, *Ma'adanei melekh*, is sometimes (e.g. in the Vilna edn. of the Talmud) rejected in favour of the title *Ma'adanei yom tov* (for that reason, I have used the abbreviation *MYT* in the notes to the present work). The origin of this change seems to be the questions that were raised after Heller's imprisonment in 1629 as to the appropriateness of the original royal title. See *Megilat eivah*, 32. To compound the confusion, one of the two sections of *Ma'adanei melekh*, entitled *Divrei ḥamudot*, is often referred to as *Leḥem ḥamudot*, a phrase from Daniel 10: 3 (e.g. even in the Yiddish *Megilat eivah*: Erik, 'Memoirs', 201).

[23] In the following generation, *Ma'adanei melekh* is quoted extensively (under the abbreviation *lamed-ḥet*, for *Leḥem ḥamudot*) in two commentaries on *Shulḥan arukh*, 'Oraḥ ḥayim', *Magen avraham* by Abraham Gombiner and *Eliyah rabah* by Elijah Spira. On the halakhic tradition of Prague (Jaffe, Heller, Spira), see n. 34 below. For appreciations by 18th- and 19th-c. halakhists, see Maimon (ed.), *In Honour of Yom-Tov*, 107–8.

[24] On the conflict over the *Shulḥan arukh*, see Tchernowitz, *Rabbinic Authorities* (Heller is discussed on pp. 132–7); Twersky, 'The *Shulḥan 'Aruk*', 148; Toledano, 'When and Where', 184–9; the collection of sources in Siev, *Rabbi Moses Isserles*, 286–96; and my article, 'Reception'.

was noted that Heller had opposed the attempt to canonize Rashi's Talmud commentary and raise it to a position of unquestioned authority. So now did he oppose the system of authoritative legal interpretation constructed by the greatest halakhist of the early modern period, Joseph Caro.

The Talmud is a text riddled with difficulties; it is brimful of apparent contradictions, and its authors seem all too frequently to wish to complicate legal issues rather than resolve them. Which interpretation of the Talmud should be authoritative? Caro believed that halakhic decisions should be based on consideration of the works of three great medieval halakhists, three 'pillars' of Jewish law. Following any opinion on which two of the three agreed would offer a straight path through the multitude of conflicting medieval interpretations of Talmud. The three works Caro proposed were the Talmud *Digest* (*Hilkhot*) of Isaac Alfasi (d. 1103); Maimonides' code of the law, the *Mishneh torah*, also from the twelfth century; and another law code, the *Arba'ah turim* (Four Columns), compiled in the mid-fourteenth century by Jacob ben Asher (*c.*1280–*c.*1340), the son of the Rosh.[25]

Heller's riposte to Caro began by following an argument first proposed by Isserles. Jewish law, Isserles claimed, quoting various talmudic passages, must follow the most recent authorities (in Hebrew, the *aḥaronim*, or in Aramaic, the *batra'ei*).[26] The most authoritative of Caro's three pillars, Heller noted, would therefore be the last to be written, Jacob ben Asher's *Arba'ah turim*.

However, Heller gave Isserles' argument a novel twist. Since all rabbinic law is based on the words of the Talmud, every code of rabbinic law, Heller asserted, must be based on some form of Talmud exegesis. The decisions of the *Arba'ah turim* cannot be truly authoritative, for that law code is merely a compilation of the decisions reached exegetically by Rabbi Jacob's father, the Rosh, in his talmudic *Digest* (known as *Piskot harosh* or *Hilkhot harosh*).

According to Heller, Jewish law stems entirely from correct talmudic interpretation. The mainstream of the Jewish legal tradition therefore runs not through codes but through Talmud commentaries and supercommentaries.[27] In this he was once more following the Maharal, who in turn had developed the position taken by Solomon Luria, Isserles' cousin and chief opponent.[28] Indeed, the Talmud itself is

[25] On Caro's system of three pillars, see Toledano, 'When and Where', 184–5.

[26] See Isserles, introduction to the *Mapah* (his commentary on the *Shulḥan arukh*). On this principle see also Rafeld, 'Principle', 119–40.

[27] The distinction between codes and commentaries parallels the institutional distinction between the court and the school, between the *dayan* and the *rosh yeshivah*. Note also *MalYT* 10: 6, where Heller argues that Rashi is a 'commentator' and not a 'decisor' (*pareshan velo paskan*).

[28] See Luria, *Yam shel shelomoh*, introd. This approach to Jewish law has a long history before the 17th c.; the criticisms of the *Shulḥan arukh* are very similar to criticisms of Maimonides' *Mishneh torah*. See Twersky, *Rabad of Posquières*, 132–3.

authoritative, according to this view, because it is the correct interpretation of the Torah.[29]

Heller concluded that the Rosh's *Digest* should be the authoritative commentary on the Talmud. As noted above, *Ma'adanei melekh* is a commentary on this work. He thought that the *Digest* should be the standard textbook from which Jewish law is to be studied (as it was in his yeshiva) and also the standard judicial text on the basis of which the law should be decided. 'Run and seize it', he wrote, 'because it is the chosen one.'

Heller's decision was a conservative one. For a number of generations, Ashkenazi halakhic scholars had relied on the authority of about a half a dozen works, mostly of the Tosafist school. These included the *Sefer mitsvot gadol* (Great Book of Commandments), the *Sefer mitsvot katan* (Small Book of Commandments), the *Mordekhai*, and also the *Arba'ah turim* and the Rosh's *Digest*. Faced with competition from the new *Shulḥan arukh* all of these works were fast falling from favour, and indeed going out of print. Heller's efforts on behalf of the Rosh closely paralleled the campaign of Baruch ben David of Gniezno to promote the *Mordekhai* as an authoritative text, and the efforts of Joel Sirkes in the 1630s to promote the *Arba'ah turim*.[30]

The weakness of Heller's argument on behalf of the Rosh, however, is apparent. If the Rosh's commentary is authoritative because he lived centuries after Alfasi and Maimonides, then a Talmud commentary of even later authorities such as Solomon Luria's *Yam shel shelomoh* (Solomon's Sea), a section of which was published in Prague in 1616, should be more authoritative still.[31] Had Heller himself written a Talmud commentary, for that matter, that would have been the most recent authority of all. He had an explanation, however, of why he had not chosen that path: it was because he considered a Talmud commentary impractical and inconvenient for the purpose of determining practical rulings. It is no more possible to derive Jewish law in practice directly from the Talmud than from the Mishnah or from the Bible itself. Against Solomon Luria (and the Maharal), Heller argued that a two-layered process of normative interpretation and super-

[29] As Heller himself says in the Yiddish version of *Megilat eivah* (quoted above, Ch. 4 n. 52). Like his contemporary Sir Edward Coke in England, who also rejected codification in favour of commentary, Heller presented the authority of ancient law as absolute. On Coke, see Helgerson, *Forms of Nationhood*, 63–104.

[30] See the introduction to Baruch b. David of Gniezno, *Gedulat mordekhai*, 5–7, discussed in Reiner, 'Changes', 15 ff.

[31] Indeed, in the 1620s Isaiah Horowitz had suggested that Solomon Luria might indeed be the *batra'ah*, the most recent and hence the most authoritative talmudic authority (while arguing that, in spite of this, Isserles was the most authoritative). Isaiah's father Abraham Horowitz had claimed that Isserles was the *batra'ah*. See I. Horowitz, *Shenei luḥot haberit*, i. 54*a*–*b*; the concluding appendix in A. Horowitz, *Emek berakhah*, 116*b*.

interpretation, of commentary and commentary on commentary, was needed to fill the gap between the ancient text and its contemporary application.

This answer is not completely satisfying either; it is strange for Heller to claim that a fourteenth-century rabbi could be 'the most recent authority'. His argument is not altogether straightforward and is clearly designed to support a conclusion chosen partly on other grounds.

One factor that Heller did not deign to mention in his introduction was that no part of the Talmud itself could be printed in Prague at any time in the sixteenth or seventeenth centuries because of Church opposition and censorship. The Rosh's *Digest* therefore served as a substitute for the Talmud itself.[32] Heller frames this difference, however, as an advantage: the full Talmud text is pedagogically unsuited for teaching practical law.

Class bias may also have shaped Heller's argument. Opposition to the *Shulḥan arukh* may be seen partly as an effort to maintain the monopoly of halakhic decision-making in the hands of those scions of wealthy families, such as Heller, who had been trained from their youth in the complexities of talmudic interpretation. To maintain that monopoly, talmudists attacked those who would simply decide law from a law code.[33]

Furthermore, the *Shulḥan arukh* had been opposed by the rabbis of Germany and Prague for two generations on the grounds of local or regional autonomy. Prague, indeed, continued to be a bastion of opposition to the *Shulḥan arukh* until the end of the seventeenth century. Part of the attraction of the Rosh was surely his German birth and his support for German custom.[34]

Heller carefully steered clear, however, of appealing to any such class or local loyalties. In contrast to Isserles (and several of Isserles' students, such as Mordechai Jaffe), whose argument against Caro's authority had been based on the differences between Sefardi and Ashkenazi customs, Heller made no argument of purely ethnic or local application, and made no reference to *minhag* (custom). Like Solomon Luria, he argued that the same laws, interpreted correctly, apply to all Jews.

Once again, Heller may be contrasted to his cousin Isaiah Horowitz. Like Heller, Horowitz was for most of his life a follower of Solomon Luria and the Maharal in their opposition to Isserles. His project of a supercommentary on the

32 See Burnett, 'Regulation of Hebrew Printing'.

33 See Reiner, 'Changes', 45–7; id., 'Ashkenazi Elite'.

34 On German Jewish opposition to the *Shulḥan arukh*, see Zimmer, *Embers of the Sages*, 177–240 (note esp. Hayim b. Bezalel on the Rosh, p. 314); Davis, 'Reception'. There were attempts in Prague to promote M. Jaffe's *Levush* (Jaffe was a Prague native). The work was reprinted twice in Prague in the early 17th c. (1609 and 1622–4), while the *Shulḥan arukh* was not printed there until 1688–95. See Tchernowitz, *Rabbinic Authorities*, 185–6 on *Eliyah rabah* by the Prague rabbi Elijah Spira, which was written about 1690 as a commentary on the *Levush* but published in the 18th c. as a commentary on the *Shulḥan arukh*.

fourteenth-century Talmud commentary of Mordekhai ben Hillel closely parallels Heller's project of a commentary on the Rosh. Yet by 1626 Horowitz was led by the increasing popularity of the *Shulḥan arukh* to alter his views. In his *Shenei luḥot haberit* he wrote:

> [Isserles'] coinage has been accepted, and we must follow his opinions and render decisions in accordance with his views. Doubtless he merited this from heaven, just as the House of Hillel did. . . . In the Diaspora, in the lands of the Polish Crown, in Bohemia, Moravia, and Germany, the [practice] has spread to render decisions in accordance with his views. . . . In this generation, we follow the opinions of Rabbi Moses Isserles, and who shall permit what he forbade?[35]

Heller, by contrast, continued to oppose the blanket endorsement of the 'coinage' of Isserles or the *Shulḥan arukh*.

ON HUMILITY

Across the river from Prague's Jewish quarter, close to the imperial palace, stands another palace, built in the 1620s by General Albrecht von Wallenstein, then at the height of his power as vanquisher of the Protestants and conqueror of Germany. His downfall would come in the 1630s; the palace is a monument to his brief glory. Outside it is a garden, and in the garden a row of statues. One is of a mighty warhorse, rearing up as it is attacked by a serpent. To the seventeenth-century eye the allegory would have been clear: the serpent is pride.[36]

One revealing passage in which Heller rejected the view of the Rosh is in his 1619 commentary on 'Nezikin' concerning the supreme ideal of religious behaviour.[37] He commented on a passage in which the Talmud quotes from Isaiah 61: 1: 'The LORD has anointed me to bring good tidings to the humble'. The Rosh interpreted the passage to mean that humility is greater than piety. Heller disagreed. For him, the highest virtue was lovingkindness (in Hebrew, *ḥesed*) that culminates in personal revelation. He commented on Psalms 89: 20: 'then Thou spokest in vision to Your pious ones'. The pious one (in Hebrew, the *ḥasid*) is greater than the humble man, Heller argued. The *ḥasid* needs no promise of future happiness. 'The good news of redemption', Heller wrote,

> is given by the prophet to the humble, not because the humble are greater, but because the pious do not require it. For what greater and higher reward can be given to a person for his work in this world than to see the beauty of the LORD (Psalm 27: 4), to hear His word, to be the seer of a vision?

[35] *Shenei luḥot haberit*, i. 54*a–b* (Sha'ar ha'otiyot, 'Kedushah').

[36] See Scholten (ed.), *Adriaen de Vries*, 234.

[37] *MYT*(*PH*), *AZ*, p. 158 n. 6.

INTERPRETATIONS AND DECISIONS

In the mid-seventeenth century, both Jews and Christians felt anxious about the hierarchy of values; that anxiety extended to the relative authority of books of religion, morality, and law. 'We like security', wrote Pascal, a generation after Heller. 'We like the pope to be infallible in matters of faith and the grave doctors to be so in moral questions so that we can feel reassured.'[38] Heller's friend and colleague Pinhas Horowitz was later said to have 'followed the rulings [of the Rosh] as if they were given at Sinai'.[39] In spite of the rhetoric of his introduction, however, Heller himself did not treat the Rosh's rulings with such deference and did not regard the *Digest* as above question; that was so only for the Bible and the Talmud.

Among the many types of comments, notes, and glosses used by medieval Jews, one is the *hasagah*—the adversarial comment that questions or contradicts the text on which it comments. Heller wrote an entire work of *hasagot*, *Malbushei yom tov*, on the halakhic sections of Mordechai Jaffe's *Levush*.[40] A few of Heller's comments on the Rosh were also *hasagot*. In a variety of cases, he rejected the Rosh's views (one comment of this type is the discussion of humility and piety just quoted; another, in which he questioned the Rosh's distinction between Trinitarianism and polytheism, is discussed in Chapter 5 above).[41]

The Torah, wrote Isaiah Horowitz in the introduction to *Shenei luḥot haberit*, is based on free will—not because one is permitted to disobey it, but because the interpretative process is open. The choice of what the Torah means is ultimately voluntary.[42] Heller, as noted, followed the halakhic school of thought of Solomon Luria and the Maharal, whose view was different: for them, Torah has an intrinsic meaning that is not created voluntarily. In *Tosafot yom tov* Heller offered a distinction: whereas midrashic interpretation was free, *peshat*, the simple meaning of the text, was fixed. Law was based on *peshat*, particularly the *peshat* of the Talmud.

We have already discussed a number of cases in which Heller's legal decisions were arguably based on adherence to the plain meaning of the Talmud—for example, his definition (following Maimonides) of Christianity as a polytheistic religion and his rejection of certain kabbalistic customs and stringencies.[43] There are many

[38] *Pensées*, no. 516, p. 212.

[39] Yair Bacharach, quoted in Muneles, *Inscriptions*, 328, from *She'elot uteshuvot ḥavot ya'ir*, no. 123. Note also the Maharal's comment that the Rosh's *Digest* should have been published alongside the Talmud itself, instead of Tosafot: quoted in Assaf, *Sources*, 48; cf. Reiner, 'Changes', 60 n. 85; Beit Halevi, *Life of Heller*, 22.

[40] On the nature of *hasagot*, see Twersky, *Rabad of Posquières*, 128–97.

[41] See e.g. *MYT (DH)*, *Ḥulin*, p. 371 n. 25 (waiting between meat and milk); *Ber.*, p. 11 n. 82 (text of blessing on Torah study).

[42] *Shenei luḥot haberit*, 14*a* (in the section 'Beit yisra'el').

[43] See above, pp. 60–1, 96.

more such examples in *Ma'adanei melekh*. In one series of comments, Heller puts together an anthology of ancient rabbinic sayings on table manners, which he presents with a minimum of interpretation.[44]

The 'simple meaning' of the Talmud text, however is not identical with the Talmud text itself; it allows for a wealth of legal distinctions and subdistinctions, definitions and sub-definitions. For example, the Rosh quoted from the Talmud the saying of Rabbi Huna that one must recite a blessing each morning before reading the Bible. In interpreting this requirement, Heller first quoted Jacob Landau, a fifteenth-century authority, who argued that the blessing is required before *studying* the Bible, but one may *recite* biblical verses within prayers before saying the blessing. (Caro, Heller noted, disagreed with this distinction, but Isserles codified it.) Furthermore, Nissim Gerondi (the Ran; *c*.1310–*c*.1375), suggested that one is allowed to rule on halakhic matters and inform others of the decision before reciting the blessing, so long as one does not explain the reasoning of the decision.[45]

In a later chapter, Heller discusses a different blessing, that to be recited by one who sees the 'Great Sea'. Here the problem is one of definition. Joseph Caro had claimed that the 'Great Sea' was the Mediterranean, but Heller very neatly showed that Caro had based his opinion on a faulty text of a responsum by the Rosh; Heller corrected the text and argued in favour of the Rosh's view that the 'Great Sea' is the Ocean itself, the sea 'that surrounds the entire world'.[46]

In a third comment, Heller argued by analogy that a room in which a husband and wife sleep together is not required, and is often not permitted, to have a *mezuzah* on the doorpost. The Talmud rules that rooms where women bathe do not require *mezuzot*, because nakedness is shameful; so too a bedroom should not require one, he argued, because the sexual act is at least as shameful as bathing.[47]

These exegetical arguments, however, in spite of their straightforward character, may well make one suspect that in fact Horowitz was correct, and that meaning is established only by the reader. In his decision concerning the 'Great Sea', Heller himself admitted that in the Bible, the 'Great Sea' is clearly the Mediterranean; he is forced to argue that, here as elsewhere, biblical and talmudic usage differ. In his decision on the bedroom *mezuzah*, which adds a major exception, mentioned nowhere in the Talmud, to the laws of *mezuzot*, the entire argument depends on Heller's feeling that sex is shameful. The interpretative process is never mechanical; therefore authority can never be wholly rooted in the text.

[44] *MYT(DH)*, *Ḥul.*, p. 377 nn. 92–100.

[45] *MYT(DH)*, *Ber.*, p. 11 n. 78.

[46] *MYT(DH)*, *Ber.*, p. 74 n. 37. Cf. *Tos YT*, *Ber.* 9: 2; M. Roth, 'Notes', 95.

[47] *MYT(DH)*, *Mezuzot* (printed in the Vilna Talmud after tractate *Menaḥot*), p. 233 n. 46. Cf. Gombiner, *Magen avraham* on *Shulḥan arukh*, 'Oraḥ ḥayim' 40: 2.

THE CONSTITUTIONS OF THE JEWS

The role of the rabbinate in the seventeenth century was shaped by several conflicting theories, none of them fully explicit.[48]

The first of these was the theory of communal democracy. According to this theory, modelled on contemporary notions of city government in Germany and elsewhere, each local Jewish community comprised a self-governing polity. Authority was vested in the community, and hence in the representatives of the community, the *rashim vetovim* or communal council. Tellingly, the word *kehilah* was used interchangeably for the community with all of its members, or for the council itself. The council, in principle, would be elected democratically each year on the basis of an adult male franchise.[49]

In practice, among Jews as among Christians, the franchise was not universal, and Jewish communal government in many places, such as Frankfurt, devolved upon a small merchant aristocracy. Indeed, the principle of rule by the wealthiest and the best born was not without its defenders in Ashkenazi Jewry in this period.[50] Although the Horowitzes' attempt to capture official control of the Prague community had been fought off in the 1530s, the Prague *kehilah* in 1627 was still firmly under the control of the wealthiest families.

The Ashkenazi rabbinate was typically subject to the rule of the elected communal government; the *kehilah* appointed the rabbis, not vice versa. Indeed, in some places the rabbinate was little more than a mere instrument of the *kehilah*, called on to perform some sacral duties. The hard-won independence of the Christian clergy, partial though it was, was not shared by the rabbinate.[51]

Among Jews as among Christians, however, the theory and practice of representative communal rule, whether avowedly democratic or self-consciously oligarchic or aristocratic, coexisted uneasily with monarchical political theories.[52]

'Who are the kings? The rabbis' is a medieval Jewish saying, repeated endlessly in Jewish writings of this period.[53] Rabbinic Judaism is in principle theocratic; that

[48] See generally Elazar and S. A. Cohen, *Jewish Polity*. Note the triplex, somewhat different from ours, offered by Cohen in *The Three Crowns*.

[49] On the forms and theory of communal self-government among Ashkenazi Jews in this period, see Rosman, 'The Autonomous Community', 79–94, and also Friedrichs, 'Jews in the Imperial Cities', 275–88. Cf., for an earlier period, Kanarfogel, 'Unanimity'. See also Scribner (ed.), *Germany*, i. 310–15 ('Urban Communities'). Note also the cautionary remarks on the concept of medieval community in Bell, *Sacred Communities*, 149–53.

[50] This is the thesis worked out by H. H. Ben-Sasson in his *Theory and Practice*.

[51] See Zimmer, *Embers of the Sages*, 14–19, 29–42, 254. Cf. Forster, 'Clericalism and Communalism'.

[52] Note particularly the early modern conflicts of custom and royal absolutism (or custom and Roman law): see Strauss, *Law, Resistance, and the State*, 96–115; Skinner, *Foundations*, ii. 261–2.

[53] It is based on a passage in the Talmud (BT *Git.* 62*a*).

is, it vests all authority within the Jewish community in the Torah, in divine law, and hence in the rabbis as interpreters of the law. In the sixteenth century, moreover, there was a marked tendency within the Ashkenazi rabbinate towards the concentration of rabbinic authority (at least locally, within a town or a region) in the figure of a single chief rabbi.[54]

Support for the monarchical rabbi's claim to authority came from the medieval Jewish philosophers. The mainstream of Jewish philosophy, influenced by Maimonides, accepted a Neoplatonic theory of the philosopher-king rabbi.[55] As the Maharal commented, 'There must be one king and no more, for if there are two, how will [the kingdom] be bound together?'[56] Joseph ben Isaac Halevi shared this philosophical tradition. 'Homer the Greek poet', Halevi quoted from the Italian Jewish scholar, Azariah dei Rossi (*c.*1511–*c.*1578),

> in the second book of the Iliad said that kingship at all times hates division and loves unity.[57] . . . And Curtius in his book on the subject of the empire said that it is proper that there be one sun in the world and one king in a land.[58]

As there is one God in the universe and one sun in the heavens, so must there be only a single monarch. In the Jewish communities of the early seventeenth century, that monarch could only be the rabbi.

Medieval and early modern Jews had a horror of dissension—*maḥloket*, as it is called in Hebrew. Before the gradual legitimation of political parties and party systems in Europe (and America), mainly in the nineteenth century, division into 'parties', that is, into factions, was seen by both Jews and Christians as something immoral and dangerous.[59]

In a theocracy, consensus is achieved through obedience: to God, to the Torah, and to the rabbi. In a traditional lay communal government, on the other hand, it was achieved largely by the rule of *minhag*, local custom. Members of the community could all agree that everything would be done the way that it had always been done. There is of course a certain tension between rabbinical authority and established custom, and the rabbis of Friedberg, near Frankfurt, for example, were contractually prohibited from changing any local *minhag*.[60]

[54] Reiner, 'Changes', 35–6.

[55] Cf. Melamed, 'Attitude towards Democracy'; Funkenstein, *Perceptions*, 155–68.

[56] Maharal, *Gur aryeh* on Num. 28: 15.

[57] In Odysseus' speech, bk. ii, ll. 203–6: 'Lordship for many is no good thing. Let there be one ruler, one king' (Lattimore's translation).

[58] *Givat hamoreh*, 29*a*.

[59] Cf. Sartori, *Parties and Party Systems*, i. 3–13 ('From Faction to Party').

[60] For the Friedberg contract, see Kober (ed.), 'Documents', 45–6. The concern of the Friedberg *kehilah* may have been specifically the integrity of German customs rejected by Polish-trained rabbis. Cf. Zimmer, *Embers of the Sages*, 254. Note the tension between established practice and rabbinic law in the Nikolsburg wine controversy (above, Ch. 5), and in the Maharal's educational

The Jewish communities of the early modern period, one might say, had three constitutions. The first was the Torah, the constitution of rabbinical rule. The second was *minhag*, custom, and the associated notion of lay communal self-government. But we must not neglect a third theory, a third source of authority, and a third constitution. In this view, authority within the Jewish community belonged ultimately to the king—a Christian though he might be—and by extension to his appointed servants, be these feudal lords and royal officials or Jewish *kehilot* and rabbis. This last theory, of course, had considerable basis in political fact. The involvement of the non-Jewish authorities in Jewish self-government was pervasive and unavoidable. Heller's own election as rabbi of Prague had probably required a letter of imperial approval.[61] The written constitution of the Jewish community, in this view, consisted of such letters and written privileges.

These three constitutions allowed the existence, correspondingly, of three leadership groups within the Jewish community: the rabbis, the *kehilah* council, and the *shtadlan*. Of these, the rabbi was rarely the most powerful.

THE TITLE PAGE

In the publication of a law book, authorship and authority are closely intertwined. The title page of the 1628 volume of *Ma'adanei melekh*, published while Heller was chief rabbi, hints at his position in the community as it was viewed by the printer. Rabbi Asher's name is prominently displayed in large, ornamental letters. Below this we read 'with the commentary of Rashi'; only then is Heller's commentary mentioned: 'and with the commentary *Ma'adanei melekh*'.

Heller's name is then given, followed by 'son-in-law of the distinguished Rabbi Moses Aaron Ashkenazi of blessed memory', in tiny letters. Heller was not a native of Prague and his credentials in the Prague community still depended to some extent on his late father-in-law's status as a leader of the *kehilah*.[62]

Descriptions of the two parts of *Ma'adanei melekh* are arranged in two inverted triangles followed by the tractates included in this volume, listed in tiny print. The printer's name appears in larger print, with the place of publication, Prague, below. As is standard in Hebrew books of this period, the place is followed by the name of the monarch: 'His Majesty Ferdinand'. Rabbinical leadership, communal leadership, and the Christian king all share the title page.

reforms. On the conflict of lay and rabbinic authority, see also H. H. Ben-Sasson, *Theory and Practice*, 194–228.

[61] See the letter of appointment for Ephraim of Luntshits in Bondy and Dworsky (eds.), *Zur Geschichte der Juden*, 786.

[62] Heller's father-in-law is also named on the title pages of *Tosafot yom tov*.

At the bottom of the page comes the date written as 'Friday of the week in which the weekly Torah reading includes the verse: "I will make peace in the land" ' (Lev. 26: 6)—a heartfelt prayer added by the printer.

LETTER TO FRANKFURT, 1628

The pressures of war were being felt in another Jewish community as well that year. Beginning in 1615 and throughout the 1620s, the Jewish community of Frankfurt am Main, shaken by its expulsion during the 1614 Fettmilch riots, and oppressed by war taxes, was racked by dissension over the form of communal government. In Adar (February/March) 1628 Heller wrote a letter to Frankfurt which shows him at his most political and confident.[63]

Authority over Frankfurt's Jewish community was monopolized by a small group of prominent families; positions on the ruling board, the *ḥavruta*, were held for life, and the body was self-perpetuating. Inspired, ironically, by the democratic tendencies of the Fettmilch uprising, an opposing group agitated for an elected, broadly based Jewish communal government. After a number of unsuccessful attempts at compromise and arbitration between the two groups, the city council of Frankfurt was brought into the controversy. Later the imperial government in Vienna became involved.

Rabbis from outside Frankfurt also entered the fray: the Va'ad Arba Aratsot (Council of Four Lands) in Poland became involved and wrote to the Frankfurt community, urging it to resolve the conflict, and it also wrote to Heller, urging him to take steps. After some months, he finally acceded.[64]

Heller's letter, after the usual elaborate forms of address ('To the holy community of Frankfurt, to the dear and the beloved, the righteous and good, who sit in the city gate, the mighty, the heroes', etc.) moved quickly to the topic of the letters he had received from the rabbis of Poland. They had asked him, Heller revealed, to put the leaders of Frankfurt Jewry under *ḥerem*: they had also offered to support his *ḥerem* and to announce the names of the transgressors at the fairs in Poland. The rabbis of Poland were particularly incensed at those 'whose hands have been raised to bring profane things into the Temple court', that is, the Frankfurt Jews who had invited the Christian authorities to intervene in an internal Jewish matter. Heller emphasized the dangers of communal division, particularly during wartime:

> Out of this has come much stumbling and ruin and destruction and division which should not have been. . . . For are we not burdened by the yoke of this bitter and painful exile? Are we not weighed down by the troubles that arise and spread out over all our

[63] On the Frankfurt controversy, see Hailperin, 'Controversy'; cf. Kracauer, *Geschichte der Juden*, i. 398–410; ii. 1–14; Rosman, 'Authority of the Council', 11–17; Friedrichs, 'Jews in the Imperial Cities', 282–5.

[64] Heller's letter is in Hailperin, 'Controversy', 130–2.

people, for our sins, and by the many calamities and catastrophes that have come upon us and upon you? Even if this were a season of life, and we were united, we would still be fearful of those . . . who rise in every generation to destroy us, were it not for our Father in Heaven. . . . How much more so in this season of death, if we are separated and divided in our opinions?

He exhorted the Frankfurt Jews to resolve their differences:

For you dwell like us under the rule of our master, His Highness the Emperor. . . . And since we have heard from various people, travellers and passers-by, many trustworthy souls, that your entire intention has been to establish matters justly, and to make a rule by which the appointment might be made in the manner of the other holy communities, therefore do this and live. You see that our sole intention is for the sake of Heaven, to make peace in the land, and not, God forbid, to exalt ourselves, nor to assert any authority over you.

He summoned the two parties, nevertheless, to send plenipotentiaries to Prague, where his court would arbitrate the dispute. 'For there is no doubt in our minds that we will find a compromise that will be good for you for ever until the Coming of the Messiah, Amen.' He threatened them once again with *ḥerem* if they did not obey, and again mentioned the rabbis of Poland, concluding,

Rely on us as on yourselves, that we do not seek anything except truth and your best good, nothing else. Therefore listen and may your souls live, 'and say of the cleaving, it is good' (Isa. 41: 7).

The words of one who seeks peace and seeks good, your beloved,

Yom-Tov, called Lipmann, the son of my father,
my teacher . . . Rabbi Nathan of blessed memory
Levi Heller Friday 26 Adar 1628

In this letter Heller played all his cards. He drew on the support of the Polish rabbinate; he appealed to the piety of the Frankfurt Jews and also to their self-interest; he threatened them with *ḥerem* and with public humiliation, and appealed to their desire for consensus. He did not, significantly, appeal to the force of age-old custom. The consensus that he was offering would be achieved by obedience to the rabbi-monarch.

Heller was using the rabbinic instrument of *ḥerem* to try to assert control in an area of law—the arrangement of communal government—which was usually left to the lay leadership. He was also attempting to exercise influence from afar (as were the rabbis of Poland), thus implicitly opposing the theory of local communal self-rule.[65]

[65] On the question of the political relations of large and small Jewish communities, see Nadav, 'Authority'. On the later development of the position of Landrabbiner in Bohemia, see Jakobovits, 'Das Prager und Böhmische Landesrabbinat'.

This was not the first time that Heller had asserted the authority of the Prague rabbinate over the Jews of other places. He had intervened in a case in Swabia, rather to the annoyance of the local rabbi there.[66] In another case, in 1627, he had asserted his authority over the Jewish community of the Silesian town of Głogów (Glogau). He wrote on behalf of a certain Yudel, who had complained that the community of Głogów was acting against him high-handedly, refusing to submit their suit to a rabbinical court or to accept binding arbitration. Heller wrote to the Jews of Głogów, threatening them with *ḥerem* if the case were not brought within eight days to a rabbinical court either in Prague or in Poznań. He added that it would be best that they come to Prague, and noted that the Prague Jewish community had shortly before been given authority over Silesian Jewry in some matters of taxation.[67]

For we dwell in the same kingdom and have the same king. Especially now, since letters have come from our emissaries at the royal court [reporting] that the king and our(!) counsellors are making Silesia tributary to us in the payment of taxes, the greatest rabbinical court of the kingdom's cities is here.[68]

The question of local autonomy and centralized control was the focus of bitter and violent dispute among Christians in the Habsburg empire during the Thirty Years War. In his letter to Głogów, Heller argued in effect that the centralizing efforts of the Habsburg monarchs had brought about a parallel centralization of rabbinical authority in the Habsburg Crown lands. As chief rabbi of Prague, Heller now had a claim to be chief rabbi of Silesia as well. Perhaps inconsistently, he was arguing from what I have called the third Jewish constitution—that is, he claimed authority over the Jews of Silesia based on the grant of power from the Christian king.

In his letter to the Jews of Frankfurt, Heller stopped short of asserting direct authority over them; indeed, he admitted explicitly that he had no such authority. The Jews of Germany in the seventeenth century did not have a central organization comparable to the Council of Four Lands in Poland. The attempt in 1603 to establish a council of German rabbis had been unsuccessful. Frankfurt, however, had much the largest Jewish community in Germany proper, and its rabbis exercised some degree of authority over Jews throughout Germany.[69] But Heller suggested strongly that it was the rabbi of Prague who ought to be the highest rabbinical authority for all the Jews of the empire.

[66] See Zimmer, *Embers of the Sages*, 153. My argument parallels Zimmer's there (pp. 140–56). Prague rabbis (among others) also interceded in the 1616 case discussed on pp. 224–7.

[67] The official letter giving the Prague Jews this authority was not written until January 1628, several months after Heller's letter. See Wolf (ed.), *Ferdinand II und die Juden*, 47–8, document vii.

[68] Heller's letter to the Jewish community of Głogów, dated Monday, [4] Elul (16 Aug.) 1627, was published in Perles, 'Urkunden'. Cf. Hailperin (ed.), *Documents*, 52–3.

[69] See Zimmer, *Embers of the Sages*, 254, 260, and generally pp. 109–76.

Heller's plea fell on deaf ears, and the Jews of Frankfurt did not send plenipotentiaries to Prague. By the time the letter arrived, the rabbis of Poland had already carried out their threat to place the Frankfurt communal leaders under a *ḥerem*. Heller's delay had thus reduced the strength of his position. Rather than his mediation, it was the decision by the Frankfurt city fathers to imprison some of the Jewish communal leaders that caused the Frankfurt Jews to reach a final compromise in May 1628.

By 1628, eight years of repeated Habsburg victories seemed to some at the imperial court to have revived the possibility of effective control of the entire empire. Indeed, Emperor Ferdinand, emboldened by signs that he took to indicate providential guidance and favour and by his ardent desire to serve God, was beginning to feel the hubris of power and success.

Heller, a loyal ally of the Habsburgs, shared a little in their hubris. His threat of *ḥerem* carried few terrors for the Frankfurt Jews. Nor did Heller realize that, in little more than a year, communal dissension much like that in Frankfurt would divide the Jews of Prague. Like the Habsburgs, he overestimated the power of the clergy over the laity, and he misjudged the strength of his position within his community—a failure common to so many of the leaders of that generation.

EIGHT

The Trial

THE ARREST

THE imperial judge came to the Jewish quarter of Prague in the late afternoon of 4 Tamuz, towards the end of June 1629.[1] Heller was not at home. 'Perhaps he is in the House of Study,' someone told the judge, 'but if your honour wishes to speak with him, he will surely come to your honour's home.' 'No,' said the judge, 'I will go to see him.'

Heller was on his way to synagogue when he heard that the judge had come to the Jewish quarter, seeking him. He said the evening prayers, and returned home. He brought with him the leadership of the Prague Jewish community, so as not to face the judge alone. Shortly afterwards, the judge arrived in Heller's street by carriage. He spent a few minutes in another house close by and then came to Heller's door.

Some time between 1644 and 1648, Heller recorded the events of his trial (as well as some later events in his life) in a memoir that he called *Megilat eivah* (The Scroll of Enmity). The name is a play on *Megilat eikhah*, the biblical book of Lamentations. Heller's account is essentially our sole source of knowledge of the whole train of events. This is how he tells the story:

He came to the house where I lived and sent . . . to ask permission to enter the apartment. We asked him . . . to come in. He came in and shook hands pleasantly with each of us. I had prepared two chairs, and he motioned me to sit at his right hand, while he sat on my left. And we sat together, speaking about this and about that. Then he said, sir, I must speak with you privately. And we went into my study. But I had already been alerted that

[1] Except where otherwise noted, the entire account of Heller's arrest, imprisonment, and release is derived from Heller's own *Megilat eivah*. Heller's narrative follows the chronological sequence of events in an uncomplicated way, and I have not marked page references. Important supporting evidence is published in Wolf (ed.), *Ferdinand II und die Juden*, 49–50; A. Z. Schwarz, 'Zum Prozess'; and in Valdštejn, *Deník*, 290, 295. No other records of the case itself have been published, and there are none in the HHStA in Vienna. One may compare in a general way the 1664 imprisonment of Heller's successor in the Prague rabbinate, Simon Spira-Wedeles. See Jakobovits, 'Die Erlebnisse'. On Ferdinand II's Jewish policy, see the documents in Wolf (ed.), *Ferdinand II und die Juden*; Lewysohn, 'Kaiserliches Schreiben', 377–9.

very day by letters from Vienna that His Highness the emperor had commanded the viceroy in Prague to have me taken to Vienna in irons. . . . So I answered him, sir, would you please discuss these things with me at Jacob Bassevi's house?[2]

They went to Bassevi's house. The judge suggested that they should go in his carriage. Heller insisted that he would prefer to go on foot—not out of humility, as he explains carefully to the reader, 'but out of fear . . . that once in his carriage, I would be taken to prison and not to Bassevi's house'. The judge said that he would go on foot as well, and the communal leaders went with them.

There too he set me on his right hand and chatted a little. Then he told Rabbi Jacob [Bassevi] . . . to come with him into a side room. And when they were there, he said, 'I cannot tell the whole story to the rabbi, because I believe that he is a good man. So I will tell you, sir, since you will know how to break the news to the rabbi, in order not to frighten him too much.'[3]

The judge told Bassevi that he had been ordered to arrest Heller. Bassevi asked the judge if he would wait a little while, so that a few men could be sent to the Oberstburggraf (the viceroy), the highest imperial authority in Prague, to ask for clemency. The judge agreed. Two men were sent, David Luria and Hene Weisels.[4]

The viceroy's residence was in the Kleinseit, across the Vltava. And when they came to the house, the gate was shut and locked, for it was already night time. And they knocked on the gate, but there was no answer, for inside they were fast asleep.

But they did not go away. They kept knocking on the gate, until finally the chamberlain of His Highness, the viceroy, who was keeping watch that night . . . heard the knocking, and looked out the window. And he said, What do you mean, knocking so loud? . . .

And they asked him to open the gate, for they were Jewish leaders, sent to the lord viceroy on an urgent matter. And when he opened the gate, they asked him to wake the viceroy, saying that they had to speak to him on a matter of life and death. And he went straight into the bedroom and woke the viceroy. And he said to him, The Jewish elders wish to speak with you, lord, and they say it is a matter of life and death. And he said, Let them in.

And when they entered, they fell on their knees, and said to him, Our lord sent the imperial judge to arrest our rabbi and to take him to Vienna under a heavy guard. 'But where shall we hide our shame?' (2 Sam. 13: 13) For our enemies will say, Is this not their greatest man? This must mean that the Jews have rebelled against His Majesty the

[2] *Megilat eivah*, 30. The translations from *Megilat eivah* are my own, from the Hebrew text. I have also consulted Leo Schwarz's translation, in his *Memoirs of My People*, and the Yiddish versions of *Megilat eivah*. See also n. 36 below.

[3] *Megilat eivah*, 30.

[4] David Luria (Karpel) was an elder of the community (Spiegel, 'Die Prager Juden', 136, 185). On Hene Weisels (d. 1668), see Hailperin MS, p. 90. Hene b. Baruch Weisels, who was a signatory of the Prague *takanot* of 1579, was presumably his grandfather: see Bondy and Dworsky (eds.), *Zur Geschichte der Juden*, 558 (no. 772).

emperor, and that is why their head has been arrested. And so in every city where they hear this, they will attack the Jews.[5]

The Oberstburggraf, Adam von Waldstein (Wallenstein), a cousin of General Albrecht von Wallenstein, was sympathetic. He gave permission for Heller to remain free overnight, and he agreed the next day to let Heller go to Vienna freely and without any guard. The *kehilah* would stand as guarantors, under the threat of severe penalties ('their necks and their lands', as von Waldstein wrote in his diary), that Heller would appear promptly at the imperial court in Vienna.[6]

IN THE PRISON OF VIENNA

What was Heller charged with? Nothing in particular. In the seventeenth century, one did not need to be charged with a crime in order to be arrested on royal or imperial orders. A man would be arrested first; the precise nature of his crime would be defined later, after the authorities had investigated what he had done wrong.

Heller's belief, though, was that he had been denounced by his opponents among the Prague Jews.[7] A controversy had developed in Prague, similar to and perhaps inspired by that in Frankfurt. In summer 1629 the Jewish community of Prague was struggling under the burden of special war taxes. Should the new tax burden be spread equally, as a poll tax, or proportionately to wealth? This problem has been discussed above, in relation to the case of the Nikolsburg wine monopoly. Controversies over the tax burden had sparked a broader struggle for dominance between factions in the Prague Jewish community. The factions were named 'the elders' and 'the troubled'; later in the 1630s they developed into Bassevian and anti-Bassevian parties. Heller (in spite of the efforts that he speaks of 'to draw near and not to make distant') was identified with the 'elder', Bassevian party, the party of the existing leadership, whose choice of tax system favoured the wealthy.[8]

The 'troubled party', frustrated by a system of communal governance under which they were excluded from power, had appealed to the emperor. Only seven weeks before Heller's arrest, on 2 May, the imperial court had responded, sending a strongly worded rescript to the 'rabbi and elders' of the Prague Jewish community.[9] The imperial letter chastised the *kehilah* for 'gross inequities' in the dis-

[5] *Megilat eivah*, 31.

[6] See Valdštejn, *Deník*, 290 (26 June 1629): 'Dnes vezli toho Žida rabi Lipmana do Vídně Jeho Milosti Císařské a zapsali se pod ztracením hrdla i statku, že ho dostaví v 6 dnech.'

[7] See *Megilat eivah*, 29–30, discussed below, p. 148.

[8] See Spiegel, 'Die Prager Juden', 146–76; Putík, 'Prague Jewish Community', 66–71.

[9] See Wolf (ed.), *Ferdinand II und die Juden*, 49–50, document no. 9, Letter 'An die Eltisten vnd den Rabbiner zu Prag bei Verthailung der Steuern die Armen nicht zu bedrücken', discussed in Spiegel, 'Die Prager Juden', 147–9.

tribution of taxes. Furthermore, the letter charged, the *kehilah*'s opponents ('the troubled party') were being intimidated with threats of *ḥerem* and imprisonment. Now, Heller supposed, the opposition party had turned the tables, and caused him to be arrested.

Heller arrived in Vienna, without his family but with Hene Weisels for company, on Sunday, about noon, not quite a week after the arrest. That day, they went to present themselves before the imperial vice-chancellor, Peter Heinrich von Stralendorf, but he was not in; Heller returned the next day.

Von Stralendorf, a member of the privy council, was born into imperial service: his father had been vice-chancellor under Rudolf II. Aged 49 and unmarried, he was a talented bureaucrat and court official, and a devout Catholic.[10] Heller wrote:

> He spoke to me harshly in the name of the emperor concerning the book of Rabenu Asher that I had published with my double commentary. . . . For the emperor had been told that I had written there against their religion. He spoke at length in the same vein.
>
> And I answered, God forbid that your servant would do such a wicked thing, Neither I nor any book of ours has a word of anything of what my lord says. For all of our books concern the Talmud, which, according to our religion, is a commentary on the Bible and the beliefs that the Torah commands. That which is forbidden as 'idolatry' is only actual idolatry, and what the Talmud says refers only to that. All the sages and writers of books since the Talmud was written are forbidden to depart from its teachings.[11]

The vice-chancellor sent Heller back to his inn and warned him on no account to leave it.

> And when I beseeched him, he said that the wish of His Majesty the emperor had been to have me arrested immediately and taken to prison. But he had spoken on my behalf, that I should not be put in prison.[12]

Heller went back to his inn. He waited a full week, as the mills of the imperial bureaucracy turned.

When Heller and the vice-chancellor met, how would each have perceived the other? The vice-chancellor saw a man of 50 years—just his own age—a father, a scholar somewhat out of his depth. He saw a Jew, a rabbi—but what was that? A useful ally and a friend of the banker Bassevi? Or a blasphemer, a Pharisee doomed to hell? Heller saw another middle-aged man, devoted to the imperial service. Did he see a representative of legitimate and responsible authority, a pious man (albeit a Christian), with whom a few words of sense or a tearful entreaty might be enough

[10] See H. F. Schwarz, *The Imperial Privy Council*, 361–2, on Stralendorf. Hailperin identifies the 'chancellor' spoken of here in *Megilat eivah* as Johann Baptista Verda von Werdenburg, on whom see Schwarz, pp. 383–5.

[11] *Megilat eivah*, 31–2.

[12] Ibid. 32.

to clear up the entire incident? Or did he see a man of violence, a cruel persecutor, a Haman?[13] History is constituted of such meetings and mismeetings.

Heller's answer to the vice-chancellor on the question of the Talmud, Christianity, and 'idolatry', it must be said, was politic and cautious—he was in an extremely dangerous situation. It was even eloquent, but it was not entirely forthright. As mentioned in Chapter 5, Heller had indeed argued in the 1619 volume of *Ma'adanei melekh* that Christianity was subject to the laws governing idolatry. In the Middle Ages, some talmudists, including the Rosh himself, had argued that it was not, arguing for a legal distinction between polytheism and Trinitarian beliefs. This was the position that Heller stated to Stralendorf, though he himself had rejected this distinction.

On Sunday 17 Tamuz, a day of misfortunes in Jewish tradition, a Vienna city judge came to Heller's inn with two men. He had a writ from the vice-chancellor to put Heller in the city's prison, in the common cell. Some of the leaders of the Vienna Jewish community escorted him there ('They talked with me to give me strength'). Once he had entered the prison, however, no one was allowed in with him, or even to speak with him; 'but the prisoners who were there treated me with respect and served me.' Heller credits this kind treatment to the grace of God. It says much for the Christian decency of the Viennese convicts. He does not mention whether the Jewish elders of Vienna had gone as far as to suggest to the prisoners that respectful behaviour could earn them a little money.

On the next day (it was now two weeks since the arrest, nearly the middle of July), Heller was moved to a room in the house of the superior city judge, and was permitted to receive visitors. On Tuesday, the Jewish community contrived to have him removed from the jurisdiction of the city to that of the imperial court, to a room in the chambers of the Hofprofos (the imperial court bailiff) where he was given a bed, a chair, a table, and a lamp: 'The gaoler was kind to me, and did not keep anything from me that I desired.' The general rule of the period was that money could buy decent treatment in prison,[14] unless, that is, one were tortured. Torture was an ordinary part of judicial investigation in the Holy Roman Empire from the time of the Black Death in 1349 until the eighteenth century. Heller would surely have recalled that in 1602, when Jewish leaders of Prague were accused of murder and the Maharal and others had been put into prison, Israel Henlisch had been tortured to death. Even under Rudolph, the Prague Jews were

[13] A Jewish convert to Christianity contrasted these two views in 1654, complaining that Jews sometimes will celebrate the death 'of a godly and just magistrate . . . that is an enemy to them', and call him Haman: Isaiah, *Vindication*, 56–7.

[14] The different versions of *Megilat eivah* differ slightly in their description of Heller's transfers between places of imprisonment. ŽMP MS 157, pp. 28–9, speaks of a transfer to the debtors' prison.

not safe from danger. The fear of torture could not have been far from Heller's mind.[15] Torture was also a standard type of punishment in this period. He might possibly have been able to recall that in Wallerstein in 1583, when he was 5 years old, Count Wilhelm had executed a Jewish thief named Abraham Hans. A church chronicler wrote, 'He had him hung by the feet, and under him, he put a hungry dog. [The thief] lived twelve hours from 7 December until 8 December.'[16]

Heller may also have known a story told by Abraham Horowitz in his ethical will about a doctor who is imprisoned. The doctor remarks that he has seven medicines. The first is hope. The second is the faith that God can save him; the third, belief that he will save him. The fourth is the recognition that his sins are being punished; the fifth, belief that suffering atones for sins. The sixth is the acknowledgement that the situation could be still worse. The last is the admission that there is nothing to be done but to hope.[17]

On the next day, Wednesday 20 Tamuz, Heller was taken to be tried by a special imperial commission.[18] Like bureaucracies everywhere and at all times, including judicial bureaucracies, the men on the imperial commission seem to have been only slightly interested in the case before them. Heller was brought in; they asked him some desultory questions.

The commission included scholars—Christian Hebraists such as the imperial librarian Sebastian Tengnagel and the convert Paul Joseph bar Zadok, who had been given the task of reading Heller's books and checking them for blasphemies against Christianity.[19] Not very imaginatively, they had looked at the first page, but they had found material there for their purpose. They discussed Heller's introduction to *Ma'adanei melekh*. 'Why do you praise the Talmud?', they asked. Had not the Pope, 'who is the spiritual father of all the emperors, and whom they must all obey, commanded that the Talmud be burnt'?

[15] On the 1602 incident, see A. David (ed.), *Hebrew Chronicle*, 55–8. Note *Tos YT*, *Ned.* 10: 3, in which Heller quotes a sermon of the Maharal that clearly refers to the incident: 'one who informs on others will himself be informed on'. The trial may have been the occasion for the Prague community's surprising request for financial aid from the German Jewish communities, which triggered the 1603 rabbinical conference in Frankfurt. On the use of torture as a means of investigation, see generally Langbein, *Prosecuting Crime*; van Dülmen, *Theatre of Horror*, 13–23, 77–81. See also Boes, 'Jews in the Criminal-Justice System', 418–19.

[16] Müller, 'Aus fünf Jahrhunderten', 171. Cf. Glanz, '"Jewish Execution"'; Ulbricht, 'Criminality and Punishment', 68.

[17] A. Horowitz, *Yesh noḥalin*, ed. Waldman, ch. 11, pp. 235–7; the story is also quoted in Glueckel bat Judah Leib, *Life of Glückel*, 5–7.

[18] On the commission, see A. Z. Schwarz, 'Zum Prozess'. The date is given in some manuscripts and editions as Thursday 21st. See Hailperin MS, p. 93 n. 1.

[19] See A. Z. Schwarz, 'Zum Prozess'. On Tengnagel, see id. (ed.), 'Aus der Brief-Sammlung Sebastian Tengnagels', and the references in id., *Die hebräischen Handschriften*.

Indeed, the Talmud had been burnt in Rome in 1553. Responding to the papal initiative, all the Hebrew books in Prague had been confiscated in 1560 by imperial order and taken to Vienna. They were later returned. The Habsburg Counter-Reformation was ambivalent in its enforcement of the full rigour of papal policy in this area, as in many others.[20]

Heller reports that he answered that the Talmud was the summation of the Oral Torah, that Jews were bound by their religion to obey it, and that 'he had praised it to the people of his nation'. He pleaded, in a word, for religious toleration, for permission to maintain the Jewish religion as a separate religious body, bound by its own laws, traditions, and values.

The commission then asked why he had written against the Christian religion. Religious tolerance, even were it to be granted to Heller and to the Jews, did not include permission to blaspheme the governing religion, and religious toleration was of course in short supply in Vienna in the middle of the Thirty Years War. Heller had not tried to veil his devotion to the Talmud, but he continued, very sensibly, to hide the strength of his opposition to Christianity. He gave the same answer to the commission that he had given to the vice-chancellor, namely that there was no discussion of Christianity in any of his works, and that all references to 'foreign religions' were to ancient paganism.

Having answered the commission's questions, Heller was returned to his confinement.

DELIVERANCE

Fear, even panic, must have seized the Jewish communities in Prague, Vienna, and elsewhere when Heller was arrested. Were other rabbis or communal leaders going to be arrested? Was there going to be an expulsion? Confiscations? Riots and massacres? Did the emperor now suspect the Jews of being in league with the Protestants?[21] A month later in Alsace, on the other side of the empire, a Jew by the name of Asher ben Eliezer Halevi wrote in his diary that the emperor had been pressed to destroy 'all the commentaries on the Torah, and also the Mishnah and the Talmud, God forbid'.[22]

Years before Ferdinand became emperor, when he was still the archduke of Inner Austria and a young man, he had expelled the Protestant preachers and made

[20] See Stow, 'The Burning of the Talmud'. On the 1560 incident, see A. David (ed.), *Hebrew Chronicle*, 47. For general information on the religious policy of Ferdinand, see e.g. Bireley, *Religion and Politics*.

[21] Cardinal Scaglia suggested such a combination of Jews and heretics in his letter of Nov. 1629; see Scaglia, 'Letter', quoted in Stow, 'The Burning of the Talmud', 444–51. Cf. below, n. 51.

[22] Asher b. Eliezer Halevi, *Zikhronot*, 27: '[God] set bears loose upon us', he wrote (cf. BT *San.* 107*b*).

bonfires of Protestant books.[23] When Protestantism was suppressed in Bohemia after the battle of White Mountain in 1620, censorship of books and the expulsion of Protestant preachers were also crucial parts of the Counter-Reformation efforts.[24] In 1626 Ferdinand had made a special decree against the blasphemous anti-Christian contents of Jewish books, with the Talmud specially in mind.[25] A general prohibition on Jewish books, while an extreme move, was not out of the question.[26]

Shortly after Heller's appearance before the imperial commission, the verdict was rendered. The copies of *Ma'adanei melekh* would be collected and burned, and Heller was fined 12,000 reichsthalers in cash—a small fortune, about twenty times what he provided for his daughter's dowry.[27] But he could appeal the verdict in a *supplicatio* to the emperor, and he did so: 12,000 reichsthalers, he wrote, was far more money than he possessed or could raise.

About a week later, on the sabbath 1 Av (21 July), the *shtadlanim*, who had been working the imperial court on Heller's behalf, were warned by the vice-chancellor that the fine would not be reduced, and that if the money were not immediately forthcoming, Heller would be taken to each of the three public squares in Vienna, stripped naked, and beaten, and then the same would be done in Prague. The threat was not an empty one, but the *shtadlanim* were not easily frightened.

Shtadlanim, Isaiah Horowitz wrote in his *Shenei luḥot haberit*, are brave men: 'Even if they are rebuked or cast aside, they return. This is the pillar of our existence in exile.' In the eternal conflict between Judaism and Christianity, Horowitz wrote, the Jews have many weapons: in the spiritual realm, prayer, charity, and repentance; in the temporal realm, entreaties, bribes, and war. But in our own day, Horowitz added, when there are no Jewish armies, the equivalent to war is the work of the *shtadlanim*.[28] In *Tosafot yom tov*, Heller too had expressed his admiration of *shtadlanim*. They fulfil an important religious function, he quoted from an earlier commentary; they are to be compared to Mordechai in the book of Esther, or to Rabbi Judah the Prince himself.[29]

Heller reports the negotiation in *Megilat eivah*. The vice-chancellor warned that Heller would be

> a shame and a disgrace to all the Jews, for such a thing as this had not been done since the beginning of the Jewish exile. And what will those who see it say, when they see the shame done to the chief rabbi of the greatest city, and a city with so many Jews?

23 See Franzl, *Ferdinand II*, 63–70, on the suppression of Protestantism in Inner Austria.

24 See Gindely, *Gegenreformation*, esp. pp. 117–19; Bohatcová, 'Book-Printing', 332–8.

25 See A. Z. Schwarz, 'Zum Prozess', 206.

26 See Burnett, 'Regulation of Hebrew Printing', 329–48.

27 Different texts of *Megilat eivah* refer alternatively to reichsthalers, Rheinesthalers, and gulden.

28 *Shenei luḥot haberit*, iii. 25*a* (Torah shebikhetav, Parashat 'Vayishlaḥ').

29 *Tos YT*, *Avot* 2: 3.

The vice-chancellor was playing to the same fear of the mob that the Prague elders had expressed in their night-time appeal to the viceroy in Prague: 'And the *shtadlanim* dropped to their knees and said, But he cannot pay such a large fine as the emperor commands.'

The vice-chancellor was not to be put aside so easily (it was, of course, possible that some fraction of the fine would go to the vice-chancellor himself). He answered, Heller tells us, 'Some of your people say that [Heller] is a very rich man, and that the fine is only a fifth of what he is worth.'[30]

The negotiations continued on Sunday and Monday. The *shtadlanim* held firm. The Jewish religion, they said, forbids payment of exorbitant ransoms; 12,000 reichsthalers was too much. On Tuesday, the vice-chancellor suggested that 10,000 reichsthalers might possibly be enough. He suggested that he personally would be willing to reduce the fine to that amount, although the emperor was adamant about receiving the full amount. And he argued that Heller would not have to pay the fine himself; the whole community, even distant communities in the land of the Turks, would help to pay the fine. On Thursday, a sum of 10,000 reichsthalers was agreed, and with some further negotiation a schedule of payment was worked out. Of these 10,000 reichsthalers, 2,000 would be paid immediately in cash. Another 1,000 would be paid within six weeks, at which time Heller would be released from prison. Then every three months for twenty-one months, he would pay a further 1,000 reichsthalers, giving a total of 10,000 reichsthalers. In addition, the copies of *Ma'adanei melekh* would not be burnt, but only censored.

Thus, in the end, it was something like the panic of the Prague Jews in 1618 and 1620. There was a great deal of fear but the damage was restricted. There were no confiscations, no expulsions, and, especially, there were no book burnings. Heller himself was not executed or tortured, but fined; the fine was large but not astronomical.

As the vice-chancellor had surmised, Heller had help in paying even this lesser fine. The first 2,000 reichsthalers were paid by Jacob Bassevi with a letter of account. The leaders of the Vienna community volunteered another 700. Heller's in-law Hanokh Schick chipped in with 100 reichsthalers.[31] His son-in-law Wolf Slawis also pitched in; so did Hene Weisels, who had accompanied Heller from Prague to Vienna, and others.

In the meantime, however, another problem had arisen for Heller. In Prague, the conflict over the distribution of taxes in the Jewish community had intensified. Heller's opponents within the Prague Jewish community took the opportunity of his arrest to try to have him removed from the chief rabbinate. One of the authori-

[30] *Megilat eivah*, 33.

[31] On Schick, see Hailperin MS, p. 94 n. 3.

ties in Prague (Heller is somewhat vague here) sent a letter to the imperial court, recommending that Heller be deprived of the rabbinate. On 18 Av the vice-chancellor acceded to the request, and told the *shtadlanim* in Vienna that Heller was to be removed from his position as chief rabbi.[32]

Although Heller attributed motives of pure malice to his opponents, we can afford to be more sympathetic. In August 1629 the conflict in the Prague Jewish community was just turning from the issue of taxes to the more basic issue of communal governance. The opposition party demanded new communal elders and a new system of elections that would guarantee representation to the poorer Jews.[33] It is not surprising that they also wanted a new chief rabbi. Furthermore, Prague Jews of both parties might easily have felt that Heller's position with the imperial authorities had been irreversibly compromised, and that to reinstate him would be a needless risk for the Prague community.

Heller naturally saw it differently:

> This was worse for me than any of the other things that had come on me. And I felt shamed and in great distress, because there was nothing left to me by which I could earn a living. But God, may He be blessed, gave me strength and firmness to bear patiently all of my troubles.[34]

Heller was released from prison on 28 Av, about the middle of August, having suffered altogether forty days of imprisonment. However, he stayed in Vienna for another month, until after Rosh Hashanah. On the eve of Yom Kippur (26 September) he returned to Prague, and immediately fell sick. He was bed-ridden, he tells us, for three months.

To pay the fine, Heller and Rachel were forced to convert their loans into cash, and to sell their assets: their silver and their house in Prague. In a formal transfer witnessed by Meir Katzenstein, they also sold his two seats at the front of the Pinkas synagogue and Rachel's seat at the front of the women's gallery.[35] All of this was not enough. Their sons contributed; so did Jacob Bassevi's son Abraham; the Prague *kehilah* gave the last 250 reichsthalers. The imperial official who was placed in charge of collecting the fine was sympathetic. 'When he came to my house, I told him the whole story, and tears poured out of my eyes, while my wife, the modest Mistress Rachel, also wept.' In summer 1631 the fine was completely paid off. Heller was once more free to leave Prague and to resume his career in the rabbinate.

[32] Cf. Adam von Valdštejn's diary entry for 30 September 1629, in Valdštejn, *Deník*, 295: 'Dostal sem psaní od Jeho Milosti Císařské strany Židův o rovnost strany contribucí a o toho Lipmona rabino, aby pokutu složili a více aby rabín nebyl.'

[33] See Spiegel, 'Die Prager Juden', 147–9; Putík, 'Prague Jewish Community', 66–8.

[34] *Megilat eivah*, 34.

[35] *Pinkas hamekomot* of the Pinkas Shul, 59–60.

EXPLANATIONS

Megilat eivah is not only a record of what happened to Heller in 1629; it is also record of how he interpreted these events, and what lessons he took or did not take away from them.[36] This is an aspect that is at least as important to our understanding of Heller as the question of how he interpreted sacred texts.

The late Professor Jacob Katz, the doyen of the study of traditional Ashkenazi Judaism, in an article on the massacres of 1648 wrote that Ashkenazi Jews were not 'realists'. Heller provides Katz with some of his most important evidence of the lack of realism on the part of the rabbis of 1648.[37]

Katz focuses especially on the question of historical causation. The rabbis of 1648, he argues, and Heller in particular, saw the causation of events within a religious framework. They saw historical events as the actions of an all-seeing God, misfortunes as punishment of sin, and good fortune as divine favour. All of this is no doubt very pious. But the rabbis of 1648 did not, so Katz insists, give any explanation of events in natural terms, in terms of human motivation and the natural consequences of human actions.

I discuss Heller's view of the massacres of 1648 in Chapter 12. However, my earlier discussion of the Jewish narrations of the events of 1618–20 has shown that Katz's generalization is only partly correct. Heller's liturgical poems did indeed interpret events as the actions of divine providence: troubles as divine punishments, deliverance as the answer to prayers. But in the Hebrew prose account the only causes suggested for misfortune were the war and the revolt themselves, while the protection of the Jews of Prague was presented as the result of Emperor Ferdinand's command to his troops. Thus the two accounts, published together but written in different literary genres, presented different frameworks for the interpretation of events. The Jews of Prague were capable of both, and saw no great conflict between them.

What framework of causation do we find in *Megilat eivah*, a work that was completed no more than four years before the 1648 massacres? I shall focus on the two events in the story whose causes stand in special need of explanation: Heller's

[36] Most of the published Hebrew editions of *Megilat eivah*, beginning with the 1880 edn. published in Vilna, include a section at the end which purports to be an account of Heller's deliverance, written by Heller's son Samuel. The story that Samuel tells has a quality reminiscent of Dumas and *The Three Musketeers*: he saves a young woman from a bull, and her husband, the French ambassador, intercedes on behalf of Rabbi Yom-Tov. Alas, the document is a forgery, as the great bibliographer Moritz Steinschneider noted (*Geschichtliteratur*, 118). Samuel's story is based on a short story written by Ludwig Philippson (1811–89), a rabbi and journalist and the author of a series of Jewish historical novelettes and stories for young readers.

[37] See J. Katz, 'Between 1096 and 1648'. Note Abraham David's argument for the accuracy of the anonymous Prague Hebrew chronicle of 1615; id., *Hebrew Chronicle*, 9.

arrest and his release. Beginning with his release, let us first consider what Heller did *not* write. There is no question that while he was in prison Heller prayed that he might be freed. That is, he prayed, and then his prayers were answered. One might suppose that he would present the events in that guise, just as he did after the events of 1620. He did not: he never mentioned prayers, either his own or those of the Jewish community on his behalf. Likewise, although Heller surely confessed his sins and did penance while he was in prison, he did not mention it. One might suppose, in short, that Heller would present his release from prison as a divine reward for some virtuous act, whether his or someone else's. He did not.

This should not really surprise us. In several places in his writings, Heller endorsed the talmudic saying, 'There is no reward in this world for the performance of the commandments.'[38] The lack of correspondence between merit and this-worldly reward is not a modern discovery.

Heller's explanation for his release seems instead almost petty. He discussed in considerable detail the efforts of the *shtadlanim*, the lobbyists of the Jewish community at court. Heller did not give all of the details, and in fact may not have known them all, but the general picture is quite clear. The *shtadlanim* did their job: they gave out presents (or bribes, depending on your point of view), they flattered, they made promises, they pleaded, they negotiated. Heller did not say in *Megilat eivah* whether prayer is effective (elsewhere he stated that it is, as mentioned earlier), but he showed clearly that lobbying works. If it be asked what Heller learned from this experience, this might be one answer.

The other major event in the story, and the causes that Heller suggested for it must now be examined. Why was he arrested in the first place? The answer to this question is more complicated: Heller actually gave three different explanations for his arrest, in different places in *Megilat eivah*. But, here again, the answers that he did not give should be considered, as well as those that he did. One might suppose, first of all, that he would interpret his arrest as a divine punishment for some sin that he himself had committed. He did not do this. Just as he did not understand his release as a reward for virtue, so he did not interpret his arrest as a punishment for sin.[39] One might also suppose that he would blame the emperor or at least the imperial court for his arrest; he might even have suggested that Emperor

[38] *Sekhar mitsvah behai alma leika* (BT *Ḥul.* 142*a*); *MYT* (*PH*), *San.* p. 238 n. 6. Cf. *MYT* (*MM*), *Ber.* p. 36 n. 50; *Tos YT*, *Avot* 2: 1, 2: 6, 2: 16, 4: 9, 5: 19; cf. *Avot* 5: 8; Joseph Halevi, *Givat hamoreh*, 27*b*.

[39] In *Tos YT*, *Avot* 4: 11, Heller had distinguished two causes of misfortune: calamities that come about on account of sin, and others that 'break forth and come according to the custom of the universe . . . that is, the accidents and evil that occur in the universe'. See Maimonides, *Guide*, 3: 12; cf. BT *BK* 80*b*. It would appear that Heller regarded his imprisonment as a calamity of the second type.

Ferdinand was a tyrant—after all, Europe was full of men much like Heller who thought this. Or else one might suppose that Heller would blame his arrest on the simple fact that the emperor was a Christian. Christians do not like Jews, he might have thought, and they do things like arresting rabbis.

Heller wrote none of these things. Instead, he gave this explanation for his arrest, at the beginning of *Megilat eivah*:

> There had been a great war in Bohemia for ten years [1618–28], because its people had rebelled against His Highness, Emperor Matthias and after him His Highness, Emperor Ferdinand [II]. . . . Because of this, livelihoods were shaken, while taxes and compulsory assessments had been increased. Therefore, the people of the [Prague] community were forced to borrow money at high interest. And when the time came to repay [the loans], division [*maḥloket*] increased in Israel on the question of distribution of the tax burden, and hearts were divided and the close became distant. And they made conspiracies in private and some even in public. And all the efforts that I made to draw near and not to repel, both with soft words and with hard ones, were to no avail.[40]

Controversy was of course nothing new to the Jewish community of Prague. In earlier days, in the mid-sixteenth century, the community had been known for its incessant quarrelling and feuding. 'There is always violence and dissension in its streets', wrote Naftali Hirtz of Brest-Litovsk.[41] We recall the bitter dispute between the Horowitzes and their opponents in the sixteenth century, including the 1559 conflict between Abraham Horowitz and Joseph Ashkenazi over philosophy.[42]

Heller knew that, as chief rabbi, he had to remain impartial, but his family ties, his personal ties, and perhaps his financial ties as well made it difficult to do so. He was a friend of Bassevi, and a member of the Horowitz family. Heller made enemies within the community, and it was those Jewish enemies—not Emperor Ferdinand and not the non-Jews—whom he blamed first for his arrest. 'There was strife and war [*tsank un krig*]' in the Jewish community of Prague, Heller wrote in the Yiddish version of *Megilat eivah*. The 'hatred' in the title of the work is not between non-Jews and Jews, but between Jews and other Jews.

Heller chose to stress the Jewish communal conflict concerning taxes as a causal factor, placing it at the beginning of his story. If the question of what he learned from his experience were to be raised again, it might be answered that he learned anew the dangers of factionalism within the Jewish community.[43]

[40] *Megilat eivah*, 29–30.

[41] *She'elot uteshuvot harema*, 94, no. 14.

[42] Note the discussion of faction formation along clan rather than class lines in Luebke, 'Terms of Loyalty'.

[43] See H. H. Ben-Sasson's long discussion in *Theory and Practice*, 235–7, 242–8, and note also the passage from the Maharal quoted and discussed in Ben-Sasson, 'The Reformation', 305 n. 189. Cf.

Of Heller's several explanations of his arrest, modern historians would as a rule no doubt prefer this one, which involves impersonal forces, material interests, and class conflicts or factional conflicts, to the others. His second explanation, a story of false rumours, offended dignity, and vengeance, gave the events a Shakespearean quality. The story was told, partly by Heller and partly to him, after his release from Vienna prison. He writes:

After much investigation, I discovered who had opposed me and who was responsible for all this. It was a certain important nobleman, favoured by the emperor. I came before him on the Fast of Gedaliah [3 Tishrei] . . . and he told me the reason for his hatred and enmity towards me. 'It was told to me that you boasted before the viceroy [von Liechtenstein] in Prague that you had bested me in [religious] debates while you were rabbi in Vienna.'

I answered him: 'Now my lord may . . . judge from this how my opponents have treated me, and how they have lied. . . . For I left [Vienna] with ten carriages, and with them many . . . soldiers to act as guards along the highways. Let them come and testify for me when it was that I left. It was near Passover, and the viceroy was already dead and buried some months since.'

Then his heart changed, and he said, '. . . My house is open to you. Come to me whenever you wish and I will help you . . .'[44]

As Israel Hailperin has plausibly suggested, the unnamed nobleman with whom Heller had this enlightening conversation may have been a priest, perhaps a Jesuit. This would explain the implication that he was in a position to have disputed religious questions with Heller and the claim that he had the ear of the emperor, for the Jesuits were indeed among Ferdinand's most important advisers.[45]

There is no way to confirm or to contradict the veracity of Heller's story. Nor can we know whether his nemesis was really motivated merely by personal pique based on a mistaken and perhaps malicious rumour. One can note that Liechtenstein, to whom Heller is said to have boasted, was one of the business partners of

BT *Yoma* 9*b* on the causes of the destruction of the Second Temple, including 'causeless hatred'. Rashi on Song of Songs 6: 12 blames the Exile on the sin of *maḥloket*, rife among the Hasmonaean kings. Isserles, in his responsum no. 63 (quoted in Siev, *Rabbi Moses Isserles*, 202), blames the misfortunes of Bohemian Jewry about 1560 on *maḥloket*; cf. Josel of Rosheim, *Historical Writings*, 212, 300. Cf. Heller on *maḥloket* in *TosYT*, *Yev.* 1: 4 and *Avot* 1: 8, quoting the Maharal; *Leket shoshanim*, ch. 24, fo. 134*b*, and the discussion in my thesis, pp. 494–9. Cf. also Friedrichs, 'Jews in the Imperial Cities', 282 ff.: 'Politics is primarily a process of conflict resolution.'

44 *Megilat eivah*, 34–5.

45 His speech (not quoted here) also has a religious tone: see below, p. 202. On the Jesuits at Ferdinand's court, see Bireley, *Religion and Politics*. Professor Stephen Burnett has suggested (in private correspondence) that if Heller's unnamed opponent was a Jesuit, then he might have been either Valentinus Joannides or Henry Phillipi 'Prescensis', professor of Hebrew at Graz (in Ferdinand's home duchy of Inner Austria) and later at Vienna and Prague.

his patron Jacob Bassevi. There were surely Habsburg courtiers eager to believe the worst of the Heller–Bassevi–Liechtenstein group.

My concern, however, is as much with Heller's perception as with the true causation of events. Having rejected the option of blaming Emperor Ferdinand, one might suppose that Heller would be drawn to the conventional stereotype of a good king misled by wicked courtiers, and that he would place blame squarely on this Christian gentleman. On the contrary, he drew the man in a sympathetic light. (I shall return to the question of Heller's depiction of the nobleman in Chapter 11.)

In Heller's view, the vengeance taken by this well-connected courtier, whom in reality he had not harmed, whom he calls a nobleman, and who was perhaps a Jesuit, is part of the explanation. It is not, however, in his view, the ultimate explanation of events. The courtier has either been misled intentionally, in which case other parties with other motives are responsible, or else the affair is a dreadful accident, and then one must see in it the hand of providence, stretched out against the Torah and its scholars.

In another place in *Megilat eivah*, at the end of the narrative of his arrest and release in a passage in which he reflects on the meaning of his experiences, Heller presents a third explanation of his arrest, describing it as an action of divine providence. He quotes a story which originally appeared in a medieval halakhic work and relates it to his misfortunes:

[Once] during a time of persecutions, the authorities decreed that on the fifth of Tamuz, all the holy writings of the Jews would be burned. And the sages of that generation asked a 'dream question' [a question to be answered by spirits in a dream] . . . and the answer was 'This is the law of the Torah' (Num. 19: 2). [That is: it is a decree of Heaven against the Torah.] . . .

And I thought . . . that the decree was originally made against my books [as well] . . . to destroy them, and because of them I was forced on the fifth of Tamuz to leave my house in Prague and travel to the court of the emperor . . . And [the dream] spoke once, but it referred both to the earlier decree and also to this decree.[46]

The story of the dream question derives from a thirteenth-century Italian compendium of Jewish prayer laws and customs called *Shibolei haleket*, by Zedekiah ben Abraham Anav, and the event that it describes is the burning of the Talmud in Paris in 1240. Heller, who had heard the story only at second hand, may or may not have known this.[47]

Heller's arrest, imprisonment, the threatened burning of his book, and his dismissal from office were parts of a larger campaign aimed at the conversion of the

[46] *Megilat eivah*, 35.

[47] See the note by the editor of the 1836 edn. of *Megilat eivah*. The story appears in Anav, *Shibolei haleket*, 252. On the tradition that the anniversary was an unlucky day, see Kook, 'Friday'.

Prague Jews. The Hebrew press in Prague was actually closed for several years,[48] and Jews in Prague and elsewhere were forced to attend special Christian sermons.[49] Heller's friend and colleague on the Prague rabbinical court, Pinhas Horowitz, was thrown into prison in November 1630 for opposing the programme of conversion.[50] The Roman Inquisition was involved; in November 1629 Cardinal Scaglia wrote to the papal nuncio in Vienna, requesting that he urge Emperor Ferdinand ('an emperor of singular piety and zeal', Scaglia wrote) to ban the Talmud utterly throughout his domains.[51] The policy resembles Ferdinand's 1596 suppression of Protestant religion in Inner Austria; there too, as mentioned earlier, a three-pronged policy of book-burnings, forced attendance at sermons, and the expulsion of clergymen had been used.[52]

The imperial court had found the Jews to be useful allies. In the aftermath of its victories on the battlefield, however, by 1629 the Habsburg court felt strong enough to dispense with some of its more dubious allies. Many of its allies in Germany had been alienated by punitive anti-Protestant policies. The great quasi-Catholic general Wallenstein was dismissed in 1630. His erstwhile partner, Heller's defender Jacob Bassevi, was arrested in February 1631.[53] Heller did not include any of these facts, many of them surely familiar to him, in his narrative. He narrowed the bounds of his story, focusing exclusively on his own personal misfortune and deliverance. He refused to present Habsburg anti-Jewish policies, and particularly the suggested suppression of the Talmud, as an important factor in his own arrest or release. He focused his criticism, perhaps unfairly, on his opponents within the Prague Jewish community and on the danger of factionalism.

In this third explanation, using the story of the Talmud burning in Paris, Heller suggested that the major attack was on Jewish *books*, and only secondarily on himself as a Jewish writer. He portrayed this attack, however, not as a decree of the Catholic Church nor of the pious Emperor Ferdinand, but as a *divine* decree. It is as if he regarded the Church and its supporters as a natural force, akin to an earthquake or a stormy sea.

48 Baron, *Social and Religious History of the Jews*, xiv. 240. L. Zunz, 'Annalen der hebräischen Typographie' does not list any works published between 1629 and 1640. Cf. Putík, 'Prague Jewish Community', 26–37.

49 See Prokeš and Blaschka, 'Antisemitismus', 49–94 ('Das Prager Ghetto und die Christliche Gesellschaft im Zeitraum der Weissenbergen-schlacht bis zur grossen Pest im Jahre 1680'); on conversion sermons, see Pribram (ed.), *Urkunden und Akten*, i. 107–12.

50 Prokeš and Blaschka, 'Antisemitismus', 60, 88 n. 22.

51 Scaglia's letter appears in Albizzi, *De inconstantia*, pt. 1: 'De inconstantia in fide', 296–8, and is discussed in Stow, 'The Burning of the Talmud', 444–51. Cf. Scaglia's discussion of the censorship of Jewish books in University of Pennsylvania MS Codex 602 (formerly MS Lea 184), 40 ff.

52 See Franzl, *Ferdinand II*, 63–70. Cf. Bireley, *Religion and Politics*, 14.

53 Spiegel, 'Die Prager Juden', 141.

ON POLITICS

The failure to investigate or even to perceive the natural causes of historical events is only half of the lack of 'realism' in traditional Ashkenazi Judaism, as Jacob Katz presents it. The second and more significant half is that traditional Askhenazi Jews, Katz claims, were unable to learn anything from history or to draw any lessons for the future, even from shocking and catastrophic events.

It has been demonstrated that the portrait of Heller as unconcerned with historical causation is not correct. But what, if anything, did he learn from his arrest, imprisonment, and release?

Two parts of the answer have already been discussed. The events reinforced his opinions that Jewish lobbying at court worked and that *maḥloket*, factionalism in the Jewish community, was dangerous. The danger of factionalism is the explicit moral of *Megilat eivah*, signalled in the title. However, it can hardly be said that he learned these two rules of thumb from events. His concern with factionalism came to the fore at least twice in the years before his arrest: it is the theme both of his final comment in *Tosafot yom tov* and of his letter to the Jews of Frankfurt. He was entirely convinced of the danger of factionalism before his arrest had ever taken place; indeed, as I have remarked, it was a truism within European culture in general. Nor would anyone in the seventeenth century have had to look very far for confirmation: religious conflict had brought Germany to the brink of ruin. There is no reason to doubt that the first principle—the usefulness of lobbying—was also a rule that Heller had learned early in life, in the home of his grandfather.

Heller did not learn from history; Katz is correct in that regard. He was a rationalist in a medieval mode. His model of science did not involve empirical research, nor did he believe that particular events could teach new political principles. Rather than learning anything new, he interpreted events in light of certain practical rules of politics of whose value he was convinced. The events, in turn, confirmed his belief in those rules.[54]

Heller was confirmed in his belief in a third principle as well, another political rule of thumb to which he had been inclined before his imprisonment. Surprisingly, after his arrest as before it, he remained inclined towards a relatively optimistic view of the relations between Jews and Christians. In particular, he remained very loyal to the Habsburg monarchy. Far from blaming the Christians for their part in the events in *Megilat eivah*, he mostly took pains to paint them in the most favourable possible light, as described above. He emphasized how polite they all were, how well they all treated him, and how respectfully they all spoke to him. The imperial judges and the Oberstburggraf in Prague, the anonymous

[54] On the exemplary theory of history-writing in this period, see Nadel, 'Philosophy of History'.

nobleman with whom Heller spoke after his release, the city gaoler in Vienna, and even the prisoners in the Vienna city gaol—all the non-Jews in the story (except for Stralendorf)—treated Heller well, and he emphasized it at every point.

At one point he even went so far as to quote an official letter in which Emperor Ferdinand told him that, although he really deserved to be executed, his punishment had been reduced to a fine of 12,000 reichsthalers (as we have seen, this was later reduced to 10,000). Heller quoted from the letter: he had been pardoned because the emperor was merciful and came from 'a dynasty of merciful kings'.

Why did Heller want his readers to know that Ferdinand, a man who ordered a major conversionary offensive against the Jews, and who was regarded by some of his contemporaries as a cruel tyrant, congratulated himself and his ancestors for being so merciful? It is easy to understand why the imperial chancery declared that Heller's pardon, for crimes that were largely imaginary, had been out of Ferdinand's 'deep graciousness', but why did Heller repeat these pious phrases? Clearly he did so because to a large extent he believed them. He had believed them in 1620 and he was not disillusioned by the events of 1629. In Heller's view, the Habsburg dynasty was merciful towards the Jews, and Ferdinand himself was a good king.[55]

Heller seems to have had no detailed knowledge of the workings of the imperial court in Vienna. He had read no works of political theory as such, neither Plato's *Republic* nor Jean Bodin's sixteenth-century *République*. His ideas about politics, like those of most early modern Jews, came down to a few very basic assumptions—but the same could be said of most Christians in the early modern period, and even of Emperor Ferdinand himself.[56]

The danger of factionalism, the effectiveness of lobbying at court, and the fundamental goodness of the king: these were the three basic assumptions that had guided Jewish political activity for fifty years and more, from the 1570s or even before, in achieving political success. Heller was convinced that they were of essential and immutable validity.

AGAIN ON NON-JEWS

A question that was discussed in an earlier chapter—Heller's view of non-Jews—may be reconsidered here. In *Tosafot yom tov*, he had rejected the notion that non-Jews are evil, that the difference between Jews and non-Jews is the ethical dualism of good versus evil. Similarly, in *Megilat eivah* few if any of the non-Jews are

[55] My argument here closely parallels Yerushalmi's demonstration of the monarchism of ibn Verga: Yerushalmi, *Lisbon Massacre*. Cf. also Carlebach, 'Between History and Myth'.

[56] Evans, 'The Imperial Vision', 85.

portrayed as evil. However, Heller did endorse a different contrast between Jews and non-Jews—not an ethical dualism but a metaphysical one, the dualism of heaven and earth. He had claimed that non-Jews are less perfect intellectually than Jews, and that while they have the potential to serve God (without being Jews), they do not *know* God. It could be anticipated, then, that Heller would depict non-Jews as earthy or ignorant in some way, and Jews as in some way superior. Rereading *Megilat eivah* with this in mind, we are not disappointed.

Megilat eivah may be read, in fact, as a comedy, with the non-Jews cast as comic fools and the Jews as comic heroes. From beginning to end, all the Christians—the polite ones as well as the rude ones, both high-born and low-born—are depicted as lacking knowledge. They do not understand the true nature of the events they are involved in; they are ignorant of Jews in general and of Heller in particular.

Heller's Jewish opponents, on the other hand, are presented as tricksters manipulating the unwitting non-Jews. Furthermore, his allies, the *shtadlanim*, while not described as deceitful like his opponents, also influence the Christians with their words and eloquence. The Christians in the work may be powerful, but they are not eloquent; they do not convince anyone.

Heller portrayed himself as eloquent as well, and, if not as a trickster—he did not accuse himself of lying—it could be said that he portrayed himself as choosing his words prudently. It will be recalled that his explanation of why he was innocent of blasphemy (his comments concerned only 'idolatry' and Christians are not idolaters) did not correspond to the opinion expressed in the first volume of *Ma'adanei yom tov*.

In another respect, however, *Megilat eivah* presented non-Jews in an entirely different light than in his earlier work. In Heller's rabbinic works, 'gentiles' are always a broad, undifferentiated category. In a sermon that will be discussed in the next chapter, he explicitly stated in one place that 'There is no difference among any of mankind except Jacob alone; the others are all united.' But immediately he backed away from this extreme claim: 'Although today there are differences among them as well', he wrote, 'in ancient times . . . it was not so.'[57]

In *Megilat eivah*, however, he depicted the Christian characters as diverse individuals. Each character is to some degree a stereotype in himself; Heller's talents of literary characterization were limited, and the work was, one may suggest again, intended partly as comedy. The arrogant privy counsellor, the susceptible gaoler, the capricious Polish nobleman who appears in a later part of the memoir—each

[57] *Derush ḥidushei halevanah*, 38. The passage involves a contrast of Jacob and Esau, and Heller may have been apologetic about his use of 'Esau' as a symbol of all non-Jews, rather than merely Christians or Rome, as is customary. The Maharal distinguished sharply between Christianity and Islam: see above, p. 94. The notion of the uniformity of ancient paganism appears in Maimonides, *Guide*, iii. 29.

one is a well-known character type. However, they are different character types, with Heller allowing each one to act and even speak in character. In *Megilat eivah*, for the first time in his writings, Heller recognized non-Jews as individuals.[58]

A DAY OF REMEMBRANCE

The theological explanation that Heller gave for the deliverance of his books from the flames suggested that he regarded that event (or non-event) as a quasi-miracle, a 'shaking of the spheres', a special reward of the virtuous in defiance of astrological Fate. As in his plague sermon of 1625, this led Heller back again to the question of proper human response to divine action. Once again, as in 1625, Heller was concerned by the ambiguous quality of the experience of 'deliverance'. 'Deliverance' is not without a price, not without sorrow. In 1625, his sorrow had been for the sufferings of others; now it was for his own troubles. He had escaped with his life, but he had lost his wealth, his job, and his home.

Heller quoted a question that a sixteenth-century exegete, Eliezer Ashkenazi, had posed in his commentary on Esther. Since the victory of the Hasmonaeans involved much greater and more public miracles than the victory of the Jews over Haman, why does the Purim celebration include a feast, while the required Hanukah observances do not? Heller approved of Ashkenazi's answer: the joy of the Hasmonaean victories was less because there were so many Jewish victims of that war.[59]

As in 1625, Heller found expression for his mixed emotions in ritual innovation. 'Many of our people', he wrote, 'when they are saved from death, make a feast-day.' Unable to overlook his sorrow, however, Heller instituted a fast-day instead, as a family ritual. The fast would be observed on 5 Tamuz, the day on which he was arrested, from sunrise until after evening prayers. A family member who is sick or weak, or a pregnant or nursing woman, need not observe the fast, but must instead give some money to charity. This ritual should be observed by all of his descendants and all of their spouses in every generation, Heller wrote, 'until the coming of the messiah'.

[58] On the question of differentiated images of non-Jews among Ashkenazi Jews of this period, cf. H. H. Ben-Sasson, 'Jews and Christian Sectarians'; note the sympathy towards Anabaptists in A. David (ed.), *Hebrew Chronicle*, 8; N. Z. Davis, *Women on the Margins*, 40–1, 211.

[59] *Megilat eivah*, 36.

PART III

CHANGE AND DEFEAT 1631–1654

NINE

The Sermon

FROM PRAGUE TO POLAND

In the summer of 1631 Heller and his family joined the mass of emigrants and exiles whom the troubles of war and religious strife had cast on to the highways of Europe. Deprived of his position as rabbi of Prague, he resolved to seek new employment and to make a new life in Poland.[1] Before he left Prague, he preached a farewell sermon in the Meisel Synagogue. The Torah reading for the day included the story of the twelve men whom Moses sent to spy out the Land of Israel; Heller must have felt that he too was at the border of a new land.

From Prague, he went first to the Polish city of Lublin, where his 15-year-old son Abraham was to marry Esther, the daughter of Yehiel Luria. Yehiel's father, Solomon Luria, a doctor in Lublin, was a relative of the talmudist Solomon Luria. The Luria family laid claim to a lineage that they traced back to Rashi himself; no better-born family existed in Ashkenazi Jewish society.[2]

For Heller, these weeks in Lublin were something like a vacation or even a sabbatical, both institutions that were unknown in the Jewish communities of the seventeenth century. For the only time in his adult life, he was free from the responsibilities of work and also from those of managing a household. He was not a man to spend a month in idleness or merely enjoying the pleasures of the table or the game board. He could not be kept away long from books, and soon he was back to tutoring the bridegroom Abraham. Their topic was astronomy.

Father and son studied the workings of the Hebrew calendar, as explained by Maimonides in his *Mishneh torah*. When they came to the end of their sessions together, Heller was inspired to write a commentary on the material that they had

[1] By 'Poland' I frequently mean the Polish–Lithuanian Commonwealth, a kingdom that included various areas that were not ethnically Polish and are not today in Poland. About half of Heller's years in 'Poland' were spent in what is today the Ukraine. On the waves of expulsion of Protestants from Prague in the 1620s, see e.g. Palmitessa, 'House, Home, and Neighborhood', 374–5. On Jewish refugees in this period, see Hailperin, 'Jewish Refugees'.

[2] *Megilat eivah*, 36. On the Lurias, see A. Epstein, 'Luria Family'.

just studied, a commentary that he called *Parashat hahodesh* (Portion of the Month). In the introduction to the work, he addressed his son:

I know you well, [and I know] that your intention was . . . not to boast that you know more than other people your age or even older than you . . . but only to know and to understand God's commandments. As the sages have written . . . 'a man is commanded to reckon the seasons and the stars' (BT *Shabat* 75*a*). . . . We must recognize that [the stars] did not come into being by necessity or logical requirement or emanation, but God, who unites all things, gave to each one its unique movement, voluntarily and not out of the necessity of the required order. For behold, they have no order or nature.[3]

Heller was aware of the new astronomy of Copernicus and Tycho Brahe, as will shortly be seen; he was particularly aware of and concerned about Tycho's claim that the heavens are not eternal, as Aristotle believed, but changing. In *Parashat hahodesh*, however, there is no reference to the new astronomy. Maimonides' Ptolemaic-Aristotelian astronomy is the sole framework of explanation.[4]

What did Heller see, as he looked up from Lublin's narrow streets and observed the star-filled sky? Did he see the eternal spheres of Aristotle's cosmos, moving in their unchanging, circular paths, signalling to the wise astronomer the existence of a First Cause? Or did he see the changing celestial world of rising and falling stars, of spheres 'without order and nature'? Perhaps he saw the second, and perhaps he was afraid; but he assured his son that the chaos of the heavens was a sign of a higher Unity.

Heller's wife Rachel, who was surely not pleased with the move to Poland, returned from Lublin to Prague. The three youngest daughters had been left there; Rachel hoped to return, marry them off quickly, and then rejoin her husband in Poland. But again war interfered. In September 1631 the imperial troops were defeated by the Swedes, and the army of Saxony invaded Bohemia. By the time Rachel arrived in Vienna, Prague was under siege. She stayed with her married daughter Nechle in Vienna and waited. General Wallenstein, called out of retirement, defeated the Saxons in May 1632, and Rachel continued on to Prague where she matched her daughter Doberish with the grandson of Jacob Bassevi. In August 1632, after a year's separation she and her husband were reunited.

During this period Heller himself had gone to Brest-Litovsk in Lithuania, where his son Liva lived. In the autumn of 1631, the rabbi of Brest honoured Heller

[3] Introduction to 'Parashat hahodesh': MS Oxford-Bodleian Heb. 2271, fo. 23*a*–*b*.

[4] The same is true of the calendrical astronomy of the other Ashkenazi rabbis of Heller's generation; cf. Langermann, 'Astronomy'. The great Polish astronomer Jan Brożek, although he personally accepted the Copernican system, taught the Ptolemaic system in his classes at the University of Cracow: see Weintraub, 'Commonwealth', 23–4. On Brożek's contact with Jews, see Hailperin, 'Between Brożek and Delmedigo'.

by allowing him to give the most important sermon of the year, on the Sabbath of Repentance, immediately prior to Yom Kippur. 'I preached very well', Heller writes.[5]

'THE LESSENING OF THE MOON'

Heller was proud of the sermons that he gave; he wrote some of them out, and to some he gave titles. One surviving example is entitled *Derush ḥidushei halevanah* (Sermon of Comments on the Creation of the Moon). It was written some time after Heller left Prague.[6]

According to a legend in the Babylonian Talmud, the sun and the moon were once equal. For that reason, in the story of the creation of the sun and the moon in the book of Genesis, they are initially called 'the two great lights': both were at first equally great. But the moon asked God, 'Can two kings wear a single crown?' (that is, how can the sun and I rule equally together?). So God ordered the moon to lessen itself. On this account, the moon is called 'the lesser light' later in the same verse. The moon, however, protested to God, 'Master of the universe, must I make myself smaller because I suggested to you something sensible?' So God conceded, 'Very well. Go and rule by day as well as by night.'[7]

In his sermon, Heller combined the exegesis of this peculiar and difficult talmudic legend with a discussion of the new astronomy of Tycho Brahe. The new astronomy was at once exciting and disturbing to men like Heller, brought up in the Aristotelian world-view. One may conjecture that its topic was brought to his mind by his study of astronomy with his son in Lublin.[8]

He also took the occasion to debate with his teacher, the Maharal, on the meaning of individuality and difference. The legend also allowed Heller to reflect on the consequences of slander and *maḥloket*, and on the religious problem of suffering,

[5] *Megilat eivah*, 36–7. In the Yiddish *Megilat eivah*, Heller writes that he delivered an 'important' (*ḥashuvdike*) sermon in Brest-Litovsk.

[6] The sermon is not dated, but a reference to the Maharal as 'r. liva perag' (*Derush ḥidushei halevanah*, 15) suggests that it was written after Heller left Prague. It is remotely possible that the sermon was delivered earlier, during Heller's years in Vienna. I published an earlier version of this and the following sections of this chapter in an article entitled 'Ashkenazic Rationalism', which was in turn based on a lecture delivered at a conference held in May 1995 entitled Jewish Responses to Early Modern Science: Jewish Treatments of Science from *De revolutionibus* to the *Principia* and Beyond, and sponsored by Tel Aviv University and the Van Leer Foundation in Jerusalem.

[7] See BT *Ḥul.* 60*b*; cf. Ginzberg, *Legends*, i. 23–4; and in the notes, v. 34–6 n. 100. My translation is based on that of William Braude, in his translation of Bialik and Ravnitsky (eds.), *The Book of Legends*, 11.

[8] On Jewish responses to science in the early modern period, see Ruderman, *Jewish Thought and Scientific Discovery*. On Ashkenazi attitudes to the new astronomy, see J. Davis, 'Ashkenazic Rationalism'; Efron, 'Irenism and Natural Philosophy'; D. Fishman, 'Rabbi Moshe Isserles'; and Reiner, 'Attitude of Ashkenazi Society', and the literature cited there.

loss, and change, questions of great personal relevance to him. The extensive homily he composed moves back and forth between scientific, ethical, and theological topics, and brings together many of the themes considered in this study.

Heller began with the question of interpretative norms. How literally should talmudic legends such as this one be taken? Heller focused particularly on the question of kabbalistic interpretation, as he had done elsewhere. The legend of the lessening of the moon, he noted, plays an important role in kabbalah. The moon is kabbalistically interpreted as the Shekhinah, or Malkhut, the lowest of the ten *sefirot*. The 'lessening of the moon' therefore parallels or represents what is called 'the exile of the Shekhinah', namely the disruption, as it were, of the intra-divine unity of the higher and lower *sefirot*, and particularly the separation of the *sefirah* of the Shekhinah from the *sefirah* of Tiferet, symbolized by the sun. Heller referred to the chapter on the lessening of the moon in Cordovero's *Pardes rimonim*. (It is worth emphasizing again that he considered Cordovero, not Isaac Luria, to be the most important recent kabbalist.)

As he had insisted in *Tosafot yom tov* and again in *Ma'adanei melekh*, Heller reasserted that every biblical and talmudic passage, however difficult its plain sense may seem, must also have a valid, public, non-kabbalistic meaning. It may be given an esoteric kabbalistic interpretation as well, but that cannot be the only meaning of the passage.[9] Furthermore, he decried those who had begun to discuss kabbalistic secrets in public sermons:

> We have no interest in expounding hidden things in public. . . . Although there are certain preachers who permit themselves to preach on the topic of *gilgul*, because, as Rabbi Isaac Abarbanel explained, certain ancient philosophers [i.e. Pythagoras] believed in it, I do not agree with this lenient view, because those philosophers, although they may have believed in [*gilgul*], did not know whose, or what, or why, or on account of what [souls are reincarnated], or many hidden things.

Heller cited Levi ibn Habib, a sixteenth-century Sefardi rabbi who had also prohibited kabbalistic sermons. He continued:

> Even worse are certain preachers who make *gilgulim* according to their own arguments, from hints that they find for themselves in Scripture. Those who hear them accept these hints as if they were handed down from Sinai, but it is not so.[10]

Without naming names (to which he was often averse) Heller was clearly referring here to kabbalistic preachers of the school of Nathan ben Solomon Spira, *rosh*

[9] On the kabbalistic interpretation of the legend, cf. I. Horowitz, *Shenei luḥot haberit*, iii. 32*b* ('Torah or' on Exodus). Horowitz, like Heller, insists on the literal truth as well as the kabbalistic significance of the legend, as discussed in Ch. 3. Cf. *MYT* (*MM*), *Ber.* p. 5 n. 50. Heller stresses there and elsewhere that every passage in rabbinic literature has a public, *peshat* interpretation. His interpretation quotes 'natural scientists' on the topic of the factors that determine the sex of a child.

[10] *Derush ḥidushei halevanah*, 3.

yeshivah in Cracow and the author of a kabbalistic work called *Megaleh amukot* (Revealer of the Depths). Spira was extraordinarily concerned with the question of *gilgul*, and the scriptural proofs that he offers are often based on *gematriyot*, the numerical values of letters.[11]

Heller turned the tables on the kabbalists in this sermon. Far from giving a kabbalistic interpretation of the talmudic passage, he provided instead a non-kabbalistic interpretation of two Zohar texts on the lessening of the moon. The Zohar, he demonstrated, like any other midrash, can be and must be interpreted in simple, transparent terms in a public sermon.[12]

Having rejected a kabbalistic line of interpretation, Heller discussed another exegetical method—philosophical-allegorical interpretation. Did the moon really shrink? Did it truly have these little conversations with God? Or was this only a fable, an allegory? Isaac Arama (*c.*1420–94) and Eliezer Ashkenazi (1513–85), Bible exegetes with a philosophical tendency, offered allegorical interpretations of the legend, which Heller summarized. Arama suggested two interpretations, both allegorical. In the first, he interpreted the story as a discussion in which God refutes the Epicurean philosophers, symbolized by the moon. In the second, the moon symbolizes the Jewish people and the story is an allegory of Jewish history; this was also the view taken by Eliezer Ashkenazi. But Heller rejected the allegorical approach as well. 'My heart tells me', he wrote, 'that the reader himself will understand how distant this is from the meaning of these passages.'[13]

Ashkenazi Judaism had a history of opposition to allegorical interpretation, regarding allegory throughout most of the Middle Ages as a Christian mode of interpretation and a source of heresy. Alongside this, however, there was a series of Ashkenazi efforts at allegorical interpretation, beginning with those of the Hasidei Ashkenaz in medieval Germany, and continuing, closer to Heller's time, with Moses Isserles' interpretation of the book of Esther. Outright opposition to allegorical interpretation was no longer possible by Heller's day—too many rabbis of unimpeachable orthodoxy had made use of it—but a certain wariness, like Heller's, was common.[14]

As to the truth of the legend, Heller wrote:

Whether all the details of this passage are true, whether these questions and answers occurred between the moon and the Holy One, blessed be He, in this way, or whether it is only an imaginative interpretation [of Scripture], out of which one may derive lessons—

[11] On Spira, see Horodetsky, *Jewish Mysticism*, iv. 129–40, and Liebes, 'The Prophet Jonah', 274–303.

[12] *Derush ḥidushei halevanah*, 9–11. The non-kabbalistic interpretation of the Zohar is quite common in sermons of this period. See e.g. Chajes, *Paḥad yitsḥak* or Nantua, *Kol yehudah*.

[13] *Derush ḥidushei halevanah*, 25.

[14] See Davis, 'Philosophy, Dogma, and Exegesis', 212–20; Elbaum, 'R. Judah Loewe's Attitude'; Kaplan, 'Rationalism and Rabbinic Culture', 224–60.

these possibilities depend on whether the celestial bodies are rational living bodies or not. . . . If, as Maimonides believes, the spheres and the celestial bodies are rational living things, then it may be that these questions and answers occurred in reality and not only in the imagination of the author of the passage speaking for a certain useful purpose or purposes. . . . Or else, if they are not rational living things, then the author of the passage did conceive these things in his imagination. In either case, everything is according to its simple sense.[15]

He thus expressed neutrality on the issue of literal truth. He was willing to treat the story as a fable, and argued that its literal truth was largely immaterial: his own exegesis focused on its ethical meaning, as will be seen. Nevertheless, he insists that it is neither a kabbalistic allegory nor a philosophical one, and that the whole story, or at least some historical kernel, might be literally true. The moon is the real moon, the sun the real sun, and the legend is in some sense astronomically correct: the moon was truly lessened early in the history of the universe.[16]

MIDRASHIC NATURAL HISTORY

Let us digress briefly here from Heller's sermon, and turn to another, earlier passage, in which he addressed questions of the relation of Torah and science, and of change in nature.

In 1625 or 1626, when Heller was rabbi in Vienna, his wife's cousin, a doctor named Aaron Lucerna who was a graduate of the University of Padua, came to him with a conundrum.[17] Lucerna brought him a fish, an animal with the unlikely name, so Heller wrote, of the *stincus marinus* and asked him whether this fish was kosher or not. Heller wrote:

The *stincus marinus* . . . is found in the Spanish Sea. It is poisonous, but pharmacists know ways to remove the poison, and then they make medicines from its flesh. It has a spine and its head is wide and it has scales over all its body, but it has no fins at all: only four legs, like the legs of a land animal. . . . And I was very puzzled by this.[18]

[15] *Derush ḥidushei halevanah*, 29. Cf. Maimonides, *Guide*, ii. 5.

[16] Compare the position on literal interpretation taken by Eliezer Ashkenazi in his Bible commentary *Ma'asei hashem*, discussed in Cooper, 'Sixteenth Century Biblical Commentary'.

[17] On Aaron Lucerna, see Daniel Carpi, 'Jews with Medical Degrees', 89–90. A letter that Lucerna wrote to his wife appears in Landau and Wachstein (eds.), *Jüdische Privatbriefe*, 4–7, and is translated in Kobler (ed. and trans.), *Letters*, ii. 456–8. Aaron's father was the private doctor of Emperor Matthias I. As Hailperin notes (MS, p. 26), a number of medical, philosophical, and astronomical manuscripts owned by Aaron's brother, Leo Lucerna, are listed in A. Z. Schwarz, *Die hebräischen Handschriften*.

[18] *MYT (MM) Ḥul.*, 335 n. 5. Cf. Teomim, *Peri megadim* on *Shulḥan arukh*, 'Yoreh de'ah' 83: 3. Cf. also D. Kaufmann, 'Jair Hayyim Bacharach', 511. I have discussed the case in 'Ashkenazic Rationalism', 612–15, and from another point of view in my article, 'Philosophy and the Law'.

What made the case a puzzling one was a certain passage in the Talmud. The Bible and Jewish law declare that every kosher fish must have both scales and fins. The Talmud, in one place, adds the observation that everything that has scales also has fins; hence everything that has scales is kosher. The *stincus marinus* had scales, but where were its fins? It had none; apparently, a living contradiction of the Talmud.

Heller wrote that he gave Lucerna two answers, an immediate answer and then a more considered one. His first answer was that this fish must be a new type of fish that had not existed at the time of the Talmud. He bolstered his argument with a reference to a passage in the midrashic text *Genesis Rabbah* that speaks of the creation of new seas. The problem of fossils, as it was discussed in the seventeenth century, connected the question of new animal species to that of new seas.[19]

Just as they have spoken in *Genesis Rabbah* of the seas that the Holy One, blessed be He, did not create during the six days of creation, so this species came into being after our sages of blessed memory received the principle that 'whatever has scales, has fins'.

Heller's first explanation thus offered a story, a history, indeed a natural history, based on a talmudic text: in a word, a midrashic natural history. Isaak Heinemann's characterization of midrash as 'creative historiography' comes to mind.[20] His second answer created instead a verbal or taxonomic distinction, which he used to reinterpret the talmudic text. Subtle distinctions were very much favoured among Ashkenazi rabbis in this period, and it is no wonder that Heller ultimately preferred his second answer. The distinction was between 'fish' and 'sea animals'. Every 'fish' that has scales has fins. But the *stincus marinus*, although it was a 'sea animal', was not a 'fish', and the talmudic dictum therefore did not apply to it. Speaking from the point of view of later science, it would appear that here Heller had intuitively reached the correct solution, for the *stincus* is clearly a reptile, perhaps a type of skink.

The development, or as it were the evolution, of new species of animals was not a traditional Jewish concept. Nor, two centuries before Darwin, was it a focus of religious controversy. Heller's comment suggested a (surprisingly modern) picture of an animal world subject to historical change. On the other hand, he never considered the possibility that, unknown to the authors of the Talmud, in ancient times *stinci marini* (if that is the plural) were already swimming and living out their

[19] The reference appears to be to *Genesis Rabbah* 42: 5, on the destruction of Sodom and the creation of the Dead Sea. Cf. Gans, *Tsemaḥ david*, pt. 2, first item (ed. Breuer, p. 168). It is hard to see why Heller would support an assertion about new species with a prooftext that speaks of new seas, were it not for the fossil connection. Heller may mean to suggest that the animal world was created with pure species, but that subsequent joining and combining has created monsters and mixed species such as this stincus.

[20] Heinemann, *The Midrashic Method*. On Heinemann's theory of midrash, see Boyarin, *Intertextuality*, 1–11.

brief aquatic lives in the Spanish Sea. Heller did not allow the possibility, that is, that the *stincus marinus* had been newly discovered.

ON THE NEW ASTRONOMY

We return to the history of the moon. In his sermon, Heller worked up gradually to an account of the moon's origin. He first suggested interpretations of the non-talmudic accounts of the moon's lessening. Thus, for example, he interpreted the versions of the story in the Zohar (reading the Zohar non-kabbalistically, as he had declared that he would) to mean that the moon was indeed physically lowered from its original orbit, and that it also suffered a loss of its 'influence'.[21]

The talmudic legend, the normative meaning of Scripture, and likewise the astronomical fact, Heller declared, goes beyond the account in the Zohar. Not only was the moon physically removed from a higher orbit to a lower one, but it suffered a loss of brightness, and furthermore became physically smaller than the sun. It will not escape the attentive reader that Heller has read a good deal into the talmudic passage.[22]

The view that Heller attributed to the Talmud conflicted, he knew, with the Aristotelian view that the stars are eternal and unchanging. 'The substance of the spheres cannot be the object of any action and cannot change', Joseph ben Isaac Halevi had written in *Givat hamoreh*; the Aristotelian moon does not have any 'origin' in the chronological sense.[23]

Heller came back to the question, therefore, of the literal truth of the story. According to the teachings of Aristotelian science, the talmudic story, as Heller has interpreted it, cannot be literally true. He therefore grounded the literal belief in the story in the new astronomy of Tycho Brahe and his followers, 'the modern scholars [*aḥaronim*], close to our time', as he wrote. Heller left the 'modern' astronomers unnamed; Ashkenazi rabbis were extremely reluctant to cite the names of Christians in their works. But, quoting the view attributed in the Talmud (*Pesaḥim* 94*b*) to the 'sages of Israel' that *galgal kavua umazalot ḥozerin*, 'the orb is fixed but the stars move', Heller endorsed the new astronomers' conception of changing heavens and permeable spheres.[24]

Heller's framework of discourse was exegetical. Ideas that were not to be found in some way in ancient or in medieval Jewish texts had no foothold in his world.

[21] *Derush ḥidushei halevanah*, 9–11. [22] Ibid. 49–50. [23] *Givat hamoreh*, 8*a*.

[24] *Derush ḥidushei halevanah*, 52. The text at this point was difficult for the editor to read, and many words are missing; nevertheless, the general trend of the argument is not hard to follow. I discuss this passage at greater length in 'Ashkenazic Rationalism', 620–1. Note Gans's apology for naming non-Jews in *Neḥmad vena'im*, 9*b*. Heller's reference to Tycho was first brought to scholarly attention, so far as I know, in Panitz, 'New Heavens', 30.

Read into the talmudic text, however, the changing Tychonian heavens could take their place as the capstone of Heller's sermon.[25]

Heller did not endorse Copernicus's view that the earth revolves around the sun. In fact, the entire question of geocentrism or helicocentrism does not seem to have interested him much, and his sermon assumed a geocentric view of the universe. What concerned him, rather, was whether the celestial bodies are unchanging crystalline spheres, or whether the stars and planets are distinct from the spheres, and hence subject to change. Following Tycho and Kepler, he asserted that they do change.

Heller was regarded by his Jewish contemporaries as an expert in astronomy. Menahem Mendl Krochmal wrote, 'The paths of the sky are well-known to . . . the author of *Tosafot yom tov*, and [he is] expert in the secrets of calculating the calendar.'[26] Heller was interested in scientific questions and aware of some of the scientific controversies and problems of his day. His discussion of the *stincus marinus* suggests some knowledge of seventeenth-century thinking about the problem of fossils. In another passage in his writings he quotes the twelfth-century philosopher Judah Halevi's attack in the *Kuzari* on alchemists who claim to be able to measure heat. While his attack was misguided (thermometers were not impossible; Galileo is sometimes credited with the invention), Heller's concern for an issue at the forefront of physics in his day is impressive.[27]

The dimensions of Heller's scientific knowledge should not be exaggerated. Astronomy was the only science that he knew at all well. He knew nothing, for example, of the new mathematics of the sixteenth century; there is not even any evidence that he knew algebra.

He was ambivalent, moreover, about reading books written by Christians, as discussed above. The Ptolemaic-Aristotelian astronomy that he learned as a young man in the 1590s was based largely, perhaps entirely, on medieval Hebrew scientific texts. (He does, it is true, refer in one place to astral observations that he made himself.[28]) He seems to have known no Latin,[29] and his knowledge of the new astronomy may have been limited to the information available in two Hebrew books, *Sefer elim* (Book of the Mighty Ones) by Joseph Solomon Delmedigo

[25] Cf. Howell, 'Role of Biblical Interpretation'; Grant, *In Defense*; Kelter, 'The Refusal to Accommodate'. Like Heller, Cardinal Bellarmine opposed the doctrine of the perfect ether on exegetical grounds.

[26] *sod ha'ibur*; cf. BT *Ber.* 58*b*. From Krochmal, *She'elot uteshuvot tsemaḥ tsedek*, no. 14, quoted in M. Roth, 'Notes', 108.

[27] Heller, *Torat ha'asham*, 103–4. I have discussed the passage in 'Ashkenazic Rationalism', 610–12. In *Sefer elim* by Joseph Solomon Delmedigo, a student of Galileo, a book which Heller had read, there is a short discussion (p. 180 of the section 'Gevurot hashem') of the expansion of liquids when heated, together with a brief description and diagram of an early thermometer.

[28] MS Oxford-Bodleian Heb. 2271, fos. 52*b*–53*a*.

[29] See above, Ch. 5 n. 26.

(1591–1655), a Jewish student of Galileo, published in 1629, and *Magen david* (Star of David) by David Gans.

This entire final passage of Heller's sermon is in fact based on a passage in David Gans's book. Gans, too, associated Tycho's new astronomy with the talmudic saying that 'the orb is fixed but the stars move'. Indeed, Gans claimed that Tycho himself had cited the talmudic rabbis as precursors.[30]

Heller read Gans's book in manuscript in 1612, but he was only gradually convinced of Tycho's position. This may be seen from two significantly different comments that he made on the nature of comets, one in 1614 and the other in 1628: In *Tosafot yom tov*, published in 1614, Heller cited only Maimonides' view of the nature of comets: the Aristotelian view that comets are not stars, that they are atmospheric, not celestial, phenomena. Discussing the same text in *Ma'adanei melekh*, however, in 1628, Heller repeated the Aristotelian view but added a possible alternative opinion, namely that comets are indeed celestial objects (a view he attributed to Rashi). Heller's opinions had no doubt been influenced in the meantime by the well-publicized dispute between Kepler and Galileo on the topic of comets between 1618 and 1623[31] (it is at least remotely possible that Heller had actually met Kepler during the latter's years in Prague[32]).

In 1598 Heller had affirmed his belief in the perfect ether and the unchanging spheres,[33] and reaffirmed it in 1614. In 1628 he expressed doubt. In the 1630s, in middle age, he finally embraced the notion of change in the heavens.

ON CHANGE

Two types of change are thus discussed together in Heller's sermon. The first is the lowering, darkening, and shrinking of the moon; the second is the discovery of astral change by the new astronomers. Heller affirmed the first, but claimed that

[30] See Gans, *Neḥmad vena'im*, sect. 25, p. 16*b*, discussed in Neher, *Jewish Thought and the Scientific Revolution*, 216–28. Cf. Isserles, *Meḥir yayin* on Esther 2: 8.

[31] See *MYT* (*MM*), *Ber*. p. 74 n. 10, written in 1628; contrast *Tos YT*, *Ber*. 9: 2. The passages are discussed at greater length in Davis, 'Ashkenazic Rationalism', 615–16. Both theories of the nature of comets are discussed in Delmedigo, *Sefer elim*, in the section 'Ma'ayan ḥatum', 71–3, but that work appeared a full year after Heller's *Ma'adanei melekh*. Note, however, that Delmedigo was writing on the topic of comets in letters as early as 1619 or 1620. See Barzilay, *Del Medigo*, 161–3.

[32] Kepler escaped the plague of 1606 in the village of Kolín. See Caspar, *Kepler*, 177. He was cheek by jowl with the leaders of the Prague Jewish community, perhaps including Heller, who were also escaping the plague. One of them was inspired to write a work on the Jewish calendar: MS Oxford-Bodleian Heb. 746/4. Cf. Ephraim of Luntshits's introduction to *Amudei shesh*.

[33] Commentary on *Beḥinat olam*, 5: 3: 16 (p. 58).

the second was not altogether real: the new astronomers had merely rediscovered what the biblical and talmudic authors already knew.

As described in Chapter 2, several Jewish scholars in Prague, Heller among them, expressed their belief in intellectual progress, the dwarf on the giant's shoulders.[34] For instance, shortly after his exile from Prague in 1612, Joseph ben Isaac declared in a sermon in Brest-Litovsk that the science of astronomy was still open to improvement. The discovery of the New World, he argued, had revealed one of the deficiencies in medieval cosmology: '[astronomy] has not yet been perfected as have the other sciences. . . . We have found inhabited lands in a region, called the "New World", which the astronomers had stated could not be inhabited'.[35]

Heller echoed this theme of intellectual progress in several places in his writings. He argued, for instance, that since the Hebrew grammar by Samuel Archivolti was the most recent, it was also the most dependable: 'Since "the last is always dearest", therefore it is an established principle in all the laws of the Torah that "the law follows the most recent authority".[36] . . . And similarly in every generation and in every science.'[37] However, truth to tell, Heller's sense of progressive change was weak. For instance, the process of technological progress, which forms so large a part of our sense of the passage of time, seems not to have been important to him.[38] He did not give speeches like that of the worthy Dornavius, rector of the gymnasium in Görlitz in Silesia, who in 1617 spoke in praise of 'all manner of scientific, scholarly, technological and industrial progress . . . [including] the telescope . . . logarithms . . . exploration . . . [and] the pocket watch'.[39] He was unaware that eyeglasses and astrolabes were medieval inventions and hence should not appear in mishnaic lists of implements.[40] However, he was aware of certain socio-

[34] See above, pp. 46–7.

[35] *Ketonet pasim*, ch. 9, 13*a*–*b*. On the scientific issue, see Headley, 'Venetian Celebration'. Joseph's argument here echoes the Maharal's argument for the superiority of Torah, in *Netivot olam*, 'Netiv hatorah', ch. 14. The Maharal contrasts the disagreement among the astronomers with the authoritative tradition of the Torah, which does not admit of disagreement. See the discussion of the passage in Neher, *Jewish Thought and the Scientific Revolution*, 210–11.

[36] On this legal principle, see above, Ch. 7 n. 26.

[37] *Leket shoshanim*, MS Opp. 703, fo. 122*a*. Note also *Tos YT*, *Avot* 4: 1, where Heller quotes the Maharal to the effect that a good student will naturally know more than his teacher.

[38] Contrast, two generations after Heller, Glueckel's sense of historical change, including both cultural and economic or technological change: see Glueckel bat Judah Leib, *Life*, 14 (manners), 15, 32 (prices, taxes, and wealth), 32 (mail coaches). Heller's contemporary Delmedigo uses human technical progress as an argument for creation (if mankind has existed an infinite length of time, the sciences should already have been perfected). See *Sefer elim*, 86. (A similar argument is used by Gersonides: see Sirat, *History of Jewish Philosophy*, 306.)

[39] Weeks, *Boehme*, 96.

[40] *Tos YT*, *Kel.* 16: 8 (astrolabe), 30: 2 (eyeglasses). Note the comment of Lipschütz, *Tiferet yisra'el* on the latter passage.

logical differences between the Jews of his own day and their talmudic and medieval ancestors.[41] He believed, for example, that Jewish women of his day were better educated than those of the twelfth century, the time of the Tosafists.[42]

There was, however, only one epochal, historical change that was truly meaningful to Heller: the beginning of the exile and loss of Jewish sovereignty after the end of the biblical period.[43] Nor did he foresee any epochal change before the coming of the messiah. He could thus express confidence that the family ritual that he had created should be observed until that time.

More vivid, then, than his awareness of epochal change was his sense of the impermanence, change, and flux that permeate the world—the random succession of years of dearth or plenty, of weak or strong monarchs. That theme dominates his first work, his commentary on *Beḥinat olam*: 'There is no man who is not subject to the terrors and frights of unfaithful time, as it says in *Musar hapilosofim*, in the letter of King Alexander to his mother.'[44] Time, time itself, is terrifying; time brings all men low, changes all fortunes.[45]

[41] See e.g. *MalYT* 3: 11: 'the nature of the lands or of the times is different'; *MalYT* 288: 5 (meaning of dreams). Cf. *MYT* (*MM*), *Ber.*, p. 68 n. 3 (danger of 'pairs'), and *MYT* (*DH*), *Ber.*, p. 75 n. 62: our bath-houses are constructed differently from talmudic bath-houses and are safer than they were. On historicist arguments in halakhah (the halakhic argument of 'changes in nature', which underlies Heller's argument here), see J. Roth, *The Halakhic Process*, 237–47. On the general question of historicism among 17th-c. talmudists, cf. Safran, 'Leone da Modena's Historical Thinking'.

[42] Today, he wrote, most Jewish women can read Hebrew letters and know some Hebrew words: *MYT* (*DH*), *Ber.*, p. 59 n. 15, and *MalYT* 199. On views of halakhic change among the 16th- and 17th-c. Polish rabbinate, see H. H. Ben-Sasson, *Theory and Practice*, 19 ff. According to Isaiah Horowitz, the tendency towards stringency is a law of Jewish history, a process that will culminate in the messianic era: I. Horowitz, *Shenei luḥot haberit*, i. 18*b*–19*a* (discussed in Ben-Sasson, *Theory and Practice*, 19–21); cf. Zimmer, *Embers of the Sages*, 258. Note also Horowitz's concept of stages of the Torah and the messianic Torah: *Shenei luḥot haberit* i. 43*a*.

[43] Cf. above, Ch. 8 n. 57, on Heller's contrast between the unity of ancient non-Jews and the diversity of contemporary ones.

[44] Commentary on *Beḥinat olam*, 1: 1: 14 (p. 11). In *TosYT*, *Yad.* 4: 5, Heller quotes Maimonides' comment that Hebrew square lettering is called *ashurit* ('Assyrian') because it is happy (*me'ushar*), in the sense that it does not change. Cf. *TosYT*, *Avot* 3: 5.

[45] On the same theme, the poem *Begidat hazeman* ('The Treachery of Time'), by a certain Matityah, was published in Prague in 1615. The theme is a favourite of Baroque authors: see e.g. Hill and Caracciolo-Trejo (eds.), *Baroque Poetry*, 174–220: 'The passage of the years, the documentation of the decay of physique, awareness of all that represented by such symbols as the clock, the sundial, the hourglass, these are the subjects which seem most to have fired the imagination.' Cf. Burke, 'Tradition and Experience', 137–44. See also the poem on time by the Lithuanian Karaite scholar Joseph b. Mordechai Malinowski (*fl.* 1600), 'Ma'asar'. Malinowski wrote the poem in Turkic; it was translated into Hebrew by his pupil, Zerah b. Nathan.

THE MAHARAL AND THE ILLUSION OF SELF

For Heller, the astronomical event—the lessening of the physical size of the moon, and its lowering into its present orbit—is only part of the story of 'the lessening of the moon', and perhaps the less important part at that. The story also has a moral component. As he wrote in his introduction, the attribution to the moon of moral qualities, thought, intention, speech, and sin may not be literally true, but they are an essential part of the story. Here he disagreed with an interpretation of the legend given by the Maharal, calling attention to the disagreement by apologizing for it elaborately. By contrast it may be recalled that in the passage in *Tosafot yom tov* on the humanity of non-Jews, Heller had not named the Maharal as the interpreter with whom he disagreed. Twenty years had given him self-confidence.

Since I know that . . . the great sage, our teacher Liva Prague, of blessed memory, studied every science, I opened his book *Gur aryeh* [Lion Cub]. And I found what I sought, for he explains the passage [in BT *Ḥulin*]. But [his explanation] did not fill my desire. Therefore I shall present his words and answer him. Although 'one does not answer the lion after his death' (BT *Gitin* 83*b*), 'it is Torah and study I must' (BT *Berakhot* 62*a*). I took the example of our forefathers and our rabbis of blessed memory in my hand, that every later one turns to the earlier one and if he has an answer in his hand, he should not be silent or refrain from answering; and those who see will choose the best.[46]

Heller's disagreement with the Maharal was over God's first intention in creating the moon. The Maharal's view is that God first intended that the moon and sun should be equal or indeed identical. It was only the moon's actions, its sins, that frustrated that intention and caused the moon to be diminished. Heller's position, however, was that God's first intention was to create the moon as it is now, distinct from and lesser than the sun. As he phrases it, 'At the beginning of the [divine] thought, it was intended by Him, may He be exalted, that there should be lack and lessening. And at the time of action it was made so.'[47] And again: 'The spelling of the biblical text [the Masorah] points clearly to my interpretation . . . that the lessening was necessary even if she [the moon] had not complained.'[48] Thus, according to Heller, evil and suffering, lack and inequality are necessary and divinely willed concomitants of the process of creation. They are not the result of sin.

The disagreement between Heller and the Maharal was not 'factual'—did the moon sin or not? Heller agreed with the Maharal that (in the legend) the moon did sin, and, likewise, that people sin. The question here is one of causation. Was the lessening of the moon a punishment for a sin that the moon committed? Heller claimed that it was not.

[46] *Derush ḥidushei halevanah*, 15. [47] Ibid. 49. [48] Ibid. 50.

The question here is in fact nothing less than the theological problem of suffering. The Maharal argued that suffering should ultimately be understood as punishment for sin. Heller denied this. Suffering, decline, and 'lessening' are the divinely decreed destiny of all material beings. They do not depend on and are not caused by sin; nor can they ultimately be prevented by righteous actions. Heller's position resembles that of Maimonides: the limitations of matter are the ultimate explanation for both suffering and moral evil.[49]

Although Heller's explicit disagreement here is with the Maharal, he was surely aware that he was disagreeing as well with kabbalists such as Isaiah Horowitz. Death, Horowitz wrote, is not the natural fate of man. Man's nature is to be immortal; only sin causes death. In *Tosafot yom tov*, Heller took issue with this paradoxical view of death, and, implicitly, he does so here again.[50]

The problem of suffering is perhaps the central intellectual problem of Judaism. It was a field crowded by Heller's day with many suggestions and conceptualizations.[51] He found room, though, to add a special contribution: the notion that before Adam's sin, even before Adam's creation, there was already suffering and lessening, namely, the lessening of the moon.[52]

The Maharal's view is perhaps more profound than Heller's. We should not take too simplistic a view of the Maharal's assertion that the moon's lessening was punishment for its sin. The conflicts over kabbalah and within kabbalah, as noted above, were in part conflicts over conceptions of the self. The Maharal asserts that the primordial sin, the sin of the moon, is the illusion of self. For him, the goal of life is spiritual self-annihilation. To grasp the Torah is to abandon the illusion of self. The moon, asserting itself to be separate from the sun, declared itself to be less than the sun. The sin carries its punishment within it.[53]

For Heller, however, the self, which is symbolized here by the separation of the moon from the sun, the experiencing, suffering, historical self, is no sin. It is a divinely willed reality.

THE ACCEPTANCE OF SUFFERING

But if the primordial sin is not self-consciousness, then what is it? What sin did the moon commit? (Heller, to repeat, accepted that the moon did commit a sin.) What is sinful in the moon's query, 'Can two kings wear the same crown?'

[49] Compare Heller's disagreement with the Maharal in *Tos YT*, *Avot* 4: 11.

[50] *Tos YT*, *Avot* 4: 22; *Shenei luḥot haberit*, i. 17*b*.

[51] See e.g. Elman, 'Suffering'; Kraemer, *Responses*; Leaman, *Evil and Suffering*.

[52] Heller also discusses the problem of the suffering of the righteous in *Tos YT*, *Kid.* 1: 10 (the righteous are punished to perfect their souls); *Avot* 5: 19 (the righteous are content with little).

[53] Cf. Safran, 'Maharal and Early Hasidism', 56.

For Heller, the sin was the moon's refusal to accept her condition, her misfortune, her refusal of what in medieval Hebrew is called *kabalat yisurin* ('acceptance of suffering'). *Kabalat yisurin* did not mean for Heller, as it did for some Ashkenazi rabbis of his day, voluntary asceticism of self-inflicted pain, fasting or lashes or rolling in the snow.[54] Rather, it meant patient acceptance of the suffering and pain that life brings to each of us, whether we want them or not.[55] The lessening of the moon, as noted, is a parable of the problem of evil; not unnaturally, Heller associated it with the figure of Job. Both the moon and Job were made to suffer without any intervening sin; but both of them, according to Heller, refused to accept their suffering as they should have, and that was a sin.

But the moon then added a further sin, of incitement and divisiveness, of *kitrug* and *maḥloket*. The moon, in Heller's interpretation, asked for the sun to be reduced in its place. In the pattern that he found in the legend of the moon's lessening, misfortune (*yisurin*) engenders envy, and envy engenders enmity and hatred.

For Heller, the causal nexus between suffering and sin is the place where, more than any other, human free will operates. Through the acceptance of suffering, we break the circle. Refusing to react to suffering with sin we do not end suffering, but we may end sin.

The manuscript of the *Derush*, near the end, where Heller discusses the subject of *maḥloket* most fully, was so damaged that its nineteenth-century editor Shemariah Zuckerman, a descendant of Heller's, could neither read nor reconstruct many of the words. However, as he remarked, it was not difficult to grasp the sense of Heller's comment.[56] Heller writes:

> Just as [*Genesis Rabbah* 4: 8 explains that] on the second day, Scripture does not say 'it was good' at all, because *maḥloket* was created on that day, as it is written, ['And let it divide the waters from the waters' (Gen. 1: 6)], so I say that on account of the complaint [of the moon], which is . . . the lights are not mentioned in the same verse as 'it was good'. . . .
>
> And the midrash that I have mentioned ends: '[If concerning a *maḥloket*, namely the creation of the firmament] which was a benefit for the world and its inhabitants [Scripture does not say, "and it was good"], how much more so would this be true of [a *maḥloket* that is harmful] to the world?'[57]

The sermon doubtless ended with the standard peroration on messianic themes. The text is lost, but it is easy to imagine the form that it took: the hope that, in the

[54] See Elbaum, *Penance and Penitence*.

[55] 'Bontsche the Silent', in I. L. Peretz's story of that name, is a later literary representation of this religious ideal. As a modern liberal or socialist, Peretz was ambivalent about its value.

[56] *Derush ḥidushei halevanah*, 54.

[57] Ibid. 53.

messianic future, the moon would be restored to its former place and glory, and with it Israel and man.

A lengthy sermon like this moves in part through associative connections that are loose and subjective. Heller drew many of his deepest personal concerns into the sermon: the teachings of the Maharal, the legitimacy of a sense of self, the problem of suffering, and here the sin of *maḥloket*. The form of the sermon allowed him to address these concerns with the guidance of Scripture.

It is clear that the pattern that Heller found here in the talmudic legend is identical to that which he found in his own experiences in 1629, as he narrated them in *Megilat eivah*, namely misfortune engendering division. The moon symbolizes Jacob, David, and by extension, the Jewish people. Here he returned quietly to the allegorical mode of interpretation that he had earlier rejected.

The stories in the Torah testify concerning [Jacob], and likewise concerning David, in the stories about him and also in his Psalms, how many evils and hardships (Ps. 71: 20) occurred to him. By their nature, they rose and fell and were overtaken by misfortunes, like the moon, that now shines and now is dark.[58]

Heller did not say, but we may understand, that, at some level, the moon also symbolized his opponents among the Jews of Prague: lessened, exiled, envious, sinful. The moon's lessening, that led it to denounce the sun and cause *maḥloket*, is parallel to the war and heavy taxes that, in Heller's view, led the Prague community into *maḥloket*, and moved some Jews to denounce Heller at the imperial court. Struggling with his sense of loss, his sense of shame, his guilt, and his anger, Heller fixed on a talmudic passage that would allow him to express his emotions in a public sphere that rarely permitted emotional expression.

But beyond that, I am convinced, at a deeper, unspoken, unsayable level, the lessened moon, the Tychonian moon—and the reference to the astronomer is Heller's own—lowered and reduced in size and in brightness, symbolized for Heller his own changing self: his falling away from high office to the common prison of Vienna, his suffering, his anger and his patience, his losses, and his personal exile.

[58] *Derush ḥidushei halevanah*, 38–9.

TEN

Attacks and Retreats

TO THE EDGE OF EUROPE

DURING that same High Holiday season of 1631 when Heller preached so well in Brest-Litovsk, he accepted the offer of a rabbinical position in the town of Nemirov (Nemyriv). Nemirov was a small town, although a wealthy one. The Jewish community there had been founded quite recently; the first written reference to it is from 1603.[1] Heller did not know, of course, that its name would soon become a watchword for Jewish martyrdom. Nemirov was on the eastern frontier of Jewish settlement in the Ukraine, on what was at that time the very edge of Europe.

Before leaving Prague, Heller had succeeded, after great effort, in securing imperial permission to serve as rabbi elsewhere in the German empire.[2] Yet he chose in the end to move to Poland. The course of the war in Germany was no doubt responsible for his change of plans. Whereas early in 1630 the war appeared to be coming to a successful end, from the Habsburg point of view, by spring 1631 the Swedish invasion was under way, and the Habsburg armies had been defeated. Germany was once again a battleground.

In 1631 Poland (that is, the Polish–Lithuanian Commonwealth) was by contrast a peaceful land. Although, by the 1630s, religions tensions were mounting between Catholics and Protestants, and between Catholics and Orthodox Christians, Poland continued to profess the principle of religious tolerance, as it had for sixty years; thus far it had escaped the religious wars that were consuming France, Germany, and Bohemia.[3]

The stately synagogues, a few of which are still standing, are monuments to the wealth and dignity of the Jewish communities of Poland in this period: one is the synagogue of the wealthy Isaac Yekels in Cracow, of which Manasseh ben Israel

[1] Ettinger, 'Jewish Participation', 117. Nemirov in the Ukraine is not to be confused with Niemirów in Poland.

[2] *Megilat eivah*, p. 36.

[3] See Tazbir, *State without Stakes*; Opalinski, 'Local Diets'.

reported that 'it stood him in one hundred thousand Francs, and is worth many tons of gold'.[4]

Polish prosperity in the early seventeenth century was based in large part on the grain trade. For Heller, an important consequence of this flourishing trade was the Polish colonization of the Ukraine. Officially made a part of the Polish Crown lands in 1569, the Ukraine was the land of opportunity (not to say opportunism) for Polish noblemen and merchants, Catholics, Protestants, and Jews.[5] Nemirov was a boom town.

To appreciate the journey from Prague to Nemirov from Heller's point of view, his mental geography must be considered. Prague, when he lived there, was more closely tied to western than to eastern Europe; also, of course, Heller had spent the early years of his life in Germany proper. In *Tosafot yom tov*, he wrote in one place of 'the lands that are around us: Germany, France, Spain, and Italy'.[6] Nemirov was a very distant place.

But Heller had no real conception of regions called 'western Europe' or 'eastern Europe', and hardly any of a continent called 'Europe'. The geographical categories that he used, rather, were 'the West' and 'the East'. 'The East', the lands of Islam, started at the border of the Ottoman empire. For example, he writes that the Jewish community of Cracow was 'the greatest and most important . . . in all the lands of the West'.[7] By 'the West', Heller meant the lands of Christianity, including Poland and including Nemirov; but Nemirov, in an area subject to recurrent attacks by the Muslim Tatars, was near the border.

Although he was only marginally aware of cultural differences between one century and another, Heller was quite aware of the differences between places and regions. In a delightful comment in a work called *Malbushei yom tov*, he remarked on the difference between 'our' gabled roofs and the domed roofs that he thought were typical of the Land of Israel; because of this, he argued, the Hebrew letter *ḥet*, which is shaped like a house with a little roof, should be written with a domed 'roof', not a gabled one.[8] In another comment, explaining a mishnaic list of articles of clothing (the Mishnah is fascinated by the sheer variety of human artefacts), he

[4] Manasseh b. Israel, 'To his Highnesse', 12. The meaning of 'stood him in' is uncertain. The most likely sense, given in *OED*, is 'to loan or wager money': thus Yekels, after building the synagogue, borrowed this sum with the synagogue as security.

[5] See Sysyn, *Between Poland and the Ukraine*, 24–5.

[6] *Tos YT*, *Git.* 9: 6.

[7] *Megilat eivah*, p. 39. Hale, *Civilization*, 1–51, has a long essay on the development of 'Europe' as a geographical concept. Heller had seen world maps (see *Tos YT*, *Ḥal.* 4: 10 and *MYT* (*DH*), *Ber.*, p. 74 n. 37), and read David Gans's geography, discussed in Neher, *Jewish Thought and the Scientific Revolution*, 95–165, and Efron, 'David ben Shlomo Gans'. Cf. *Tos YT*, *San.* 4: 3, which discusses the problem (previously addressed by Azariah dei Rossi, the Maharal, and Gans) of whether and in what sense Jerusalem is the 'centre of the world'. Cf. Neher, *Jewish Thought*, 157–60.

[8] *MalYT* 36: 1.

noted the difference between German and Polish trousers; in another place, the difference between German and Polish bread.[9]

There was much that was strange in this land. Heller seems to have been shocked, for example, by the Polish Jewish custom of salting (or '*kashering*') their meat as they travelled by covering it with salt, wrapping it in a piece of linen cloth, and taking it in the wagon. In Prague, Heller had published a special Yiddish broadsheet, called *Berit melaḥ* (Covenant of Salt), on ritual salting—and this was not how it should be done. Ritual salting, he insisted to his householders, could only be done in a sieve or on a slanted board. This custom of doing it on the move 'should be suppressed completely'.[10]

The Jews of Nemirov, it is true, did speak German—that is, Judaeo-German, Yiddish. But they spoke it, Heller complained, with a thick accent; ten years later, in 1641, he was still complaining about it.[11]

There was something else in Nemirov neither truly strange nor quite familiar—aspects of life that must have reminded Heller of his early years in Wallerstein. Like Wallerstein, and unlike Prague with its 60,000 inhabitants, Nemirov was a small town. (Even in Prague, to be sure, urban life in the seventeenth century was in no respect as 'urban' as it would become in later centuries.) A new home will inevitably remind us of our childhood; the experience of helplessness coupled with the experience of discovery is the very essence of childhood.

The image prevalent today of pre-modern Ashkenazi Jews, especially Polish Jews, is based mostly on the nineteenth-century *shtetl*. There is much to recommend such a view. Jewish life in eastern Europe remained fairly stable from the mid-seventeenth to the mid-nineteenth centuries. Here is the synagogue where everyone prays; there is the poor man saying psalms, and the rich man buying a synagogue honour; there are the women in the marketplace and the rabbi in his study. It may be a century earlier or later. The seasons pass. It is a timeless way of life that is passed from generation to generation, and that has itself no sense of the passage of history.[12] But there were also a number of significant differences between 1630 and 1850. In 1850, the Jews of eastern Europe were religiously divided and poorly organized; in 1630, they were united and highly organized. There was an elaborate system of *kehilot*, linked by councils, and culminating in the central Council of the Four Lands.[13] In 1850, the Jews of eastern Europe were politically powerless, or nearly so; Poland was no longer a state and the Jews had little influence in St Petersburg. In 1630, Jews were still a major support of the Polish state.

9 *Tos YT*, *Shab.* 16: 4 (trousers); *Torat ha'asham*, 172 (bread).

10 *Torat ha'asham*, 15 (salting). Note also the much more significant difference concerning the purchase of rabbinical office, which will be discussed later in this chapter.

11 *She'elat gitin*, 2a.

12 Cf. the emphasis on cyclical, natural time in traditional society in Bogucka, *Lost World*.

13 See e.g. Polonsky *et al.* (eds.), *The Jews in Old Poland*, 93–165.

Finally, and most important: in 1850, the great mass of the Jews of eastern Europe, the Ostjuden, were technologically and culturally backward, even compared to the upper classes of Warsaw, but especially as compared to the middle classes of London, Paris, and Berlin. In 1630, the cultural and technological divisions between western and eastern Europe were rarely noticed.[14] By 1670, a Jewish satirist in Prague could contrast the wealthy but ignorant German Jews with the scholarly, pious, but wretchedly poor Jewish refugees from the wars in Poland. The anonymous satirist remarked, though, that the contrast could not have been made a generation before. In 1630, the modernization of the German Jews and their cultural distancing from Polish Jews had scarcely begun.[15]

Heller must surely have been alarmed by the violent tenor of life in this frontier region: the raids of Tatars, the rebellions of Cossack troops, and the rage of Polish noblemen.[16] He may also have experienced some discomfort in adapting from life in Prague to life in Nemirov—some absence of luxuries, some roughness of manners. These may indeed have been among the reasons that he did not remain in Nemirov any longer than he had to. But he did not feel, as would a Jew who moved from Prague to Nemirov in the nineteenth century (or more likely, from Nemirov to Prague), that he was moving from one world to another, from one century to another.

AGAIN ON THE *SHULḤAN ARUKH*

After only three years in Nemirov, Heller left in 1634 to become chief rabbi in a larger city farther from the frontier—Volodymyr, which the Jews called Lodmir or Ludmir.[17] Ludmir, an old Jewish community dating back to the thirteenth century, was one of the chief cities of the region of Volhynia, between the Ukraine and Poland.[18]

Heller's major written work from his years in Ludmir is a book written about 1639, called *Torat ha'asham* (The Law of the Guilt Offering). *Torat ha'asham* is a

[14] Mączak, 'Progress and Underdevelopment'.

[15] Weinreich (ed.), 'Di bashraybung'. The satirist points out that in the previous generation it was German Jews who sought refuge in Poland—as had Heller. Abraham b. Samuel Ashkenazi makes the same remark in his chronicle of the massacres of 1648, *Tsa'ar bat rabim*, in Gurland (ed.), *On the History*, pt. 4, p. 19. On the differences between Polish and German Jewry in this period, see Hundert, 'Comparative Perspectives', esp. p. 105 n. 12. Note also S. P. Rabbinowitz's argument (against Heinrich Graetz) that the differences between German and Polish Jews in this period were small, published in Rabbinowitz's Hebrew edn. of Graetz's history, *Divrei yemei yisra'el*, pt. 8, bk. 1, pp. 157–9; cf. pp. 119–24.

[16] See Ettinger, 'Legal and Social Status', 122–7; Sysyn, *Between Poland and the Ukraine*, 24–5.

[17] *Megilat eivah*, p. 37.

[18] On the Jewish community of Volodymyr, see *Volodymyr Memorial Book*; Ettinger, 'Legal and Social Status', 115–30; Tikhomirov, *Towns of Ancient Rus*, 338–9. On Volhynia in this period, see Sysyn, *Between Poland and the Ukraine*, 38–43.

commentary on *Torat haḥatat* (The Law of the Sin Offering), a small codification of the laws of *kashrut* by Moses Isserles. In the progression of Heller's halakhic writings, *Torah ha'asham* marked the end of a gradual defeat.

Heller started out, it will be recalled, after completing *Tosafot yom tov*, to write a Talmud commentary that would also lay out Jewish law as it was applied in his own day. Quickly, perhaps even before he started, he gave up that ambition. He no longer believed, if he had every truly believed, that a simple Talmud commentary could serve the function of detailing present-day law. Instead he decided to write a commentary on the Rosh's *Digest* of the Talmud.

For the second volume of *Ma'adanei melekh* in 1628, however, Heller gave up the plan of a simple commentary. He revised the format of his commentary, and decided to split it into two parts. One part would discuss exegetical issues, while the other part would lay out the law in practice. Although he continued to insist in the introduction on the superiority of commentaries to codes, he no longer believed that a single commentary—on any text at all, it would appear—could perform both the function of Talmud exegesis and that of legal decision.

Ma'adanei melekh was never finished. In 1628 Heller outlined five parts, to cover the entire range of talmudic law; but only two parts, the volume published in 1619 and the second volume of 1628, were ever published or (so it would appear) ever completed. Like many other rabbinic writers, Heller was defeated by the sheer extent of the Talmud, a text too extensive and too problematic to be explained in its entirety.

Instead, in *Torat ha'asham* Heller decided to review the laws of *kashrut*, which he had already treated in the second volume of *Ma'adanei melekh*, in his commentary on tractate *Ḥulin*. The substance of his legal views had not undergone any major changes. In *Torat ha'asham*, he chose, however, to recast them in a new form. He abandoned his opposition to Isserles' project of codification. Isserles' *Torat ha'ḥatat* is a legal code, and Heller's *Torat ha'asham* is thus a commentary on a legal code, the very form that he had rejected with such eloquence a decade earlier.

Stubbornly, he continued to avoid the *Shulḥan arukh* itself. Nor did he restrict his urge to criticize Isserles' rulings. He quoted Solomon Luria's criticism of his cousin: '[Isserles] made up compromises and customs himself and he cannot be relied upon at all, unless one carefully checks his opinions.'[19] Like nearly all of Isserles' early commentators, Heller found fault with his views in many places. In spite of that, *Torat ha'asham* co-operated in the establishment of Isserles as the essential halakhic authority for Polish Jewry, and Isserles' works as the decisive Ashkenazi statement of Jewish law in practice.[20]

[19] *Torat ha'asham*, 185.

[20] Heller's new attitude was also signalled in an approbation that he wrote in 1646 for *Naḥalat tsevi*, a commentary on the *Shulḥan arukh*, in which he described the latter as 'the book from which legal decisions go out to the entire House of Israel'.

Heller had made an accommodation to the *Shulḥan arukh*, just as Isaiah Horowitz had done fifteen years before. Living in Prague, in the Maharal's city, he had had no reason to admit the halakhic authority of Isserles, the rabbi of Cracow. Did not Prague have a larger and more ancient Jewish community? But here in Poland, in Isserles' country, Heller bowed to his legal presence.

With this change in Heller's attitude towards codification came also a changed attitude towards custom, *minhag*. This is natural, since as a codifier Isserles made Ashkenazi custom the baseline of his legal rulings. Although *minhag* plays a certain role in Heller's decisions in *Ma'adanei melekh* (as for instance in his lenient ruling on non-Jewish bread), it is a small one.[21] Like Solomon Luria, Heller defended the authority of the medieval rabbis of Germany and northern France, of Rashi, the Tosafists, and the Rosh, by arguing that their interpretations of the Talmud agreed with the Talmud's plain meaning, and ought (ideally) to be binding on all Jews everywhere. Heller did not adopt Isserles' more modest argument that there is a body of special customs or talmudic interpretations binding only Ashkenazi and not Sefardi Jews.[22]

Eventually, however, Heller came to accept Isserles' view. In 1649 he gave a final and full endorsement to Isserles' conception of *minhag ashkenaz*. His conversion was complete. 'We are the descendants', he wrote, 'of the Jews of France and Germany, and we decide questions of halakhah in accordance with their opinions, as the *gaon* . . . Rabbi Moses Isserles wrote in his introduction to the *Shulḥan arukh*.'[23]

Torat ha'asham remained unpublished for more than three hundred years. It survived in a single manuscript in the Bodleian Library in Oxford, a manuscript which had been part of the library of David Oppenheimer, chief rabbi of Prague at the beginning of the eighteenth century. This single surviving manuscript is, alas,

[21] Note *MYT* (*MM*), *Ber.*, p. 24 n. 5: a custom that contravenes the Talmud may be supported on the basis of the Tosefta.

[22] See the introductions to Isserles' commentary on the *Shulḥan arukh*, and to his *Torat haḥatat*: 'If a man were to decide the law following [Caro's] opinions . . . he would contradict all of the customs that are followed in these lands.' Similarly, in his introduction to *Darkhei mosheh*, he wrote '[Caro] contradicts all of the customs that are observed in these lands.' Cf. also *Darkhei mosheh*, 'Yoreh de'ah' 35: 7. On Isserles' view of custom, see Siev, *Rabbi Moses Isserles*, 219–26; J. Ben-Sasson, *The Thought of R. Moses Isserles*, 265–8. On medieval Ashkenazi views of the force of custom, see Denari, *Ashkenazi Rabbis*, 192 ff.; Woolf, 'Authority of Custom'. Note also Kelley, 'Second Nature'; Strauss, *Law, Resistance, and the State*, 86–7; Bogucka, *Lost World*.

[23] *She'elot uteshuvot ge'onei batra'ei*, ed. Elijah b. Moses of Pińczów (*editio princeps* Turka, 1764), no. 10. The responsum discusses a case of an *agunah*, a woman with a husband who is presumed but not proven to be dead. Note also Heller's concern for the force of custom in his responsum on announcing the equinox, written in this period; Krochmal, *She'elot uteshuvot tsemaḥ tsedek* (Altdorf, 1766), no. 14. I discuss this responsum at length in my dissertation, pp. 461–3; cf. Davis, 'Philosophy and the Law', 274 n. 31.

lacking the first several pages:[24] the entire introduction is missing. Heller entitled this introduction *Kelalei hora'at isur veheter* (The General Principles of Prohibition and Permission). It was described in the late seventeenth century by the bibliographer Shabetai Bass as a treatment of the crucial problem in Jewish law of deciding questions that are disputed among the medieval talmudists.

One passage from the lost introduction is quoted by Heller himself, later on in *Torat ha'asham*. In it, he discusses the origins and the authority of *minhag*, and takes a crucial step in the direction of Isserles' view of custom:

> Every region, every land, and every city must follow the opinions of . . . the rabbi, who was the first leader [*manhig*] of that place, and of 'the judge who shall be in their days' (Deut. 17: 9), when the latter court is not greater [than the former] in Torah and in number, and in this era, when there is no priest or anointed judge in Jerusalem.[25]

For Heller, as for Isserles, the power of *minhag* is not based on the authority of the community as such. It is based rather on the authority of its initial legislator, its *manhig*. Heller assumes as a historical fact that *minhagim* were established not by the common people, nor by the community as a whole, but by the first rabbis of the community. His conception of *minhag*, one could say, is rabbinical-monarchical rather than democratic. It reflects the Platonic theories of the legislator applied to Judaism by the medieval Jewish philosophers, rather than the communitarian impulses of the medieval Ashkenazi rabbis.[26]

The relevance of this conception to Heller's own situation in the Ukraine should not be overlooked. Here new communities were being established, local institutions were being created, and local customs were gaining the force of age-old practice. Heller knew himself to be a *manhig*, a maker of customs.

ON HONOUR

The life of the Ashkenazi Jewish communities was guided by many fundamental values. Many (such as charity, prayer, and Torah study) were emphasized in the Talmud, but there was at least one towards which rabbinic tradition is at best ambivalent. That value is honour, in Hebrew, *kavod*.[27]

[24] See the editors' introduction in *Torat ha'asham*. David Oppenheimer was the grandson of Heller's cousin Simeon Wolf Oppenheim of Worms.

[25] *Torat ha'asham*, 360.

[26] Cf. *Tos YT*, *Meg*. 4: 3. On these two theories of custom, see Woolf, 'Authority of Custom', 62–3. The theory of custom which relegates the people to a passive role, accepting the customs that have been decreed for them, can be compared to the state of mind that made *cuius regio, eius religio* seem such a reasonable principle to 16th-c. men.

[27] On Jewish concepts of honour and deference, see N. Z. Davis, *Women on the Margins*, 34–6; Jütte, 'Ehre und Ehrverlust'; Hundert, 'Decline of Deference'; Zimmer, *Embers of the Sages*, *passim*, e.g. pp. 47, 55. Cf. Backmann *et al.* (eds.), *Ehrkonzepte*.

The demand for honour, many Jewish moralists of the period charged, disrupted the other values of Ashkenazi Judaism. It distorted the goals of Torah education, limited the devoutness of prayer, and undermined the justice meted out by rabbinical courts.[28] *Kavod*, Heller wrote in 1617, engenders hatred among mankind, because those who pursue honour, while outwardly they may be shown deference, are secretly despised and derided.[29]

The struggle to achieve and preserve personal and family honour was not a mere temptation; it was one of the pillars of Ashkenazi Judaism. Heller, a Jewish orphan from a small German market town, was no stranger to the pursuit against which he warned. By birth he belonged to the Jewish social elite of the Habsburg empire, including Prague. By arranging strategic matches for his children, moreover, he had formed ties with many of the wealthiest and most respected Jewish families in Poland. He was very proud of these matches and of his relations by marriage, as is shown by the extensive and mostly quite unnecessary references to them in *Megilat eivah*. One passage in *Torat ha'asham*, however, suggests that by the late 1630s Heller no longer entirely identified himself with the wealthy as a class.[30] The comment springs from a very minor law concerning cooking on the sabbath. In his comment, Heller lays out the divisions of Jewish society as he saw them.

He first quotes a rule that allows a certain leniency in the laws of preparing meat on the sabbath to those who must show special respect towards their guests. He then quotes the comment of Jacob Moellin (Maharil; *c.*1360–1427) who ruled that hospitality for the poor does not fall under this law (it falls under the laws of charity). This rule of sabbath hospitality, according to Moellin applies only to guests who are 'wealthy and honoured'.[31] Heller explains: 'wealthy and honoured' does not include those whose deeds are not worthy of honour, even if they are wealthy. They do not deserve special hospitality. In Prague, it had always been his assumption that wealth and lineage went (for the most part) hand in hand. He was faced in Poland, however, by another element of Jewish society: the tax-farmers, so-called arendators, a group of wealthy Jews whose lineage he neither knew nor respected, and whose claim to honour he was inclined to question. Heller claims, without any apparent textual support, that Moellin did not mean to exclude 'those who are worthy of respect, who are not rich', that is, the pious and learned poor,

[28] See Bettan, 'Sermons', 454–68; H. H. Ben-Sasson, 'Wealth and Poverty', 142–66; Rabinowitz, *Portraits of Preachers*, 137–41.

[29] *Tos YT*, *Avot* 4: 21. There is something prophetic in his remark, in light of the bitter opposition that he suddenly encountered in 1629.

[30] *Torat ha'asham*, pp. 32–3.

[31] Note also the comment of Hayim b. Bezalel (writing in Germany in 1575) in his introduction to *Vikuah mayim hayim*, printed in Tchernowitz, *Rabbinic Authorities*, iii. 98: 'The argument of the honour due to guests no longer applies today, because most guests are not worthy of honour. Would only that [the host] need not fear when they enter the house!'

and 'decent people of good families'. Hospitality is theirs for the taking. The only group which Moellin recommended for charity and excluded from the laws of 'hospitality', he claims, are 'decent people of poor families'. Poor sinners, he ruled somewhat harshly, are not even deserving of charity.[32]

Heller thus established a number of rankings within Jewish society: the sinful poor or rich—not deserving of either charity or hospitality; the decent poor—deserving of generosity and charity, but not honour; the poor who are pious and learned or of good families, and the wealthy, if they are not sinful—both deserving of respect and hospitality. That is, he inserted into Moellin's simple twofold division of society a third class: Jews who are pious or learned or of good families, but who are not themselves wealthy. They too, he claimed, are deserving not merely of charity, but of honour.

Heller, who was perhaps no longer a wealthy man, did not now identify himself with the wealthiest Jews, but rather with 'the learned, the pious, and decent people of good families'. His new support for the *Shulḥan arukh*, a work that had always been popular outside the rabbinical aristocracy, fits this shift of class allegiance.

Indeed, Heller would shortly deliver an attack on some of the wealthiest Jews of Poland and their pretensions to communal leadership. He convinced first the rabbis of Volhynia and then the rabbis of all of Poland that they should renew the prohibition on the purchase of rabbinical office from non-Jewish officials.

THE BAN ON THE PURCHASE OF RABBINICAL OFFICE

In Iyar (April/May) 1640 Heller addressed the annual gathering of the rabbis of Volhynia.

I rose up 'like one who is awakened from sleep' to renew all that . . . the great rabbis of the land [had decreed] prohibiting the purchase of the rabbinate from local [non-Jewish] officials, as it was once done in the days of the High Priests [who purchased their position from the Romans]. Therefore the sages of that generation decreed bans and . . . curses . . . and decrees and fines. . . . But these bans were breached time after time. . . .

And so I . . . together with the leaders of the region [of Volhynia] made a decree supporting all the words of the earlier rabbis. And we added to them, for the earlier rabbis [had made a ban] only on those who themselves purchased the rabbinate . . . but I brought together all of these leaders and we extended all of the decrees to those who allow themselves to be appointed to such a position [after it had been purchased].

And . . . when the heads of the four chief communities of Volhynia (namely Ludmir, Ostroh, Kremenets, and Lutsk) were gathered together at the council . . . the heads of the yeshivas of the four communities and the communal leaders . . . reissued the laws. . . . And then in Jarosław, where many of the heads of yeshivas [of Poland] were gathered,

[32] Cf. the discussion of distinctions between 'deserving' and 'undeserving' poor in 17th-c. Europe: Parker, *Europe in Crisis*, 28–36.

together with the leaders of the Four Lands . . . it was recorded in the Pinkas [register] of the Land, signed by the rabbis and heads of yeshivas . . . that the rabbinate may not be purchased.[33]

The well-informed Amsterdam rabbi Manasseh ben Israel, describing the Jews of the world to Oliver Cromwell in 1655, contrasted the German Jews with the Jews of Poland, who 'have the jurisdiction to judge among themselves all causes, both Criminal and Civil'.[34] Although Jews in all parts of Europe throughout the Middle Ages enjoyed some degree of autonomy, the self-government exercised by the Polish Jews, through institutions such as the Council of the Four Lands, was extraordinary. In certain localities, as the traveller Fynes Moryson noted in 1592, the Jews comprised the majority of the population.[35]

In the sixteenth century, as the Askhenazi rabbinate became regularized and professionalized, it came to be seen as a potential source of income and object of patronage, just as posts within the Christian clergy were often regarded. Christian nobles were happy to sell rabbinical positions in their dominions to their Jewish clients. However, just as the Counter-Reformation Church prohibited the sale or purchase of Church offices (in Church law, this is the sin of 'simony'), so was the right to appoint rabbis contested by local Jewish communal governments.[36]

Thirty rabbis, including Mordechai Jaffe, Ephraim of Luntshits, Meir of Lublin, Samuel Edels, and the young Isaiah Horowitz, had signed a *ḥerem*, a ban, against the purchase of rabbinical positions in 1587. The *ḥerem* was repeated in 1590 and in 1597. After that, however, the decree had not been renewed. Heller states that these pronouncements had become ineffective. 'In the eyes of the common people', he writes, 'they were a joke and a laughing-stock.'[37]

Heller's 1640 decree attempted to give teeth to the earlier prohibition. The earlier decree had threatened with *ḥerem* the purchaser of the rabbinical office; but he was typically a wealthy Jew, an arendator, often a client of a powerful Polish lord, who could flout the authority of the *ḥerem*. The new decree now also threatened with *ḥerem* the rabbi who had been appointed by the purchaser, a more vulnerable figure.

There is no reason to doubt Heller's testimony concerning the infractions of the earlier *ḥerem*. Neither is there any reason to suppose, however, that the 1640 decree

33 *Megilat eivah*, 37–8.

34 Manasseh b. Israel, 'To his Highnesse', 12.

35 Moryson, *Shakespeare's Europe*, 488.

36 The Council of Trent in 1563 (Session 24: 14 and 18) tightened the existing laws against sale and purchase of ecclesiastical offices, and made additional rules to improve the qualifications of the clergy. Noble patrons were allowed to control many ecclesiastical appointments; they were not in principle allowed to sell them.

37 The bans of the Council of Four Lands were published by Hailperin in *Documents*, 62–5. On purchase of rabbinic office, see H. H. Ben-Sasson, *Theory and Practice*, 221–8; Assaf, 'History of the Rabbinate', 34–41; Reiner, 'Changes', 47 ff.; Rosman, *The Lords' Jews*, 200; Schochet, *Bach*, 25; Zimmer, *Embers of the Sages*, 159, 261–2.

was very much more effective or very much less quixotic than its predecessor. Shabetai Horowitz, Isaiah's son, complained towards the end of the 1640s that the rule was still being ignored. The rabbinical pronouncement demanded internal Jewish discipline that did not exist.[38]

Quickly, Heller became embroiled in disputes. He wrote, 'Everything that I did added to my enemies. . . . and the close became far and the far off were brought together, and they wished to remove me from the rabbinate.'[39] Documents from 1640 and 1641, preserved in a unique manuscript published in the nineteenth century, cast light on the opposition to Heller.[40] As rabbi of Ludmir, he tried to remove a certain Rabbi Josel from his position as rabbi of Lokacze, a small town south-west of Ludmir. In Ludmir, as in Prague, Heller believed in the authority of larger Jewish communities and their rabbis over smaller communities. Josel of Lokacze responded that Heller had a personal grudge against him and should have disqualified himself from the case; furthermore that he, Josel, had been appointed as rabbi *by the community* of Lokacze for another two years; furthermore that Heller would not show him the testimony or the evidence against him in the case; furthermore that he, Josel, had considerable outstanding loans in Lokacze which he was now unable to collect.

The rabbinical court in Ostroh, having heard these complaints against Heller, wrote to him in early August 1640, warning him to desist, and to allow Josel to serve as rabbi in Lokacze until the end of his term, and even half a year longer, in order to be able to collect his debts. The rabbis of Ostroh commanded Heller to do nothing until the next rabbinical council at the Jarosław fair. The rabbinical courts of Kremenets and Lutsk, the other major communities in Volhynia besides Ludmir itself, supported the rabbis of Ostroh. The rabbis of Kremenets appealed to Heller's humility and also, much as Heller himself had done in his letter to Frankfurt in 1628, to the need to avoid conflict and *maḥloket*.

As a halakhic question, the matter once again involved the authority of Moses Isserles, concerning which we have, over and over, seen Heller's ambivalence. In one of his responsa, Isserles had recognized the legitimacy of non-Jewish

38 Shabetai Horowitz's comment is in *Vavei ha'amudim*, printed at the end of I. Horowitz, *Shenei luḥot haberit*, 23*b*.

39 *Megilat eivah*, 38. Note Heller's language of 'the far-off brought together'; this seems to recur in his understanding of the causation of misfortune. Note particularly his stress on the alliance of Cossacks and Tatars in 1648. Communal tensions seem to be reflected again in Heller's responsum in *Eitan ha'ezraḥi*, nos. 9–10. The incident seems very complicated, but Heller writes, 'That man who caused *maḥloket* caused it to himself, for no one supported him at that time. And I did not open my mouth against him, and I was appeased without any payment of money, God forbid, and I did not even wish to be appeased with words.'

40 Brann, 'Additions'. Heller's letter is on pp. 275–7. Hailperin copies the texts with some useful annotations (MS, pp. 115–22).

appointments to the rabbinate, arguing that (in the famous talmudic phrase) 'the law of the kingdom is the law'.[41] The courts of Ostroh, Lutsk, and Kremenets were apparently following Isserles' opinion.

They may also have felt that they were following the lead of Joel Sirkes, the late rabbi of Cracow and the leading talmudist of his generation, who had also not opposed the purchase of the rabbinate, but had actually argued that a rabbi ought to be a wealthy man. 'A *rosh yeshivah*', Sirkes wrote, 'who equals a high priest or a king, needs to be wealthy in order that his teachings be respected.'[42] Sirkes died in Adar (March) 1640; the timing of Heller's initiative, only months after Sirkes' death, may not have been coincidental.[43] It is curious, though, and perhaps significant, that David ben Samuel Halevi (*c.*1586–1667), one of the major talmudists in Ostroh, did not sign the letter to Heller. David ben Samuel later wrote the *Turei zahav*, a major commentary on the *Shulḥan arukh*; he was the son-in-law of Joel Sirkes, and in 1640 he was, as it were, his father-in-law's heir apparent.[44]

Heller's response is dated 25 Tevet (7 January) 1641—five months later. In it he denied that Josel had ever been appointed by his community. If he had, why didn't he have any writ of appointment to show? Furthermore, he never refused to show Josel any testimony; on the contrary, he had ordered that it be shown to him. Furthermore (I am skipping some of his arguments) was not Josel free to collect his debts even if he was not rabbi of the community? What sort of people were the Jews of Lokacze if they were not to be trusted to pay back their debts? Furthermore, Heller wrote he and Josel were 'not in the same category at all' and should not be held equally responsible for the conflict. 'I have been sitting quietly', Heller writes, 'and my work is the yoke of the Torah and the yoke of the community.'

Events, furthermore, had proved Heller right, he claimed, for later on Josel appeared at the rabbinical meeting in Beresteczko and said nothing. Furthermore, he (Heller) had been personally insulted, in public letters, and for no reason. And also any fool would know (Heller uses a talmudic phrase, 'any reed-cutter in a bog') that a personal enemy must disqualify himself from acting as a judge in a court case. He had no personal antagonism to Josel. The letter from the rabbis of Lutsk, on the other hand 'seems to have been written while they were asleep' (another talmudic phrase). In conclusion, the truth of the matter was that the whole incident

[41] Isserles, *She'elot uteshuvot harema*, no. 123 (discussed by Siev on pp. 60–3 and in id., *Rabbi Moses Isserles*, 119–24.). Note Isserles' references, repeated by Heller in *Megilat eivah*, to the ancient High Priests who purchased their office.

[42] Sirkes, *Bayit ḥadash*, 'Yoreh de'ah', para. 246; cf. id., *She'elot uteshuvot habaḥ hayeshanot*, no. 52.

[43] On the date of Sirkes' death, see Schochet, *Bach*, 20 n. 5.

[44] See Brann's note, 'Additions', 273 n. 4. Hailperin (MS, p. 117 n. 2) suggests that David was simply not a member of the rabbinic court of Ostroh, and so naturally did not sign the letter. Note David b. Samuel, *Turei zahav*, 'Yoreh de'ah', 246. On David b. Samuel, see Schochet, *Taz*.

concerned the purchase of the rabbinate, which the rabbis of Ostroh, Lutsk, and Kremenets had all joined Heller in prohibiting. And finally, Heller concluded, on 10 Kislev (November/December) (six weeks before Heller's letter), twenty householders of the community of Lokacze had chosen a new rabbi: a member of a good family, Solomon ben Nathan Spira, son of the great kabbalist and scholar of Cracow. 'Today', Heller wrote, 'the messengers have gone after the rabbi.'

Heller had waited until after the election to send his response to the surrounding communities. He had also waited until his own position in Ludmir was secure. On 1 Shevat (12 January) 1641, a week after he wrote this letter, he recorded in *Megilat eivah*, he was hired by the Ludmir community for an additional term of three years.[45]

A year before the conclusion of his term, however, in spring 1643, Heller again found himself in difficulties, this time with the Polish authorities. A royal official, perhaps the *voivode* of Volhynia, a nobleman named Adam Sanguszko, announced that Heller must leave Ludmir. Sanguszko (if that is who it was), Heller writes in *Megilat eivah*, had received an unsigned letter accusing Heller of defaming Christianity, reviving and perhaps expanding on the accusations of 1629.[46] He would arrive in Ludmir in two days, on his way to Warsaw, the official warned; by that time, Heller should be gone.[47]

True to his general view of the causation of events in his life, Heller was certain that the letter had been written by his Jewish opponents, who, he was sure, unable to have his rabbinical contract terminated by the Ludmir community, had finally turned to the Polish authorities. They were presumably not averse to involving non-Jews in rabbinical affairs—that had been cause of the argument in the first place.

From another point of view, however, the incident can be taken as a sign of the increased tension between Christians and Jews in Ludmir, and indeed throughout Poland. In 1639 and 1640 there had been conflicts between the Jews and the Catholic clergy in Ludmir, and attacks on Jews by Catholic students had become frequent.[48]

On 29 Sivan (14 June) 1643, Heller went to stay with his grandson outside town, in the village of Turisk. Already in distress, he was cast into despair a few days later by the news of his daughter Doberish's death. However, a reprieve was quickly

[45] *Megilat eivah*, 38.

[46] Letter: Yiddish *Megilat eivah* in ŽMP MS 157, p. 47 and MS 347, p. 21. On the active administrative role often taken by a *voivode* in the 17th c. in matters regarding the Jewish community, see B. Cohen, 'Jurisdiction'; Grodziski, 'Kraków Voivode's Jurisdiction'.

[47] On Sanguszko, see the article in *Polski Słownik Biograficzny*. It is remotely possible that there is surviving material relevant to the incident in the Sanguszko archives.

[48] Ettinger, 'Legal and Social Status', 125–6.

negotiated by the *shtadlanim*, giving him six weeks to return to Ludmir, pack his things and order his affairs before leaving. The local Jewish communities rallied to his aid; the rabbinical courts of Ostroh, Lutsk, and Kremenets now sent letters of support, and further negotiations, while Heller was off at another grandson's wedding in Chełm, brought about an annulment of Heller's expulsion.[49]

This brush with Polish officialdom was rather different from Heller's imprisonment and trial twelve years before. In 1643 he was never formally charged with a crime; in the end, he suffered neither imprisonment, nor a fine, nor removal from office. Yet the parallels between the two events impressed him more than the differences. There was a coincidence of dates. On 5 Tamuz (22 June), the date of his arrest in Prague, the lord of Ludmir, as yet unappeased, had passed through Turisk, where Heller was staying, and he had feared for his life.[50]

Heller was also inclined to think that there was also a parallel in causation. Once again, conflict within the community, *maḥloket*, had led him to be denounced to the non-Jewish authorities, and this had brought about his misfortune.

Why did Heller care so much about the sale or purchase of rabbinical office? Now as before, he was a supporter (as well as of course an employee) of the *kehilot*. He felt that the *kehilah* governments (and with them, the Council of the Four Lands, which was the union of Polish *kehilot*) should control rabbinical appointments. He did not approve of the alliance that had been formed in the smaller Polish and Ukrainian towns between the Polish noblemen, their Jewish clients, the arendators (a group from whom, as we saw earlier, Heller felt alienated), and the arendators' chosen rabbis, whom he regarded as typically unqualified.[51]

Though he emerged here as a champion of democratic rule in the *kehilot*, we have seen that Heller did not place much value on democracy as such. Rather, as he saw it, the arrangements among these three groups violated three principles: the autonomy of the Jewish community, the principle that rabbis should be properly qualified, and the requirement that rabbinical judges should be impartial. These concerns were close to his heart, as they had been to the Maharal's. Heller thought that his opponents were partisan; as his letter reveals, he was stung when he in turn was accused of bias and conflict of interest.[52]

[49] *Megilat eivah*, 38–9.

[50] See Yiddish *Megilat eivah*, ŽMP MS 157, p. 49.

[51] On this alliance, see Rosman, *The Lords' Jews*, 198–203. On the contrast of royal cities and private cities, and the position of the rabbinate in each one, cf. J. Goldberg, *Jewish Society*, 146–50.

[52] See e.g. Heller's comment in *Tos YT*, *Avot* 1: 6; cf. also *Tos YT*, *Edu.* 8: 7. On the Maharal, see Hailperin (ed.), *Legislation*, p. 60 n. 1 (cf. p. 97); Sherwin, *Mystical Theology*, 167. Note the 1579 Prague document against the appointment of rabbis by non-Jews: Bondy and Dworsky (eds.), *Zur Geschichte der Juden*, 558 (no. 772). Heller's position closely parallels that of his contemporary, Samuel Edels, who had been the rabbi of Ostroh until his death in 1632: see Horodetsky, *History of the Rabbinate*, 188. Siev asserts, as do Assaf and others, that, being a recent immigrant, Heller was

But these motivations, whether principled or partisan, were intertwined for Heller with a more purely personal motive. He associated his fight over purchase of the rabbinate with his arrest and imprisonment in Vienna years before, and closely identified his opponents in Ludmir with his opponents in Prague. Having been only a few years earlier the victim of the intervention of the imperial court in the politics of the Prague Jewish community and having himself been expelled from office by non-Jewish authorities, Heller had reason to oppose non-Jewish involvement in rabbinical elections. His anger at his Prague opponents is palpable throughout *Megilat eivah*; it spilled over into resentment of Polish Jews who negotiate with Christian authorities to control appointments to rabbinical office.

In his youth, Heller wrote in his commentary on *Beḥinat olam* that the perfect man, the *shalem*, can perform miracles; he can change the very course of the stars in the heavens.[53] Heller thought that the workings of circumstance and divine providence had given him the power to determine the shape of new Jewish communities. In establishing the rules of the new synagogue in Vienna, and in fighting for Jewish communal control of rabbinical appointments in Volhynia and the Ukraine, he thought that he was moulding the shape of generations to come, establishing patterns that would become ingrained customs.

Is there any need to stress again the vanity of such an ambition? Heller fought many battles and lost most of them, but that is perhaps the mark of a spiritual leader. 'They live in failure', writes Buber: 'It is for them to fight and not to conquer. . . . The real way from the creation to the kingdom is trodden not on the surface of success, but in the depths of failure.'[54]

THE PERMISSION TO PUBLISH KABBALAH

Heller changed his views a number of times during the 1630s and 1640s. He took an aggressive stand against some of the wealthiest Jews in Poland. He accepted the authority of Isserles and the principle of legal codification. He came to rely more strongly than he had on the force of custom. One last change, perhaps the most significant, completes this picture of shift and motion: Heller's reversal of his stand on the publication of kabbalistic material. What he had earlier condemned, he now permitted.

In 1646 a German kabbalist named Naftali ben Jacob Bacharach submitted for the approval of the rabbis of Poland and Germany a work of Lurianic kabbalah

unused to the Polish pattern of purchase of rabbinical office, and so was outraged. This claim has some support in Heller's emphasis (in one of the manuscripts of the Yiddish *Megilat eivah*) on Poland as locus of purchase of rabbinical office: ŽMP MS 157, p. 44.

[53] Commentary on Bedersi, 1: 2: 4; p. 12; cf. *Derush ḥidushei halevanah*, 41.

[54] *Writings*, 224.

entitled *Emek hamelekh* (The Valley of the King). This was the first extensive published exposition of Lurianic doctrine, and includes, among other things, a very strongly worded attack on Jews who seek to prevent kabbalistic wisdom from reaching the people—that is, on rabbis such as Heller.[55]

The work drew enthusiastic approbations, such as the one from Naftali ben Isaac Bonn of Mainz: '[The author] rose to Heaven, to the halls of the Divine Chariot. . . . Matters that the Ancient of Days [*atik yomin*—God] hid are revealed to him, to benefit the people, to bring into the light the hidden wisdom.'[56] Shabetai Sheftel ben Isaiah Horowitz also praised the book warmly: '[The author] has surely drawn from the treasures of . . . Rabbi Isaac Luria, the man of God . . . and understood his secrets clearly. [Therefore] it is proper to print [this book]. Happy is the eye that has seen these things!'

Heller, in an act of great self-effacement and restraint, also wrote an approbation for the book. It was less enthusiastic than the others. Significantly, he made no reference to Isaac Luria. He wrote:

> There is an old controversy among the sages of the generations before us, whether the secrets of the kabbalah should be preached in public or not. But an exception may be made for the matter of *gilgul*, because although . . . [Rabbi Levi] ibn Habib [*c.*1483–*c.*1545] forbids it to be preached in public, I have seen that the wise man . . . Rabbi Isaac Abarbanel . . . states that many of the ancient Greek philosophers through their speculations on nature discovered the matter of *gilgul*. Therefore one may say that [*gilgul*] is not in a class with the other secrets of the kabbalah, and that it is proper to reveal it. Therefore, when I saw the book written by the exalted scholar . . . Rabbi Naftali Hirtz ben . . . Jacob Elhanan . . . whose book arouses hearts not to sin, and if they have sinned to turn in repentance, and furthermore contains the matter of *gilgulim*—therefore I said that this book should be permitted to be printed, so that the sinners should see it and be shamed, and all the people will see and read, and will not sin more.

This argument is the precise reverse of the position that he took in his sermon on the lessening of the moon. There too he had referred to Ibn Habib and Abarbanel. But whereas in his sermon he *accepted* Ibn Habib's ruling that *gilgul* may not be made a subject for public preaching, here he *rejects* Ibn Habib's opinion.

The decision to write the approbation was one for which Heller was criticized by one of his protégés some years later. Berekhiah Berakh ben Isaac Eizik, Heller's son-in-law's brother-in-law, was the Jewish preacher of Cracow. In 1662, in the aftermath of the massacres of 1648, he placed the blame on the many sins of Polish Jewry. He attacked various groups: for instance, arendators, rabbis who purchased their positions from Polish authorities (thus continuing Heller's battle on that

[55] See N. Bacharach, *Emek hamelekh*, p. 7*a*, in the second introduction; Scholem, *Sabbatai Sevi*, 68–71; Liebes, 'Life, Writings, and Kabbalistic Teachings'.

[56] Cf. BT *Pes.* 119*a*.

issue), and kabbalists who published kabbalistic secrets; but Berakhiah Berakh also sharply criticized the rabbis who had given permission for kabbalistic books to be published.[57]

In adopting this new leniency,[58] Heller was influenced, first and foremost, by his times. The movement towards publication and popularization of kabbalah was the general characteristic of Jewish culture of the seventeenth century. As more and more kabbalistic material began to appear in print in works of many different genres—sermons, ethical handbooks, Torah commentaries—the inhibitions on publishing such material grew gradually weaker; Heller too finally reversed his stand and permitted the publication of *Emek hamelekh*.

If he had been a man who was easily swayed, then this explanation would be sufficient to explain his change of heart. But that is not the case. He was, on the contrary, self-confident and even obstinate. It is not convincing to suggest that he was moved only by others, by the example of rabbis such as Joel Sirkes or Shabetai Horowitz. It was suggested earlier that in Poland Heller may have begun to identify with the class of 'those who are worthy of respect, who are not rich', and that this may explain to some degree his acceptance of the *Shulḥan arukh*. Similarly here, his acceptance of the popularization of kabbalah may stem from his new social perspective.

We owe it to Heller, however, to look again carefully at his approbation. It focuses on two points: the philosophical value of the doctrine of *gilgul* and the moral value of kabbalistic teachings. If kabbalah is in fact an ancient philosophy that does indeed motivate men and women to acts of piety and saintliness, why then should works such as this one not be published?

The philosopher Spinoza, still a young man at the time of Heller's death, rejected the melancholy of guilt and chastised the weak habit of regret. In Heller's day, this Spinozan doctrine was not yet known (it was not widely accepted until the twentieth century), and contrition, that is, repentance (*teshuvah*), was still highly valued. At the age of nearly 70, Heller changed his mind and repented the vehemence of his opposition to some kabbalists. He wrote that Bacharach's book 'rouses hearts . . . to turn in repentance'; it may be suggested that the heart that it turned was Heller's own.[59]

[57] See Berakhiah Berakh b. Isaac Eizik, *Zera berakh*, introd. On Berakhiah, see H. H. Ben-Sasson, *Theory and Practice*, 50–1, 194–6; Scholem, *Sabbatai Sevi*, 86–7, 602, 627.

[58] On the similar about-face of Elijah of Izmir, *c.*1674, see Saperstein (ed.), *Jewish Preaching*, 309.

[59] On the 17th-c. image of the 'penitent philosopher', or the philosopher turned kabbalist, see the discussion and the sources cited in my thesis, pp. 334–7.

ELEVEN

A Rabbi's Autobiography

THE CORONATION, 1644

On a Saturday night in late winter 1644, the *kehilah* government of Cracow met in the council chamber which was above the old synagogue and elected the new chief rabbi. They sent the three senior *gaba'im* and the communal servants with torches in their hands to announce their decision to Heller.

When I came in, they stood up and said to me, *Mazal tov*! And they seated me on the throne. The *parnas* said to me, We have unanimously agreed that there shall be none like our lord, and we have accepted His Great Torahness as president of the rabbinical court.[1]

And Heller answered with a few words ('few in number, great in value', he says), and a little prayer that his rule would find divine favour.

Although Cracow was by this time in decline, its Jewish community was still pre-eminent in Poland, and its chief rabbi the first among equals in the Polish rabbinate.[2] Being elected the president of the rabbinical court of Cracow was, in Heller's eyes, the conclusion of his trial, the completion of his deliverance; it was the happy ending of his life, of his long quest for rank, dignity, and honour. He felt, in the midst of his growing family, busy with his work in the pious community of Cracow, that nothing was now missing from his life.[3]

'The crown', he wrote, taking over a talmudic phrase with an appropriately royal motif, 'returned to its former dignity.' He now felt that he was finally able to

[1] *Megilat eivah*, 40. Compare the elements of the royal coronation: grand entry, coronation proper, and homage; see Ochmann, 'Coronation'. Heller had come to Cracow the previous autumn when he had been elected to be co-rabbi together with Joshua b. Joseph.

[2] The basic work on the Cracow Jews of this period is Bałaban, *History*: the members of the Cracow *kehilah* government during these years are listed on p. 261. Additional archival material on Heller's rabbinic activities in Cracow probably exists in the *Acta Palatinalia Iudaica Cracoviensia: Varia* 12 (1642–7).

[3] Heller wrote in a responsum, 'The men of the towns around the holy community of Cracow beset me . . . with their legal cases, so that I nearly have no time to sleep': Rapoport, *She'elot uteshuvot eitan ha'ezraḥi*, no. 7.

establish a thanksgiving feast for his deliverance in 1629. His descendants continue to celebrate it to this day, on the first day of the festive month of Adar.[4]

DELIVERANCE NARRATIVE AND AUTOBIOGRAPHY

This coronation ceremony is the final scene of *Megilat eivah*, Heller's autobiographical memoir.

Writing is based on speech; first-person narrative is one of the most natural types of writing, and one of the oldest.[5] There are ancient Jewish autobiographies: in the Bible, parts of the book of Nehemiah are written in the first person. Nevertheless, the genre was not well regarded in the Middle Ages; it was thought to smack of pride. The genres of autobiography and memoir first became important in Christian Europe in the sixteenth and seventeenth centuries; diary-keeping also became more common in this period. This is an aspect of what has been called the Renaissance discovery of the individual.[6]

Among Jews as well, autobiography and first-person narratives of all kinds were marginal genres throughout the Middle Ages.[7] Beginning in the sixteenth century, however, there are a substantial number of memoirs and first-person narratives by Ashkenazi Jews.[8] In particular, there is a group of memoirs, many of them from

[4] Note that the date of the feast, unlike that of the fast that Heller had established for 5 Tamuz, was not the anniversary of the event.

[5] Georg Misch begins his multi-volume *Geschichte der Autobiographie* with ancient Egypt; in contrast, Roy Pascal begins with St Augustine in *Design and Truth*.

[6] Note the comment in Finkelstein, *Akiba*, pp. ix–xi. The moral disapproval of autobiography continued among Jews until the 19th c.; as Moseley notes, none was published (except 'Megilat r. me'ir'): see Moseley, 'Jewish Autobiography' 220–1. The phrase 'discovery of the individual' was coined by Jacob Burckhardt in his 1860 classic, *Civilization of the Renaissance in Italy*. For a recent treatment, see J. Martin, 'Inventing Sincerity'. On early modern autobiographies, see Amelang, *Flight of Icarus*. David Sabean stresses the many types of self-conception, and the conflicts among them, in European culture of the early modern period: see id., 'Production of the Self'.

[7] Certain examples do exist, such as Petahiah of Regensburg's narrative of his pilgrimage to the land of Israel, and a very brief anonymous memoir of a German Jew, written about 1380. See Yuval, 'A German-Jewish Autobiography'.

[8] On Jewish autobiographies of the early modern period, see Moseley, 'Jewish Autobiography', which discusses *Megilat eivah* on pp. 191–206. Cf. also Zinberg, *History*, vi. 99–101, vii. 236–7; Erik, *History of Yiddish Literature*, 394–420; N. Z. Davis, 'Fame and Secrecy', and her discussion of Glueckel's memoir in her *Women on the Margins*, 5–62; Schacter, 'History and Memory'. See also Shatzky, 'Jewish Memoir Literature'. Besides those memoirs listed in the next few notes, note Josel of Rosheim's 'Diary' (in a wonderful edition by Chava Fraenkel-Goldschmidt), and, from the 18th c., the autobiographies of Jacob Emden (discussed at length by Moseley), Solomon Maimon, and Ber of Birkenthal. For bibliography, see also Schacter, 'History and Memory', 444 n. 6. There is also a substantial number of memoirs by apostate Ashkenazi Jews, although they do not concern us here: see Carlebach, 'Converts'.

Prague, beginning in the seventeenth century, that share a common form and theme. The focus of each narrative is a danger—often, but not always, imprisonment—that the author underwent, and the story of how he escaped it. This group of writings, to which *Megilat eivah* obviously belongs, may be called deliverance narratives.[9] Some, like Heller's, were written to be read by families at annual family celebrations.[10]

The deliverance narrative has close ties to another biographical genre, namely martyrology.[11] Meir Kadosh, for example, began his story with a riddle: how did he acquire his peculiar name, 'Meir the Martyr', when he was clearly still alive? He answered with the story of how, as a young student, he was kidnapped by a Polish nobleman near the town of Oswięcim.[12] Hanokh Altshuler, the *shamash* of one of the Prague synagogues in the 1620s, wrote another, about his brush with the law in a case of stolen tapestries. Likewise, towards the beginning of the eighteenth century, the grandfather of Solomon Maimon preceded his grandson, author of a classic autobiography of the Haskalah, in committing to writing the story of his misfortunes and escapes.[13]

[9] See Moseley, 'Jewish Autobiography', 202–5. On the custom of special 'Purims', as they were called, and the scrolls that were written for these celebrations (initially communal rather than family celebrations), see the article 'Purim' in the *Jewish Encyclopedia*.

[10] Some were purely oral texts. For example, the story of Joshua Edels of Prague and his imprisonment in the 1640s was first written down by a descendant of Edels in 1833: see Edeles, *Megilat r. yehoshua edeles*. It is similarly possible that Heller's memoir existed originally as an oral text—the earliest manuscripts date from the 18th c.—or particularly that the Yiddish text, before it was written down, may have been for some generations an oral text parallel to the written Hebrew text.

[11] These personal deliverance narratives are parallel, as Jacob Shatzky (in his 1944 article in *Yivo-bleter*) and others have noted, to the Ashkenazi Jewish histories and historical poems from this period that narrate the dangers and deliverance of whole communities, such as the community of Frankfurt in 1614, or Heller's thanksgiving poems from 1620. On the poems, see e.g. Turniansky, 'Yiddish "Historical" Songs'. On Judah Leib b. Joshua Heschel, *Milḥamah beshalom* (narrative of the siege of Prague in 1648), see Šedinová, 'Hebrew Literature', 38–57.

[12] Oswięcim later achieved notoriety under the name of Auschwitz. Meir b. Yehiel Hakadosh's memoir, 'Megilat r. me'ir', was written and (exceptionally) published in Cracow in 1632, and reprinted in 1903.

[13] 'The Story of the Tapestry' [Megilat purei hakela'im] by Hanokh b. Moses Altshuler was written about 1623; cf. Sadek, 'Die Yiddische Version'. Maimon's grandfather appears in Maimon, *Solomon Maimon*, 7. Other examples include (from the early 18th c.) the story of Samuel Taussig, *Megilat shmu'el*. Other family *megilot* from Prague, most from the 18th c., are listed by S. H. Lieben in his introduction to *Megilat shmu'el*, 308–12. Cf. also Sadek, 'From the MSS Collections', 16–19. The *megilah* of the Behrend family of Leipzig, from about 1730, also belongs to the genre of imprisonment stories. It was translated from Yiddish to German by Jost (see Behrend family, 'Eine familien-Megillah'). Abraham b. Joseph Segal apparently wrote a memoir of deliverance in the 1650s; he mentions it in his introduction to his commentary on *Megilat ta'anit*, but it is not extant. Note also the deliverance themes in the late 17th-c. memoir of Phoebus (Feivel) Gans of Minden (dis-

Megilat eivah, in some long-vanished initial draft, may have been a simple deliverance narrative. The hero (Heller) fell into danger and he was saved. That is, he was imprisoned in Vienna and eventually released. The present form of *Megilat eivah* is, however, a double deliverance narrative. The extension of the narrative focuses on a repetition of that pattern of deliverance. In Ludmir Heller was once again in danger, but communal action saved him, and he returned triumphantly to Ludmir as he had once returned to Prague.

But he did not leave matters there. *Megilat eivah* does not end with his return to Ludmir, but continues with the story of his election to the rabbinate in Cracow, and closes with the scene of his formal appointment and acceptance. This closing scene completes the story and gives it a rounded and circular form. The pattern of rise and fall begun in the first section reaches its conclusion here, as Heller emphasized.

One should not anachronistically suppose that in *Megilat eivah* Heller intended to write an 'autobiography' in the modern sense, that is, to give a 'full account' of his life.[14] He did not include any facts about his childhood (as another seventeenth-century Jew, Glueckel of Hameln, did in her wonderful memoir) or about his father (as he had in his introduction to *Ma'adanei melekh*).[15] Neither in *Megilat eivah* nor in any of his other writings did he mention his mother. Indeed, apart from a list of the works that he wrote, he included virtually nothing of his life before his arrest, that is, before he was 50 years old. He was not telling the story of his formative years, but rather the misfortunes of a grown man.

Thus Heller was not telling his whole story: there are patterns of deliberate silence in *Megilat eivah*.[16] Indeed, he made his concern for appropriate silence explicit: twice, he quoted the biblical verse, 'A prudent man concealeth shame' (Prov. 12: 16) to justify his omission of the names of his Jewish opponents from the narrative.[17] Moreover, those names were not the only ones that he concealed. He also did not record the name of any of the non-Jews who appear in the narrative,

cussed in Zimmer, *Embers of the Sages*, 157–74), in the anonymous late 17th-c. fragment published by Alexander Marx (id. (ed.), 'A Seventeenth Century Autobiography'), and in Glueckel's memoirs themselves. Note also the deliverance themes in the early 19th-c. memoir of Moses Sofer, *Sefer zikaron*.

[14] This is the thrust of Moseley's argument; he attributes the notion of a 'full account' to Rousseau, and dates it to the 18th c. Cf. the discussion in Amelang, *Flight of Icarus*, introd. However, note Juda Mehler's professed goal of recording 'everything that has happened to me since I became a man' (by which, as he immediately explains, he means 'since I was married'): see his autobiographical introduction to *Shevet yehudah*, in Bloch, 'Vielbegehrter Rabbiner', 131.

[15] On the absence of the self as a child before Rousseau, see Moseley, 'Jewish Autobiography', 24–47.

[16] Cf. R. Pascal, *Design and Truth*, 62–70, on reticence and memory; Amelang, *Flight of Icarus*, 117–29, on silences in early modern artisan autobiographies.

[17] *Megilat eivah*, 30, 34.

except that of the emperor himself (in Chapter 8, I discussed other omissions from Heller's narrative: for example, neither the arrest of his patron Jacob Bassevi nor that of his colleague Pinhas Horowitz are mentioned).[18] There is so much that Heller did not recount: the foul and sweet smells of city streets, the beadle summoning the men to morning prayers, the indistinct letters of a Hebrew book read by candlelight, the all-pervasive darkness of the night hours, the infirmities of his ageing body. But one must not expect Heller to write like a nineteenth-century novelist.[19]

The historian Peter Burke discerns two main types of silence in early modern Europe: the silence of respect and the silence of discretion.[20] Heller was discrete. He mentioned that, to pay his fine to the emperor, he was forced to sell his house; he did not mention that he sold it to his son.[21]

This is not to mention aspects of life, such as bodily emissions, concerning which modesty and good taste commanded silence. While it may be supposed that the common Vienna prison was not an entirely pleasant place to spend a night, or, to take a second example, that during his long illness Heller suffered various symptoms of disease, he spared his readers all these memories. His rabbinic works, like other rabbinic works and the Talmud itself, are very selective in their choice of topics, but their silences are very different from those of *Megilat eivah*. In his halakhic writings, Heller felt a responsibility, for example, to discuss the disposal of infant faeces on the sabbath. The *kashrut* of maggoty food, including both the food items and the maggots themselves, deserved several extensive discussions. So did a wide variety of sexual matters.[22] In *Megilat eivah*, however, Heller did not include any such details: there are no maggots, and indeed there is not even any eating.

A different sort of modesty affected Heller in another way: he never described his own appearance or anyone else's. Here again, moral scruples may account in part for the silence. Portraiture was an art rejected by traditional Ashkenazi Judaism. For Heller, physical description, even in words, may have suggested vanity and even lewdness.

Megilat eivah, as already noted, exists in two versions, Hebrew and Yiddish.[23] Each version, each language, has its own silences. Heller was accompanied to

[18] See above, p. 151.

[19] For a discussion of what is missing in 16th-c. travel accounts (e.g. peasants), see Halperin, 'Foreign Travel Accounts', 96–8, 110–11.

[20] Burke, 'Notes'. Cf. J. Martin, 'Inventing Sincerity'.

[21] See *Megilat eivah*, 36; Muneles (ed.), *Inscriptions*, 323.

[22] By the 17th c. rabbinic literature had begun to be criticized for its obscenity: see *Kol sakhal*, attributed to Leone da Modena, in T. Fishman, *Shaking the Pillars*, 157; cf. Rivkin, *Leon da Modena*, 129.

[23] The Hebrew version has been published many times, the Yiddish version only once, in a short-lived Yiddish periodical in the 1920s. See the Bibliography of Heller's works below, items 31 and 32.

Vienna by a servant; the servant appears in the Yiddish version, but not in the Hebrew one.[24] Heller pleaded for a favour from the Vienna city judge with prayers and also with a bribe; the pleas appear in the Hebrew version, the bribe only in the Yiddish version.[25] In general, the Yiddish version is more detailed and more circumstantial than the Hebrew one, but there are some exceptions: the Hebrew text is more detailed, for example, in its description of Heller's writings.[26]

One aspect of autobiography, a crucial part of the Western tradition since Augustine's *Confessions*, is lacking from *Megilat eivah*: the probing of conscience. In this, he was at one with most other seventeenth-century Ashkenazi Jewish memoirists.[27] Only Glueckel made some efforts in this vein. Abraham Horowitz suggested that one should keep a diary, which he calls a *megilat setarim*, a scroll of secrets, in which to record all one's sins. Given the obviously private and possibly scandalous character of such a diary, it is not surprising that none survive.[28]

Heller was not able to conceal his vices, notably ambition, sublimated as rabbinical ambition, and pride, sublimated into the pride of Torah. Nevertheless, in *Megilat eivah*, and in his other writings as well, he declined to remember his sins. Nor was he concerned, even slightly, with the theme of temptation; the fundamental puritan theme of deliverance from sin appears neither in *Megilat eivah* nor in any of the other Ashkenazi deliverance narratives.[29] 'The prudent man', it may be recalled, 'concealeth shame.'

ON SILENCE

Another sort of silence is that of the Stoic. An ancient tradition links silence and misfortune. 'Let him sit alone in silence', writes the author of Lamentations (3: 28). Job's comforters are silent for seven days before they speak.[30]

The philosophy of the Stoics enjoyed a revival in Europe in the early seventeenth century, supported by writers and thinkers such as the French essayist Michel de Montaigne, the Spanish satirist Quevedo, the German poet Martin Opitz, and especially the Dutch scholar Justus Lipsius. Parallel to this current of thought, Heller placed some emphasis on the Stoic elements of rabbinic and medieval Judaism, as is evident in his sermon on the lessening of the moon.

[24] Yiddish *Megilat eivah* in Erik, 'Memoirs', 202, ŽMP MS 157, p. 29.

[25] Yiddish *Megilat eivah* in ŽMP MS 347, p. 11.

[26] The two versions are compared by Erik, *History of Yiddish Literature*, 414–19.

[27] Cf. R. Pascal, *Design and Truth*, 24: 'Most medieval religious autobiographies fail to relate meaningfully outer event and inner experience.' See also Schiffman, 'Renaissance Historicism'.

[28] See the introduction to *Berit avraham*. Jacob Emden's memoir may show the influence of this category of writing.

[29] See Shea, *Spiritual Autobiography*.

[30] Cf. David b. Samuel, 'Magen david', 6*a*. On the types of Jewish silence, cf. the section on silence in I. Horowitz, *Shenei luḥot haberit*, 'Sha'ar ha'otiyot', *shetikah* (i. 77*b*–79*a*).

Unlike many modern readers, Heller was rarely struck by moral compunctions in reading rabbinic texts. For example, the strict punishments that are theoretically prescribed in rabbinic literature for certain infractions of ritual law, such as the death penalty for sabbath-breaking, do not seem to have struck him as cruel or unfair. Neither did the unequal treatment of men and women in Jewish law evoke from him any signs of discomfort or hesitation.[31]

But one mishnaic rule that truly disturbed him is the rule that on the sabbath a mourner may not tear his garments. It is not the special stringency that disturbed him, but rather the suggestion that, were it not the sabbath, a person would be allowed to vent feelings of anger and grief in this way. Heller was convinced that such permission would be highly improper.

Maimonides wrote that . . . when a man tears his garment, he calms his anger. But it would appear that this is prohibited, because we have learned explicitly in the Mishnah, at the end of tractate *Berakhot* (9: 5), that 'a person is required to bless [God for] evil tidings just as one blesses [God for] good tidings', and [Maimonides] explained there that [one must bless God for evil tidings] joyfully with a happy heart, repressing his anger.[32]

Jewish Stoics do not refrain from tears but from expressions of anger. Heller was not ashamed to write twice in *Megilat eivah* that he had wept, but he was deeply and bitterly ashamed of his anger, which he strove, quite unsuccessfully, to hide.[33]

Heller believed that personal sorrows should be met not with anger but with joy. It is clear from any number of passages in *Megilat eivah* and elsewhere that he did not succeed in living up to this ideal. Indeed, as is clear both in *Megilat eivah* and in his plague sermon in 1625, he hesitated to celebrate even miracles with unalloyed joy when deliverances were joined to sorrows.

He knew the pain of a bereaved father. His daughter Nechle died in 1632, and his daughter Doberish in 1641.[34] In 1639, moreover, his daughters Reyzel and Nisel, together with three of his grandchildren, died in Prague in a plague that devastated the entire Prague Jewish community. He failed to record their deaths in *Megilat eivah*, but in an uncommon—within his time and culture, almost unparalleled—gesture, he personally wrote their epitaph as an outpouring of personal grief:

[31] The unequal treatment of Jews and non-Jews in certain aspects of the law, surprisingly, did call forth such a response. Heller quoted Maimonides' apologetic justification of these inequalities: *Tos YT*, *BK* 4: 3. Cf. Emanuel, 'Attitude', 51.

[32] *Tos YT*, *Shab.* 13: 3. Cf. *Tos YT*, *Ber.* 9: 5.

[33] See *Megilat eivah*, 29, 36. Gaukroger, *Descartes*, 18–19, notes an early 17th-c. fashion for melancholy states of mind.

[34] See Muneles, *Inscriptions*, 323; Wachstein (ed.), *Inschriften*, i. 143; *Megilat eivah*, 38.

My daughter, my daughter, the pious Reyzel
My daughter, my daughter, the pious Nisel,
Bring me two eyes like two fountains, that for each of you a fountain will flow.
But how will I be comforted or cease?
When I remember my grandsons Moses and Simhah ['Joy'],
All joy is darkened to me,
And when I think of my grandson Gottred, my heartache is great.
With this I will close: may their souls be bound in the bond of eternal life,
But I will be in mourning and wailing, until I merit the day of resurrection.[35]

FAMILY

Heller's essential desire in *Megilat eivah*, as noted above, was to tell a story of deliverance. Superimposed on that narrative framework, however, is a more complex portrayal of the self in a strikingly modern vein, divided between career and home, between a succession of rabbinical jobs, each one listed and commented on, and (especially in the second half of the work) his life as a family patriarch.

It is a measure of the importance of family for Heller that he included in *Megilat eivah* many details about his family life. This is especially marked in light of his extreme selectivity in regard to the details that he included in that work. *Megilat eivah* was of course written to be read by his family at the annual family celebration that he established, and that fact too suggests the extent to which he saw himself as a member of his family.[36] It should be noted, however, that Heller's family does not appear in the first half of the narrative, that is, before his release from prison in Vienna.[37] In the second half of the work, on the other hand, it is mentioned frequently and prominently, on several occasions in contexts that digress from the main plotline. Heller's relationship to his family had changed over the years.

The family is, of course, an educational grouping as well as a biological or an economic one. Nor is this task merely incidental to it; it is at the very centre of a notion of a family that children are not merely fed, but taught. For Heller, as a rabbi and a scholar, education was primarily book learning, the study of Torah. In several passages in *Tosafot yom tov*, however, written when he was in his thirties and his children were still young, Heller presented Torah and family as adversaries. In

[35] The epitaph is published in Muneles (ed.), *Inscriptions*, 321–4.

[36] Cf. also the discussions above of Heller's activities within the Horowitz family (above, pp. 25–6), and his designation as 'the son-in-law of R. Aaron' on the title pages of *Tosafot yom tov* and *Ma'adanei yom tov* (above, pp. 131–2). Note too the regards that he sent to his cousin Mirel Wallerstein at the end of his letter to Aunt Edel (above, p. 103), as well as his regards to his son and his in-laws in Lvov in two of his responsa: Rapoport, *She'elot uteshuvot eitan ha'ezrahi*, nos. 7, 9, and his prayer for his family in the poem that he placed at the end of *Tosafot yom tov*.

[37] Pinhas Horowitz the elder of Cracow, whose relationship to Heller (through Rachel) is spelled out by him, is mentioned in the dream question story in *Megilat eivah*, 35.

one place, for example, he argued against the Rosh's view that the court should compel a young man to take a wife if he has passed the age of 20, saying that the man should be allowed to continue to study unmarried, if that was his wish. Clearly Heller, who had himself married before the age of 20, believed that a man who begins to earn a living and raise a family risks abandoning the study of Torah.[38] He was proud that he could afford an apartment with a study, a room where he could leave his family behind and let someone else (his wife, his in-laws, the wet-nurse) take care of the children.[39] Even when he had been a young yeshiva student, to begin study was to leave the family behind and to go elsewhere, even to another city; Heller himself probably left his family in Wallerstein when he went to study with Jacob Günzburg.

Heller taught his children himself—as we have seen, this included Hebrew grammar—and so succeeded, even in these early years, in joining family and Torah. When he began to teach students in his home, moreover, he embraced another family, not of blood relations but of students—boys who sat at his table, ate his food, and were entrusted to his care. He writes that he was 'a father to them',[40] and in his introduction to the tractate *Avot* (Fathers) he repeated with a certain pride the medieval commonplace that teachers are the true parents.

As his own sons grew to maturity, however, his study with them grew as well. His oldest son, Moses, helped read the proofs for *Tosafot yom tov*; the proofs of the 1619 volume of *Ma'adanei melekh* were read by Liva, while those of the 1628 volume were read by his youngest son, Abraham. The second edition of *Tosafot yom tov* was proof-read by his son-in-law Zevi Hirsch Melis, the husband of his daughter Rebecca.[41]

It will be recalled that Heller studied astronomy with Abraham at the time of the latter's wedding. Later, he seems to have studied the Jerusalem Talmud with Abraham and Liva. In one place, he actually refers to a commentary that Abraham, then in his twenties, wrote on the Jerusalem Talmud, one of the first Ashkenazi commentaries on this work and a praiseworthy contribution to the revival of neglected ancient Jewish texts.[42] The members of Heller's family ceased to be a distraction from the study of Torah and became instead companions for him as a

[38] See *TosYT*, introd. to *Yev*. Cf. *TosYT*, *Avot* 1: 5, 3: 7.

[39] See *Megilat eivah*, 26.

[40] Yiddish *Megilat eivah* in Erik, 'Memoirs', 192.

[41] See Hailperin MS, pp. 45–6, 101 n. 3.

[42] *TosYT*, *Sot*. 9: 1; cf. *Peah* 6: 2, *MS* 5: 6, *Men*. 7: 3, *Torat ha'asham*, 187; and see J. M. Zunz, *City of Righteousness*, 101. Abraham Heller's commentary, which may have been a very slight work, was never published, and the manuscript, like so many others, was lost. Ginzberg (*Commentary*, 121), in his survey of commentaries on the Jerusalem Talmud, expresses doubt that Abraham Heller ever actually wrote the commentary; he suggests that the work may only have been planned. This seems unnecessary. David Darshan, a student of Isserles, wrote a commentary on the Jerusalem Talmud in the mid-16th c.: see Darshan, *Shir hama'alot*, 25.

Torah scholar. He quoted each of his sons (but, regrettably, none of his daughters) in his later writings.[43]

Much of the discussion of his children in *Megilat eivah* concerns the topic of marrying them off. Chapter 6 described him negotiating one marriage in 1619, and Rachel enjoying Esther's successful match.[44] The later matches were also well made, from Heller's point of view—that is, his sons, daughters, and grandchildren were married into wealthy and distinguished families. The Heller family also pursued the strategy of settling in diverse cities and countries. The eldest, Moses, remained in Prague, while Nechle moved to Vienna; Liva and Samuel were in Brest-Litovsk, Doberish in Cracow, and Abraham in Lublin.[45]

Heller was also active as a grandfather. He seems to have been fond of his daughter Nisel's son Nathan, and mentions specially in *Megilat eivah* that he went to Nathan's wedding in Chełm. Nathan was named after Heller's father (the custom among Ashkenazi Jews is to name children after departed relatives), and was something of a scholar; Heller quoted him in one place in his writings.[46]

Two other grandchildren are mentioned in *Megilat eivah*. After their daughter Doberish's death, Heller and his wife raised two of Doberish's daughters, named Reyzel and Nisel after their aunts.[47] Truly his life had come full circle, from his childhood as an orphan raised by his grandfather to being a grandfather raising his orphaned grandchildren.

ON HIMSELF

We must now raise the question: how did Heller perceive himself? How did he depict himself in *Megilat eivah*?

I have already noted that he did not intend to give a complete account of his life. On the other hand, however, he did not present himself merely as a cipher. In addition to portraying himself as the victim of religious persecution and as the recipient of special divine favour—as the stereotypical hero, that is, of a deliverance narrative—he also depicted himself as a professional rabbi, advancing his career in a series of jobs, and as a family patriarch, marrying off children and mourning them.

[43] References to Heller's sons in the 2nd edn. of *Tosafot yom tov* are collected in J. M. Zunz, *City of Righteousness*, 101, Beit Halevi, *Life of Heller*, 38, and Hakohen, 'His Books', 156. One may add that Heller quotes Liva in *Torat ha'asham*, 187.

[44] See above, pp. 103–4.

[45] On the strategy of dispersal, see N. Z. Davis, *Women on the Margins*, 13. On Heller's son Samuel, see Hailperin MS, p. 38 n. 5, quoting Feinstein, *City of Fame*, 120. Is Abraham Heller the same as Abraham Heller of Frankfurt, the Jewish doctor who applied for an imperial Passbrief on 14 Oct. 1636 (listed in the HHStA records)?

[46] 'Notes on *Tur* and *Shulḥan arukh*, "Even ha'ezer"', published with *Ḥidushei harashba* on tractate *Ketuvot*, para. 170.

[47] *Megilat eivah*, 39. On the adoption of grandchildren, cf. Gaukroger, *Descartes*, 23.

To understand his self-portrait, I must begin, however, with another individual, the man whom Heller cast in *Megilat eivah* as his true nemesis, the Viennese 'nobleman' with whom he arranged an interview after being released from prison. As noted in Chapter 8, this man may have been a Jesuit. In the Hebrew text Heller called him, *sar ḥashuv, nasu panim etsel hakeisar* ('an important nobleman favoured by the emperor'), and in the Yiddish, *ayn groser mekhtiger her* ('a great and powerful gentleman').[48]

Let us recall the scene, only part of which was quoted above.[49] The nobleman refused to help Heller, and accused him of having once made a boast at his expense. Heller responded that he could not have done so, since the man to whom he was said to have made the boast, Count von Liechtenstein, was already dead and not available for conversation at the time of the supposed boast.

At that point, as Heller recounted, the attitude of the nobleman changed. He still refused to help Heller return to his post as the rabbi of Prague, but he suggested instead that Heller 'could serve the Almighty in some other profession'. Heller answered that he could not change professions, and so the conversation moved to a short discussion of the rabbinical job market. The nobleman suggested that Heller find a rabbinical post in Germany; Heller countered that on account of the war, Germany was now too expensive a place to live. The nobleman concluded the interview by assuring Heller that his (the nobleman's) house was always open to him, and by giving him the pious advice to be patient with his misfortunes. Heller left, as he tells us, with proper bows and obeisances.

It is surely unnecessary to point out that Heller portrayed his nemesis as mild-mannered, even apologetic. It is a surprise to the reader; perhaps it was a surprise to Heller himself when it happened. Indeed, he portrayed the nobleman as being pious, that is, concerned with the worship of the Almighty; he is actually said to recognize that Heller can serve the Almighty, as a Jew and perhaps even as a rabbi. The nobleman's view is the precise mirror-image of Heller's view of non-Jews as expressed in *Tosafot yom tov*.

The non-Jews in *Megilat eivah*, as noted in Chapter 8, are mostly depicted as being somewhat stupid. Did Heller depict himself as cleverer than this 'groser mekhtiger her'? He did. The Christian was deceived and Heller corrected him. The Christian then tried to be helpful, but his suggestion—a career in Germany—was not a good one (particularly with the hindsight of the 1640s). Furthermore, Heller's answer to him on the question of von Liechtenstein seems cagey (though perhaps I am here being too suspicious). He said only that when he returned to Prague, von Liechtenstein was dead; he did not say whether he had made a similar boast to someone else.

48 Ibid. 34; Yiddish *Megilat eivah*, ed. Erik, 206.

49 See above, pp. 149–50.

Why did Heller include this particular scene in *Megilat eivah*? The interview was fruitless, uneventful, even banal. What meaning did it carry for Heller or for his readers?

To answer this question we must glance at another rabbinic memoir, Leone da Modena's *Ḥayei yehudah* (Life of Judah), written in the same period as *Megilat eivah*. In *Ḥayei yehudah*, Christians usually appear to confirm da Modena's dignity and prestige. They applaud his sermons and read his books. One of the great moments of da Modena's life, as he narrated it in his memoir, was the day that a member of the French royal family came to hear him preach.[50]

Heller was moved by the same desire to record the honour and deference that he had received from non-Jews of high or even low rank. The Prague Jews, Fynes Moryson had once written, 'live in exceeding contempt, hearing nothinge but reproches from the people'.[51] Not so. Heller noted that the imperial judge asked him to sit at his right hand. He may have been alarmed, but he could not help but be flattered when the imperial vice-chancellor exaggerated his wealth and treated him as a great Jewish leader, assuring the sceptical *shtadlanim* that even the Jews of Turkey would contribute to Heller's ransom. The powerful Viennese gentleman allowed him an interview and spoke to him with respect. Heller wished to convey to his readers, including his family, that he was an important man who talked to powerful noblemen, a man who had received a pardon from the emperor himself. He had *kavod*; he had honour.[52]

The Viennese nobleman was also concerned with honour—so Heller depicted him. It upset him that Heller might have bragged about besting him in debate, or might have scorned or belittled him. He is depicted in three dimensions. He is a religious man; he is a political agent, a man with the ear of the emperor; and he is a man of honour, to whom Heller, at the end of the scene, pays deference.

The entire plot of *Megilat eivah*, or at least its first half, revolves around these same three axes. Heller, as shown above in Chapter 8, gave three explanations of his arrest. One was religious, providential: a divine *gezerah* against the Torah. Another was political: the Thirty Years War caused political dissension within the Prague Jewish community. The third explanation was that given by the Vienna nobleman, whose story made the plot hinge on a question of honour.

An answer can now be suggested to the question of how Heller saw himself. He viewed himself along these same three axes. His rabbinical career carried all three meanings for him—religious, political, and social-hierarchical. He saw himself as a man close to God, an embodiment of Torah; as a man active in communal politics,

[50] See Leone da Modena, *Autobiography*, 131; cf. pp. 78, 80, 96, 107, 109, 117, 121, 128, 143, 146–7, 151, 171.

[51] Moryson, *Shakespeare's Europe*, 490.

[52] Heller's dry recounting of his rabbinical posts and his discussions of the lineage of his in-laws made the same point.

trying to hold together a divided community; and also not least as a man of honour. In the Viennese nobleman Heller drew a kind of mirror-image of himself; no mere stereotype, not a complete picture but a faithful one of a proud man, who taught but never fully learned the lesson of patience.

TWELVE

The Massacres of 1648

THE TWENTIETH DAY OF SIVAN

IN spring and summer 1648 the Cossack uprising led by Bogdan Chmielnicki brought massacres and violence to the Ukraine and Poland. Among the victims of the Cossacks and their allies were thousands, even tens of thousands, of Jews in Poland and the Ukraine. Thousands more may have died in the famine and the plagues that accompanied and followed the insurrection. Nemirov, where Heller had so recently been rabbi, was among the first towns to be put to the sword, on 20 Sivan (10 June) 1648. It was followed by Tulczyn, Bar, Polonnoye, and many, many other communities. Ludmir and Lutsk were not spared; Lvov suffered a devastating siege; even Lublin was threatened before the Cossacks withdrew behind the Dnieper that winter. The war and the massacres began again in 1649 and continued sporadically through the next decade.[1]

Forty years later, the Shabatean visionary Mordechai Ashkenazi thought that

Earlier versions of this chapter were delivered as lectures at the Tauber Institute of Brandeis University and the conference at Bar Ilan University on 'Gezerot taḥ–tat: European Jewry in 1648–49: Contexts and Consequences'. The author is indebted to the audiences at both lectures, and to the organizers of the conference.–

[1] Many of the Hebrew chronicles and poems on the 1648 massacres are collected in Gurland, *On the History*. Note also the liturgical poems on the massacres by David b. Samuel, 'Magen david', 4*a*–6*a*. There is an extensive scholarly literature on the massacres, as well as an enormous literature on the rebellion in general. See the historiographical surveys in Raba, *Between Remembrance and Denial*; Basarab, *Pereiaslav 1654*; and Bacon, ' "The House of Hannover" '. We look forward to the appearance of Frank Sysyn's full history of the 1648 Cossack rebellion. A special issue of *Jewish History* on the events of 1648 appeared while the present book was in proof; it is an essential starting point for future research, and considerably revises our understanding of events. 17th-c. Jewish descriptions of the massacres (including Heller's) are discussed in Raba, *Between Remembrance and Denial*, 37–70. See also Fram, 'Reappraisal'; J. Katz, 'More'; Fram, 'And Still a Gap Exists'; and id., 'Creating a Tale'. The Hebrew chronicles of the massacres and their authors are described in Malachi, 'Chroniclers'; Weinryb, 'Hebrew Chronicles'. On the responses of the Jewish community to the massacres, see Hailperin, 'Captivity and Redemption'. Note also J. Katz, 'Between 1096 and 1648'; Nadav, 'Jewish Community of Nemyriv'; Bacon and Rosman, 'A "Chosen" Community'; Rosman, 'Image of Poland'; Roskies, *Against the Apocalypse*, 48–52; Alan Mintz, *Hurban*, 102–5.

his *magid*, his instructing angel, still wept for the 1648 massacres.[2] Heller thought that they were the worst calamity to befall the Jews since the Romans destroyed the Second Temple, worse than the Crusades. He may well have been correct: the slaughter was on a scale that the Jews had not known for centuries and that would not be repeated until the twentieth century.

FASTING AND SILENCE

Some time after the first series of massacres, in 1650, during a break in the fighting, the Jewish community of Poland began to seek ways to commemorate these events. Shabetai Kohen, a young and brilliant talmudist in Vilna, suggested, and the Council of the Four Lands adopted, an annual fast-day.[3] Massacres in many different communities had taken place on many different days, but 20 Sivan, the anniversary of the massacre in Nemirov, was chosen as a general fast-day for all the Jews of Poland and the Ukraine.

Certain details of the 1650 decision suggest Heller's involvement. Shabetai Kohen was a protégé of his,[4] and Heller had lived in Nemirov for three years.[5] The arguments made for choosing 20 Sivan seem to repeat those made by Heller in *Megilat eivah*. The fast-day that he created on the anniversary of his arrest in 1629 provided a model for the commemoration of the 1648 massacres.[6]

[2] Scholem, *Dreams*, 86. Scholem misreads *zot hashanah*, literally 'this year', as a reference to 1695–6. It is actually the name of the year: *zot* = 408.

[3] See Shabetai b. Me'ir Hakohen, *Megilat eifah*, 255; Hailperin, *Documents*, 77–8. The two texts echo one another. Although Shabetai seems to claim that he acted on his own initiative in instituting the fast-day, it is possible that the council suggested and adopted the fast-day, and that Shabetai then went further and declared it binding on his family both inside and outside Poland.

[4] Heller's relation to Shabetai Hakohen may be gauged from the approbation that he gave to the latter's *Siftei kohen*, and still more so from the notes that Heller added to the text of *Siftei kohen*. The title of Shabetai's *Megilat eifah* seems more than coincidentally close to *Megilat eivah*.

[5] Note also the reference to the massacre of Nemirov in connection with Heller's 'Mi sheberakh' (below, n. 6).

[6] Note also the annual day of mourning declared in Cracow in 1637 in memory of the seven martyrs of that year: see the document in Wettstein, *Ancient Matters*, 15. But the choice of 20 Sivan is backed by two arguments strangely reminiscent of Heller's reasoning in *Megilat eivah*: an argument from medieval precedent backed up by an argument that the fast-day commemorates the beginning of the misfortune. Shabetai Kohen and the Council of Four Lands both argued that 20 Sivan had been declared as a fast-day on an earlier occasion (the martyrdom of the Jews of Blois in 1171). This medieval precedent is reminiscent of Heller's remarks concerning 'Thursday of Parashat Ḥukat' as a day of bad omen (see above, Ch. 8 nn. 46–7). Heller was influenced by that precedent when he chose the date of his arrest (rather than, say, the date that he was put in prison) as the date of the fast-day. It is also the beginning of his narrative in *Megilat eivah*. Similarly, it was argued that the massacre of Nemirov was the beginning of the 1648 massacres. It was indeed the first town in which Jews were massacred, but it was preceded by massacres of village Jews, and the

Even before the declaration of the annual fast-day, however, he had responded to the 1648 massacres with innovations in ritual. 'As soon as the terrible massacre of the holy community of Great Nemirov was known in the holy community of Cracow', that is, almost at the very beginning of the troubles in 1648, he instituted a short blessing, a special *Mi sheberakh*, to be recited every sabbath and holiday during morning services in the synagogues of Cracow on behalf of those who do not hold private conversations during the prayer service.[7]

At times of danger, penitence was the rule.[8] Heller's new blessing is comparable to the great penitence instituted at the same time by the kabbalist and visionary Samson of Ostropol in an attempt to avert misfortune.[9] He knew the victims of Nemirov, we must assume, and must have sat with them when they were in mourning. Now he was mourning them. It was noted in Chapter 11 that Heller believed in principle that he should 'bless [God for] evil tidings joyfully with a happy heart'. This he did not have the strength to do in 1648; he had only the strength to be silent. That was his message to the Jews of Cracow: remain silent.

Concerns about talking during the prayer service were common in the sixteenth and seventeenth centuries. The great kabbalists Isaac Luria and Moses Cordovero, for instance, had warned their followers against it.[10] Just a year or two before the massacres, Shabetai Horowitz had included talking during the prayer service among his criticisms of Polish Jewry.[11] 'Woe to them and woe to their souls!' wrote

designation as the 'beginning' is once again somewhat arbitrary. It is not, for instance, the beginning of Hannover's chronicle. Note also that Shabetai refers to the fast-day as a family fast-day—along the lines of Heller's—rather than a communal one. I am indebted to Jacob J. Schacter's illuminating discussion of this material, and look forward to his forthcoming article on the 20 Sivan fast-day.

[7] Heller's blessing and its superscription are reprinted in Haberman, 'Liturgical and Other Poems', 141. On the fight of Cracow rabbis, including Joel Sirkes and others, against conversations in synagogue, see Bialer, 'Cracow', 132–3. Loud praying is defended by Heller in *MalYT* 100: 2. The noisiness of synagogues was frequently remarked on by non-Jews. See e.g. Comenius, *Labyrinth*, 51: '[The Jews], wagging their heads, mumbled something in a low voice; or arising and stopping their ears, they opened their mouths wide and gave out sounds not unlike those of howling wolves.'

[8] There is no reason to believe, incidentally, that Heller thought that the massacres had been a punishment for this sin in particular (any more than he thought that the Vienna plague of 1625 was a punishment for not reciting *Oreḥot ḥayim*). Heller's view of the causes of the massacres will be discussed below.

[9] 'It did not help', the chronicler Nathan Hannover reported gloomily concerning R. Samson's effort, 'for the evil decree had already been sealed': Hannover, *Yeven metsulah*, 47–8; cf. A. Ashkenazi, *Tsa'ar bat rabim*, 19. For prophylactic penance, see also Hahn, *Yosef omets*, p. x.

[10] See Fine (trans. and ed.), *Safed Spirituality*, 35 (no. 9), 72 (no. 25); cf. p. 45 (no. 20). Cf. Hahn, *Yosef omets*, 5; Glueckel bat Judah Leib, *Life*, 10. Note also *Oreḥot ḥayim*, attributed to the Rosh (and translated by Heller), nos. 14, 50; and cf. Kanarfogel, *'Peering through the Lattices'*, 83.

[11] 'Vavei ha'amudim', end of ch. 10, in I. Horowitz, *Shenei luḥot haberit*, ii.13*a*.

Horowitz. 'How will their prayers ascend to Heaven?' Prayers must be said with devotion, if God is to listen to them. Heller believed in miracles, and he believed in the possible efficacy of prayer.[12]

The form of Heller's change, his *takanah*, however, is somewhat surprising. Contrast the suggestion of Shabetai Horowitz: 'It would be proper for every community . . . to designate men who will reprove those who converse with many threats and embarrass them publicly.' In the synagogues of Prague, Horowitz and Heller no doubt remembered, those who gossiped with their neighbours were to be evicted by the *gaba'im*.[13] Clearly, Heller instituted a blessing rather than a system of fines because he wished to enact a response that would be pious but not punitive. Blessings for the virtuous, not curses for the wicked, were to be the order of the day.

One historian reports a legend that Heller, seeking guidance on how to respond to the massacres, made use of a traditional Ashkenazi Jewish magical ceremony, known as a *she'elat ḥalom*, a dream question. In this ceremony, a question is asked before one goes to sleep, and in a dream that night, an answer comes from a departed soul.[14] Although this incident is merely imagined, it is well imagined. Heller did believe in ghosts and specifically in dream questions, as witnessed by the story of a medieval dream question that he tells in *Megilat eivah*. It is possible that in these desperate and frightful times, he sought guidance from the world of ghosts. Indeed, perhaps this legend should be embroidered a little. It may be speculated, somewhat fancifully perhaps, that Heller addressed his question to the spirit of the Maharal.

The new custom that Heller instituted (to return from legend to fact) was inspired by two of the Maharal's teachings. Like other rabbis whom I have mentioned, the Maharal was distressed by talk during the prayer services. Moreover he instituted in Nikolsburg, as mentioned in Chapter 5, just such a *Mi sheberakh* as this one, on behalf of those who do not drink non-Jewish wine.[15]

Heller's response to the events was a public act, but it was also an act with a deep

[12] See *Tos YT, Kid.* 4: 14, discussed above, Ch. 6, pp. 111–12. Note also Heller's comments in the printer's introduction to his poems on the ancient prayers as a ladder raising one's prayers to Heaven: see Haberman, 'Liturgical and Other Poems', 126.

[13] See the 1640 model rabbinical contract from Prague, in J. Katz, 'On the History of the Rabbinate', 292–3. Cf. the 1620 rules from Zolkiew, which decree a fine for every violation of the rule of silence; Cygielman, *Jews of Poland and Lithuania*, 509 (from S. Buber, *Kiryah nisgavah*, 84).

[14] Beit Halevi, *Life of Heller*, 29. Beit Halevi refers to the remark by Jacob Joseph b. Judah in the late 18th c., in the introduction to his *Sefer rav yeivi*, that Heller's decision was inspired. However, Jacob Joseph does not refer to a dream question, which thus appears to be Beit Halevi's own addition to the story. See Trachtenberg, *Jewish Magic and Superstition*, 241 on dream questions.

[15] See Tsevi Jaffe, 'Ruling', fos. 296*b*–297*a*, which refers to the Maharal (as well as Luntshits) in this connection. Note also the Maharal's objections to private conversations during the sermon; 'Derush na'eh leshabat shuvah', in *Derashot maharal*, 4. On the Maharal's 'Mi sheberakh', see above, Ch. 5 n. 4.

private meaning. At the end of his life, he once again drew inspiration from the teachings of the man whom for many years, until he was more than 60 years old, he would not call his teacher, the man whom he admired, perhaps, above all others—the Maharal.

TWO KINDS OF MESSIANISM

Heller was not permitted to remain silent. He was asked to write a liturgical poem to be recited in the synagogues each year on 20 Sivan, the day that the rabbis of Poland had set aside as an annual fast-day. He was reminded that he had written poems of this type for the Prague Jews, after the Battle of White Mountain in 1620.

At first, he refused. It was his opinion, he wrote back, that God should be addressed in ancient words. The poems written in commemoration of earlier massacres would be sufficient for the new fast-day. The medieval poems, written at the time of the massacres of the Crusades, would serve 'as a ladder' leading the prayers of the Polish Jews to heaven.

On second thoughts, however, Heller wrote, he had decided that perhaps a combination of old and new verses would be best. He appended seven new verses to a poem by Eliezer ben Nathan (*c.*1090–*c.*1170).[16] The first three verses were narrative. The last four—more than half of what he wrote—concerned the theme of messianism and messianic expectations.

Questions of messianism were at the forefront of Jewish life during the years following the massacres of 1648. Many Jews regarded them as *ḥevlei mashiaḥ*, the apocalyptic precursors to the predestined messianic advent.[17] Calls for messianic vengeance against the non-Jews or the Christians were made by many Jews in the years following the massacres, by figures such as Israel of Bełżyce and Shabetai Horowitz, or, decades later, Nathan of Gaza and Shabetai Tsevi.[18] Heller's main

[16] The story of Heller's hesitations in writing his two poems is in the printer's introduction, which apparently quotes from a letter that Heller sent to the printer; Haberman, 'Liturgical and Other Poems', 126–8.

[17] On the prediction (based on the writings of Cordovero, interpreting a passage from the Zohar), see Scholem, *Sabbatai Sevi*, 88–93. Cf. Silver, *Messianic Speculation*, 185–6. Heller probably chose this particular poem by Eliezer b. Nathan (after a laborious search, he tells us in the printer's introduction) because it too shares the theme of disappointed messianism. Cf. also Bacon and Rosman, 'A "Chosen" Community', 212. Joshua Heschel of Lublin, *Ḥanukat hatorah*, 44 (discussed by Scholem) asserted that the *peshat*(!) of the verse in Leviticus indicated that the messiah should have come in 1648.

[18] See Saperstein (ed.), *Jewish Preaching*, 290, 300; Gurland (ed.), *On the History*, pt. 3, pp. 24, 27; A. Ashkenazi, *Tsa'ar bat rabim*, *passim*; decree of 1650, in Hailperin (ed.), *Jews in Poland*, ii. 256. On the theme of messianic vengeance in Sabbatianism, see Scholem, *Sabbatai Sevi*, 592; Barnai, 'Outbreak'. Even a casual reference to a martyr was customarily followed in the early modern period by the phase 'may the Lord avenge his blood'.

purpose in his poem was to deny that belief. He pointed to the failure of messianic predictions in the past,[19] and emphasized that the year 1648 had itself been anticipated falsely as the year of the messianic redemption.

> In the years 408 [= 1648] and 409,
>   we, the seed of your lovers, were very much smitten,
> Though we hoped that in the year 408,
>   each man would return to his possessions
> From the land of our captivity.[20]

Heller denied altogether that the date of the messianic advent is revealed anywhere in Scripture:[21] '[God] has not revealed his heart's thought to his lip, [to reveal] when He will fulfil [His promise].' As is clear from his earlier writings, he did not believe in predestination.[22] Furthermore, in his poem, he made no call for messianic vengeance, and indeed excised such a call from the poem of Eliezer ben Nathan. Justifying his high-handed editing, he spoke of *darkhei shalom*, the 'ways of peace'.[23] Rejecting the fatalistic premises and the violence of what may be called 'apocalyptic messianism', he preached rather 'prophetic messianism', that is, the ability of sincere repentance to bring the messiah at any time. Heller quoted from a talmudic legend the messiah's own promise to Rabbi Joshua ben Levi: I will come 'Today, if you listen to [my] voice' (Ps. 95: 6).[24]

[19] For Heller's own messianic expectations, see *Tos YT*, *Avot* 5: 2: the destruction of the Second Temple in 68 CE (3828 AM) is half-way between the Flood (1656 AM) and the coming of the messiah, which should then be in 6000 AM, i.e. 2240 CE. Cf. BT *San.* 97*a*–*b*, *AZ* 9*a* and *Tos YT*, *Tam.* 7: 4. See Silver, *Messianic Speculation*, 185–6 (Silver misinterprets the passage as a reference to the date 1648). Heller presumably felt, however, that the messiah could come at any time. Cf. Berekhiah Berakh b. Isaac Eizik, *Zera berakh*, pt. 2, 2*a*. See also Carlebach, 'Between History and Hope', 51 ff. Heller's refers to Solomon Molcho as a simple martyr rather as a (failed) messianic figure (on the passage, see above, Ch. 3, n. 25). The 1614 introduction to *Tosafot yom tov*, however, suggests a messianic motivation for the study of Mishnah (see above, Ch. 4, n. 15), while Heller's *Tsurat habayit* of 1602 treats a messianic theme; it is at least remotely possible that Heller shared in the messianic expectations for the date 1615 expressed by Kitzingen, *Ḥag pesaḥ*, at the end of the book. Cf. Tamar, 'Eschatological Calculations'.

[20] Cf. Isa. 41: 8; Lev. 25: 10; Jer. 30: 10.

[21] Cf. Jacob Boehme's rejection of apocalyptic calculation in the 1620s. See Weeks, *Boehme*, 139.

[22] See *Tos YT*, *Avot* 5: 6; cf. commentary on *Beḥinat olam* 8: 2: 7, p. 75.

[23] The full text of Eliezer b. Nathan's poem is in Bernfeld (ed.), *Book of Tears*, i. 208–9. The purpose of the excision was probably not to 'make room' for Heller's verses (they could have been added without 'making room') but to remove this theme. Heller's reference to 'the ways of peace' is quoted in the printer's introduction. There is also no call for vengeance in Heller's 'El malei raḥamim' (Haberman, 'Liturgical and Other Poems', 139–41). On the theme of vengeance, cf. Bacon and Rosman, 'A "Chosen" Community', 218, and for this theme in medieval Jewish messianism, see Yuval, 'The Vengeance and the Curse', 34–45, and the discussion of Yuval's views in *Zion*, 59 (1994), nos. 2–3; Berger, 'On the Image'.

[24] See BT *San.* 98*a*. Cf. M. Buber, 'Prophecy'; Russell, *Method and Meaning*.

DEMONIZING THE COSSACKS

Heller's 1650 poem, or half-poem, did not satisfy his audience. In 1651 the communal leadership of Cracow pressured him; eventually 'he nodded and said that one does not refuse great men'.[25] He wrote a new poem of seventeen verses, based mostly on a chronicle of the massacres by Gabriel ben Joshua Schossburg, called *Petaḥ teshuvah* (Gate of Repentance), published in Amsterdam the previous year.

Of the many Jewish liturgical poems written after the massacres, none focused to such a degree on the horrifying stories of the massacres themselves. Heller's first poem, with its emphasis on messianism and theology, in no way prepares us for this second one. It is an extensive recounting of sadism, violent cruelty, and murder: women and men hung in synagogues, blinded, drowned, and crushed alive, children brutally skewered, pregnant women cut open and their foetuses ripped out; cannibalism; men cut open, their innards ripped out and the corpses of cats sewn inside them.[26] Heller catalogued the types of suffering: mutilation, rape, exile and flight, forced conversion, plague and sickness, poverty, captivity, and slavery.

In Heller's poem, all is topsy-turvy. In the baroque style of his age, and in common with the Yiddish *Gzeire lid* (massacre song), cruel mockery and bitter irony claim his attention. Friend (*ohev*) becomes foe (*oyev*), Heller writes. The serf is now the master; the master is now the slave. The dead are left unburied; the living are buried alive. Jews are slaughtered, and their chests opened and lungs examined; this one is kosher, cries the murderer, this one is not kosher. The enemies do not only mock the laws of *kashrut*; in a mockery of the quality of mercy itself, they blind parents *after* killing their children in front of them. The very pigs and dogs, stepping carefully around corpses in the streets, put to shame the inhumanity of the murderers.

But there was a crowning irony: Heller emphasized in this poem, as he had in the first poem, that 1648 was predicted as the year of the coming of the messiah; but instead of the messiah, there was 'thick darkness as darkness itself, deep darkness without order'.

Heller's poem is one of the most graphic and violent works in all of early modern Hebrew literature. One could hardly believe that such a work could be written at all in the elevated diction of the Hebrew liturgical poetry of the period.

25 From the printer's introduction: Haberman, 'Liturgical and Other Poems', 126.

26 Almost all of the specific details in Heller's poem are taken from Schossburg, *Petaḥ teshuvah*. In a general way, one may compare the stories of horrors that circulated throughout Europe during the Thirty Years War. Note, for example, the stories of cannibalism discussed (and dismissed for the most part) in Ergang, *Myth*, 4–17. See also Yakovenko, 'The Events of 1648'.

Heller did not initially want to write his second poem, and perhaps he should not have.[27]

In keeping with the poem's dark tone, Heller's theology also took on apocalyptic overtones. He prayed now to God to be 'jealous', a biblical word associated with punishment of the wicked. Moreover, he no longer asked that the messianic era be given as a reward for righteousness; he now wrote of it as a deserved recompense for suffering.

Heller's presentation of events, full of details of horrors, was also full of silences. In 1648 Jews were far from being the only victims of violence: Poles and Ukrainians were also massacred in huge numbers.[28] The chronicler Nathan Hannover, whose catalogue of types of torture and murder is otherwise very similar to Heller's poem, adds that 'they did the same to the gentiles who were Polish, and especially to the priests and monks'.[29] Heller, however, did not mention the suffering of groups other than Jews. He hardly even alluded in his second poem, as he had in his first, to the general state of war and rebellion. Amazingly, in a note to the printer of both poems, Heller wrote that the events of 1648 were different from those in Prague in 1620 in that the suffering in 1620 was not restricted to Jews.[30]

Nathan Hannover also stressed that a number of Jewish communities were successful in defending themselves together with their Polish allies: 'In the strong fortified city of Kamieniec-Podolski . . . the nobles and the Jews defended themselves and fired upon their enemies with big cannons, inflicting heavy losses upon them.'[31]

[27] The literary historian Simon Bernstein, who called Heller's poem a classic of Hebrew literature, compared it to Bialik's 'The City of Slaughter' (Bialik's poem was written as the opposite of Heller's); Bernstein, *In the Visions*, 204–5. Heller's poem resembled Joseph Mazel's Yiddish 'Gzeyre Lid' (massacre poem). On the conventions of Hebrew and Jewish vernacular martyrology in the Middle Ages, see Einbinder, 'Troyes Laments'.

[28] Hailperin, *Jews and Judaism*, 220 n. 46. Cf. Sysyn, 'Seventeenth Century Views on the Causes of the Khmel'nyts'kyi Uprising', 447: 'Each group in the fragmented society of the Ukrainian lands wrote about its own fate and ignored that of others.'

[29] Hannover, *Yeven metsulah*, 32. On slaughter and cruel murder of Poles and Catholic priests, see ibid. 35–6, 42–3, 53, 57, 59, 64, 70; on slaughter and famine among Ukrainians, see ibid. 44, 58, 75–6. J. Katz, 'Between 1096 and 1648', 330, notes Hannover's emphasis on the 'common destiny of the Poles and Jews'. Meir of Szczebrzeszyn also emphasized this theme, as well as the theme of Jewish self-defence, albeit not to the same degree as Hannover: see his *Tsok ha'itim*, 8–9, 15–16, 18 (self-defence), 8–9, 18 (killing of Poles), 21 (killing of Ukrainians). Schossburg, *Petaḥ teshuvah* mentioned them, particularly as part of the story of the Jews of Tulczyn (pp. 39–40, cf. p. 51; but see also pp. 43–4), but did not emphasize these themes.

[30] Haberman, 'Liturgical and Other Poems', 126.

[31] Hannover, *Yeven metsulah*, 63. Cf. Horn, 'Jewish Participation'. On Jewish self-defence, see Hannover, *Yeven metsulah*, 37, 40, 63, 71, 80, and on the general theme of self-defence, 58, 60–2. The story of the Jews of Tulczyn as told by Hannover, whether or not it is historically accurate, seems to reflect a genuine disagreement on the relative value of self-defence and voluntary martyrdom.

Heller refrained from mentioning the participation of Jews in military actions together with the Poles.

In his second poem, Jewish suffering, and especially Jewish martyrdom, was the only story.[32] In 1648, claimed Heller in his letter to the printer, the massacres, 'like the misfortunes that have befallen us since the days of the destruction [of the Temple] . . . were on account of the hatred against us. For they wanted to kill us to carry out vengeance with sword and slaughter.'[33] In the poems, however, even the motive of vengeance is left unsaid. The murderers' hatred for the Jewish religion, indicated by their desecration of synagogues, Torah scrolls, and Jewish books, and by the forced conversion of some of the victims, is left entirely unexplained. It is portrayed as intrinsic, almost instinctive.[34]

Heller's demonized portrait of the massacres' perpetrators did not stem, we know, from a generalized hatred of non-Jews. His sympathetic view of non-Jews has been described, and in *Megilat eivah* he depicts Christians for the most part as good-natured men carrying out unpleasant duties, rather than as being motivated by hatred for Judaism. But from Cossack and Tatar soldiery Heller expected only savagery.[35]

THE ABSENCE OF THE KING

Modern historians have focused mainly on three groups of causes of the massacres of Jews in 1648. First, there are the general roots of the Cossack uprising and its violence, particularly the underlying conflicts between Catholics and Greek Orthodox, between Poles and Ukrainians, between the nobility and the Cossacks, and between landowners and peasants. Second is the long tradition of Christian anti-Judaism, which made Jews a likely target of any outbreak of violence in early modern Europe. And finally there are the roots, mainly economic, of the specific antagonism of Cossacks and Ukrainian peasants towards the Jews, who were wealthier than they and had power over them in various ways.[36]

[32] See J. Katz, 'Between 1096 and 1648', 335; Mintz, *Hurban*, 104–5; Fram, 'Reappraisal', 179–81; Fram, 'Creating a Tale', 89–112. As these scholars all point out, one must keep in mind the broad Ashkenazi definition of a 'martyr', namely any Jew murdered by a non-Jew. Only one of Heller's seventeen verses depicts voluntary martyrdom.

[33] See the printer's introduction; Haberman, 'Liturgical and Other Poems', 126.

[34] See J. Katz, 'Between 1096 and 1648', 332.

[35] Cf. Weinryb, *Jews of Poland*, 200. Heller may have differentiated 'non-Jews' along both social and ethnic lines. Most of the non-Jews depicted in *Megilat eivah* are of high social class, but note the favourable depiction of the criminals with whom Heller was gaoled in Vienna (p. 32). On the attitudes of west Europeans in this period towards eastern Europe, see Halperin, 'Foreign Travel Accounts'.

[36] Sysyn, 'Seventeenth Century Views on the Causes of the Khmel'nyts'kyi Uprising'. Cf. Fram, 'Reappraisal', 169–76; Sysyn, 'The Khmel'nyts'kyi Uprising', 125–31; Bacon, ' "The House of Hannover" ', 187–91.

Of these three groups of causes, the most important, in the view of contemporary historians, indeed perhaps the only important one, is the first group, the general roots of the uprising. There is little evidence that the Jews were singled out for attack in 1648. They were killed alongside Poles, noblemen, Catholic priests, and even sometimes Greek Orthodox Ukrainian burghers. The 1648 massacres were not pogroms (although they may have played a role in inspiring the pogroms of later periods), and it is not clear to what extent anti-Jewish attitudes played a role in their causation.[37]

Among the seventeenth-century Jewish chroniclers, Nathan Hannover stressed the general causes of the uprising, while also touching on the other two groups of causes that I have mentioned. He began the chronicle long before the massacres, with the ascension of Sigismund III to the Polish throne. 'He was a merciful and proper king, who loved justice and loved the Jews', Hannover wrote. But King Sigismund oppressed 'the Greek nation', that is, the Greek Orthodox.

And then the Greek nation became poorer and more lowly and despised, and they became male and female slaves to the Poles and the Jews, *lehavdil* [not to compare the two]. . . . And the dukes and the other noblemen greatly oppressed the Greek nation, 'and they made their life bitter with hard work and mortar and brick and every sort of work, at home and in the field' (Exod. 1: 4). . . . So low were they, that almost every other nation ruled over them, even that nation that is the most oppressed of nations, [the Jews].[38]

Some seventeenth-century Poles, however, emphasizing the last of our three groups of causes, the specific complaints of the Cossacks and Ukrainians against the Jews, blamed the Jews for the entire Cossack revolt. Hence the 1648 massacres, far from engendering sympathy for Jews among Poles, may have had the reverse effect.[39]

Other seventeenth-century Jews, however, offered explanations of an entirely different, theological or metaphysical type, not favoured by modern historians. The itinerant preacher and kabbalist Israel ben Benjamin, in a sermon in the town of Bełżyce in 1648, used the framework of Lurianic kabbalah to explain the massacres. He began with the traditional paradigm of suffering caused by sin, but immediately gave it a new twist. The 'Greek nation' (the Greek Orthodox Ukrainians), Israel ben Benjamin argued, is attached metaphysically to a particular evil 'shell' or *kelipah*, called 'Nogah' (Venus). This 'shell' more than other 'shells', and hence the Greek nation more than other nations, is affected by the deeds of the Jews. When the Jews sin, therefore, the 'shell' Nogah 'becomes cruel', and then the

[37] See the articles in the special issue of *Jewish History*, 17/2 (2003), on 'Gezerot ta" h'. We look forward to the articles of Serhii Plokhy and Olexij Tolotchko.

[38] Hannover, *Yeven metsulah*, 20.

[39] See Sysyn, 'A Curse on Both their Houses', p. xix; Raba, *Between Remembrance and Denial*, 108–11, 125, 131, 191.

Greek nation treat the Jews with cruelty. In this version of things, the line of causation runs from the Jewish sin to the shell 'Nogah' to Greek cruelty; divine intervention as traditionally conceived is absent.[40]

In his poems on the 1648 massacres, Shabetai Horowitz, by contrast, expressed his faith in the simple Deuteronomic paradigm: suffering is caused by sin, and demands repentance. Chapter 10 discussed Berekhiah Berakh ben Isaac's expanded treatment of this theme in 1662, in which he detailed the groups of sinners (such as Jewish tax-farmers and scholars who publicize kabbalistic secrets) and the particular sins that had caused the massacres.

Other Jews of that generation denied that the victims of the massacres should be blamed. The chronicler Abraham ben Samuel Ashkenazi, author of *Tsa'ar bat rabim*, claimed that the victims, the pious Jews of Poland, had not been punished for their sins at all. They were innocent of sin, and had suffered for the sins of others; as the Talmud says, 'The righteous are held liable for the sin of the generation' (BT *Shabat* 33*b*).[41] Nathan Hannover, whose eulogy of Polish Jewry was discussed in my Introduction, took the same view.[42]

How did Heller explain the massacres? In his first poem, like most writers of liturgical poems, Heller suggested that the massacres were a punishment of Jewish sin, for which he begged God's forgiveness.[43] He also insisted on the surprising and sudden character of the events:

> In Poland, the lands of the Crown,
> we had long dwelt in peaceful repose
> Until a great upheaval began within it.

In his second poem on the 1648 massacres, however, the language of sin and forgiveness vanished. In their place came the notion of God's absence.[44] 'Is it not because my God is not in my midst that these evils have befallen me?', Heller asked, quoting the book of Deuteronomy (31: 17). Divine absence rather than divine punishment is the view suggested by Maimonidean philosophy, which identifies all suffering as privation and disorder.

[40] The sermon of Israel b. Benjamin of Bełżyce is translated in Saperstein (ed.), *Jewish Preaching*, 289–300.

[41] See A. Ashkenazi, *Tsa'ar bat rabim*, 13.

[42] Hannover, *Yeven metsulah*, 82. On this passage, see J. Katz, 'Between 1096 and 1648', 335; Bacon and Rosman, 'A "Chosen" Community', 216.

[43] In Heller's second verse, he wrote, 'holy communities were destroyed for [their] sins', and he asked for forgiveness in the penultimate verse.

[44] Jewish sin is a major theme of Heller's source, Schossburg's *Petaḥ teshuvah* (literally, 'The Doorway of Repentance'): see pp. 32, 33–4, 36–7, 46, 49. Samuel Halevi, in his liturgical poem (in Gurland (ed.), *On the History*, pt. 2, pp. 20–1), which he based closely on Heller's second poem, felt compelled to add the theme of sin: 'Sins and iniquities prevailed and they are gone over our heads (Ps. 38: 5).'

In this same poem, however, Heller also offered explanations for the events, using natural (that is, political) terms.[45] As in his earlier writings, he viewed events within each of these two frameworks, political as well as providential.

Modern and liberal historians tend to look at events from the point of view of revolutionaries, and to focus on the grievances that motivate revolutions and uprisings. Hannover followed this tendency; it may not be coincidental that he had spent time in Amsterdam and Venice, centres of European anti-monarchical and republican thought, before writing his chronicle. Heller, however, was apparently unconcerned with the question why the Cossacks wished to revolt against the Poles. He did not rehearse any of the grievances that led to the rebellion. Similarly, in 1620, he had not mentioned any of the grievances of the Protestants in Prague.

Heller's explanatory focus was instead on the rebels' opportunity, on the question of how the uprising was able to achieve so much success. He suggested two causes: first, the alliance of the Cossacks and Tatars, and second, the absence of the Polish king:

> When the men of Greece joined with the men of Kedar
> And there was no king in the land,
> they burst through and destroyed every bound.
> Destruction follows upon destruction,
> calamity upon calamity.

Poland in the seventeenth century was an elective, not an inherited, monarchy. When the Polish king, Władysław, died suddenly just as the massacres were beginning, the monarchy was left vacant for fully six months until his brother Jan Casimir, was elected as his successor—six months in which the Jews were massacred. The fact that massacres happened during the interregnum is mentioned not only by Heller but by many of the Hebrew chronicles, and in a surprising number of the liturgical poems written to commemorate the massacres.[46]

Both of his explanations fit well with one of his most basic moral and political assumptions about the world.[47] Tatars and Cossacks were well known to be enemies ('cats and dogs', as Hannover wrote),[48] but co-operation between enemies makes

[45] As noted in Bernstein, *In the Visions*, 204.

[46] See Gurland, *On the History*, pt. 1, p. 13 (the *kinah* of Ephraim b. Joseph), p. 15 (the *kinah* of Hanokh b. Abraham of Gniezno), pt. 4, p. 20 (the *kinah* of Samuel Halevi), and in A. Ashkenazi, *Tsa'ar bat rabim*. Shabetai b. Meir emphasized the death of the king in a passage quoted below; he pointed out, however, that the massacres began before Władysław died, and so inserts a note of caution as to the explanatory force of the king's death. Cf. Raba, *Between Remembrance and Denial*, 54–5. Note that the absence of the monarch is also mentioned in the Hebrew prose account of the Defenestration of Prague; Haberman, 'Liturgical and Other Poems', 131.

[47] On monarchism among early modern Jewish historians and its tenacity in the face of apparent anti-Judaism among monarchs, see above, Ch. 8 n. 55. Cf. Luebke, ' "Naive Monarchism" '.

[48] In Hannover's introduction to *Yeven metsulah*.

them strong. Likewise, division within a community makes it weak. Without the uniting presence of the king, the kingdom may be expected to dissolve into its constituent parts.

Another Jewish chronicler of the massacres was Shabetai Kohen of Vilna. The Cossacks, he wrote,

raised up their hand against the king and his noblemen and officers, that is, King Władysław, who was a good king [*melekh kasher*], who should be counted among the righteous, for he was always kind and gracious to the Jews, and upheld his covenant with them.[49]

It was on the day of the first massacres, Shabetai wrote, that

the king 'was gathered to his people' (Gen. 49: 29) and his soul departed . . . while he was in Lithuania . . . close to the city of Vilna. . . . And we, the people of the Lord . . . cried and mourned for His Highness, the king, may he rest in peace.[50]

The Jews of Vilna did not yet know about the massacres that were occurring hundreds of miles to the south (like Heller, Shabetai focused on the irony of events). The Jews were weeping because the good King Władysław had died.

Who is loyal? Who is disloyal? According to Shabetai, the weeping Jews were loyal and the Cossacks were disloyal; 'they broke their covenant', he wrote in the same passage. King Władysław was also loyal—loyal to the Jews, wrote Shabetai: 'he upheld his covenant with them.'

Many observers of the catastrophes and wars of the mid-seventeenth century, not only Jews, drew the conclusion that what was needed was a stronger monarchy. The best known of these was the political philosopher Thomas Hobbes, an exact contemporary of Heller. Hobbes lived through the bloodshed of the English Civil War and concluded that the solution to disorder lay in a strong central government. Heller was not Hobbes, but he reacted in a similar way to the events in Poland, locating the fault in the weakness of the monarchy. Loyal to the Habsburg politics of his youth and middle age, a good son of the 'Age of Absolutism', Heller continued to support the Habsburgs' allies and close kin, the Vasa kings of Poland.[51]

[49] The designation *melekh kasher* is from the Talmud (*RH* 3*b*), where it is applied to King Cyrus of Persia. See I. Horowitz's discussion of Cyrus in id., *Shenei luḥot haberit*, iii. 11*a* ('Lekh lekha'), note.

[50] Shabetai b. Meir Hakohen, *Megilat eifah*.

[51] Monarchism and anti-monarchism as competing political trends in the Polish–Lithuanian Commonwealth in this period are discussed in Frost, *After the Deluge*. Cf. id., '"Initium Calamitatis Regni"', 184: 'Poles [in 1648] did not believe that their monarchy was a cipher, even if subsequent historians have so determined.' The connection between the Habsburgs and the Vasas is stressed by Hannover; the first line of *Yeven metsulah* records the wedding of King Sigismund of Poland and the Habsburg princess, Anne of Austria.

The policies of the Jewish community in Poland in the years following 1648 were also based on the continuing fear of expulsion, a traditional threat but a very real one, as the 1656 expulsion of the Unitarians ('Arians') demonstrated. Once again, close alignment with the Crown and continued lobbying were regarded as the most effective defence.[52]

The events of 1648 suggested to Heller and to the other Jewish survivors no political programme superior to that in which they already believed: the avoidance of conflict within the community, the lobbying of non-Jewish authorities, and support for the king. In spite of demonstrating the limited effectiveness of traditional Jewish policies, the massacres of 1648 actually reinforced the principles on which they were based. Had not conflict within the Polish state brought catastrophe upon that state, as well as upon the Jews? Had not the death of the king robbed the Jews of their defence?

A case in Cracow in 1648 or 1649 suggests the lengths to which Heller and the Jewish community were willing to go to maintain good relations with the Polish authorities. A certain Jew had converted to Christianity out of fear and possibly constraint. Now safe in Cracow, he came to the ghetto and wished to return to Judaism. The Christian authorities in the city, however, demanded him back. Paying little heed to the talmudic principles involved in the case, the rabbis of Cracow, with Heller at their head, turned the refugee away. The Cracow Jews were patient; they were waiting for the new Polish monarch, Jan Casimir, to grant a general permission for converted Jews to return to Judaism, as he did in 1649 and 1650.[53]

But Jan Casimir and his army were not loyal to the Jews. In 1655, the year after Heller's death, the Swedes, victorious in Germany, invaded Poland. During the Polish–Swedish war, a Polish army loyal to Jan Casimir carried out a further series of massacres of the Jews of Poland.[54] Heller, now beyond the reach of armies and persecutors, did not have to face the true failure of his generation's policy, the failure to secure the goodwill of the Polish armies. These second massacres, perpetrated not by the enemies of the Polish Crown but by its servitors, inspired no Jewish chronicles and indeed were barely recollected either in the later seventeenth century or afterwards. Indeed, the rabbinate and the Jewish community had no political response to them, but only a dream of the Anointed One of God.

[52] See Hailperin, 'Threatened Expulsion'.

[53] N. N. Kahana, *She'elot uteshuvot divrei renanah*, no. 54 (p. 243); cf. Fram, 'Perception and Reception'. The 1650 permission to return to Judaism is discussed in Fram, 'And Still a Gap Exists', 36.

[54] See Hundert, *Jews in a Polish Private Town*, 26–30.

'YOU HAVE BECOME A PLAGUE'

The difficult topic of Heller's relationship with God has been left to this point in the narrative, close to the end of his life.

God appears and reappears over fifty years of Heller's writings. As in any rabbinic writer—one might almost say, any religious writer—images of immanence and transcendence, of closeness and distance, appear side by side. While both appear to express sincere religious emotion, Heller's expressions of God's immanence are more conventional, but certain of his expressions of God's transcendence are more radical and novel.

In *Leket shoshanim*, Heller claimed that God is absolutely transcendent, standing in no relation to man or to the world, not even, strictly speaking, the relation of Creator. He is beyond all language; no word of the Torah truly refers to him. Yet he may join with man in the kiss of mystic unity.[55]

Only God is free, Heller wrote in *Tosafot yom tov*. He is an absolute unity and therefore he is changeless. In another comment in *Tosafot yom tov*, Heller examined the Ineffable Name of God, the Tetragrammaton. Departing from the common view that associates the name with the verb 'to be', Heller quoted his friend Meir Bach that the name is related to the verb 'to fear'; its meaning is that 'God will one day set his fear upon all of Creation.'[56]

In 1631 Heller gave his son a proof that God exists: he must exist because the world lacks rational order and cannot be the result of logical necessity. Heller called God the *meyaḥed*, the Uniter who is also the Particularizer.

Heller was very concerned, as noted earlier, with the problems of providence and reward. God is good, he emphasized in a number of places in *Tosafot yom tov*; even the forty years that the children of Israel spent wandering in the desert were a positive gift.[57] God answers prayers, Heller insisted in a passage in *Tosafot yom tov* (discussed in Chapter 6). In 1621 he wrote that God had answered the prayers of the Jews of Prague. In 1625, and again in 1629, he responded to God's deliverance with hesitant thanksgiving. In 1628, in his letter to the Jews of Frankfurt, he spoke of God's protection of the Jews, without which they could not survive in exile.

God is not simply just, Heller quoted approvingly in *Ma'adanei melekh* in 1628; he is Justice. He is not simply wise; he is Wisdom itself.[58] Suffering must not be made a cause of complaint against God. In his sermon on the lessening of the moon, Heller criticized Job for doubting God's justice.

[55] Cf. the commentary on Bedersi (14: 1: 1 [p. 107]); *TosYT*, *RH* 1: 2.

[56] *TosYT*, *AZ* 1: 3, *Suk*. 4: 5.

[57] On God's goodness, see *TosYT*, *Avot* 2: 4, *Ta'an*. 3: 8; cf. *MYT* (*MM*), *Ber*., p. 6 n. 60: 'We do not say that God "destroyed" the Temple, because He does only good and not evil.' On the forty years in the desert, see *TosYT*, *Sot*. 1: 9.

[58] *MYT* (*MM*), *Ber*., p. 12 n. 3.

But, in 1650, did he now avoid such doubts himself? It has already been noted that Heller wrote initially to the printer that he did not wish to write any poems. The old poems were sufficient; God should be addressed with ancient words. As we have seen, however, he let himself be persuaded that he should write new poems. In the first poem (or, as we saw, half-poem), many of the earlier themes and epithets were repeated. 'Good You are', he wrote, 'and You do good to the small and the great.'

> He is called when He is near, and He may be found when we search for
> Him and seek Him.
> To those who send me may the mouth of the LORD say, 'I have forgiven'
> (Num. 14: 20) and to me may He answer, 'according to your words'
> (Num. 14: 20)
> The Messiah and the messenger Elijah: this one shall redeem us, and that
> one shall appear first to announce it.
> Awesome, high, and holy, living and present, the LORD is our God.

These conventional expressions of God's goodness and closeness are absent, however, from Heller's second poem. To whom, to what, may God be compared? 'He is unto me as a bear in wait, as a lion in the secret places', wrote the author of Lamentations (3: 10) in a verse that David ben Samuel quoted in his 1648 poem.[59]

Heller, in his second poem on the 1648 massacres—what might be called his catalogue of suffering—went further. He had intended, perhaps, to write, 'You have *sent* a plague against your people', or something of that sort. But his pen moved of itself, as it were, and Heller made the phrase into a metaphor for God, who is beyond all comparison, a new metaphor, closer to his own experience. Heller, who had lived through numerous plagues, who had lost two children to the plague, wrote:

> You have become a plague to your people.

LETTER TO CHĘCINY, 1651

We have only scant records of Heller's activities in the six years that he lived after the massacres. These years saw continued sufferings—invasions, massacres, and plagues—throughout the Polish Commonwealth.

One responsum that survives is from 1649. A longstanding tradition in Jewish law states that a husband's death must be legally certified for the widow to remarry. Heller adjudicated one case in which the circumstantial evidence that the husband had died was judged to be sufficient for the death to be regarded as certain.[60]

[59] 'Magen david', 5b.

[60] *She'elot uteshuvot ge'onei batra'ei*, no. 10.

Another document of Heller's, recorded in one of the *pinkasim* (registers) of the synagogues of Cracow, concerns a Jew named Meir ben Asher Lemil, who fled to Poland from the Ukraine: '[Meir] wept copiously . . . and cried in the bitterness of his soul . . . "I have sinned before the LORD, the God of Hosts".' Meir confessed to the sins of 'spilling semen because of evil thoughts and touching a . . . married woman, although I did not have any sexual intercourse with her, God forbid'. Meir had performed a penance set for him by two rabbis, but, he said, 'This was not sufficient for me, when I see that the LORD's anger has raged against His people Israel. For I said, Perhaps my sins caused all of this.'

Meir, poor soul, had blamed the massacres on his own sin, and so he had performed a second penance. Heller joined with other Polish rabbis in issuing a writ to protect Meir and his honour against the ill reputation that might follow him on account of his confessed sins:

> All the gates are locked except the gates of oppression—that is, oppressive words, such as 'Remember your former deeds'. . . . And even more so [is it forbidden to] spread rumours exaggerating what happened, for that is not only oppression but slander which has no basis. [Slander] also has no remedy, neither contrition nor confession nor penances and fines; the only [remedy is] to ask forgiveness, in public up to three times, from the one who has been insulted. In particular, this God-fearing man, who has made a great . . . penance, Rabbi Meir by name . . . whose repentance an angel has reached out to accept. Therefore . . . every man and woman . . . must guard his honour, and not oppress him, neither by word or hint, neither him nor any of his family.[61]

In 1652, in his annual public sermon on the sabbath before Passover, Heller chose the topic of the ten plagues. The sermon is not extant, and we do not know its precise contents. Did it hint at the wreaking of divine vengeance on the persecutors of the Jews, pointing to the fate of the Egyptians who had enslaved, tortured, and slaughtered them? Or did it, portraying the ten plagues in an exegetical panoply of suffering, reflect on the sufferings that the Jews of Poland had undergone in recent years, or indeed in recent weeks? The year 1652 was another plague year in Cracow. Heller may have offered, as he did in 1625 in Vienna, some response that Jews might make to a plague, based on the example of biblical Israel.[62]

One of the last extant pieces of writing by Heller is a partly illegible letter to the Jewish community of Chęciny in Poland, dated 20 Tishrei (5 October) 1651, six

[61] Wettstein, 'Antiquities from Old Registers', 615–16. The Cracow *pinkasim* were all lost and presumably destroyed during the Holocaust; Wettstein's transcriptions, scattered in various Hebrew periodicals, are all that remain.

[62] See Heller's marginal note in his copy of *Sefer maharil*; S. Cohen, 'From the Library', 105–7. The ten plagues were also the topic of his 1644 Passover sermon: see *Tos YT*, *Avot* 5: 4. On the plague of 1652, see Hailperin, *Jews and Judaism*, 256; Raba, *Between Remembrance and Denial*, 157.

months before this sermon.[63] The letter concerns a communal controversy, a *maḥloket*. A time of misfortune, Heller believed, will be a time of controversy. The details of the conflict, apparently between the community of Chęciny and that of Pińczów, are entirely lost, but it is clear that once again, Heller attempted to resolve the conflict amicably but forcefully.

To the dearly beloved, great men, men of good name . . . the heads and leaders of the holy community of Chęciny.

. . . Those letters reached me and I read them twice. I also listened at length to those dear ones who brought them. . . . And I discussed with them . . . and I answered them as they will tell you . . . I still stand upon my watch, as your eyes see truly. . . . But I was not able . . . Perhaps God will grant . . . the controversy, and each man will go in peace . . . and the heads . . . of the holy community of Pińczów will come to me, I shall say that they have 'cut the shoots' (BT *Ḥagigah* 14*b*) through this controversy . . . the heads of the [Four] Lands . . . great expense . . . to pursue peace, to bring hearts close . . .

The words of one who speaks peace and seeks good,
Yom-Tov, called Lipmann Levi Heller

Heller died nearly three years later, on 6 Elul (19 August) 1654. He was buried in the cemetery of the Remu Synagogue in Cracow, where his grave may still be seen.[64] There is a reliable report from the early years of the eighteenth century that he died 'without leaving behind even enough money to buy a shroud'.[65] He died a year before the sack of Jewish Cracow, two years before the massacre of the Jews of Chęciny.[66]

Strangely, the name inscribed on his tombstone is Gershom Saul Yom-Tov Lipmann Heller. That is also how he signed his name on his last printed halakhic

[63] Letter to Chęciny, in Hailperin (ed.), *Documents*, 493. A responsum by Heller, written a few months before the letter to Chęciny, deals with the case of a butcher in Leszno. The responsum, dated 24 Tamuz (13 July) 1651, is copied in the responsa of the rabbi of Leszno, Isaac Eulenburg (d. 1657), MS Oxford-Bodleian Heb. 840, fos. 12*a*–13*a*. It was published in *Moriah*, 15 (1986–7), nos. 7–10, pp. 32–4. A second copy of the same responsum is in Eulenburg's miscellaneous writings, MS Oxford-Bodleian Heb. 2214/2, fos. 31*b*–32*a*. It is followed by Eulenburg's own decision in the same case (fos. 32*b*–33*a*) and other material on the same incident (fos. 33*b*–34*b*, 44*a*–47*b*).

[64] Heller's epitaph is in Friedberg (ed.), *Jewish Epitaphs*, 13. The present gravestone is not the original one, but the inscription has been preserved.

[65] Margaliot, *Ḥiburei likutim*, introd.; cf. Berekhiah Berakh b. Isaac Eizik, *Zera berakh*, both quoted in Hailperin MS, p. 54 n. 2. The Jews of Cracow were extremely hard pressed for money in the 1650s, just at the same moment that infinite demands were suddenly made on their charity. Add to this a long personal illness, and it is easy to see how Heller's modest wealth might well have been exhausted by the time of his death. In 1654, there was no money to pay the *dayanim* in Poznań: see Avron (ed.), *Pinkas hakesherim*, 144.

[66] On Cracow, see Bałaban, 'The Jews of Cracow'; on Chęciny, see Hundert, *Jews in a Polish Private Town*, 26–30.

decision as well, written a month before his death (appropriately, it concerns the laws of mourning).[67] It has been suggested plausibly that his name was officially changed during his illness, a custom recommended in the Talmud.[68] The name 'Gershom' has a poignant fittingness for Heller in Poland: as it is written in the Bible, 'He called his name Gershom, for he said, I have been a stranger in a strange land' (Exod. 2: 22).

After Heller's death, his wife Rachel returned from Cracow to Prague, to escape the fearful conditions in the Polish city, and to return to her kin and her firstborn son. She died there on 1 December just a few months after her husband. They had been married for about sixty years.[69]

In Venice, Moses Zacuto (*c.*1620–1697), a talmudist, kabbalist, and poet, wrote a eulogy for Heller:

> His heart studied every mystery and every secret, and
> everything that the heart of man requires . . .
> Who can be compared to him, who ascended
> to the heavens above and did not fall or limp?
> Who is like him who dived to the depths
> of the great abyss and did not drown?
> Who is like him who wandered to the ends
> of the earth and did not settle?[70]

[67] Heller's comments on the mourner's kaddish were published in Buchner, *Oreḥot ḥayim* (repr. in *Moriah*, 14 (1985–6), nos. 9–10, pp. 18–19). His approbation for Buchner's *Oreḥot ḥayim*, dated 21 Av (4 Aug.) 1654, appears on pp. 20–1.

[68] BT *RH* 16*b*. Cf. J. M. Zunz, *City of Righteousness*, 96.

[69] Rachel's epitaph is in Muneles (ed.), *Inscriptions*, 329.

[70] Zacuto's eulogy is in a manuscript collection of his eulogies: JTS MS E.N. Adler 378, microfilm no. 3545 (Makhon Letatslumei Kitvei Yad, no. 29350).

Yom-Tov Lipmann Heller's Extant Works and Writings

For further bibliographical details, see Israel Hailperin, 'A Bibliography of the Writings of Rabbi Yom-Tov Lipmann Heller', *Kiryat sefer*, 7 (1930), 140–8, and my own 'Corrections and Additions to Israel Hailperin's "Bibliography of the Writings of R. Yom Tov Lipman Heller"', in Joseph Davis, 'R. Yom Tov Lipman Heller, Joseph b. Isaac ha-Levi, and Rationalism in Ashkenazic Jewish Culture 1550–1650' (Ph.D. diss., Harvard University, 1990), 518–25.

Commentaries and Notes

1. Commentary on Yedaiah Bedersi, *Beḥinat olam* (Prague, 1598). I have used the Zhitomir 1858 edition.
2. *Tsurat beit hamikdash* (or *Tsurat habayit*) (Prague, 1602). I have used the edition by Nehemiah Malin (Jerusalem, 1970).
3. Approbation and notes in *Givat hamoreh* (Prague, 1611) by Joseph b. Isaac Halevi of Lithuania. *Givat hamoreh* has been reprinted in a new photo-offset edition (New York, 1994).
4. *Tosafot yom tov* (Prague, 1614–17; 2nd rev. edn., Cracow, 1643–4). I have used the Vilna (Romm), 1908 edition (based on the Cracow edition), frequently reprinted.
5. *Ma'adanei yom tov* on Seder 'Nezikin' (Prague, 1619). Originally entitled *Pilpula ḥarifta*. I have used the edition in the standard Vilna (Romm) text of the Babylonian Talmud, frequently reprinted.
6. *Ma'adanei yom tov* on tractates *Berakhot*, *Ḥulin*, *Nidah*, etc. (Prague, 1628). Originally entitled *Ma'adanei melekh* and *Divrei ḥamudot*; also known as *Leḥem ḥamudot*. I have used the edition published in the standard Vilna (Romm) text of the Babylonian Talmud. Note that 'Hilkhot sefer torah' etc. are published with tractate *Menaḥot*.
7. *Malbushei yom tov* on *Shulḥan arukh*, 'Oraḥ ḥayim', ed. Isaac Feigenbaum, 2 vols. (Warsaw, 1893–5). A manuscript in the Bodleian Library, Oxford (Heb. 741) differs slightly from the printed text. The manuscript continues with Heller's comments on 'Even ha'ezer', which correspond closely to no. 8, below.
8. 'Notes on *Tur* and *Shulḥan arukh*, "Even ha'ezer"', published with *Ḥidushei harashba* on tractate *Ketuvot* (Metz, 1768).
9. Supercommentary on Ibn Ezra's commentary on the Torah and the Five Scrolls, published (from the Bodleian manuscript) with a short commentary under the title *Ma'amar yom tov* by Abraham Heller, a descendant of the author (Jerusalem, 1989). The beginning (Gen. 1: 1–31: 53) was also published by Naftali Ben-Menahem,

'R. Yom-Tov Lipmann Heller's Commentary on Ibn Ezra's Commentary on the Torah' [Perush r. yom-tov lipman heler al ibn ezra al hatorah], in Judah Leib Hakohen Maimon (ed.), *In Honour of Yom-Tov* (Jerusalem, 1956), 196–214.

10. *Leket shoshanim*, commentary on the Hebrew grammar, *Arugat habosem*, by Samuel Archivolti. It has not been published: MS Oxford-Bodleian Heb. 2271.

11. *Torat ha'asham*, commentary on *Torat haḥatat* by Moses Isserles, was published from the Bodleian manuscript by David and Samson Heller, descendants of the author (Jerusalem, 1977).

12. *Parashat haḥodesh*, commentary on Maimonides, *Mishneh torah*, 'Laws of the Sanctification of the New Moon', has not been published. It is extant in two manuscripts, both in the Bodleian Library, Oxford: Heb. 631/1 and Heb. 2271/2.

13. Marginal notes in the British Library copies of *Sefer naftulei elokim*, by Naftali Treves (a supercommentary on Bahya b. Asher's commentary on the Torah), and *Imrei shefer* by Nathan b. Samson Spira (a supercommentary on Rashi's commentary on the Torah) were published by 'the Greenwald family' (London, 1958).

14. MS Oxford-Bodleian Heb. 775 includes a note (fo. 119*b*) on 'Yoreh de'ah', para. 374, copied from 'the writing of . . . R. Lipmann, the author of *Tosafot yom tov*, in his *Shulḥan arukh*'.

15. MS Ansbach VIb 136/1 is attributed tentatively to Heller by the cataloguers of the Makhon Letatslumei Kitvei Yad of the Hebrew University and Jewish National Library in Jerusalem. The work is a collection of *hasagot* (objections) to *Sefer me'irat einayim* (*Sema*) by Joshua b. Alexander Falk, which is a commentary on 'Ḥoshen mishpat', the fourth section of the *Shulḥan arukh*.

16. Some marginal notes by Heller in his copy of *Sefer maharil* (Cremona, 1566) by Jacob Moellin, now in the HUC–Klar Library in Cincinnati, were published by Simon Cohen, 'From the Library of Yom Tob Lipmann Heller', *Studies in Jewish Booklore and Bibliography*, 1 (1954), 103–7.

17. MS Bar Ilan 842 is a copy of the anonymous kabbalistic work, *Sefer hapeliyah*, made, according to the colophon, by 'Moses b. Jacob . . . of Bystřice, scribe of R. Loewe . . . for R. Yom Tov called Lipmann b. Nathan Heller of Wallerstein'. There are a few marginal notes in the book, besides those of the scribe himself; they may be by Heller.

Responsa and Halakhic Decisions

18. Responsum in Menahem Mendl Krochmal, *She'elot uteshuvot tsemaḥ tsedek* (Altdorf, 1766), no. 14.

19. Responsa in *She'elot uteshuvot ge'onei batra'ei*, ed. Elijah b. Moses of Pińczów (Turka, 1764), nos. 1, 10, and 18.

20. Responsum in Joshua b. Joseph, *She'elot uteshuvot penei yehoshua* (Amsterdam, 1715), no. 53. The same case also appears in Nathan Neta Kahana, *She'elot uteshuvot divrei renanah*, ed. Isaac Herskovitz (New York, 1984), 127–8.

21. In Joel Sirkes, *She'elot uteshuvot bayit ḥadash haḥadashot* (Korets, 1785), no. 27 by Sirkes answers Heller's letter in *She'elot uteshuvot ge'onei batra'ei*, no. 18; no. 28, by Heller, continues the dispute.

22. Responsa in *She'elot uteshuvot eitan ha'ezraḥi* by Abraham Rapoport (Ostroh, 1796), nos. 7, 9, 10, and 40.

23. Heller's responsum on the Nikolsburg wine controversy of 1616 is among those in Aryeh Pisek, *Sefer dimyon aryeh* (Prague, 1616).

24. A responsum sent by Heller to Isaac Eulenburg, the rabbi of Leszno (d. 1657), dated 24 Tamuz 1651, was published in *Moriah*, 15/7–10 (1987), 32–4, from the manuscript of Eulenburg's responsa, MS Oxford-Bodleian Heb. 840 fos. 12*a*–13*a*. A second copy of the same responsum is in Eulenburg's miscellaneous writings, MS Oxford-Bodleian Heb. 2214/2 fos. 31*b*–32*a*. It is followed by Eulenburg's own decision in the same case (fos. 32*b*–33*a*) and other material on the same incident (fos. 33*b*–34*b* and 44*a*–47*b*).

25. *She'elat gitin* on the spelling of names for bills of divorce: MS Oxford-Bodleian Heb. 808/1.

26. As noted by Hailperin (Hailperin MS, p. 29 n. 1), a section of the *takanot* that Heller wrote in 1625 for the Vienna Jewish community (mentioned in *Megilat eivah*) is quoted in Menahem Mendl Krochmal, *She'elot uteshuvot tsemaḥ tsedek* (Altdorf, 1766), no. 37.

27. Heller signed a decision of the Council of Four Lands, published in Israel Hailperin (ed.), *Documents of the Council of Four Lands* (Jerusalem, 1946), 71–3; also in S. Dubnow (ed.), *Pinkas hamedinah o pinkas va'ad hakehilot harashiyot bimedinat lita* (Berlin, 1925), 279. It is dated 2 Nisan 1644.

Sermons

28. Heller's *Derush* on 'Ḥayei sarah' (Gen. 23: 1–25 :18), together with his Yiddish translation of *Oreḥot ḥayim*, attributed to Asher b. Yehiel (Prague, 1626). The sermon was reprinted under the title of *Ma'amar hahoda'ah vehatakanah* in a new edition of *Oreḥot ḥayim*, ed. Meir Malin (Jerusalem, 1987).

29. *Derush ḥidushei halevanah* (Vilna, 1866). The sermon on the lessening of the moon. A photo-offset edition appeared in Jerusalem, 1973.

Poetry

30. All of Heller's poetry, including variant readings, was reprinted in an edition by Abraham Haberman, 'The Liturgical and Other Poems of R. Yom-Tov Lipmann Heller' [Piyutav veshirav shel r. yom tov lipman heler], in Judah Leib Hakohen Maimon (ed.), *In Honour of Yom-Tov* (Jerusalem, 1956), 125–45. Included are Heller's opening and closing poems in some of his published books, his *seliḥot* on the events in Prague in 1618 and 1620 (Prague, ?1621), and his *seliḥot* and prayers on

the massacres of 1648 (Cracow, 1650). Haberman also included the prose material that was printed together with the *seliḥot*, including a short halakhic discussion by Heller.

31. *Megilat eivah* (Hebrew). Heller's memoir exists in a number of manuscripts and printed editions, as well as many translations. The first printed edition is that of Breslau, 1836. (The 1790 edition listed tentatively by Hailperin does not exist.) The various editions from 1836 to 1897 are listed and described in G. Kisch, 'Die Megillat Eba'. The Makhon Letatslumei Kitvei Yad in Jerusalem has microfilms of seven Hebrew manuscripts of *Megilat eivah*: JTS Mic. 3741, JTS Mic. 3778 (dated 1836), Oxford-Bodleian Heb. 414/2 (dated 1756), Oxford-Bodleian Heb. 2246/4, Amsterdam-Rosenthal 218, Warsaw 465, and Jerusalem-Samuel Safrai 1/3. Additionally, two Prague manuscripts are listed in Sadek, 'From the MSS Collections', 16–17, as Inv. no. 170188 (Cat. MS 29), dated 1773, and Inv. no. 170356 (Cat. MS 156), dated 1796.

    References in the notes of this work are to the text published by Judah Leib Hakohen Maimon, 'R. Yom-Tov Lipmann Heller', in id. (ed.), *In Honour of Yom-Tov* (Jerusalem, 1956), 28–40.

    There are several translations of *Megilat eivah* into various languages (including Judaeo-Arabic). A relatively recent English translation is that of Chaim Lipschitz and Neil Rosenstein, *The Feast and the Fast* (New York, 1984), which includes some useful genealogical tables of the Heller family.

32. *Megilat eivah* (Yiddish). The Yiddish text was published by Max Erik on the basis of MS Oxford-Bodleian Heb. 2209 in 'Memoirs of the Tosafot Yom Tov'. There are three other manuscripts of the Yiddish text: Jewish Theological Seminary Mic. 3779 (dated 1759), whose text is very close to Erik's, and ŽMP MSS 157 and 347, whose texts, while similar to each other, differ materially from Erik's.

Approbations

33. To the prospectus of David Gans, *Magen david* (Prague, 1612). There is a unique copy in the Bodleian Library, Oxford.
34. To Solomon Luria, *Yam shel shelomoh* on BT *BK* (Prague, 1616), signed by Heller together with the five other members of the Prague rabbinical courts.
35. To Isaac b. Samuel, *Siaḥ yitsḥak* (Prague, 1627).
36. To Isaiah Horowitz, *Sha'ar hashamayim* (Amsterdam, 1717), written in 1636.
37. To Yedidiah Gottlieb, *Ahavat hashem* (Cracow, 1641).
38. To Judah b. Joseph Nantua, *Kol yehudah* (Prague, 1641).
39. To Jacob ibn Habib, *Ein ya'akov* (Cracow, 1643), signed by Heller among others: reprinted in Israel Hailperin (ed.), *Documents of the Council of Four Lands* (Jerusalem, 1946), 67.
40. To Yedidiah Gottlieb, *Shir yedidut* (Cracow, 1644).

41. To Jacob David b. Isaac of Chęciny, *Perush al hamesorah* (Lublin, 1644). Printed again in the Amsterdam, 1651 edition, entitled *Ta'amei hamesorah.*

42. To Eliezer b. Samuel Ashkenazi, *Damesek eli'ezer* (Lublin, 1646).

43. To Shabetai b. Meir Kohen, *Siftei kohen* (Cracow, 1646). Heller also added some comments of his own within the text, e.g. at 'Yoreh de'ah', 66: 12.

44. To Berekhiah Berakh b. Isaac Eizik, *Zera berakh* (Cracow, 1646).

45. To Tsevi b. Joseph Hakohen, *Naḥalat tsevi* (Cracow, 1646).

46. To Eliezer b. Menahem Sternberg, *Petaḥ einayim* (Cracow, 1647).

47. To Naftali b. Jacob Elhanan Bacharach, *Emek hamelekh* (Amsterdam, 1648).

48. To Sa'adiah b. Aaron Halovna, *Mishnat ḥasidim* (Amsterdam, 1651).

49. To Hayim Buchner, *Oreḥot ḥayim* (Cracow, 1654), and a *pesak din* on mourning during *yom tov*, published in *Oreḥot ḥayim*, both reprinted in *Moriah*, 14 (1986), nos. 5–8, pp. 20–1, and nos. 9–10, pp. 18–19, ed. Yitshak Yudlov *et al.*

Letters

50. Heller's letter to his wife's aunt Edel, dated 22 Nov. 1619, appears in A. Landau and B. Wachstein (eds.), *Jüdische Privatbriefe aus dem Jahre* 1619 (Vienna, 1911). Heller's letter is in the Hebrew section, pp. 28–9. There is a transcription into Latin letters on p. 49, and a facsimile reproduction. Rachel's letter is on p. 29 (transcribed p. 50). Heller is also referred to in several other letters in the collection.

51. Heller's letter to the Jewish community of Głogów (Glogau), dated Monday [4] Elul (16 Aug.) 1627, published by J. Perles, 'Urkunden zur Geschichte der jüdischen Provinzial-synoden in Polen', *Monatsschrift für Geschichte und Wissenschaft des Judentums*, 16 (1867), 306–7. Cf. Israel Hailperin (ed.), *Documents of the Council of Four Lands* (Jerusalem, 1946), 52–3.

52. Heller's letter to the Jewish community of Frankfurt am Main, published in Israel Hailperin, 'The Controversy over Communal Elections in Frankfurt am Main and its Echoes in Poland and Bohemia' [Maḥloket al bereirat hakahal befrankfurt demain veheideha befolin], *Zion*, 21 (1956), 86–8; repr. in id., *Jews and Judaism in Eastern Europe* (Jerusalem, 1969), 130–2.

53. Letters to and from Heller, concerning a controversy over the rabbinate in Lokacze, dated Tevet (Jan./Feb.) 1641, were published in M. Brann, 'Additions à l'autobiographie de Lipman Heller', *Revue des Études Juives*, 21 (1890), 272–7.

54. Heller's letter to the Jewish community of Chęciny, dated 20 Tishrei (5 Oct.) 1651, was published from Heller's autograph copy in Israel Hailperin (ed.), *Documents of the Council of Four Lands* (Jerusalem, 1946), 493.

Miscellaneous

55. *Berit melaḥ*, a Yiddish broadsheet on the laws of salting meat (Prague, ?1628).

56. Heller's Yiddish translation of *Oreḥot ḥayim* was reprinted together with the Hebrew text of *Oreḥot ḥayim* and a literal Hebrew retranslation of Heller's translation by 'descendants of Rabenu *Tosafot yom tov*' (Benei Berak, 1986).

57. Heller's epitaphs for his daughters and grandchildren, published in Otto Muneles, *The Inscriptions of the Old Jewish Cemetery of Prague* (Jerusalem, 1988), 321–4.

58. Among the material copied by F. Wettstein from the (now lost) *pinkasim* of the synagogues of Cracow is a document written by Heller in 1650 to protect the reputation of a penitent, Meir b. Asher Lemil of Russia: 'Antiquities from Old Registers on the History of the Jews in Poland, Especially Cracow' [Kadmoniyot mipinkase'ot yeshanim lekorot yisra'el befolin bikhelal uvikerako biferat], *Otsar hasifrut*, 4 (1892), 615–16.

59. Also copied by Wettstein from the Cracow *pinkasim* is a contract of sale (perhaps actually a loan in the form of a sale and buy-back) signed by Heller, published in F. Wettstein, 'Conversations from Old Cracow Copied from the Registers' [Siḥot mini kedem: mu'atakot mipinkasei kerako], *Hatsofeh leḥokhmat yisra'el*, 4 (1915), 172–3.

60. Oral tradition, quoted in Aaron Samuel Kaidanover, *Birkat hazevaḥ* (Amsterdam, 1669), 162*b*.

61. Oral tradition, quoted by Moses b. Aaron Zevi Hirsh Kats, a grandson of Heller's, in his *Asefat hakohen* (repr. Bartfeld, 1906), 45*a–b*.

62. A 1648 or 1649 decision by Heller's court in Cracow is mentioned in Nathan Neta Kahana of Ostroh, *She'elot uteshuvot divrei renanah*, ed. Isaac Herskovitz (New York, 1984), no. 54.

63. A decision by Heller concerning the 'blessing on the sun' is mentioned in Isaac b. Abraham of Poznań, *She'elot uteshuvot rabenu yitsḥak hagadol mipozna* (Jerusalem, 1982), no. 5 (p. 8).

Heller's Lost Writings

Much of Heller's writing is lost, including sermons, responsa, letters, etc. Specific mention can be made of the following items:

64. Heller's supercommentary on Bahya b. Asher's Torah commentary, entitled *Tuv ta'am* (mentioned in *Megilat eivah*).

65. *Ma'adanei yom tov* on Sedarim 'Mo'ed' and 'Nashim'. Also: *Kitsur ma'adanei yom tov* (a digest of his decisions in the work) and a second edition of his *Pilpula ḥarifta* (mentioned in *Tosafot yom tov*, *Arakhin* 1: 4).

66. *Malbushei yom tov* on *Shulḥan arukh*, 'Yoreh de'ah' and 'Ḥoshen mishpat'.

67. In his bibliography of Heller's works, Hailperin lists the introduction to *Torat ha'asham* as a separate work, *Darkhei hora'ah*. The introduction was still extant in the late seventeenth century, but was subsequently separated from the rest of the manuscript and lost.

68. Heller wrote marginal notes to works such as *Netivot olam* by the Maharal of Prague (see *Malbushei yom tov*, 1: 2), the responsa of Solomon Luria (see *Malbushei yom tov*, 554), and undoubtedly many other works as well. As Hailperin notes in his bibliography, Heller's marginal notes in his copy of a geography of the land of Israel, *Kaftor vaferaḥ* by Eshtor Haparhi were extant as late as the nineteenth century.

69. It is clear that Heller wrote many more responsa than those that are extant. A collection of his responsa may still have been extant in the late seventeenth century.

70. Likewise, Heller wrote sermons each year. In his *Derush ḥidushei halevanah* (see above, no. 29), p. 51, Heller refers to 'a sermon which discusses . . . the six days of creation, which I called *Havayot hayesodot* ["The Beings of the Elements"]'. In a marginal note to *Sefer maharil* (see above, no. 16) Heller refers to two other sermons to which he gave names, and which he apparently wrote out as well. The first, called *Torah kedumah*, was given in Cracow on the second sabbath before Passover, 1649; the second, the following week, was called *Minḥah arevah*, after the first two words of the *haftarah* portion (Malachi 3: 4) on which the sermon was based.

71. The documents that Heller sent to the imperial courts in 1629 in connection with his trial are also mentioned in *Megilat eivah*. Additional archival material on Heller's rabbinical activities in Cracow may exist in the Acta Palatinalia Iudaica Cracoviensia: Varia 12 (1642–7), now in the Archiwum Miasta i Wojewodztwa of Cracow.

Bibliography

A bibliography of secondary literature relevant to this study (including a list of a number of other useful bibliographical guides) has already been published in Joseph Davis, 'The Cultural and Intellectual History of Ashkenazic Jews 1500–1750: A Selective Bibliography and Essay', *Leo Baeck Institute Yearbook*, 38 (1993), 343–86.

Anon., comments on Maimonides, *Mishneh torah*, 'Laws of the Sanctification of the New Moon', written 1606, MS Oxford-Bodleian Heb. 746/4.

Anon., 'Purims, Special', *Encyclopaedia Judaica* (Jerusalem, 1971), xiii, cols. 1395–1400.

Anon., 'The Rules of the Maharal of Prague in the Altneushul' [Takanot maharal miperag beveit hakeneset alt-noi], *Panim me'irot*, 26 (1992), 3–6.

Anon., 'Sefer alilot devarim', rationalist polemic and satire, ed. Raphael Kircheim, *Otsar neḥmad*, 4 (1864), 177–214.

AARON SAMUEL B. MOSES OF KREMENETS (KRZEMIENIEC), *Nishmat adam*, on kabbalah (Hanau, 1611; repr. Zhitomir, 1863).

ABRAHAMS, ISRAEL (ed.), *Hebrew Ethical Wills*, 2 vols. (Philadelphia, Pa., 1926).

ADINI, UZIEL, 'Education for Perfection: Traces of the Educational Philosophies of the Maharal of Prague and Jan Amos Comenius' [Ḥinukh el shelemut: be'ikvot mishnatam haḥinukhit shel hamaharal miperag ve'amos komenius], *Shevilei haḥinukh*, 37 (1974), 102–11.

ADLER, SIMON (ed.), 'Das älteste Judicial-Protokoll des jüdischen Gemeinde-Archives in Prag (1682)', *Jahrbuch der Gesellschaft für Geschichte der Juden in der Čechoslovakischen Republik*, 3 (1931), 217–56.

ALBECK, HANOKH, *Introduction to the Mishnah* [Mavo lamishnah] (Jerusalem, 1967).

——*Six Orders of the Mishnah* [Shishah sidrei mishnah meforashim biyedei ḥanokh albek], 6 vols. (Tel Aviv, 1952–9).

ALTMANN, ALEXANDER, 'The Ladder of Ascension', in id., *Studies in Religious Philosophy and Mysticism* (London 1969), 53–70.

ALTSHULER, DAVID (ed.), *The Precious Legacy: Judaic Treasures from the Czechoslovak State Collections* (New York, 1983).

ALTSHULER (PERLES), ELEAZER, *Dikdek yitsḥak*, on grammar, MS Oxford-Bodleian Heb. 1497/1.

——*Naḥalat avot*, commentary on Song of Songs, MS Oxford-Bodleian Heb. 358.

ALTSHULER, HANOKH B. MOSES, 'Megilat purei hakela'im', deliverance narrative, ed. Alexander Kisch, in *Jubelschrift zum siebzigsten Geburtstage des Prof. Dr. H. Graetz* (Breslau, 1887), Heb. sect. 48–53.

ALTSHULER, NAFTALI B. ASHER, *Ayalah sheluḥah*, Bible commentary (Cracow, 1593).

AMELANG, JAMES, *The Flight of Icarus: Artisan Autobiography in Early Modern Europe* (Stanford, Calif., 1998).

——(ed.), *A Journal of the Plague Year: The Diary of the Barcelona Tanner Miquel Parets 1651* (Oxford, 1991).

ANAV, ZEDEKIAH B. ABRAHAM, *Shibolei haleket*, ed. Solomon Buber (Vilna, 1886).

ARISTOTLE, *Works*, ed. W. D. Ross (Oxford, 1913).

ASHER B. ELIEZER HALEVI OF REICHSHOFEN, *Zikhronot*, diary, ed. Moses Ginsburger (Berlin, 1913).

ASHKENAZI, ABRAHAM B. SAMUEL, *Tsa'ar bat rabim*, chronicle, in Hayim Jonah Gurland (ed.), *On the History of the Persecution of Jews* (Przemysl, Cracow, and Odessa, 1886–92; repr. Jerusalem, 1972, Brooklyn, NY, 1993), pt. 4.

ASHKENAZI, JOSEPH B. JOSEPH, anti-rationalist tract, ed. Gershom Scholem, in id., 'New Information Concerning R. Joseph Ashkenazi, the Tanna of Safed', *Tarbiz*, 28 (1958), 59–89, 201–35.

ASHKENAZI, JUDAH B. NATHAN, notes on the Jewish calendar and lunar astronomy, published with Mordechai Jaffe, *Levush eder hayakar* (Lublin, 1594; repr. New York, 1965).

ASHKENAZI, MORDECHAI, *The Dreams of the Shabatean Rabbi Mordechai Ashkenazi* [Ḥalomotav shel hashabeta'i r. mordekhai ashkenazi], ed. Gershom Scholem (Jerusalem, 1938).

ASHTOR, ELIYAHU, 'Ibrāhīm ibn Ya'qūb', in Cecil Roth (ed.), *The World History of the Jewish People*, 2nd ser., vol. ii: *The Dark Ages: Jews in Christian Europe* (Ramat Gan, 1966), 305–8.

——*The Jews of Moslem Spain*, trans. Aaron and Jenny Klein, 2 vols. (Philadelphia, Pa., 1979).

ASSAF, SIMHAH, 'On the History of the Rabbinate in Germany, Poland, and Lithuania' [Lekorot harabanut be'ashkenaz, polaniyah, velita], in id., *In the Tents of Jacob*, 27–65.

——*In the Tents of Jacob* [Be'ohalei ya'akov] (Jerusalem, 1943).

——(ed.), *Sources for the History of Jewish Education* [Mekorot letoledot haḥinukh beyisra'el], vol. i (Jerusalem, 1954).

AVRON, DOV (ed.), *Pinkas hakesherim shel kehilat pozna*, registers of the Jewish community of Poznań (Jerusalem, 1966).

AZULAI, ABRAHAM, *Ahavah bata'anugim: peirush limesekhet eduyot shel r. avraham azulai*, commentary on tractate *Eduyot* of the Mishnah, ed. Dov Zlotnick, *Meḥkarim umekorot*, 1 (1978), 1–122.

BACHARACH, NAFTALI, *Emek hamelekh*, on kabbalah (Amsterdam, 1648; repr. Israel, n.d.).

BACHARACH, YAIR B. MOSES, *She'elot uteshuvot ḥavot ya'ir*, responsa (New York, n.d.).

BACKMANN, SIBYLLE, *et al.* (eds.), *Ehrkonzepte in der frühen Neuzeit: Identitäten und Abgrenzungen* (Berlin, 1998).

BACON, GERSHON, '"The House of Hannover": *Gezeirot tah* in Modern Jewish Historical Writing', *Jewish History*, 17 (2003), 179–206.

——and MOSHE ROSMAN, 'A "Chosen" Community in Straits: The Jews of Poland after the Massacres of 1648' [Kehilah 'nivḥeret' bametsukah: yahadut polin be'ikvot gezerot taḥ–tat], in Shmuel Almog and Michael Heyd (eds.), *Re'ayon habeḥirah beyisra'el uva'amim* (Jerusalem, 1991), 207–19.

BAŁABAN, MAJER, *History of the Jews in Cracow and Kazimierz* [Historia Żydów w Krakowie i na Kazimierzu], vol. i (Cracow, 1931); published earlier as *Dzieje Żydów w Krakowie* (Cracow, 1912).

——'The Jews of Cracow during the Swedish Invasion' [Yehudei kerako biyemei hakibush hashevedi], *Hatsefirah*, 49 (25 Nov. 1926), 5; 61 (10 Dec. 1926), 5; 67 (16 Dec. 1926), 4–5; 73 (24 Dec. 1926), 4.

BARNAI, JACOB, 'The Outbreak of Sabbateanism: The Eastern European Factor', *Journal of Jewish Thought and Philosophy*, 4 (1994), 171–83.

BARON, SALO, 'Ghetto and Emancipation: Shall We Revise the Traditional View?', *Menorah Journal*, 14 (1928), 515–26.

——*Social and Religious History of the Jews*, 2nd edn., vol. xiv: *Catholic Restoration and Wars of Religion* (New York, 1967); vol. xvi: *Poland–Lithuania 1500–1650* (New York, 1976).

BARUCH B. DAVID OF GNIEZNO, *Gedulat mordekhai*, commentary on Mordechai b. Hillel, *Sefer mordekhai* (Hanau, 1615; repr. Jerusalem, 1991).

BARZILAY (EISENSTEIN), ISAAC, 'The Italian and Berlin Haskalah: Parallels and Differences', *Proceedings of the American Academy for Jewish Research*, 29 (1961), 17–54.

——*Yosef Shlomo Del Medigo: His Life and Times* (Leiden, 1974).

BASARAB, JOHN, *Pereiaslav 1654: A Historiographical Study* (Edmonton, 1982).

BASS, MENDEL, rabbinic contract, 1644, *Kerem shelomoh*, 5/3 (43) (1982), 54–5.

BAUMINGER, ARYEH, *et al.* (eds.), *Cracow [Memorial] Book: A City and Mother in Israel* [Sefer kraka: ir va'em beyisra'el] (Jerusalem, 1959).

BECK, LEWIS WHITE, *Early German Philosophy: Kant and his Predecessors* (Cambridge, Mass., 1969).

Behrend family, 'Eine familien-Megillah aus der ersten hälfte des 18. Jahrhunderts', ed. J. M. Jost, *Jahrbuch für die Geschichte der Juden und des Judenthums*, 2 (1861), 39–82.

BEIT HALEVI, ISRAEL DAVID, *The Life of R. Yom Tov Lipmann Heller* [Toledot r. yom tov lipman heler] (Tel Aviv, 1954).

BELL, DEAN PHILLIP, 'Creating a Jewish History of Early Modern Germany', *Shofar*, 15 (1996), 119–28.

——*Sacred Communities: Jewish and Christian Identities in Fifteenth-Century Germany* (Leiden, 2001).

BEN-SASSON, HAIM HILLEL, 'Concepts and Reality in Jewish History in the Later Middle Ages' [Musagim umetsi'ut bahistoriyah hayehudit beshilhei yemei habeinayim], review of Jacob Katz, *Masoret umashber*, *Tarbiz*, 29 (1959), 297–312.

——'Horowitz, Horwitz, or Hurwitz: Rabbi Isaiah ben Rabbi Abraham Halevi' [Horovits, horvits, o hurvits: r. yeshayahu ben r. avraham halevi], *Entsiklopediyah ivrit* (Jerusalem, 1961), vol. xiii, cols. 943–6.

——'Jews and Christian Sectarians: Existential Similarity and Dialectical Tensions in Sixteenth Century Moravia and Poland–Lithuania', *Viator*, 4 (1973), 369–85.

——'The Reformation in Contemporary Jewish Eyes', *Proceedings of the Israel Academy of Sciences and Humanities*, 4 (1971), 239–326.

——'Response' [to Jacob Katz, 'On Halakhah and *Derush* as a Historical Source'], *Tarbiz*, 30 (1960), 69–72.

——*Theory and Practice: The Social Attitudes of the Jews of Poland in the Later Middle Ages* [Hagut vehanhagah: hashkefoteihem haḥevratiyot shel yehudei polin beshilhei yemei habeinayim] (Jerusalem, 1959).

——'Wealth and Poverty in the Teaching of the Preacher R. Ephraim of Leczyca' [Osher ve'oni bemishnato shel hamokhiaḥ r. efrayim ish lenchits], *Zion*, 19 (1954), 142–66.

BEN-SASSON, JONAH, *The Thought of R. Moses Isserles* [Mishnato ha'iyunit shel harema] (Jerusalem, 1984).

BEN-SHLOMO, JOSEPH, *The Theology of R. Moses Cordovero* [Torat ha'elohut shel r. mosheh kordovero] (Jerusalem, 1965).

BENAYAHU, MEIR, *Sefer toledot ha'ari: Its Textual History and its Historical Merit* [Sefer toledot ha'ari: gilgulei nusḥa'otav ve'erko mibeḥinah historit] (Jerusalem, 1967).

BENEDICT, PHILIP, 'Bibliothèques protestants et catholiques à Metz au XVIIe siècle', *Annales ESC*, 40 (1985), 343–70.

BEREKHIAH BERAKH B. ISAAC EIZIK, *Zera berakh*, sermons, pt. 2 (Amsterdam, 1662).

BERGER, DAVID, 'Miracles and Natural Order in Nahmanides', in Isadore Twersky (ed.), *Rabbi Moses Nahmanides (Ramban): Explorations in his Religious and Literary Virtuosity* (Cambridge, Mass., 1983), 113–28.

——'On the Image and Ultimate Fate of the Gentiles in Ashkenazic Polemical Literature' [Al tadmitam vegoralam shel hagoyim besifrut hapulmus ha'ashkenazit], in Yom Tov Assis *et al.* (eds.), *Yehudim mul hatselav: gezeirot tatnu* [= 1096] *bahalakhah, bahistoriyah, uvahistoriyografiyah* (Jerusalem, 2000), 74–91.

BERLINER, ABRAHAM (ed.), 'Sefer hazkarat neshamot: kehilat varmaisa', memorial book of the Jewish community of Worms, *Kovets al yad*, 3 (1887), 3–62.

BERNFELD, SIMON (ed.), *The Book of Tears* [Sefer hadema'ot], Jewish martyrological writings, 3 vols. (Berlin, 1926).

BERNSTEIN, SIMON, *In the Visions of Generations* [Beḥazon hadorot] (New York, 1928).

BETTAN, ISRAEL, 'The Sermons of Ephraim Luntshitz', *HUCA* 8–9 (1932), 443–80; repr. in id., *Studies in Jewish Preaching: Middle Ages* (Cincinnati, Ohio, 1939), 273–316.

BIALER, JUDAH LEIB, 'Cracow, Chosen City' [Kraka, ir segulah], in A. Bauminger *et al.* (eds.), *Cracow [Memorial] Book: A City and Mother in Israel* (Jerusalem, 1959), 126–66.

BIALIK, H. N., and Y. H. RAVNITSKY (eds.), *The Book of Legends*, trans. William Braude (New York, 1992).

BIRELEY, ROBERT, SJ, *Religion and Politics in the Age of the Counterreformation: Emperor Ferdinand II, William Lamormaini SJ, and the Formation of Imperial Policy* (University of North Carolina [Chapel Hill], 1981).

BLOCH, PHILIPP, 'Der Streit um den Moreh des Maimonides in Posen', *Monatsschrift für Geschichte und Wissenschaft des Judentums*, 47 (1903), 153–69, 263–79, 346–7.

——'Vielbegehrter Rabbiner des Rheingaues, Juda Mehler Reutlingen', in *Beiträge zur Geschichte der deutschen Juden: Festschrift zum siebzigsten Geburtstage Martin Philippsons* (Leipzig, 1916), 114–34.

BOES, MARIA, 'Jews in the Criminal-Justice System of Early Modern Germany', *Journal of Interdisciplinary History*, 30 (1999), 407–35.

BOGUCKA, MARIA, *The Lost World of the 'Sarmatians': Custom as the Regulator of Polish Social Life in Early Modern Times* (Warsaw, 1996).

BOHATCOVÁ, MIRJAM, 'Book-Printing and Other Forms of Publishing in Prague 1550–1650', in Fučiková, Eliška *et al.* (eds.), *Rudolf II and Prague: The Court and the City* (London, 1997), 332–9.

BONAMI, DAVID, 'The Theological Ideas in the Hiddushei Aggadot of Maharsha' (Doctor of Hebrew Literature diss., Jewish Theological Seminary, New York, 1976).

BONDY, GOTTLIEB, and FRANZ DWORSKY (eds.), *Zur Geschichte der Juden in Böhmen, Mähren, und Schlesien von 906 bis 1620* (Prague, 1906).

BONFIL, ROBERT (REUVEN), 'How Golden was the Age of the Renaissance in Jewish Historiography', *History and Theory*, 27 (1988), 78–102; repr. in David Ruderman (ed.), *Essential Papers on Jewish Culture in Renaissance and Baroque Italy* (New York, 1992), 219–51.

——*Rabbis and Jewish Communities in Renaissance Italy*, trans. Jonathan Chapman (Oxford, 1990); 1st pub. as *Harabanut be'italiyah bitekufat harenesans* (Jerusalem, 1979).

BOYARIN, DANIEL, *Intertextuality and the Reading of Midrash* (Bloomington, Ind., 1990).

BRANN, MARCUS, 'Additions à l'autobiographie de Lipman Heller', *Revue des Études Juives*, 21 (1890), 270–7.

BREUER, EDWARD, 'In Defense of Tradition: The Masoretic Text and its Rabbinic Interpretation in the Early Rabbinic Haskalah' (Ph.D. diss., Harvard University, 1990).

BREUER, MORDECHAI, 'Ashkenazi Yeshivot in the Later Middle Ages' [Yeshivot ashkenaziyot beshilhei yemei habeinayim] (Ph.D. diss., Hebrew University of Jerusalem, 1967).

——'The Debate of the Maharal of Prague with the Christians: A New Look at *Sefer be'er hagolah*' [Vikuḥo shel maharal miperag im hanotsrim: mabat ḥadash al sefer be'er hagolah], *Tarbiz*, 55 (1986), 253–60.

——'The Early Modern Period', in Michael Meyer and Michael Brenner (eds.), *German-Jewish History in Modern Times*, vol. i (New York, 1996), 79–260.

——'Modernism and Traditionalism in Sixteenth Century Jewish Historiography: A Study of David Gans' Tzemah David', in Bernard Cooperman (ed.), *Jewish Thought in the Sixteenth Century* (Cambridge, Mass., 1983), 49–88.

——'A Sketch of R. David Gans, the Author of Tsemah David' [Kavim lidemuto shel r. david gans, ba'al tsemaḥ david], *Bar Ilan*, 11 (1974), 97–118.

BRIK, AVRAHAM, 'R. Eleazar Altshul-Perles: A Scholar and Kabbalist of the Seventeenth Century' [R. elazar altshul-perles: gaon umekubal bame'ah hasheva-esreh], *Shanah beshanah* (1989), 482–91 (1990), 365–77.

BRODY, HEINRICH, *Die Handschriften der Prager jüdische Gemeindebibliothek* (Prague, 1911).

——'A Manuscript Miscellany', *Jewish Quarterly Review*, 13 (1922), 53–98.

BROYDE, MICHAEL, 'The Obligation to Encourage Gentiles to Observe the "Seven Noahide Laws"' [Ḥovatam shel yehudim le'oded shemirat sheva mitsvot benei noaḥ al yedei nokhrim], *Dinei yisra'el*, 19 (1998), 87–111.

BUBER, MARTIN, 'Prophecy, Apocalyptic, and the Historical Hour', in id., *On the Bible*, ed. Nahum Glatzer (New York, 1968), 172–87.

——*The Writings of Martin Buber*, ed. Will Herberg (New York, 1956).

BUBER, SOLOMON, *Anshei shem*, history of the rabbinate and community of Lvov (Cracow, 1895).

——*Kiryah nisgavah*, history of the rabbinate and community of Żółkiew (Zholkva) (Cracow, 1903).

BUCHEN, IRVING H., '*Satan in Goray* and the Progression of Possession', in id., *Isaac Bashevis Singer and the Eternal Past* (New York, 1968), 83–97.

BUCHNER, HAYIM, *Oreḥot ḥayim* (Cracow, 1654), halakhic booklet, sections ed. Yitshak Yudlov, in *Moriah*, 14 (1985–6), nos. 5–8, pp. 17–25; nos. 9–10, pp. 18–22.

BURKE, PETER, 'Notes for a Social History of Silence in Early Modern Europe', in id., *The Art of Conversation* (Ithaca, NY, 1993), 123–43.

BURKE, PETER, 'Tradition and Experience: The Idea of Decline from Bruni to Gibbon', *Daedalus*, 105/3 (1976), 137–52.

BURNETT, STEPHEN G., 'The Regulation of Hebrew Printing in Germany 1555–1630: Confessional Politics and the Limits of Jewish Toleration', in Max Reinhart (ed.), *Infinite Boundaries: Order, Disorder, and Reorder in Early Modern German Culture* (Kirksville, Mo., 1998), 329–48.

CAÑIZARES ESGUERRA, JORGE, 'New World, New Stars: Patriotic Astrology and the Invention of Indian and Creole Bodies in Colonial South America 1600–1650', *American Historical Review*, 104 (1999), 33–68.

CARLEBACH, ELISHEVA, 'Between History and Hope: Jewish Messianism in Ashkenaz and Sepharad' (Selmanowitz Lecture, Touro College, 1998).

——'Between History and Myth: The Regensburg Expulsion in Josel of Rosheim's Sefer ha-Miknah', in Elisheva Carlebach, John Efron, and David Myers (eds.), *Jewish History and Jewish Memory: Essays in Honor of Yosef Hayim Yerushalmi* (Hanover, NH, 1998), 40–53.

——'Converts and their Narratives in Early Modern Germany: The Case of Friedrich Albrecht Christiani', *Leo Baeck Institute Year Book*, 40 (1995), 65–84.

CARO, JOSEPH, *Beit yosef*, commentary on Jacob b. Asher, *Arba'ah turim*, published in standard editions of the latter.

——*Shulḥan arukh*, 1st edn., with commentary of Moses Isserles (Cracow, 1577; repr. Jerusalem, 1974).

CARPI, DANIEL, 'Jews with Medical Degrees from the University of Padua' [Yehudim ba'alei to'ar doktor lirefu'ah befaduah], in Carpi *et al.* (eds.), *Scritti in memoria di Nathan Cassuto* (Jerusalem, 1986), Hebrew section pp. 62–91.

CASPAR, MAX, *Kepler*, trans. and ed. C. Doris Hellman (London, 1959).

CASSIRER, ERNST, *et al.* (eds.), *Renaissance Philosophy of Man* (Chicago, 1945).

CHAJES (or HAYES), ISAAC, *Paḥad yitsḥak*, commentary on aggadic portions of BT *Gitin* (Lublin, 1573).

CHAJES, J. H., 'Judgments Sweetened: Possession and Exorcism in Early Modern Jewish Culture', *Journal of Early Modern History*, 1 (1997), 124–69.

CHAZAN, ROBERT, 'The Timebound and the Timeless: Medieval Jewish Narration of Events', *History and Memory*, 6 (1994), 5–34.

CIPOLLA, CARLO, *Faith, Reason, and the Plague in Seventeenth Century Tuscany*, trans. Muriel Kittel (Ithaca, NY, 1977).

——*Fighting the Plague in Seventeenth Century Italy* (Madison, Wis., 1981).

COHEN, BENJAMIN, 'The Jurisdiction of the Wojewoda over the Jews in "Old" Poland' [Hayurisdiktsiyah havoyevodit legabei hayehudim befolin ha'yeshanah'], in Shmuel Yeivin (ed.), *Sefer rafa'el mahler* (Tel Aviv, 1974), 47–66.

COHEN, GERSHON, 'On the History of the Conflict over Gentile Wine in Italy: Some Sources' [Letoledot hapulmus al setam-yeinam be'italiyah umekorotav], *Sinai*, 77 (1975), 62–90.

COHEN, SIMON, 'From the Library of Yom Tob Lipmann Heller', *Studies in Jewish Booklore and Bibliography*, 1 (1954), 103–7.

COHEN, STUART A., *The Three Crowns: Structures of Communal Politics in Early Rabbinic Jewry* (Cambridge, 1990).

COLORNI, ABRAHAM, *Scotographia o vero scienza di scrivere oscuro . . .* (Prague, 1593).

COMENIUS, JAN, *The Labyrinth of the World*, trans. Matthew Spinka (Ann Arbor, Mich., 1972).

COOPER, ALAN, 'An Extraordinary Sixteenth Century Biblical Commentary: Eliezer Ashkenazi on the Song of Moses', in Barry Walfish (ed.), *Frank Talmage Memorial Volume*, vol. i (Haifa, 1993), 129–50.

CYGIELMAN, SHMUEL ARTHUR (ed.), *The Jews of Poland and Lithuania before 1648* [Yehudei polin velita ad shenat taḥ] (Jerusalem, 1991). A section of the work is trans. as id., *Jewish Autonomy in Poland and Lithuania until 1648* (Jerusalem, 1997).

DAN, JOSEPH, *The Hebrew Story in the Middle Ages* [Hasipur ha'ivri biyemei habeinayim] (Jerusalem, 1974).

—— *The Mystical Teachings of Hasidei Ashkenaz* [Torat hasod shel ḥasidut ashkenaz] (Jerusalem, 1968).

—— '"No Evil Descends from Heaven": Sixteenth Century Jewish Concepts of Evil', in Bernard Cooperman (ed.), *Jewish Thought in the Sixteenth Century* (Cambridge, Mass., 1983), 89–105.

DANBY, HERBERT (trans.), *The Mishnah* (Oxford, 1933).

DARSHAN, DAVID, *Shir haMa'alot L'David and Ktav Hitnazzelut L'Darshanim*, on preaching, ed. and trans. Hayim Goren Perelmuter (Cincinnati, Ohio, 1984).

DAVID, ABRAHAM (ed.), *A Hebrew Chronicle from Prague, c.1615*, trans. Leon J. Weinberger and Dena Ordan (Tuscaloosa, Ala., 1993); the Hebrew text appeared as *A Hebrew Chronicle from Prague from the Early Seventeenth Century* [Keronikah ivrit miperag mereshit hame'ah ha-17] (Jerusalem, 1984).

DAVID, ZDENEK V., 'Jews in Sixteenth Century Czech Historiography: The "Czech Chronicle" of Václav Hájek of Libocany', *East European Jewish Affairs*, 25 (1995), 25–42.

DAVID B. JACOB OF SZCZEBRZESZYN, *Perush al targum yonatan vetargum yerushalmi*, commentary on minor Targumim (Prague, 1609).

DAVID B. SAMUEL, 'Magen david', liturgical poetry, in Menahem Mendel Biber (ed.), *Yalkut menaḥem* (Vilna, 1903), 4*a*–6*a*.

——'Takanot hataz', local by-laws for the Jews of Uherský Brod, ed. Abraham Judah Frankel-Grun, *Hatsofeh leḥokhmat yisra'el*, 3 (1913), 188–90.

—— *Turei zahav*, commentary on *Shulḥan arukh*, printed in the standard editions.

DAVID OF LANDSHUT *see* F. KLEIN-FRANKE

DAVIDSON, HERBERT, 'Medieval Jewish Philosophy in the Sixteenth Century', in Bernard Cooperman (ed.), *Jewish Thought in the Sixteenth Century* (Cambridge, Mass., 1983), 106–45.

DAVIS, JOSEPH, 'Ashkenazic Rationalism and Midrashic Natural History: Responses to the New Science in the Works of Rabbi Yom Tov Lipmann Heller (1578–1654)', *Science in Context*, 10 (1997), 605–26.

——'The Cultural and Intellectual History of Ashkenazic Jews 1500–1750: A Selective Bibliography and Essay', *Leo Baeck Institute Yearbook*, 38 (1993), 343–86.

——'A German-Jewish Woman Scholar of the Early Sixteenth Century', in Rela Geffen and Marsha Edelman (eds.), *Freedom and Responsibility: Exploring the Challenges of Jewish Continuity*, Gratz College centennial volume (New York, 1999), 101–10.

——'Philosophy, Dogma, and Exegesis in Medieval Ashkenazic Judaism: The Evidence of *Sefer Hadrat Qodesh*', *Association of Jewish Studies Review*, 18 (1993), 195–222.

——'Philosophy and the Law in the Writings of R. Yom Tov Lipman Heller', in Isadore Twersky and Jay Harris (eds.), *Studies in Medieval Jewish History and Literature*, vol. iii (Cambridge, Mass., 2000), 249–80.

——'R. Yom Tov Lipman Heller, Joseph b. Isaac ha-Levi, and Rationalism in Ashkenazic Jewish Culture 1550–1650' (Ph.D. diss., Harvard University, 1990).

——'The Reception of the *Shulhan 'Arukh* and the Formation of Ashkenazic Jewish Identity', *Association of Jewish Studies Review*, 26 (2002), 251–76.

——'The "Ten Questions" of Eliezer Eilburg and the Problem of Jewish Unbelief in the Sixteenth Century', *Jewish Quarterly Review*, 91 (2001), 293–336.

DAVIS, NATALIE ZEMON, 'Fame and Secrecy: Leon Modena's *Life* as an Early Modern Autobiography', in Mark Cohen (ed. and trans.), *The Autobiography of a Seventeenth Century Venetian Rabbi: Leon Modena's Life of Judah* (Princeton, NJ, 1988), 50–70; also pub. in *History and Theory*, 27 (1988), 103–18.

——'Printing and the People', in ead., *Society and Culture in Early Modern France* (Stanford, Calif., 1975), 189–226.

——*Women on the Margins: Three Seventeenth-Century Lives* (Cambridge, Mass., 1995).

DAXELMÜLLER, CHRISTOPH, 'Organizational Forms of Jewish Popular Culture since the Middle Ages', in R. Po-Chia Hsia and Harmut Lehmann (eds.), *In and Out of the Ghetto: Jewish–Gentile Relations in Late Medieval and Early Modern Germany* (Cambridge, 1995), 29–48.

DE VIGUERIE, JEAN, 'Le Miracle dans la France du XVIIe siècle', *Dix-Septième Siècle*, 35 (1983), 313–32.

DEGANI, BEN ZION, 'The Structure of World History and the Redemption of the Jews in *Tsemaḥ david* by R. David Gans' [Hamivneh shel hahistoriyah ha'olamit uge'ulat yisra'el betsemaḥ david ler. david gans], *Zion*, 45 (1980), 173–200.

DEKKER, THOMAS, 'The wonderfull yeare', in *The Plague Pamphlets of Thomas Dekker*, ed. F. P. Wilson (Oxford, 1925; repr. St Clair Shores, Mich., 1971).

DELMEDIGO, JOSEPH SOLOMON, *Sefer elim*, on science, religion, and metaphysics (Amsterdam, 1629; Odessa, 1864).

DEMETZ, PETER, 'Die Legende vom Magischen Prag', in Amy Cohn and Elisabeth

Strenger (eds.), *Brücken über dem Abgrund: Festschrift für Harry Zohn* (Munich, 1994), 367–82.

——*Prague in Black and Gold: Scenes from the Life of a European City* (New York, 1997).

DENARI, YEDIDYAH, *Ashkenazi Rabbis of the Later Middle Ages* [Ḥakhmei ashkenaz beshilhei yemei habeinayim] (Jerusalem, 1984).

DIRLMEIER, ULF, and GERHARD FOUQUET, 'Diet and Consumption', in Bob Scribner (ed.), *Germany: A New Social and Economic History*, vol. i: *1450–1630* (London, 1996), 85–111.

DONNE, JOHN, *Sermons*, ed. Evelyn M. Simpson and George R. Potter, vol. vi (Berkeley, Calif., 1953), 349–64 (sermon 18, 15 Jan. 1626).

DUBITSKY, YISRAEL, 'Matter and Form: A Critically Annotated Bibliography of Studies on Rabbi Judah Loew, or Maharal of Prague, Printed between 1972 and 1996' (Master of Library Science diss., City University of New York, 1995).

DUBNOW, SIMON, *History of the Jews in Russia and Poland*, trans. Israel Friedlaender, 3 vols. (Philadelphia, Pa., 1916).

——(ed.), *Pinkas hamedinah o pinkas va'ad hakehilot harashiyot bimedinat lita*, records of the Jewish Council of Lithuania (Berlin, 1925).

EDELES, JOSHUA, *Megilat r. yehoshua edeles* (ŽMP MS 255), deliverance narrative, written by a descendant on the basis of oral traditions in 1833.

EDELS, SAMUEL B. JUDAH (MAHARSHA), *Ḥidushei agadot vehalakhot*, Talmud commentary, printed in the Vilna Talmud.

EFRON, NOAH, 'Irenism and Natural Philosophy in Rudolfine Prague: The Case of David Gans', *Science in Context*, 10 (1997), 627–49.

——'Liberal Arts, Eirenism and Jews in Rudolfine Prague', in Jaroslav Folta (ed.), *Science and Technology in Rudolfinian Times* (Prague, 1997) [= Acta historiae rerum naturalium necnon technicarum, NS 1 (1997)], 24–35.

——'Rabbi David ben Shlomo Gans and Natural Philosophy in Seventeenth-Century Prague' (Ph.D. diss., Tel Aviv University, 1997).

EIDELBERG, SHLOMO, *R. Juspa, Shamash of Warmaisa (Worms): Jewish Life in Seventeenth-Century Worms* [R. yuzpa shamash dikehilat varmaysa: olam yehudeiha bame'ah ha-17], full text in English and in Hebrew (Jerusalem, 1991).

EILBURG, ELIEZER B. ABRAHAM, *Eser she'elot*, questions on Judaism, JTS MS microfilm no. 2323, fos. 45–77.

EINBINDER, SUSAN, 'The Troyes Laments: Jewish Martyrology in Hebrew and Old French', *Viator*, 30 (1999), 201–30.

ELAZAR, DANIEL J., and STUART A. COHEN, *The Jewish Polity: Jewish Political Organization from Biblical Times to the Present* (Bloomington, Ind., 1985).

ELBAUM, JACOB, 'The Influence of Spanish-Jewish Culture on the Jews of Ashkenaz and Poland in the Fifteenth–Seventeenth Centuries', in Joseph Dan (ed.), *Binah: Studies in Jewish History, Thought, and Culture*, vol. iii (Westport, Conn., 1994),

179–97; 1st pub. as 'Kesharei tarbut bein yehudei polin ve'ashkenaz levein yehudei italiyah bame'ah ha-16', *Gal-ed*, 7–8 (1985), 11–40.

ELBAUM, JACOB, 'More on the Image of the Dwarf and the Giant' [Od al mashal hananas veha'anak], *Sinai*, 77 (1975), 287.

——*Openness and Insularity: The Spiritual-Literary Culture of Polish Jews in the Later Sixteenth Century* [Petiḥut vehistagrut: hayetsirah haruḥanit-hasifrutit befolin uve'aratsot ashkenaz beshilhei hame'ah hashesh-esreh] (Jerusalem, 1990).

——*Penance and Penitence: Studies in the Penitential Systems of the Rabbis of Germany and Poland 1348–1648* [Teshuvat halev vekabalat yisurin: iyunim beshitot hateshuvah shel ḥakhmei ashkenaz ufolin 1348–1648] (Jerusalem, 1992).

——'R. Judah Loewe's Attitude to Aggadah', *Scripta Hierosolymitana*, 22 (1971), 28–47.

ELMAN, YAAKOV, '"It is no empty thing": Nahmanides and the Search for Omnisignificance', *Torah u-Madda Journal*, 4 (1993), 1–63.

——'The Suffering of the Righteous in Palestinian and Babylonian Sources', *Jewish Quarterly Review*, 80 (1990), 315–39.

EMANUEL, YONAH, 'The Attitude towards Gentile and Secular Learning in the Works of the Author of *Tosafot Yom Tov*' [Hayaḥas le'umot ha'olam uleḥokhmot kelaliyot besifrei ba'al hatosafot yom tov], *Hama'ayan*, 4/2 (1964), 50–9.

——'Rashi's Torah Commentary and its Supercommentaries in *Tosafot Yom Tov*' [Perush rashi al hatorah umefarashav betosafot yom tov], in Esriel Hildesheimer and Kalman Kahana (eds.), *Memorial Book for Jacob Jehiel Weinberg* [Sefer zikaron leya'akov yeḥi'el veinberg] (Jerusalem, 1970), 443–6.

EPHRAIM SOLOMON B. AARON OF LUNTSHITS, *Amudei shesh*, ethics (Warsaw, 1875; repr. Brooklyn, NY, 1976).

EPSTEIN, ABRAHAM, 'The Luria Family' [Mishpaḥat luria], in Abraham M. Haberman (ed.), *Kitvei avraham epstein*, vol. i (Jerusalem, 1950), 309–53.

EPSTEIN, JACOB NAHUM, *Introduction to the Text of the Mishnah* [Mavo lenusaḥ hamishnah] (Jerusalem, 1948).

ERGANG, ROBERT, *The Myth of the All-Destructive Fury of the Thirty Years' War* (Pocono Pines, Pa., 1956).

ERIK, MAX (pseud.; Zalman Merkin), *The History of Yiddish Literature: From Earliest Times until the Period of the Enlightenment* [Di geshikhte fun der yidisher literatur fun di eltste tsaytn biz der haskole-tkufe] (Warsaw, 1928).

——'The Memoirs of the Tosafot Yom Tov: A Seventeenth-Century Yiddish manuscript of *Megilat eivah*' [Di memuarn fun dem tosfes yontef: a yidisher ksav-yad fun der 'megiles eyve' fun dem 17tn yorhundert], *Arkhiv far yidisher shprakhvisnshaft, literatur-forshung, un etnologie*, ed. Noah (Nojach) Prylucki, 1 (1926–33), 179–217.

ETKES, IMMANUEL, 'Magic and *Ba'alei-Shem* in Ashkenazi Society at the Turn of the Eighteenth Century' [Mekomam shel hamagiyah uva'alei hashem baḥevrah ha'ashkenazit bemifneh hame'ot ha-17–ha-18], *Zion*, 60 (1995), 69–104.

ETTINGER, SHMUEL, 'Jewish Participation in the Colonization of the Ukraine' [Ḥelkam shel hayehudim bekolonizatsiyah shel ukra'inah 1569–1648], *Zion*, 21 (1956), 107–42.

——'The Legal and Social Status of the Jews of Ukraine from the Fifteenth Century to the Cossack Uprising of 1648', *Journal of Ukrainian Studies*, 17 (1992), 107–40; 1st pub. in *Zion*, 20 (1955), 128–52.

EUCHEL, ISAAC, and MENAHEM MENDL BRESLAU, 'The Stream of Besor' [prospectus of *Hame'asef*, 13 Apr. 1783], trans. Laura Sachs, in Paul Mendes-Flohr and Jehuda Reinharz (eds.), *The Jew in the Modern World*, 2nd edn. (Oxford, 1995), 80–3.

EVANS, R. J. W., 'The Imperial Vision', in Geoffrey Parker (ed.), *The Thirty Years War*, rev. edn. (London, 1987; repr. New York, 1993), 83–8.

——*Rudolph II and his World* (Oxford, 1973).

EVENETT, H. OUTRAM, *The Spirit of the Counter-Reformation*, ed. John Bossy (Cambridge, 1968).

FAIERSTEIN, MORRIS, ' "God's Need for the Commandments" in Medieval Kabbalah', *Conservative Judaism*, 36 (1982), 45–59.

FARINE, AVIGDOR, 'Charity and Study Societies in Europe of the Sixteenth–Eighteenth Centuries', *Jewish Quarterly Review*, 64 (1973), 16–47, 164–75.

FEINSTEIN, ARYEH LEIB, *City of Fame* [Ir tehilah], history of the Jews of Brest-Litovsk (Warsaw, 1886).

FERGUSON, WALLACE, *The Renaissance in Historical Thought: Five Centuries of Interpretation* (Cambridge, Mass., 1948).

FINE, LAWRENCE, 'The Art of Metoposcopy: A Study in Isaac Luria's Charismatic Knowledge', *Association of Jewish Studies Review*, 11 (1986), 79–101; repr. in id. (ed.), *Essential Papers on Kabbalah* (New York, 1995), 315–37.

——'Maggidic Revelation in the Teachings of Isaac Luria', in Jehuda Reinharz *et al.* (eds.), *Mystics, Philosophers, and Politicians: Essays in Jewish Intellectual History in Honor of Alexander Altmann* (Durham, NC, 1982), 141–58.

——'Recitation of Mishnah as a Vehicle for Mystical Inspiration: A Contemplative Technique Taught by Hayyim Vital', *Revue des Études Juives*, 141 (1982), 183–99.

——(ed. and trans.), *Safed Spirituality* (New York, 1984).

FINKELSTEIN, LOUIS, *Akiba: Scholar, Saint, and Martyr* (New York, 1936).

——*Sifra on Leviticus*, vol. i (New York, 1989).

FISHMAN, DAVID, 'Rabbi Moshe Isserles and the Study of Science among Polish Rabbis', *Science in Context*, 10 (1997), 571–88.

FISHMAN, JUDAH LEIB HAKOHEN *see* MAIMON, JUDAH LEIB HAKOHEN

FISHMAN, TALYA, *Shaking the Pillars of Exile: 'Voice of a Fool', an Early Modern Jewish Critique of Rabbinic Culture* (Stanford, Calif., 1997).

FLATTO, SHARON, 'Prague's Rabbinic Culture: The Concealed and Revealed in Ezekiel Landau's Writings' (Ph.D. diss., Yale University, 2000).

FOGELMAN, MORDECHAI, 'Observations on his Commentary on the Mishnah' [Birurim leperusho lamishnah], in Judah Leib Hakohen Maimon (ed.), *In Honour of Yom-Tov* (Jerusalem, 1956), 215–20.

FORSTER, MARC, 'Clericalism and Communalism', in Max Reinhart (ed.), *Infinite Boundaries: Order, Disorder, and Reorder in Early Modern German Culture*, Sixteenth-Century Essays and Studies 40 (Kirksville, Mo., 1998), 55–75.

FRAM, EDWARD, 'And Still a Gap Exists between 1096 and 1648' [Ve'adayin ein bein tatnu letaḥ–tat], response to Jacob Katz, 'More on "Between 1096 and 1648"', *Zion*, 62 (1997), 31–46.

——'Between 1096 and 1648: A Reappraisal' [Bein tatnu letaḥ-tat: iyun meḥadash], *Zion*, 61 (1996), 159–82.

——'Creating a Tale of Martyrdom in Tulczyn, 1648', in Elisheva Carlebach, John Efron, and David Myers (eds.), *Jewish History and Jewish Memory: Essays in Honor of Yosef Hayim Yerushalmi* (Hanover, NH, 1998), 89–112.

——*Ideals Face Reality: Jewish Law and Life in Poland 1550–1655* (Cincinnati, Ohio, 1997).

——'Perception and Reception of Repentant Apostates in Medieval Ashkenaz and Premodern Poland', *Association of Jewish Studies Review*, 21 (1996), 319–39.

FRÄNKLIN (WALLERSTEIN), ABRAHAM B. JACOB, [legal documents], Haus- Hof- und Staatsarchiv (Vienna), Alte Prager Akten box no. 85, fos. 242–9.

FRANZL, JOHANN, *Ferdinand II: Kaiser im Zwiespalt der Zeit* (Graz, 1978).

FRIEDBERG, BERNHARD (HAYIM), *History of Hebrew Printing in Poland* [Toledot hadefus ha'ivri befolaniyah], rev. edn. (Tel Aviv, 1950).

——(ed.), *Jewish Epitaphs* [Luḥot zikaron] (Frankfurt am Main, 1904; repr. Israel, 1969).

FRIEDLAND, SH., 'A Family Megilah from Prague, 1732' [A prager familyen-megile funem yor 1732], *Yivo-bleter*, 13 (1938), 69–76.

FRIEDMAN, JEROME, *The Most Ancient Testimony: Sixteenth-Century Christian Hebraica in the Age of Renaissance Nostalgia* (Athens, Ohio, 1983).

FRIEDMAN, PHILIP, 'Polish Jewish Historiography between the Two Wars (1918–1939)', *Jewish Social Studies*, 11 (1949), 373–408.

FRIEDRICHS, CHRISTOPHER R., 'Anti-Jewish Politics in Early Modern Germany: The Uprising in Worms, 1613–17', *Central European History*, 23 (1990), 91–152.

——'Jews in the Imperial Cities: A Political Perspective', in R. Po-Chia Hsia and Harmut Lehmann (eds.), *In and Out of the Ghetto: Jewish-Gentile Relations in Late Medieval and Early Modern Germany* (Cambridge, 1995), 278–88.

——'Politics or Pogrom? The Fettmilch Uprising in German and Jewish History', *Central European History*, 19 (1986), 186–228.

——*Urban Society in an Age of War: Nördlingen 1580–1720* (Princeton, NJ, 1979).

FROST, ROBERT I., *After the Deluge: Poland–Lithuania and the Second Northern War 1655–1660* (Cambridge, 1993).

——'"Initium Calamitatis Regni"? John Casimir and Monarchical Power in Poland–Lithuania 1648–1668', *European History Quarterly*, 16 (1986), 181–208.

FUČIKOVÁ, ELIŠKA, *et al.* (eds.), *Rudolf II and Prague: The Court and the City* (London, 1997).

FUNKENSTEIN, AMOS, *Perceptions of Jewish History* (Berkeley, Calif., 1993); 1st pub. as *Tadmit vetoda'ah historit bayahadut uvisevivutah hatarbutit* (Tel Aviv, 1991).

GANS, DAVID, *Magen david*, prospectus for id., *Neḥmad vena'im* (Prague, 1612).

——*Neḥmad vena'im*, astronomical and cosmographic textbook (Jessnitz, 1743; repr. Brooklyn, 1990).

——*Tsemaḥ david*, chronicle, ed. Mordechai Breuer (Jerusalem, 1983).

GANS, PHOEBUS (FEIVEL) OF MINDEN, 'Zikhronot', deliverance narrative and memoir, ed. David Kaufmann in his edition of Glueckel's autobiography, *Zikhronot marat glikl hamil* (Frankfurt am Main, 1896), 334–400.

GASTER, MOSES, 'The Maasehbuch and the Brantspiegel', in Salo Baron and Alexander Marx (eds.), *Jewish Studies in Memory of George A. Kohut* (New York, 1935), 270–8.

GAUKROGER, STEPHEN, *Descartes: An Intellectual Biography* (Oxford, 1995).

GETZ, BERAKH B. ELIAKIM, *Zera berakh shelishi*, sermons on Genesis (Halle, 1714).

GINDELY, ANTONIN, *Geschichte der Gegenreformation in Böhmen*, ed. Theodor Tupetz (Leipzig, 1894).

GINZBERG, LOUIS, *Commentary on the Talmud Yerushalmi* [Perushim veḥidushim biyerushalmi], vol. i (New York, 1941).

——*Legends of the Jews*, 7 vols. (Philadelphia, Pa., 1909–38).

GLANZ, RUDOLF, 'The "Jewish Execution" in Medieval Germany', *Jewish Social Studies*, 5 (1943), 3–26.

GLUECKEL BAT JUDAH LEIB, *The Life of Glückel of Hameln 1646–1724: Written by Herself*, trans. Beth-Zion Abrahams (London, 1962).

GOETSCHEL, ROLAND, 'The Maharal of Prague and the Kabbalah', in Karl Grözinger and Joseph Dan (eds.), *Mysticism, Magic, and Kabbalah in Ashkenazi Judaism* (Berlin, 1995), 172–80.

GOLD, HUGO (ed.), *Die Juden und Judengemeinden den Mährens in Vergangenheit und Gegenwart* (Brünn, 1929).

GOLDBERG, JACOB, *Jewish Society in the Polish-Lithuanian Commonwealth* [Haḥevrah hayehudit bemamlekhet polin-lita], trans. Zofiyah Lasman (Jerusalem, 1999).

GOLDBERG, SYLVIE ANNE, *Crossing the Jabbok: Illness and Death in Ashkenazi Judaism in Sixteenth- through Nineteenth-Century Prague* (Berkeley, Calif., 1995).

GOLDSMITH, ARNOLD D., *The Golem Remembered 1909–1980: Variations of a Jewish Legend* (Detroit, 1981).

GOMBINER, ABRAHAM, *Magen avraham*, commentary on *Shulḥan arukh*, 'Oraḥ ḥayim', published in the standard editions.

GOODMAN, AILENE, 'Explorations of a Baroque Motif: The Plague in Selected Seventeenth Century English and German Literature' (Ph.D. diss., University of Maryland, 1981).

GOTTESDIENER (OVADIAH), ABRAHAM, *Maharal: His Life, his Times, and his Teachings* [Hamaharal: ḥayav, tekufato, vetorato] (Jerusalem, 1976); 1st pub. as 'The Lion of the Sages of Prague' [Ha'ari shebeḥakhmei perag], *Azkarah*, 4 (1937), 253–443.

GRAETZ, HEINRICH, *Geschichte der Juden*, 3rd edn., ed. Marcus Brann, 11 vols. (Leipzig, 1897); pub. in Eng. as *History of the Jews*, trans. Bella Loewy, 6 vols. (Philadelphia, Pa., 1891–8); pub. in Heb. as *Divrei yemei yisra'el*, trans. and ed. Saul Pinhas Rabbinowitz, 8 vols. (Warsaw, 1893–1911).

GRAFTON, ANTHONY, *Defenders of the Text: The Traditions of Scholarship in an Age of Science 1450–1800* (Cambridge, Mass., 1991).

——'Humanism and Science', in id., *Defenders of the Text*, 178–203.

——*Joseph Scaliger: A Study in the History of Classical Scholarship*, 2 vols. (Oxford, 1983–93).

——'Renaissance Readers and Ancient Texts: Comments on Some Commentaries', *Renaissance Quarterly*, 38 (1985), 615–49.

GRANT, EDWARD, *In Defense of the Earth's Centrality and Immobility: Scholastic Reactions to Copernicanism in the Seventeenth Century*, Transactions of the American Philosophical Society 74, pt. 4 (Philadelphia, 1984).

GREENBERG, MOSHE, 'You are Called "Man" . . .' [Atem keruyim adam . . .], in id., *Al hamikra ve'al hayahadut: kovets ketavim*, ed. Avraham Shapira (Tel Aviv, 1984), 55–67.

GRIES, ZE'EV, *The Literature of Pious Customs: Its History and its Place in Early Hasidism* [Sifrut hahanhagot: toledoteiha umekomah beḥayei ḥasidei r. yisra'el ba'al shem-tov] (Jerusalem, 1989).

GRODZISKI, STANISŁAW, 'The Krakow Voivode's Jurisdiction over Jews', in Antony Polonsky *et al.* (eds.), *The Jews in Old Poland 1000–1795* (London, 1993), 199–218.

GROSS, BENJAMIN, 'Importance de la notion de miracle dans la théologie du Maharal', in Eliane Amado Lévy-Valenci *et al.* (eds.), *Mélanges André Neher* (Paris, 1975), 95–102.

GRÜNENWALD, ELISABETH, 'Zur Geschichte von Burg und Markt Wallerstein', *Nordschwaben*, 6/1 (1978), 2–9.

GRUNWALD, MAX, *Geschichte der Juden in Wien 1625–1740* (Vienna, 1913).

GUGGENHEIM, YACOV, 'Meetings on the Road: Encounters between German Jews and Christians at the Margins of Society', in R. Po-Chia Hsia and Harmut Lehmann (eds.), *In and Out of the Ghetto: Jewish–Gentile Relations in Late Medieval and Early Modern Germany* (Cambridge, 1995), 125–36.

GURLAND, HAYIM JONAH (ed.), *On the History of the Persecution of Jews* [Lekorot hagezerot al yisra'el] (Przemysl, Cracow, and Odessa, 1886–92; repr. Jerusalem, 1972).

HABERMAN, ABRAHAM M., 'The Liturgical and Other Poems of R. Yom-Tov Lipmann Heller' [Piyutav veshirav shel r. yom tov lipman heler], in Judah Leib Hakohen Maimon (ed.), *In Honour of Yom-Tov* (Jerusalem, 1956), 125–45.

HADDA, JANET, *Isaac Bashevis Singer: A Life* (Oxford, 1997).

HAGIZ, JACOB B. SAMUEL, *Ets ḥayim*, commentary on the Mishnah (Verona, 1650).

HAHN, JOSEPH, *Yosef omets*, pietistic work (Frankfurt am Main, 1928).

HAILPERIN (HALPERN), ISRAEL, 'Between Brożek and Delmedigo', in Meir Ben-Horin *et al.* (eds.), *Studies and Essays in Honor of Abraham A. Neuman* (Leiden, 1962), 640–9; repr. in Hailperin, *Jews and Judaism in Eastern Europe*, 388–93.

——'A Bibliography of the Writings of Rabbi Yom-Tov Lipmann Heller' [Ḥiburei rabi yom-tov lipman heler ukhetavav], *Kiryat sefer*, 7 (1930), 140–8.

——'Captivity and Redemption of Captives during the Persecutions in the Ukraine and Lithuania 1648–1660' [Sheviyah ufedut bigezerot ukrainah velita shemi-shenat taḥ [1648] ve'ad shenat takh [1660]], in id., *Jews and Judaism in Eastern Europe*, 212–49; 1st pub. in *Zion*, 25 (1960), 17–56.

——'The Controversy over Communal Elections in Frankfurt am Main and its Echoes in Poland and Bohemia' [Maḥloket al bereirat hakahal befrankfurt demain veheidehah befolin uvihem], in id., *Jews and Judaism in Eastern Europe*, 108–35; 1st pub. in *Zion*, 21 (1956), 64–91.

——'Jewish Refugees of the Thirty Years War in Eastern Europe' [Pelitim yehudiyim shel milḥemet sheloshim hashanah bemizraḥah shel eiropah], in id., *Jews and Judaism in Eastern Europe*, 197–211; 1st pub. in *Zion*, 27 (1962), 199–215.

——*Jews and Judaism in Eastern Europe* [Yehudim veyahadut bemizraḥ eiropah] (Jerusalem, 1969).

——'Rabbi Yom Tov Lipmann Heller (Tosafot Yom Tov): A Monograph with Sources, Tables, and Illustrations' [Rabi yom-tov lipman heler (tosafot yom tov): monografiyah betseruf mekorot, tavelot, vetsiyurim], MS, Dinur Institute, Jerusalem, *c.*1932.

——'The Threatened Expulsion of the Jews of Poland–Lithuania in the Later Seventeenth Century' [Al sakanat gerush likhelal yisra'el befolin velita bamaḥatsit hasheniyah shel hame'ah ha-17], in id., *Jews and Judaism in Eastern Europe*, 266–76; 1st pub. in *Zion*, 17 (1952), 65–74.

——(ed.), *Documents of the Council of Four Lands* [Pinkas va'ad arba aratsot] (Jerusalem, 1946); 2nd edn., ed. Israel Hailperin and Israel Bartal (Jerusalem, 1990).

——(ed.), *The Jews in Poland* [Beit yisra'el befolin], vol. ii (Jerusalem, 1954).

——(ed.), *Legislation of the Jewish Council of Moravia 1650–1745* [Takanot medinat mehren [5]410-[5]505] (Jerusalem, 1951).

HAKOHEN, MORDECHAI, 'His Books and Method of Study' [Sefarav veshitot limudo], in Judah Leib Hakohen Maimon (ed.), *In Honour of Yom-Tov* (Jerusalem, 1956), 146–91.

——*Great Men and their Times* [Ishim utekufot] (Jerusalem, 1977).

HALE, JOHN, *Civilization of Europe in the Renaissance* (New York, 1994).

HALIVNI, DAVID WEISS, *Peshat and Derash: Plain and Applied Meaning in Rabbinic Exegesis* (New York, 1991).

HALPERIN, CHARLES J., 'Sixteenth Century Foreign Travel Accounts to Muscovy: A Methodological Excursus', *The Sixteenth Century Journal*, 6 (1975), 89–111.

HANKE, LEWIS, *Aristotle and the American Indians* (Chicago, 1959).

HANNOVER, NATHAN NETA, *Yeven metsulah*, chronicle of the 1648 massacres, ed. Israel Hailperin (Tel Aviv, 1966); Eng. trans. by Abraham J. Mesch, *Abyss of Despair* (New York, 1950).

Harvard Ukrainian Studies, 8/1–2 (1984): special issue on Peter Mohyla.

Harvard Ukrainian Studies, 10/3–4 (1986): special issue on 'Concepts of Nationhood in Early Modern Eastern Europe', ed. Ivo Banac and Frank Sysyn.

HAYIM B. BEZALEL, introduction to *Vikuaḥ mayim ḥayim*, on dietary laws, in Chaim Tchernowitz, *History of Rabbinic Authorities since the Middle Ages*, vol. iii (New York, 1947), 93–100; also pub. in Eric Zimmer, *Embers of the Sages* (Jerusalem, 1999), 307–17.

HEADLEY, JOHN, 'The Sixteenth Century Venetian Celebration of the Earth's Total Habitability: The Issue of the Fully Habitable World for Renaissance Europe', *Journal of World History*, 8 (1997), 1–29.

HEINEMANN, ISAAK, *The Midrashic Method* [Darkhei ha'agadah], 2nd edn. (Jerusalem, 1954).

HELGERSON, RICHARD, *Forms of Nationhood: The Elizabethan Writing of England* (Chicago, 1992).

HELLER, MARVIN J., 'Observations on a Little Known Edition of Tractate Niddah (Prague, *c.*1608) and its Relationship to the Talmudic Methodology of the Maharal of Prague', *Torah u-Madda Journal*, 8 (1998), 134–50.

HELLIN, ELHANAN B. ABRAHAM, 'Megilat vints', historical poem, in David Gans, *Tsemaḥ david* (Offenbach, 1768); also printed in Avraham Kahana, *Sifrut hahistoriyah hayisra'elit*, vol. ii (Warsaw, 1923), 182–93; new edn., ed. and trans. Rivka Kern Ulmer (Frankfurt, 2001).

HENDERSON, JOHN B., *Scripture, Canon, and Commentary: A Comparison of Confucian and Western Exegesis* (Princeton, NJ, 1991).

HEŘMAN, JAN, 'La Communauté juive de Prague et sa structure au commencement des temps modernes: La Première Moitié du seizième siècle', *Judaica Bohemiae*, 5 (1960), 31–70.

HESCHEL, ABRAHAM JOSHUA, *The Earth is the Lord's: The Inner World of the Jew in Eastern Europe* (New York, 1950).

HILL, JOHN PETER, and ENRIQUE CARACCIOLO-TREJO (ed. and trans.), *Baroque Poetry* (London, 1975).

HILLERBRAND, HANS, 'The "Other" in the Age of Reformation: Reflections on Social Control and Deviance in the Sixteenth Century', in Max Reinhart (ed.), *Infinite Boundaries: Order, Disorder, and Reorder in Early Modern German Culture* (Kirksville, Mo., 1998), 245–70.

HIRSCHLER, SHIMON (ed.), 'These Are the Ancient Rules of the Lion . . . the Maharal of Prague' [Eleh hatakanot hayeshanot meha'ari . . . maharal miperag], *Kol torah*, 18 (1985), 57–63.

HORN, MAURYCY, 'Jewish Participation in Polish Wars during the Sixteenth and Seventeenth Centuries' [Der onteyl fun yidn in di milkhomes fun poyln in XVI un XVII yorhundert], *Bleter far Geshikhte*, 19 (1980), 49–88.

HORODETSKY, SAMUEL ABBA, 'Günzburg-Ulma, Jakob ben Ascher Aaron', in *Encyclopedia Judaica* (Berlin, 1931), vol. vii, col. 735.

——*Jewish Mysticism* [Hamistorin beyisra'el], vol. iv (Tel Aviv, 1961).

——'Mysticism in Polish Judaism 1540–1740' [Hazeramim hamistoriyim bekerev yehudei polin 5300–5500], *He'atid*, 5 (1913), 105–31; also pub. in German as *Mystisch-religiöse Strömungen unter den Juden in Polen im 16.–18. Jahrhundert: Inaugural-Dissertation* (Bern, 1912; repr. New York, 1980).

——*On the History of the Rabbinate* [Lekorot harabanut] (Warsaw, 1911).

——'R. Solomon Luria and the Kabbalah' [Hareshal vehakabalah], *Hagoren*, 1 (1898), 95–9.

HOROVITZ, MARKUS, *The Rabbis of Frankfurt* [Rabanei frankfurt], ed. Joseph Unna (Jerusalem, 1972).

HOROWITZ, ABRAHAM, *Berit avraham*, on repentance (Lublin, 1577).

——*Emek berakhah*, on the laws of blessings (Cracow, 1597).

——1559 tract in defence of Maimonides, ed. Phillip Bloch, in id., 'Der Streit um den Moreh des Maimonides in Posen', *Monatsschrift für Geschichte und Wissenschaft des Judentums*, 47 (1903), 153–69, 263–79, 346–7.

——*Ḥesed avraham*, commentary on Maimonides, *Shemoneh perakim*, 1st edn. (Lublin, 1577); 2nd edn. (Cracow, 1602); appears in the Vilna Talmud.

——*Yesh noḥalin*, ethical will (Warsaw, 1873; repr. Tiberias, 1965); ed. Hayim Waldman (Jerusalem, 1992).

HOROWITZ, CARMI, *The Jewish Sermon in Fourteenth Century Spain* (Cambridge, Mass., 1989).

HOROWITZ, ELLIOTT, 'Jewish Confraternities in Seventeenth Century Verona: A Study in the Social History of Piety' (Ph.D. diss., Yale University, 1982).

——'Masters and Servant-Girls in European Jewish Society from the Middle Ages to the Early Modern Period' [Bein adonim limesharetot baḥevrah hayehudit ha'eiropit bein yemei habeinayim lereshit ha'et haḥadashah], in Israel Bartal and Isaiah

Gafni (eds.), *Eros, Marriage, and Transgression: Essays on the History of Sexuality and the Family* [Eros, erusin, ve'isurin: miniyut umishpaḥah bahistoriyah] (Jerusalem, 1998), 193–211.

HOROWITZ, ISAIAH B. ABRAHAM, [rabbinic contract, Frankfurt am Main, 1606], in Markus Horovitz, *Rabanei frankfurt*, ed. Joseph Unna (Jerusalem, 1972), 322–4; repr. in Eugene Newman, *The Life and Teachings of Isaiah Horowitz* (London, 1972), 200–1, and trans. pp. 38–41.

——*Sha'ar hashamayim*, commentary on the prayer book (Amsterdam, 1717).

——*Shenei luḥot haberit*, 3 vols. in 1 (Józefów, 1878); 4 vols. in 2 (Warsaw, 1862; repr. Jerusalem, 1980); 1st section pub. as *The Generations of Adam*, trans. Miles Krassen (New York, 1996).

HOROWITZ, SHABETAI B. AKIBA, *Shefa tal*, on kabbalah (Hanau, 1612; repr. Jerusalem, 1971).

HOROWITZ, SHABETAI B. ISAIAH, *Vavei ha'amudim*, on ethics, pub. at the end of Isaiah Horowitz, *Shenei luḥot haberit* (Amsterdam, 1648/9) and in subsequent edns. Sections are translated in *Hebrew Ethical Wills*, ed. and trans. Israel Abrahams (Philadelphia, Pa., 1926), 255–7.

HOWELL, KENNETH, 'The Role of Biblical Interpretation in the Cosmology of Tycho Brahe', *Studies in the History and Philosophy of Science*, 29 (1998), 515–37.

HSIA, R. PO-CHIA, 'The Jews and the Emperors', in Charles W. Ingrao (ed.), *State and Society in Early Modern Austria* (West Lafayette, Ind., 1994), 71–9.

——'Printing, Censorship, and Antisemitism in Reformation Germany', in Philip N. Bebb and Sherrin Marshall (eds.), *The Process of Change in Early Modern Europe: Essays in Honor of Miriam Usher Chrisman* (Athens, Ohio, 1988), 135–78.

——*Society and Religion in Münster 1535–1618* (Princeton, NJ, 1984).

——and HARMUT LEHMANN (eds.), *In and Out of the Ghetto: Jewish–Gentile Relations in Late Medieval and Early Modern Germany* (Cambridge, 1995).

HUNDERT, GERSHON, 'An Advantage to Peculiarity? The Case of the Polish Commonwealth', *Association of Jewish Studies Review*, 6 (1981), 21–38.

——'Comparative Perspectives on Economy and Society: The Jews of the Polish–Lithuanian Commonwealth—A Comment', in R. Po-Chia Hsia and Harmut Lehmann (eds.), *In and Out of the Ghetto: Jewish–Gentile Relations in Late Medieval and Early Modern Germany* (Cambridge, 1995), 103–8.

——'The Decline of Deference among the Jews of Poland–Lithuania' [Shekiat yirat kavod bikehilat beit yisra'el befolin-lita], *Bar Ilan*, 24–5 (1989), 41–50.

——*The Jews in a Polish Private Town: The Case of Opatów in the Eighteenth Century* (Baltimore, Md., 1992).

HUSS, BOAZ, '*Sefer ha-Zohar* as a Canonical, Sacred, and Holy Text: Changing Perspectives on the Book of Splendor between the Thirteenth and Eighteenth Centuries', *Journal of Jewish Thought and Philosophy*, 7 (1998), 257–307.

IBN YAHYA, GEDALIAH, *Shalshelet hakabalah*, chronicle (Jerusalem, 1962).

IDEL, MOSHE, 'Differing Conceptions of Kabbalah in the Early 17th Century', in Isadore Twersky and Bernard Septimus (eds.), *Jewish Thought in the Seventeenth Century* (Cambridge, Mass., 1987), 137–200.

——'Magic Temples and Cities in the Middle Ages and the Renaissance', *Jerusalem Studies in Arabic and Islam*, 3 (1981–2), 185–9.

——' "One from a Family, Two from a Clan": The Diffusion of Lurianic Kabbalah and Sabbatianism: A Reexamination', *Jewish History*, 7/2 (1993), 79–104.

——'Particularism and Universalism in Kabbalah 1480–1650', in David Ruderman (ed.), *Essential Papers on Jewish Culture in Renaissance and Baroque Italy* (New York, 1992), 324–44.

——'Solomon Molkho as Magician' [Shelomoh Molekho kemagikon], *Sefunot*, 18 (1985), 193–219.

ISAAC B. SAMUEL HALEVI OF POZNAŃ, *Siaḥ yitsḥak* (Prague, 1627).

ISAIAH OR JESAJA, PAUL (Eliezer b. Isaiah Hakohen), *Vindication of the Christians Messias* (London, 1654).

ISRAEL, JONATHAN, 'Central European Jewry during the Thirty Years War', *Central European History*, 16 (1983), 3–30.

——*European Jewry in the Age of Mercantilism 1550–1750*, rev. edn. (Oxford, 1989).

ISRAEL B. BENJAMIN OF BEŁŻYCE, [sermon, 1648], in Marc Saperstein (ed. and trans.), *Jewish Preaching 1200–1800: An Anthology* (Princeton, NJ, 1989), 286–300.

ISSERLES, MOSES B. ISRAEL, *Darkhei mosheh*, commentary on Jacob b. Asher, *Arba'ah turim*; printed in many editions of the latter.

——*Mapah*, commentary on Joseph Caro, *Shulḥan arukh*, printed in the standard editions.

——*Meḥir yayin*, commentary on Esther (repr. New York, 1983).

——*She'elot uteshuvot harema*, responsa, ed. Asher Siev (Jerusalem, 1971).

——*Torat haḥatat*, on the dietary laws, in *Ḥamishah sefarim niftaḥim* (Żółkiew, 1857).

——*Torat ha'olah*, allegorical interpretation of the Temple, 3 vols. in 2 (Prague, 1854).

JACOB JOSEPH B. JUDAH OF OSTROH, *Sefer rav yeivi* (Brody, 1857).

JAFFE, MORDECHAI B. ABRAHAM, *Levush*, 9 vols. in 6 (New York, 1962–5).

——*et al.*, 'Pesakim bidevar ḥalitsah pesulah', responsa on a case of refusal of levirate marriage (Prague, 1609); ed. Moshe Friedman, *Moriah*, 15/3–4 (1987), 24–39.

JAFFE, TSEVI B. ABRAHAM KALONYMOS, 'Ruling on the Prevention of Talking during Prayer' [Pesak din al meniat hadibur bishe'at tefilah], MS Oxford-Bodleian Heb. 908, fos. 296*b*–297*a*.

JAKOBOVITS, TOBIAS, 'Die Erlebnisse des Oberrabbiners Simon Spira-Wedeles in Prag [1640–1679]', *Jahrbuch der Gesellschaft für Geschichte der Juden in der Čechoslovakischen Republik*, 4 (1932), 253–95.

——'Das Prager und Böhmische Landesrabbinat: Ende des siebzehnten und Anfang des achtzehnten Jahrhunderts', *Jahrbuch der Gesellschaft für Geschichte der Juden in der Čechoslovakischen Republik*, 5 (1933), 79–136.

JANSSEN, JOHANNES, *A History of the German People at the End of the Middle Ages*, ed. Ludwig Pastor, trans. M. Christie, 14 vols. (London, 1909).

JASTROW, MARCUS, *A Dictionary of the Targumim, the Talmud Babli and Yerushalmi, and the Midrashic Literature* (New York, 1886–1903; repr. 1996).

Jewish History, 17/2 (2003), special issue on '*Gezeirot Ta"h*: Jews Cossacks, Poles and Peasants in 1648 Ukraine'.

JOSEL (JOSEPH) B. GERSHON OF ROSHEIM, 'Diary' [Journal de Joselman de Rosheim], ed. Isidor Kracauer, *Revue des Études Juives*, 16 (1888), 84–105.

——*Historical Writings* [Ketavim historiyim], ed. Chava Fraenkel-Goldschmidt (Jerusalem, 1996).

——*Sefer hamiknah*, miscellany, mostly a copy of Abraham Bibago, *Derekh emunah*, ed. Chava Fraenkel-Goldschmidt (Jerusalem, 1970).

JOSEPH B. ISAAC HALEVI, *Givat hamoreh*, revision of Maimonides' proofs of God's existence (Prague, 1611; repr. Brooklyn, NY, 1994).

——*Ketonet pasim*, sermon (Lublin, 1614).

JOSEPH B. MOSES OF KREMENETS (KRZEMIENIEC), *Bi'urei rashi*, supercommentary on Rashi's Torah commentary (Prague, 1614).

JOSHUA B. JOSEPH, *Meginei shelomoh*, defence of Rashi's Talmud commentary (Amsterdam, 1715).

JOSHUA HESCHEL B. JACOB OF LUBLIN, *Ḥanukat hatorah*, commentary on the Torah, ed. Hanokh Henikh Ersohn (Piotrków, 1900).

JUDAH LEIB B. BEZALEL OF PRAGUE *see* MAHARAL

JUDAH LEIB B. JOSHUA HESCHEL, *Milḥamah beshalom*, chronicle of the siege of Prague, 1648, ed. Johann Wagenseil, in id., *Exercitationes sex* (Altdorf, 1689), 99–159.

JUSPA (JOSEPH), SHAMES OF WORMS, 'Customs of the Holy Community of Worms', in Shlomo Eidelberg, *R. Juspa, Shammash of Varmaisa (Worms): Jewish Life in Seventeenth Century Worms* (Jerusalem, 1991).

JÜTTE, ROBERT, 'Ehre und Ehrverlust im spätmittelalterlichen und frühneuzeitlichen Judentum', in Klaus Schreiner and Gerd Schwerhoff (eds.), *Verletzte Ehre: Ehrkonflikte in Gesellschaften des Mittelalters und der Frühen Neuzeit* (Cologne, 1995), 144–65.

KAHANA, AVRAHAM (ed.), *Jewish Historical Literature* [Sifrut hahistoriyah hayisra'elit], vol. ii (Warsaw, 1923).

KAHANA, NATHAN NETA OF OSTROH, *She'elot uteshuvot divrei renanah*, responsa, ed. Isaac Herskovitz (New York, 1984).

KAIDANOVER, AARON SAMUEL, *Birkat hazevaḥ*, Talmud commentary (Amsterdam, 1669).

KANARFOGEL, EPHRAIM, 'On the Role of Bible Study in Medieval Ashkenaz', in Barry Walfish (ed.), *Frank Talmage Memorial Volume*, vol. i (Haifa, 1993), 151–66.

——*'Peering through the Lattices': Mystical, Magical and Pietistic Dimensions in the Tosafist Period* (Detroit, 2000).

——'Unanimity, Majority, and Communal Government in Ashkenaz during the High Middle Ages: A Reassessment', *Proceedings of the American Academy for Jewish Research*, 58 (1992), 79–106.

KAPLAN, LAWRENCE, 'Rationalism and Rabbinic Culture in Sixteenth Century Eastern Europe: R. Mordecai Jaffe's Levush Pinat Yikrat' (Ph.D. diss., Harvard University, 1975).

KASHER, MENAHEM M., 'Some Notes' [He'arot aḥadot], in Judah Leib Hakohen Maimon (ed.), *In Honour of Yom-Tov* (Jerusalem, 1956), 192–5.

KATZ, JACOB, 'Between 1096 and 1648' [Bein tatnu letaḥ–tat], in Shmuel Ettinger *et al.* (eds.), *Sefer yovel leyitsḥak baer* (Jerusalem, 1961), 318–37.

——*Exclusiveness and Tolerance: Studies in Jewish–Gentile Relations in Medieval and Modern Times* (Oxford, 1961); 1st pub. as *Bein yehudim lagoyim* (Jerusalem, 1961).

——*Halakhah and Kabbalah: Studies in the History of Judaism in its Social Setting* [Halakhah vekabalah: meḥkarim betoledot dat yisra'el al madoreiha vezikatah haḥevratit] (Jerusalem, 1984); sections are translated in Katz, *Divine Law in Human Hands: Case Studies in Halakhic Flexibility* (Jerusalem, 1998).

——'Marriage and Private Life at the End of the Middle Ages' [Nisu'in veḥayei ishut bemotsei yemei habeinayim], *Zion*, 10 (1946), 21–54.

——'More on "Between 1096 and 1648"' [Od al "Bein tatnu letaḥ–tat"]; response to Edward Fram, 'Between 1096 and 1648: A Reappraisal', *Zion*, 62 (1997), 23–9.

——'On Halakhah and *Derush* as a Historical Source' [Al halakhah uderush kemakor histori]; response to Haim Ben-Sasson, 'Concepts and Reality', *Tarbiz*, 30 (1960), 62–8.

——'On the History of the Rabbinate in the Later Middle Ages' [Letoledot harabanut bemotsei yemei habeinayim], in E. Z. Melamed (ed.), *Sefer zikaron levinyamin de vries* (Jerusalem, 1969), 281–94.

——'The Stories of Three Apologetic Dicta' [Sheloshah mishpatim apologetiyim begilguleihem], *Zion*, 23–4 (1958), 174–93.

——*Tradition and Crisis: Jewish Society at the End of the Middle Ages*, trans. Bernard Cooperman (New York, 1993); 1st pub. as *Masoret umashber: haḥevrah hayehudit bemotsei yemei habeinayim* (Jerusalem, 1958).

KATZ, NAFTALI B. ISAAC, Letter to his wife, pub. in 'Mikhtav me'et r. naftali kats av beit din befinsk delita le'ishto', ed. Ephraim Kupfer, *Gal-ed*, 3 (1976), 315–18.

KATZENELLENBOGEN, ISAAC B. MOSES, *Moledot yitsḥak*, on the Jewish calendar (Prague, 1623).

KAUFMANN, DAVID, 'Jair Hayyim Bacharach', *Jewish Quarterly Review*, OS 3 (1891), 292–313, 485–536.

——*Die letzte Vertreibung der Juden aus Wien und Niederösterreich. Ihre Vorgeschichte (1625–1670) und ihre Opfer* (Vienna, 1899).

——'Der zweite Corrector der Claudius'schen hebräischen Bibel, Dr. med. Leo Simon, Rabbiner von Mainz', *Zeitschrift der Deutschen Morgenländischen Gesellschaft*, 45 (1891), 493–504.

KAUFMANN, THOMAS D., *The School of Prague: Painting at the Court of Rudolf II* (Chicago, 1988).

KELLEY, DONALD R., 'Second Nature: The Idea of Custom in European Law, Society, and Culture', in Anthony Grafton and Ann Blair (eds.), *The Transmission of Culture in Early Modern Europe* (Philadelphia, Pa., 1990), 131–72.

KELLNER, MENAHEM, *Maimonides on the 'Decline of the Generations' and the Nature of Rabbinic Authority* (Albany, NY, 1996).

KELTER, IRVING A., 'The Refusal to Accommodate: Jesuit Exegetes and the Copernican System', *The Sixteenth Century Journal*, 26 (1995), 273–83.

KESTENBERG-GLADSTEIN, RUTH, 'Bassevi of Treuenberg, Jacob', *Encyclopaedia Judaica*, vol. iv, cols. 316–17.

——'Bohemia', in Cecil Roth (ed.), *The World History of the Jewish People*, 2nd ser., vol. ii: *The Dark Ages: Jews in Christian Europe* (Ramat Gan, 1966), 309–12.

KIEFER, FREDERICK, *Fortune and Elizabethan Tragedy* (San Marino, Calif., 1983).

KIENER, RONALD, 'The Status of Astrology in the Early Kabbalah from the Sefer Yesirah to the Zohar', *Jerusalem Studies in Jewish Thought*, 6/3–4 (1987), Eng. sect., pp. 1–42.

KIESSLING, ROLF (ed.), *Judengemeinden in Schwaben im Kontext des Alten Reiches* (Berlin, 1995).

KIEVAL, HILLEL, 'Pursuing the Golem of Prague: Jewish Culture and the Invention of a Tradition', *Modern Judaism*, 17 (1997), 1–20.

KISCH, ALEXANDER, 'Die Prager Judenstadt während der Schlacht am weissen Berge', *Allgemeine Zeitung des Judenthums*, 56 (1892), 400–3.

KISCH, BRUNO, 'History of the Jewish Pharmacy Judenapotheke in Prague', *Historia Judaica*, 8 (1946), 149–79.

KISCH, GUIDO, 'Die Megillat Eba in Seligmann Kisch's Uebersetzung', *Jahrbuch der Gesellschaft für Geschichte der Juden in der Čechoslovakischen Republik*, 1 (1929), 426–34.

KITZINGEN, JACOB, *Ḥag pesaḥ*, on the Passover seder; final section on messianism (Cracow, 1597).

KLEINBERGER, AARON FRITZ, 'The Didactics of Rabbi Loew of Prague', *Scripta Hierosolymitana*, 13 (1963), 32–55.

——*The Educational Philosophy of the Maharal of Prague* [Maḥashavto hapedogogit shel hamaharal miperag] (Jerusalem, 1962).

——'Jewish Education in Central and Eastern Europe from the Sixteenth to the Eighteenth Centuries' [Haḥinukh hayehudi bame'ot ha-16–ha-18: merkaz eiropah umizraḥah], in Martin Buber (ed.), *Entsiklopediyah ḥinukhit* (Jerusalem, 1964), vol. iii, cols. 382–405.

KLEIN-FRANKE, F., 'An Unknown Jewish Translation of *Kitab al-tib* by Al-razi' [Tirgum yehudi bilti noda shel kitab al-tib al-mansuri li'al razi], *Kiryat sefer*, 44 (1969), 436–41.

KLEMPERER, GUTMANN, 'The Rabbis of Prague', *Historia Judaica*, 12 (1950), 52–66, 143–52; 13 (1951), 55–82.

KOBER, ADOLF (ed.), 'Documents selected from the Pinkas of Friedberg, a former Free City in Western Germany', *Proceedings of the American Academy for Jewish Research*, 17 (1947), 20–59.

KOBLER, FRANZ (ed. and trans.), *Letters of Jews through the Ages*, 2 vols. (Philadelphia, Pa., 1953–4).

KOCHER, PAUL H., *Science and Religion in Elizabethan England* (New York, 1969).

KOHEN, MENAHEM, 'Text Criticism and Belief in the Letter-Perfect Text of Scripture' [Ha'idiah bidevar kedushat hanusaḥ le'otiyotav uvikoret hatekst], in Uriel Simon (ed.), *The Bible and Us* [Hamikra ve'anaḥnu] (Tel Aviv, 1979), 42–69.

KOOK, S. H., 'Friday of the Synagogue Reading "Hukat"' [Yom hashishi parashat ḥukat], *Edut*, 2 (1947), 281–3.

KOPPELMAN, JACOB B. SAMUEL BUNAM, *Ohel ya'akov*, commentary on Joseph Albo, *Sefer ha'ikarim* (Freiburg, 1584).

——*Omek halakhah*, comments on laws and Talmud passages requiring mathematical calculations or scientific information (Cracow, 1593).

KRACAUER, ISIDOR, *Geschichte der Juden in Frankfurt am Main 1150–1824*, 2 vols. (Frankfurt, 1925–7).

KRAEMER, DAVID, *Responses to Suffering in Classical Rabbinic Literature* (Oxford, 1995).

KROCHMAL, MENAHEM MENDEL, *She'elot uteshuvot tsemaḥ tsedek* (Altdorf, 1766).

KUGEL, JAMES, *The Idea of Biblical Poetry: Parallelism and its History* (New Haven, Conn., 1981).

KULKA, OTTO DOV, 'Comenius and Maharal: The Historical Background of the Parallels in their Teaching', *Judaica Bohemiae*, 27 (1991), 17–30; 1st pub. as 'Hareka hahistori shel mishnato hale'umit vehaḥinukhit shel hamaharal miperag', *Zion*, 50 (1985), 277–320.

KUPFER, EPHRAIM, 'The Cultural Image of Ashkenazi Judaism in the Fourteenth and Fifteenth Centuries' [Lidemutah hatarbutit shel yahadut ashkenaz veḥakhameiha bame'ah ha-14–15], *Tarbiz*, 42 (1972), 113–47.

——and BEDŘICH MARK, 'The Renaissance in Italy and Poland and its Influence on the Jews' [Der renesans in italye un in poyln un zayn virkung oyf di yidn], *Bleter far Geshikhte*, 6/4 (1953), 4–99.

LANDAU, ALFRED, and BERNHARD WACHSTEIN (eds.), *Jüdische Privatbriefe aus dem Jahre 1619* (Vienna, 1911).

LANGBEIN, JOHN H., *Prosecuting Crime in the Renaissance: England, Germany, France* (Cambridge, Mass., 1974).

LANGERMANN, Y. TZVI, 'The Astronomy of R. Moses Isserles', in Sabetai Ungurn (ed.), *Physics, Cosmology, and Astronomy 1300–1700: Tension and Accommodation* (Dordrecht, 1991), 83–98.

——'*Tekunat ha-Hawayah* by Meir b. Moses Judah Loeb Neumark of Nicolsburg (1703)', *Aleph*, 1 (2001), 328–32.

LAPLANCHE, FRANÇOIS, 'Tradition et modernité au XVIIe siècle: L'Exegèse biblique des Protestants français', *Annales ESC*, 40 (1985), 463–88.

LAWEE, ERIC, 'On the Threshold of the Renaissance: New Methods and Sensibilities in the Biblical Commentaries of Isaac Abarbanel', *Viator*, 26 (1995), 283–319.

LEAMAN, OLIVER, *Evil and Suffering in Jewish Philosophy* (Cambridge, 1995).

LEINER, YERUHAM, 'R. Solomon Luria and Kabbalah' [Hamaharshal vehakabalah], *Sinai*, 44 (1959), 224–9.

LEVINE, HILLEL, '"Dwarfs on the Shoulders of Giants": A Case Study in the Impact of Modernization on the Social Epistemology of Judaism', *Jewish Social Studies*, 40 (1978), 63–73.

LEWYSOHN, L., 'Kaiserliches Schreiben Betreffs der Belastigungen der Wormser Juden durch Cinquartierungen und andere Auslagen', *Jahrbuch für die Geschichte der Juden und des Judenthums*, 2 (1861), 377–9.

LIEBEN, KOPPELMAN (ed.), *Gal-Ed: A Collection of 170 Tombstones from the Prague Cemetery* [Gal-ed: kovets me'ah veshivim kitvei luḥot avnei zikaron bisdeh hakevurah perag] (Prague, 1856).

LIEBEN, S. H., 'Der hebräische Buchdruck in Prag', in S. Steinherz (ed.), *Juden in Prag* (Prague, 1927), 88–106.

LIEBES, YEHUDA, 'Mysticism and Reality: Towards a Portrait of the Martyr and Kabbalist, R. Samson Ostropoler', in Isadore Twersky and Bernard Septimus (eds.), *Jewish Thought in the Seventeenth Century* (Cambridge, Mass., 1987), 221–56; 1st pub. as 'Ḥalom umetsiut: lidemuto shel hakadosh hamekubal r. shimshon me'ostropoliyah', *Tarbiz*, 52 (1982), 83–110, 661–4.

——'On the Life, Writings, and Kabbalistic Teachings of [Naftali Bacharach], Author of *Emek hamelekh*' [Lidemuto, ketavav, vekabalato shel ba'al emek hamelekh], *Meḥkerei yerushalayim bemaḥshevet yisra'el*, 11 (1993), 101–37.

——'The Prophet Jonah as Messiah son of Joseph' [Yonah ben amitai kemashiaḥ ben yosef], *Meḥkerei yerushalayim bemaḥshevet yisra'el*, 3 (1984), 274–311.

——'Ha-Tikkun ha-Kelali of Rabbi Nahman of Bratslav and its Sabbatean Links', in id., *Studies in Jewish Myth and Jewish Messianism* (Albany, NY, 1993), 115–50; 1st pub. as 'Hatikun hakelali shel r. nahman miberaslav veyaḥaso leshabta'ut', *Zion*, 45 (1980), 201–45.

LIPSCHUETZ, MOSES B. NOAH ISAAC, *Leḥem mishneh*, commentary on the Mishnah (Cracow, 1636).

LIPSCHÜTZ, ISRAEL, *Tiferet yisra'el*, commentary on the Mishnah, printed in many editions of the latter.

LISKER, ABRAHAM B. HAYIM, *Be'er avraham*, Mishnah commentary (Cracow, 1683).

LÖWENSTEIN, LEOPOLD, 'Günzburg und die schwäbischen Gemeinden', *Blätter für Jüdische Geschichte und Literatur*, 1 (1900), 9–10, 25–7, 41–3, 57–9; 2 (1901), 25–7, 33–5, 41–4, 49–51, 57–9; 3 (1902), 4–6, 21–4, 56–8.

LUEBKE, DAVID MARTIN, '"Naive Monarchism" and Marian Veneration in Early Modern Germany', *Past and Present*, 154 (1997), 71–106.

——'Terms of Loyalty: Factional Politics in a Single German Village (Nöggenschwihl, 1725–1745)', in Max Reinhart (ed.), *Infinite Boundaries: Order, Disorder, and Reorder in Early Modern German Culture* (Kirksville, Mo., 1998), 77–100.

LURIA, SOLOMON B. YEHIEL, *Yam shel shelomoh*, commentary on various tractates of the Talmud, 7 vols. (1616–1850; repr. in 3 vols. New York, 1953).

MACLEAN, IAN, *Interpretation and Meaning in the Renaissance: The Case of Law* (Cambridge, 1992).

MĄCZAK, ANTONI, 'Progress and Underdevelopment in the Eyes of Renaissance and Baroque Man', *Studia Historiae Oeconomicae*, 9 (1974), 77–94.

MAHARAL (JUDAH LEIB B. BEZALEL OF PRAGUE), *Derashot maharal miperag*, collected sermons (Jerusalem, 1968).

——*Derekh haḥayim*, commentary on Mishnah, *Pirkei avot*, ed. Hayim Pardes (Tel Aviv, 1975).

——*Gevurot hashem*, on the Exodus (Jerusalem, 1971).

——*Gur aryeh*, supercommentary on Rashi's Torah commentary, in Joshua Gershon Munk (ed.), *Arba'ah perushim al perush rashi* (Jerusalem, 1958).

——Letter, Haus- Hof- und Staatsarchiv (Vienna), Alte Prager Akten, box 84, fo. 547*b*.

——*Netivot olam*, ethics (New York, 1969); ed. Hayim Pardes, 2 vols. (Tel Aviv, 1982–8).

——'Teshuvot maharal miperag', responsa, ed. Yitshak Yudlov, in Yosef Buksboim (ed.), *Memorial Book in Honour of Ya'akov Betzalel Zholty* [Sefer zikaron likhvodo shel ya'akov betsalel zholti] (Jerusalem, 1987), 264–96.

——*Tiferet yisra'el*, essay on Torah, ed. Hayim Pardes (Tel Aviv, 1969).

MAHARSHA *see* EDELS

MAIMON, JUDAH LEIB HAKOHEN (ed.), *In Honour of Yom-Tov: Studies in Honour of the 300th Anniversary of the Death of Rabbi Yom-Tov Lipmann Heller* [Likhvod yom tov: ma'amarim umeḥkarim ad shelosh me'ot shanah lifetirato shel rabenu yom tov lipman heler] (Jerusalem, 1956).

MAIMON, SOLOMON, *Solomon Maimon: An Autobiography*, trans. J. Clark Murray, ed. Moses Hadas (New York, 1947).

MAIMONIDES, MOSES, *Guide of the Perplexed* [Moreh nevukhim], trans. Shlomo Pines (Chicago, 1963).

MALACHI, A. R., 'The Chroniclers of the Massacres of 1648' [Roshmei gezerot taḥ], *Sefer hashanah liyehudei amerikah*, 10–11 (1949), 425–44.

MALINOWSKI, JOSEPH B. MORDECHAI, 'Ma'asar ha'of utefisato', poem, trans. Zerah b. Nathan, in Jacob Mann, *Texts and Studies in Jewish History and Literature*, vol. ii (Philadelphia, Pa., 1935), 1228–9.

MANASSEH B. ISRAEL, from his letter 'To his Highnesse the Lord Protector of the Commonwealth of England, Scotland, and Ireland', repr. in Paul Mendes-Flohr and Jehuda Reinharz (eds.), *The Jew in the Modern World*, 2nd edn. (Oxford, 1995), 10–13.

MANN, COLO, *Wallenstein*, trans. C. Kessler (London, 1976).

MANN, VIVIAN, and RICHARD COHEN (eds.), *From Court Jews to the Rothschilds: Art, Patronage, and Power 1600–1800* (Munich, 1996).

MANOAH HENDL B. SHEMARIAH, *Mano'aḥ halevavot*, commentary on Bahya ibn Pakuda, *Ḥovot halevavot* (Lublin, 1596).

MARGALIOT, ZELIG, *Ḥiburei likutim*, comments on talmudic passages (Venice, 1715).

MARTIN, A. LYNN, *Plague? Jesuit Accounts of Epidemic Disease in the Sixteenth Century* (Kirksville, Mo., 1996).

MARTIN, JOHN, 'Inventing Sincerity, Refashioning Prudence: The Discovery of the Individual in Renaissance Europe', *American Historical Review*, 102 (1997), 1308–42.

MARX, ALEXANDER (ed.), 'A Seventeenth Century Autobiography: A Picture of Jewish Life in Bohemia and Moravia', *Jewish Quarterly Review*, 8 (1918), 269–304, 476; repr. in id., *Studies in Jewish History and Booklore* (New York, 1944), 178–97.

MAZEL, JOSEPH B. ELEAZAR LIPMANN ASHKENAZI OF PROSSNITZ, 'Gzeyre lid', song on the massacres of 1648 (1st edn. Prague, 1648); ed. Max Weinreich, in 'Tsvey yidishe kines oyf khmelnitskis gzeyres', in id., *Bilder fun der Yidisher Literatur-Geshikhte* (Vilna, 1928), 199–211.

MEHLER REUTLINGEN, JUDA, autobiographical introd. to *Shevut yehudah*, *see* Phillip Bloch, 'Vielbegehrter Rabbiner'.

MEIR B. LEIB OZERS, *Sefer olat tamid*, collection of midrashic and kabbalistic dicta, MS Oxford-Bodleian Heb. 925.

MEIR OF SZCZEBRZESZYN, *Tsok ha'itim*, chronicle of the massacres of 1648 (Cracow, 1650); repr. in Moshe Rosman (ed.), *Sipurei hagezerot bishenot taḥ vetat* (Jerusalem, 1982), 1–22.

MEIR B. YEHIEL HAKADOSH, 'Megilat r. me'ir', deliverance narrative, *Kovets al yad*, 10 (1903), 1–16.

MELAMED, AVRAHAM, 'The Attitude towards Democracy in Medieval Jewish Philosophy', *Jewish Political Studies Review*, 5 (1993), 33–56.

MENDEL ISAAC OF CRACOW, 'An Unknown Letter by Mendel Isaac of Cracow to Rudolph II' [An umbakanter briv fun Mendl Yitskhok fun kroke tsum kayzer Rudolf], ed. Nathan Michael Gelber, *Yivo-bleter*, 11 (1937), 401–5.

MERTON, ROBERT, *On the Shoulders of Giants: A Shandean Postscript* (New York, 1965).

MEYER, MICHAEL, 'When Does the Modern Period of Jewish History Begin?', *Judaism*, 24 (1975), 329–38.

——and MICHAEL BRENNER (eds.), *German-Jewish History in Modern Times*, vol. i, trans. William Templer (New York, 1996).

MINTZ, ADAM, 'The Jews of Prague and the Battle of White Mountain', unpublished seminar paper.

MINTZ, ALAN, *Hurban: Responses to Catastrophe in Hebrew Literature* (New York, 1984).

MISCH, GEORG, *Geschichte der Autobiographie*, 2nd edn. (Leipzig, 1931).

MODENA, LEONE DA, *Ari nohem*, against kabbalah, ed. Nehemiah Libowitz (Jerusalem, 1929).

——*The Autobiography of a Seventeenth Century Venetian Rabbi: Leon Modena's Life of Judah*, ed. and trans. Mark Cohen (Princeton, NJ, 1988).

——*Ḥayei yehudah*, ed. Daniel Carpi (Tel Aviv, 1985).

——[attributed], *Kol sakhal*, ed. and trans. Talya Fishman as *Shaking the Pillars of Exile. 'Voice of a Fool': An Early Modern Jewish Critique of Rabbinic Culture* (Stanford, Calif., 1997).

MORRIS, MICHAEL W., and KAIPING PENG, 'Culture and Cause: American and Chinese Attributions for Social and Physical Events', *Journal of Personality and Social Psychology*, 67 (1994), 949–71.

MORYSON, FYNES, *An Itinerary containing his Ten Yeeres Travell through the Twelve Dominions of Germany, Bohmerland, etc.* (Glasgow, 1907).

——*Shakespeare's Europe: A Survey of the Condition of Europe at the End of the 16th Century, being Unpublished Chapters of Fynes Moryson's Itinerary (1617)*, ed. Charles Hughes, 2nd edn. (New York, 1967).

MOSELEY, MARCUS, 'Jewish Autobiography in Eastern Europe: The Pre-History of a Literary Genre' (Ph.D. diss., University of Oxford, 1990).

MÜLLER, L., 'Aus fünf Jahrhunderten: Beiträge zur Geschichte der jüdischen Gemeinden im Riess', *Zeitschrift des Historischen Vereins für Schwaben und Neuburg*, 25 (1898), 1–124; 26 (1899), 81–182.

MUNELES, OTTO, *Bibliographical Survey of Jewish Prague* (Prague, 1952).

——'From the Archives of the State Jewish Museum', in Rudolf Iltis (ed.), *Jewish Studies: Essays in Honour of the Very Reverend Dr Gustav Sacher, Chief Rabbi of Prague* (Prague, 1955), 100–7.

——(ed.), *The Inscriptions of the Old Jewish Cemetery of Prague* [Ketovot mibeit ha'almin hayehudi he'atik biferag] (Jerusalem, 1988).

——(ed.), *The Prague Ghetto in the Renaissance Period* (Prague, 1965).

MUNK, BARUKH, *History of the Munk Family* [Toledot mishpaḥat munk] (Jerusalem, 1985).

MUNZAR, JAN, 'Weather Patterns in Czechoslovakia during the Years 1588–1598', in Burkhard Frenzel *et al.* (eds.), *European Climate Reconstructed from Documentary Data* (Stuttgart, 1992), 51–6.

MYERS, DAVID, *Re-Inventing the Jewish Past: European Jewish Intellectuals and the Zionist Return into History* (Oxford, 1995).

NADAV, MORDECHAI, 'The Authority of the Jewish Community of Tykocin over the Jewish Communities and Settlements in its Hinterland' [Teḥumei shelitatah shel kehilat tiktin al hakehilot vehayishuvim bisevivoteiha], *Gal-ed*, 11 (1989), 13–25.

——'The Jewish Community of Nemyriv in 1648: Their Massacre and Loyalty Oath to the Cossacks', *Harvard Ukrainian Studies*, 8 (1984), 376–87; 1st pub. in Heb. in *Zion*, 47 (1982), 77–82.

NADEL, GEORGE, 'Philosophy of History before Historicism', *History and Theory*, 3 (1964), 291–315.

NANTUA, JUDAH LEIB B. JOSEPH ROFE, *Kol yehudah*, sermons (Prague, 1641).

NEHER, ANDRÉ, *David Gans: Disciple du Maharal, assistant de Tycho Brahe et de Jean Kepler* (Paris, 1974); English edn.: *Jewish Thought and the Scientific Revolution of the Sixteenth Century*, trans. D. Maisel (Oxford, 1986).

——*Le Puits de l'exil: La Théologie dialectique du Maharal de Prague (1512–1609)* (Paris, 1966).

——'New Material on David Gans as an Astronomer' [Ḥomer ḥadash al david gans ketokhen], *Tarbiz*, 45 (1975), 138–47.

NEHORAI, MICHAEL, 'Nahmanides' and Judah Halevi's Theories of Miracles' [Torat hanes etsel haramban vezikatah ler. yehudah halevi], *Da'at*, 17 (1986), 23–31.

NEUBAUER, ADOLPH, *Catalogue of the Hebrew Manuscripts in the Bodleian Library* (Oxford, 1886).

NEWMAN, EUGENE, *The Life and Teachings of Isaiah Horowitz* (London, 1972).

NIGER, SHMUEL, 'On *Satan in Goray*', trans. Joseph Landis, *Yiddish*, 6/2–3 (1985) 73–80.

NISBET, ROBERT, *History of the Idea of Progress* (New York, 1990).

OCHMANN, STEFANIA, 'The Coronation of John Casimir in 1649' [Koronacja Jana Kazimierza w roku 1649], *Odrodzenie i Reformacja w Polsce*, 28 (1983), 135–59.

OPALINSKI, EDWARD, 'The Local Diets and Religious Tolerance in the Polish Commonwealth 1587–1648', *Acta Poloniae Historica*, 74 (1996), 22–44; 1st pub. as 'Sejmiki szlacheckie wobec kwestii tolerancji religijnej w latach 1587–1648', *Odrodzenie i Reformacja w Polsce*, 34 (1989), 21–40.

OPHIR, BARUCH TSEVI, *et al.* (eds.), *Memorial Book of Jewish Communities: Germany; Bavaria* [Pinkas hakehilot: germaniyah: bavariyah] (Jerusalem, 1972).

PACHTER, MORDECHAI, '*Sefer reshit ḥokhmah* by R. Elijah di Vidas and its Epitomes' [Sefer reshit ḥokhmah ler. eliyahu di vidas vekitsurav], *Kiryat sefer*, 47 (1972), 686–710.

PALMITESSA, JAMES R., 'House, Home, and Neighborhood on the Eve of White Mountain: Material Culture and Daily Life in the New City of Prague 1547–1611' (Ph.D. diss., New York University, 1995).

——'The Prague Uprising of 1611: Property, Politics, and Catholic Renewal in the Early Years of Habsburg Rule', *Central European History*, 31 (1998), 299–328.

PANITZ, MICHAEL, 'New Heavens and a New Earth: Seventeenth to Nineteenth Century Jewish Responses to the New Astronomy', *Conservative Judaism*, 40/2 (1988), 28–42.

PARKER, GEOFFREY, *Europe in Crisis 1598–1648* (Ithaca, NY, 1979).

——(ed.), *The Thirty Years War*, rev. edn. (London, 1987; repr. New York, 1993).

PASCAL, BLAISE, *Pensées*, trans. A. J. Krailsheimer (London, 1966).

PASCAL, ROY, *Design and Truth in Autobiography* (Cambridge, Mass., 1960).

PERLES, JOSEPH, 'Urkunden zur Geschichte der jüdischen Provinzial-Synoden . . . in Polen', *Monatsschrift für Geschichte und Wissenschaft des Judentums*, 16 (1867), 108–11, 152–5, 222, 226, 304–8, 343–8.

PETERS, F. E. (ed. and trans.), *Judaism, Christianity, and Islam*, 3 vols. (Princeton, NJ, 1990).

PETERSEN, PETER, *Geschichte der Aristotelischen Philosophie im Protestantischen Deutschland* (Leipzig, 1921).

PFAFFENHOFEN, ALEXANDER B. ISAAC, *Sefer masah umerivah*, debate poem of poor man versus rich man, ed. Chava Turniansky (Jerusalem, 1985).

PIEKARZ, MENDEL, *The Beginnings of Hasidism: Intellectual Trends in the Homiletical-Ethical Literature* [Biyemei tsemiḥat haḥasidut: megamot ra'ayoniyot besifrut derush umusar] (Jerusalem, 1978).

Pinkas hamekomot, register of the Pinkas Shul, ŽMP, inv. 44.960.

PISEK, ARYEH LEIB, *Dimyon aryeh*, responsum on the Nikolsburg wine controversy (Prague, 1616).

POLONSKY, ANTONY, JAKUB BASISTA, and ANDRZEJ LINK-LENCZOWSKI (eds.), *The Jews in Old Poland 1000–1795* (London, 1993).

Polski słownik Biograficzny (Warsaw, 1935–).

POPKIN, RICHARD, *The History of Scepticism from Erasmus to Spinoza* (Berkeley, Calif., 1979).

POPPER, WILHELM, 'Les Juifs de Prague pendant la Guerre de Trente Ans', *Revue des Études Juives*, 29 (1894), 127–41; 30 (1895), 79–93.

PORGES, MOSES B. ISRAEL NAFTALI, *Darkhei tsiyon*, guide for travellers to the Land of Israel, trans. J. D. Wilhelm, in Abraham Yaari (ed.), *Journeys in the Land of Israel* [Masa'ot erets yisra'el] (Tel Aviv, 1946), 267–304.

PORTALEONE, ABRAHAM, *Shiltei hagiborim*, on the Temple (Mantua, 1612).

PORTER, ROY, and MIKULÁS TEICH (eds.), *The Renaissance in National Context* (Cambridge, 1992).

PRESS, VOLKER, 'Kaiser Rudolph II. und der Zusammenschluss der deutschen Judenheit: Die sogenannte Frankfurter rabbinerverschwörung von 1603 und ihre Folgen', in Alfred Haverkamp (ed.), *Zur Geschichte der Juden in Deutschland des späten Mittelalters und der frühen Neuzeit* (Stuttgart, 1981), 243–93.

PREUS, JAMES SAMUEL, *From Shadow to Promise: Old Testament Interpretation from Augustine to the Young Luther* (Cambridge, Mass., 1969).

PRIBRAM, ALFRED FRANCIS (ed.), *Urkunden und Akten zur Geschichte der Juden in Wien*, 2 vols. (Vienna, 1918).

PROKEŠ, JAROSLAV, and ANTON BLASCHKA, 'Der Antisemitismus der Behörden und das Prager Ghetto in nachweissbergischen Zeit', *Jahrbuch der Gesellschaft für Geschichte der Juden in der Čechoslovakischen Republik*, 1 (1929), 41–262.

PUTÍK, ALEXANDR, 'The Origin of the Symbols of the Prague Jewish Town: The Banner of the Old-New Synagogue, David's Shield, and the "Swedish" Hat', *Judaica Bohemiae*, 29 (1993), 4–37.

——'The Prague Jewish Community in the Late Seventeenth and Early Eighteenth Centuries', *Judaica Bohemiae*, 35 (2000), 4–140.

RABA, JOEL, *Between Remembrance and Denial: The Fate of the Jews in the Wars of the Polish Commonwealth during the Mid-Seventeenth Century as Shown in Contemporary Writings and Historical Research* (New York, 1995).

RABBINOWITZ, SAUL PINHAS, *Traces of Free-Thinking in the Polish Rabbinate* [Ikvot shel ḥofesh de'ot barabanut shel polin], trans. Y. D. Abramski (Jerusalem, 1959); 1st pub. as 'Slyedi svobodomisliya v Polskom ravvinizmye XVI vyeka', *Evreiskaia Starina*, 3 (1911), 3–18.

RABINOWITZ, HAYIM REUBEN, *Portraits of Preachers* [Deyokna'ot shel darshanim] (Jerusalem, 1967).

RAFELD, MEIR, 'Certain Kabbalistic Elements in the Halakhic Teachings of R. Solomon Luria' [Al me'at sheki'in kabaliyim bemishnat hahilkhatit shel hamaharshal], *Da'at*, 36 (1996), 15–34.

——'The Complex Legal History of a Controversial Dictum' [Gilgulah hahilkhati hamefutal shel memrah redufah], *Dinei yisra'el*, 19 (1998), 241–51.

——'The Principle that "The Law Follows the Most Recent Authorities" in the Writings of Sixteenth- and Seventeenth-Century German and Polish Rabbis: Sources and Branches' ['Hilkheta kevatra'ei' etsel ḥakhmei ashkenaz ufolin bame'ot ha-15–16: mekorot usefiḥin], *Sidra*, 8 (1992), 119–40.

RAPOPORT, ABRAHAM, *She'elot uteshuvot eitan ha'ezraḥi*, responsa (Ostroh, 1796; repr. Jerusalem, 1968).

RAPPEL, DOV (ed.), *The Seven Sciences: The Jewish Debate over Secular Education before the Enlightenment* [Sheva haḥokhmot: havikuaḥ al limudei ḥol besifrut haḥinukh hayehudit ad reshit hahaskalah] (Jerusalem, 1990).

——(ed.), *The Debate over Pilpul* [Havikuaḥ al hapilpul] (Tel Aviv, 1979).

RAVID, BENJAMIN, '"Kosher Bread" in Baroque Venice', *Italia*, 6 (1987), 20–9.

REIF, STEFAN, *Shabbethai Sofer and his Prayer Book* (Cambridge, 1979).

REINER, ELHANAN, 'The Ashkenazi Elite at the Beginning of the Modern Era: Manuscript vs. Printed Book', *Polin*, 10 (1997), 85–97.

——'The Attitude of Ashkenazi Society to the New Science in the Sixteenth Century', *Science in Context*, 10 (1997), 589–603.

——'A Biography of an Agent of Culture: Eleazar Altschul of Prague and his Literary Activity', in Michael Graetz (ed.), *Schöpferische Momente des europäischen Judentums in der frühen Neuzeit* (Heidelberg, 2000), 229–47.

——'Changes in Polish and German Yeshivot in the Sixteenth and Seventeenth Centuries and the Controversy over Pilpul' [Temurot biyeshivot polin ve'ashkenaz bame'ot ha-16–ha-17 vehavikuaḥ al hapilpul], in Israel Bartal *et al.* (eds.), *'According to the Custom of Ashkenaz and Poland': Studies in Jewish Culture in Honour of Chone Shmeruk* [Keminhag ashkenaz ufolin: sefer yovel lekhone shmeruk: kovets meḥkarim betarbut yehudit] (Jerusalem, 1993), 9–80.

——'Wealth, Social Status, and Torah Study: The Kloyz in Eastern Europe in the Seventeenth and Eighteenth Centuries' [Hon, ma'amad ḥevrati, vetalmud torah: hakloiz baḥevrah hayehudit bemizraḥ eiropah bame'ot ha-17–18], *Zion*, 58 (1993), 287–328.

RIVKIN, ELLIS, *Leon da Modena and the Kol Sakhal* (Cincinnati, Ohio, 1952).

RIVKIND, ISAAC (ed.), 'A Pamphlet of Regulations from Prague' [Kuntres takanot prag], *Reshumot*, 4 (1926), 345–52.

ROBINSON, IRA, 'Moses Cordovero and Kabbalistic Education in the Sixteenth Century', *Judaism*, 39 (1990), 155–62.

ROSENBERG, SHALOM, 'Exile and Redemption in Jewish Thought in the Sixteenth Century: Contending Conceptions', in Bernard Cooperman (ed.), *Jewish Thought in the Sixteenth Century* (Cambridge, Mass., 1983), 399–430.

ROSENFELD, MOSHE N., '*The Brantspiegel*: An Unknown Edition and the Identity of its Author' [Der brant shpigel: mahadurah bilti noda'at shel hasefer vezihui meḥabero], *Kiryat sefer*, 55 (1980), 617–21.

ROSKIES, DAVID, *Against the Apocalypse: Responses to Catastrophe in Modern Jewish Culture* (Cambridge, Mass., 1984).

ROSMAN, MOSHE (MURRAY), 'The Authority of the Council of Four Lands outside Poland' [Samkhut shel va'ad arba aratsot miḥuts lefolin], *Bar Ilan*, 24–5 (1989), 11–30.

——'The Autonomous Community: Patterns of Organization and Leadership' [Kehilot uva'adim: defusei irgun vehanhagah], in Immanuel Etkes *et al.* (eds.), *Poland:*

Topics in the History and Culture of the Jews of Eastern Europe [Polin: perakim betoledot yehudei mizraḥ-eiropah vetarbutam], 10 vols. in 7 (Tel Aviv, 1991), iii–iv. 73–154.

ROSMAN, MOSHE, 'The Image of Poland as a Center of Torah Study after the Massacres of 1648' [Demuyav shel beit yisra'el befolin kemerkaz torah aḥarei gezerot taḥ vetat], *Zion*, 51 (1986), 435–48.

—— *The Lords' Jews: Magnate–Jewish Relations in the Polish–Lithuanian Commonwealth during the Eighteenth Century* (Cambridge, Mass., 1990).

—— 'A Minority Views the Majority: Jewish Attitudes towards the Polish–Lithuanian Commonwealth and Interaction with Poles', *Polin*, 4 (1989), 31–41.

ROSS, CHERYL LYNN, 'The Plague of *The Alchemist*', *Renaissance Quarterly*, 41 (1988), 439–58.

ROSS, TAMAR, 'Miracles as an Additional Dimension in the Thought of the Maharal of Prague' [Hanes kemeimad nosaf behagut hamaharal miperag], *Da'at*, 17 (1986), 81–96.

ROSSI, AZARIAH DEI, *Me'or einayim*, ed. David Cassel (Vilna, 1866; repr. Jerusalem, 1970).

ROTH, CECIL, 'The Amazing Abraham Colorni', in id., *Personalities and Events in Jewish History* (Philadelphia, Pa., 1961), 296–304.

ROTH, JOEL, *The Halakhic Process: A Systemic Analysis* (New York, 1986).

ROTH, MESHULAM, 'Notes on the Books of the Tosafot Yom Tov' [He'arot lesifrei hatosafot yom tov], in Judah Leib Hakohen Maimon (ed.), *In Honour of Yom-Tov* (Jerusalem, 1956), 70–109.

ROWAN, STEVEN, 'Jurists and the Printing Press in Germany: The First Century', in Gerald Tyson and Sylvia Wagonheim (eds.), *Print and Culture in the Renaissance: Essays on the Advent of Printing in Europe* (Newark, Del., 1986), 74–89.

—— *Law and Jurisprudence in the Sixteenth Century: An Introductory Bibliography* (Sixteenth Century Bibliography 26) (St Louis, Mo., 1986).

RUDERMAN, DAVID B., *Jewish Thought and Scientific Discovery in Early Modern Europe* (New Haven, Conn., 1995).

RUSSELL, D. S., *The Method and Meaning of Jewish Apocalyptic* 200 BC–100 AD (Philadelphia, Pa., 1964).

SABEAN, DAVID, 'The Production of the Self during the Age of Confessionalism', *Central European History*, 29 (1996), 1–18.

SACK, BRACHA, 'The Influence of Cordovero on Seventeenth Century Jewish Thought', in Isadore Twersky and Bernard Septimus (eds.), *Jewish Thought in the Seventeenth Century* (Cambridge, Mass., 1987), 365–80.

SADEK, VLADIMIR, 'Étendard et Robe de Salomon Molkho', *Judaica Bohemiae*, 16 (1980), 64.

—— 'From the MSS Collections of the State Jewish Museum (MSS of Historical Content)', *Judaica Bohemiae*, 9 (1973), 16–22.

——'Social Aspects in the Work of Prague R. Löw (Maharal) 1512–1609', *Judaica Bohemiae*, 19 (1983), 3–21.

——'Le Système cosmologique de Shabtaj ben Akiba Horowitz (vers 1565–1619)', *Judaica Bohemiae*, 3 (1967), 18–25.

——'Die Yiddische Version der Familienmegila "Vorhangpurim" aus dem Jahre 1623', *Judaica Bohemiae*, 4 (1968), 73–8.

SAFRAN, BEZALEL, 'Leone da Modena's Historical Thinking', in Isadore Twersky and Bernard Septimus (eds.), *Jewish Thought in the Seventeenth Century* (Cambridge, Mass., 1987), 381–98.

——'Maharal and Early Hasidism', in id. (ed.), *Hasidism: Continuity and Transition* (Cambridge, Mass. 1988), 47–144.

SAMUEL BEN ISAAC DI UCEDA, *Midrash shmuel*, commentary on *Pirkei avot* (Venice, 1579).

SAPERSTEIN, MARC, 'The *Hesped* as Historical Record and Art-Form: Saul Levi Morteira's Eulogies for Dr David Farar', in id., *'Your Voice Like a Ram's Horn': Themes and Texts in Traditional Jewish Preaching* (Cincinnati, Oh., 1996), 367–410.

——(ed. and trans.), *Jewish Preaching 1200–1800: An Anthology* (New Haven, Conn., 1989).

SARTORI, GIOVANNI, *Parties and Party Systems*, vol. i (Cambridge, 1976).

SCAGLIA, DESIDERIO, letter, in Francesco Albizzi, *De Inconstantia in Jure* (Amsterdam, 1683), pt. 1: *De Inconstantia in Fide*, 296–8.

——*Prattica per le cause del Sant' Offizio*, University of Pennsylvania MS Codex 602 (formerly MS Lea 184).

SCHACTER, JACOB J., 'History and Memory of Self: The Autobiography of Rabbi Jacob Emden', in Elisheva Carlebach, John Efron, and David Myers (eds.), *Jewish History and Jewish Memory: Essays in Honor of Yosef Hayim Yerushalmi* (Hanover, NH, 1998), 428–52.

——'Rabbi Jacob Emden: Life and Major Works' (Ph.D. diss., Harvard University, 1988).

SCHECHTER, SOLOMON, 'Leopold Zunz', in id., *Studies in Judaism*, 3rd ser. (Philadelphia, Pa., 1924), 84–142.

SCHIFF, MEIR B. JACOB, Talmud commentary, printed in the Vilna Talmud.

SCHIFFMAN, ZACHARY SAYRE, 'Renaissance Historicism Reconsidered', *History and Theory*, 24 (1985), 170–82.

SCHMITT, CHARLES B., 'Philosophy and Science in Sixteenth Century Universities: Some Preliminary Comments', in John E. Murdoch and Edith D. Sylla (eds.), *The Cultural Context of Medieval Learning*, Boston Studies in the Philosophy of Science 26 (Dordrecht/Boston, 1975), 485–530.

SCHOCHET, ELIJAH J., *Bach: Rabbi Joel Sirkes: His Life, Works and Times* (New York, 1971).

——*Taz: Rabbi David Halevi, c.1586–1667* (New York, 1979).

SCHOLEM, GERSHOM, *The Dreams of the Shabatean Rabbi Mordechai Ashkenazi* [Ḥalomotav shel hashabeta'i r. mordekhai ashkenazi] (Jerusalem, 1938).

——'From Philosopher to Kabbalist' [Meḥoker limekubal], *Tarbiz*, 6 (1935), 334–42.

——*Kabbalah* (Jerusalem, 1974).

——'New Information Concerning R. Joseph Ashkenazi, the Tanna of Safed' [Yediot ḥadashot al r. yosef ashkenazi hatana mitsefat], *Tarbiz*, 28 (1958), 59–89, 201–35.

——*Sabbatai Sevi: The Mystical Messiah*, trans. R. J. Zvi Werblowsky (Princeton, NJ, 1973).

——'The Sabbatian Movement in Poland' [Hatenuah hashabta'it befolin], in Israel Hailperin (ed.), *Beit yisra'el befolin*, vol. ii (Jerusalem, 1954), 36–76; repr. in Scholem, *Studies and Texts on the History of Sabbatianism* [Meḥkarim umekorot letoledot hashabta'ut] (Jerusalem, 1974), 68–140; French trans.: 'Le Mouvement sabbataïste en Pologne', *Revue de l'Histoire des Religions*, 143 (1953), 30–90, 209–32; 144 (1953), 42–77.

——'Transmigration of Souls' [Gilgul], in id., *Pirkei yesod behavanat hakabalah usemaleiha* (Jerusalem, 1977), 308–57.

——(ed.), 'Sabbatian Miscellany' [Likutim shabtayim], *Zion*, 10 (1945), 140–8.

SCHOLTEN, FRITS (ed.), *Adriaen de Vries 1556–1626* (Los Angeles, 2000).

SCHORN-SCHÜTTE, LUISE, 'The Christian Clergy in the Early Modern Holy Roman Empire: A Comparative Social Study', *The Sixteenth Century Journal*, 29 (1998), 717–32.

SCHORSCH, ISMAR, 'The Myth of Sephardic Supremacy', *Leo Baeck Institute Year Book*, 34 (1989), 47–66.

——*On the History of the Political Judgment of the Jew*, Leo Baeck Memorial Lecture 20 (New York, 1976).

SCHOSSBERG, GABRIEL BEN JOSHUA, *Petaḥ teshuvah*, chronicle of the 1648 massacres (Amsterdam, 1650–1); repr. in Hayim Jonah Gurland (ed.), *On the History of the Persecution of Jews* (Przemysl, Cracow, and Odessa, 1886–92; repr. Jerusalem, 1972), pt. 5, pp. 29–54.

SCHWARZ, ARTHUR Z., *Die hebräischen Handschriften der Nationalbibliothek in Wien* (Vienna, 1925).

——'Zum Prozess der Lipman Heller', in Josef Fischer *et al.* (eds.), *Festskrift [David] Simonsen* (Copenhagen, 1923), 206–12.

——(ed.), 'Aus der Brief-Sammlung Sebastian Tengnagels', *Zeitschrift für Hebräische Bibliographie*, 20 (1917), 72–6.

SCHWARZ, HENRY F., *The Imperial Privy Council in the Seventeenth Century* (Cambridge, Mass., 1943).

SCHWARZ, IGNAZ, *Das Wiener Ghetto* (Vienna, 1909).

SCHWARZ, LEO W. (ed. and trans.), *Memoirs of My People* (Philadelphia, Pa., 1943).

SCHWARZFUCHS, SIMON, *A Concise History of the Rabbinate* (London, 1993).

SCHWARZSCHILD, STEVEN, and HENRY SCHWARZSCHILD, 'Two Lives in the Jewish Frühaufklärung: Raphael Levi Hannover and Moses Abraham Wolff', *Leo Baeck Institute Year Book*, 29 (1984), 229–76.

SCRIBNER, BOB, 'Preconditions of Tolerance and Intolerance in Sixteenth Century Germany', in Ole Peter Grell and Bob Scribner (eds.), *Tolerance and Intolerance in the European Reformation* (Cambridge, 1996), 32–47.

——(ed.), *Germany: A New Social and Economic History*, vol. i: *1450–1630* (London, 1996).

ŠEDINOVÁ, JIŘINA, 'Czech History as Reflected in the Historical Work by David Gans', *Judaica Bohemiae*, 8 (1972), 74–83.

——'Hebrew Literature as a Source of Information on the Czech History of the First Half of the 17th Century: The Reflection of Events in Contemporary Hebrew Literature', *Judaica Bohemiae*, 20 (1984), 3–30; 23 (1987), 38–57.

——'Literary Structure of the Seventeenth Century Hebrew Lyrico-Epic Poetry', *Judaica Bohemiae*, 25 (1989), 82–106.

——'Non-Jewish Sources in the Chronicle by David Gans, *Tsemach David*', *Judaica Bohemiae*, 8 (1972), 3–15.

——'Old Czech Legends in the Work of David Gans', *Judaica Bohemiae*, 14 (1978), 89–112.

SEGAL, ABRAHAM B. JOSEPH, commentary on *Megilat ta'anit*, published in *Megilat ta'anit* (Amsterdam, 1659).

SEGAL, LESTER A., *Historical Consciousness and Religious Tradition in Azariah de' Rossi's Me'or Einayim* (Philadelphia, Pa., 1989).

SEPTIMUS, BERNARD, *Hispano-Jewish Society in Transition: The Career and Controversies of R. Meir Abulafia* (Cambridge, Mass., 1980).

SHABETAI B. MEIR HAKOHEN, *Megilat eifah*, chronicle of the massacres of 1648, in Israel Hailperin (ed.), *The Jews in Poland*, vol. ii (Jerusalem, 1954), 252–5.

SHAPIRO, MARC, 'The Last Word in Jewish Theology?: Maimonides' Thirteen Principles', *Torah u-Madda Journal*, 4 (1993), 187–242.

SHATZ, RIVKAH, 'The Maharal: Between Existence and Eschatology' [Torat hamaharal: bein ekhzistentsiyah le'eskhatologiyah], in Zevi Baras (ed.), *Meshiḥiyut ve'eskhatologiyah: kovets ma'amarim* (Jerusalem, 1984), 301–22; also pub. in *Kivunim*, 8 (1980), 11–28.

SHATZKY, JACOB, 'Jewish Memoir Literature' [Memuarn-literatur bay yidn], review of Leo W. Schwarz, *Memoirs of My People*, *Yivo-bleter*, 23 (1944), 389–95.

SHEA, DANIEL B. JR., *Spiritual Autobiography in Early America* (Princeton, NJ, 1968).

SHEFFER, ANNE, 'Beyond Heder, Haskalah, and Honeybees: Genius and Gender in the Education of Seventeenth- and Eighteenth-Century Judeo-German Women', in Peter J. Haas (ed.), *Recovering the Role of Women: Power and Authority in Rabbinic Jewish Society* (Atlanta, Ga., 1993), 85–112.

SHERWIN, BYRON L., *Mystical Theology and Social Dissent: The Life and Works of Judah Loew of Prague* (East Brunswick, NJ, 1982).

SHMERUK, KHONE, 'The First Jewish Woman Writer in Poland: Rebecca bat Meir Tiktiner and her Works' [Hasoferet hayehudit harishonah befolin: rivkah bat me'ir tiktiner veḥibureiha], *Gal-ed*, 4–5 (1978), 13–23.

—— *Yiddish Literature: Topics in its History* [Sifrut yidish: perakim letoledoteiha] (Tel Aviv, 1978).

SHMIDMAN, MICHAEL, 'On Maimonides' "Conversion" to Kabbalah', in Isadore Twersky (ed.), *Studies in Medieval Jewish History and Literature*, vol. ii (Cambridge, Mass., 1984), 384–6.

SHOHAT, AZRIEL, *Changing Times: The Beginnings of the Enlightenment among German Jewry* [Im ḥilufei tekufot: reshit hahaskalah beyahadut germaniyah] (Jerusalem, 1960).

——'Study Societies in the Seventeenth and Eighteenth Centuries in the Land of Israel, Poland, and Germany' [Ḥevrot-limud bame'ot 17–18 be'erets yisra'el, befolin, uvegermaniyah], *Haḥinukh*, 28 (1956), 404–18.

SHULMAN, NISSON, *Authority and Community: Polish Jewry in the Sixteenth Century* (New York, 1985).

SHULVASS, MOSES, 'Ashkenazic Jewry in Italy', *YIVO Annual of Jewish Social Science*, 7 (1952), 110–31; 1st pub. as 'Dos ashkenazishe yidntum in italye', *Yivo-bleter*, 34 (1950), 157–81.

SHUMAKER, WAYNE, 'John Dee's Conversations with Angels', in id., *Renaissance Curiosa* (Binghamton, NY, 1982), 15–52.

SIEGMUND, STEPHANIE, 'La vita nei ghetti', in Corradi Vivanti (ed.), *La storia d'Italia*, 11: *Gli ebrei in Italia* (Turin, 1996), 845–92.

SIEV (ZIV), ASHER, *Rabbi Moses Isserles* [Rabenu mosheh iserles (Rema)] (New York, 1972).

SILVER, ABBA HILLEL, *A History of Messianic Speculation in Israel* (New York, 1927).

SINGER, ISAAC BASHEVIS, *Satan in Goray*, trans. Jacob Sloan (New York, 1955).

SIRAT, COLETTE, *A History of Jewish Philosophy in the Middle Ages*, trans. M. Reich (Cambridge, 1985).

SIRKES, JOEL B. SAMUEL, *Bayit ḥadash*, commentary on Jacob b. Asher, *Arba'ah turim*, printed in standard editions.

——*She'elot uteshuvot baḥ haḥadashot*, responsa (Jerusalem, 1959).

——*She'elot uteshuvot bayit ḥadash hayeshanot*, responsa (Ostroh, 1834).

SKINNER, QUENTIN, *The Foundations of Modern Political Thought*, 2 vols. (Cambridge, 1978).

SOFER, MOSES, *Sefer zikaron* (Vienna, 1863), memoirs; partial trans.: *Pressburg under Siege*, trans. Avraham Yaakov Finkel (New York, 1991).

SPICER, JOANEATH, 'The Star of David and Jewish Culture in Prague around 1600,

Reflected in Drawings of Roelandt Savery and Paulus van Vianen', *The Journal of the Walters Art Gallery*, 54 (1996), 203–24.

SPIEGEL, KÄTHE, 'Die Prager Juden zur Zeit des dreissigjährigen Krieges', in Samuel Steinherz (ed.), *Die Juden in Prag* (Prague, 1927), 107–86.

SPINOZA, BARUCH, *Theologico-Political Tractatus*, trans. R. H. M. Elwes (London, 1883).

SPIRA, ELIJAH BEN BENJAMIN WOLF, *Eliyah rabah*, commentary on Mordechai Jaffe, *Levush*, 'Oraḥ ḥayim' (Jerusalem, 1999).

ŠRONĚK, MICHAL, 'Sculpture and Painting in Prague, 1550–1650', in Eliška Fučiková *et al.* (eds.), *Rudolf II and Prague: The Court and the City* (London, 1997), 353–75.

STANISLAWSKI, MICHAEL, 'The State of the Debate over Sabbatianism in Poland: A Review of the Sources', in Harold B. Segel *et al.* (eds.), *Poles and Jews: Myth and Reality in the Historical Context* (New York, 1986), 58–69.

STARN, RANDOLPH, 'Renaissance Redux', *American Historical Review*, 103 (1998), 122–4.

STEINMETZ, DAVID (ed.), *The Bible in the Sixteenth Century* (Durham, NC, 1990).

STEINSCHNEIDER, MORITZ, *Die Geschichtliteratur der Juden* (Frankfurt am Main, 1905).

STONE, LAWRENCE, *The Crisis of the Aristocracy 1558–1641* (Oxford, 1965).

STOW, KENNETH, 'The Burning of the Talmud in 1553 in the Light of Sixteenth Century Catholic Attitudes towards the Talmud', *Bibliothèque d'Humanisme et Renaissance*, 34 (1972), 435–59.

STRAUSS, GERALD, *Law, Resistance, and the State: The Opposition to Roman Law in Reformation Germany* (Princeton, NJ, 1986).

ŠULER, B., 'Ein Maimonides-Streit in Prag in sechzehnten Jahrhundert', *Jahrbuch der Gesellschaft für Geschichte der Juden in der Čechoslovakischen Republik*, 7 (1935), 411–20.

SUSSMAN, JACOB, 'Manuscripts and Textual Traditions of the Mishnah' [Kitvei yad umesoret nusaḥ shel hamishnah], *Seventh World Congress of Jewish Studies* (1977) (Jerusalem, 1980), vol. iii, pp. 215–50.

SYKES, DAVID, 'Discrepancies between Maimonides and his Halakhic Sources' [Setiyotav shel harambam mimekorotav behalakhah], *Dinei yisra'el*, 13–14 (1988), 113–51.

SYSYN, FRANK, *Between Poland and the Ukraine: The Dilemma of Adam Kysil 1600–1653* (Cambridge, Mass., 1985).

——'A Curse on Both their Houses: Catholic Attitudes towards the Jews and Eastern Orthodox during the Khmel'nyts'kyi Uprising in Father Pawel Ruszel's *Fawor Niebieski*', in Shmuel Almog *et al.* (eds.), *Israel and the Nations: Essays in Honour of Shmuel Ettinger* [Bein yisra'el la'umot: kovets ma'amarim shai lishemuel etinger] (Jerusalem, 1987), Eng. section, pp. xi–xxiv.

SYSYN, FRANK, 'The Khmel'nyts'kyi Uprising: A Characterization of the Ukrainian Revolt', *Jewish History*, 17 (2003) 115–39.

——'Seventeenth Century Views on the Causes of the Khmel'nyts'kyi Uprising: An Examination of the "Discourse on the Present Cossack or Peasant War"', *Harvard Ukrainian Studies*, 5 (1981), 430–66.

TAMAR, DAVID, 'Eschatological Calculations in *Ḥag pesaḥ* [by R. Jacob Kitzingen]' [Ḥishuvei hakets baḥibur ḥag pesaḥ], *Sinai*, 100 (1987), 131–8.

TA-SHEMA, ISRAEL, 'Torah Study as a Social and Religious Problem in *Sefer ḥasidim*: Criticism of the Tosafistic Method in Thirteenth-Century Germany' [Mitsvat talmud-torah kive'ayah ḥevratit-datit besefer ḥasidim: levikoret shitat hatosafot be'ashkenaz bame'ah ha-13], *Bar-Ilan Annual*, 14–15 (1977), 98–113.

TAUSSIG, SAMUEL, *Megilat shemuel*, deliverance narrative; German trans. 'Megillath Samuel', ed. and trans. S. H. Lieben, *Jahrbuch der Gesellschaft für Geschichte der Juden in der Čechoslovakischen Republik*, 9 (1938), 307–39.

TAZBIR, JANUSZ, *State without Stakes: Polish Religious Toleration in the Sixteenth and Seventeenth Centuries*, trans. A. Jordan (New York, 1973).

TCHERNOWITZ, CHAIM, *History of Rabbinic Authorities since the Middle Ages* [Toledot haposekim], 3 vols. (New York, 1947).

TEOMIM, JOSEPH, *Peri megadim* [= *Siftei da'at* and *Mishbetsot zahav*, twin supercommentaries on *Siftei kohen* and *Turei zahav*, commentaries on the *Shulḥan arukh*], printed in standard editions of the *Shulḥan arukh*.

THOREN, VICTOR, *The Lord of Uraniborg: A Biography of Tycho Brahe* (Cambridge, 1990).

TIKHOMIROV, MIKHAIL, *The Towns of Ancient Rus*, trans. Y. Sdobnikov, ed. D. Skvirsky (Moscow, 1959).

TIROSH-ROTHSCHILD, HAVA, *Between Worlds: The Life and Thought of Rabbi David ben Judah Messer Leon* (Albany, NY, 1991).

TISHBY, ISAIAH, *Paths of Faith and Heresy* [Netivei emunah uminut] (Tel Aviv, 1964).

——*The Wisdom of the Zohar*, trans. David Goldstein, 3 vols. (London, 1989).

TOEGEL, MIROSLAV (ed.), *Documenta Bohemia Bellum Tricennale Illustrantia*, vol. ii (Prague, 1972).

TOLEDANO, JACOB, 'When and Where was the Authority of the *Shulḥan arukh* Accepted?' [Matai uve'elu mekomot nitkabel hashulḥan arukh lehalakhah pesukah], in Yitshak Raphael (ed.), *Rabbi Joseph Karo: Studies in the Teachings of the Author of the Shulḥan arukh* (Jerusalem, 1969), 184–8.

TRACHTENBERG, JOSHUA, *Jewish Magic and Superstition: A Study in Folk Religion* (New York, 1939).

TURNIANSKY, CHAVA, 'An Unknown Historical Song Concerning the Events in Frankfurt am Main 1612–1616' [An umbakant historish lid vegn di gesheenisn in Frankfurt de-Mayn 1612–1616], *Ninth World Congress of Jewish Studies* (1985) (Jerusalem, 1986), Div. C, Heb. section, 423–48.

——'Yiddish "Historical" Songs as Sources for the History of Jews in Pre-Partition Poland', *Polin*, 4 (1989), 42–53.

TWERSKY, ISADORE, 'Law and Spirituality in the Seventeenth Century: A Case Study in R. Yair Hayyim Bacharach', in I. Twersky and Bernard Septimus (eds.), *Jewish Thought in the Seventeenth Century* (Cambridge, Mass., 1987), 447–67.

——*Rabad of Posquières: A Twelfth-Century Talmudist*, rev. edn. (Philadelphia, Pa., 1980).

——'The *Shulḥan 'Arukh*: Enduring Code of Jewish Law', *Judaism*, 16 (1967), 141–58; repr. in Judah Goldin (ed.), *The Jewish Expression* (New Haven, Conn., 1976), 322–43.

——'Talmudists, Philosophers, Kabbalists: The Quest for Spirituality in the Sixteenth Century', in Bernard Cooperman (ed.), *Jewish Thought in the Sixteenth Century* (Cambridge, Mass., 1983), 431–87.

ULBRICHT, OTTO, 'Criminality and Punishment of the Jews in the Early Modern Period', in R. Po-Chia Hsia and Harmut Lehmann (eds.), *In and Out of the Ghetto: Jewish–Gentile Relations in Late Medieval and Early Modern Germany* (Cambridge, 1995), 49–70.

URBACH, EPHRAIM ELIMELEKH, *The Tosafists* [Ba'alei hatosafot], 4th edn., 2 vols. (Jerusalem, 1980).

VALDŠTEJN (WALLENSTEIN), ADAM OF, *Deník rudolfinského dvořana, Adam mladšíz Valdštejna 1602–1633*, diary, ed. Marie Koldinská and Petr Mat'a (Prague, 1997).

VAN DÜLMEN, RICHARD, *Theatre of Horror: Crime and Punishment in Early Modern Germany*, trans. Elisabeth Neu (Cambridge, 1990).

VOGLER, BERNARD, *Le Clergé protestant rhénan au siècle de la Réforme (1555–1619)* (Paris, 1976).

VOLAVKOVÁ, HANA, *The Pinkas Synagogue* (Prague, 1955).

Volodymyr memorial book [Pinkas ludmir: sefer zikaron likehilat ludmir] (Tel Aviv, 1962).

VON KRUSENSTJERN, BENIGNA, and HANS MEDICK (eds.), *Zwischen Alltag und Katastrophe: Der Dreissigjährige Krieg aus der Nähe* (Göttingen, 1999).

WACHSTEIN, BERNHARD (ed.), *Die Inschriften des Alten Judenfriedhofes in Wien* (Vienna, 1912).

WALLENSTEIN, ADAM OF *see* VALDŠTEJN, ADAM OF

WALSHAM, ALEXANDRA, *Providence in Early Modern Europe* (Oxford, 2000).

WEEKS, ANDREW, *Boehme: An Intellectual Biography* (Albany, NY, 1991).

WEINBERG, JOANNA, 'Azariah de' Rossi and Septuagint Traditions', *Italia*, 5 (1985), 7–35.

WEINGARTEN, SHMUEL HAKOHEN, 'The Tombstone of R. Moses Levi Heller Wallerstein' [Matsevato shel r. mosheh heler valershtain], in Judah Leib Hakohen Maimon (ed.), *In Honour of Yom-Tov* (Jerusalem, 1956), 221–3.

WEINREICH, MAX (ed.), 'Di bashraybung fun ashkenaz un polak', debate poem of a German, a Polish, and a Czech Jew (Prague, *c.*1675), in id., 'Two Yiddish Satiric Poems about Jews' [Tsvey yidishe shpotlider oyf yidn], *YIVO Filologishe Shriftn*, 3 (1929), 537–54.

WEINRYB, BERNARD, 'The Hebrew Chronicles on Bohdan Khmel'nyts'kyi and the Cossack–Polish War', *Harvard Ukrainian Studies*, 1 (1977), 153–77.

——*The Jews of Poland: A Social and Economic History of the Jewish Community of Poland from 1100 to 1800* (Philadelphia, Pa., 1973).

WEINTRAUB, WIKTOR, 'The [Polish–Lithuanian] Commonwealth and the Book *De Revolutionibus*', *Polish Studies*, 18/3 (1973), 19–24.

WERBLOWSKY, R. J. ZWI, *Joseph Karo: Lawyer and Mystic*, rev. edn. (Philadelphia, Pa., 1977).

WETTSTEIN, FEIVEL (ed.), *Ancient Matters from the Registers of the Jewish Community of Cracow* [Devarim atikim mipinkasei hakahal bikerako] (Cracow, 1900).

——'Antiquities from Old Registers on the History of the Jews in Poland, Especially Cracow' [Kadmoniyot mipinkase'ot yeshanim lekorot yisra'el befolin bikhelal uvikerako biferat], *Otsar hasifrut*, 4 (1892), 577–642; also pub. as book (Cracow, 1892).

——'Conversations from Old Cracow Copied from the Registers' [Siḥot mini kedem: muatakot mipinkasei kerako], *Hatsofeh leḥokhmat yisra'el*, 4 (1915), 166–86.

——'From the Registers of the Jewish Community of Cracow on the History of the Jewish People and its Sages' [Mipinkasei hakahal bikerako lekorot yisra'el veḥakhamav], in Marcus Brann (ed.), *Gedenkbuch zur Erinnerung an David Kaufmann* (Breslau, 1900), 69–84.

——'Treasures from the Registers of the Jewish Community of Cracow' [Divrei ḥefets mipinkasei hakahal bikerako], *Me'asef*, 1 (1902), 7–78.

WIESNER, MERRY E., 'Paternalism in Practice: The Control of Servants and Prostitutes in Early Modern German Cities', in Philip N. Bebb and Sherrin Marshall (eds.), *The Process of Change in Early Modern Europe: Essays in Honor of Miriam Usher Chrisman* (Athens, Ohio, 1988), 179–200.

WISCHNITZER, MARK, 'A Friday in 1619: Letters of Jews in Prague to Jews in Vienna' (Russian), *Evreiskaia Starina*, 2 (1910), 636–47.

WOLF, GERSON (ed.), *Ferdinand II und die Juden* (Vienna, 1859); also pub. as 'Die Juden unter Ferdinand II', *Jahrbuch für die Geschichte der Juden und des Judenthums*, 1 (1860), 217–86.

WOLFSBERG, YESHAYAHU, 'R. Yom-Tov Lipmann Halevi Heller', in Judah Leib Hakohen Maimon (ed.), *In Honour of Yom-Tov* (Jerusalem, 1956), 119–24.

WOLFSON, ELLIOT, 'The Influence of Isaac Luria on Isaiah Horowitz' [Hashpa'at ha'ari al hashelah], *Meḥkerei yerushalayim bemaḥshevet yisra'el*, 10 (1992), 423–49.

WOOLF, JEFFREY, 'The Authority of Custom in the Responsa of R. Joseph Colon (Maharik)', *Dinei yisra'el*, 19 (1998), Eng. section, pp. 43–73.

YAKOVENKO, NATALIA, 'The Events of 1648–1649: Contemporary Reports and the Problem of Verification', *Jewish History*, 17 (2003), 165–78.

YATES, FRANCES, *The Art of Memory* (London, 1966).

—— *The Occult Philosophy in Elizabethan England* (London, 1979).

YEHIEL MIKHEL THE SCRIBE IN CRACOW, poem on the plague of 1623, in Feivel Wettstein, 'Antiquities Copied from the Records of the Jewish Community of Cracow' [Divrei kedem mipinkasei hakahal bikerako], *Luaḥ sha'ashuim*, 1 (1902), 193–7.

YERUSHALMI, YOSEF HAYIM, *The Lisbon Massacre of 1506 and the Royal Image in the Shebet Yehudah*, *HUCA* supplement 1 (Cincinnati, Ohio, 1976).

——*Zakhor: Jewish History and Jewish Memory* (Seattle, Wash., 1982).

YUVAL, ISRAEL J., 'A German-Jewish Autobiography of the Fourteenth Century', in Joseph Dan (ed.), *Binah: Studies in Jewish History, Thought, and Culture*, vol. iii: *Jewish Intellectual History in the Middle Ages* (Westport, Conn., 1994), 79–99; 1st pub. in Heb. in *Tarbiz*, 55 (1986), 541–66.

——*Sages in their Generation: The Religious Leadership of the Jews of Germany in the Later Middle Ages* [Ḥakhamim bedoram: hamanhigut haruḥanit shel yehudei germaniyah beshilhei yemei habeinayim] (Jerusalem, 1989).

——'The Vengeance and the Curse, the Blood and the Libel' [Hanakam vehakelalah, hadam veha'alilah], *Zion*, 58 (1993), 33–90.

ZACUTO, MOSES, eulogy for Heller, in the manuscript collection of his eulogies: Jewish Theological Seminary MS E. N. Adler 378; Jewish Theological Seminary microfilm no. 3545.

——Letter on non-Jewish wine, *Kerem shelomoh*, 5/8 (1982), p. 24.

ZAIMAN, JOEL, 'The Traditional Study of the Mishnah', in Jacob Neusner (ed.), *The Study of Ancient Judaism: Mishnah, Midrash, Siddur*, vol. i (New York, 1988), 27–35.

ZAPALAC, KRISTIN E. S., '"With a Morsel of Bread": Delineating Differences in the Jewish and Christian Communities of Regensburg Before the Pogrom of 1519', in Max Reinhart (ed.), *Infinite Boundaries: Order, Disorder, and Reorder in Early Modern German Culture* (Kirksville, Mo., 1998), 271–90.

ZEILLER, MARTIN, *Topographia Germaniae: Schwaben* (Frankfurt am Main, 1653; repr. Kassel, 1960).

ZIMMER, ERIC (YITSHAK), *Embers of the Sages: Topics in the History of the German Rabbinate in the Sixteenth and Seventeenth Centuries* [Gaḥalatan shel ḥakhamim: perakim betoledot harabanut begermaniyah bame'ah hashesh-esreh uvame'ah hasheva-esreh] (Jerusalem, 1999).

——'R. Eliakim Gottschalk and his Debate with R. Isaiah Horowitz' [R. elyakim gotshalk uvikuḥo im hashelah], *Sinai*, 88 (1981), 138–54.

ZIMMER, ERIC, 'R. Jacob Reiner, Chief Rabbi of Swabia in the Sixteenth Century' [R. ya'akov reiner: rav hamedinah shel shevaben bame'ah ha-16], *Sinai*, 87 (1980), 119–34.

——(ed.), *History of the German Rabbinate in the Sixteenth Century: The Conflict between the Rabbis of Frankfurt and Swabia 1564–1565* [Mitoledot harabanut begermaniyah bame'ah ha-16: hasikhsukh bein rabanei frankfurt lerabanei shevaben 324–325] (Jerusalem, 1984).

——(ed. and trans.), *Jewish Synods in Germany during the Late Middle Ages (1286–1603)* (New York, 1978).

ZINBERG, ISRAEL, *A History of Jewish Literature*, trans. Bernard Martin, 12 vols. (Cleveland, Ohio, 1972–8); 1st pub. as *Geshikhte fun der literatur bay yidn*, 8 vols. (New York, 1943).

ZIVITOFSKY, ARI, 'Is Turkey Kosher?', *Journal of Halacha and Contemporary Society*, 35 (1998), 79–110.

ZLOTNICK, DOV, 'The Commentary of R. Abraham Azulai to the Mishnah', *Proceedings of the American Academy for Jewish Research*, 40 (1972), 147–68.

——'On the Origins and History of the Saying of "The Dwarf and the Giant"' [Al mekor hamashal 'hananas vehe'anak' vegilgulo], *Sinai*, 77 (1975), 184–9.

ZUNZ, J. M., *City of Righteousness: History of the Rabbis of Cracow* [Ir hatsedek: toledot rabanei ir kerako] (Lvov, 1874).

ZUNZ, LEOPOLD, 'Annalen der hebräischen Typographie von Prag vom Jahre 1513 zum Jahre 1657', in id., *Zur Geschichte und Literatur*, 2nd edn. (Berlin, 1919), 268–303.

——'Das Gedächtniss der Gerechten', in id., *Zur Geschichte und Literatur*, 2nd edn. (Berlin, 1919), 304–459.

Index of Personal Names

A

Aaron Samuel of Kremenets 59, 75 n., 94 n.
Abarbanel, Isaac 45 n., 74 n., 162, 190
Abraham Hans (thief) 141
Abraham Hayim of Opatów 102–3
Adeni, Solomon 68 n.
Akiba 93–5
Albo, Joseph 40 n.
Alfasi, Isaac 123
Altschul, Moses 28
Altshuler, Hanokh ben Moses 194
Altshuler, Naftali 39, 48 n.
Altshuler Perles, Eleazar 28
Anav, Zedekiah ben Abraham 150
Arama, Isaac 63 n., 163
Archivolti, Samuel 55–6, 169
Ari, the, *see* Luria, Isaac
Aristotle and Aristotelianism 36, 39 n., 40, 43–5, 50, 64, 90 n., 91, 94, 159–60, 166
Asher ben Eliezer Halevi of Reichshofen 117 n., 142
Asher ben Yehiel, *see* Rosh
Ashkenazi, Abraham ben Samuel 178 n., 207 n., 209 n., 215–16
Ashkenazi, Bezalel 68
Ashkenazi, Eliezer 30, 155, 163, 164 n.
Ashkenazi, Joseph 43, 53, 68, 148
Ashkenazi, Judah ben Nathan 33 n.
Ashkenazi, Mordechai 205–6
Ashkenazi, Moses Aaron 7, 9, 23, 25, 131, 199 n.
Averroes 44–5, 91 n.
Azulai, Abraham 46 n., 68 n.

B

Bach, Meir 81, 219
Bacharach, Naftali ben Jacob 15, 60, 189–91
Bacharach, Yair Hayim 42 n., 164 n.
Bahya ben Asher 54–5, 81, 122
Bahya ibn Pakuda 34, 40 n., 42
Bar Zadok, Paul Joseph 141
Bartenura, Obadiah, *see* Bertinoro, Obadiah of
Baruch ben David of Gniezno 124
Bass, Mendel 117 n.
Bassevi, Abraham ben Jacob 145
Bassevi, Jacob 112–13, 117, 137–9, 144, 150–1, 160, 196
Bassevi, Samuel (Heller's son-in-law) 160
Bedersi, Jedaiah, *see Heller Index*: writings: *Beḥinat olam*
Bella bat Jacob, *see* Teitsch, Bella
Bellarmine, Robert 70, 167 n.
Ben-Sasson, Haim Hillel 6–8
Berakhyah Berakh ben Isaac 14 n., 190–1, 210 n., 215, 222 n.
Bertinoro, Obadiah of 51 n., 68, 73–4, 78–80
Bialik, Hayim Nahman 212 n.
Boehme, Jacob 102, 210 n.
Bonn, Naftali ben Isaac 190
Brahe, Tycho 27–8, 35, 44, 111 n., 160, 166–8, 174
Brożek (Bruscius), Jan 160 n.

C

Caro, Joseph:
  halakhic authority, his view of 123–6, 180 n.
  halakhic views of 60, 89 n., 128
  and Mishnah 69 n.
Chajes, Isaac 40, 163 n.
Cohen, Tobias 42 n.
Colorni, Abraham 27–8
Comenius, John 34, 204 n.
Cordovero, Moses 52–6, 59–60, 69, 162, 207, 209 n.
Crescas, Hasdai 44

D

da Modena, Leone, *see* Modena, Leone da
Darshan, David 200
David of Landshut 114
David ben Samuel (the Taz) 57 n., 186, 197 n., 220
David of Szczebrzeszyn 67
de Vries, Adriaen 126
Dee, John 27, 58 n.
dei Rossi, Azariah, *see* Rossi, Azariah dei
Dekker, Thomas 47
Delmedigo, Joseph Solomon 167–8, 169 n.
Dietrichstein, Cardinal Franz von 85
Dietrichstein, Maximilian von 84–5
Donne, John 113, 115
Dornavius (Dornau), Caspar 169

E

Edels, Joshua 194 n.
Edels, Samuel 60, 184, 188 n.
Eilburg, Eliezer 41, 72
Eisenstadt, Moses ben Hayim 42 n.
Eleazar ben Dinai (ancient Jewish bandit) 71
Eliezer ben Nathan (Ra'avan) 209–10
Elijah of Izmir 191 n.
Elizabeth of Bohemia 104
Emden, Jacob 193 n., 197 n.
Ephraim ben Joseph (liturgical poet) 216 n.
Ephraim of Luntshits 28
  appointment of 131 n.
  death of 106
  and Halevi, Joseph ben Isaac 44, 46
  and Maharal 69
  on Mishnah study and *Tosafot yom tov* 69 n.
  in Nikolsburg tax case 86
  and penitential rules (1611) 48
  in plague (1606) 47 n., 168 n.
  as preacher 113
  purchase of rabbinical office, opposes 184
  as rabbinic activist 30, 69
  on silence during prayer 208 n.
  as social critic 4–5, 8, 26, 85
  and thanksgiving day (1611) 107
Eshtor Haparhi 75 n.
Euclid 45 n., 74, 90–1
Eulenburg, Isaac 222 n.
Eybeschuetz, Baer 42 n.

F

Falaquera, Shem Tov ben Joseph 40 n.
Farrar (Farar), David 53–4, 58, 77 n.
Ferdinand II 106–9, 117, 131, 133–53
  conversion campaign (1629–31) 142–3, 150–1, 153
  and Habsburg Jewish policy 21 n.
  Heller's loyalty to 108–9, 133–5, 147–53
  Prague Jews, intervention in dispute among (1629) 138–9, 145
  Prague Jews, protection of (1620) 106–8, 146
  procession in honour of (1623) 109 n., 117
  Protestantism, suppression of 142–3, 151, 159 n.
  Talmud, suppression of (1626) 143
  on title page of *Ma'adanei yom tov* (1628) 131
  and the trial of Heller (1629) 136–45
  Vienna Jewish community, granted toleration by 113
Fränklin family 23
Fränklin, Abraham (Heller's cousin) 9, 20
Fränklin, Lipmann (Heller's cousin) 20 n., 22
Fränklin, Moses (Heller's grandfather) 20, 22 n., 89, 152
Frederick V, elector palatine, king of Bohemia 104, 106, 108–9

G

Gabbai, Isaac 68
Galileo Galilei 167–8
Gans, David:
  astrology, rejection of 111
  and astronomy 28, 55 n., 90, 166 n., 168, 176 n.
  and Brahe, Tycho 28, 168
  on the Maharal's interview with Rudolph II 22 n.
  on new seas 165 n.
  on non-Jews 90, 92, 95 n., 168
  on Prague 27 n.
  on progress 46
  quotes non-Jewish authors 90, 166 n.
  on toleration of Jews in 16th c. 21 n.
Gedaliah of Worms 108
Gersonides 35, 91, 169 n.
Glückel bat Judah of Hameln 51, 169 n., 195, 197, 207 n.
Gombiner, Abraham 111 n., 122 n.
Graetz, Heinrich 5–6, 14
Günzburg, Jacob 24, 31, 55 n., 200
Günzburg, Simon 20
Gutman, Leb, and Sarel bat Moses 104

H

Hagiz, Jacob ben Samuel 68 n.
Hahn, Juspa 107 n., 207 n.
Hailperin, Israel vii, 8
Hakohen, Isaac ben Samson, *see* Isaac ben Samson Hakohen
Hakohen, Shabetai ben Meir, *see* Shabetai ben Meir Hakohen
Halevi, Joseph ben Isaac, *see* Joseph ben Isaac Halevi
Halevi, Judah 167
Halevi, Samuel, *see* Samuel Halevi
Hameln, Hayim 51
Hammerschlag, Hanokh 102, 104
Hammerschlag, Rikel and Zangwill 102
Hanau, Solomon 42 n.
Hannover, Nathan Neta 4–5, 206 n., 207 n., 212, 214–16, 217 n.
Hannover, Raphael Levi 42 n.
Hanokh ben Abraham of Gniezno 216 n.
Hanokh ben Isaac (letter-writer, 1619) 102, 104

Hayat, Judah 93
Hayim ben Bezalel 88 n., 95 n., 125 n., 182 n.
Hayim ben Isaac Hakohen 117 n.
Hefets, Enshchen (Asher) 81
Heller, Joseph (Heller's brother) 20 n.
Heller, Moses (Heller's grandfather), *see* Fränklin, Moses
Heller, Nathan (Heller's father) 19, 201
Heller, Rachel (Rachel Munk, Heller's wife) 5, 23–5, 145, 160, 200–1, 223
Heller, Yom-Tov Lipmann, *see Heller Index*
Heller, Yom-Tov Lipmann, children of:
  Abraham 25, 159–60, 200–1
  Doberish 25, 160, 187, 198, 201
  Esther 25, 104, 201
  Liva 25, 160, 200–1
  Moses 25, 196, 200–1, 223
  Nechle 25, 103, 160, 198
  Nisel 25, 103, 198–9
  Rebecca 25, 160, 200
  Reyzel 25, 160, 198–9
  Samuel 25, 146 n., 199 n., 201
Heller, Yom-Tov Lipmann, grandchildren of:
  Gottred 198–9
  Mikhel (in Turisk) 187
  Moses 198–9
  Nathan 188, 201
  Nisel 201
  Reyzel 201
  Simhah 198–9
Hellin, Elhanan ben Abraham 105
Henlisch, Israel 140
Hobbes, Thomas 217
Horodetsky, Samuel 6
Horowitz family 9, 25–6, 43, 129
Horowitz, Abraham:
  Ashkenazi, Joseph, controversy with 43, 53, 148
  on diaries of sins 197
  and Horowitz, Isaiah 53
  on Isserles, authority of 124 n.
  on magnetism 40
  Maimonides' *Eight Chapters*, his commentary on 40–1
  on prayer, purpose of 63 n.
  prisoner, his story of the 141
  questions of philosophy, his list of 41, 53
  on quoting non-Jews by name 90 n.
Horowitz, Hezekiah ben Asher 102
Horowitz, Isaiah 51–4
  and Heller: approbation for *Tosafot yom tov* 66; Heller's opinion of Horowitz 52
  and kabbalah 51–2, 55, 62, 191
  life: and his father (Abraham Horowitz) 53; *ḥerem* on purchase of rabbinical office (1587) 184; Frankfurt contract (1606) 119; appointed rabbi in Prague (1614) 51; Nikolsburg tax case (1616) 86; *sandek* (godfather) at circumcision (1619) 102; Prague thanksgiving day (1620) 106; emigration to Land of Israel (1621) 52
  and the Maharal 69
  popularity and influence of 51
  radicalism of 53, 170 n.
  views: on *agadah*, literal truth of 162 n.; on bread, non-Jewish 88; 'commandments serve God's needs' 63 n.; on death and immortality 172; on evil thoughts, elevation of 54; on free will 52, 128; on halakhah, history of 170 n.; on halakhah and interpretation of Torah 128; on 'lessening of the moon' 162 n.; on messianism 170 n.; on Mishnah 69 n., 70–1; on name of God 76 n.; on non-Jews 94 n., 95 n., 143, 217 n.; against philosophy 43 n., 52–4; on Rashi 78; on *shtadlanim* 143; on *Shulḥan arukh*, authority of 125–6, 180; on silence, types of 197 n.; on wine, non-Jewish 86
  writings: prayer book 51–2; *Shenei luḥot haberit* 51, 59; supercommentary on Mordechai ben Hillel 125–6
Horowitz, Pinhas, of Cracow 86 n., 199 n.
Horowitz, Pinhas, rabbi in Prague 81, 86–7, 128, 151, 196
Horowitz, Shabetai Sheftel ben Akiba 28, 55 n., 59
Horowitz, Shabetai Sheftel ben Isaiah 30 n., 58 n., 60, 69 n., 78, 185, 190, 207–9, 215
Horowitz, Solomon Zalman ben Isaiah 104
Hunain ibn Isaac 34, 90, 170
Hundert, Gershon 12

I

Ibn Ezra, Abraham 35, 72–3
  see also Heller Index: writings and sermons: Ibn Ezra
Ibn Gabbai, Meir 53, 55
Ibn Habib, Levi 162, 190
Ibrahim ben Ya'qub 26
Isaac of Corbeil 124
Isaac ben Samson Hakohen 22–3 n., 28, 46, 86 n.
Isaac ben Samuel of Acre 55
Isaac ben Samuel Halevi of Poznań 121
Isaac ben Solomon of Brest-Litovsk 44 n.
Isaac ben Yekutiel Kuskis 28
Isaiah (Jesaja), Paul 140 n.

Israel ben Benjamin of Bełżyce 209, 214–15
Israel, Jonathan 12
Isserles, Moses:
on allegorical interpretation 31–2, 163
on Ashkenazi custom 125, 180–1
and astronomy 33 n., 168 n.
authority of 123–6, 179–81, 185–6, 189
on Bohemia and Moravia, Jews of 83 n., 148 n.
on education 31–2
on end of universe 45 n.
on factionalism as cause of misfortune 148 n.
halakhic views of: on Bible verses, recitation of 128; on chicken and cheese 60 n.; on Christianity, status of 96 n.; on non-Jews, reading books by 91; on rabbinate, non-Jewish appointments to 185–6
and harmonization of halakhic views 74
on kabbalah 60, 63
and philosophy, Jewish 40, 42–3
on purpose of commandments 40
on science and metaphysics 43, 91
writings: *Mapah* (commentary on *Shulḥan arukh*) 123–6; *Meḥir yayin* (commentary on Esther) 163; *Torat haḥatat* (code of laws on *kashrut*) 178–9; *Torat ha'olah* (Temple, interpretation of) 31–2

J
Jacob ben Asher (the Tur) 123–4
Jaffe, Mordechai:
halakhic code of (*Levush*) 66 n., 122 n., 125
and Jewish philosophy 40–1, 111 n.
on progress 46
against purchase of rabbinical office 184
on Torah and 'seven sciences' 33–4, 64–5
Jan Casimir of Poland 216, 218
Jedaiah Hapenini (Jedaiah Bedersi), *see Heller Index*: writings: *Beḥinat olam*
Joannides, Valentinus 149 n.
John Casimir of Poland, *see* Jan Casimir
Jonathan ben Israel of Ruzhany 42 n.
Jonson, Ben 48
Joseph (Josel) ben Gerson of Rosheim 148 n., 193 n.
Joseph ben Isaac Halevi 44–50
on America, discovery of 169
and Aristotelianism 44–5, 58 n., 166, 169
on astronomy 44, 166, 169
born in Brest-Litovsk 44
on divine reward and punishment 147 n.
as 'dwarf on the shoulders of a giant' 46–7, 169
on education, Jewish (Torah study) 120
exile from Prague 48–50
and Heller 45–7, 50, 58 n.
on infinite succession of worlds 44–5
and Intellects, Averroes' theory of 58 n.
on magnetism 40 n.
on Maimonides 44 n., 64 n.
on monarchy 130
opponents of Jewish philosophy, his typology of 49
quotes Rossi, Azariah dei 130
writings: *Givat hamoreh* 44–7; *Ketonet pasim* 48–9; 'Treatise on Divine Unity' 50, 97 n.
Joseph ben Issachar 28
Joseph (Josel) of Lokacze (Lokachi) 185–7
Joseph (Yehosef) ibn Shraga 35
Josephus and Josippon 74, 89 n.
Joshua ben Joseph of Cracow 67 n., 78, 192 n.
Joshua Heschel of Lublin 209 n.
Journet, Noël 73 n.
Judah the Prince 30–1, 70, 76, 143
Judah Loew ben Bezalel, *see* Maharal of Prague
Juspa, *shamash* of Worms 107–8, 117 n.

K
Kadosh, Meir 194
Kaidanover, Aaron Samuel 72
Kalonymos ben Kalonymos 40 n.
Karo, Joseph, *see* Caro, Joseph
Karpel, David, *see* Luria, David
Katz, Gerson ben Solomon Popper 44 n.
Katz, Jacob 6, 10–13, 15, 146, 152
Katz, Naftali ben Isaac 103 n.
Katz, Zanvill 71, 81
Katzenellenbogen, Isaac 109 n.
Katzenstein, Meir 145
Kepler, Johannes 27, 44, 168
Kimhi, David 35
Kitzingen, Jacob 210 n.
Kitzingen, Joseph 19
Kohen, Moses 81
Kohen, Shabetai (the Shakh), *see* Shabetai ben Meir Hakohen
Kolinsky (Kelin) family 19–20
Komensky, Jan, *see* Comenius, John
Koppelman, Jacob 32 n., 40, 46
Krochmal, Menahem Mendl 66 n., 167
Kupfer, Ephraim 6–7

L
La Peyrère, Isaac 72
Landau, Jacob (the Agur) 128
Lawrence of Brindisi 47
Łęczyca, Ephraim of, *see* Ephraim of Luntshits
Levi ben Gershom, *see* Gersonides

Levi, Isaac 81
Levush, *see* Jaffe, Mordechai
Liechtenstein, Karl von 149, 202
Lipschitz, Isserl and Malka 103–4
Lipschitz, Mordechai 46, 86–7
Lipschuetz, Moses ben Noah Isaac 68 n.
Lisker, Abraham ben Hayim 68 n.
Loew of Prague, *see* Maharal of Prague
Lucerna, Aaron and Leo 164–5
Luntshits, Ephraim of, *see* Ephraim of Luntshits
Luria family 159
Luria (Karpel), David 137
Luria, Esther bat Yehiel (Heller's daughter-in-law) 159
Luria, Isaac 52–3, 55, 58, 160, 189–91, 207, 214
Luria, Solomon (doctor in Lublin) 159
Luria, Solomon ben Jehiel:
 authority of 124
 on German Jews 83 n.
 halakhic authority, view of 123–7, 180
 and Isserles, Moses 42–3, 91, 124 n., 179
 on kabbalah and halakhah 60
 on non-Jews, teaching Torah to 95 n.
 on study of philosophy 42–3, 91
Luria, Yehiel ben Solomon 159

M

Magen Avraham, *see* Gombiner, Abraham
Maharal of Prague (Judah Loew ben Bezalel) 21–2, 29–31, 68–9, 93–4, 110–11, 123–5, 171–2, 208
 as aristocrat, rabbinic 9
 his circle of scholars 27–9
 family and descendants: Bacharach, Yair (great-grandson) 42 n., 164 n.; Fränklin, Abraham (son-in-law) 9, 20; Hayim ben Bezalel (brother) 88 n., 95 n., 125 n., 182 n.; Hayim ben Isaac Hakohen (grandson) 117 n.; Isaac ben Samson Hakohen (son-in-law) 22–3 n., 28, 46, 86 n.; Katz, Naftali ben Isaac (grandson) 103 n.; Wallerstein, Henele bat Abraham (granddaughter) 103; Wallerstein, Jacob Koppel (grandson) 103 n.; Wallerstein, Mirel (granddaughter) 103, 199 n.; Wallerstein, Samuel ben Abraham (grandson) 103
 and *golem* legend 29, 57
 as halakhist 30, 31 n., 180
 and kabbalah 63, 84 n.
 life 29; controversies 30, 49–50; death 47; establishes Prague *ḥevrot* 69, 81; imprisoned (1602) 140–1; *kloyz* (college) of 29, 31; in Nikolsburg 84; meets Rudolph II (1592) 22
 as 'the Lion' 29, 171
 and printing 78, 91 n., 121
 views: on *agadah*, interpretation of 30; on astrology 111; on astronomy, uncertainty in 169 n.; on creation of the moon 171–2; on education 30–5, 40, 68–9, 120, 127 n., 169 n.; on eras of Jewish history 21; on factionalism 98 n., 148 n.; on halakhic authority and codification 9, 123–5, 127; on Islam and Christianity 94; on Israel, land of 52 n.; on Jerusalem 176 n.; on martyrs 22; on miracles and nature 94, 110–11; on Mishnah study 68–9, 78 n.; on monarchs 130; on Moravia, Jews of 83 n.; on non-Jews 83 n., 84, 91 n., 94–5; on opposites 94; on philosophy, Jewish 9, 30, 49–50, 63; on *pilpul* 73, 120; proof of God's existence 49; on rabbis, qualifications of 188; on Rashi and Tosafot 78; on religious conflict 98 n.; on revelation, divine 20 n.; on rich and poor 30, 69; on the Rosh 127 n.; on science vs. metaphysics 91, 169 n.; on self, illusion of 29, 161, 171–2; on silence during prayer 208; on the soul and the angels 37; on wine, non-Jewish 84
 writings: *agunah*, responsum concerning 31 n.; *Be'er hagolah* 30; commentary on *Ẓera'im* and *Tohorot* 78 n.; *Derekh haḥayim* (*Avot* commentary) 30, 94; *Gevurot hashem*, introduction to 110; *Gur aryeh* (Rashi supercommentary) 77 n., 171; sermons and eulogies 21, 141 n.; *takanot* and liturgical innovations 30, 84, 208; *Tiferet yisrael* 37
Maharil, *see* Moellin, Jacob
Maharsha, *see* Edels, Samuel
Maharshal, *see* Luria, Solomon
Maimon, Solomon 193 n., 194
Maimonides, Moses:
 on anger 198
 and astronomy 159, 164, 168
 on Christianity 97
 and clockmaker, God as 40
 and codification of law 123
 on duration of the universe 45 n.
 of food, importance of 88
 on happiness and change 170 n.
 on language 76
 on magic 57
 and Moses, compared 46, 49
 negative theology 64
 on non-Jews 92, 95, 97, 198 n.

Maimonides, Moses (*cont.*):
on praises of God 62
on prayer, purpose of 63
on progress 46
proofs of God's existence 44
on rabbis and philosopher-kings 30
on suffering and evil 172, 198, 215
on unity, divine 97
writings: *Eight Chapters* (introduction to *Avot* commentary) 40 n.; Mishnah commentary 68, 74, 76–7, 80; *Mishneh torah* 42 n., 47 n., 76–7, 123, 159; *Moreh nevukhim* 7, 33–4, 36, 40–6, 64, 80, 95; Thirteen Principles of Faith 7, 36
see also Subject Index: philosophy, Jewish
Malinowski, Joseph ben Mordechai 170 n.
Manasseh ben Israel 21, 93 n., 175, 184
Manoah Hendl ben Shemariah of Beresteczko 40 n.
Mansfeld, Peter Ernest 109 n.
Matityah 170 n.
Matthias I (Habsburg emperor) 101, 148
Mazel, Joseph ben Eleazar Ashkenazi of Prossnitz 211, 212 n.
Mehler, Juda 195 n.
Meir ben Asher Lemil of Ukraine 221
Meir Hakadosh, *see* Kadosh, Meir
Meir of Lublin 184
Meir of Rothenburg 82
Meir of Szczebrzeszyn 212 n.
Meisel, Mordechai, and family 25, 27
see also Subject Index: Prague: Meisel synagogue
Melis, Zevi Hirsch (Heller's son-in-law) 200
Mendel Isaac of Cracow (engineer) 28 n.
Mendelssohn, Moses 14, 77 n.
Modena, Leone da (Leon) 53, 58 n., 73 n., 91 n., 196 n., 203
Moellin, Jacob (Maharil) 182–3
Mohyla, Peter 34
Molcho, Solomon 56–7, 210 n.
Montalto, Elijah 58
Mordechai ben Hillel ('the Mordechai') 124, 126
Mordechai of Nelle 27
Morin, Jean 72
Moryson, Fynes 23, 26–8, 88, 184, 203
Moses of Coucy 124
Moses ben David Segal 86
Moses ben Isaiah Menahem (Moses Mendels) 117 n.
Moses ben Jacob of Bystřice (scribe in Prague) 81 n.
Munk, Moses Aaron, *see* Ashkenazi, Moses Aaron

N

Naftali Hirtz of Brest Litovsk 148
Nahmanides, Moses 55, 111
Nantua, Judah 163 n.
Nathan of Gaza 209
Neumark, Meir ben Moses Judah Leb of Nikolsburg 42 n.
Niderlander, Ephraim ben Abraham 28
Nissim Gerondi 121, 128

O

Oettingen-Wallerstein, Friedrich V of 22
Oettingen-Wallerstein, Wilhelm III of 141
Oppenheim, Simeon Wolf 20, 68 n., 81
Oppenheimer, David 180
Ostropoler, Samson, *see* Samson of Ostropol
Ozers, Meir ben Leb Anshel 93

P

Pascal, Blaise 127
Peretz, Isaac Leib 173 n.
Pfaffenhofen, Alexander 85–6
Philippson, Ludwig 146 n.
Phillipi (Prescensis), Henry 149 n.
Pisek, Aryeh Leb 84–6
Plato and Platonism 33, 37, 45 n., 57, 130, 153, 181
Porges, Moses 66 n.
Portaleone, Abraham 61 n.
Pythagoras 162, 190–1

R

Rabbinowitz, Saul Pinhas 6–7
Rambam, *see* Maimonides
Ramban, *see* Nahmanides
Rapoport, Abraham 29, 67 n.
Rashi:
authority of 77–9, 180
Bible commentary of 148 n.
Joshua ben Joseph, deathbed apparition to 78
and Luria family 159
Mishnah and Sifra, knowledge of 68 n.
on Noahide laws 93
philosophy and astronomy, knowledge of 41 n., 79 n., 168
in Prague, legend of 26
Talmud commentary of 77–9, 120, 123, 131
Torah commentary of 33, 35, 77 n.
Razi, al-, Hebrew translation of 114
Reiner, Elhanan 8–9

Rivkes, Moses 93 n.
Rosh:
authority of *Digest* (*Piskei harosh*) 120–9, 131, 180
on Christianity, halakhic status of 96, 140
halakhic opinions of 96–7, 127–8, 140, 199–200
Oreḥot ḥayim, attributed to 116
philosophy, Jewish, opposition to 42 n.
on pride and humility 126
responsa of 80
Rossi, Azariah dei 30, 46 n., 115 n., 130, 176 n.
Rudolph II 21–2, 26–8, 47, 139–40

S
Sa'adiah Gaon 35
Salmasius, Claudius 67
Samson of Ostropol 92 n., 207
Samson of Sens 41 n., 42 n., 68 n.
Samuel ben Gabriel (letter-writer, 1619) 102
Samuel Halevi (liturgical poet) 216 n.
Sanguszko, Adam 187–8
Savery, Roelandt 87
Scaglia, Cardinal Desiderio 142 n., 151
Schick, Hanokh (Heller's in-law) 144
Schiff, Meir 111 n.
Schossburg, Gabriel ben Joshua 211, 212 n., 215 n.
Shabetai ben Meir Hakohen (the Shakh) 206, 216 n., 217
Shakh, the, *see* Shabetai ben Meir Hakohen
Shamash, Juspa, *see* Juspa, *shamash* of Worms
Shelah, the, *see* Horowitz, Isaiah
Sigismund III of Poland 214, 217 n.
Singer, Isaac Bashevis 13–15
Sirkes, Joel:
family of 102
and Horowitz, Isaiah 52
on non-Jewish bread 89 n.
on philosophy and kabbalah 53–4, 58, 191
as rabbinic activist 30 n.
on silence during prayer 207 n.
and the *Turim* 124
on wealth and the rabbinate 186
Slawis, Wolf (Heller's son-in-law) 144
Sofer (Schreiber), Moses (the Hatam Sofer) 195 n.
Solomon ben Hayim (letter-writer, 1619) 102
Solomon ben Judah Leibush of Lublin 53
Solomon Zalman ben Joel of Brest-Litovsk 25 n.
Spinoza, Baruch 11 n., 15, 44, 53, 110 n., 191
Spira, Elijah ben Benjamin Wolf 122 n., 125 n.
Spira, Nathan, the Elder 80
Spira, Nathan ben Solomon 55 n., 76, 92 n., 162–3, 187
Spira, Solomon ben Nathan 187
Spira-Wedeles, Simon 136 n.
Stralendorf, Peter Heinrich von 139–40, 143–5, 153–4

T
Taku, Moses 42 n.
Taz, the, *see* David ben Samuel
Teitsch, Bella bat Jacob (recipient of 1619 letter) 102
Tengnagel, Sebastian 28 n., 141
Teomim, Edel 102–4, 199 n.
Teomim, Moses Aaron, *see* Ashkenazi, Moses Aaron
Tiktiner, Rebecca 28
Treves, Naftali 55, 59
Tsevi, Shabetai 13–15, 42 n., 53, 56, 209

U
Uceda, Samuel di 89 n., 118 n., 120 n.
Ulma, Hayim (book-collector) 80 n.

V
Valdštejn, *see* Wallenstein
Van Vianen, Paulus 87

W
Wallenstein (Valdštejn), Adam von 137–8, 145 n., 152
Wallenstein, Albrecht von 112, 126, 151, 160
Wallerstein, *see* Fränklin family; Fränklin, Abraham; Fränklin , Lipmann; Fränklin, Moses
Wallerstein, Henele bat Abraham 103
Wallerstein, Jacob Koppel 103 n.
Wallerstein, Mirel 103, 199 n.
Wallerstein, Samuel ben Abraham 103
Weisels, Hene (Hanokh) 137, 139, 144
Werdenburg, Johann Baptista Verda von 139 n.
Władysław IV of Poland 11, 216–17

Y
Yehiel Mikhel the Scribe in Cracow 114
Yekels, Isaac 175
Yerushalmi, Yosef 13
Yudel (Jew in Głogów) 134

Z
Zacuto, Moses 84 n., 223
Zevi, Sabbatai, *see* Tsevi, Shabetai

Index of References to Yom-Tov Lipmann Heller

astronomy:
approbation for David Gans 90
in *Behinat olam* commentary 36
changes views on 168
and proof of God's existence 36–7, 160, 219
Ptolemaic and Brahian 160, 166–8
required by halakhah 90, 160
in sermon on lessening of moon 161–74
study of 5, 90, 167–8
teaches son Abraham 159–61
children and grandchildren 25, 103–4, 159–60, 187–8, 198–201, 223
defeats of, summary 4, 15
descendants:
Epstein, Nahman 57 n.
Hailperin, Israel vii, 8
Heller, Abraham 225
Heller, David and Samson 226
Kaunfer, Marcia Lapidus vii
Roth, Meshulam 57 n.
Zuckerman, Shemariah 173
education 5, 34–5, 121–2
astrology, study of 111 n.
astronomy, study of 5, 36, 90, 167–8
Bible, study of 35, 80
erudition and memorization 79–81
geometry and arithmetic, study of 5, 74–5, 167
grandfather (Moses Fränklin), study with 20
Hebrew grammar, study of 55, 120 n.
in *hevrot* 31 n., 69, 81
Jerusalem Talmud, study of 200
Jewish philosophy, study of 34, 45, 50
kabbalah, study of 34, 54–5
languages, knowledge of 67, 89, 167
at yeshiva of Jacob Günzburg 24, 31, 200
eulogy for 223
family fast and feast, annual 155, 193–4, 206
family 19–26, 35–6, 51–3, 101–4, 144–5, 155, 159–60, 192–201
adoption of grandchildren among 20, 201
birth of children 25
children's education and Torah study 55 n., 199–200
cousins 20, 22, 24 n., 82, 103, 199 n.
daughters 25, 103–4, 160, 187, 198–201; their marriages 103–4, 144, 160, 200
death and mourning 19, 198–9
father (Nathan Heller) 19, 195
father-in-law, *see Names Index*: Ashkenazi, Moses
grandfather; *see Names Index*: Fränklin, Moses
in-laws 25–6, 52–3, 103, 144, 159, 182, 190–1, 199 n., 200, 203
marriages arranged 7, 103, 159, 182
in *Megilat eivah* 192–201
mother 19, 195
servant 197
strategic dispersal of children 201
and synagogue 25
visits among 160
weddings of 104, 159–60, 188, 200–1
wife (Rachel Munk) 5, 23–5, 145, 160, 200–1, 223
gravestone 1, 222–3
halakhic opinions:
agunah 31 n., 180 n., 220
apostates, return to Judaism 218
astronomy, study of 90, 160
Barukh she'amar 60 n.
bed, positioning of 91 n., 162 n.
blessing on 'Great Sea' 128
blessing on Torah study 127 n., 128
chicken, eating after cheese 60–1
Christian trinitarianism 96–7, 127, 139
copyright 80
custom, authority of 133–4, 180–1
debtors' prison 5
equinox, announcement of 180 n.
eucharist in houses owned by Jews 96–7
hand-washing, disposing of water 60
havdalah spices, myrtle in 60
hospitality and charity 182–3
jurisdiction of Prague court 134
kabbalah, public teaching of 162, 189–91
Kaddish in Aramaic 60 n.
kashering meat, *see* sabbath laws: salting meat
Kedushah said out loud 60 n.
maggoty food: eating 196; selling 88

magic, permissibility of 57
mezuzah, bedroom 128
miracles, thanksgiving for 115
non-Jewish books, reading 89–91
non-Jewish bread 88, 180
non-Jewish wine 87
non-Jews, teaching ethics to 95
prayers, adding to set praises 62
rabbinical office, purchase of 183–7
sabbath laws: disposal of infant faeces 196; salting meat for honoured guests 9, 182–3; weaving 79
salted fish, *kashrut* of 88
salting meat (kashering) 177
sea animals, categories of 165
Shema, how to read 60 n.
stincus marinus, *kashrut* of 164–6
synagogue, twelve windows in 60
table manners 128
taxation of Nikolsburg wine 86–7
tefillin on *ḥol hamo'ed* 61 n.
thanksgiving blessing on miracles 111
Torah reading, saying with *ḥazan* 60 n.
Torah scrolls, ink for 60
turkey, *kashrut* of vii
in historiography, modern Jewish 5–6, 8, 13
interpretation by, *see Subject Index*: biblical characters and events; biblical verses; Mishnah passages; talmudic passages
as kabbalist 54–62
letters:
to Aunt Edel (1619) 103–4, 199 n.
to Chęciny Jewish community (1651) 221–2
to Cracow publisher (1651) 12–13, 80, 209, 212
to Frankfurt Jewish community (1628) 10, 132–5, 219
to Głogów Jewish community (1627) 134
to Kremenets, Lutsk, and Ostroh (1641) 186–7
to Oppenheim, Simeon Wolf (1616) 82

LIFE:
summary 2–4
1578–1617:
born 19
orphan raised by grandfather 20
at yeshiva of Jacob Günzburg 24, 31, 200
moves to Prague 27
marriage to Rachel Munk 23–4
member of Pinkas Shul 7, 25
children born 25
serves on Prague rabbinical court 25–6, 121
buys apartment 35–6
writes commentary to *Beḥinat olam*, 1598 36–8
meets the Maharal 30–1
writes *Tsurat beit hamikdash*, 1602 61, 81
studies kabbalah 54
studies with Joseph ben Isaac 45
teaches children 55 n., 120
studies in *ḥevrah Mishnayot* 31 n., 69, 81
writes *Tosafot yom tov* 66
Nikolsburg wine tax case (1616) 83–7
completes *Tosafot yom tov* 97
1618–31:
war begins 101
runs private yeshiva 74, 102, 119–20, 124, 200
writes *Ma'adanei melekh* on *Nezikin* 121
daughters' marriages 103–4, 144, 160, 200
Battle of White Mountain (1620) 12, 106–9
rabbi of Nikolsburg (1624) 87, 113
rabbi of Vienna 113–16, 149, 163–4, 227 no. 26
survives plague (1625) 113–16
makes innovation in Vienna liturgy 116
chief rabbi of Prague (1627–9) 19, 117–35, 149
writes second volume of *Ma'adanei melekh* 19, 122
intervenes in Frankfurt communal dispute 10, 132–5
controversy over tax distribution in Prague 10, 138–9
arrested (1629) 136–8
imprisoned in Vienna 11, 139–45, 189, 196
tried by imperial commission 141–3
deposed from Prague rabbinate 144–5, 189
interview with Vienna nobleman 149–50, 202–4
returns to Prague; falls ill 145, 196
institutes family fast-day 155
pays fine 145, 196
permitted to enter rabbinate in Germany 175
1631–54:
leaves Prague 159
son Abraham's marriage in Lublin 159
teaches Abraham astronomy 159–60
preaches in Brest-Litovsk 160, 175
rabbi in Nemirov 67 n., 174–8, 205–7
rabbi in Ludmir 31 n., 60, 178–89
studies with his sons 200–1
bereaved in plague (1639) 198–9
ban on purchase of rabbinical office (1640) 8–9, 183–7
controversy with Josel of Lokacze 185–7
contract renewed in Ludmir 187
denounced in Ludmir 187

life, 1631–54 (*cont.*):
adopts two granddaughters 13, 201
rosh yeshiva in Cracow (autumn 1643) 67 n., 192 n.
appointed chief rabbi of Cracow (1644) 192
institutes family feast 193
Megilat eivah 195, 199
permits kabbalistic publication 15, 189–91
and 1648 massacres 10–15, 185 n., 205–24
institutes blessing for those who are silent 207–9
and 20 Sivan fast-day 206
contrasts 1648 with 1620: 12, 212, 216
decisions, sermons, and letters (1648–54) 218, 220–2
final sickness and death (1654) 9, 222–3

liturgical innovations 115–16, 207–9
and the Maharal 30–1, 68–9, 171–2, 208–9
early influence of the Maharal 20 n.
on the lessening of the moon 171–2
on miracles 110–11
and Mishnah study 68–9
on non-Jewish wine 87
on non-Jews 93–4
on the rabbinate, qualifications of 188
and rabbinic activism 119–21
as rabbinic aristocrats 9
on the self 171–2
on the *Shulḥan arukh* and halakhic codes 123–5
on silence during prayer 208–9
on talmudic interpretation 127
names of 19, 25, 67, 222–3
reading and personal library 79–81
reputation and legends about 5, 57, 66–7, 191, 208, 223
sermons, *see* writings and sermons
social status 7–9, 19–20, 23–6, 102–4, 131–2, 138, 181–3, 201–4
views:
on *agadah*, literal truth of 162–4, 166–7
on angels 37, 57–9
on anger 7, 198
on animals and seas, new 13, 164–6
on Ashkenazi Jews, origins of 180
on astrology 36–7, 111, 155
on astronomy 36–7, 159–74
on Bible, letter-perfection of 72
on body, human 36
on Catholic Church 151
on causation 10, 109–12, 146–52, 171–2, 185 n., 203, 207 n.
on childhood, age, and middle age 36, 121, 195
on Chmielnitsky massacres, *see separate sub-entry below*: on Gezeirot Tah Vetat
on Christianity and Trinitarianism 91, 96–7, 139–40, 142, 147–55, 187, 213
on comets, nature of 168
on Cordovero, Moses 54–5, 162
on Cossacks and Tatars 185 n., 211–13, 216
on Cracow 176, 192
on Creation 64, 160–8
on Crusader massacres of 1096: 12, 206, 209, 213
on Czech Protestants and Frederick of Bohemia 108–9
on death 19, 172, 199
on Defenestration of Prague 107–9
on demons 37–8
on *devekut* and mystical kiss 56
on disease 37–8
on dogma 36, 64
on dreams 38, 150, 208
on 'East' and 'West' 66, 176–8
on education 64–5, 74–5, 90, 119–20, 124, 160, 169–71, 199–201
on factionalism (*mahloket*) 10, 14–15, 97–8, 132–5, 148, 151–2, 161, 173–4, 216–18, 222
on family: his immediate 199–201; his in-laws and extended family 52, 82, 103, 203 n.
on family and Torah study 199–201
on his father (Nathan Heller) 19, 195
on food 37, 88, 196
on free will 37, 160, 210
on freedom of interpretation 76–7, 171
on geometry and Euclid 5, 36, 90–1
on Gezeirot Tah Vetat 10–13, 185 n., 205–21
on ghosts 57 n.
on *gilgul* 37, 58–9, 75–6, 162, 190–1
on God, absence of 215
on God, attributes of 56, 62, 64, 219–20
on God and language 64, 219
on God, name of 76, 219
on God, proofs of the existence of 36–7, 160, 219
on grammar, study of 120–1, 169
on Habsburg monarchs 10, 107–9, 133–5, 217
on halakhic authority 122–9, 132–5, 178–81
on halakhic questions, *see separate entry*
on Hanukah and Purim 155
on hasid (the pious man) 126
on heat, measurement of 167
on himself 19, 115, 174, 181, 193–7, 201–4
on historical change 12–13, 37, 164–70, 206, 212, 218

on history, lessons of 152, 218
on honour 9, 182–3, 201–4, 221
on Horowitz, Isaiah 52
on individual self 57–9, 171–2
on Israel, Land of 52 n., 176
on Isserles, Moses 74, 179–80
on kabbalah 5–6, 37, 54–65, 75–6, 162–3, 189–91
on language 64, 76
on Luria, Isaac 55, 162, 190
on magic 56–9, 155
on the Maharal 30–1, 69, 87, 94–5, 171, 188, 208–9
on Maimonides 46, 64, 74, 95, 123, 163–4, 168
on mathematics 91
on messianism 37, 95, 209–10
on miracles 109–16, 155, 189
on monarchy 10–11, 153, 216–18
on moon, creation of 161–74
on names and naming 19, 71, 223
on New Astronomy 160, 166–9
on non-Jews 37, 92–5, 107–9, 139–40, 153–5, 170 n., 202–3, 209–18
on order and chaos 36–7, 160, 211, 219
on peace and war 97–8, 105–6, 210
on *peshat* 5, 61–2, 70–9, 128–9, 162–3
on philosophy 34–8, 45–7, 50–2, 55, 62–5, 89–95, 109–12, 163–4
on *pilpul* 5, 73–4, 120
on plague 115, 220
on political theory 10–11, 152–3, 215–18
on Prague 27, 134–5
on prayer 5, 108, 111–12, 147, 206–9
on predestination and divine foreknowledge 37, 210
on pride and humility 98, 126, 160, 211
on progress 46–7, 165–70
on providence 110–12, 150–1
on rabbinate 119–21, 134, 145, 148, 181, 188, 201–4
on Rashi 77–9, 123 n.
on rebellion 108–9, 216–17
on repentance 190–1, 210, 221
on revelation 20
on reward and punishment 108, 110–12, 126, 146–8, 212, 215, 219
on the Rosh 120, 123–9, 180
on Satan 37, 71
on sexuality 36 n., 37–8, 129
on *shtadlanim* 143, 147, 152
on *Shulḥan arukh* and halakhic codes 5, 9, 122–6, 179–80
on silence 63–4, 195–8, 207–9
on sin 37, 71, 120 n., 171–2, 190–1
on 1648 massacres, *see separate sub-entry above*: on Gezeirot Tah Vetat
on social classes, categories of 9, 182–3, 213
on soul, origin of 37, 57–9, 63
on spheres, celestial, nature of 36, 160, 166–8
on suffering, acceptance of 145, 161, 171–4, 207
on Talmud 76–7, 123–4, 139, 142
on tears and crying 198
on *teshuvah*, *see* repentance
on thanksgiving 111, 114–16, 140, 155, 192–3
on Thirty Years War 12, 105–9, 114–16, 133–4, 148, 202
on thoughts, secret 57–9
on time and change 13, 37–8, 170
on toleration of Judaism 142
on Torah: authorship of 72–3; infinite meanings of 77 n.; Torah and peace 97–8, 210; Torah and 'seven sciences' 64–5
on Tosafot 77–9
on Ukraine 176–8
on wealth 9, 36, 38, 111–12, 182–3
on White Mountain, Battle of 12, 106–9, 147, 209, 212
on women 36, 71
on Zohar 60–2
writings and sermons:
Beḥinat olam, commentary on 20, 34–8, 58, 93 n., 111 n., 122, 168, 170, 189, 219 n.
epitaph of daughters Reyzel and Nisel 198–9
Ibn Ezra, commentary on 56 n., 72–3, 77 n., 110, 111 n., 120 n.
Kelalei hora'at isur veheter 181
Leket shoshanim 55–6, 63–4, 120, 169, 219
letters, *see separate entry*
Ma'adanei melekh: censorship of 122 n., 142–4; on Christianity 96–7, 139–40; as double commentary 121, 124–5, 179; first volume (1619) 88–9, 121, 200; halakhic opinions in 127–9; in Heller's trial 122 n., 139–44; introduction to 19, 121–6, 195; on kabbalah 57–65; on peace 105–6; proof-readers of (Liva and Abraham Heller) 200; scientific questions in 164–6, 168; second volume (1628) 122, 179; on theology 57–9, 62–5, 126, 219; title 74 n., 122 n.; title page (1628) 131–2, 199 n.; work left unfinished 179
Malbushei yom tov 127, 176
marginalia 55–6, 67 n., 80–1, 222–3

writings and sermons (*cont.*):
Megilat eivah: events in 54–5, 119–20, 136–61, 175, 183–9, 192–204; explanatory frameworks in 146–51, 188, 203; family in 199–201; genre and structure of 152, 182, 189, 193–7, 199, 203–4; and Heller family feast and fast 155, 192–4, 199, 206 n.; non-Jews in 146–55, 201–4; omissions in 151, 195–7; as portrayal of self 195–7, 199, 201–4; second section (story of Samuel Heller) 146 n.; title 136, 152, 206 n.; Yiddish version of 140 n., 148, 161 n., 187–8, 196–7, 200 n., 202
Oreḥot ḥayim, Yiddish translation of 116, 121
Parashat haḥodesh (on calendrical astronomy) 72 n., 159–60
poem on Battle of White Mountain 107–8, 147, 219
poem on Defenestration of Prague 108–9
poems on 1648 massacres (1651) 209–16, 220; Cossacks and Tatars, portrayal of 211–13, 216; explanations of events in 215–17; horrors and ironies in 211–12; *Petaḥ teshuvah*, based on 211; suffering of non-Jews ignored 12, 212–14
responsa 31 n., 86–7, 89 n., 180, 199 n., 220, 222 n.
salting meat, broadsheet on 121, 177
Sefer naftali, notes on 55–6
sermons 113, 160, 231 no. 70; in Brest-Litovsk (1631) 160–1; farewell sermon (Prague, 1631) 159; on *Ḥayei sarah* (Vienna, 1625) 113–16, 155, 219; at installation ceremony (Cracow, 1644) 192; on 'lessening of the moon' 161–74; on Ten Plagues 221
She'elat gitin 19, 177
Torat ha'asham (on laws of *kashrut*) 72 n., 167, 178–83
Tosafot yom tov 66–82, 89–95, 97–8, 111–12, 122, 168; and artefacts in the Mishnah 79, 169, 176; and Bertinoro 78–80; closing poem of 199 n.; concluding comment of 97–8; Euclid in 74–5, 90; geography in 75, 176 n.; and *ḥevrot* 69, 81; introduction of 30; Josephus in 74; kabbalah in 75–6; and Maimonides 74, 76–7; non-Jews in 74–5, 89–95; and *peshat* 70–9; and *pilpul* 74; popularity of 66–7, 122; proof-reader (Moses Heller) 200; questions unanswered in 67; quotations of oral teachings in 81; and Rashi and Tosafot 77–9; and revival of Mishnah study 67–9; and science 74–5, 90, 168; second edition 67, 200, 201 n.; as supercommentary 66, 74, 80; textual emendation in 66, 71–2; and textual omnisignificance 71; title 66; title page 131 n., 199 n.
Tsurat beit hamikdash (*Tsurat habayit*) 27, 61, 81, 121
Tuv ta'am (supercommentary on Bahya ben Asher) 54–5, 122

Index of Subjects

A

agadah:
allegorical or literal interpretation of 30–3, 53, 74, 162–4
commentaries on 28
creative historiography in 165
and halakhah 61 n., 77
and kabbalah 59, 162–3
and *peshat* 77
and science 163–8
see also biblical characters and events; talmudic passages, interpreted and applied
alchemy 27, 34, 167
Alexander the Great, letter of 170
allegory 31–3, 126, 163–4
Altneushul 29–30, 119
Amsterdam 53, 211, 216
Ancona 41
angels 37, 57–9, 107
see also demons; *magidim*
antisemitism, *see* Jews, as perceived by non-Jews; Jews, persecution of
art 36, 87, 126, 196
astrology 36, 45 n., 110–11, 114, 155, 166
astronomy:
Aristotelian 36, 40, 44, 159–60, 166
comets, nature of 168
geocentrism and heliocentrism 167
halakhic status of 90, 160
and midrash 166, 174
moon, origin of 166
new astronomy of 16th–17th cc. 44, 160, 166–9
progress in 46
spheres, nature of 36, 160, 164
study by Ashkenazi Jews 5, 33, 41, 42 n., 44, 46 n., 79 n., 159–74
at University of Cracow 160 n.
see also astrology; *Heller Index*: astronomy
Austria, Inner 143, 151
autobiographies and memoirs, Jewish 193–7
see also Heller Index: writings and sermons: *Megilat eivah*
autonomy, Jewish, see *kehilah*

B

Baptists (Anabaptists), Jewish views of 155 n.
Bar (town in Ukraine) 205
Bashraybung fun ashkenaz un polak 178
Begidat hazeman (poem) 170 n.
Beḥinat olam, *see Heller Index under* writings and sermons
beit din (*bes din*), *see* rabbis: courts
Berdichev, Society of Woodchoppers for the Study of Mishnah 69
Beresteczko (Berestechko) 186
Bible:
commentaries on 28, 35, 54–5, 67, 72–3, 76, 77 n., 80, 162–4
infinite meanings of 77 n., 127
kabbalistic interpretation of 54–5, 61, 76
literal and allegorical interpretation of 7, 41, 163–4
Masoretic text of 41, 72, 171
morality of biblical heroes 41
Mosaic authorship of the Torah 72–3
Rashi's Torah commentary, canonization of 77 n.
'seventy faces of Torah' 76
study of 33, 35, 39, 54, 80, 128
textual variants of 72
biblical characters and events, interpretations of:
Abraham, Isaac, and Jacob 56 n.
Adam 31, 172
Balaam 94 n.
creation of firmament 173
creation of moon and sun 161–74
Cyrus, king of Persia 217 n.
David and the book of Psalms 174
Edom and Ishmael 94
Eliezer (servant of Abraham) 114–15
Elijah the Prophet 220
Esther 163
Eve 71
Flood 210 n.
Haman 140 n.
Hezekiah, king of Judah 89
Jacob 174
Jacob and Esau 37 n., 154 n., 143
Jacob's ladder 33, 122
Jehosaphat, king of Judah 73

biblical characters and events (*cont.*):
Job 173, 197, 219
Joseph and his brothers 46, 49
Joshua in Gibeon 110
Laban 94 n.
Lamentations 136, 197, 220
Lot 94 n.
Mordechai 143
Pharaoh 94 n., 110
Purim 106, 155
Ruth 94 n.
slavery in Egypt 214
Sodom, destruction of 165
Song of Songs 56, 61 n., 114
Temple, Ezekiel's vision of the rebuilt 61
Ten Plagues 110, 113 n., 221
Tower of Babel 56
wilderness, Israelites in 219
biblical verses, interpretations of:
Gen. 1: 27, 'The image of God' 95
Gen. 36: 31, 'These are the kings of Edom' 73
Exod. 2: 22, 'Stranger in a strange land' 223
Lev. 16: 3, 'With this shall Aaron come' 206 n., 209 n.
Lev. 26: 6, 'I will make peace in the land' 132
Num. 19: 2, 'This is the law of the Torah' 150
Deut. 4: 4, 'You who cleave to the Lord' 56
Deut. 31: 17 'God is not in my midst' 215
Isa. 32: 17, 'Work of righteousness shall be peace' 105–6
Isa. 41: 7, 'Say of the cleaving, it is good' 133
Isa. 61: 1, 'to bring good tidings to the humble' 126
Isa. 65: 1, 'I called, here I am' 49
Jer. 14: 19, 'But behold there was terror' 107
Jer. 17: 9–10, 'The heart . . . who can know it?' 58
Ps. 27: 4, 'to see the beauty of the LORD' 126
Ps. 29: 11, 'God has granted strength to his people' 97–8
Ps. 89: 20, 'You spoke in vision to your pious ones' 126
Ps. 95: 6, 'Today, if you listen to His voice' 210
Prov. 2: 16–19, the adulterous woman 53
Prov. 6: 7, 'The ant has no chief' 72
Prov. 8: 8, 'All the words are in righteousness' 64, 76 n.
Prov. 9: 1, 'She has hewn her seven pillars' 65
Prov. 12: 16, 'A prudent man concealeth shame' 195, 197
Prov. 29: 3, 'Keeps company with harlots' 39
Prov. 31: 10, 'Woman of valour' 114
Lam. 3: 10, 'a bear in wait' 220
Eccles. 2: 13, 'The advantage of light over darkness' 64
2 Chron. 6: 30, 'You alone have known the heart' 58
Blois 206
'Book of Creation', see *Sefer yetsirah*
books, *see* manuscripts; printing
bread, non-Jewish 88–9, 180
Brest-Litovsk (Brest, Brisk, Brzesć) 44, 48, 160, 169, 201

C

captives, redemption of 102, 144
Catholic Church:
clergy of, violence against 105, 212
and conversion of the Jews 142–3, 150–1, 153
episcopal activism in 30 n.
Hebraists, Christian 28 n., 141–2, 149 n.
Jesuits 34 n., 85 n., 149, 202
and loans at interest, Jewish 21
in Ludmir 187
and miracles 107, 110
Pascal on 127
Prague, archiepiscopal synod of 24 n., 48 n., 87 n., 95 n.
Protestantism, suppression of 142–3, 151, 159 n.
Talmud, suppression of 125, 139–43, 150–1
Trent, Council of 184 n.
see also Christianity, Jewish views of
causation:
of catastrophes and changes 37
early modern theories of 10–11, 109–12, 146
of erotic dreams 38
the First Cause 33, 36
of Heller's arrest and release 138, 146–51, 187–8, 203
of magnetism 40
of messianic deliverance 210
of plague 114
of sin and suffering 171–2
of 1648 massacres 10–11, 207 n., 213–18, 221
see also free will
charity 5, 24, 102, 155, 182, 222 n.
Chęciny 221–2
Chełm 188
children 20, 25, 36, 101–4, 159–60, 198–201, 211
Chmielnitsky massacres, *see* Gezeirot Tah Vetat
Christianity, Jewish views of 94–8, 139–40, 142, 151, 155 n., 187, 213–15
see also non-Jews, Jewish attitudes towards

circumcision 43, 102
community, Jewish, see *kehilah*
confraternity, see *ḥevrah*
Cossacks 178, 185 n., 205, 211–17
Council of Four Lands (Va'ad Arba Aratsot) 10, 14, 132, 134, 177, 183–4, 188, 206, 209 n., 222
court Jews, see *shtadlanim*; *Names Index*: Bassevi, Jacob; Meisel, Mordechai
court, rabbinical (*beit din*), *see* rabbis: courts
Cracow, Jewish (Kazimierz):
  authority over other Polish communities 222
  cemetery of, old Jewish 1, 222
  educational rules of 114 n.
  everyday life in 114
  Heller in 118 n., 192–3, 206–23
  Heller's view of 176, 192
  installation of rabbi in 192
  Isaac Yekels, synagogue of 175–6
  Joshua ben Joseph, death of 78
  kehilah, rules of 5 n., 114 n., 117 n.
  legends of 57 n.
  mourning, annual day of 206 n. 6
  philosophy, study of Jewish 39
  plague (1623) 47, 114
  plague (1652) 221
  preacher of, *see Names Index*: Berakhyah Berakh ben Isaac
  sack (1655) 222
  silence during prayer 207–9
  1648–50, events during 207–9, 211–18
  synagogues 175–6, 207–9
  see also Names Index: Isserles, Moses
Creation, *see* theology and dogma
Crusades and 1096 Rhineland massacres 12, 206, 209
custom (*minhag*), conceptions of 85, 88–9, 125, 130–1, 180–1

D

David, Star of 87, 90
deliverance narratives 106–9, 193–7
  see also Heller Index: writings: *Megilat eivah*
demons 37–8, 57
dietary laws, see *kashrut*
'Duties of the Heart', *see Names Index*: Bahya ibn Pakuda
dwarf on the shoulders of a giant 46–7, 169

E

education, Jewish (Torah study) 4–8, 30–6, 39–45, 52–4, 67–9, 120–1, 199–201
  astronomy, study of 5, 33–4, 36, 90, 159–60, 167–8
  Bible, study of 33, 35, 39, 54, 80, 128
  Bible–Mishnah–Talmud sequence 33, 35, 121
  Cracow educational rules 114 n.
  geography, study of 75, 90 n., 128, 176
  geometry and arithmetic, study of 5, 28, 74–5, 167
  halakhah, study of 33, 120, 124
  Hebrew grammar, study of 28, 33–4, 55, 120–1, 169
  for the Heller children 55 n., 199–201
  in *ḥevrot* 31 n., 69, 81
  kabbalah, study of 33–4, 37, 54–5, 59
  memorization in 69, 79–81
  Mishnah, study of 33, 67–9, 81
  non-Jewish books, study of 43–5, 89–91
  non-Jews, teaching Torah to 95
  philosophy, study of 5–8, 15, 28 n., 39–45, 52–4, 64–5, 91
  pilpul 5–6, 14, 33, 73–4, 120
  reform of, 16th–17th cc. 15, 30–5, 40–1, 43, 69, 81, 114 n., 119–21
  and 'seven sciences' 28 n., 33–4, 48–9, 64–5
  and social class 8–9, 125, 191
  Talmud, study of 33–5, 43 n., 67–8, 74, 119–20, 124–5, 200
  yeshivas: of Cracow 67 n., 192 n.; of Günzburg, Jacob 24, 31, 200; of Heller (*c.*1620) 74, 102, 119–20, 124, 200; *kloyz* of the Maharal 29, 31; of Prague 136
Enlightenment, *see* Haskalah
everyday life:
  badge, Jewish 87
  bandits, robbers, and thieves 22, 37, 141, 182 n., 194
  bath-houses 170 n.
  bread and bakeries 88–9
  circumcision 102
  clothing and textiles 24–5, 36, 79, 87, 174
  in Cracow (1623) 114
  dancing 23
  debtors' prison 5, 140 n.
  disease 37, 145
  doctors 23, 28, 39, 53–4, 114, 159, 164
  dreams 38, 150, 208
  eyeglasses and astrolabes 169
  fears, typical early modern Jewish 37–8, 104–6, 142–4, 218
  food 88–9, 174
  games 36
  gifts and bribes 25, 82, 140, 143–5, 147, 197
  gravestones and epitaphs 1, 24, 198–9, 222
  hospitality 182–3
  housing 26–7, 35–6, 136–7, 145, 176

everyday life (*cont.*):
inns 83 n., 88, 96–7, 144
lending and debt 5, 22–3, 118 n., 175 n., 185–6
medicine and remedies 57 n., 114, 164
Megilat eivah depicts 195–7, 199
melancholy and tears 198
mills 36
music 23, 117, 207 n.
naming 19, 23, 25, 67, 90–1, 118, 166, 195, 201, 223
oral culture 81, 194 n., 208
in Poland and Ukraine (*c.*1630) 175–8
in Prague and Vienna (1619) 101–4
processions 117
reading 79–81, 89–91
servants 5, 48, 197
sin 4–5, 47–8, 83–4, 90, 114, 132–3, 183, 190–1, 197, 221
streets 20, 26–7, 113
technological change 169
visions, deathbed 78
weather 35–7
weddings 23–4
wine 85–6; monopoly 84–5
see also rich and poor
evil and suffering:
causation of 37–8, 146–51, 171–2, 187–8, 203, 213–17, 221
literary responses to 102–3, 114–16, 172–4, 198–9, 209–16
political responses to 133, 152–3, 217–18
ritual and halakhic responses to 102, 115–16, 155, 206–9, 220–3
spiritual responses to 38, 114, 141, 172–4, 197–8, 219–20
'Examination of the World', *see Heller Index*: writings: *Beḥinat olam*
excommunication, see *ḥerem*

F

family, *see* children; women; *Heller Index*: family
fast instituted by Heller 154
Fettmilch uprising 105, 132
Frankfurt am Main, Jews of:
controversy over *kehilah* governance 10, 129, 132–5, 138, 185, 219
and Fettmilch uprising 105, 132
Günzburg controversy 20
Hayim ben Isaac Hakohen 117 n.
Heller, Abraham 201 n.
rabbinic conference (1603) 24 n., 134, 141 n.
rabbis, contract of 117–19
free will 37, 52, 127, 160, 210
Freiburg 40 n.
Friedberg 24 n., 84 n., 117 n., 130

G

Gehinnom, *see* heaven and hell
geometry 5, 36, 74–5
Germany and Habsburg empire, Jews of:
autobiographies and memoirs of 193–7
centralization and local autonomy of 129–35
conversion offensive against 142–3, 150–1, 153
court Jews and *shtadlanim* 9–11, 21–2, 84–5, 131, 134, 138–9, 143–7, 152–4
expulsions of 21, 104–5
halakhic traditions of 88–9, 124–6, 131, 179–80
historiography of 4–15, 21 n.
pietism of 24, 51, 84 n., 116, 207 n.
and Poland, Jews of 5–6, 132–5, 177–8, 184, 188
political successes of 21–2, 27, 105–8, 112–13, 144, 152–3
rabbinic conferences 24 n., 84 n., 134
rich and poor 85–6, 129–35, 182 n.
Rudolph II 21, 26–8, 47, 139–40
Shulḥan arukh, reception of 5, 8, 15, 122–6
and Talmud censorship 125, 139–43, 150–1
taxation of 6, 10, 83–7, 134, 138–9, 148
urban rebellions and riots 47, 104–9
views of Manasseh ben Israel on 21
views of Moses Isserles on 83 n., 148 n.
views of Solomon Luria on 83 n.
Wallerstein 19–23, 89, 141, 177, 200
see also Frankfurt am Main; Prague; Vienna; *Names Index*: Ferdinand II
Germany and Habsburg empire, officials of:
Hofpropos (imperial court bailiff) 140
imperial commission 141–2
imperial judge (Prague) 136–7
imperial vice-chancellor 136–40, 143–4
Oberstburggraf (Bohemian viceroy) 137–8, 145 n., 149, 152, 201–2
Reichshofrat 22
Gezeirot Tah Vetat (massacres of 1648) 10–15, 205–22
and *agunot*, releasing 220
amnesty (1650) 218
and blessing for those who are silent during prayer 207–9
causes and explanations of 10–11, 146, 207 n., 213–18, 221
chronicles of, 17th-c. 4–5, 211–12, 214–18
gezeirah, concept of 111, 150–1

historiography of, modern 10–15, 146, 205 n., 213–14
Jewish self-defence in 212–13
liturgical poetry on 209–16, 220
and messianism 10, 14–15, 209–12, 218, 220
and monarchism 216–18
Nemirov, massacre of 175, 205–8
plague (1652) 221
Poles and Ukrainians, massacre and torture of 12, 212, 214
refugees from 178
repentance and blame after 190–1, 207, 214–15, 221
and 1655–6 massacres 218, 222
Tulczyn, massacre of 205, 212 n.
and 20 Sivan fast-day 206
Władisław IV, death of 216–17
see also Heller Index: writings: poems on 1648 massacres

ghosts and apparitions 57 n., 78, 208
gilgul (transmigration of souls) 37, 58–9, 69 n., 75–6, 162–3, 190–1
Głogów (Glogau) 134
golem 28–9, 35, 57
Greek alphabet and language 41 n., 66–7
'Guide of the Perplexed' (*Moreh nevukhim*), *see Names Index*: Maimonides: writings
Gzeire lid, *see Names Index*: Mazel, Joseph ben Eleazar

H

Habsburg empire, *see* Germany and Habsburg empire
halakhah:
and *agadah* 61 n., 77
Ashkenazi and Sefardi traditions of 125–6, 178–81
and authority of rabbis 129–31
and class difference 5, 83–7, 125, 182–3
codification of, and the *Shulḥan arukh* 122–9, 179–81
custom (*minhag*), conceptions of 85, 88–9, 125, 130–1, 180–1
German and Polish traditions of 125, 131, 179–80
historical argument in 169–70
Isserles, Moses, authority of 123–6, 179–81, 185–6, 189
and Jewish difference 83–91
and kabbalah 60–2
'the law follows the most recent authority' 123–6
Luria, Solomon, school of 122–9, 180
in messianic age 53, 170 n.
mitsvot, purpose of 40
Prague tradition of 122 n., 125 n., 179–80
the Rosh, authority of 123–5, 127–9
and science 42–3, 90–1, 164–6
and talmudic interpretation 77–9, 122–9
see also rabbis: courts; *Heller Index*: halakhic opinions

Hanau 40 n.
Hanukah, festival of 155
Hasidei Ashkenaz 30 n., 59 n., 163
hasidism 92
Haskalah (Jewish Enlightenment) 1, 5, 14, 77 n., 91–2, 194
heaven and hell 92–3, 139
Hebrew grammar 28, 33–4, 55, 76, 120–1, 169
Hebrew language and alphabet 33–4, 89, 102, 120–1, 170 n., 176
Hebrew poetry:
liturgical 106–9, 114, 117 n., 209–16, 220
non-liturgical 34, 36–8, 85–6, 170 n., 194 n., 199, 223
Hebrew, mishnaic 76
ḥerem 54, 84 n., 105, 118–19, 132–5, 139, 183–5
ḥevrah, *ḥevrot* 4, 30, 69, 81
historiography, modern Jewish 4–15
foundation stories in 14–15
of Gezeirot Tah Vetat 10–15
by Graetz, Heinrich, and S. P. Rabbinowitz 5–7, 14
by Hailperin, Israel vii, 8
by Katz, Jacob 6–7, 10–11
lachrymosity in 11–13
of Prague Jews 27 n.
rabbinic biography in 1–2
and *Satan in Goray* 13–15
social history in 8–10
stages of 4
Zionist 10–11

historiography, traditional Jewish:
and *agadah*, literal interpretation of 30, 53, 74, 77, 162–4
and ahistoricism 13, 34, 177
foundation myths in 14, 170, 180–1
of Gezeirot Tah Vetat 4–5, 12, 206, 211–17
Jewish and non-Jewish history in 92
messianism, 17th-c. debate on 15, 53, 170 n., 209–10
miraculous deliverance in 107–8, 194 n.
monarchism in 153 n., 216–17
periodization and 14, 21, 170, 206
of Prague Jews (1618–20) 101, 106–9

historiography, traditional Jewish (*cont.*):
and progress 46, 166–70
of rabbinic literature 123–4, 170
realism of 146–53
of 1655–6 massacres 218
see also causation; *Names Index*: Gans, David
honour (*kavod*) 7, 9, 24, 117–18, 143–4, 181–3, 192, 203–4, 221
and explanation of events 149–50, 203
Heller on 182–3, 221
Ḥovot halevavot, *see Names Index*: Bahya ibn Pakuda

I
individual, the:
and autobiography 193–7
dimensions of 201–4
discovery of 1, 193
and ghosts 57 n.
and kabbalah 58–9
non-Jews as 154–5
and origin of soul 37, 58, 63
secret thoughts of 57–9
spiritual annihilation of 171–2
see also *gilgul*
interpretation and *peshat* 5, 14, 60–2, 70–9, 128–9, 162–3, 209 n.
see also *agadah*; Bible: literal and allegorical interpretation; biblical characters and events; biblical verses; Mishnah: interpretation of; Mishnah passages; talmudic passages
Israel, land of 43, 52–3, 66, 67 n., 68 n., 69 n., 176, 193 n.
Italy, Jews of 22, 27, 30, 39 n., 91 n.

J
Jarosław 183, 185
Jerusalem 176 n.
Jews, as perceived by non-Jews 92, 139, 202–3
by anonymous nobleman in Vienna 202–3
by Comenius, John 204 n.
in Cracow plague (1623) 47
in Gezeirot Tah Vetat 214
by Moryson, Fynes 23, 26–8, 88, 102 n., 184, 203
by Savery, Roelandt 87
Jews, persecution of:
conversion offensive, Habsburg 142–3, 150–1, 153
eras of 21
expulsion 21, 104–5, 108–9, 187–8, 218
and *gezeirot*, concept of 111, 150–1
ghettoization 22–3, 24 n., 26–7, 48 n., 87, 95 n., 113
imprisonment and kidnap 102, 135–6, 140, 151, 194, 196
Jewish badge 87
and lachrymosity in Jewish historiography 11–13
martyrdom 22, 175, 194, 206 n., 212–13
riot and urban violence 104–9, 132, 138, 187
torture 140–1, 211
see also Gezeirot Tah Vetat
Jews, socio-economic status of, *see* rich and poor

K
kabbalah 5–6, 8–9, 14, 28, 33–4, 51–65, 75–6, 162–3, 189–91
in Ashkenazi culture, medieval 59 n.
Cordovero as authority on 52–6, 162
doctrines: 'awakening' of God 56; 'clothing' of the rabbis 56; 'commandments serve God's needs' 63; *devekut* and mystical kiss 56; four worlds 56; *gilgul* 37, 58–9, 69 n., 75–6, 162–3, 190–1; infinite meanings of Torah 77 n.; *kavanot* in prayer 62; concerning non-Jews 92–3; rabbis, ancient, images of 75; 'returning light' 56; sabbatical cycles 45 n.; *sefirot* 56, 97, 162, 190; soul, origin of 37, 57–9, 63; 'sparks' and 'shells' 214–15
and ethics 51, 54, 56, 59
and halakhah 60–1, 127
and heresy 53
legends concerning kabbalists 56–8
lessening of the moon, interpretation of 162–3
Lurianic 52, 55, 189–91, 214–15
and midrash 59
and Mishnah 68–9, 75–6
opposition to popularization of 6, 8, 59–60, 162–3, 189–91
and philosophy 6, 53–4, 59, 63–5, 162, 191
in Prague 28
and prayer 62–3
radicalism in 53–4, 60
rise in 17th c. 54, 58–62, 162–3, 189–91
1648 massacres, interpretation of 214–15
and wine, non-Jewish 84 n.
see also Zohar; *Names Index*: Horowitz, Isaiah
Kamenets-Podolsk (Kamieniec) 212
kashrut:
of bread, non-Jewish 88–9, 180
and butcher, unreliable 222 n.
of chicken after cheese 60–1
of fish 83 n., 88
Heller's book on (*Torat ha'asham*) 176–83

Heller's study of 80
and inns, food in 83 n., 88
of maggoty food 88, 196
of milk, non-Jewish 84 n.
mockery of 88, 211
and salting meat 176–7
of *stincus marinus* 164–6
of turkey vii
of wine, non-Jewish 83–7
Kazimierz, *see* Cracow, Jewish
kavod (*koved*), *see* honour
kehilah, *kehilot*:
of Chęciny and Pińczów 222
constitutional theories of 85 n., 129–31, 181
of Cracow 5 n., 114 n., 117 n., 192, 206–8, 211
elections in 117, 129, 132, 145
of Frankfurt am Main 119, 129, 132–5
institutions of 4–5
jurisdiction of 132–5, 183–9, 222
kehilah, meaning of term 129
legislation of 5 n., 30, 48, 84 n., 107, 115–16, 184–8, 206–8, 227 no. 26
of Lokacze 185–7
of Ludmir (Volodymir) 185, 187–8
and monarchism 10–11, 21, 107–9, 133–5, 153, 216–18; rabbinic 130
of Nikolsburg 83–7
personnel of 8, 28, 57, 102, 114, 118, 192, 194
in Poland 175, 177, 183–9
political rules of thumb in 10, 129–35, 152–3, 188–9, 216–18
of Poznań 118 n., 134, 222 n.
privileges of 84–5, 113, 131, 134
and rabbinate 8, 30, 69, 117–21, 129–35, 183–9, 192
rich and poor in, *see separate entry*
social conflict in 7–9, 14–15, 20, 25, 83–7, 129, 132–5, 138–9, 144–5, 148, 152–3, 183–9, 216–18, 222
taxation in 83–7, 118–19, 134, 138–9, 145, 148
of Vienna 113, 116, 227 no. 26
of Żółkiew 208 n.
see also Council of Four Lands; *ḥerem*
Kolín 168 n.
Kraków, *see* Cracow
Kremenets (Kremianets, Krzeminiec) 183, 185
Kuzari, *see Names Index*: Halevi, Judah

L

Latin language 34, 89, 114, 167
law, Jewish, *see* halakhah
law, Roman 21–2, 73 n.
Leszno (Lissa) 222 n.
letters, Prague–Vienna (Nov. 1619) 24 n., 101–4, 164 n., 199 n.
Lissa, *see* Leszno
Lithuania, *see* Brest-Litovsk; Vilna
lobbying, see *shtadlanim*
Lokacze (Lokachi) 185–7
Lublin 40, 159–61, 205
Ludmir (Lodmir, Vladimir Volynski, Volodymir, Włodomierz Wolinsky) 178, 183, 185–9, 196, 205
Lutsk (Łuck) 183, 185–8, 205
Lvov (Lemberg, Lviv, Lwów) 20 n., 29, 199, 205

M

Maccabees, book of 89 n.
magic:
at court of Rudolph II 27
of divine names 56–7
dream question 150, 208
efficacy of 53
of names, giving and changing 19, 223
permissibility of 57
see also astrology; *golem*
magidim (instructing angels) 57–9, 69 n., 206
Maimonidean controversies, *see* philosophy, Jewish: opposition
Mantua 26 n., 56, 84 n.
manuscripts 55, 66–7, 72, 80–2, 168, 173, 180
see also scribes
martyrdom 22, 175, 194, 206 n., 212–13
mathematics, *see* education, Jewish: geometry and arithmetic
Me'asef (18th-c. Hebrew journal) 1
Megaleh amukot, the, *see Names Index*: Spira, Nathan ben Solomon
memoirs 193–7
messianism:
faith in 10, 37, 133, 155, 170, 173–4, 218, 220
and Gezeirot Tah Vetat 10, 14–15, 209–12, 218, 220
Heller's views concerning 37, 95, 209–10
17th-c. debate concerning 15, 170 n., 209–10
Shabatean movement 13–15, 42 n., 53, 56, 209
midrash, see *agadah*
Mikulov, *see* Nikolsburg
minhag, *see* custom
miracles:
during the early 17th c. 107–8, 110, 115, 155
ritual responses to 114–16, 155, 198
theories of 109–12, 155
Mishnah 66–82
artefacts listed in 79, 169, 176
and Caro, Joseph 69 n.

Mishnah (*cont.*):
commentaries on 67–9, 81; of Bertinoro 68, 73–4, 78–80; of Maimonides 68, 74, 76–7, 80; of Meir of Rothenburg 82; of Simeon Wolf Oppenheim 82; supercommentaries on 81
conclusion of 97–8
as divinely inspired 70–1
geography in 75, 176 n.
geometry in 74–5, 90
Greek loanwords in 66–7
Hebrew of 76
interpretation of: and omnisignificance 70–6; *peshat* in 70–9; *pilpul* and 73–4; of Rashi and Tosafot 77–9; talmudic (normative) 76–7
kabbalah and 62, 75–6
manuscripts and printed editions of 66–8, 72, 80 n.
and messianism 210 n.
miracles in 110 n.
non-Jews in 92–7
study of 33, 35, 67–9, 81, 121, 210 n.
textual emendation of 70–2
tractates of, sequence 71
see also Heller Index: writings: *Tosafot yom tov*
Mishnah passages, interpreted:
Ber. 1: 5, 'as a man of seventy years' 110 n.
Ber. 2: 1, 'between paragraphs, he may greet' 74 n.
Ber. 2: 6, 'delicate' 76 n.
Ber. 5: 4, 'if he is certain' 61 n.
Ber. 9: 2, 'one who sees the Great Sea' 75 n.
Ber. 9: 2, 'on comets' 168
Ber. 9: 5, 'required to bless evil tidings' 198
Demai 2: 4, 'wholesale merchants' 67 n.
Ter. 1: 1, 'they must give heave offering' 76 n.
Kil. 3: 1, 'a garden six handbreadths square' 74
Kil. 5: 5, 'renders forty-five vines unfit' 74, 91 n.
Shev. 6: 1, 'from the land of Israel to Keziv' 75 n.
Ḥal. 4: 10, 'the men of Alexandria' 75 n., 90 n., 176 n.
Bik. 3: 3, 'the rulers, the prefects' 71
Shab. 1: 11, 'Rabbi Judah says' 71
Shab. 13: 2, 'two loops in the heddles' 79
Shab. 13: 3, 'one who tears his garment' 198
Shab. 16: 4, 'eighteen garments' 176 n.
Eruv. 10: 1, 'one who found tefillin' 74 n.
Pes. 3: 8, 'Mount Scopus' 75 n.
Pes. 4: 9, 'book of medicine' 89
Pes. 8: 1, 'guardians' 67 n.
Shek. 6: 3, 'thirteen gates of the Temple' 74, 89 n.
Yoma 1: 1, 1: 7, High Priest on Yom Kippur 31
Yoma 6: 2, 'they have sinned' 72 n.
Suk. 4: 5, name of God 76, 81 n., 219
RH 1: 2, 'on Rosh Hashanah' 111 n.
RH 2: 4, 'Where were the bonfire signals?' 75 n.
Ta'an. 3: 8, 'but not for too much rain' 219 n.
Meg. 4: 3, 'They may not recite the Shema' 181 n.
Meg. 4: 9, 'he is to be silenced' 77 n.
Ḥag. 2: 1, 'work of the Divine Chariot' 57
Yev. 1: 4, 'Even though these declared' 149 n.
Yev. 2: 8, 'the oldest brother is commanded' 77 n.
Yev. 8: 6, '*androginos*' 67 n.
Ket. 6: 1, 'objects found by the wife' 75 n.
Naz. 5: 5, 'May I be a Nazirite' 76–7
Sot. 1: 9, 'And likewise in repaying good' 219
Sot. 9: 9, Teḥinah ben Perishah 71–2, 81 n.
Kid. 1: 10, 'his days are lengthened' 172 n.
Kid. 4: 14, 'all is according to his merits' 111–12, 208
BK 1: 1, 'injury' 76 n.
BK 4: 3, 'If an ox of an Israelite' 95 n., 198 n.
BK 8: 7, '"return the man's wife" (Gen. 20: 7)' 77 n.
Sanh. 4: 3, 'seated in a semicircle' 176 n.
Sanh. 10: 3, 'The generation of the Flood' 93
Makot 3: 1, 'They who are to be beaten' 67 n.
Eduyot 8: 7, 'Ben Zion brought in by force' 188 n.
AZ 1: 3, 'the calends' 67 n., 219 n.
AZ 1: 9 'he might bring in items of idolatry' 96
AZ 2: 5, '"Your love is better than wine" (S. of S. 1: 2)' 81 n.
Avot, title of tractate 200
Avot 1: 1, 'teach many students' 120 n.
Avot 1: 2, 1: 18, six pillars 4
Avot 1: 3, 'Do not be like servants' 95 n.
Avot 1: 4, 'sit in the dust of their feet' 120 n.
Avot 1: 5, 'a man who converses with his wife' 200 n.
Avot 1: 6, 'get yourself a colleague' 120 n., 188 n.
Avot 1: 8, 'do not be like a lawyer' 26 n.
Avot 2: 1, 'you do not know the reward of *mitsvot*' 147 n.
Avot 2: 2, 'study of Torah and worldly labour' 120 n.

Avot 2: 3, 'be careful of the government' 143 n.
Avot 2: 4, 'do not separate yourself' 219 n.
Avot 2: 5, 'not everyone who does much business' 118 n.
Avot 2: 6, Hillel and the skull 75–6, 147
Avot 2: 7, 'more flesh, more worms' 57 n.
Avot 2: 16, 'the reward of the righteous' 147 n.
Avot 3: 5, 'the yoke of the kingdom' 170 n.
Avot 3: 7, 'one who leaves aside his study' 200 n.
Avot 3: 9, 'he whose wisdom comes before' 120 n.
Avot 3: 10, 'his wisdom will endure' 95 n.
Avot 3: 14, 'Beloved is man' 93–5
Avot 3: 15, 'All is foreseen' 37 n.
Avot 3: 17, 'If there is not Torah' 120 n.
Avot 3: 18, '*gematriyot*' 120 n.
Avot 4: 1, '"From all my teachers" (Ps. 119: 99)' 169 n.
Avot 4: 1, 'who conquers his impulse' 120 n.
Avot 4: 2, 'just as the weightiest' 120 n.
Avot 4: 9, 'He who fulfils the Torah in poverty' 147 n.
Avot 4: 11, 'a shield against misfortune' 147 n., 172 n.,
Avot 4: 21, 'Envy, lust, and honour' 182
Avot 4: 22, 'The dead will be resurrected' 172 n.
Avot 5: 2, 'Ten generations' 210 n.
Avot 5: 6, 'Ten things were created' 37 n. 76 n., 210 n.
Avot 5: 8, 'Plague comes' 147 n.
Avot 5: 19, 'eat in this world' 147 n., 172 n.
Avot 5: 22, 'There is no better quality' 89 n.
Men. 4: 4, 'dedicated' 120 n.
Tamid 7: 4, 'rest in eternal life' 210 n.
Midot 1: 3, 'the Kiponos Gate' 67 n.
Midot 3: 1, 'in the shape of a *gamma*' 67 n.
Kelim 14: 8, 'in the shape of a *gamma*' 67 n.
Kelim 16: 8, 'the sword' 72 n.
Kelim 16: 8, '*sakoratia*' (astrolabe) 169
Kelim 20: 7, 'in the form of a Greek *chi*' 67 n.
Kelim 23: 3, '*kumpon*' (arena) 67 n.
Kelim 30: 2, '*aspaklaryah*' (mirror, eyeglasses) 169
Ohilot 18: 7, dwelling-places of idolaters 94 n.
Neg. 6: 6, '*bohak*' (skin discoloration) 91
Nid. 2: 5, '*prozdor*' (vestibule) 67 n.
Nid. 5: 9, 'twenty years old' 72 n.
Nid. 8: 1, '*torfah*' (her private parts) 67 n.
Yad. 4: 5, the ancient Hebrew alphabet 170 n.
Uktsin 3: 12, 'peace' 97–8

mitnagedim 92
monarchism 10–11, 21, 107–9, 130, 133–5, 153, 216–18
Moravia, Jews of 83 n., 126
  see also Nikolsburg
Moreh nevukhim, *see Names Index*: Maimonides: writings
Munich 48 n.
Münster 85 n.
Musarei hapilosofim 34, 90, 170
mysticism, Jewish, *see* kabbalah

N

Nemirov (Nemyriv) 67 n., 175–8, 205–7
Neoplatonism, *see Names Index*: Plato
neo-Stoicism, *see* Stoicism
Nikolsburg (Mikulov), Jews of:
  Heller as rabbi of 87, 113
  letters from Prague to (1619) 102–4
  the Maharal in 29–30, 84, 208
  privileges of 84–5
  wine tax controversy among 83–7, 131 n., 138
non-Jews, Jewish attitudes towards 83–98, 146–55, 202–3, 209–18
  and autonomy, Jewish 129–35, 143, 185–6
  bread and food of 83 n., 84 n., 88–9
  and Christianity 96–7, 139–40, 142, 151, 187, 213
  comic view of 92, 153–5, 202
  Cossacks and Tatars 176, 178, 185 n., 205, 211–17
  demonization of 92–3, 211–13
  differentiation among 94, 154–5, 213
  discrimination against 198
  in heaven and hell 92–3
  history of non-Jews 92, 106–9, 212–17
  and honour 202–4
  humanity of non-Jews 92–5
  as individuals 154–5
  Islam and Christianity 94, 154, 176
  knowledge and service of God among 95, 202
  messianic fate of non-Jews 37, 95, 209–10
  and miracles 94, 110
  monarchs 10–11, 21, 107–9, 131, 133–5, 153, 216–18
  naming and quoting by name 44–5, 90–1, 130, 166, 170, 195–6
  noblemen 22, 131, 136–40, 149, 152–5, 201–4, 217–18
  philosophers and scientists 39, 43–50, 64–5, 74–5, 90, 93 n., 160–2, 168, 190–1
  printers 91 n.
  reading books by 43–5, 89–91

non-Jews, Jewish attitudes towards (*cont.*):
suffering of non-Jews 12, 114–16, 212–14
teaching Torah to 95
weddings, Jewish, attendance at 23–4
wine made or touched by 83–7
and women, Jewish 48, 50, 84 n.
Nördlingen 21–3, 90, 103

O

Oreḥot ḥayim 116, 121, 207 n.
Ostroh (Ostrog) 183, 185–8
Oswięcim (Auschwitz) 194
Ottoman empire ('lands of the Turks') 66, 176, 203

P

Padua, University of 23, 39, 164
Pardes rimonim, *see Names Index*: Cordovero, Moses
Paris, burning of Talmud in (1240) 150–1
peshat, *see* interpretation
philosophy, Jewish 5–8, 30–54, 63–5, 89–97, 130, 163–4
and kabbalah 49, 51–5, 59, 63–4, 190–1
opposition to among Ashkenazi Jews: Altshuler, Naftali (1593) 39; Ashkenazi, Joseph (1559) 43; Joseph Halevi, exile of (1612) 48–50; Horowitz, Isaiah (*c.*1623) 52–3; Luria, Solomon (*c.*1560) 42–3; the Maharal (*c.*1600) 30; *Moreh nevukhim*, ban on (1232) 7, 42; Sirkes, Joel (1618) 53–4; 13th–14th cc. 42 n.; typology of 49
'the penitent philosopher' 64 n., 191
study of among pre-modern Ashkenazi Jews 39–54; absence in 11th c. 41; decline of (1620–90) 15, 42, 54; efflorescence of (1550–1620) 6–8, 39–43; by Joseph ben Isaac Halevi (*c.*1611–14) 44–50; by Heller (*c.*1595–1612) 34, 45; historiography of 5–8; in Prague and Regensburg (*c.*1400) 6, 42; publication of classic works (1590–1620) 39–40, 42; revival of (after 1690) 42; *see also* astronomy; science, natural; theology
piety and pietism 4–5, 24, 102–4
asceticism 24, 173, 221
captives, redemption of 102, 144
charity (*tsedakah*) 4, 24–5, 102, 144, 155, 181–3, 222 n.
Hannover's 'six pillars' 4
kabbalistic 60–1, 189–91
and non-Jews, attitudes towards 48–50, 83–97
pietistic literature: *Emek hamelekh* 189–91; *Oreḥot ḥayim* 116, 121, 207 n.; in Prague (*c.*1600) 28; *Shenei luḥot haberit* 51, 59
and plague 35, 48, 114–16
repentance and penance (*teshuvah*) 48, 173, 190–1, 207, 210, 215, 221
suffering, acceptance of 38, 141, 173, 198, 202, 219
thanksgiving 103–7, 114–16, 155, 192–4
women, pious 24–5, 28, 121
see also *ḥevrah*; prayer
pilpul 5–6, 14, 33, 73–4, 120
Pińczów 222
Pirkei avot, *see* Mishnah passages, interpreted
plague 13, 35, 47–8, 110, 113–16, 198–9, 205, 220–1
and class differences 47–8
explanation of 114
Heller's sermons on 113–16, 155, 219, 221
poetry, *see* Hebrew poetry; Yiddish language
Polish–Lithuanian Commonwealth, Jews of:
arendators (tax-farmers) 182, 190, 215
autobiographies of 193–4
Cracow, pre-eminence of 192
critiques of, 17th-c. Jewish 4, 69 n., 114, 185, 190, 207, 215
customs and halakhic traditions of 125–6, 176–81, 206–9
Czarniecki (1655–6) massacres of 218, 222
everyday life in 175–8, 187
expulsion of, threatened 218
and German Jews, contrasted 5–6, 135, 177–8, 184, 188
historiography of 4–15
institutions of 4, 69
kehilot of 5 n., 114 n., 117–18 nn., 185–8, 192, 206–8, 211
Manasseh ben Israel on 175, 184
Moryson, Fynes on 184 n.
neighborhoods of 23 n.
origins and foundation stories of 180
piety and pietism among 4, 69, 221
in Prague and Vienna 28–9, 44–50, 102
printing by 39–40, 42, 67 n., 80, 124, 189–91, 200
purchase of rabbinical office 183–91
and Shabatean movement 14–15, 205–6, 209–10, 218
in 1650 and 1850, contrasted 177
Torah scholarship of 30–3, 39–43, 48, 68, 78, 91–2, 122–6, 159–64, 178–80, 184–6, 191, 200
and voivode, authority of 187

Yiddish of 177
see also Gezeirot Tah Vetat
political theory, traditional Jewish, see *kehilah*; *shtadlanim*
Polonnoye 205
Poznań 118 n., 134, 222 n.
see also Names Index: Horowitz, Shabetai Sheftel ben Isaiah
Prague and Prague Jews:
Altneushul 29–30, 119
authority over other communities 132–5
Bassevian and anti-Bassevian parties 138
chronicler of, anonymous Hebrew (*c*.1615) 107, 146 n., 155 n.
Church of the Holy Spirit 23, 36
deliverance narratives of 106–9, 193–4
descriptions and views of Prague: by Gans, David (1592) 27 n.; by Heller (1602) 27, 36; by Moryson, Fynes (1592) 26–7; by Naftali Hirtz of Brest Litovsk 148; by Rapoport, Abraham 29
doctors, Jewish 23, 28
drawings of, by Savery and Van Vianen 87
elections of 117, 145
everyday life of 23–7, 36–8, 87, 101–4
halakhic traditions of 122 n., 135 n., 180
ḥevrot of 69, 81
historiography of 27 n.
history: origins (10th c.) 26; Jewish rationalism (14th c.) 6, 42; Horowitz controversy (1530s) 25, 129, 148; expulsions (1541, 1561) 104, 148 n.; Maimonidean controversy (1559) 43, 148; Hebrew books confiscated (1560) 142; Maharal in Prague (1573–1609) 30; communal governance regulated (1579) 30, 188 n.; description by Fynes Moryson (1592) 26–7; plague (1598) 35; Jewish leaders arrested (1602) 140–1; archiepiscopal synod (1605) 24 n., 48 n., 87 n., 95 n.; plague (1606) 47, 168 n.; Passau war (1611) 47, 107; plague (1611) 47–8; penitential rules (1611) 48; Joseph ben Isaac Halevi (1611–12) 44–50; defenestration (1618) 101, 109; threat of expulsion (1618) 108–9; iconoclasm (1619) 97; coronation of Frederick (1619) 104; Battle of White Mountain, and sack (1620) 12, 106–9, 144; procession (1623) 109 n., 117; Jewish quarter expanded (1623–4) 113; plague (1625) 113 n.; communal controversy (1629) 138–9, 145, 148, 188–9; trial of Heller (1629) 136–45; conversion campaign (1630) 150–1; siege by Saxon army (1631) 160; plague (1639) 198–9, 220
hospital, Jewish 23 n.
Italian Jews in 26 n., 27
Jewish badge in 87
Jewish quarter (ghetto, Josefstadt) 26–7, 113
legends of 26, 29, 56–7
letters from Prague to Vienna (1619) 101–4
libraries and book collections (17th c.) 80 n.
Maharal, *kloyz* of 29, 31
Mala Strana (Kleinseit) 26, 126, 137
Meisel family 25, 27
Meisel synagogue 27, 102, 119, 159
Mishnah *ḥevrot* 69, 81
Pinkas Shul 7, 9, 25, 56–7, 119, 145
plague in 35, 47–8, 113 n., 168 n., 198–9, 220
population of 26–7, 177
printing in 28 n., 39–40, 46, 121, 125, 151, 170 n.
rabbinical court of 25–6, 86–7, 118 n., 121
rabbis of, contracts and duties of 117–19
Rashi in Prague, legend of 26
Rudolph II, court of 22, 26–8
scholars in circle of the Maharal 27–9
synagogues in 119, 208; *see also separate sub-entries for* Altneushul, Meisel synagogue, Pinkas Shul
taxes of 118–19, 134, 138–9, 145, 148
thanksgiving days ('special Purims') of 106–7, 155, 194
Wallenstein palace 126
weddings, Jewish (1592) 23–4
yeshiva of Heller (*c*.1620) 74, 102, 119–20, 124, 200
yeshiva of Prague 136
see also *golem*; *Names Index*: Bassevi, Jacob; Maharal
prayer:
additions to set prayers 61
blessing on Torah study 20, 127–8
efficacy of 52, 111–12, 208
on gemstone given to Rudolph II 22 n.
halakhot concerning 60–1, 111, 127–8
Havdalah blessing, interpretation of 64–5
ḥevrot for 69
Horowitz, Isaiah, prayer book of 51–2
informal and occasional 35–6, 104, 132, 192, 199
innovations in 61, 84, 105, 115–16, 207–9
interpretation of 62
kabbalistic 51–2, 59, 61–2
kavanah in 62

prayer *(cont.)*:
liturgical poetry 106–9, 114, 117 n., 209–16, 220
loud 207 n.
Mi sheberakh, Heller's (Cracow) 207–8
Mi sheberakh, the Maharal's (Nikolsburg) 84, 208
Oreḥot ḥayim, recital of (Vienna) 115–16
and plague 35, 48, 115, 117 n.
and powerlessness 10
purpose of 62–3
silence during 207–9
among 'six pillars' of Judaism 4
and social status 7
of thanksgiving 106–7, 111, 115
tikun ḥatsot 59, 62
see also synagogue
preaching, *see* sermons
printing:
of autobiography 193 n.
and censorship 125, 141–3, 151
and copyright 80
and erudition 79–81
of halakhic codes 124–5
ink, paper, and typeface 66
of Jewish philosophy 39–40, 42, 52
of kabbalah 52, 189–91
and marginalia 81
of Mishnah 66–8
by non-Jewish printers 91 n.
and oral culture 81
and proof-readers 200
and rabbinic activism 120–1
and reading barriers 91
of Talmud 78 n., 125, 143, 151
title pages 131–2
progress, conceptions of 44–6, 165–70
providence, divine, *see* causation; miracles
Purims, special 106–7, 155, 194

R

rabbis, rabbinate:
activist model of 30, 69, 119–21, 183–7
ancient, images of 30–1, 69 n., 70, 74 n., 75
appointment and hiring of 8, 117, 149, 175, 187
arrest of 136, 140, 151, 196
authority of 129–31, 181, 183–5
autobiography of 192–204
biography of 1–2
careers of 113, 192–3, 202
centralization of 130, 134–5, 185–7, 221–2
conferences of, German 24 n., 84 n., 134
conflict and *maḥloket* among 97–8, 130, 173–4, 181, 183–9
contracts, salaries, and duties of 117–19, 222
courts, rabbinic 4, 25–6, 85–7, 121, 132–5, 139, 181, 183–9
historiography of 5–11
installation ceremony for 192
legends of 75
as monarchs 130
partiality and impartiality of 5, 26, 119, 148, 185–6, 188–9
professionalization of 9, 118 n., 184, 188
purchase of office by 8, 183–9
Renaissance model of 31–5, 51
social status of 7–9, 26, 118–19, 181–3, 203–4
see also education, Jewish; *kehilah*; sermons
Renaissance 31–2, 51, 67, 193
rich and poor:
classifications of 8–9, 182
conflict of 5, 7–9, 14–15, 83–7, 132–5, 138–9, 144–5, 148, 152–3
creditors and debtors 5, 22–3, 185–6
critiques of wealth 4, 30, 36, 69 n., 114, 185, 190, 207, 215
and education, Jewish 8, 33 n.
endogamy among 159
in Frankfurt Jewry 129, 132–5
in German Jewry 85–6, 129–31, 182 n.
Heller's attitudes towards 36, 86–7, 143, 182–3, 201–4, 211
in Jewish historiography 8–9
in Nikolsburg Jewry 83–7
and non-Jews, Jewish attitudes towards 202–4, 213 n.
and plague 47–8
polarization of 9
in Polish Jewry 4–15, 114, 175–6, 182–90, 213–15, 222
in Prague Jewry 30, 47–8, 117–19, 125–6, 138–9, 145, 148
synagogue seating of 7
taxation of 83–7, 138–9, 145, 148
and wine-drinking 85–6
see also *kehilah*: social conflict in
Ruaḥ ḥen 39–40

S

Sabbatian movement, *see Names Index*: Tsevi, Shabetai
Safed (Tsefat) 43, 52, 68–9
Satan 37, 71
Satan in Goray, *see Names Index*: Singer, Isaac Bashevis

science, natural:
alchemy 27, 34, 167
Aristotelian 36–7, 91 n., 162 n.
earthquake 115
habitability of the entire world 169
and halakhah 42–3, 90–1
magnetism 40
and mathematics 91, 167
measurement of heat 167
and metaphysics 43, 91
in Mishnah 75
new animals and new seas 13, 164–6
north wind and conception 91 n., 162 n.
progress in 46, 166–70
skin discoloration 91 n.
stincus marinus, classification of 166–70
study of 'seven sciences' 28 n., 49, 64–5
superiority of Torah to 48–9, 64–5
see also astronomy
scribes 8, 28, 102, 114, 118
Sefardi Jews 5, 41, 125–6, 180
Sefer alilot devarim 78 n.
Sefer hapeliyah 81 n.
Sefer mitsvot gadol (*Semag*) 124
Sefer mitsvot katan (*Semak*) 124
Sefer naftali 55, 59
Sefer yetsirah 57
self-government, Jewish, see *kehilah*
sermons:
of Chajes, Isaac 40
Christian 47, 115, 151
of Ephraim of Luntshits 4–5, 8, 30, 69, 113
Heller's experience reflected in his 115, 174
Heller's knowledge of text editing seen in 72 n.
of Horowitz, Isaiah 51
of Israel of Bełżyce 214–15
of Joseph ben Isaac Halevi 48–9
kabbalistic 8, 162–3, 191, 214–15
of the Maharal 21, 30, 141 n., 208 n.
of Modena, Leone da 203
of Nantua, Judah 163 n.
and rabbinic activism 30, 69
silence during 208 n.
Zohar in 163
see also Heller Index: writings: sermons
Shabatean movement, *see Names Index*: Tsevi, Shabetai
shamashim (beadles) 8, 57, 107–8, 117 n., 118, 194
Shelah, Shenei luḥot haberit 55, 59
see also Names Index: Horowitz, Isaiah
shtadlanim 10–11, 84–5, 131, 134, 138–9, 143–7, 152–4, 187–8, 218
Shulḥan arukh, reception of 5, 8, 15, 122–6, 178–81, 183
Sifra 61, 68 n.
silence:
and divine transcendence 63–4
modest and prudent 195–7
and mourning 197–9
during prayer service 207–9
during sermon 208 n.
Silesia, Jews of 41, 134, 169
1648, massacres of, *see* Gezeirot Tah Vetat
social classes and social criticism, *see* rich and poor
soferim, *see* scribes
stincus marinus 164–6
Stoicism and neo-Stoicism 197–8
Sulzbach, Jewish printing in 42
Swabia, Jews of 19–23, 134
synagogue:
as communal expense 87
desecration of 211, 213
as fortress 12
gaba'im (deacons) of 118, 192, 208
gifts to 25
governance of 25
honours, purchase of 177
mortgage of 175 n.
permission to build 27 n., 113
portraits of Jews in 87
and rabbis 7, 118–19
relics in 56–7
seating in 7, 145
weddings and circumcisions in 23–4, 102
women's gallery in 145
of Yekels, Isaac (Cracow) 175
see also Prague: Altneushul, Pinkas Shul; prayer

T

Talmud Bavli (Babylonian Talmud):
burning of 141–2, 150–1
censorship and suppression of 125, 139–43
commentaries on 77–9, 123–9
Heller's view of 76–7, 123–4, 139, 142
letter-perfection of 71 n.
moral compunctions in regard to 198
obscenity, accused of 196
and *pilpul* 5–6, 73–4, 119–20
study of 33–5, 43 n., 67–8, 74, 119–20, 200
and Zohar 60–1
see also *agadah*; Mishnah
Talmud Yerushalmi (Jerusalem Talmud) 200

talmudic passages, interpreted and applied:
Ber. 5*b*, 'One who places his bed' 91 n., 162 n.
Ber. 8*a*, 'the day the Temple was destroyed' 219 n.
Ber. 10*b*, 'There is no artist' 36
Ber. 11*b*, blessing on Torah study 127 n., 128
Ber. 12*b*, 'King of justice' 219
Ber. 14*b*, repeating the last words of Shema 60 n.
Ber. 21*b*, recital of Kedushah 60 n.
Ber. 33*b*, additions to set prayers 62
Ber. 34*b*, 'a building with windows' 60
Ber. 54*a*, 'a miracle' 111
Ber. 54*b*, 'Four must give thanks' 111
Ber. 57*b*, conversion of the non-Jews 95 n.
Ber. 58*a*, 'sages of the non-Jews' 65 n., 93 n.
Ber. 60*a*, 'a bathhouse' 170 n.
Shab. 12*b*, 'a man should not pray . . . in Aramaic' 60 n.
Shab. 33*b*, miracle of Rabbi Simeon bar Yohai 115
Shab. 33*b*, 'the sin of the generation' 215
Shab. 75*a*, 'commanded to reckon the . . . stars' 160
Shab. 116*a*, 'philosopher' 41 n.
Pes. 94*b*, 'the orb is fixed but the stars move' 166–8
Pes. 110*a*, 'danger of pairs' 170 n.
RH 3*b*, 'a fit king' 217
RH 16*b*, changing names in a sickness 223
Yoma 9*a*, 18*a*, buying the office of high priest 183, 186 n.
Yoma 11*a*, 'exempt from the law of *mezuzah*' 128
Yoma 69*b*, 'The crown returned to its former dignity' 192
Suk. 26*b*, a short nap 61 n.
Meg. 9*a*, the Septuagint and the ways of peace 210
MK 19*a*, tefillin on *ḥol hamo'ed* 61 n.
Ḥag. 13*a*, 'We have no concern for secret things' 63
Ḥag. 13*a*, 'One may not teach the secrets of Torah' 59–60, 162–3, 189–91
Ḥag. 13*a*, 'One may not teach Torah to non-Jews' 95
Ḥag. 14*b*, 'cut the shoots' 222
Sot. 38*b*, 'One who blesses is blessed' 63
Sot. 49*b*, 'Greek wisdom' 41 n.
Git. 19*a*, ink 60
Git. 62*a*, 'Who are the kings? The rabbis' 49, 130
Git. 83*b*, 'one does not answer the lion after his death' 171
BK 60*a*, 'the Destroying Angel' 12, 105, 212
BK 113*a*, 'the law of the land is the law' 186
BM 59*b*, 'the gates of oppressive words' 221
BM 68*a*, 'lest the door be shut to borrowers' 5
BM 114*b*, 'You are called man' 94 n.
BB 15*a*, 'Satan is the evil inclination' 37
Sanh. 33*a*, 'reed-cutters in a bog' 186
Sanh. 63*b*, 'partnership with an idolater' 96
Sanh. 65*b*, Rabbi Hanina and the *golem*-calf 57 n.
Sanh. 95*a*, Eliezer and the 'shortening of the way' 115
Sanh. 98*a*, Joshua ben Levi and the messiah 210
Sanh. 100*a*, 'one who starves himself in this world' 147
Sanh. 106*b*, 'God searches the heart' 87
AZ 7*b*, dealing with non-Jews on Sundays 96
AZ 19*b*, 'forty years old' 121
AZ 20*b*, 'humility is greatest' 126
AZ 35*b*, non-Jewish bread 88
AZ 54*b*, 'philosopher' 41 n.
Ḥulin 60*b*, lessening of the moon 161–74
Ḥulin 66*b*, 'whatever has scales, has fins' 164–6
Ḥulin 67*b*, maggoty food 88, 196
Ḥulin 104*b*, chicken and cheese 60–1
Ḥulin 142*a*, 'no reward in this world' 147
Arakhin 29*a*, 'a *perutah*' 89 n.
see also Mishnah, interpretation of
Targum 35, 72, 80
Tatars 176, 178
taxation, Jewish communal:
equity and inequity in 6, 85, 138, 148
Nikolsburg wine tax 83–7
Prague war tax 10, 138–9, 148
rabbis exempt from 118
Silesia 134
systems of 85
Temple, Jerusalem:
destruction of 14, 181, 206, 210 n., 213, 219 n.
diagram of, Heller's 61 n.
Ezekiel's vision of 61
High Priests and purchase of office 183, 186
Isserles's interpretation of 31–2
as metaphor for Jewish community 132
study of in 16th and 17th cc. 61 n.
teshuvah, *see* piety and pietism: repentance
thanksgiving, rituals of 106–7, 111, 115, 155, 192–5, 219

theology and dogma, Jewish:
Bible, letter-perfection of 72
Creation, the 41, 64, 160–8, 169 n., 171–2
freedom and free will 37, 52, 76–7, 127, 160, 171, 210
goodness of God 56, 103–4, 219
and heresy 43, 54, 163
images and names for God: attributes, divine 56, 62, 64, 219–20; clockmaker 40; First Cause 33, 36; and ineffability, divine 63–4, 219; intellect 32 n.; mankind as divine image 95; particularizer 160; plague 220; *Shem hameforash* (Tetragrammaton) 76, 219
incorporeality, divine 40
miracles 109–12, 114–16, 155, 189
Mosaic authorship of Torah 72–3
Moses as most perfect man 46
non-Jewish knowledge of God 95
perfection, infinite 44
predestination and divine foreknowledge 37, 210
proofs of God's existence 36–7, 43–4, 160, 219
resurrection of the dead 37, 41, 199
revelation and inspiration, divine 20, 52, 70
reward and punishment 47, 108, 110–12, 114, 126, 146–8, 190–1, 207 n., 212, 215, 219
sin 37, 53, 71, 85, 88, 147, 171–4, 214–15
soul, origin in God 37, 57–9, 63
Talmud, letter-perfection of 71
Thirteen Principles of Maimonides 7, 36
transcendence and immanence 63–4, 215, 219
unity of God 97
universe, end of 44
wisdom of God 36–7, 219
see also angels; kabbalah; messianism
Thirty Years War:
Defenestration of Prague (1618) 101–9
everyday life during 101–4, 112–21
expulsions and refugees in 102–3, 108, 159
Frederick and Elizabeth, coronation of 104
Heller's views of 12, 105–9, 114–16, 133–4, 148, 202
imperial victories (1620s) 135, 151
inflation (1620–3) 112
Mansfeld, Peter Ernst 109 n.
Moravia, campaigns in (1618–20) 101–4
Polish–Habsburg alliance 217
rabbinic job market during 175, 202
Saxon invasion of Bohemia (1631) 160
Silesia, Habsburg conquest of 134
small nations in 112
suffering and horrors during 12, 112, 115, 211 n.
Swedish invasion 175
taxes during 138, 148
Vienna, attack on (1619) 102
Wallenstein, Albrecht von 112, 126, 151, 160
Wallerstein castle destroyed (1648) 22
White Mountain, Battle of 12, 106–9, 144, 146–7, 209, 212
see also Names Index: Ferdinand II
toleration, religious:
Habsburg empire 11, 20–3
Polish–Lithuanian Commonwealth 12, 175
Prague 26–7
see also Jews, persecution of
Torah, study of, *see* education, Jewish
Torat kohanim, *see* Sifra
torture 140–1, 211–12
Tosafists, Tosafot 41 n., 57, 77–9, 95, 120, 180
Tosefta 61, 180 n.
transmigration of souls, see *gilgul*
tsedakah, *see* charity
Tsefat, *see* Safed
tsitsit 56–7
Tulczyn (Tulchin) 205, 212 n.
Turim, *see Names Index*: Jacob ben Asher
Turisk (Turzisk) 187
turkey, *kashrut* of vii

U
Ukraine 174–8
grievances of Christians against Jews in 96–7
Kiev Academy 34
see also Gezeirot Tah Vetat; Ludmir
Unitarians, Polish, expulsion of 218
Ushpitzin, *see* Oświęcim

V
Va'ad Arba Aratsot, *see* Council of Four Lands
Venice 53, 58, 216
Vienna:
Christian Hebraists in 28 n., 141–2, 149 n.
Heller imprisoned in 136–45
Heller as rabbi of 113–16, 149, 155, 163–4, 189
Jewish quarter (Leopoldstadt) 11, 113
letters from Prague (1619) 101–4
Lucerna, Aaron, and Leo in 163–4
Nechle Heller in 103, 160, 201
plague (1625) 113–16, 155, 207 n., 219
takanot of 189, 227 no. 26
Wallerstein (Fränklin), Abraham in 9
see also Germany and Habsburg empire, Jews of

Vilna (Vilnius) 217
Volhynia, *see* Ludmir
Volodymir , *see* Ludmir

W

Wallerstein (town) 19–23, 89, 141, 177, 200
Warsaw 187
Wettenhausen (village in Swabia) 22
White Mountain, Battle of 12, 106–9, 144, 146–7, 209, 212
Włodomierz Wolinsky, *see* Ludmir
women:
- *agunah* 31 n., 180 n., 220
- chaperoning of 48, 50, 84 n.
- and Cracow plague, 1623 114
- Glückel of Hameln 169 n., 195, 197, 207 n.
- and Heller family feast and fast 155
- Heller's wife and daughters, *see Heller Index under* family
- kabbalistic study by 59
- literacy of 170
- naming ceremony for 118
- as pedlars 48, 50
- piety of 24, 28, 121
- and Prague–Vienna letters (1619) 101–4
- servant girls 5, 48
- synagogue gallery for 145
- Tiktiner, Rebecca 28
- 'whores', exile of 48
- and Yiddish books 121

Worms 19–20, 69 n., 82, 105, 107–8
- Juspa, *shamash* of Worms 107–8, 117 n.

Y

yeshiva, *see* education, Jewish: yeshivas
Yiddish language and literature:
- autobiographies and memoirs 194 n.
- *Bashraybung fun Ashkenaz un Polak* 178
- 'Bontshe the Silent' (Peretz) 173 n.
- Glückel of Hameln, memoir of 169 n., 195, 197
- *Gzeire lid* 211
- letters to Vienna (1619) 101–4
- *Megilat eivah*, Yiddish version of 140 n., 148, 161 n., 187–8, 196–7, 200 n., 202
- *Oreḥot ḥayim*, Yiddish translation of 116, 121
- Polish and German dialects 177
- in Polish–Lithuanian Commonwealth 177
- in Prague (*c.*1600) 28
- *Satan in Goray* 13–15
- *Sefer masah umerivah* (Pfaffenhofen) 85–6
- and women 121

Yom Kippur ritual, interpreted by Isserles 31–2

Z

Zohar:
- canonization and authority of 60
- date of messianic coming in 209 n.
- demon-sages in 53
- *devekut* in 56 n.
- as halakhic source 60–1
- interpreted non-kabbalistically 62, 163, 166
- and Maimonides on ineffability 64
- as midrash 61, 163
- on non-Jews 92–3, 94 n.
- publication of 59

Żółkiew (Zholkva) 48 n., 208 n.